SMP Further Mathematics Series
Differential Equations and Numerical Analysis

Andrew Paterson

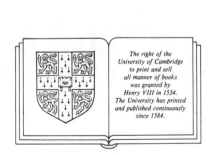

The right of the
University of Cambridge
to print and sell
all manner of books
was granted by
Henry VIII in 1534.
The University has printed
and published continuously
since 1584.

CAMBRIDGE UNIVERSITY PRESS

Cambridge

New York   Port Chester   Melbourne   Sydney

$E|510$ $/38772$

Published by the Press Syndicate of the University of Cambridge
The Pitt Building, Trumpington Street, Cambridge CB2 1RP
40 West 20th Street, New York, NY 10011-4211, USA
10 Stamford Road, Oakleigh, Melbourne 3166, Australia

First published 1991

Printed in Great Britain at the University Press, Cambridge

British Library cataloguing-in-publication data
Differential equations and numerical analysis.
1. Ordinary differential equations. Numerical solution
515.352

ISBN 0 521 40930 6

Contents

Acknowledgements

Thanks are due to various examining boards for questions used as revision exercises. Questions are reproduced by permission of:

- the University of Cambridge Local Examinations Syndicate (UCLES)
- the Oxford and Cambridge Schools Examination Board for their own examinations (O and C) and for those set for the School Mathematics Project (SMP) and the MEI Schools Project
- the Welsh Joint Education Committee (WJEC)
- the Associated Examining Board (AEB).

Each question has its source (in abbreviated form) and its year noted after it; all are A-level questions except those from AEB which are AS-level.

The University of Cambridge Local Examinations Syndicate bears no responsibility for the example answers to questions taken from its past question papers which are contained in this publication. A similar statement holds for the other examining boards named above.

Preface

Many practical applications of mathematics, from engineering and physics through to biology and agricultural science, have three phases. The first is the conversion of aspects of the subject into a mathematical form, by recognising important (and measurable) quantities, and relations between them; this is the process known as *mathematical modelling*. The second phase is the solution of simple versions of these models by exact formulas; this gives a test of the suitability of the models by seeing whether they give the right type of predictions. The third phase is the numerical solution of the full models, to give results to compare against experimental values. This book is about these three activities. Many of the models considered here will involve differential or difference equations, for which exact solution methods will be shown. Many of the situations discussed will be greatly oversimplified, since we have to keep the mathematics and the numerical work within reasonable bounds, and since we do not have the time to become experts in all the subjects where mathematics is applied.

The subject matter of this book is not modern: Newton used all the three phases outlined above. But it is new for schools, and the reason that it is now appropriate at the sixth form level is that the numerical work can be done automatically (and usually accurately) by calculators and computers. When Newton did it, the effort of doing the calculations was enormous. Now they can be done in seconds, if you have the right program and a machine to run it on.

You do not need a powerful computer or great skill as a programmer to work through this book, but you must be prepared to write short programs, and you must have some sort of computer to run them on. I used a programmable calculator (*Casio fx-700P*, using BASIC) and a graphics calculator (*Casio fx-7000G*), and found them to be sufficient, if rather slow at times. As a consequence, the numerical answers given in the book are those offered by those machines; other computers are quite likely to give slightly (or totally) different values.

This book was written for the SMP Further Mathematics series, but the material is not specifically tied to that syllabus. In an attempt to answer the 'why?' questions of numerical work as well as the 'how?' questions, there are chapters and sections of somewhat difficult or advanced theory. They are there for completeness, but you can skim through or omit much of them. What you cannot do is overlook the disasters that can happen in numerical calculation: you must always look at answers and ask if they are reasonable or if they may be rubbish because of some unforeseen quirk of the program or the machine.

The book is intended to be accessible to those with GCSE grades A to C (or equivalent). In the first third of the book no calculus is needed, and few functions

– the logarithm function does not appear until Chapter 8 and the exponential function not until Chapter 10. Matrices are a very useful tool in many of the areas discussed, but most of the sections containing matrix calculations can be omitted at a first run through the material (many students will not need more than a first run through).

The exercises are important, and so is the actual doing of calculations. It is only when you try methods on particular examples that you meet the reasons for organised computing, and the need for supporting mathematics to tell you when it can go wrong.

The outline solutions are just that. There is no room to write out full solutions, and you should be able to fill in details for yourself. When you try the revision exercises, don't jump straight to my outline solution when you get stuck; first identify and review the area of work that the question asks about. If you can't follow my solution, it may be because it is wrong – all books have errors in them. Moreover, if you have found a different or a better solution method, fine; there are often many ways of solving a problem.

My feeling is that many parts of mathematics are fun to do, in particular the modelling of a real situation and its subsequent mathematical or numerical investigation. I hope you have fun too with the material I have collected here.

This book originated in a series of meetings organised by John Hersee (then Executive Director of SMP) to review the content and direction of the Further Mathematics syllabus. After enjoyable discussions with a lively group, mainly of school teachers, a writing group was formed to produce draft material which was then tested in schools. My thanks go to Dick Russell, John Atiyah and Peter O'Grady for writing drafts of various sections, and to the schools who sent in comments on the drafts. They are, however, in no way responsible for my idiosyncratic final treatment of the material they offered. My thanks also go to the SMP Office for the assistance with the production of the final version of the text, in particular to Margaret Youngs for a great deal of typing.

Andrew Paterson

1

Simple iteration

The idea of 'iteration', of doing things repeatedly in the expectation either of getting a better and better answer or of advancing step-by-step to a desired end point, is fundamental in numerical mathematics. The idea comes up naturally in some everyday ideas, so I shall start with some of these examples.

1.1 EXAMPLES OF ITERATION

Example 1

Like everyone else, I had two parents. Each of them had two parents and so I had four grandparents; I shall call my grandparents my

ancestors at level 2.

How many ancestors at level 3 did I have? How many at level 4? How many at level n? The answers must be 8 at level 3, 16 at level 4, and 2^n at level n: each generation back doubles the number of ancestors at that level. In mathematical language

$$a_{n+1} = 2a_n$$

(or in words, ancestors at level $n + 1$ are twice ancestors at level n) which together with $a_1 = 2$ determines the value of a_n for all n by *iteration*, i.e. by going one step at a time to higher values of n.

Notice the two approaches here. We can
either do arithmetic and get a sequence of answers

$$\{2, 4, 8, 16, 32, \ldots\}$$

or look for a solution formula which gives the answers for all values of n, which here is

$$a_n = 2^n.$$

Exercise 1A

1 How many ancestors at level 30 did I have? What was the population of the world then (roughly)?

2 How thick is a sheet of paper? Is it true that if you could fold it in half (thus doubling the thickness) fifty times, it would reach the Moon?

3   Puff pastry is made, according to my recipe book, by an iterative process. Put a layer of fat between two rectangles of dough; the process you iterate is

'fold in three and roll it out to the original shape'.

What is the thickness of each fat layer after ten iterations, if it was 1 millimetre to start with? How many dough layers are there then? Do you think this model of how puff pastry is made will give accurate answers, or at least answers that are near enough right?

4   Solve the following equations (i.e. find a *formula* for a_n, u_n, v_n).

(i) $a_{n+1} = \frac{1}{2}a_n$, $a_0 = 1024$ (ii) $u_{n+1} = -u_n$, $u_1 = 3$
(iii) $v_n = kv_{n-1}$, $v_0 = A$ (iv) $a_{n+1} = a_{n-1}$, $a_0 = 2, a_1 = 0$

Example 2

One of the most common iterative processes is that of calculating interest on money. As I write, rates of interest are around 10 per cent per annum, so that if I leave £1000 in my building society for a year, I may expect to get back

$$£1000\,(1 + 10/100) = £1100.$$

Actually I am likely to get more, as most building societies calculate the interest twice a year, at half the rate. So after six months my deposit is worth

$$£1000\,(1 + 5/100) = £1050.$$

and after the full year it is worth

$$£1050\,(1 + 5/100) = £1102.5.$$

If they calculate interest monthly, as some do at present, I get even more; my return at the end of the year is then

$$£1000\,(1 + 10/1200)^{12} = £1104.71.$$

Sometimes this is described as an effective annual rate (APR) of 10.471 per cent, since that is the rate which (calculated only once in the year) would give the same return.

Exercise 1B

1   What is the effective annual rate (APR) for 10 per cent per annum calculated ('compounded') daily? Use a 365-day year.

2   A credit card company charges 2% per month on outstanding debts, and claims that this is

'equivalent to an Annual Percentage Rate (APR) of 26.8%'.

Show the calculations involved in deriving this figure.

3   A loan company charges 1% per month on the *initial* sum lent (not on the amount outstanding) when the loan is to be repaid in a year by equal monthly instalments. What is the APR in this case? What would it be if the period of the loan was five years (still with equal monthly instalments)?

4 Invest 1p today at a fixed return of 0.01% per annum above inflation; set out in your ultra-fast space ship and return (little older) to an Earth date increase by 10^6 years, to claim your investment. How much is it worth at present values?

1.2 MATHEMATICAL FORMULATION

The general mathematical form for a simple iterative process is

$$\begin{cases} u_{n+1} = f(u_n) \\ u_0 \text{ has a given value} \end{cases}$$

where u_n means the value at stage n, u_{n+1} means the value at stage $n+1$, and the value at the $(n+1)$th stage depends on the value at the nth stage (through the function f). A starting value must also be given, which is usually at $n=0$ or at $n=1$.

The examples we had before were:

(i) for ancestors

$$a_{n+1} = 2a_n, \ a_1 = 2 \ (\text{or } a_0 = 1);$$

(ii) for building society deposit d_n

$$d_{n+1} = \{1 + r/(100t)\}^t d_n$$

where r is the annual percentage rate and t is the number of calculations per year.
Try the next few examples on your calculator.

(iii) $u_{n+1} = 2/u_n$ with $u_0 = 1$;
(iv) $u_{n+1} = 4/u_n^3$ with $u_0 = 2$;
(v) $u_{n+1} = \cos u_n$ with $u_0 = 1$ (use radians).

You can see that there is quite a wide variety of responses as n increases.

(i) $a_n \to \infty$, i.e. it gets beyond (and stays beyond) any number you like as n gets large enough (you read it as 'a_n tends to infinity').
(ii) $d_n \to \infty$ (but it will take rather a long time before I become a millionaire).
(iii) $u_n = 1$ or 2 alternately.
(iv) u_n is either very small or very large, alternately.
(v) u_n approaches a fixed end value as n gets large, getting ever closer as n gets larger, i.e.

$$u_n \to 0.7390851 \ldots$$

For a fuller discussion on limits, and how to use the '$\to$' symbol properly, see (for example) *Extensions of Calculus* in this series.

Exercise 1C

1 Use your calculator to carry out these iterations.
(i) $u_{n+1} = \sqrt{(10/u_n)}$ with $u_0 = 1$;
(ii) $v_{n+1} = \sqrt{(1 + v_n)}$, $v_0 = \frac{1}{2}$, and relate the limiting value to a solution of $v = \sqrt{(1 + v)}$;

(iii) $w_{n+1} = 5 \tan w_n$, $w_0 = 0.1$.
What number have you calculated in (i)?

2   My ancestors intermarried (I know that the parents of one of my grandparents were cousins) and so the number of my *distinct* ancestors is not 2^n for all n, but less than this. Suppose I try as a model

$$\begin{cases} a_{n+1} = 2000a_n/(1000 + n^2) \\ \quad a_0 = 1. \end{cases}$$

Use your calculator (or computer) to find $a_1, a_2, \ldots, a_{20}$. Will you eventually get back to just two ancestors for a large value of n?

1.3   POPULATION MODELS

One area of serious study in which iterative methods are widely used is population dynamics, that is, the study of how and why populations change in the way they do. Let us take as an example the population of the USA from the year 1790 on, when censuses were introduced there.

Date	1790	1800	1810	1820	1830	1840
Population (million)	3.9	5.3	7.2	9.6	12.9	17.1

In 1798, Malthus suggested that populations increased proportionately to the present population (because both births and deaths should be nearly proportional to the number of people alive). That is, he was suggesting the model

$$u_{n+1} = ku_n$$

for some value of k, and some initial population u_0. You can see that the solution of this equation is (using n to number decades after 1790)

$$u_n = k^n u_0,$$

just as the number of ancestors in Section 1.1 was $2^n \times 1$. By trial and error you can find that a good fit to the above census data comes from the value $k = 1.35$, with $u_0 = 3.9$.

Date	1790	1800	1810	1820	1830	1840
Model population	3.9	5.3	7.1	9.6	13.0	17.5

However, after 1840, model and reality slowly part company.

Date	1850	1860	1870	1880	1890	1900
Real population	23.2	31.4	38.6	50.2	62.9	76.0
Model population	23.6	31.9	43.0	58.1	78.4	105.9

In 1837, Verhulst suggested that for various reasons populations tended to reach a steady level, rather than continuing to grow for ever. The model he put forward was

$$u_{n+1} = au_n - bu_n^2,$$

which is known as the 'logistic model'. You can get quite a good fit to the census figures if you take

$$a = 1.355, \ b = 0.0018, \ u_0 = 3.9,$$

but as before the model fails to give appropriate values at later dates.

Date	1880	1890	1900	1910	1920	1930	1940	1950
Real population	50.2	62.9	76.0	92.0	107	123	132	151
Model population	49.3	62.5	77.6	94.3	112	129	145	159

The fact is that human populations are never as simple as the early theories tried to make out. During the period after 1790 the USA changed its frontiers, which is not allowed for in the models, and immigration from Europe caused great changes in the population. As you might expect, modern population models are far more complicated than the ones given above: later we shall return to some of the possible changes to the models.

Exercise 1D

1 Use the given logistic model to calculate US population figures for the years 1800, 1810, ..., 1870.

2 Fit a logistic model (by trial and error) to the number of entrants for a certain A-level examination (do not expect too good a fit).

Date	1966	1967	1968	1969	1970	1971	1972	1973	1974	1975	1976	1977	1978
Number of entrants	20	33	55	120	187	289	429	491	515	542	610	661	690

On your model, what is the steady level of entrants reached after a long time? (*Hint*: try values around $a = 1.7$ and $b = 10^{-3}$ as a start.)

3 Let the number of cars on the road in the UK in the year $1974 + n$ be u_n. Old cars are scrapped, old and new are smashed in collisions or by TV stunt crews, so that there is a total loss of cars in each year which we may guess to be cu_n (with c between 0 and 1). However new cars also come on to the roads; let us suppose that about 1.8×10^6 new cars are arriving each year. Make some choices for u_0 and c and predict the total number of cars on the road five years from now.

4 In fact information on u_n and the number of new cars is collected each year, by the Society of Motor Manufacturers and Traders.

Date	1974	1975	1976	1977	1978	1979	1980	1981	1982	1983	1984
New ($\times 10^6$)	1.269	1.194	1.286	1.324	1.592	1.716	1.514	1.485	1.555	1.792	1.750
Population ($\times 10^6$)	13.95	14.06	14.372	—	14.42	14.93	15.44	15.63	16.08	16.61	17.31

Can you get a reasonable fit with a model of the form

$$u_{n+1} = (1-c)u_n + 1.2 + 0.05n$$

where the term $1.2 + 0.05n$ represents the new cars?

1.4   INSTABILITY IN ITERATIONS

When you use a computer or a calculator you can sometimes be totally surprised by the answers that you get after many iterations. This is best shown by an example.

Example 3

I programmed the iteration

$$\begin{cases} u_{n+1} = nu_n - n/(n+1) \\ \quad u_1 = 1 \end{cases}$$

on my *Casio fx*-700P. The first few results I got were

$$u_2 = 0.5 \quad u_3 = 0.3333\ldots \quad u_4 = 0.25$$

$$u_5 = 0.2 \quad u_6 = 0.1666\ldots \quad \text{and so on.}$$

Clearly what is being given is the solution

$$u_n = 1/n,$$

which you can show easily to be correct:

$$n \times 1/n - n/(n+1) = 1/(n+1)$$

$$= u_{n+1}.$$

But when I persevered with the iteration, I reached the surprising results (after lots of apparently correct ones):

$$u_{40} = -0.2236\ldots$$

$$u_{41} = -9.9231\ldots$$

$$u_{42} = -407.82\ldots$$

and after that the values became huge and negative.

Thus the calculator/computer gave the wrong values; moreover a different calculator/computer will not necessarily give you the same wrong values. I put the same program into my *Casio fx*-7000G and found

$$u_{40} = 20\,936.603\,61,$$

again after all the values up to u_{30} were correct, or very nearly so.
Even worse was to follow. I re-programmed the 7000G with

$$u_{n+1} = n(u_n - (n+1)^{-1})$$

instead of

$$u_{n+1} = nu_n - n(n+1)^{-1}$$

and got different answers again:

$$u_{18} = \quad 1.17139\ldots$$

$$u_{19} = \quad 20.1377\ldots$$

$$u_{20} = 381.666\ldots$$

We describe this sort of behaviour as 'instability'. More precisely, the iteration

$$\begin{cases} u_{n+1} = f(n)u_n + g(n) \\ \quad u_k = \text{a given value } U \text{ for some } k \end{cases}$$

is unstable if a small change in U leads to a large change in u_n.
Two questions arise naturally here:

(i)   how can we tell in advance if such an iteration is going to be unstable?
(ii) where did the small change in U arise in the example?

These two questions will be answered, one in the next chapter when we see how to solve iterations of this sort, and the other in Chapter 3 when we investigate how computers do arithmetic.

Exercise 1E

1   The iteration

$$\begin{cases} u_{n+1} = 2u_n - 1 \\ \quad u_0 = 1 \end{cases}$$

clearly has the solution $u_n = 1$ for all n. Test it for stability by using the alternative starting values

(i) $u_0 = 1 + 10^{-10}$ (ii) $u_0 = 1 - 10^{-10}$,

and running as far as u_{40} in each case.

2   Run the iteration

$$\begin{cases} u_{n+1} = nu_n - n/(n+1) \\ \quad u_1 = 1 + 10^{-10} \end{cases}$$

on a computer to verify that the iteration done in Example 3 was unstable according to the definition given.

3   Determine whether the following iterations are stable or unstable.

(i) $u_{n+1} = \frac{1}{2}u_n + 1$, $u_0 = 2$;
(ii) $v_{n+1} = \cos v_n$, $v_0 = 1$;
(iii) $w_{n+1} = n^2 w_n - n + 1/(n+1)$, $w_1 = 1$.

Note that the iteration in (ii) is of the more general form $v_{n+1} = f(v_n)$, but the definition of stability can easily be extended.

1.5   SUMMARY

There are several ideas you should take forward from this chapter.

(i) *Iteration*: stepping forward according to some formula.

(ii) *A model*: an attempt to describe some aspect of reality with tolerably simple mathematics.

(iii) *Instability*: some iterations may have a mathematically exact solution which cannot be found by computers.

You should also leave this chapter having had some practice both on your calculator and on a computer; you will be glad of it later.

2
Solving first order linear difference equations

2.1 PRELIMINARIES

This chapter is concerned with finding solution formulas for equations of the form

$$\begin{cases} u_{n+1} = k(n)u_n + c(n), \\ \text{with } u_0 \text{ or } u_1 \text{ given.} \end{cases} \tag{A}$$

In this equation $k(n)$ and $c(n)$ denote functions of n which are given; they will usually be easy functions, because the methods become intolerably complicated when they are not. Often, in fact, we shall consider $k(n)$ to be a constant; and $c(n)$ will rarely be more difficult than a quadratic in n.

You might think that these days there is little need to find solution formulas, since any given equation can be programmed easily on a computer, which will then generate the solution values. This is partly true, and in cases where a solution formula cannot be found easily, a computer solution will often be used. But there are four good reasons for seeking solution formulas as well.

(i) Computer solutions may not work, due to instability, as described in Section 1.4.

(ii) It is easier to investigate the structure and meaning of a solution formula than to investigate a large collection of numbers.

(iii) Many problems can be solved at once by means of a solution formula, whereas computer solutions must be done one-by-one.

(iv) Algebraic methods can show up valuable similarities between different areas of mathematics.

The equation in (A) above is called 'first order' because only u_{n+1} and u_n enter it, with suffixes differing by one. The equation

$$u_{n+1} = u_n - u_{n-1}$$

is an example of a second order equation: the greatest difference between suffixes is two, between $n+1$ and $n-1$. Second and higher order equations are also important, but we can get many of the major ideas by considering first order equations.

The equation in (A) is also called 'linear' because u_{n+1} and u_n appear separately and to the first power; there are no terms in u_n^2, or in $u_{n+1}u_n$, or in $\cos u_n$, and so on. For example

$$u_{n+1} = 2/u_n$$

is not linear, as u_n appears to the -1th power; similarly

$$v_{n+1} = \sqrt{(1+v_n)}$$

is not linear. But

$$a_{n+1} = 2000a_n/(1000+n^2)$$

is linear – you only look at how a_{n+1} and a_n come in, not at the function of n that multiplies a_n.

The equation in (A) is also called a 'difference equation', because it is about values of a function u_n where the integers n have a difference of one between them.

The words and ideas from this chapter will be used again repeatedly in later work. There will be second order linear difference equations; there will be first order linear differential equations, and also second order ones; there will be linear simultaneous equations. For all of these there will be important mathematical aspects in common, so this chapter is vital as a basis for later understanding.

Exercise 2A

1   Find a second order linear difference equation in Exercise 1A, question 4.
2   Find a non-linear difference equation in Section 1.3. What is its order?

2.2   TWO EXAMPLES

We shall approach the theory by way of two examples, the first numerical and the second algebraic. Numerical examples are often best done by calculator or computer, but in this case we shall do it 'by hand', to show how the calculations work.

Example 1

I need to borrow £50 000 to buy a flat; the current rate of interest is 10% (and I shall suppose I am borrowing on a fixed rate mortgage, so that this is a constant rate), and I can afford to pay £500 per month to the building society. How does my debt to them change with time?

I shall take one year as the unit of time, with interest added at the end of each year, and £1000 as the unit of money.

At the beginning of the first year I owe 50 (units of a thousand pounds), during that year I pay in 6, and at the end of the year interest of 5 is added to my debt. So at the end of the first year I owe

$$50 \times 1.1 - 6.$$

Introducing u_n to mean my debt at the end of year n,

$$u_1 = 50 \times 1.1 - 6.$$

Carry on the calculation similarly: at the end of the second year I owe

$$u_2 = (50 \times 1.1 - 6) \times 1.1 - 6,$$

and at the end of the third year my debt is

$$u_3 = \{(50 \times 1.1 - 6) \times 1.1 - 6\} \times 1.1 - 6$$
$$= 50 \times 1.1^3 - 6(1 + 1.1 + 1.1^2).$$

It looks as though

$$u_n = 50 \times 1.1^n - 6(1 + 1.1 + 1.1^2 + \ldots + 1.1^{n-1})$$

is the general result here. The difference equation appropriate for this situation is clearly

$$\begin{cases} u_{n+1} = 1.1u_n - 6, \\ \text{with } u_0 = 50, \end{cases}$$

the $1.1u_n$ giving the increase in the debt due to a 10% interest rate, and the -6 being the repayment.

Now, using the formula for the sum of a geometric progression,

$$1 + 1.1 + 1.1^2 + \ldots + 1.1^{n-1} = \frac{1.1^n - 1}{0.1},$$

so that

$$u_n = (50 - 60) \times 1.1^n + 60.$$

That is,

$$u_n = -10 \times 1.1^n + 60$$

is the solution formula for the first order linear difference equation

$$\begin{cases} u_{n+1} = 1.1u_n - 6 \\ \quad u_0 = 50. \end{cases}$$

Note the following points, which will be needed later:

(i) the coefficient 1.1 of u_n in the equation returns as the power 1.1^n in the solution;
(ii) the -6 in the equation returns, as 60, in the solution;
(iii) the initial value 50 was used in getting the coefficient of 1.1^n in the solution.

Example 2

A drug is administered to a patient every four hours. If the concentration in his blood is u_n just after the absorption of the nth dose (which is typically quite quick), then the body's biochemistry reduces the concentration to

$$ku_n$$

(where k lies between 0 and 1), just before the next dose. If the dose increases the concentration (every time the dose is given) by an amount c, then you have the equation

$$u_{n+1} = ku_n + c.$$

What needs to be known is what level is reached two or three days after the start of a course of treatment, and whether you could reach this level more quickly by starting with a double (or triple) dose.

To start with we assume the patient has a residual level (at one time-step before treatment is started)

$$u_0 = d$$

in his body from previous treatment (we can always put $d = 0$ if there has been no previous treatment). After one dose, using the difference equation, you get

$$u_1 = kd + c.$$

Keep going like this: after the second dose the level is

$$u_2 = k(kd + c) + c,$$

and after the third dose it is

$$u_3 = k\{k(kd + c) + c\} + c$$
$$= k^3 d + c(1 + k + k^2).$$

As in the last example, the form of the solution is now clear:

$$u_n = k^n d + c(1 + k + k^2 + \ldots + k^{n-1}),$$

which as before gives

$$u_n = k^n d + c\frac{1 - k^n}{1 - k}$$

since in this case $0 < k < 1$ so that $1 - k^n > 0$. Rearranging this gives

$$u_n = \left(d - \frac{c}{1-k}\right)k^n + \frac{c}{1-k}$$

as the solution of the difference equation

$$\begin{cases} u_{n+1} = ku_n + c \\ \quad u_0 = d. \end{cases}$$

This shows very clearly the roles of k, c and d in the difference equation.

Just as in the last example:

(i) the variation of u_n with n is through k^n,
(ii) the constant c returns in the constant $c/(1-k)$ in the solution,
(iii) the initial value d only appears in the coefficient of k^n.

Exercise 2B

1   Verify that

$$-10 \times 1.1^n + 60$$

satisfies both the equation

$$u_{n+1} = 1.1u_n - 6$$

and the initial condition $u_0 = 50$.

2   Similarly verify that

$$\left(d - \frac{c}{1-k}\right)k^n + \frac{c}{1-k}$$

is a correct solution to the equation in Example 2.

3   In Example 1, when is my debt to the building society equal to zero?

4   Usually building societies lend for 20 years, and adjust the monthly repayment to achieve zero debt at the end of the 20th year. If I borrowed £P at rate $r\%$, determine an equation for my monthly repayment £c.

5   For penicillin at dosages of around 10^6 'units' the value of k in Example 2 may be taken as $1/15$. Show that

$$u_n \approx 15c/14$$

for $n \geqslant 3$, provided that d is not large.

6   A longer lasting drug has $k = 3/4$. Compare the times taken to reach a minimum concentration of $2.5c$ in the blood for the two dosage systems:
   (i) $d = 0$, then a double dose, then another double dose, thereafter single doses;
   (ii) $d = 0$, then a triple dose, thereafter single doses.

2.3   COMPLEMENTARY FUNCTIONS AND PARTICULAR SOLUTIONS

Let us start again from the two examples above, and draw out some general results from what we have done.

In Example 1 we solved the problem

$$\begin{cases} u_{n+1} = 1.1u_n - 6 \\ \quad u_0 = 50, \end{cases}$$

finding that its solution was

$$u_n = -10 \times 1.1^n + 60.$$

I wish to point out four things here:

(i) $u_n = 60$ satisfies the equation

$$u_{n+1} = 1.1u_n - 6$$

but *not* the initial condition $u_0 = 50$;

(ii) $v_n = -10 \times 1.1^n$ satisfies a *reduced* equation

$$v_{n+1} = 1.1v_n;$$

(iii) the reduced equation is satisfied by

$$v_n = A \times 1.1^n$$

for any value of A;
(iv) it is only the combination

$$-10 \times 1.1^n + 60$$

that satisfies both the equation

$$u_{n+1} = 1.1u_n - 6$$

and the initial condition $u_0 = 50$.

Four similar statements are true for the case of the problem

$$\begin{cases} u_{n+1} = ku_n + c \\ \quad u_0 = d, \end{cases}$$

which was solved in Example 2.

(i) $u_n = c/(1-k)$ satisfies the equation

$$u_{n+1} = ku_n + c,$$

as you can check by substitution.

(ii) $v_n = \left(d - \dfrac{c}{1-k} \right) k^n$ satisfies the reduced equation

$$v_{n+1} = kv_n,$$

which again is easily checked by substitution.
(iii) In fact

$$v_n = Ak^n$$

satisfies the reduced equation for any A.
(iv) Only the combination

$$\left(d - \frac{c}{1-k} \right) k^n + \frac{c}{1-k}$$

satisfies both

$$u_{n+1} = ku_n + c$$

and the initial condition $u_0 = d$.

These examples, and many more like them, suggest that it will be a good move to consider the problem in three parts as follows (using Example 2 to show what is going on),

$$\begin{cases} u_{n+1} = ku_n + c \\ u_0 = d. \end{cases}$$

(a) Write down the *homogeneous equation*

$$v_{n+1} = kv_n,$$

which is found by missing out all the terms that do not involve the unknown in the equation, and then replacing u_n by v_n. The solution of this is

$$v_n = Ak^n$$

for any A, and is called the *complementary function* of the original equation.
(b) Find any *particular solution* of the full equation. In Examples 1 and 2 the particular solution was just a constant, and it could be found easily by substituting

$$u_n = D$$

(say) into the original equation, giving a value for D. For example in Example 2 this substitution gives

$$D = kD + c$$

so that $D = c/(1-k)$, as before.
(c) The *general solution* is then given as the sum of the complementary function and the particular solution. This is often written as

$$GS = CF + PS$$

for short, as the words are rather long!

You then find the value of the constant A by using the initial condition on u_0, and putting $n = 0$ into the GS. In Example 2 this gives us

$$u_0 = d = Ak^0 + D$$
$$= A + c/(1-k)$$

so that

$$A = d - c/(1-k)$$

and the (previously found) solution returns:

$$u_n = \left(d - \frac{c}{1-k}\right)k^n + \frac{c}{1-k}.$$

This method has a wide application, not only here but also in dealing with

higher order linear difference equations
linear differential equations
linear integral equations
linear algebraic equations

in fact anywhere that linearity comes in. The terminology of

complementary function
homogeneous equation
particular solution
general solution

is not completely uniform through all these areas, but the ideas are the same in all the subjects.

2.4   TWO MORE EXAMPLES

The ideas in Section 2.3 are hardly needed to solve the examples that we worked through about debt repayment and drug dosage. It is when k and c in the equation

$$u_{n+1} = ku_n + c$$

are *not* constants that the separation of the problem into three parts is a great help. Even then the determination of a particular solution may be hard if c is not a simple function of n.

The related homogeneous equation is

$$v_{n+1} = k(n)v_n,$$

that is, you keep the terms with suffixes $n+1$ and n, but not the part which has neither of them. The complementary function of this equation can be found rather easily, as follows. Clearly (putting $n=0$)

$$v_1 = k(0)v_0$$

where $k(0)$ is known for any given function k, and where v_0 is the initial value. Then (putting $n=1$)

$$v_2 = k(1)v_1 = k(1)k(0)v_0$$

so that v_2 is also known. In this manner we can build up to any term, and get

$$v_n = k(n-1)k(n-2)\ldots k(1)k(0)v_0.$$

Since the initial value for this sequence is not known, we write the complementary function as

$$v_n = Ck(n-1)k(n-2)\ldots k(1)k(0),$$

where C is some constant which is fixed later from the conditions in the problem. What we have shown is that the complementary function for such an equation can *always* be found, as a long product of values of the function k.

Example 3

We shall solve

$$\begin{cases} u_{n+1} = \dfrac{n}{n+1}u_n + \dfrac{1}{n+1}, \\ u_1 = 3. \end{cases}$$

(a) The homogeneous equation is

$$v_{n+1} = \frac{n}{n+1}v_n.$$

Using the method shown above gives, in turn,

$$v_2 = \tfrac{1}{2}v_1$$

$$v_3 = \tfrac{2}{3}v_2 = \tfrac{2}{3} \times \tfrac{1}{2}v_1 = \tfrac{1}{3}v_1$$

$$v_4 = \tfrac{3}{4}v_3 = \tfrac{1}{4}v_1$$

$$\ldots$$

$$v_n = \frac{1}{n}v_1.$$

Notice that here I did *not* start with v_0: it would have given the useless equation

$$v_1 = 0 \times v_0.$$

You always have to use your judgement, even when a method seems to be totally straightforward.

The complementary function here is therefore

$$v_n = C/n,$$

for any constant C.

(*b*) How shall I find a particular solution of this equation? At this stage the page should go blank while you spend five minutes guessing one (it can't be too hard, or it wouldn't be put in here …).

Okay, the answer is that $u_n = 1$ is a particular solution.

There is a very real problem here: if we changed roles and *you* chose a function $c(n)$ to put at the end of the equation, and *I* tried to guess a particular solution, then I should probably fail. There *are* advanced methods for finding the particular solution, and you will meet related (but easier) methods later for differential equations.

(*c*) We now have a general solution

$$u_n = C/n + 1,$$

and the initial condition gives, putting $n = 1$,

$$u_1 = 3 = C + 1,$$

so that $C = 2$. The problem is now solved:

$$u_n = 2/n + 1.$$

Example 4

Next we solve

$$\begin{cases} u_{n+1} = nu_n - n/(n+1) \\ \quad u_1 = 1, \end{cases}$$

which is an equation we saw to be unstable in Section 1.4.

(*a*) The homogeneous equation is

$$v_{n+1} = nv_n,$$

which has solution

$$v_n = C(n-1)!$$

by the method used above. The 'factorial function' is on your calculator, and is defined by

$$n! = n(n-1)(n-2)\dots 3 \times 2 \times 1,$$

with the convention that $0! = 1$.

(b) A particular solution of the equation is

$$u_n = 1/n,$$

because

$$\frac{1}{n+1} = n \times \frac{1}{n} - \frac{n}{n+1}.$$

(c) The general solution is therefore

$$u_n = C(n-1)! + 1/n.$$

Fitting the condition

$$u_1 = 1$$

gives $C = 0$, so that the solution of the problem is

$$u_n = 1/n.$$

The instability of this solution is caused by the very large size of $(n-1)!$ when n increases:

$$n = 15,\ 14! = 8.7 \times 10^{10},$$

$$n = 20,\ 19! = 1.2 \times 10^{17},$$

$$n = 25,\ 24! = 6.2 \times 10^{23}.$$

Thus if even a very small error is made in the calculation of $1/n$, this can be vastly amplified by multiplication by the factorial function.

Why does this general method always work? Let us take v_n to be a CF satisfying the equation

$$v_{n+1} = k(n)v_n,$$

with initial value C, and let w_n be a PS of the full equation, so that

$$w_{n+1} = k(n)w_n + c(n).$$

Then

$$v_{n+1} + w_{n+1} = k(n)(v_n + w_n) + c(n),$$

so that $u_n = v_n + w_n$ satisfies the full equation, and we can choose the value of C so as to fit any required value at $n=0$ or $n=1$. Hence we have indeed found a solution to the original problem. The difficulty remains of finding the PS, and we discuss this in more detail for some cases, in the next section.

Exercise 2C

1   The mortgage rate rises to 15% while you still owe £38k (i.e. £38 000) to the building society.

   (*a*)   if you can only repay £$\frac{1}{2}$k per month, how long will you have to go on paying?

   (*b*)   If the building society insists on repayment in 15 years, how much must you pay per month?

2   You pay £c per month into a pension fund, which credits interest at r% at the end of each year on your fund at the *start* of the year.

   (*a*)   How much is held in your name at the end of a working life of 40 years?

   (*b*)   The pension fund now pays you an annuity of £A per month, basing its calculations on

      (i)   receiving interest of r% at the end of each year on the balance then remaining,

      (ii)   the expectation that you will die at the end of 15 years.

Determine A in terms of c and r, and show that if $r = 3$ and you require $A = 1000$, then c needs to be 163.08. (An interest rate of 3% *above inflation* is quite realistic.)

3   Verify that the equation

$$u_{n+1} = (n+1)^{-1}u_n + n + 1$$

has particular solution $n + 1$. Solve the equation given that $u_1 = 1$.

4   Solve the equation

$$u_{n+1} = nu_n - n/(n+1)$$

with $u_9 = \frac{1}{9} - 10^{-13}$. When does u_n differ by more than 1 from $1/n$?

5   Find general solutions for

   (*a*) $u_{n+1} = 1 - u_n$

   (*b*) $u_{n+1} = (n+1)u_n + (n+1)!$.

In each case find the solution which has $u_0 = 1$, and hence find u_{10}.

6   Suppose that *both* V_n and W_n satisfy the problem

$$\begin{cases} u_{n+1} = k(n)u_n + c(n) \\ u_0 = r. \end{cases}$$

Show that U_n defined as $V_n - W_n$ satisfies the problem

$$\begin{cases} U_{n+1} = k(n)U_n \\ U_0 = 0. \end{cases}$$

Hence deduce that a first order linear difference equation has a *unique* solution, so that however you find a solution, it is bound to be the correct one. This 'uniqueness theorem' is a first example of theorems of this type; they can be proved in all areas of mathematics which are linear.

2.5   THE PARTICULAR SOLUTION

In the last section there was no difficulty in finding a formula for the complementary function, but no method was given for finding the particular solution. We face the problem now. In fact we can only find particular solutions easily for

$$u_{n+1} = k(n)u_n + c(n)$$

in very simple or special cases. However, we can usually make progress in the simpler case when k is a constant

$$u_{n+1} = ku_n + c(n),$$

at least when $c(n)$ is a reasonably simple function.

The methods available are

(*a*) use the equation to calculate u_1, u_2, u_3, u_4 and see if we can see any pattern emerging;
(*b*) use intelligent guesswork (where I must stress the intelligence);
(*c*) build up some experience of what solution fits what equation by starting with some solutions and then deducing which equations they fit.

This all seems unsatisfactorily vague; unfortunately there is no better way available at an elementary level, and in fact these methods do provide a number of useful solutions. When you get on to differential equations you will find that the corresponding problem is much simpler, though it is still often easiest to use intelligent guesswork.

Let us see how it works in practice. When we solved

$$u_{n+1} = ku_n + c$$

in Section 2.2, we used method (*a*): we guessed the answer after calculating u_1, u_2, and u_3. Could we have done it by intelligent guesswork? Well, perhaps not yet, because we do not have the experience to base a guess on. What you should notice at this stage is that the constant c on the right hand side leads to a *constant*

$$c/(1-k)$$

as the particular solution, at least in the case $k \neq 1$. Once you notice it, it should be obvious: if $u_n = a$ is the particular solution, then $u_{n+1} = a$ also, and the equation reduces to

$$a = ka + c,$$

or

$$a = c/(1-k).$$

What about the same equation with $k = 1$? The answer can't be a constant, because you would get

$$a = a + c,$$

which doesn't determine a. Back to method (*a*):

$$u_1 = u_0 + c,$$

$$u_2 = u_1 + c = u_0 + 2c,$$

$$u_3 = u_2 + c = u_0 + 3c,$$

and so on.

It looks as though the particular solution is just

$$u_n = nc,$$

and it is not hard to verify that this is indeed the case by substituting:

$$(n+1)c = nc + c.$$

The special case here has given an extra n in the answer.

Try another example:

$$u_{n+1} = ku_n + cn.$$

Pause for a moment before you go on. Can you guess (intelligently) what the particular solution might be? If not we must use method (a) again.

$$u_1 = ku_0.$$

$$u_2 = ku_1 + c = k^2u_0 + c.$$

$$u_3 = ku_2 + 2c = k^3u_0 + kc + 2c.$$

$$u_4 = ku_3 + 3c = k^4u_0 + k^2c + 2kc + 3c.$$

$$u_5 = ku_4 + 4c = k^5u_0 + k^3c + 2k^2c + 3kc + 4c.$$

By this stage I hope that you can see that *one* particular solution is

$$u_n = k^{n-2}c + 2k^{n-3}c + \ldots + (n-2)kc + (n-1)c.$$

Certainly that fits all the cases $n=1$, $n=2, \ldots, n=5$ which we have calculated. This seems to be a hopeless mess, but it can be proved that

$$k^{n-2} + 2k^{n-3} + \ldots + (n-2)k + (n-1)$$

$$= \frac{k^n}{(k-1)^2} - \frac{1}{(k-1)^2} - \frac{n}{(k-1)}$$

for $k \neq 1$. The easiest way of proving this result is by multiplying each side by $(k-1)^2$; you will find that most of the terms on the left cancel out, leaving just

$$k^n - 1 - n(k-1).$$

Alternatively this result can be proved by the method of mathematical induction. We can now rewrite our particular solution as

$$Ak^n + Bn + C$$

where the constants A, B, C are given by

$$\begin{cases} A = (1-k)^{-2}c \\ B = (1-k)^{-1}c \\ C = -(1-k)^{-2}c. \end{cases}$$

If you look back to the values u_1 to u_5 calculated above, you will see that there is already a term k^nu_0 occurring in the solution. The term Ak^n can be combined with k^nu_0 to give a complementary function Dk^n for some constant D.

Thus we have found a particular solution whose form is

$$(Bn+C)c.$$

Should you have been able to guess this, and so avoid all that work? Perhaps. What has happened is that the term not in u_n or n_{n+1}, which was nc, has led to a rather similar particular solution $(Bn+C)c$.

One more calculation before we try to generalise. The last piece of work had to be restricted to $k \neq 1$, because of the terms in $1/(1-k)$ in the answers. So what about the case $k=1$? If you can't guess what form to use for the particular solution, then we must use method (a) again, on

$$u_{n+1}=u_n+cn.$$

Working as before gives

$$u_n=u_0+c+2c+3c+4c+ \ldots +(n-1)c.$$

The terms in c add up, by taking them in pairs (c with $(n-1)c$, $2c$ with $(n-2)c$, and so on), to give

$$u_n=u_0+\tfrac{1}{2}n(n-1)c.$$

The particular solution part of this expression is

$$\tfrac{1}{2}n(n-1)c;$$

in other words, in this special case the linear term cn has led to a quadratic particular solution $\tfrac{1}{2}n(n-1)c$.

Method (b), the method of intelligent guesswork, can now be stated:

(i) look at the term (the one not in u_n) that is creating the particular solution;
(ii) try something with some as yet unknown coefficients in it, that is closely related to the term in (i);
(iii) substitute in to the original equation to find the coefficients;
(iv) if you seem to have a special case, go back to (ii), but with an extra n in what you try;
(v) if it still doesn't seem to be working, try a little more intelligence.

This method will very often give you the answer quickly; sometimes it will not work, and you will have to try methods (a) or (c).

Let us do an example. We will find the particular solution for

$$u_{n+1}=5u_n+3n+2.$$

(i) The term without u_{n+1} or u_n is $3n+2$.
(ii) Try $u_n=an+b$ as a particular solution.
(iii) Substitution gives

$$a(n+1)+b=5(an+b)+3n+2,$$

or

$$n(a-5a-3)+(a+b-5b-2)=0.$$

Now this has to be true for all n, as we are looking for a solution u_n that holds for all n, so each of the two brackets must be zero (if you don't follow this, consider the two cases $n=0$ and $n=1$, for which the equation must hold).

This gives you two equations for a and b, with solution

$$\begin{cases} a = -\frac{3}{4} \\ b = -\frac{11}{16}, \end{cases}$$

and so the particular solution is $-\frac{3}{4}n - \frac{11}{16}$. To get the general solution of course you add on the complementary function

$$A \times 5^n.$$

Try another example. Find the particular solution for

$$u_{n+1} = u_n + 3n + 2.$$

Suppose you try $an + b$ as a particular solution; then you must have

$$a(n+1) + b = an + b + 3n + 2,$$

for all n. This reduces to

$$3n - a + 2 = 0,$$

for all n, which cannot be satisfied (try $n=0$ and $n=1$ to check this). This is therefore a case of (iv) in the method of intelligent guesswork, and hence we must try

$$u_n = pn^2 + qn + r.$$

Substituting this formula into the equation gives

$$p(n+1)^2 + q(n+1) = pn^2 + qn + 3n + 2$$

for all values of n. This can be rewritten as

$$n^2(p-p) + n(2p + q - q - 3) + (p + q - 2) = 0.$$

Since it is true for all values of n (e.g. 0 and 1) you can find p and q

$$p = \frac{3}{2},\ q = \frac{1}{2}.$$

Notice that r is not determined like this; the complementary function in the case $k=1$ already contains a constant into which r can be assimilated. The general solution for the case $k=1$ is

$$u_n = A + \frac{3}{2}n^2 + \frac{1}{2}n.$$

Exercise 2D

1   Use the method of intelligent guesswork to find particular solutions for:
   (i) $u_{n+1} = 3u_n + n^2$,
   (ii) $u_{n+1} = u_n + n^2 - 1$.

2   Find the first five terms in the two equations in question 1, using $u_0 = 1$ as starting value. Solve the equations with this initial condition, and check your answers by comparing them with the terms you have found.

3   Use the method of intelligent guesswork to find particular solutions for:

(i) $u_{n+1} = -2u_n + a^n$ for $a \neq -2$,

(ii) $u_{n+1} = 2u_n + 2^n$.

You may want to work out the first few terms in each case before guessing.

4   Solve

(i) $u_{n+1} = 4u_n + \sin(\frac{1}{2}n\pi)$, $u_0 = 1$;

(ii) $u_{n+1} = u_n + \cos(\frac{1}{2}n\pi)$, $u_0 = 0$.

5   (i) Solve

$$u_{n+1} = 10u_n - n, \ u_0 = \tfrac{1}{81}.$$

(ii) Compare your results with a computer (or calculator) iteration.

(iii) Discuss the results.

6   (i) Solve the equation in Exercise 1D, question 4.

(ii) Solve the equation in Exercise 1E, question 1, for each of the alternative starting values, and show that the sum of the solutions is 2 for all n.

2.6   SUMMARY

The only first order linear difference equations that have turned out to be easy to solve are those of the form

$$u_{n+1} = ku_n + \text{easy function of } n,$$

where the easy functions of n are:

(i)   polynomials like $a + bn + cn^2$,

(ii) powers a^n,

(iii) cosines or sines.

I have found you a few other equations that can be solved in reasonably simple terms; I found them mainly by using what I called method (c) – start with the solution and find what equation it satisfies. Generally speaking the equation

$$u_{n+1} = k(n)u_n + c(n)$$

is too hard for us, and we will have to rely on a computer solution.

You need to take forward some definitions of words from this chapter:

(i) *linear*: u_n, u_{n+1} (and so on) occur as first powers only in the equation.

(ii) *first order*: the suffixes have maximum difference one.

(iii) *difference equation*: an equation involving u_n, u_{n+1}, u_{n-1} and so on.

(iv) *homogeneous equation*: miss out the terms not involving the unknown in a linear difference equation.

(v) *complementary function*: a solution of a homogeneous equation, including an (as yet) unknown constant.

(vi) *particular solution*: *any* solution of the full equation.

(vii) *general solution*: complementary function plus particular solution.

(viii) *intelligent guesswork*.

3

Numbers in computers

3.1 INTRODUCTION

Calculators do not all give the *same* answer when you do nasty pieces of arithmetic on them, and they certainly do not give *correct* answers. As I write I have four electronic calculating devices on the table. In order of increasing complexity they are:

(i) a time-piece (watch, alarm clock and stop watch) which also has a four-function calculator built into it. I shall call this 'my watch';
(ii) a scientific calculator (*Casio fx*-120) with all the usual functions, including some statistical ones. I shall call this 'my calculator';
(iii) a programmable calculator (*Casio fx*-700P) which uses BASIC, has 26 memories and allows you to write the sort of short programs needed in this book. I shall call this 'my computer', because I shall be using it mainly as that;
(iv) a graphics calculator (*Casio fx*-7000G) which displays graphs (and text), can take short programs (but not in BASIC) and which has all the usual functions (including statistical). I shall call this my 'graphics calculator', as I shall rarely use it for programming.

These generally give *different* answers for the same calculation. The example I shall use here is

$$(\sqrt{\pi})^2 - \pi.$$

The answer given by the various machines follow.

(i) After I gave it $\sqrt{\pi} = 1.7724538$, my watch did the multiplication. I then subtracted 3.1415926 from 3.1415924 (its answer) and was given 0 as the result!
(ii) My calculator gave

$$(\sqrt{\pi})^2 - \pi = -1 \times 10^{-9}.$$

(iii) My computer gave

$$(\sqrt{\pi})^2 - \pi = -5 \times 10^{-11}$$

when no intermediate answers were asked for. However, when I asked for $(\sqrt{\pi})^2$ and then subtracted π, I was given

$$(\sqrt{\pi})^2 - \pi = 4 \times 10^{-10}.$$

(iv) The graphics calculator gave

$$(\sqrt{\pi})^2 - \pi = -3 \times 10^{-12}$$

from a single calculation; but if $(\sqrt{\pi})^2$ was calculated first I was given

$$(\sqrt{\pi})^2 - \pi = 4.1 \times 10^{-10}.$$

The moral here is *not* to use a cheap calculator for everything, but to be aware that all answers given by calculators and computers are wrong, and depend on what machine you use and how you arrange the calculation. Your calculator(s) or computer are likely to give *different* answers from mine. We must hope to develop methods which will ensure that

(*a*) our answers are very close to each others',
(*b*) they are very close to the real answer.

This chapter gives a start on controlling errors, by understanding how they arise, and how they can get large.

Exercise 3A

Use any calculators and computers you can to calculate $(\sqrt{\pi})^2 - \pi$, with and without an intermediate display of $(\sqrt{\pi})^2$.

3.2   ARITHMETIC ON A CRUDE CALCULATOR

One Sunday morning I noticed on the marmalade jar in a friend's house the numbers giving the contents of the jar:

340 g   12 oz
255 ml   9 fl oz.

I recognised (being used to old fashioned units) that each column gave the density of the marmalade (relative to water); I wondered if each column gave the same value.

My watch was lying on the table, so I calculated the ratio of densities

$$(12 \times 255)/(9 \times 340).$$

With a calculator you have to choose what order you do the operations in (ordinary arithmetic is *associative*, in other words the order doesn't matter), and I did them as

$$[\{\tfrac{1}{9}/340\} \times 12] \times 255,$$

working from left to right. The display on the calculator then read

$$0.999\,702.$$

'The stupid manufacturer', I thought, 'he couldn't convert fl oz to ml accurately'. Since the Sunday paper hadn't arrived, I went on playing with my watch, and recalculated the answer as

$$\{\tfrac{12}{9}/340\} \times 255.$$

This gave me the display

$$0.999\,982\,5.$$

Light now dawned: if you factorise 340 and 255 you can show that the answer is exactly 1. So there must be something in the way that such cheap calculators operate that causes the answer to come out wrong. To find out what it was I did the operations one by one, noting the display each time.

$$\tfrac{1}{9} = 0.111\,111\,1,$$

and divide by 340 to get

$$0.000\,326\,7;$$

next multiply by 12

$$0.003\,920\,4,$$

and multiply by 255

$$0.999\,702.$$

At each stage the calculator held no extra digits in its memory, as I checked by multiplying by 10. So when the display is $0.000\,326\,7$ there are only *four* significant figures left, and the last one of them is not really correct, as you can see by using a 'proper' calculator:

$$\tfrac{1}{9}/340 = 3.267\,973\,8 \times 10^{-4}.$$

The memory also holds an extra two digits, as I found when I multiplied by 10^4 and got

$$3.267\,973\,855.$$

There are no more digits held; if you subtract 3.26 and multiply by 100 all you get is

$$0.797\,385\,5.$$

So with this order for the operations, using my watch as a calculator cannot give an answer that has more than four correct digits.

Nobody, I hope, would use a watch as a calculator to do any serious calculations. The example shows that electronic calculation need not give totally correct results, and we must investigate a little what it is that goes on in the calculator or computer, so as to be aware of the dangers.

Exercise 3B

1   What order of operations will give the best result from such a crude calculator?

2   Find the largest number whose square will be displayed as zero on this calculator.

3   Show that multiplication on this calculator is not associative, by calculating

$$0.0003 \times 0.0003 \times 2$$

in two ways.

3.3 ROUNDING AND CHOPPING

My calculator informs me that

$$\tfrac{1}{77} = 0.012\,987\,012\,(98),$$

where the two figures in brackets are held in memory, as I found by multiplying by 100. From this I deduce that it holds 10 significant digits and uses them in calculations even if it is not displaying them all.

My computer (programmable calculator) says that

$$\tfrac{1}{77} = 0.012\,987\,012\,9(9),$$

with one reserve digit. It too uses 10 significant digits, but you will notice that the last one is not the same for the two machines. My graphics calculator gives the same result as the computer with all the digits displayed.

You cannot write the full decimal form of $\tfrac{1}{77}$ as it is infinitely long, but it starts off as

$$0.012\,987\,012\,987\,012\ldots$$

You can see that my calculator has just chopped off the digits after the ten that it uses (chopping off digits is also called *truncation* of the value), whereas my computer (programmable calculator) has chosen its last digit to give the best approximation to the true value. The computer, by rounding the last digit it uses, has ensured that its maximum error is as small as possible; in the example of $\tfrac{100}{77}$ you can be sure the error is no more than 5×10^{-10}. The calculator on the other hand, could have an error of up to 10^{-9}. This doesn't mean that the calculator always produces a much worse answer. For the calculation of

$$\tfrac{15}{999} \times 100$$

the displays were

calculator	1.501 501 501
computer	1.501 501 502
with correct value	1.501 501 501 501 ...

Each is in error by about 5×10^{-10}, one by chopping off digits and one by rounding. The errors in this case are in opposite directions.

There is one further comment to be made about rounding of numbers to a given length, and that is about the treatment of numbers ending in the digit 5. In theory it would be best to round half of these up and half down (as recommended in *British Standard 1957* of 1953), so that the average error in lots of such roundings would be zero. This can be achieved by rounding to the nearest *even* digit when a 5 is to be rounded, so that, for example

$$1.005 \text{ becomes } 1.00$$
$$1.015 \text{ becomes } 1.02$$

on rounding to three significant digits. Unfortunately nobody has told my computer to do this. It rounds all numbers ending in 5 *up*, as I found by feeding in

$$1.501\,501\,501\,500\,0 \quad \text{and} \quad 1.501\,501\,500\,500\,0$$

which were stored as

$$1.501\,501\,502 \qquad \text{and} \quad 1.501\,501\,501.$$

This discussion may seem rather academic (that is, correct but of no real importance). I will show you, by examples, that the finite length of numbers stored in calculators and computers can have serious consequences.

Exercise 3C

1 Shorten the following numbers to 4 figures using (a) chopping, (b) rounding, and putting the answers in the standard form of $a \times 10^n$.
(i) $5\,623\,816$ (ii) $951\,351$ (iii) $157.618\,2$
(iv) $-5.937\,761$ (v) $-0.000\,325\,856\,4$.

2 Use 4 figure arithmetic and (a) chopping, (b) rounding, to evaluate
(i) $(6.278 \times 6.581) \div 6.429$
(ii) $6.278 \times (6.581 \div 6.429)$
(iii) $(12.388 \times 13.419) \div 5.729\,5$.
Also calculate the correct answers.

3 Experiment with your calculator(s) and computer to discover what you can about its arithmetical processes for shortening and displaying numbers.

3.4 TWO EXAMPLES OF ERRORS

Example 1

I shall use my (scientific) calculator, which only uses *ten* digits in calculations, to solve the pair of equations

$$\begin{cases} 2.281\,01x + 1.615\,14y = 2.762\,55 \\ 1.615\,14x + 1.143\,65y = 1.956\,11. \end{cases}$$

The numbers I am using only require six digits, so they can be stored in the calculator with total accuracy; when you multiply two of them the real result has eleven digits, of which only ten will be retained. The error involved here is at most 10^{-10}, which appears to be insignificantly small compared to the numbers I am working with. So I set out with hopes of finding an answer that is correct to nine or ten digits.

The calculation method is to multiply the first equation by $1.143\,65$ and the second by $1.615\,14$; subtraction then eliminates the terms in y, and you get x by a division. When I carried out this process the answer I got for x was

$$x = 9.007\,518\,796.$$

I then substituted this in the first equation to find y, with value

$$y = -11.010\,068\,679.$$

These answers are in fact much less accurate than I suggested they ought to be. The exact answers here are

$$x = 9, \ y = -11.$$

Thus in my calculated answers only the first three digits are accurate, which is far less than the accuracy to which the coefficients are given, and to which the calculator ought to be working.

You may object that the answers I have found are still quite good, accurate to about $\frac{1}{10}\%$. My reply to that is that this was a very small calculation (even if a carefully chosen one), and that if the accuracy is so badly reduced in a small calculation, how much worse could it be in doing long pieces of work on a computer?

Why has my calculation turned out so badly? To see this we need to look at the detail of the calculation. The process of eliminating y gives the equation

$$\{2.281\,01 \times 1.143\,65 - (1.615\,14)^2\}x$$

$$= 2.762\,55 \times 1.143\,65 - 1.956\,11 \times 1.615\,14$$

which the calculator reduces to

$$-1.33 \times 10^{-7}x = -1.198 \times 10^{-6}.$$

This is where the accuracy has been lost: the two parts of the coefficient of x in the previous equation are very nearly equal, and when they are subtracted most of the ten digits are zeros, leaving only three significant digits in the coefficient of x. There is a similar reduction of accuracy on the right hand side of the equation.

It is important to remember this possible source of loss of accuracy. The calculation can lose *many* significant figures of accuracy when a subtraction is done, and because you cannot usually know whether or not the numbers to be subtracted are close to one another, you do not know after a subtraction how accurate your answer will be.

Example 2

Here is another example in which subtraction leads to larger errors than you might expect. I program my computer to solve the quadratic equation

$$ax^2 + bx + c = 0$$

by means of the standard formula

$$x = \{-b \pm (b^2 - 4ac)^{1/2}\}/2a,$$

which is exactly correct as long as $a \neq 0$. Now I ask for the solutions for the case

$$a = 1,\ b = 100\,345,\ c = 1.$$

It gives me the output

$$x_1 = -1 \times 10^{-5},\ x_2 = -100\,345.$$

Neither of these is correct, as you can see by substituting them in the equation, and the reason for the lack of accuracy is the same as in the previous example: nearly equal quantities have been subtracted.

In this example the computer tells me that it has in its stores

$$\begin{cases} -b = -100\,345 \\ (b^2 - 4ac)^{1/2} = 100\,345 \end{cases}$$

and the sum of these is stored as -2×10^{-5}. In fact, $b^2 - 4ac$ is computed by the machine as $1.006\,911\,902 \times 10^{10}$, whereas b^2 would be calculated as $1.006\,911\,903 \times 10^{10}$. This collection of apparently contradictory information is made clear by another habit in some computers; they tell you what they think you need to know rather than all of what they know (just like many people). My computer (according to the manual) works 'using 12 positions ...' in 'internal operations', but 'the number of output positions is 10'.

So the value the machine actually used for the square root was

$$100\,345 - 2 \times 10^{-5},$$

which is how it gave me the approximate root

$$x_1 = -1 \times 10^{-5}.$$

The correct roots for this equation are

$$-9.9656\ldots \times 10^{-6} \quad \text{and} \quad -100\,344.999\,990\ldots;$$

a method for showing this is included in Exercise 3D.

Exercise 3D

1   If, in Example 1, you use a calculator or computer working with 12 figures, what answer should you get?

2   In Example 1, I could have eliminated x rather than y, to solve first for y. Show that my answer for y would be

$$-11.007\,518\,79,$$

and find the corresponding value for x.

3   Consider the equations

$$\begin{cases} 2x + 3y = 4 \\ 3x - 2y = 1. \end{cases}$$

Suppose that all the numbers here are *rounded* ones, so that 2 represents an original number between 1.5 and 2.5, and similarly for the others. Draw a (suitable) set of lines on graph paper (or use a graphic display) to find the region inside which the solution to the unrounded equations must lie. (Think which lines are best to draw.)

4   Suppose that the coefficients in the equations for x and y in Example 1 had been rounded to the six figures that are shown; this means that, for example, the first coefficient is only known to be between

$$2.281\,005 \text{ and } 2.281\,015,$$

with corresponding uncertainty in the others. Find out in what area of the x, y-plane the solution of the equations must lie.

5   Continue the exploration of the internal working of your calculator or computer. Here is one sample calculation for you.

Use a computer or calculator and the formula for solving a quadratic equation and see what you get for

$$x^2 - 10^6 x + 1 = 0.$$

Explain how the machine reaches its answers.

6 Suppose that the quadratic in question 5 has the *exact* solutions (or roots) P and Q. Then theory says that it can be written as

$$(x-P)(x-Q)=0.$$

When you multiply this out you obtain

$$x^2-(P+Q)x+PQ=0.$$

This must be the same equation as we started with, and so the coefficients must be identical in the two forms of the equation, so

$$\begin{cases} P+Q=10^6 \\ PQ=1. \end{cases}$$

The larger sized solution which the machine found is reasonably accurate, because no subtraction was involved in finding it; call it p. Then an equally accurate estimate of the smaller root Q is

$$1/p,$$

from the equation $PQ=1$. Apply this reasoning to the quadratic solved in Example 2.

Having found a good estimate of Q, use the equation $P+Q=10^6$ to find a better estimate of P, and do the same for the equation in Example 2.

3.5 THE COMBINATION OF ERRORS

The calculations which went wrong in the sections above were short pieces of work which were carefully designed to lead to trouble. The more normal state of affairs with computer arithmetic is to have very many calculations, each of which is liable to introduce a slight error due to rounding. In this section we shall have a look at how errors can build up when many of them are combined.

Let us start with addition. If you have two numbers like $0.875\,123\,642\,9$, each of which may be in error by up to $\frac{1}{2}\times 10^{-10}$, then the sum of the two may be in error by up to 10^{-10} in either direction, because the errors will combine if they have the same sign. Similarly if you add 100 numbers in your computer the error in the sum could be as large as 50×10^{-10} in either direction. This is the worst that could happen. It is more likely that the errors would be some positive and some negative so that they would largely cancel out. The theory of statistics can be used to estimate what the likely error is in the sum of n numbers, each of which has (independently) an error at random between $-\frac{1}{2}\times 10^{-10}$ and $+\frac{1}{2}\times 10^{-10}$. From the *Central Limit Theorem* it can be shown that the error in the sum is almost certain to have size less than $n^{1/2}\times 10^{-10}$; and it is very likely to be smaller than $(n/3)^{1/2}\times 10^{-10}$. For example, for 100 numbers added together the error:

(i)   *must* lie between -50×10^{-10} and $+50\times 10^{-10}$,
(ii) is *very likely* to lie between -6×10^{-10} and $+6\times 10^{-10}$,
(iii) is *almost certain* to lie between -10×10^{-10} and $+10\times 10^{-10}$.

Now suppose that we are running a calculation in which the correct values of two numbers are A and B. What is being held in the computer will be approximations to these, say a and b. We can define *errors* α and β by

$$\begin{cases} A = a + \alpha \\ B = b + \beta. \end{cases}$$

(These are the Greek letters 'alpha' and 'beta', from which the English word 'alphabet' is derived.) Note here that we could equally well have defined the errors to be the negatives of these, and you may meet this alternative definition in other texts.

These errors can be described in various ways. The error in a is α, but it is often useful to consider only the *size* of the error, and we then say that the *absolute error* is

$$|\alpha| = |A - a|.$$

In other circumstances it is more convenient to talk about the *relative error*, defined as

$$|\alpha/A|, \text{ for } A \neq 0.$$

Similarly the percentage error is occasionally useful, and it is taken to be 100 times the relative error. The reason for concentrating on the modulus of the various measures of error is that we are usually concerned to find an idea of how large an error can be, and its sign is often of much less importance.

We shall suppose for the moment that A and B are positive numbers, and that α and β are small errors.

If you take the sum of a and b in the computer, what are the absolute error and the relative error in the result? Leave aside for the moment any question of additional rounding errors and suppose that all calculations of addition are done exactly. Since

$$a + b = A - \alpha + B - \beta$$
$$= (A + B) - (\alpha + \beta),$$

we have that the absolute error here is

$$|\alpha + \beta|$$

and the relative error is

$$\frac{|\alpha + \beta|}{|A + B|}.$$

Clearly

$$|\alpha + \beta| \leqslant |\alpha| + |\beta|;$$

you get equality if α and β have the same sign, and otherwise two errors of opposite sign 'cancel out', at least partially. Try it with some numbers if you don't see it at once.

What about the relative error? Suppose we have

$$|\alpha/A| = r_a, \ |\beta/B| = r_b$$

as the two individual relative errors, and suppose that

$$r_a \geqslant r_b.$$

Then numerical experiment suggests that

$$r_b \leqslant \left| \frac{\alpha + \beta}{A + B} \right| \leqslant r_a,$$

and you can work through a proof of this in Exercise 3E. This is an important result: relative errors cannot increase on addition of positive numbers. The *total* error may grow, but as a proportion of the sum of the correct answers it cannot exceed the largest of the relative errors of the components in the addition.

How much of all this is true for subtraction, i.e. for addition involving negative numbers? It is still true that the total error in adding n such numbers has the error described in (i) to (iii) above. But the relative and percentage errors can become large, because the denominator $A + B$ can have a much smaller size than either A or B separately. This is what caused most of the disasters in previous sections. For example, if

$$\begin{cases} A = -1.000\,000\,108, \ B = 1.000\,000\,512, \\ \alpha = 3 \times 10^{-9}, \qquad \beta = -1 \times 10^{-9} \end{cases}$$

then the relative error is

$$(\alpha + \beta)/(A + B) = 0.004\,950\ldots,$$

which is *far* larger than the relative errors in either A or B:

$$|\alpha/A| = 3.00 \times 10^{-9}, \ |\beta/B| = 1.00 \times 10^{-9}.$$

We conclude, as we found earlier, that subtraction of nearly equal numbers can cause serious errors to arise.

What about multiplication? The product of two approximations is given in terms of the real values and the errors by

$$ab = (A - \alpha)(B - \beta)$$
$$= AB - \alpha B - \beta A + \alpha \beta$$
$$\approx AB - \alpha B - \beta A,$$

assuming that the product $\alpha \beta$ of two small errors is very much less than the other terms in the expansion. Hence the absolute error in the (approximate) product ab is

$$|AB - ab| \approx |\alpha B + \beta A|.$$

This is not a very helpful formula, and again the relative error is easier to understand. It is

$$\left| \frac{AB - ab}{AB} \right| \approx \left| \frac{\alpha}{A} + \frac{\beta}{B} \right|$$

$$\leqslant \left|\frac{\alpha}{A}\right| + \left|\frac{\beta}{B}\right|,$$

so that the relative error after a multiplication is no greater than the *sum* of the two relative errors to within a very close approximation. This is another important result; it lets us estimate the largest size for the error after a multiplication rather easily.

For example, take the values for A, B, α, β given above. For these values

$$\begin{cases} AB = -1.000\,000\,62, \\ ab = (A-\alpha)(B-\beta) = -1.000\,000\,624, \\ r_{ab} = 3.999\,997\,52 \times 10^{-9}, \\ r_a + r_b = 3.999\,999\,164 \times 10^{-9}. \end{cases}$$

Notice that the last two numbers are not exactly equal because the very small quantity

$$\alpha\beta/AB$$

has been dropped in the theory, and also because there are rounding errors in all these calculations.

Naturally, when you do many multiplications, there will be cancellation between positive and negative relative errors so that the actual final error will almost always be less than the largest value you could have. We shall not investigate the statistical behaviour of the final error.

Division gives the same result for relative errors that we have just found for multiplication. This can be seen in two ways. Firstly, division is the same as multiplication by the (multiplicative) inverse, which is just some other number to multiply by; and secondly, and more explicitly, you can show that (for $B \neq 0$)

$$\frac{a}{b} = \frac{A-\alpha}{B-\beta} \approx \frac{A}{B}\left\{1 - \frac{\alpha}{A} + \frac{\beta}{B}\right\}$$

(a proof is outlined in Exercise 3E below). Hence

$$\left|\frac{A}{B} - \frac{a}{b}\right| \approx \left|\frac{A}{B}\right| \times \left|\frac{\alpha}{A} - \frac{\beta}{B}\right|,$$

which gives the result on the relative error

$$r_{a/b} \leqslant r_a + r_b,$$

approximately, on dividing by $|A/B|$.

In the discussion on addition of positive numbers we considered both the actual error, which probably increased like $n^{1/2}$ for n additions, and the relative error, which could not exceed the largest relative error amongst the terms to be added. So far we have only considered the relative error for multiplication. The *absolute* error in the result of a multiplication such as

$$10^6 \times a = 10^6 \times (A-\alpha)$$

is of course $10^6\alpha$, which is far larger than the initial error. This will not matter if you are only concerned with the value of the product, because there will be the same number of correct figures in it, since the relative error has not increased. But if the problem you are doing requires you next to add on a rather small number b, it may get entirely lost in the enlarged error term $10^6\alpha$. So, if possible, it is better to avoid multiplication by very large numbers, or the equivalent division by very small numbers. We shall see an example in Chapter 5 where such multiplications cause a bad answer to appear.

Exercise 3E

1   Take the values

$$A=193,\ B=216,\ a=191,\ b=217$$

and calculate
(i)   the errors α and β,
(ii) the absolute errors,
(iii) the relative errors in a and b,
(iv) the absolute and relative errors in

$$a+b,\ a-b,\ ab,\ a/b.$$

2   Here is a very large addition sum for you to do on your computer, to see how the random errors give you a growing total error in the result, but not a total error that grows in a regular way. Put

$$F(r)=1+2^{-1/100}+2^{-2/100}+2^{-3/100}+\ \dots\ +2^{-(r-1)/100}.$$

Compute $F(r)$ by adding up the terms, for

$$r=100,\ 200,\ 300,\ 400,\ 500,\dots,1000,\ 2000,\ 3000.$$

You can get the correct value of $F(r)$ by noticing that it is a geometric progression, and hence has sum

$$F(r)=(1-2^{-r/100})/(1-2^{-1/100}).$$

3   Take positive numbers A, B, α, β and assume that the relative errors are related by

$$\frac{\alpha}{A}\geqslant\frac{\beta}{B},$$

i.e. $r_a\geqslant r_b$.
(i)   Show that

$$\alpha(A+B)\geqslant\alpha A+\beta A.$$

(ii) Deduce that

$$\frac{\alpha}{A}\geqslant\frac{\alpha+\beta}{A+B}.$$

(iii) Show similarly that

$$\frac{\alpha+\beta}{A+B}\geqslant\frac{\beta}{B}.$$

(iv) Use these results to prove that

$$r_b\leqslant r_{a+b}\leqslant r_a.$$

4 Take positive numbers A, B, α, β.

(i) Show that

$$\frac{A-\alpha}{B-\beta} = \frac{A(1-\alpha/A)}{B(1-\beta/B)}.$$

(ii) Suppose that $r_b = \beta/B$ is very small, and show that

$$\frac{1}{1-\beta/B} \approx 1 + \beta/B$$

by multiplying each side by $1 - \beta/B$.

(iii) Hence complete a demonstration that

$$r_{a/b} \leqslant r_a + r_b,$$

to a good approximation, when r_a and r_b are very small and neither b nor B is zero.

5 Expand $\sin(A-\alpha)$ and use the approximation $\sin\alpha \approx \alpha$ (for radian measure) to find the approximate relative error in $\sin a$.

6 The correct number A is usually *not* known, but the approximation a is known. What are the (i) absolute and (ii) relative errors in α/a as an approximation for α/A?

3.6 SUMMARY

All electronic calculation works to a finite number of decimal places, and real numbers are shortened to this length (either by rounding or by truncation); this is a source of error in calculations.

Different machines will give different answers (in general), and the longer the calculation, the further all these answers are likely to be from the correct answer.

Subtraction of nearly equal numbers can lead to the loss of many decimal places in a calculation, and this must be kept in mind in all calculations.

Formal rules can be established for the largest possible error in the result of calculations with inexact numbers. They are given in terms of the *absolute errors* and the *relative errors* of the numbers held.

(i) The *absolute* error in the result of adding any two numbers with errors is no greater than the sum of the absolute errors in those two numbers.

(ii) The *relative* error in the result of adding two *positive* numbers with errors is no greater than the larger of the relative errors of those two numbers. If the numbers have opposite signs, the relative error of the sum may be much larger than this.

(iii) the *relative* error in the result of multiplying or dividing two numbers with errors is no greater than the sum of the relative errors of the two numbers.

(iv) The *absolute* error in the result of multiplying by a large number or dividing by a small one can become large enough to obscure other numbers in a calculation.

4

Solving $f(x) = 0$ by simple iteration

This chapter is concerned with the classical problem of finding roots of equations. That is, if I am asked to find the values of x for which

$$\cos\{(1 + \sin x)^3\} - x^2 + 1.2 = 0,$$

how do I do it? By saying it is a classical problem I mean that mathematicians and users of mathematics have been seeking solution methods for a very long time, and are still doing so with ever more involved equations.

The method in this chapter is a first attempt at a solution method, using computer technology where appropriate. In outline the method is

(i) find an *approximate* solution,
(ii) find a method for improving it by successive steps of an iteration.

4.1 APPROXIMATE SOLUTIONS

Since I can see no easy way to solve such an unpleasant looking equation as

$$\cos\{(1 + \sin x)^3\} - x^2 + 1.2 = 0,$$

I reach for my graphics calculator – naturally a computer with graphics would do the job better, but all I want is an approximate solution. I program it to give me a graph of

$$y = \cos\{(1 + \sin x)^3\} - x^2 + 1.2$$

for values of x between -4 and 4, as a first try to see what the curve looks like. Having seen it, I set the program to have

$$-1.5 \leqslant x \leqslant 1.5$$
$$-2.5 \leqslant y \leqslant 2.5.$$

The result is shown in the sketch, Fig. 1.

Using the graphics calculator I quickly find that the four roots of the equation are approximately

$$-1.50, \ 0.46, \ 0.57, \ 1.28.$$

I could easily get *better* approximations to these roots by 'zooming in' near the places where the graph cuts the axis. For example, if I zoom in to the rectangle

$$0.40 \leqslant x \leqslant 0.60$$
$$-0.10 \leqslant y \leqslant 0.10,$$

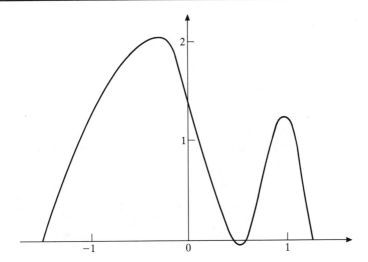

Figure 1. The curve $y=\cos\{(1+\sin x)^3\}-x^2+1.2$

I get the graph shown in the next sketch, Fig. 2, and the estimates 0.457 and 0.515 for the two roots shown.

You could continue this zooming in to get better and better approximations to the roots, but I intend to use a mathematical method of improving these approximate roots in the rest of this chapter.

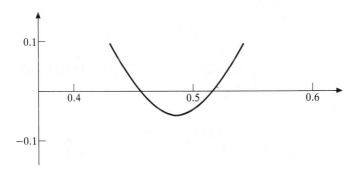

Figure 2. Detail of $y=\cos\{(1+\sin x)^3\}-x^2+1.2$

Before going on it is worth spending a short time on non-computer methods of finding approximate roots. After all, how did I decide to look at the interval

$$-4\leqslant x\leqslant 4$$

as my first guess for where the roots might be?

Method 1, signs

Find the sign of y at a selection of values of x. When there is a change of sign there must be a root of the equation. For example:

$$\begin{cases} \text{at } x=-2, \ y \text{ is negative} \\ \text{at } x=-1, \ y \text{ is positive} \end{cases}$$

and so there is a root between $x=-2$ and $x=-1$.

   The trouble with this method is that it can miss a pair of roots that are close together. For example:

$$\begin{cases} \text{at } x=0.4, \ y \text{ is positive} \\ \text{at } x=0.6, \ y \text{ is positive} \end{cases}$$

and yet there are *two* roots in between.

Method 2, sketch the graph

If you evaluate y at intervals of 0.1 along the axis you can plot points which, when joined up with a smooth curve, will give you a very good idea of the graph. This is, after all, just what the graphics program is doing, though it does it more thoroughly and quickly.

Method 3, splitting the function

Consider the *two* graphs

$$\begin{cases} y=\cos\{(1+\sin x)^3\} \\ y=x^2-1.2. \end{cases}$$

Each is easier to plot than the equation we started with. The first is not too much trouble because I know how

$$1+\sin x$$

varies as x varies, and so I should be able to sketch

$$(1+\sin x)^3,$$

and then make a fair attempt at

$$\cos\{(1+\sin x)^3\}.$$

These graphs, together with $y=x^2-1.2$ are shown in Fig. 3, and they show the approximate roots to be at

$$-1.5, \ 0.5, \ 0.5, \ 1.2.$$

This method is a bit like 'intelligent guesswork' in Chapter 2. It requires both intelligence and some luck, as not all functions will split up into two easy parts.

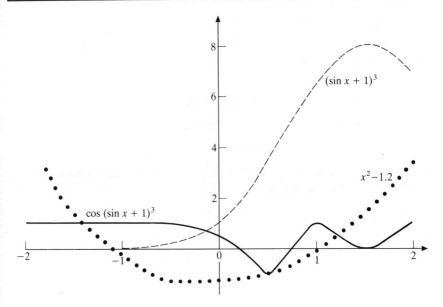

Figure 3. Constituent graphs for the splitting $x^2 - 1.2 = \cos\{(1 + \sin x)^3\}$

Exercise 4A

1   Use the method of signs, the method of graph sketching and the method of splitting (if you can) on the following equations, to find approximate roots. Also use a graphics program to confirm your results.
(i) $x^3 - 3x^2 - 9x - 4 = 0$.
(*Hint*: split this as $x^3 = 3x^2 + 9x + 4$.)
(ii) $x \cos x - \sin x = 0$.
(*Hint*: split this as $x = \tan x$.)
(iii) $9 \cos(\sin x) - 9 \sin(\cos x) - 1 = 0$.

2   The shaded part is cut off the circle in Fig. 4 by the line AB, where O is the centre of the circle. Determine the angle (degrees) such that the shaded area is equal to the area of the triangle OAB.

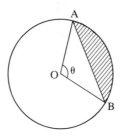

Figure 4. Two areas in a circle

3 Some equations have *double* roots, for example

$$x^2 - 10\cos x + 10 = 0$$

at $x=0$. Which methods will work best for double roots?

4.2   COBWEB AND STAIRCASE DIAGRAMS

Suppose that I want to solve the equation

$$x^4 + x^3 - 1 = 0$$

to a high degree of accuracy. What I shall do (and we shall come to the full reasons for how I make this decision, much later) is to rewrite the equation as

$$x^3(x+1) = 1$$

i.e.

$$x^3 = (x+1)^{-1}$$

or

$$x = (x+1)^{-1/3}.$$

When you sketch graphs for the two sides of this equation separately, you get Fig. 5, which shows (when drawn accurately) that there is a root near $x=0.8$ (and another near $x=-1.4$).

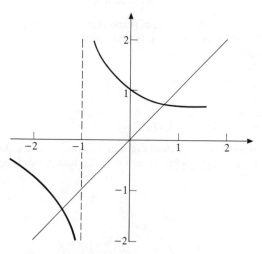

Figure 5. Graphs for $x^4 + x^3 - 1 = 0$

I am going to use the simple iteration

$$\begin{cases} x_{n+1} = (x_n+1)^{-1/3} \\ \quad x_0 = 0.8 \end{cases}$$

in an attempt to find the positive root X of the equation

$$x^4+x^3-1=0.$$

The sequence of numbers my computer generated for this iteration was as follows:

$$x_1 = 0.822\,070\,691\,4$$
$$x_2 = 0.818\,737\,958\,8$$
$$x_3 = 0.819\,237\,750\,4$$
$$x_4 = 0.819\,162\,721\,6$$
$$x_5 = 0.819\,173\,983\,2$$
$$x_6 = 0.819\,172\,292\,8$$
$$x_7 = 0.819\,172\,546\,5$$
$$x_8 = 0.819\,172\,508\,4$$
$$x_9 = 0.819\,172\,514\,1$$
$$x_{10} = 0.819\,172\,513\,3$$
$$x_{11} = 0.819\,172\,513\,4.$$

Thereafter the same value repeated itself. Is this the solution I am seeking? Yes, firstly because if I calculate $x_{11}^4+x_{11}^3-1$ I get zero, and secondly because if

$$x_{11} = (x_{11}+1)^{-1/3}$$

then

$$x_{11}^4 + x_{11}^3 - 1 = 0.$$

The geometrical interpretation of this iteration can be shown on an enlarged part of the graph near $x=0.8$, $y=0.8$ (Fig. 6).

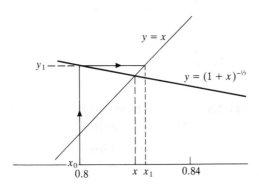

Figure 6. First step in the iteration

Starting from $x=x_0$ you go *up* to the curve

$$y=(x+1)^{-1/3}$$

to get the value

$$y_1=(x_0+1)^{-1/3}.$$

We wish this to become the next value of x we use, so we go *across* to the other graph

$$y=x$$

to make

$$y_1=x_1, \text{ i.e. } x_1=(x_0+1)^{-1/3}.$$

Then going *down* to the x-axis shows us where x_1 is, at $x\approx0.822$.

   This process of going up, across, and down is going to be repeated many times. Some of the steps are illustrated in Fig. 7. If you repeat the process enough times, it is clear that you will home in on the point where the graphs cross, i.e. at $x=X$, the solution of the equation.

   The diagram is a 'spiral' with right angled corners; it is otherwise called a 'cobweb diagram'.

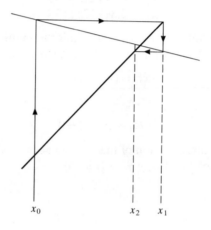

Figure 7. Cobweb diagram for $x_{n+1}=(x_n+1)^{-1/3}$

   The graphs in Figs. 5, 6 and 7 are typical for a large class of iterations, but there are many others with a rather different shape. If you try to solve the equation

$$x^3-x-1=0$$

by means of the iteration

$$\begin{cases} x_{n+1}=(x_n+1)^{1/3} \\ \quad x_0=1.4, \end{cases}$$

you get the two graphs shown in Fig. 8, with an enlarged version in Fig. 9. The sequence of moves

up to the curve

across to $y=x$

down to the x-axis

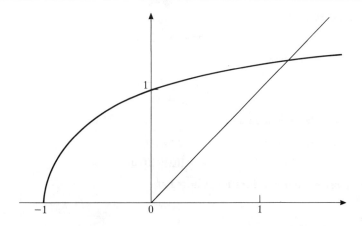

Figure 8. Graphs for the iteration $x_{n+1}=(x_n+1)^{1/3}$

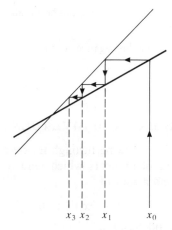

$x_3\ x_2\quad x_1\qquad\qquad x_0$

Figure 9. Staircase diagram for $x_{n+1}=(x_n+1)^{1/3}$

now generates a 'staircase diagram' instead of a cobweb diagram. In this case the staircase descends to $X = 1.324\,717\,957$. If you had started instead at $x_0 = 1.3$ the staircase would have ascended from the left towards X.

Exercise 4B

1   Solve the equation

$$x^2 - 10x + 10 = 0$$

by using the iteration

$$\begin{cases} x_{n+1} = \tfrac{1}{10}x_n^2 + 1 \\ \quad x_0 = 1. \end{cases}$$

Draw the related staircase diagram.

2   Solve the equation

$$x^2 + 2x - 1 = 0$$

by using the iteration

$$\begin{cases} x_{n+1} = \tfrac{1}{2}(1 - x_n^2) \\ \quad x_0 = 0.1. \end{cases}$$

Draw the related cobweb diagram.

3   Find the other root of

$$x^2 - 10x + 10 = 0$$

by choosing a different iteration, starting at

$$x_0 = 9.$$

4   Find approximate roots for

$$x^3 - 12x + 12 = 0$$

by the methods of Section 4.1, and choose suitable iterations to evaluate all three roots to six places of decimals.

5   Find an iterative method for the negative root of

$$x^4 + x^3 - 1 = 0.$$

4.3   CONVERGENT AND DIVERGENT ITERATIONS

You may have found while working through Exercise 4B that not all iterative schemes give a sequence of numbers which tend to the required root. For example, if you try to find a root of

$$x^3 - 12x + 12 = 0$$

near $x = 3$ by setting up the iteration

$$\begin{cases} x_{n+1} = 1 + x_n^3/12 \\ \quad x_0 = 3, \end{cases}$$

you find the sequence

$$\begin{aligned}
x_1 &= \quad 3.25 \\
x_2 &= \quad 3.8606\ldots \\
x_3 &= \quad 5.7952\ldots \\
x_4 &= \quad 17.219\ldots \\
x_5 &= 426.46\ldots
\end{aligned}$$

and so on. Fig. 10 shows that the staircase is *leaving* the root at X, not approaching it.

Similarly, if you try to solve

$$x^4 + x^3 - 1 = 0$$

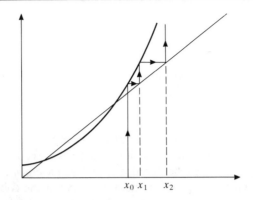

Figure 10. Divergent iteration $x_{n+1}=1+x_n^3/12$

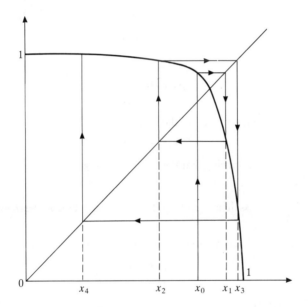

Figure 11. Diverging cobweb diagram for $x_{n+1}=(1-x_n^4)^{1/3}$

by using the iteration

$$\begin{cases} x_{n+1}=(1-x_n^4)^{1/3} \\ \quad x_0=0.8 \end{cases}$$

you get

$$x_1=0.8389\ldots$$
$$x_2=0.7961\ldots$$
$$x_3=0.8425\ldots$$
$$x_4=0.7915\ldots$$
$$x_5=0.8468\ldots$$

$$x_6 = 0.7860\ldots$$
$$x_7 = 0.8519\ldots$$
$$x_8 = 0.7793\ldots$$

and eventually after many iterations you get 0 and 1 alternately. The cobweb diagram looks like Fig. 11, where the successive points spiral *out* from the root near 0.8, and finally oscillate.

When the iterative process moves *away* from the root, as in these two examples, it is called a *divergent* iteration. In previous examples in Section 4.2 it *approached* the root, and in those cases the iteration is called *convergent*. The criterion for convergence is that the slope of the iterative curve in the cobweb or staircase diagram is less than 1 in size at (and near) the intersection of the curves. This will be proved later but is made plausible in Exercise 4C.

Exercise 4C

1   The trivial equation

$$\begin{cases} (1+\alpha)x - 1 = 0 \\ \quad \alpha \neq -1 \end{cases}$$

can be solved by iteration. Set up the iteration

$$x_{n+1} = 1 - \alpha x_n,$$

and show by careful drawing that the iteration diverges if the slope of the line

$$y = 1 - \alpha x$$

is greater than 1 or less than -1; but that it converges if the slope lies between -1 and $+1$.

2   Show the same result as in question 1 by solving the difference equation

$$\begin{cases} x_{n+1} = -\alpha x_n + 1 \\ \quad x_0 = A \end{cases}$$

for $|\alpha| > 1$ or $|\alpha| < 1$.

3   Make an argument, based on the local straightness of any (reasonable) curve and the results of this Exercise, for the statement that iterations converge if the slope has modulus less than 1.

4.4   ACCELERATION OF CONVERGENCE

If you tabulate the *errors* in Section 4.2 for the iteration

$$\begin{cases} x_{n+1} = (x_n + 1)^{-1/3} \\ \quad x_0 = 0.8 \end{cases}$$

you find the values in the table.

Iterate	Value	Error value	Error
x_0	0.8	0.091 725 134	ε_0
x_1	0.822 070 691 4	$-0.002\,898\,178\,046$	ε_1
x_2	0.818 737 958 8	$4.345\,546\,13 \times 10^{-4}$	ε_2
x_3	0.819 237 750 4	$-6.523\,696\,8 \times 10^{-5}$	ε_3
x_4	0.819 162 721 6	$9.791\,826 \times 10^{-6}$	ε_4
x_5	0.819 173 983 2	$-1.469\,755 \times 10^{-6}$	ε_5
x_6	0.819 172 292 8	$2.206\,13 \times 10^{-7}$	ε_6
x_7	0.819 172 546 5	-3.3116×10^{-8}	ε_7
x_8	0.819 172 508 4	4.973×10^{-9}	ε_8
x_9	0.819 172 514 1	-7.44×10^{-10}	ε_9
x_{10}	0.819 172 513 3	1.15×10^{-10}	ε_{10}
x_{11}	0.819 172 513 4	-2×10^{-11}	ε_{11}

(The Greek letter 'epsilon' is often used for errors.)

This does not look very promising; the errors reduce and are alternately positive and negative. But if you take the *ratios* of successive errors

$$\varepsilon_1/\varepsilon_0, \ \varepsilon_2/\varepsilon_1, \ \varepsilon_3/\varepsilon_2, \ldots$$

you get the sequence

$\varepsilon_1/\varepsilon_0$	$-0.151\,163\,17$
$\varepsilon_2/\varepsilon_1$	$-0.149\,940\,62$
$\varepsilon_3/\varepsilon_2$	$-0.150\,123\,749\,8$
$\varepsilon_4/\varepsilon_3$	$-0.150\,096\,276\,7$
$\varepsilon_5/\varepsilon_4$	$-0.150\,100\,195\,8$
$\varepsilon_6/\varepsilon_5$	$-0.150\,101\,887\,7$
$\varepsilon_7/\varepsilon_6$	$-0.150\,109\,014\,4$
$\varepsilon_8/\varepsilon_7$	$-0.150\,169\,102\,5$
$\varepsilon_9/\varepsilon_8$	$-0.149\,607\,882\,6$
$\varepsilon_{10}/\varepsilon_9$	$-0.154\,569\,892\,5$
$\varepsilon_{11}/\varepsilon_{10}$	$-0.173\,913\,043\,5$

What happens here is that the ratio of the errors settles down to be very close to

$$-0.1501,$$

until random errors in the computations become relatively large as the error approaches zero.

That is, the errors approximately satisfy the difference equation,

$$\begin{cases} \varepsilon_{n+1} = -0.1501\varepsilon_n \\ \quad \varepsilon_0 = \quad 0.0917 \end{cases}$$

This difference equation has the solution

$$\varepsilon_n = (-0.1501)^n \times 0.0917,$$

by the methods in Chapter 2, which confirms that $\varepsilon_n \to 0$ as n gets larger.

Any iteration which has the property that the modulus of the ratio of successive errors

$$\varepsilon_{n+1}/\varepsilon_n$$

tends to a constant K is called a 'first order' iterative process, if $K \neq 0$. It certainly converges if $0 < |K| < 1$ since $\varepsilon_n = K^n \varepsilon_0$, and so $\varepsilon_n \to 0$. If $|K|$ is small, the convergence is rapid; but if $|K|$ is near 1 the convergence of the iterative process is very slow, and many iterations will be needed to reach its limit, i.e. the solution of the equation being solved. There is, however, a clever technique for increasing the rate of convergence in first order processes.

Suppose we had exactly

$$\begin{cases} \varepsilon_1 = K\varepsilon_0 \text{ and } \varepsilon_2 = K\varepsilon_1 \\ \text{with } 0 < |K| < 1. \end{cases}$$

We can rewrite these as

$$X - x_1 = K(X - x_0)$$
$$X - x_2 = K(X - x_1)$$

where X is the unknown limit of the iteration. They may be rewritten again as

$$x_1 = X + K(x_0 - X)$$
$$x_2 = X + K^2(x_0 - X),$$

and we can also use the equation

$$x_0 = X + (x_0 - X).$$

From these three equations you can derive

$$x_1 - x_0 = (K - 1)(x_0 - X)$$
$$x_2 - 2x_1 + x_0 = (K^2 - 2K + 1)(x_0 - X)$$

and hence

$$\frac{(x_1 - x_0)^2}{x_2 - 2x_1 + x_0} = x_0 - X.$$

That is, from *any* three iterates x_0, x_1 and x_2 (because you can start an iteration at *any* point) you can get a good estimate of the final value X from the formula

$$X \approx x_0 - \frac{(x_1 - x_0)^2}{x_2 - 2x_1 + x_0}.$$

It is only an estimate because our assumptions that

$$\varepsilon_1 = K\varepsilon_0$$

$$\varepsilon_2 = K\varepsilon_1$$

are not quite true in any real iteration.

Apply this to the values at the start of this section. You get

$$x_1 - x_0 = \quad 0.022\,070\,691\,4$$
$$x_2 - 2x_1 + x_0 = -0.025\,403\,424$$

and

$$X \approx 0.8 + 0.019\,175\,187\,5$$
$$= 0.819\,175\,187\,5,$$

which is a much better estimate of X than any of x_0, x_1, x_2.
Apply it similarly to x_1, x_2 and x_3. This time you use

$$x_2 - x_1 = -0.003\,332\,732$$
$$x_3 - 2x_2 + x_1 = \quad 0.003\,832\,524\,2$$

and find that

$$X \approx x_1 - 0.002\,898\,116\,7$$
$$= 0.819\,172\,574$$

which has six significant figures correct, compared with our result from the iteration.

Finally, apply it to x_6, x_7 and x_8. Similar calculations show that the correction term is

$$2.205\,746\,744 \times 10^{-7}.$$

This gives

$$X \approx 0.819\,172\,513\,37\ldots$$

which agrees with our result from a continuation of the iteration.

This acceleration technique is known as *Aitken's δ^2 (or Δ^2) acceleration process*, and the reasons for the Greek deltas will appear in a later chapter. Note that it must only be applied to *first order* processes, and is best applied when $\varepsilon_{n+1}/\varepsilon_n$ has settled to an almost constant value (which you cannot really know until *after* you have solved the problem).

Exercise 4D

1   The iteration

$$\begin{cases} x_{n+1} = (1 - x_n^3)^{1/4} \\ \quad x_0 = 0.8 \end{cases}$$

is meant to find the root of

$$x^4 + x^3 - 1 = 0,$$

but it converges very slowly. Use x_{10}, x_{11} and x_{12} with Aitken's process to get a better approximation x_0^* to the root X.

2   Use x_0^* as a *new* starting point for the iteration in question 1 and calculate two iterates x_1^* and x_2^* from there. Apply Aitken's process to *these* three iterates to get an even better approximation x_0^{**} to X.

3   Assume that x_0^{**} is very close to X, and use the equation

$$x_2^* - x_0^{**} = K(x_1^* - x_0^{**})$$

to find an estimate of K in this process. Hence determine (approximately) how many iterations would be needed from x_0 to get to within 10^{-10} of X, without the use of Aitken's technique.

4.5   A DIFFICULT EXAMPLE

The example we started this chapter with was

$$\cos\{(1 + \sin x)^3\} - x^2 + 1.2 = 0,$$

and we found that it had four roots, near

$$-1.50, \ 0.46, \ 0.57, \ 1.28.$$

Can we improve these using our iterative techniques? Not easily, I am afraid.

(a)   Start by trying the iteration

$$x_{n+1} = [1.2 + \cos\{(1 + \sin x_n)^3\}]^{1/2}.$$

The results of starting at the four approximations above are as follows:
(i) $x_0 = -1.50$: the iteration goes into a cycle between $x = 1.05$ and $x = 1.47$, not converging to the root.
(ii) $x_0 = 0.46$: the iteration converges slowly.
(iii) $x_0 = 0.57$: as in (i).
(iv) $x_0 = 1.28$: as in (i).
What this means is that to get towards the other roots you need to split the equation up differently, and so get a different iteration.

(b)   You could rewrite the equation as

$$x = \sin^{-1}[\{\cos^{-1}(x^2 - 1.2)\}^{1/3} - 1]$$

and try to use this for iteration purposes. All you get is error messages on the computer, either at once or soon, as you try to find an angle whose cosine exceeds 1.

The moral of this example is that finding the correct iteration is *not* an easy problem.

4.6   SUMMARY

Using computer graphics will give approximate solutions to equations of almost any degree of complexity, and zooming in on particular regions can give good accuracy. Without using a computer the problem is much harder, but there are some techniques which can be used.

Many equations can be rewritten in the form

$$x = f(x),$$

some in many ways. The iteration

$$x_{n+1} = f(x_n),$$

when started from an approximation to a root, sometimes *converges* to the root; sometimes it will *diverge*; and sometimes it will finally *oscillate*. These behaviours can be illustrated by drawing *cobweb* or *staircase* diagrams.

Convergence of the iteration is assured by the *slope* of the iteration curve having modulus less than 1 at and near the root.

Slowly convergent *first order* iterations can often be improved by using *Aitken's δ^2 technique*.

It may be difficult to find iterations (of the type discussed) to improve all the approximate roots of an equation.

5

Gauss elimination

It is common, in applications of mathematics to real life situations, to find large sets of equations arising. In population forecasting, which is needed to cost the provision of social services in the future, you can easily get twenty equations in twenty unknowns by dividing the population into age groups of five years. Some models of this sort are discussed in Chapter 7. In economic modelling you may have to consider 100 industries, and their contribution to the overall economy; their interactions and outputs will lead to 100 equations. In engineering, the solution of a single differential equation, say in a stress calculation, may require the range to be divided into 200 points, leading to 200 linear equations relating function values. In weather forecasting for the North Atlantic and Europe you may have differential equations for ten functions (such as pressure, temperature, humidity, wind speed and direction, pollutants) at ten levels in the atmosphere and values at 10 000 points over half the northern hemisphere.

In this chapter we take a first look at the easiest sorts of equations, linear algebraic equations, such as

$$\begin{cases} 5x - 7y + 4z = 16 \\ 5x + y - 3z = 12 \\ x - y - z = 0. \end{cases}$$

This is one of the extensions of the idea of finding roots of equations, discussed in the last chapter; the extension in this case is to many equations, but they are kept to *linear* equations. The extension to many *non-linear* equations is rather difficult.

With many equations to solve it is essential to use computer methods. That means that we have to discuss the *efficiency* of any proposed method (if the Meteorological Office used inefficient equation solvers it would only manage to calculate last week's weather). We also need to discuss the *accuracy* of the computer output – the inaccuracy of a calculator solution in Section 3.4 is a warning of what can go wrong.

There are two basic approaches to solving sets of linear algebraic equations. One is a direct attack, which is described in this chapter. The other is to use an iterative method, building on our previous experience of iteration in earlier chapters; this will be deferred until Chapter 6.

I shall use computer methods in the examples we discuss. It is unreasonable to expect you to program the lengthy set of operations needed for the solution method that is to be described. However, it would be very helpful for you to have an equation solving package available; the calculations can *always* be done using a calculator, but the time needed is not time well spent, and you should get some experience of larger sets of equations than appear in the exercises.

5.1   THE SIMPLE GAUSS METHOD

If you have three (linear) simultaneous equations to solve for three unknowns, you normally proceed by eliminating one unknown at a time until you have a single equation in one unknown. This equation can then be solved easily, and then the other unknowns can be found by working back through the elimination process. For example, consider the equations quoted above:

$$\begin{cases} 5x - 7y + 4z = 16 \\ 5x + y - 3z = 12 \\ x - y - z = 0. \end{cases}$$

Subtraction of the first equation from the second gives a replacement for the second; and subtraction of $\frac{1}{5}$ of the first equation from the third gives a replacement for the third:

$$\begin{cases} 5x - 7y + 4z = 16 \\ 8y - 7z = -4 \\ 0.4y - 1.8z = -3.2. \end{cases}$$

Now subtract $\frac{1}{20}$ of the second equation from the third to replace the third equation:

$$\begin{cases} 5x - 7y + 4z = 16 \\ 8y - 7z = -4 \\ -1.45z = -3. \end{cases}$$

These equations are solved in turn as

$$\begin{cases} z = 3/1.45 = 2.0689 \dots \\ y = (7z - 4)/8 = 1.3103 \dots \\ x = (7y - 4z + 16)/5 = 3.3793 \dots, \end{cases}$$

using a calculator to get the answers.

This method of successive elimination and then solving the equations in turn is known as the (simple) *Gauss elimination* method.

The standard check at the end is to substitute the values that have been found into the equations and calculate three *residuals*. The first residual here is the correct right hand side minus its estimate:

$$16 - 5 \times 3.3793 \dots + 7 \times 1.3103 \dots - 4 \times 2.0689 \dots$$

which my calculator gave as 1×10^{-8}. Note that some texts define residuals as minus this value. In a similar way the other two residuals came out as

$$2 \times 10^{-8} \quad \text{and} \quad 1 \times 10^{-9}.$$

If the answers were exactly correct, the residuals would be zero; they are not zero here because the calculator introduced errors when it chopped (for example) the value of z to ten decimal digits. These errors have then increased as arithmetic has been done to solve for y and x and calculate the residuals, together with further chopping of answers to ten digits.

Would I get the same answers for x, y and z if I multiplied each equation by, say, 1000 before starting? Yes, of course; try it, if you don't believe me. But what about the residuals? I would now have

$$16\,000 - 5000 \times 3.3793\ldots + 7000 \times 1.3103\ldots - 4000 \times 2.0689\ldots$$

My calculator makes this residual equal to

$$1 \times 10^{-5}.$$

This does not mean the solutions are now less accurate; it just means that you must compare the residuals with the size of the terms in the equation. For the first equation it is

$$1 \times 10^{-8}/16$$

that is the better measure of the error, or

$$1 \times 10^{-8}/(5 \times 3.3793\ldots),$$

or some such quantity. These give numbers around 5×10^{-10} in size, which seems reasonable when errors up to 10^{-10} in size may have been introduced by chopping.

Unfortunately, small residuals do not necessarily mean that you have good answers. The equations

$$\begin{cases} x + \frac{1}{2}y + \frac{1}{3}z = 4 \\ \frac{1}{2}x + \frac{1}{3}y + \frac{1}{4}z = 3 \\ \frac{1}{3}x + \frac{1}{4}y + \frac{1}{5}z = 2 \end{cases}$$

have the exact solution

$$x = -12, \ y = 72, \ z = 60.$$

Let us see what happens when we use 3 digit arithmetic (not counting 0. as a digit) and rounding extra digits.

The equations are replaced by

$$\begin{cases} 1 & 0.5 & 0.333 & 4 \\ 0.5 & 0.333 & 0.25 & 3 \\ 0.333 & 0.25 & 0.2 & 2 \end{cases}$$

where I have used (essentially) matrix form to avoid writing x, y, z and $+$, $-$, $=$

all the time (computers use this sort of array to store the numbers involved). Performing the Gauss elimination procedure leads first to

$$\left\{\begin{array}{llll} 1 & 0.5 & 0.333 & 4 \\ & 0.083 & 0.083 & 1 \\ & 0.083 & 0.089 & 0.67, \end{array}\right.$$

using multipliers 0.5 and 0.333; and then to

$$\left\{\begin{array}{llll} 1 & 0.5 & 0.333 & 4 \\ & 0.083 & 0.083 & 1 \\ & & 0.006 & -0.33. \end{array}\right.$$

Note the loss of significant figures in the last equation, due to subtraction. Solving for z, y, x in turn, and still using 3 digits and rounding, gives us

$$x = -11.3, \ y = 67.1, \ z = -55.$$

Not a very good set of answers! But if you calculate the residuals, you find

$$\left\{\begin{array}{l} r_1 = 0 \\ r_2 = 0.15 \\ r_3 = -0.04, \end{array}\right.$$

which are satisfactorily small compared with the size of the terms (up to 33.6) which come into the equations.

Exercise 5A

1 Solve the equations

$$\left\{\begin{array}{l} x + \tfrac{1}{2}y + \tfrac{1}{3}z = 4 \\ \tfrac{1}{2}x + \tfrac{1}{3}y + \tfrac{1}{4}z = 3 \\ \tfrac{1}{3}x + \tfrac{1}{4}y + \tfrac{1}{5}z = 2 \end{array}\right.$$

using 4 digit arithmetic with rounding. Calculate the residuals.

2 How many multiplications and how many additions are needed (in general) to solve
(i) 3 equations in 3 unknowns using the simple Gauss method?
(ii) How many for 4 equations and unknowns?
(iii) How many for n?

3 Solve the two sets of equations, using the simple Gauss method and 4 digit arithmetic:

(a) $\left\{\begin{array}{l} \tfrac{1}{3}x + \tfrac{1}{4}y + \tfrac{1}{5}z = 2 \\ \tfrac{1}{2}x + \tfrac{1}{3}y + \tfrac{1}{4}z = 3 \\ x + \tfrac{1}{2}y + \tfrac{1}{3}z = 4 \end{array}\right.$

(b) $\left\{\begin{array}{l} \tfrac{1}{5}x + \tfrac{1}{4}y + \tfrac{1}{3}z = 2 \\ \tfrac{1}{4}x + \tfrac{1}{3}y + \tfrac{1}{2}z = 3 \\ \tfrac{1}{3}x + \tfrac{1}{2}y + z = 4. \end{array}\right.$

In each case calculate the residuals.
(c) Comment on your results, comparing them also with the results of question 1.

4 If you have access to a 'simple Gauss' computer package, use it to solve a 5×5 set of equations corresponding to those in question 1 (e.g. the first equation has coefficients $1, \frac{1}{2}, \frac{1}{3}, \frac{1}{4}, \frac{1}{5}; 4$).

5.2   PARTIAL PIVOTING

In Exercise 5A you should have found that rearranging equations gave you different answers, though in the examples done the accuracies of the answers were all about the same. I am now going to show you a set of equations where it makes a great deal of difference how you organise them.

The equations

$$\begin{cases} 10^{-6}x & + & z = 1 \\ x + 10^{-6}y & & = 1 \\ & y + 10^{-6}z = 1 \end{cases}$$

clearly have the solution

$$x = y = z = 10^6/(10^6 + 1)$$

$$= 0.999\,999\,000\,0$$

(to 10 d.p.). When I ran them on my computer using the simple Gauss program, it told me that

$$x = 1, \; y = 0, \; z = 0.999\,999.$$

This is clearly a *very* poor 'solution' of the third equation, even if it is quite good for the other two. So we can get very bad answers from the computer on some occasions. Let us follow its working to see how to avoid such poor answers, if possible.

The first reduction uses multipliers 10^6 (for the second equation) and 0 (for the third equation), giving

$$\begin{cases} 10^{-6}x & + & z = 1 \\ 10^{-6}y - 10^6 z & = 1 - 10^6 \\ & y + 10^{-6}z = 1. \end{cases}$$

The second reduction uses a multiplier of 10^6 again, and gives (in exact arithmetic)

$$\begin{cases} 10^{-6}x & + & z = 1 \\ 10^{-6}y - 10^6 z = 1 - 10^6 \\ (10^{12} + 10^{-6})z = 10^{12} - 10^6 + 1. \end{cases}$$

But my computer cannot manage numbers like $10^{12} + 10^{-6}$ or $10^{12} - 10^6 + 1$, and replaces them with 10^{12} and $10^{12} - 10^6$. So the computer now holds

$$10^{12}z = 10^{12} - 10^6$$

as its last equation, which has solution

$$z = 1 - 10^{-6} = 0.999\,999.$$

Substitution of this value of z into the modified second equation gives $y=0$, exactly; and the first equation gives $x=1$, again exactly.

The cause of all this trouble has been the use of *large* multipliers (10^6 in each case) which have caused significant figures to be lost. In turn they are due to small elements in the equations which happen to be in important places in the calculation. The result is a set of 'solutions' which are not close to the correct answers. The residuals are

$$0,\ 0,\ 0.999\,999$$

which clearly show how bad the result is, since the largest residual is the same size as the terms occurring in the equation.

In this case we can rearrange the equations very simply to get correct answers. The trouble has arisen with the 10^{-6} terms which we have used in constructing the multipliers for the elimination process. These very small terms have been on the 'leading diagonal' (from top left to bottom right); they are called *pivots* in the Gauss elimination process. In this example the 'first pivot' is the 10^{-6} which is the coefficient of x in the first equation. The 'second pivot' is the 10^{-6} which is the coefficient of y in the *modified* second equation, which was

$$10^{-6}y - 10^6 z = 1 - 10^6.$$

The 'third pivot' is the coefficient of z in the *final* form of the third equation, that is

$$10^{12} + 10^{-6}.$$

When the equations have been fully reduced the pivots are all on the leading diagonal.

We shall interchange the equations before we start the calculation, and write them as

$$\begin{cases} x + 10^{-6}y && = 1 \\ & y + 10^{-6}z = 1 \\ 10^{-6}x & + & z = 1, \end{cases}$$

by putting the first equation last. The first pivot is now 1 (the coefficient of x in the first equation), and the first reduction gives

$$\begin{cases} x + 10^{-6}y && = 1 \\ & y + 10^{-6}z = 1 \\ & -10^{-12}y + & z = 1 - 10^{-6}. \end{cases}$$

The next pivot is also 1 (the coefficient of y in the second equation), and we get

$$\begin{cases} x + 10^{-6}y && = 1 \\ & y + 10^{-6}z = 1 \\ & (1 + 10^{-18})z = 1 - 10^{-6} + 10^{-12}. \end{cases}$$

The last equation is recorded in the computer as

$$z = 1 - 10^{-6},$$

and back substitution leads in turn to

$$y = 1 - 10^{-6}$$
$$x = 1 - 10^{-6},$$

each time dropping off 10^{-12} when 1 is present, because computers can only deal with numbers of a finite length, which in the case of mine is length 12. We have now got good answers, just at the cost of rearranging the equations.

What must be done, then, is to rewrite the computer program so that it automatically rearranges the equations to avoid small pivots. This is achieved by:

(i) looking for the largest size of number (sign doesn't matter) in the column of numbers going down from the current pivot,
(ii) interchanging the equation with this largest number and the equation containing the current pivot.

In the example as it was originally written we had

$$\begin{cases} \underline{10}^{-6}x + & 0y + & 1z = 1 \\ 1x + 10^{-6}y + & 0z = 1 \\ 0x + & 1y + 10^{-6}z = 1. \end{cases}$$

The current pivot is 10^{-6} (underlined), but in the column going down from it there is a larger value (1) in the second equation. So we interchange the first equation and the second to get

$$\begin{cases} \underline{1}x + 10^{-6}y + & 0z = 1 \\ 10^{-6}x + & 0y + & 1z = 1 \\ 0x + & 1y + 10^{-6}z = 1. \end{cases}$$

Now do the reduction process once, to get to

$$\begin{cases} 1x + 10^{-6}y + & 0z = 1 \\ - \underline{10}^{-12}y + & 1z = 1 - 10^{-6} \\ {}^{1}y + 10^{-6}z = 1. \end{cases}$$

The new pivot is 10^{-12} in the second place in the second equation, because we have already dealt with the first equation and the first column. But below it there is a larger value, the 1 in the third equation. So the second and third equations must be interchanged, to get

$$\begin{cases} 1x + 10^{-6}y + & 0z = 1 \\ \underline{1}y + 10^{-6}z = 1 \\ - 10^{-12}y + & 1z = 1 - 10^{-6}, \end{cases}$$

with new second pivot 1. You then do the reduction process again, and get to the good solution we found above.

This improvement is known as (partial) pivoting, and it is usual for Gauss elimination programs for solving equations to include it.

Note that there is no advantage in just multiplying all the equations by 10^6 'to remove the small pivots'. The pivots then remain small compared to the other elements in the equations, and the problem remains.

This example is a very extreme one, with its carefully chosen entries of 10^{-6} so that a product of two (or three) of them would 'fall off the end' of what my computer would record. If your computer is more efficient than mine and uses more digits, then adjust the entries of 10^{-6} to 10^{-7} or 10^{-8} or whatever is needed. In real problems there are usually no such obvious difficulties in the statement of the equations; it is only when the computer gets well into the reduction process that something turns up which starts to lose accuracy through loss of significant information. Automatic partial pivoting is a system which deals well with the problem of small pivots in most cases.

However it does not deal with every problem. One very special case is left to the exercises, but another major problem will be discussed in the next section.

Exercise 5B

1   Review your solutions to questions 1 and 3 in Exercise 5A. You will find that one of them has (in effect) used partial pivoting. Which is it? Does it give the most accurate answers?

2   It could happen that *all* the elements in a particular column are small, and so you are bound to have a small pivot. Take as example

$$\begin{cases} 10^{-6}x + \tfrac{1}{3}y \quad\quad + \tfrac{2}{3}z = 2 \\ 10^{-12}x + \tfrac{2}{3} \times 10^{-6}y + \tfrac{1}{2}z = \tfrac{1}{7} \\ \quad\quad\quad 10^{-12}y + \tfrac{15}{13}z = \tfrac{15}{13}. \end{cases}$$

(a) Solve this set of equations (using a computer and pivoting).
(b) Show why the computer gives $z = 1$ if it is using 12 places in its arithmetic.
(c) Solve it again after interchanging the first and third columns (i.e. redefining x to be z and z to be x); this gives the largest element in the same row *or* column as the first pivot, called *full pivoting*.
(d) Solve it again after changing the variables to

$$\begin{cases} X = 10^{-6}x \\ Y = \quad y \\ Z = \quad z \end{cases}$$

and solving the new equations for X, Y, Z. (The method in (d), i.e. using variables which are all going to have the same sort of size, is the most sensible approach, so full pivoting need not be used here.)

3   How many extra steps are needed to implement partial pivoting for
   (i)   a 3×3 set of equations,
   (ii) a 4×4 set of equations,
   (iii) an $n \times n$ set of equations?

5.3   ILL-CONDITIONING

In Section 3.4 I solved the equations

$$\begin{cases} 2.281\,01x + 1.615\,14y = 2.762\,55 \\ 1.615\,14x + 1.143\,65y = 1.956\,11 \end{cases}$$

to get

$$\begin{cases} x = 9.007\,518\,796 \\ y = -11.010\,068\,679. \end{cases}$$

The true answers are

$$x = 9 \qquad y = -11.$$

When you write out the Gauss elimination routine for this example you get

$$2.281\,01 \quad 1.615\,14 \qquad 2.762\,55$$

$$0 \qquad\quad -5.8 \times 10^{-8} \quad 6.43 \times 10^{-7},$$

where I have still been using my 10 digit scientific calculator. The solution is now

$$\begin{cases} y = -11.086\,206\,89 \\ x = 9.061\,041\,46. \end{cases}$$

You can see why the calculation has been so inaccurate (and why I should only give answers correct to about 1% and not with so much spurious 'accuracy'): the second pivot is tiny, and since it has only two figures in it, it cannot be accurate to more than about 1%.

These equations are said to be *ill-conditioned*. The meaning is that you get very few accurate figures in your answer, despite working to a large number of decimal places in all the calculations. The fundamental cause has been explained already, in Section 3.4; it was the subtraction of nearly equal numbers which gave the second pivot the value

$$-5.8 \times 10^{-8},$$

with the consequent loss of all but two digits.

Even using 12 digits on my computer only gave me a value of -5.834×10^{-8} for the second pivot, and solutions

$$-11.002\,22 \ldots$$

$$9.001\,57 \ldots$$

The easiest way of detecting ill-conditioning in a set of equations is to build into the Gauss elimination a request to print out

(i)   the value of each pivot,
(ii) the product of the pivots.

If you see small pivots (small compared with the general size of the coefficients of the equations) you may expect ill-conditioning. A better test is the magnitude of the product of the pivots: if this is very small compared to a product of typical sized coefficients in the equations, one for each equation, then the system is ill-conditioned.

Ill-conditioning is related to the instability we saw in Section 1.4; in both cases the finite length of numbers used in computer arithmetic can lead to large differences from the correct solution. Let us see what happens if a very small change is made in the equations we have been discussing. As an example, I shall change the coefficient of x in the first equation by 10^{-6} to get

$$2.281\,011x + 1.615\,14y = 2.762\,55.$$

Working with 12 figures on my computer, Gauss elimination now gives

$$4.43 \times 10^{-7}y = 1.49943 \times 10^{-6}$$

for the second equation. Hence the solution is now

$$y = \quad 3.384\ldots$$

$$x = -1.185\ldots$$

This shows why ill-conditioning is so important. What look like trivial changes in the coefficients of the equations can lead to catastrophic changes in the solutions.

There is another consequence of ill-conditioning; the residuals may be very small, even if the solution is quite inaccurate. Take the original equations of this section, whose solutions are exactly $x = 9$ and $y = -11$. Substitute instead the values

$$x = 9.061 \quad \text{and} \quad y = -11.086$$

into the equations, and find the residuals to be

$$\begin{cases} r_1 = -2.3957 \times 10^{-4} \\ r_2 = -1.6964 \times 10^{-4}. \end{cases}$$

The 'solutions' are wrong by about 1%, yet the residuals are very small.

When you have only two or three equations to consider, a geometrical representation of ill-conditioning is available. The two equations of this section represent almost parallel lines (Fig. 1).

Change the slope of one of them slightly, and the point of intersection moves drastically. For three equations you have to consider three planes; taken in pairs

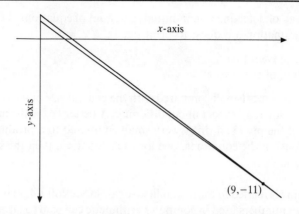

Figure 1. Two ill-conditioned equations give almost parallel lines

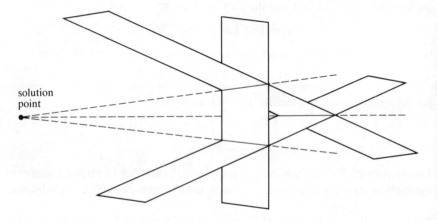

Figure 2. Three ill-conditioned equations give planes whose lines of intersection are almost parallel

they define three lines of intersection which meet at the solution point and which are nearly parallel (Fig. 2).

Exercise 5C

1 Test the equations in Exercise 5A questions 1 and 3 for ill-conditioning. Compare the product of the three pivots for each set of equations.

2 Change the right hand side of the first equation in this section to 2.76256 and solve the pair of equations for this new value. Explain your answer geometrically and algebraically.

3 Are the equations discussed in Section 5.2 ill-conditioned?

4   Test the following set of equations for ill-conditioning.

$$\begin{cases} 0.99x + 0.98y + 0.84z + 0.69t = 0.35 \\ 0.98x + 0.97y + 0.42z + 0.23t = 0.26 \\ 0.80x + 0.46y + 0.84z + 0.30t = 0.23 \\ 0.66x + 0.24y + 0.36z + 0.74t = 0.20 \end{cases}$$

5   Use a Gauss elimination package to test these equations for ill-conditioning, by calculating the product of pivots, for values of n up to 5.

$$x + \tfrac{1}{2}y + \tfrac{1}{3}z + \ldots + \frac{1}{n}w = 1$$

$$\tfrac{1}{2}x + \tfrac{1}{3}y + \tfrac{1}{4}z + \ldots + \frac{1}{n+1}w = 2$$

$$\tfrac{1}{3}x + \tfrac{1}{4}y + \tfrac{1}{5}z + \ldots + \frac{1}{n+2}w = 3$$

$$\ldots$$

$$\frac{1}{n}x + \frac{1}{n+1}y + \frac{1}{n+2}z + \ldots + \frac{1}{2n-1}w = n.$$

For $n = 5$ check the ill-conditioning by changing 5 to 5.0005 in the fifth equation and comparing the % change in the solution with the % change in the coefficient.

5.4   FURTHER DIFFICULTIES

(*a*) The equations

$$\begin{cases} \frac{1}{635}x + y = 17 \\ x + 635y = 10\,795 \end{cases}$$

are in fact the same equation, since $17 \times 635 = 10\,795$. But if I use my calculator, not having noticed that the equations are 'linearly dependent', what I get is

$$\begin{cases} 0.001\,574\,803\,149x + y = 17 \\ -2 \times 10^{-7}y = 0 \end{cases}$$

so that the 'solution' is $y = 0$, $x = 10\,795$.

This is *not* a problem that will arise often. You may be able to detect it by seeing that the second pivot here is just a rounding error, and that a large value has arisen for x because of this.

This is really a special case of ill-conditioning, but my calculator does not notice that the ill-conditioning here is total, i.e. the second pivot should be exactly zero.

(*b*) The equations

$$\begin{cases} \frac{1}{635}x + y = 17 \\ x + 635y = 10\,796 \end{cases}$$

in fact have no solution – they are *inconsistent*. If you multiply the first by 635 you get

$$x + 635y = 10\,795$$

which cannot be true as well as

$$x + 635y = 10\,796.$$

Despite this, my calculator is happy to do a Gauss elimination, giving

$$0.001\,574\,803\,149x + \qquad\quad y = 17$$
$$-2 \times 10^{-7}y = 1,$$

and so

$$y = -5 \times 10^6, \ x = 3.175\ldots \times 10^9.$$

Inconsistent sets of equations are in fact quite important, but this solution is of no value whatever. More useful 'solutions' of inconsistent equations will be described in Chapter 8. For the moment, notice the tiny pivot and the enormous solutions: these are a sign that you may have inconsistent equations.

(*c*) Question 1 in Exercise 5C should suggest to you that the magnitude of the product of the pivots is the same (to within errors due to finite length arithmetic) however you organise the calculation, and this is in fact true. This means that standard Gauss elimination, by always choosing the *largest* pivot in the current column, merely forces smaller pivots to appear later in the calculation, where they will cause trouble. It would, perhaps, be best to devise a system where all pivots were the same size. This is not necessary in practice – you can see that the solutions in Exercises 5A questions 1 and 3 are not very different, despite the differences of the pivots in the three cases. Moreover it would be very difficult to devise a means of achieving this result. So standard Gauss elimination will be left with this small defect.

Exercise 5D

1   Use 4 digit arithmetic to 'solve'

$$\begin{cases} x + \tfrac{1}{2}y + \tfrac{1}{3}z = 4 \\ \tfrac{1}{2}x + \tfrac{1}{3}y + \tfrac{1}{4}z = 3 \\ 5x + \tfrac{17}{6}y + 2z = 24. \end{cases}$$

Verify that the equations are linearly dependent.

2   Use 4 digit arithmetic to 'solve' the equations of question 1, but with 24 replaced by 24.1. Verify that the equations are in fact inconsistent.

5.5   MATRIX CONSIDERATIONS

There are advantages in using matrix notation for theoretical work, as this reduces the working to a compact form.

(*a*) The equations will be written as

$$AX = b$$

where A is (in general) an $n \times n$ matrix and X and b are column vectors ($n \times 1$ matrices). The solution process, due to faulty computer arithmetic, does not produce the solution X, but an approximation x to it, where

$$X = x + \delta x.$$

We know that substituting our 'solutions' into the equations does not satisfy them, but leaves a residual, say r, where

$$r = b - Ax$$
$$= b - A(X - \delta x).$$

Now the equations tell us that

$$b = AX,$$

and so

$$r = A\delta x.$$

This may, in principle, be solved as

$$\delta x = A^{-1} r.$$

The residuals r are always small; and if A^{-1} is not large in some sense, it follows that the errors δx in the solutions are also small. But if A^{-1} is large (in a sense to be made more definite shortly) then δx need not be small, despite r being small. This agrees with our experience of ill-conditioned sets of equations.

(*b*) A crude estimate of the 'size' of a matrix is provided by its determinant, det A, which can be evaluated as the product of the pivots in a Gauss elimination procedure *without* pivoting. Now it is a well known result (i.e. go and look elsewhere, in a book about matrices, such as *Linear Algebra and Geometry* in this series) that

$$\det(A^{-1}) = (\det A)^{-1},$$

so that δx may not be small if det A is small (i.e. if the pivots are small), even though the residuals are small.

In Gauss elimination *with* pivoting, the product of the pivots is equal to

$$(-1)^k \det A,$$

where k is the number of row interchanges that have been carried out. So it remains true that

$$|\det A| = |\text{product of pivots}|.$$

(*c*) If a matrix has a full set of independent eigenvectors, then there is a transformation (using those eigenvectors)

$$U^{-1}AU = \Lambda$$

which gives a diagonal matrix Λ composed of the eigenvectors. (Λ is the Greek capital letter 'lambda', and its lower case version is λ.) Now the determinant of Λ is just the product of its diagonal elements (it needs to have no Gaussian reduction to get it into suitable form), i.e. the product of the eigenvalues of $\mathbf{A}$. Hence

$$\det(\mathbf{U}^{-1}\mathbf{A}\mathbf{U}) = \text{product of eigenvalues.}$$

However, it is another standard result that

$$\det(\mathbf{PQ}) = (\det \mathbf{P})(\det \mathbf{Q})$$

for any square matrices of the same size, and so the product of the eigenvalues of $\mathbf{A}$ equals

$$(\det(\mathbf{U}^{-1}))(\det \mathbf{A})(\det \mathbf{U}),$$

which reduces to just $\det \mathbf{A}$. Hence if you know the eigenvalues of $\mathbf{A}$ you know its determinant.

In fact the condition for ill-conditioning is best put in terms of the eigenvalues λ of $\mathbf{A}$, as

$$|\lambda|_{\min} \ll |\lambda|_{\max}.$$

However, this is usually no help, as the determination of the eigenvalues can take a large amount of work.

Exercise 5E

1   If small changes $\delta\mathbf{A}$ and $\delta\mathbf{b}$ are made to the matrix $\mathbf{A}$ and the vector $\mathbf{b}$, show that the consequent change in the solution vector $\mathbf{X}$ (assuming totally accurate arithmetic) is given by

$$\delta\mathbf{X} \approx \mathbf{A}^{-1}(\delta\mathbf{b} - \delta\mathbf{A}\mathbf{X}).$$

Explain why large changes $\delta\mathbf{X}$ can result from small changes in $\mathbf{b}$ or in $\mathbf{A}$ in an ill-conditioned system.

2   For linearly dependent or inconsistent sets of equations one pivot is exactly zero. Deduce that one eigenvalue is zero.

5.6   SUMMARY

Solving many linear equations is important. The commonest method is a *systematic elimination* method, with *pivoting*; the *residuals* should be calculated, and the *pivots* (and their product) should be recorded.

The combination of many thousands of arithmetical operations, together with the finite length of computer arithmetic, leads to inaccurate answers. The inaccuracies are bad when the equations are *ill-conditioned*. The simplest test for ill-conditioning is to compare the size of the product of all the pivots with a product of typical sized coefficients, one for each equation: if the product of the pivots is very much the smaller, the equations are ill-conditioned. The consequence of ill-conditioning is inaccurate solutions, despite small residuals.

The condition of a set of equations $\mathbf{Ax} = \mathbf{b}$ can be discussed in terms of

(a) the *geometry* of lines, planes, or hyperplanes,
(b) the *eigenvalues* of the matrix $\mathbf{A}$.

6

Matrix iteration

Gauss elimination is a direct attack on solving sets of linear algebraic equations, but it has drawbacks:

(i) the computer program is a trouble to set up,
(ii) the number of operations in running a large set of equations is inevitably high,
(iii) there are difficulties with ill-conditioned sets of equations.

We have seen that many equations in *one* variable will respond to a solution method based on iteration. So why not try iteration on sets of linear algebraic equations? This chapter shows some methods of using iterations on matrix equations, and when they can be efficiently used.

6.1 JACOBI ITERATION

Take the set of three equations

$$\begin{cases} 5x + y - 10z = 4 \\ x - 5y + 3z = 2 \\ 10x \quad + 5z = 5 \end{cases}$$

as an example. I can rearrange them first as

$$\begin{cases} 10x \quad + 5z = 5 \\ x - 5y + 3z = 2 \\ 5x + y - 10z = 4, \end{cases}$$

where I am putting the largest possible elements on the leading diagonal, in much the same way as pivots in Gauss elimination were taken as large as possible. Then I shall rewrite these as

$$\begin{cases} x \quad + \frac{1}{2}z = \frac{1}{2} \\ -\frac{1}{5}x + y - \frac{3}{5}z = -\frac{2}{5} \\ -\frac{1}{2}x - \frac{1}{10}y + z = -\frac{2}{5}, \end{cases}$$

which makes the leading diagonal have all its coefficients just $+1$. Now I do a second rearrangement to

$$\begin{cases} x = & -\tfrac{1}{2}z + \tfrac{1}{2} \\ y = \tfrac{1}{5}x & + \tfrac{3}{5}z - \tfrac{2}{5} \\ z = \tfrac{1}{2}x + \tfrac{1}{10}y & - \tfrac{2}{5}. \end{cases}$$

This set of equations is ready for iteration, and the iteration we shall do first is *Jacobi* iteration, in which we take

$$\begin{cases} x_{n+1} = & -\tfrac{1}{2}z_n + \tfrac{1}{2} \\ y_{n+1} = \tfrac{1}{5}x_n & + \tfrac{3}{5}z_n - \tfrac{2}{5} \\ z_{n+1} = \tfrac{1}{2}x_n + \tfrac{1}{10}y_n & - \tfrac{2}{5}, \end{cases}$$

together with some sensible starting value. Since the coefficients of x_n, y_n, z_n are all moderately small (they have been *forced* to be so in the rearrangement process), we may guess that

$$x_0 = \tfrac{1}{2}, \ y_0 = -\tfrac{2}{5}, \ z_0 = -\tfrac{2}{5}$$

will be reasonable starting values.

A few iterations done by calculator give the following sequence of vectors

$$\begin{pmatrix} x_n \\ y_n \\ z_n \end{pmatrix}$$

$$\begin{pmatrix} 0.5 \\ -0.4 \\ -0.4 \end{pmatrix}, \begin{pmatrix} 0.70 \\ -0.54 \\ -0.19 \end{pmatrix}, \begin{pmatrix} 0.595 \\ -0.374 \\ -0.104 \end{pmatrix}, \begin{pmatrix} 0.5520 \\ -0.3434 \\ -0.1399 \end{pmatrix}, \begin{pmatrix} 0.56995 \\ -0.37354 \\ -0.15834 \end{pmatrix}, \begin{pmatrix} 0.57917 \\ -0.381014 \\ -0.152379 \end{pmatrix}$$

$$n=0 \qquad n=1 \qquad n=2 \qquad n=3 \qquad n=4 \qquad n=5$$

To get a long sequence of vectors it is sensible to use a computer. A simple program gave the following results.

$$\begin{pmatrix} 0.575058\ldots \\ -0.375044\ldots \\ -0.149956\ldots \end{pmatrix} \begin{pmatrix} 0.5749994\ldots \\ -0.3749988\ldots \\ -0.1499989\ldots \end{pmatrix} \begin{pmatrix} 0.5749999793 \\ -0.3749999771 \\ -0.1500000017 \end{pmatrix}$$

$$n=10 \qquad\qquad n=15 \qquad\qquad n=20$$

Clearly the iteration is converging to the correct solution, which is

$$\begin{pmatrix} X \\ Y \\ Z \end{pmatrix} = \begin{pmatrix} 0.575 \\ -0.375 \\ -0.150 \end{pmatrix}.$$

It is convenient to use matrix notation to describe Jacobi iteration. The rearrangement of the equations put them into the form

$$\mathbf{x} = \mathbf{A}\mathbf{x} + \mathbf{b},$$

where **A** was a matrix whose elements were all intended to be *less* than 1 in size. In the example we had

$$\mathbf{A} = \begin{pmatrix} 0 & 0 & -0.5 \\ 0.2 & 0 & 0.6 \\ 0.5 & 0.1 & 0 \end{pmatrix}.$$

It may not be *easy* to carry out such a rearrangement on a large set of equations, and indeed it may not even be *possible*. How can you rearrange the equations

$$\begin{cases} 3x + y + 3z = 1 \\ 3x - y + 3z = 0 \\ 3x + y - 3z = 4 \end{cases}$$

to get them into the required form with a matrix **A** whose entries are all *less* than 1 in size?

Supposing that we have reduced the equations to

$$\mathbf{x} = \mathbf{Ax} + \mathbf{b},$$

with the entries in **A** all less than 1 in modulus, then we can set up the iteration

$$\mathbf{x}_{n+1} = \mathbf{Ax}_n + \mathbf{b},$$

with some starting vector $\mathbf{x}_0$. Let us follow through a few steps of the iteration, as we did when looking for solutions in Chapter 2:

$$\mathbf{x}_1 = \mathbf{Ax}_0 + \mathbf{b},$$
$$\mathbf{x}_2 = \mathbf{Ax}_1 + \mathbf{b} = \mathbf{A}(\mathbf{Ax}_0 + \mathbf{b}) + \mathbf{b}$$
$$= \mathbf{A}^2 \mathbf{x}_0 + (\mathbf{A} + \mathbf{I})\mathbf{b},$$
$$\mathbf{x}_3 = \mathbf{Ax}_2 + \mathbf{b}$$
$$= \mathbf{A}\{\mathbf{A}^2 \mathbf{x}_0 + (\mathbf{A} + \mathbf{I})\mathbf{b}\} + \mathbf{b}$$
$$= \mathbf{A}^3 \mathbf{x}_0 + (\mathbf{A}^2 + \mathbf{A} + \mathbf{I})\mathbf{b}.$$

In this calculation **I** is the appropriately sized unit matrix, and it is clear that you will get

$$\mathbf{x}_n = \mathbf{A}^n \mathbf{x}_0 + (\mathbf{A}^{n-1} + \mathbf{A}^{n-2} + \dots + \mathbf{I})\mathbf{b}.$$

Two things are evident from this formula. First, if $\mathbf{A}^n$ does not tend to $\mathbf{0}$ as n gets large, then the iteration depends on what vector $\mathbf{x}_0$ you use as an initial guess; this cannot be right, as a set of linear equations can only have one solution. Second, the sum matrix

$$\mathbf{A}^{n-1} + \mathbf{A}^{n-2} + \dots + \mathbf{I}$$

must not continue to grow as n gets bigger and bigger, or else the iteration *cannot* converge to give a sensible result for the solution vector $\mathbf{x}$. Thus it appears that we must have

$$\mathbf{A}^n \to \mathbf{0}$$

in order to have a convergent Jacobi iteration. This is why the entries in $\mathbf{A}$ have to be made small, because otherwise there would appear to be no hope of getting $\mathbf{A}^n \to \mathbf{0}$. Moreover, it would seem that the smaller the elements in $\mathbf{A}$, the quicker the convergence would be. In the example we did above the largest sized element in $\mathbf{A}$ was 0.6, and we needed 15 iterations to get an answer accurate to 5 significant figures.

To investigate these ideas, I ran a Jacobi iteration using the matrix and vector

$$\mathbf{A} = \begin{pmatrix} 0 & a & 2a & 3a \\ -a & 0 & a & -a \\ 2a & a & 0 & 2a \\ 0 & -a & a & 0 \end{pmatrix}, \mathbf{b} = \begin{pmatrix} 1 \\ 2 \\ 3 \\ 4 \end{pmatrix}$$

for various values of a, to see how many iterations were needed to get accurate answers. My results were as follows, when I used the vector $\mathbf{b}$ as $\mathbf{x}_0$.

(i) $a = 0.05$ $n = 9$
(ii) $a = 0.10$ $n = 13$
(iii) $a = 0.20$ $n = 28$
(iv) $a = 0.25$ $n = 46$
(v) $a = 0.30$ $n = 96$
(vi) $a = 0.33$ $n = 227$

This shows clearly that the process converges rapidly when all the elements are small in size, and that when the top right element (which is the largest in this example) approaches 1, the number of iterations becomes rather large. In fact the iteration *still* converges when this element exceeds 1: there is *no* absolute requirement which says that all elements in $\mathbf{A}$ must be less than 1 in size for convergence. Two further runs gave

(vii) $a = 0.35$ $n = 1516$
(viii) $a = 0.40$ no convergence.

We will investigate convergence of Jacobi iteration more fully in Section 6.3, but it seems clear from this example that convergence occurs if $\mathbf{A}$ has elements of small size, and divergence starts when the elements of $\mathbf{A}$ (or at least some of them) reach 1 in size.

Exercise 6A

1   Rearrange the equations

$$\begin{cases} x - 2y = -2 \\ 2x + y = 2 \end{cases}$$

for Jacobi iteration. How many iterations are needed to get a solution with 6 significant figures correct? Start with $x_0 = y_0 = 1$.

2 Solve the equations

(i) $\begin{cases} 10x + 8y + z = -7 \\ 4x + 10y - 5z = 2 \\ 10x + 2y + 20z = 3 \end{cases}$

(ii) $\begin{cases} 7x + 3y + 2z = 13 \\ 2x - y + 5z = 12 \\ x + 4y - z = 8 \end{cases}$

by Jacobi iteration, giving the number of iterations needed for 6 significant figure accuracy.

3 The equations

$$\begin{cases} 5x - 7y + 4z = 16 \\ 5x + y - 5z = 12 \\ x - y - z = 0 \end{cases}$$

were solved by Gauss elimination in Section 5.1. Can you solve them by Jacobi iteration? If so, about how many iterations do you guess will be needed for 6 significant figure accuracy? See how long it takes to get one figure fixed, and then two, and then guess.

4 Show that

$$(A - I)(A^{n-1} + A^{n-2} + \ldots + A + I) = A^n - I.$$

Hence deduce the sum of the 'geometric progression'

$$A^{n-1} + A^{n-2} + \ldots + A + I.$$

What does it tend to, as n gets very large, if $A^n \to 0$? Deduce that the Jacobi iteration has as its limiting vector

$$x = (I - A)^{-1} b.$$

Does this satisfy the equation $x = Ax + b$?

5 Iterations of the form

$$Dx_{n+1} = Ax_n + b$$

where D is a simple matrix, i.e. one for which the equations

$$Dx = k$$

can be easily solved, are sometimes called Jacobi iterations. Find the corresponding 'proper' Jacobi form when D is a diagonal matrix.

6.2 GAUSS–SEIDEL ITERATION

The first Jacobi iteration that we did in Section 6.1 used the equations

$$\begin{cases} x_{n+1} = & \tfrac{1}{2}z_n + \tfrac{1}{2} \\ y_{n+1} = \tfrac{1}{5}x_n & + \tfrac{3}{5}z_n - \tfrac{2}{5} \\ z_{n+1} = \tfrac{1}{2}x_n + \tfrac{1}{10}y_n & - \tfrac{2}{5}. \end{cases}$$

In this method we used the *old* values of x, y, z consistently on the right hand side, but there is no reason to do this. After all, when the first equation has been solved we have found what is presumably a better value, x_{n+1}, to replace x_n with. Why not do so in the remaining equations? This leads to *Gauss–Seidel* iteration, which for this example is

$$\begin{cases} x_{n+1} = & -\frac{1}{2}z_n + \frac{1}{2} \\ y_{n+1} = \frac{1}{5}x_{n+1} & +\frac{3}{5}z_n - \frac{2}{5} \\ z_{n+1} = \frac{1}{2}x_{n+1} + \frac{1}{10}y_{n+1} & -\frac{2}{5}. \end{cases}$$

That is, the new values are used as soon as they are ready, in all subsequent equations. The first few vectors, starting as before from

$$\mathbf{x}_0 = \begin{pmatrix} 0.5 \\ -0.4 \\ -0.4 \end{pmatrix},$$

are

$$\mathbf{x}_1 = \begin{pmatrix} 0.7 \\ -0.5 \\ -0.1 \end{pmatrix}, \mathbf{x}_2 = \begin{pmatrix} 0.55 \\ -0.35 \\ -0.16 \end{pmatrix}, \mathbf{x}_3 = \begin{pmatrix} 0.58 \\ -0.38 \\ -0.148 \end{pmatrix}, \mathbf{x}_4 = \begin{pmatrix} 0.574 \\ -0.374 \\ -0.1504 \end{pmatrix}.$$

Therefore you find

$$\mathbf{x}_{10} = \begin{pmatrix} 0.574\,999\,936 \\ -0.374\,999\,936 \\ -0.150\,000\,025\,6 \end{pmatrix},$$

and this is already very close to the true answer. For this example the Gauss–Seidel method has converged considerably faster than the Jacobi iteration.

In matrix notation, we have

$$\mathbf{x} = \mathbf{Ax} + \mathbf{b},$$

and then we split $\mathbf{A}$ into a 'lower triangular' part $\mathbf{L}$ and an 'upper triangular' part $\mathbf{U}$ so as to get the iteration

$$\mathbf{x}_{n+1} = \mathbf{Lx}_{n+1} + \mathbf{Ux}_n + \mathbf{b}.$$

In this example we had

$$\mathbf{L} = \begin{pmatrix} 0 & 0 & 0 \\ 0.2 & 0 & 0 \\ 0.5 & 0.1 & 0 \end{pmatrix}, \mathbf{U} = \begin{pmatrix} 0 & 0 & -0.5 \\ 0 & 0 & 0.6 \\ 0 & 0 & 0 \end{pmatrix}.$$

The entries in $\mathbf{L}$ are all *below* the principal diagonal from top left to bottom right, while the elements in $\mathbf{U}$ are all above that diagonal.

You can therefore write this iteration as

$$(\mathbf{I} - \mathbf{L})\mathbf{x}_{n+1} = \mathbf{U}\mathbf{x}_n + \mathbf{b}$$

or

$$\mathbf{x}_{n+1} = (\mathbf{I} - \mathbf{L})^{-1}\mathbf{U}\mathbf{x}_n + (\mathbf{I} - \mathbf{L})^{-1}\mathbf{b}.$$

It is thus of the same form as the Jacobi iteration, but with $\mathbf{A}$ replaced by $(\mathbf{I} - \mathbf{L})^{-1}\mathbf{U}$, and $\mathbf{b}$ replaced by $(\mathbf{I} - \mathbf{L})^{-1}\mathbf{b}$. However, you do not need to calculate $(\mathbf{I} - \mathbf{L})^{-1}\mathbf{U}$ or $(\mathbf{I} - \mathbf{L})^{-1}\mathbf{b}$ in order to run the iteration, you just need to use the latest available values of x, y, z.

Thus the convergence of Gauss–Seidel iteration will depend on whether

$$\{(\mathbf{I} - \mathbf{L})^{-1}\mathbf{U}\}^n \to 0;$$

this corresponds to the condition that $\mathbf{A}^n \to 0$ for Jacobi iteration to converge.

Let us try again the example

$$\mathbf{A} = \begin{pmatrix} 0 & a & 2a & 3a \\ -a & 0 & a & -a \\ 2a & a & 0 & a \\ 0 & -a & a & 0 \end{pmatrix}, \mathbf{b} = \begin{pmatrix} 1 \\ 2 \\ 3 \\ 4 \end{pmatrix}$$

to see what improvement Gauss–Seidel iteration makes. I again used the vector $\mathbf{b}$ as the starting vector $\mathbf{x}_0$ of the iteration, and found the following,

(i) $a = 0.25$ $n = 23$
(ii) $a = 0.3$ $n = 47$
(iii) $a = 0.33$ $n = 110$
(iv) $a = 0.35$ $n = 728$
(v) $a = 0.40$ no convergence.

You can see that for each value of a that I tested, the iteration gets to the end in about half the number of steps than were needed in Jacobi iteration. Gauss–Seidel is *usually* (though not always) better than Jacobi iteration. Notice that Gauss–Seidel in this example has not converged over a larger range of a; there is bound to be some change, because

$$(\mathbf{I} - \mathbf{L})^{-1}\mathbf{U} \neq \mathbf{A},$$

but it has not been detected in this experiment.

Exercise 6B

1   Use Gauss–Seidel iteration on the equations in Exercise 6A, question 2. How many iterations do you need this time for 6 figure accuracy?

2   Repeat question 3 of Exercise 6A using Gauss–Seidel iteration.

3   A set of four equations in four unknowns has been arranged as

$$\mathbf{x} = \mathbf{A}\mathbf{x} + \mathbf{b},$$

with the elements of **A** all being small. How many multiplications and how many additions are needed for each step of

(i) Jacobi iteration,
(ii) Gauss–Seidel iteration?

How many for an $n \times n$ matrix **A**? Compare the computing cost of solving n equations

(a) directly using Gauss elimination;
(b) iteratively using 20 steps of the Gauss–Seidel method.

(Remember that some elements of **A** are *always* zero.)

4   Go back to the ill-conditioned set of equations in Section 5.3. Try using Jacobi and Gauss–Seidel iteration to solve these equations.

5   Consider the equations

$$\begin{cases} x + py = b \\ qx + y = c \end{cases}$$

where p and q are both less than 1 in modulus. Write them in the form

$$(\mathbf{I} - \mathbf{L})x = \mathbf{U}x + \mathbf{b}$$

ready for Gauss–Seidel iteration. Calculate

$$(\mathbf{I} - \mathbf{L})^{-1}$$

and

$$(\mathbf{I} - \mathbf{L})^{-1}\mathbf{U}.$$

Show that

$$\{((\mathbf{I} - \mathbf{L})^{-1})\mathbf{U}\}^n \to \mathbf{0}.$$

6   Show that if p and q in question 5 are both very close to 1, the equations are ill-conditioned. Show that Gauss–Seidel convergence is then very slow.

7   As in Exercise 6A, question 5, pseudo-Gauss–Seidel iterations

$$\mathbf{D}x_{n+1} = \mathbf{L}x_{n+1} + \mathbf{U}x_n + \mathbf{b}$$

can be considered. Show how to convert this equation to a proper Gauss–Seidel iteration when **D** is a matrix with zeros above the principal diagonal.

6.3 CONVERGENCE

We have seen that, when the matrix **A** has small elements, both Jacobi and Gauss–Seidel iterations arrive at the correct solution (to within the limits of computer arithmetic). That is, they converge to the solution. We now need to think about three sorts of question.

(a) How can we measure this convergence? It is not a simple question since the iterates and solution are all *vectors* which may have 10 or 20 components.
(b) How fast is the convergence, in the examples we have seen and in general?
(c) Are there any useful theorems that tell you when, and how fast, the iterations will converge to the answer?

(a) Measuring convergence

Think back to what we did in Section 4.4 for iterations of the form

$$x_{n+1} = f(x_n),$$

which were converging to a solution X. We defined the errors at each iteration by

$$\varepsilon_n = X - x_n,$$

and convergence meant that

$$|\varepsilon_n| \to 0$$

as n gets large. In the present context we have an iteration

$$\mathbf{x}_{n+1} = \mathbf{A}\mathbf{x}_n$$

converging to a solution vector $\mathbf{X}$, and we can define a *vector* of errors

$$\boldsymbol{\varepsilon}_n = \mathbf{X} - \mathbf{x}_n.$$

For example if you are dealing with four equations with the four unknowns $x, y, z,$ t, and solution X, Y, Z, T, then we have

$$\mathbf{x}_n = \begin{pmatrix} x_n \\ y_n \\ z_n \\ t_n \end{pmatrix} \quad \text{and} \quad \boldsymbol{\varepsilon}_n = \begin{pmatrix} X - x_n \\ Y - y_n \\ Z - z_n \\ T - t_n \end{pmatrix}.$$

These vectors $\mathbf{x}_n$, $\mathbf{X}$ and $\boldsymbol{\varepsilon}_n$ are 'four-dimensional' vectors, with properties very like those of ordinary (geometrical) vectors in two or three dimensions. In particular, they have a 'length' derived from 'Pythagoras' theorem':

$$\text{length of } \mathbf{x}_n = \{x_n^2 + y_n^2 + z_n^2 + t_n^2\}^{1/2}.$$

This gives a first way of measuring convergence, for it is clear that

(i) if $\boldsymbol{\varepsilon}_n \to \mathbf{0}$ (i.e. all its components individually $\to 0$) then the length of $\boldsymbol{\varepsilon}_n \to 0$ also,
(ii) if the length of $\boldsymbol{\varepsilon}_n \to 0$ then also $\boldsymbol{\varepsilon}_n \to \mathbf{0}$ (i.e. each component $\to 0$).

It is convenient to have a symbol for 'length', and it is usual to put

$$|\boldsymbol{\varepsilon}_n| = \text{length of } \boldsymbol{\varepsilon}_n$$

for the square root of the sum of the squares of the components of $\boldsymbol{\varepsilon}_n$.

But this is not the *only* useful way of measuring the size of $\boldsymbol{\varepsilon}_n$. You could just as well take the element of $\boldsymbol{\varepsilon}_n$ which has *largest* size; if it is approaching zero, then so clearly is the whole of $\boldsymbol{\varepsilon}_n$. You could otherwise take the sum of the sizes of the elements of $\boldsymbol{\varepsilon}_n$ as a measure of how near $\boldsymbol{\varepsilon}_n$ is to the zero vector; again, if this is approaching zero, so must the vector $\boldsymbol{\varepsilon}_n$ be approaching the zero vector.

These are three examples of what are called *norms* of vectors. The notation usually used is

$$
\begin{cases}
\|\varepsilon_n\|_2 \text{ for what we have called length,} \\
\|\varepsilon_n\|_\infty \text{ for the largest sized element,} \\
\|\varepsilon_n\|_1 \text{ for the sum of moduli of elements}
\end{cases}
$$

(read as 'the 2 norm of ε_n', and so on).

It is clearly time to see this in action. I shall use the first example of Jacobi iteration from Section 6.1. First I shall look at the lengths of the error vectors. Since in this example the solution vector is

$$
\mathbf{X} = \begin{pmatrix} X \\ Y \\ Z \end{pmatrix} = \begin{pmatrix} 0.575 \\ -0.375 \\ -0.150 \end{pmatrix},
$$

we have

$$
\varepsilon_0 = \begin{pmatrix} X - x_0 \\ Y - y_0 \\ Z - z_0 \end{pmatrix} = \begin{pmatrix} 0.075 \\ 0.025 \\ 0.250 \end{pmatrix}
$$

so that

$$
\|\varepsilon_0\|_2 = |\varepsilon_0| = \{(X - x_0)^2 + (Y - y_0)^2 + (Z - z_0)^2\}^{1/2} = 0.2622
$$

to 4 significant figures. Similar calculations give the sequence of error lengths

n	$|\varepsilon_n|$
1	0.2108
2	0.05017
3	0.04037
4	9.858×10^{-3}
5	7.695×10^{-3}
6	1.992×10^{-3}
10	8.516×10^{-5}
15	1.671×10^{-6}
20	3.096×10^{-8}

Similarly, if you use the largest sized element in ε_n (the *infinity norm*) as a measure of how big ε_n is, you get the following sequence.

n	$\|\varepsilon_n\|_\infty$
0	0.250
1	0.165
2	0.046
3	0.0316
4	8.34×10^{-3}
5	6.014×10^{-3}
6	1.484×10^{-3}
10	5.828×10^{-5}
15	5.541×10^{-7}
20	2.292×10^{-8}

There is no great difference from the sequence of lengths, and we shall usually use lengths when we are talking about convergence. The calculation of the other convergence measure, the sum of the sizes of the components of ε_n (the 1 norm) is left to the exercises.

You will notice that both sequences of measures for the error decrease, but not in a very regular fashion.

(b) Rate of convergence

In Section 4.4 the rate of convergence was estimated by taking values of the ratio

$$\varepsilon_{n+1}/\varepsilon_n,$$

and we found that, for a range of values of n, this became very close to

$$-0.1501.$$

This let us talk about first order processes for which

$$\varepsilon_{n+1}/\varepsilon_n \to K, \; K \neq 0,$$

as n gets large. What are the corresponding ideas here?

Let us look at the example again. When you calculate the ratio of lengths

$$|\varepsilon_{n+1}|/|\varepsilon_n|,$$

which seems a reasonable generalisation, you get

n	ratio
0	0.8040
1	0.2380
2	0.8047
3	0.2442
4	0.7806
5	0.2589

(using 4 s.f. in the ratios). You also get

n	5	10	15
$\lvert\varepsilon_{n+5}\rvert/\lvert\varepsilon_n\rvert$	0.01107	0.01962	0.01853

and this should be about K^5 if $\lvert\varepsilon_{n+1}\rvert/\lvert\varepsilon_n\rvert$ is tending to a constant K. It appears that, using this measure of convergence, there is something like a first order process with an average value of the constant

$$K \approx 0.45,$$

after a period of considerable fluctuation at the start.

Why is there such fluctuation here, when in Section 4.4 the decrease of ε_n was by a very nearly constant factor on each iteration? We can understand this to some extent geometrically, especially in this three dimensional case. Start from the iteration equation

$$\mathbf{x}_{n+1} = \mathbf{A}\mathbf{x}_n + \mathbf{b}.$$

Now since $\mathbf{X}$ is the correct solution of this we must have

$$\mathbf{X} = \mathbf{A}\mathbf{X} + \mathbf{b}.$$

Subtract these to find

$$\varepsilon_{n+1} = \mathbf{X} - \mathbf{x}_{n+1} = \mathbf{A}(\mathbf{X} - \mathbf{x}_n) = \mathbf{A}\varepsilon_n.$$

The matrix $\mathbf{A}$ is performing some selection of operations like

rotations, reflections, shears

on any vector it operates on, as well as a set of three contractions along some directions, and these contractions are not necessarily of equal size. Thus if ε_n happens to be lined up with a direction associated with a *large* contraction, it will generate a vector ε_{n+1} of much smaller size. But if it happens to be near a direction of *lesser* contraction, the corresponding ε_{n+1} will have a length only slightly shorter than that of ε_n. Life in three dimensions is much more complicated than in only one dimension!

Exercise 6C

1   Use the equations of Exercise 6A question 1 and Jacobi iteration to generate a sequence of error vectors ε_n. Plot the first 6 on graph paper. What is the geometrical effect of the matrix $\mathbf{A}$ in this example?

2   Use the equations of Exercise 6A, question 2(ii) and Jacobi iteration to generate a sequence of error vectors ε_n, $n = 0$ to 10. Calculate the corresponding values for

(i) $\lvert\varepsilon_n\rvert = \lVert\varepsilon_n\rVert_2$, the length of ε_n;
(ii) $\lVert\varepsilon_n\rVert_1$, the sum of the sizes of the components of ε_n;
(iii) $\lVert\varepsilon_n\rVert_\infty$, the largest of the sizes of the components of ε_n.

3   Calculate the errors ε_n, $n=0$ to 4, for the equations (from Section 6.1)

$$\begin{cases} x_{n+1} = & -\tfrac{1}{2}z_n + \tfrac{1}{2} \\ y_{n+1} = \tfrac{1}{5}x_{n+1} & +\tfrac{3}{5}z_n - \tfrac{2}{5} \\ z_{n+1} = \tfrac{1}{2}x_{n+1} + \tfrac{1}{10}y_{n+1} & -\tfrac{2}{5} \end{cases}$$

and determine the rate-of-convergence constant K for this iteration.

4   Calculate the 1 norm $\|\varepsilon_n\|_1$ for the iterates in the first example in Section 6.1.

5   Show that, in the iteration $\mathbf{x}_{n+1} = \mathbf{A}\mathbf{x}_n + \mathbf{b}$,

$$\varepsilon_n = \mathbf{A}^n\varepsilon_0$$

and hence prove that $\mathbf{A}^n \to \mathbf{0}$ is needed for an iterative process to converge.

(c)   Theorems on convergence

The remaining question on convergence was, what theorems are there? I do not expect that you will want to study all the proofs in detail, so I am putting the results first, and putting some proofs in the exercises.

> Theorem 6.1   If the largest row sum of moduli of elements in $\mathbf{A}$ is *less* than 1, then both the Jacobi and Gauss–Seidel iterations using $\mathbf{A}$ converge.

Example 1.1

The matrix

$$\mathbf{A} = \begin{pmatrix} 0 & 0 & -0.5 \\ 0.2 & 0 & 0.6 \\ 0.5 & 0.1 & 0 \end{pmatrix}$$

was used in Sections 6.1 and 6.2. The row sums of moduli of elements are

$$\text{first row: } |0| + |0| + |-0.5| = 0.5$$
$$\text{second row: } |0.2| + |0| + |0.6| = 0.8$$
$$\text{third row: } |0.5| + |0.1| + |0| = 0.6$$

The largest of these is 0.8, which is indeed less than 1. This agrees with the fact that both iterations converged.

Example 1.2

The matrix

$$\mathbf{A} = \begin{pmatrix} 0 & 0.25 & 0.5 & 0.75 \\ -0.25 & 0 & 0.25 & -0.25 \\ 0.5 & 0.25 & 0 & 0.5 \\ 0 & -0.25 & 0.25 & 0 \end{pmatrix}$$

was also used in each section. The two iteration schemes both converged. The largest row sum of moduli of elements is provided by the first row:

$$|0| + |0.25| + |0.5| + |0.75| = 1.5.$$

This is greater than 1, but that does *not* contradict the theorem, which does *not* say that

$$\text{convergence} \Rightarrow \text{row sum} < 1.$$

As this example shows, convergence may well happen with a largest row sum of moduli *greater* than 1; the theorem merely says that you cannot be *certain* of convergence using this test unless the row sums of moduli are all less than 1.

Theorem 6.2   If the largest column sum of moduli of elements of **A** is less than 1, then both Jacobi and Gauss–Seidel iterations converge.

Example 2.1

If you use the matrix

$$A = \begin{pmatrix} 0 & 0.6 & -0.7 \\ -0.5 & 0 & 0.1 \\ 0.2 & 0.3 & 0 \end{pmatrix}$$

for either iteration method, then you will get convergence, because the column sums of moduli are

$$\text{column 1: } |0| \quad + |-0.5| + |0.2| = 0.7$$
$$\text{column 2: } |0.6| \quad + |0| \quad + |0.3| = 0.9$$
$$\text{column 3: } |-0.7| + |0.1| \quad + |0| \quad = 0.8$$

The largest of these is 0.9, which is less than 1. Note that Theorem 6.1 tells you nothing here, as the top row sum of moduli exceeds 1.

Example 2.2

For the matrix in Example 1.1 the third column sum of moduli is 1.1, so Theorem 6.2 tells you nothing about the convergence of the iterations.

Example 2.3

For the matrix in Example 1.2 you get no information from either of Theorems 6.1 or 6.2. Yet both iteration schemes converge, as we have seen.

Theorem 6.3   (*a*) Jacobi iteration converges if and only if all the eigenvalues of **A** have modulus less than 1.
(*b*) Gauss–Seidel iteration converges if and only if all the eigenvalues of $(\mathbf{I} - \mathbf{L})^{-1}\mathbf{U}$ have modulus less than 1.

These are very precise tests, which *can* be read either way round; for example

(moduli of eigenvalues < 1) ⇒ (Jacobi converges)

and also

(Jacobi converges) ⇒ (moduli of eigenvalues < 1).

Example 3.1

The eigenvalues λ of the matrix

$$\begin{pmatrix} 0 & a & 2a & 3a \\ -a & 0 & a & -a \\ 2a & a & 0 & 2a \\ 0 & -a & a & 0 \end{pmatrix}$$

satisfy the equation

$$\lambda^4 - 7a^2\lambda^2 - 6a^3\lambda + 9a^4 = 0$$

(see *Linear Algebra and Geometry* in this series, for how to derive it). When I put the corresponding equation for $\mu = \lambda/a$ (this is the Greek letter 'mu') on my graphics calculator, I found that it had two real roots, at

$$\mu \approx 2.828 \quad \text{and} \quad 0.8085.$$

Since

$$(\mu - 2.828)(\mu - 0.8085)$$

must be a factor of

$$\mu^4 - 7\mu^2 - 6\mu + 9 = 0,$$

the other factor works out as

$$\mu^2 + 3.637\mu + 3.936.$$

The other two roots are therefore

$$\mu \approx -1.818 \pm 1.258j$$

$$= 2.211 \, (\cos\alpha \pm j\sin\alpha)$$

where $\alpha = 145.3^0$ and $j = \sqrt{(-1)}$.

The moduli of the four eigenvalues are consequently

$$2.828a, \, 2.211a \text{ (twice)}, \, 0.8085a.$$

These are all less than 1 if

$$a < 0.354,$$

which agrees well with our discovery that Jacobi iteration converged (very slowly) for

$$a = 0.35.$$

This theorem looks as though it will be a great deal of trouble to apply, since the equation for the eigenvalues λ is hard to find and hard to solve, especially for matrices of large size. This problem can be overcome, as we shall see in the next section.

Exercise 6D

1 Use the theorems of this section to show that the equations of Exercise 6A, question 2, give convergent Jacobi and Gauss–Seidel iterations.

2 Use the theorems of this section to show that the equations of Exercise 6A, question 3, give a convergent Jacobi iteration.

3 Use the theorems of this section to find for what values of p and q the Gauss–Seidel iteration for question 5 of Exercise 6B converges.

4 Suppose that there is a matrix U such that

$$A = U\Lambda U^{-1}$$

where Λ is a diagonal matrix composed of eigenvalues of A. Show that

$$A^n = U\Lambda^n U^{-1}$$

where Λ^n is a diagonal matrix composed of nth powers of eigenvalues of A. Hence show that

$$A^n \to 0$$

as n gets large, and that Jacobi iteration converges, if all the eigenvalues are less than 1 in modulus. (For the existence of U see *Linear Algebra and Geometry* in this series, and other texts.)

5 Suppose that the largest row sum of moduli of elements for the matrix A is

$$C < 1.$$

Given that

$$\varepsilon_{n+1} = A\varepsilon_n,$$

show that the largest modulus component of ε_{n+1} has modulus less than C times the largest modulus component of ε_n. Hence show that the corresponding Jacobi iteration converges.

6 Suppose that the largest column sum of moduli of elements for the matrix A is

$$K < 1.$$

Given that

$$\varepsilon_{n+1} = A\varepsilon_n,$$

show that the sum of the moduli of the components of ε_{n+1} is less than K times the sum of the moduli of the components of ε_n. Hence show that the corresponding Jacobi iteration converges.

7 Prove results corresponding to questions 4, 5 and 6 for Gauss–Seidel iterations.

6.4   THE EIGENVALUE OF LARGEST MODULUS

It is only the eigenvalue of largest modulus that is needed in Theorem 6.3 for testing the convergence of a Jacobi or Gauss–Seidel iteration, and we can determine whether this modulus is greater or less than 1 quite easily.

> **Theorem 6.4**   If λ is the eigenvalue of largest modulus of the matrix $\mathbf{A}$ and $\mathbf{u}$ is (almost) any vector, then
>
> $$|\mathbf{A}^{n+1}\mathbf{u}|/|\mathbf{A}^n\mathbf{u}| \to |\lambda|$$
>
> as n gets large. The exceptional vectors are those perpendicular to the corresponding eigenvector of $\mathbf{A}$.

Example 4.1

Take

$$\mathbf{A} = \begin{pmatrix} 0 & 0.4 & 0.8 & 1.2 \\ -0.4 & 0 & 0.4 & -0.4 \\ 0.8 & 0.4 & 0 & 0.4 \\ 0 & -0.4 & 0.4 & 0 \end{pmatrix}$$

and take

$$\mathbf{u} = \begin{pmatrix} 1 \\ 1 \\ 1 \\ 1 \end{pmatrix}.$$

Then the sequence of numbers $|\mathbf{A}^{n+1}\mathbf{u}|/|\mathbf{A}^n\mathbf{u}|$ is (keeping 4 s.f.)

n	values
0	1.456
1	0.775
2	1.164
3	1.120
4	0.888

n	5	10	15	20	25
values	1.245	1.110	1.067	1.055	1.052

It looks as though $|\lambda|$ for the eigenvalue of largest modulus is about 1.05. This agrees with (slowly) divergent Jacobi iteration for this case.

Example 4.2

The matrix

$$A = \begin{pmatrix} 0 & 0 & -0.5 \\ 0.2 & 0 & 0.6 \\ 0.5 & 0.1 & 0 \end{pmatrix}$$

has already been shown to give convergent Jacobi iteration (by the row sum test). Therefore we know, from Theorem 6.3 above, that the eigenvalue of largest modulus has modulus less than 1. Let us try to find it by iteration. Use the initial vector

$$\mathbf{u} = \begin{pmatrix} 1 \\ 1 \\ 1 \end{pmatrix}$$

and iterate as before. The sequence of iterates

$$|A^{n+1}\mathbf{u}|/|A^n\mathbf{u}|$$

does not converge, and in fact seems to oscillate randomly between about 0.24 and 0.80. The reason for this is that the equation for the eigenvalues λ in this case is

$$\lambda^3 + 0.19\lambda + 0.01 = 0.$$

The real root here (from my graphics plotter) is at

$$\lambda = -0.051$$

and hence the equation factorises as

$$(\lambda^2 - 0.051\lambda + 0.196)(\lambda + 0.051) = 0.$$

Consequently the other two roots are

$$\lambda = 0.026 \pm 0.442j$$

approximately, which have modulus 0.443. The maximum value of $|\lambda|$ is indeed less than 1, but Theorem 6.4 does not apply as there is not a *single* eigenvalue of largest modulus. You need a more refined theorem than Theorem 6.4 to deal with this case, and you will have to find that in more specialised texts.

Exercise 6E

1   Find the modulus of the eigenvalue of largest modulus for

$$A = \begin{pmatrix} 0 & 1 & 1 \\ 1 & 0 & 1 \\ 0 & 1 & 0 \end{pmatrix}$$

by iteration.

2   The sequence of iterates in Example 4.1 is a convergent first order process. Use Aitken's acceleration technique on the values for $n = 10, 15, 20$ to find a good value of the limit $|\lambda|_{max}$.

3   Construct a proof of Theorem 6.4, using

$$\mathbf{u} = \alpha \mathbf{e}_1 + \beta \mathbf{e}_2 + \ldots + \nu \mathbf{e}_m$$

where $\mathbf{e}_i$ are eigenvectors of $\mathbf{A}$. (ν is the Greek letter 'nu'.)

6.5   ITERATION OR ELIMINATION?

If you are presented with a set of, say, 20 equations in 20 unknowns, should you use Gauss elimination or a version of iteration?

The first question to ask is this. Is the matrix of the equations going to give a form

$$\mathbf{x} = \mathbf{A}\mathbf{x} + \mathbf{b}$$

with $\mathbf{A}$ having small entries? If the entries are not small, then the iterative processes we have been discussing are unlikely to converge and you *have* to use Gauss elimination.

If the answer to the first question is yes, you need to know approximately how many iterations will be needed for convergence. This may be estimated from sums of row moduli, or sums of column moduli, or largest eigenvalue modulus. If these are around $\frac{1}{2}$ in size, then each iteration will reduce one of the error norms by about $\frac{1}{2}$, so that to gain three extra places of accuracy you need about 10 iterations. But if they are about $\frac{1}{10}$ in size, then each iteration gives an extra place of accuracy. You can see this happening in the second example in Section 6.1, where

$$a = 0.33 \text{ needed 227 iterations,}$$

while

$$a = 0.20 \text{ needed 28 iterations,}$$

and

$$a = 0.05 \text{ needed 9 iterations.}$$

The largest modulus eigenvalues in the three cases were 0.933, 0.566 and 0.141 respectively, and all of 0.933^{227}, 0.566^{28}, 0.141^9 are less than 1.5×10^{-7}.

It may still be that iteration seems to need more computer arithmetical operations if the number of iterations exceeds the number of variables in the equations (see the estimates in question 3 of Exercise 6B and question 2 of Exercise 5A). However there are some classes of problems (notably to do with solving differential equations with conditions given at more than one point) where the matrix $\mathbf{A}$ is 'sparse', having far fewer than 400 non-zero entries in a 20×20 matrix, in some organised way. The number of operations can then be reduced by not doing the ones involving zeros.

Exercise 6F

1   For what values of a would you certainly prefer Gauss elimination to iteration for the
equations

$$\begin{pmatrix} 1 & a & 2a & 3a \\ -a & 1 & a & -a \\ 2a & a & 1 & 2a \\ 0 & -a & a & 1 \end{pmatrix} \begin{pmatrix} x \\ y \\ z \\ t \end{pmatrix} = \begin{pmatrix} 1 \\ 2 \\ 3 \\ 4 \end{pmatrix}?$$

2   This matrix **A** is sparse:

$$A = \begin{pmatrix} 1 & 0.1 & 0 & 0 & 0 & 0 \\ 0.1 & 1 & 0.2 & 0 & 0 & 0 \\ 0 & 0.2 & 1 & 0.3 & 0 & 0 \\ 0 & 0 & 0.3 & 1 & 0.4 & 0 \\ 0 & 0 & 0 & 0.4 & 1 & 0.5 \\ 0 & 0 & 0 & 0 & 0.5 & 1 \end{pmatrix}.$$

Would you use iteration or elimination to solve

$$Ax = b?$$

6.6   LESLIE MATRICES

One practical example of matrix iteration, not necessarily of the types studied
above, is provided by the study of population. Let us start with a simple example.

The Ministry of Pensions and Education in Ruritania needs to be able to plan
for the future, in a crude way at least (since, by Murphy's Law, all forecasts are
wrong). They divide the population for planning purposes into

$$\begin{cases} s_n & \text{people of school age in year } n \\ w_n & \text{people of working age in year } n \\ p_n & \text{people of pension age in year } n. \end{cases}$$

Since those under school age do not yet have the vote in Ruritania, they are not
counted. As school age is from 5 to 25 (including universities, youth training and
sponsored holidays in Spain) it is reckoned that each year $\frac{1}{20}$ of the group become
workers. There is also an increase in this age group as babies reach school age,
and this is assumed to take place at a rate of $\frac{1}{30}$ times the number of workers, per
year. It follows that next year's number of school age people is

$$s_{n+1} = s_n - s_n/20 + w_n/30.$$

If the population is to be predicted from present levels you must also have an
equation for the changes in w_n. Now, working life is from 25 to 55, so it is assumed
that each year $\frac{1}{30}$ of the workers become pensioners (nobody dies early in

Ruritania, it is far too well organised for that). The equation for workers is therefore

$$w_{n+1} = w_n - w_n/30 + s_n/20.$$

Finally the pensioners equation just reflects the transfer of $\frac{1}{20}$ workers to pension age and the death rate of pensioners, which is $\frac{1}{20}$.

$$p_{n+1} = p_n - p_n/20 + w_n/30.$$

The census in 1990 gave the values (in hundreds of thousands)

$$s_0 = 20, \ w_0 = 40, \ p_0 = 20.$$

The Ruritanian Ministry got out its computer to set up the calculation for the next 30 years, to determine how much would be needed from the Gross National Product to maintain schools and pay pensions, and therefore how much could be paid to the workers. They found:

n	0	5	10	15	20	25	30
s_n	20	21.4	22.3	22.9	23.3	23.5	23.7
w_n	40	38.6	37.7	37.1	36.7	36.5	36.3
p_n	20	21.4	22.3	22.9	23.3	23.5	23.7

Further calculation showed that the population would eventually become steady at (24, 36, 24); but long before that the birth and death rates are likely to have changed, so you cannot rely on such a long term prediction. The shorter term conclusion here is that the number of dependents (school age plus pensioners) is increasing, and the number of workers (who provide the money) is decreasing. So either the workers should retain less money, or support for dependants should be reduced.

The iteration in their forecast is, in matrix form

$$\begin{pmatrix} s_{n+1} \\ w_{n+1} \\ p_{n+1} \end{pmatrix} = \begin{pmatrix} \frac{19}{20} & \frac{1}{30} & 0 \\ \frac{1}{20} & \frac{29}{30} & 0 \\ 0 & \frac{1}{30} & \frac{19}{20} \end{pmatrix} \begin{pmatrix} s_n \\ w_n \\ p_n \end{pmatrix}.$$

This is not much like the iterations in Sections 6.1 and 6.2, in that the matrix has elements nearly equal to 1 down its principal diagonal; there is also no vector of constants on the right hand side of the equation, though this could be brought into the model by postulating some emigration or immigration.

This type of model was brought into population studies, in a matrix formulation, by Leslie (a zoologist), and this sort of matrix which represents birth, death and transfer processes in a population is called a *Leslie matrix*.

The general Leslie matrix model for the population of Britain would be

$$\mathbf{x}_{n+1} = \mathbf{L}\mathbf{x}_n + \mathbf{m}_n,$$

where $\mathbf{x}_n$ would be a vector with (say) 100 elements, one for each year of life, and where $\mathbf{m}_n$ would be a net immigration vector. Unfortunately the entries in $\mathbf{L}$ (the Leslie matrix) would not be constants: birth and death rates change over the years, in an unpredictable fashion (when will a cure for AIDS be discovered?), so prediction for many years ahead is an uncertain process.

You can easily see that $\mathbf{L}$ is a very sparse matrix; take for example the row of $\mathbf{L}$ that refers to 18 year olds in a model for Britain – next year 99.9% of them have become 19 year olds and 0.1% have died in motor cycle (and other) accidents, but none have become any other age, so there is only *one* non-zero entry in that row.

The population structure varies considerably between countries. The table below gives some idea of this, with each population divided into six age groups. The figures are percentages for that country.

Age group	0–14	15–29	30–44	45–59	60–74	$\geqslant 75$
Ethiopia	43.5	27.0	16.3	8.8	3.7	0.7
Guyana	47.1	25.1	13.4	9.0	4.4	1.0
India	41.9	24.1	17.8	10.2	4.9	1.1
USA	28.6	24.0	17.0	16.3	10.4	3.7
UK, 1911	30.8	26.6	21.2	13.3	6.7	1.5
UK, 1971	24.1	21.0	17.6	18.3	14.3	4.7

The figures are mainly for the last census before 1980. They show the high mortality at early ages, and the short expected life span in the Third World countries. These populations are far too complicated for us to model here, but it is an important activity if any economic forecasting is to be done.

We can analyse the Ruritanian Leslie matrix, with which we started this section, quite fully by matrix methods. The matrix is

$$\mathbf{L} = \begin{pmatrix} \frac{19}{20} & \frac{1}{30} & 0 \\ \frac{1}{20} & \frac{29}{30} & 0 \\ 0 & \frac{1}{30} & \frac{19}{20} \end{pmatrix},$$

which has eigenvalues

$$\lambda_1 = 1, \ \lambda_2 = \tfrac{19}{20}, \ \lambda_3 = \tfrac{11}{12}.$$

The three corresponding eigenvectors are any constants times

$$\mathbf{e}_1 = \begin{pmatrix} 2 \\ 3 \\ 2 \end{pmatrix}, \ \mathbf{e}_2 = \begin{pmatrix} 0 \\ 0 \\ 1 \end{pmatrix}, \ \mathbf{e}_3 = \begin{pmatrix} 2 \\ -2 \\ 1 \end{pmatrix}$$

(see *Linear Algebra and Geometry* for the method of finding the eigenvectors).

The meaning here is that if you have any population vector which is proportional to $(2 \ 3 \ 2)^T$, then the next year, after the Leslie matrix has acted on it, it will have the same values because it corresponds to an eigenvalue of 1. But if you start with a population vector proportional to one of the other eigenvectors (or to a mixture of them), then the next year you will have a smaller total population because the other eigenvalues are smaller than 1.

Let us see this in action. The census figures for 1990 (year 0) gave $\mathbf{u}_0 = (20 \ 40 \ 20)^T$. This vector can be rewritten

$$\mathbf{u}_0 = 12 \begin{pmatrix} 2 \\ 3 \\ 2 \end{pmatrix} - 2 \begin{pmatrix} 0 \\ 0 \\ 1 \end{pmatrix} - 2 \begin{pmatrix} 2 \\ -2 \\ 1 \end{pmatrix}.$$

Apply the Leslie matrix once to get the figures for the population in 1991; because $\mathbf{Le}_1 = 1\mathbf{e}_1$, and $\mathbf{Le}_2 = \frac{19}{20}\mathbf{e}_2$, and $\mathbf{Le}_3 = \frac{11}{12}\mathbf{e}_3$, we find

$$\mathbf{u}_1 = 12 \begin{pmatrix} 2 \\ 3 \\ 2 \end{pmatrix} - \frac{19}{10} \begin{pmatrix} 0 \\ 0 \\ 1 \end{pmatrix} - \frac{11}{6} \begin{pmatrix} 2 \\ -2 \\ 1 \end{pmatrix} = \begin{pmatrix} 20.3 \\ 39.7 \\ 20.3 \end{pmatrix}.$$

If you apply the Leslie matrix n times, then each time brings the corresponding eigenvalue as a factor to each vector and you end up with

$$\mathbf{u}_n = 12 \times 1^n \begin{pmatrix} 2 \\ 3 \\ 2 \end{pmatrix} - 2 \times (\tfrac{19}{20})^n \begin{pmatrix} 0 \\ 0 \\ 1 \end{pmatrix} - 2 \times (\tfrac{11}{12})^n \begin{pmatrix} 2 \\ -2 \\ 1 \end{pmatrix}.$$

Now as n gets large $(\tfrac{19}{20})^n$ and $(\tfrac{11}{12})^n$ both get very small, and so the population finally approaches $(24 \ 36 \ 24)^T$. But it takes a very long time to reach this population vector because you need a really very large value of n before $(\tfrac{19}{20})^n$ is small: $n = 100$ gives 6×10^{-3}.

Now you could have started with *any* initial population vector, and represented it in terms of the three eigenvectors. There is a theorem that shows that three such vectors form a basis for the space $\mathbb{R}^3$. Consequently after a large number of years the population vector is bound to approach some constant times $(2 \ 3 \ 2)^T$ for this particular Leslie matrix.

Suppose you have some other Leslie matrix (of any size, not just 3×3); then a similar calculation will show you that:

(i) if one eigenvalue is 1 and the others all have modulus smaller than 1, then the eventual population vector is proportional to the eigenvector whose eigenvalue is 1;

(ii) if all the eigenvalues are less than 1 in modulus, then the population will die out completely;

(iii) if there is an eigenvalue larger than 1, then the population will increase without limit.

Note that the eigenvalues need not always be real and positive, as they were in this example.

Exercise 6G

1   Vary the Ruritanian planning model to allow for
(i) a birthrate of $\frac{1}{25}$ in place of $\frac{1}{30}$;
(ii) a net emigration rate per year of 1% of the workers and 1% of the school population.
  Compute the population forward for at least 20 years starting from

$$s_0 = 20, \ w_0 = 20, \ p_0 = 20.$$

2   Burmese beetles live at most three years (according to Bernardelli who investigated them, and published his results in 1941). They breed only when fully mature, at the end of their third year, when each beetle lays eggs which will produce six new beetles at the start of the next year. By the end of their first year only $\frac{1}{3}$ of the new beetles are surviving; by the end of the second year half of these survivors have died. Set up the Leslie matrix, and determine the fate of colonies whose initial populations are
(a) 1000 first year, 300 second year and 100 third year beetles;
(b) 1200 first year, 400 second year and 200 third year beetles.

3   If you kept the beetles in captivity you might expect different results, for example because of better food supply and fewer predators. Assume that the new Leslie matrix is

$$\begin{pmatrix} 0 & 1 & 3 \\ \frac{1}{2} & 0 & 0 \\ 0 & \frac{1}{3} & 0 \end{pmatrix}.$$

Write this as a series of statements about survival and reproduction. Follow the history of initial populations whose components are
(i) 1000, 300, 100   (ii) 1200, 400, 200.

4   Investigate the properties of the Leslie matrix

$$\mathbf{L} = \begin{pmatrix} 0.9 & c & 0 \\ 0.1 & 0.9 & 0 \\ 0 & 0.1 & 0.9 \end{pmatrix},$$

for the cases (i) $c = 0.1$ (ii) $c = 0.11$ (iii) $c = 0.09$.

5   Show that the eigenvalues for the captive Burmese beetles are 1, and two complex numbers with modulus less than 1. Verify that the computer runs you did earlier for this model agree with the theory for such a set of eigenvalues.

6   Investigate the matrix for Burmese beetles in the wild from question 2.

6.7   SUMMARY

(a)   *Jacobi* iteration uses equations in the form

$$\mathbf{x} = \mathbf{A}\mathbf{x} + \mathbf{b},$$

where $\mathbf{A}$ has small (off diagonal) elements, to set up the iteration

$$\mathbf{x}_{n+1} = \mathbf{A}\mathbf{x}_n + \mathbf{b},$$

and it converges if $\mathbf{A}^n \rightarrow \mathbf{0}$.

(b) *Gauss–Seidel* iteration uses equations

$$\mathbf{x} = \mathbf{Lx} + \mathbf{Ux} + \mathbf{b}$$

where **L** is lower triangular and **U** is upper triangular (and **L** and **U** are small) to set up the iteration

$$\mathbf{x}_{n+1} = \mathbf{Lx}_{n+1} + \mathbf{Ux}_n + \mathbf{b},$$

and it converges if

$$\{(\mathbf{I} - \mathbf{L})^{-1}\mathbf{U}\}^n \to 0.$$

(c) Convergence is assured for these iterative solutions by three methods
   (i)   a test on row sums of moduli (Theorem 6.1)
   (ii) a test on column sums of moduli (Theorem 6.2)
   (iii) a test on moduli of eigenvalues (Theorem 6.3).

(d) Measures for use in convergence are the *norms*
   (i)   the *length* of the error vector, $\|\boldsymbol{\varepsilon}_n\|_2$
   (ii) the *maximum of the modulus* for components of the error vector, $\|\boldsymbol{\varepsilon}_n\|_\infty$
   (iii) the *sum of the moduli* of the components of the error vector, $\|\boldsymbol{\varepsilon}_n\|_1$.

(e) The maximum of the modulus of the eigenvalues can usually be found by an iterative process.

(f) Iteration is a good method of solving equations when the test quantities in (c) are small, and particularly so for *sparse* matrices.

(g) In population studies the iterating matrix is called a *Leslie matrix*. The eigenvalues and eigenvectors of this matrix determine how the population changes. In particular the eigenvalue of largest modulus determines the ultimate size of the population, with extinction if $|\lambda|_{\max} < 1$.

7

Two-variable iterations

In this chapter I shall bring together ideas from several previous chapters:

(i) from Chapter 4, iterations

$$x_{n+1} = f(x_n)$$

to solve the equation

$$x = f(x);$$

(ii) from Chapter 6, iterations involving many variables

$$\mathbf{x}_{n+1} = \mathbf{A}\mathbf{x}_n + \mathbf{b}$$

to solve matrix equations for a vector $\mathbf{x}$;

(iii) from Chapters 1, 2 and 6, the use of mathematical equations as a model for real systems so as to obtain predictions;

(iv) from Chapter 2 the solution of simple difference equations.

7.1 FREE NEWSPAPERS

(a) The model

I intend to set up a *very* simple model of the competition between two free newspapers. There will be several places where you may think that the model could be improved, but I would rather start with the easiest possible version.

Suppose that in week n, newspaper A gives out u_n copies and newspaper B gives out v_n copies. Suppose also that their costs are (roughly) proportional to their circulations, so that for A the cost of production is αu_n while for B it is βv_n (they may not be equally efficient, so you will often have $\alpha \neq \beta$). Such newspapers survive on advertising, and money is mainly given by advertisers in relation to the amount of exposure their product or service receives. If the *total* advertising revenue that is available is £K per week, and if it is divided in proportion to circulation, then A will get

$$£Ku_n/(u_n + v_n)$$

in advertising revenue, while B gets

$$£Kv_n/(u_n + v_n).$$

This means that A's net income is

$$Ku_n/(u_n + v_n) - \alpha u_n,$$

and B's net income is similarly

$$Kv_n/(u_n + v_n) - \beta v_n.$$

These incomes are mainly used to finance the production of the next week's newspapers, so that next week's printing for A can be at most

$$u_{n+1} = \{Ku_n/(u_n + v_n) - \alpha u_n\}/\alpha$$

as that uses up all of the income from the previous week. I propose, therefore, to investigate the model

$$\begin{cases} u_{n+1} = au_n/(u_n + v_n) - u_n \\ v_{n+1} = bv_n/(u_n + v_n) - v_n, \end{cases}$$

where $a = K/\alpha$ and $b = K/\beta$. My plan is to follow the growth or decay of these two newspapers as they compete for advertising money.

After I have done this, you may ask whether the results I find are in accordance with reality. If not, we had better rethink the model to put in one or more of the many aspects of running a newspaper that have so far been left out. It would, however, be a mistake to try to put everything into a first model; it would probably then have too many constants to be estimated in the equation, and it would be easy to lose sight of the major aspects of the competitive struggle in a mass of detail. Two of the main rules for constructing mathematical models are

(i) keep it as simple as you dare to start with,
(ii) make changes when the results don't match reality.

In the model I have constructed there are *four* constants to choose

$$a, b, u_0, v_0.$$

As a first example let us put

$$a = 310, \ b = 300, \ u_0 = v_0 = 100.$$

This corresponds to newspaper A being slightly more efficient, and both starting with the same level of production. My computer output gave the following figures.

n	10	20	30	40	...	100	101	102
u_n	136	164	182	193	...	203	107	203
v_n	65	38	20	10	...	0	0	0

That is, it looks as though a slight difference in efficiency leads to a rapid decline of the less efficient newspaper, but not to a steady value of u.

The same decline takes place even if B starts with a rather larger production, to try to capture more of the advertising revenue. With a and b as above and with $u_0 = 50$, $v_0 = 150$ I found:

n	10	20	30	40
u_n	82	119	152	176
v_n	119	83	51	28

It looks as though this model predicts the triumph of the more efficient in the end, whatever the starting values: that seems a reasonable result to find, so the model is performing as one would expect.

The case of equally efficient newspapers is interesting, and shows us the way into the mathematics of the situation. I did some computer runs with $a = b = 300$, and found the following results.

(i) For $u_0 = v_0 = 75$, I found $u_n = v_n = 75$ for all n.
(ii) For $u_0 = v_0 = 100$, I found that (u_n, v_n) alternated between $(100, 100)$ and $(50, 50)$.
(iii) For $u_0 = 120$ and $v_0 = 50$, I found that (u_n, v_n) alternated between $(120, 50)$ and $(91.7\ldots, 38.2\ldots)$.

In none of the trials was one of the newspapers eliminated, which is reasonable if they are equally efficient; but also you may note that u_n/v_n is a constant, i.e. it does not change as n increases.

(b)   The mathematical analysis

We will start the mathematical analysis of the model in (a) above by looking at the case $a = b$. The equations are then

$$\begin{cases} u_{n+1} = au_n/(u_n + v_n) - u_n \\ v_{n+1} = av_n/(u_n + v_n) - v_n, \end{cases}$$

and if you put

$$v_n = pu_n$$

for a constant value of p (because u_n/v_n was found to be constant in the trials described above), you just get the one equation

$$u_{n+1} = a/(1 + p) - U_n.$$

This is a linear first order difference equation. Its complementary function, from the homogeneous equation

$$U_{n+1} = -U_n$$

is just

$$C(-1)^n;$$

its particular integral is the constant D which satisfies

$$D = \frac{a}{1+p} - D;$$

hence its general solution is

$$u_n = C(-1)^n + \frac{a}{2(1+p)}.$$

And if you use the initial value u_0 when $n=0$ you find, finally,

$$\begin{cases} u_n = \left\{ u_0 - \dfrac{a}{2(1+p)} \right\}(-1)^n + \dfrac{a}{2(1+p)} \\ v_n = pu_n \\ p = v_0/u_0. \end{cases}$$

You may check that you get the behaviour described in (a) from this solution.

Now let us return to the case of *unequal* efficiencies, and rewrite the equations in terms of α, β and K (in place of a and b), as

$$\begin{cases} \alpha u_{n+1} = K u_n/(u_n+v_n) - \alpha u_n \\ \beta v_{n+1} = K v_n/(u_n+v_n) - \beta v_n. \end{cases}$$

When you add these you get

$$\alpha u_{n+1} + \beta v_{n+1} = K - (\alpha u_n + \beta v_n).$$

This is now made much simpler if you change to the unknown

$$w_n = \alpha u_n + \beta v_n.$$

The equation reduces to the easy difference equation

$$w_{n+1} = K - w_n.$$

The solution, using the standard method, is

$$w_n = \tfrac{1}{2}K + (\alpha u_0 + \beta v_0 - \tfrac{1}{2}K)(-1)^n.$$

In this case it is not easy to find u_n and v_n separately, but we can get some idea of what is going on from our computer runs and by plotting points as a 'graph'. Let us plot the pair of numbers

$$(u_n, v_n)$$

as a point by having u and v axes as shown in Fig. 1.

I did a (carefully chosen) computer run with

$$a = 330,\ b = 300,\ u_0 = 55,\ v_0 = 100$$

and got the succession of points shown, where the value of n is given beside each point. The values I chose gave me just

$$w_n = \text{constant},$$

or

$$\alpha u_n + \beta v_n = \text{constant},$$

and so all the points lie on a straight line.

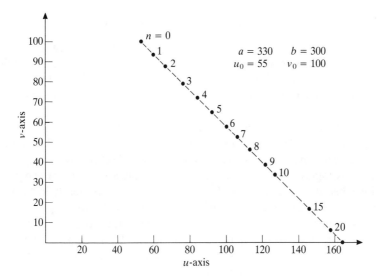

Figure 1. Competition between unequally efficient newspapers

In the general case the value of w_n alternates between

$$\alpha u_0 + \beta v_0$$

when $n = 0, 2, 4, 6, \ldots$ and

$$K - (\alpha u_0 + \beta v_0)$$

when $n = 1, 3, 5, 7, \ldots$ That is, the points lie alternately on the *two* straight lines

$$\begin{cases} \alpha u + \beta v = \alpha u_0 + \beta v_0 \\ \alpha u + \beta v = K - (\alpha u_0 + \beta v_0). \end{cases}$$

For example, if you take the case

$$a = 310,\ b = 300,\ u_0 = 90,\ v_0 = 110$$

the first few results for u_n and v_n are as follows.

n	0	1	2	3	4	5
u_n	90	50	97	53	105	57
v_n	110	55	103	51	96	48

If you plot these points you will find the two straight lines, with points alternately on one line and the other.

(c)   Discussion of the model

The model is undoubtedly inadequate, because the two free newspapers in my area continue to exist, and I cannot believe they are exactly equally efficient. However the model that I have constructed has some plausibility, and gives interesting results. Certainly I do not have the information to construct a more realistic model.

Our analysis of free newspapers has shown that the less efficient one is quite quickly eliminated. This is an example of an important biological law, known as the *Principle of competitive exclusion*. This is to the effect that if two species have the same ecological niche (i.e. the same food supply and the same geographical location) then the less efficient will soon disappear. Consequently in Nature you never find two species with exactly the same niche. When you apply this idea to newspaper companies, you will soon see that each paper tries to set its own style so as to attract a loyal readership (this is its 'food supply'). To increase circulation, and so boost profits, they try to steal other papers' readership, with £10^6 Bingo, or special photographs.

Exercise 7A

1   For the given newspaper model try the extreme case

$$a = 310, \ b = 300, \ u_0 = 5, \ v_0 = 195$$

to show that extremely unequal starting values cannot save a slightly less efficient newspaper (according to this model).

2   A 'steady state solution' is one that does not alter as n increases, so that

$$u_{n+1} = u_n, \ v_{n+1} = v_n, \text{ for all } n.$$

Find the steady state solutions of the given newspaper model. Confirm these answers with computer runs.

3   For the case of equal efficiencies, set up and solve the equation for z_n defined as $u_n + v_n$. Check that your solution agrees with the results given above.

4   In the special case

$$a = 330, \ b = 300, \ u_0 = 55, \ v_0 = 100$$

show that the straight line graph is

$$10u_n + 11v_n = 1650.$$

Use this equation to eliminate v_n from the first of the model equations, that is, to get an equation relating u_{n+1} and u_n. Can you solve it?

7.2   ARMS RACES

War and the arms race have provided mathematicians with material from which to construct models, with the intention of showing why or how past events have occurred.

The model constructed by Richardson in 1939 to discuss arms races was actually in terms of differential equations; but there are advantages in discussing it here, because decisions on defence spending (in peace time) are usually made annually, rather than continuously. Figures for the 1909–1914 arms race are readily available and are used here.

We shall let x_n be the defence budget for the France–Russia alliance in the year $1909 + n$, and y_n be the similar budget for the alliance of Germany and Austria-Hungary. The model is based on the following ideas.

(i) The budget x_n was increased if y_n was perceived to be 'too large for safety', but the increase was moderated if x_n was already so large that 'more could not be afforded'.
(ii) There was an allowance for a general fear and hatred of the other side: since prejudices die hard this was taken to be about constant.
(iii) Trade with the other side was held to be a factor which reduced fear and hatred; this too was nearly constant.

The budget increases were therefore modelled by the equations

$$\begin{cases} x_{n+1} - x_n = -ax_n + ky_n + g \\ y_{n+1} - y_n = -by_n + lx_n + h. \end{cases}$$

The first terms on the right represent a desire to spend money on other purposes; the second terms represent a fear of the other side's armaments; the third terms represent hate, reduced by trade.

Actual defence budgets were as follows (in millions of £s).

Year	1909	1910	1911	1912	1913
France + ally	115.3	119.4	127.8	145.0	166.7
Germany + ally	83.9	85.4	87.1	93.7	122.3
Total	199.2	204.8	214.9	238.7	289.0
Increase		5.6	10.1	23.8	50.3

Let us start by considering the row of totals. You get a good fit if you take $a = b = 0.20$ and $k = l = 1.40$. Adding the model equations then gives

$$x_{n+1} + y_{n+1} - x_n - y_n = 1.20 \, (x_n + y_n) + g + h.$$

The left hand side of this equation corresponds to the row marked 'increases', and plotting the increases against the totals gives a good straight line, with slope about 1.20 and intercept about 195 on the totals axis. This means that $g + h$ must have value about -232.8.

The individual budgets are fitted rather less well by taking

$$g = -90 \quad \text{and} \quad h = -143.$$

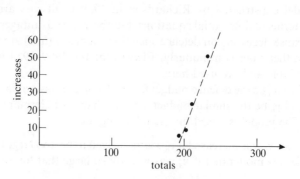

Figure 2. Budget increases and total budgets

Year	1909	1910	1911	1912	1913
F–R, model	115.3	119.7	125.5	140.6	172.5
G–AH, model	83.9	85.5	93.0	107.1	139.6

It is difficult to be sure that the model above is doing more than just fit to the available figures, especially since there are six constants to choose in the model, and only twelve experimental points. Wars are usually preceded by a build up in armaments, but the model above gives an impossibly rapid increase if you let it continue for a few more years. The present arms race has been continuing now for over 40 years without either leading to a major war or to total bankruptcy for one side; it seems likely that the modelling that Richardson did is not appropriate now, even if it fitted the figures in 1909–1913. However, as I write in 1990, the arms race may be ending due to the imminent economic collapse of one side, at least partly due to excessive spending on arms.

Exercise 7B

1   Is there a sensible steady state solution

$$x_n = X, \; y_n = Y, \text{ for all } n$$

to Richardson's equations? Is it stable, i.e. if you take

$$x_0 = X + \delta, \; y_0 = Y + \varepsilon$$

with δ and ε very small, do x_n and y_n remain close to X and Y respectively, as n increases? Use the values

$$a = 0.2, \; b = 0.25, \; k = 1.4, \; l = 1.5$$

$$g = -90, \; h = -143$$

if you prefer computer runs to algebra.

2 Solve the model equation

$$x_{n+1} + y_{n+1} - x_n - y_n = 1.20(x_n + y_n) - 233$$

by putting

$$w_n = x_n + y_n,$$

and taking w_0 to be 199.

3 Try Richardson's model with

$$a = b = 0.2 \quad \text{and} \quad k = l = 1.4$$

and taking $g = -90$, $h = -143$. Run both versions forward to 1918, assuming that no war occurred. Interpret your results.

4 Find a linear first order difference equation for z_n, defined as

$$z_n = x_n - y_n,$$

and solve it, in the case $a = b = 0.2$, $k = l = 1.4$, $g = -90$, $h = -143$.

Hence determine both x_n and y_n as functions of n.

(This method of 'linear combinations' of the two variables will recur in later work.)

7.3 THE BATTLE OF IWO JIMA

(a) The battle and the model

In 1916 Lanchester made an interesting model for how battles of long duration progressed. In it he assumed that the loss of men on day n of the battle was proportional to the strength of the opposing forces; and that reinforcements could arrive to maintain the fighting numbers. This gave him equations

$$\begin{cases} x_{n+1} = x_n - ay_n + f(n) \\ y_{n+1} = y_n - bx_n + g(n). \end{cases}$$

Here $f(n)$ and $g(n)$ are the reinforcements to the two sides at the end of day n, and the constants a and b represent the effectiveness of the two sides in destroying their opponents.

Let us apply this model to the battle of Iwo Jima (an island some 1000 km south of Japan) which took place in 1945. In total about 73 000 Americans and 21 500 Japanese were involved. On day 1 the battle started with

$$\begin{cases} x_1 = 54\,000 \text{ Americans} \\ y_1 = 21\,500 \text{ Japanese}. \end{cases}$$

American reinforcements were 6000 on day 3 and 13 000 on day 6; there were no other reinforcements. Using Lanchester's model with

$$a = 0.055 \quad \text{and} \quad b = 0.010$$

enables you to calculate the values of x_n and y_n on subsequent days. You may be surprised by the wide disparity between the efficiencies of the Americans (0.010) and the Japanese (0.055); this is due to the difficulty of attacking a well-prepared fortress, from the sea.

The first few steps of the calculation give the following values for the remaining combatants on each side (in thousands).

Day	1	2	3	4	5	6	7
x_n	54.0	52.8	57.6	56.5	55.4	67.3	66.3
y_n	21.5	21.0	20.5	19.9	19.3	18.7	18.0

The reinforcements have been assumed to join in the fighting on the day of landing. You can continue the calculation, but it is clear what will happen: the Japanese lose about 600 men a day until there are none left (on day 36), while the Americans start by losing at a rate of 350 a day and end with a very small loss rate. The battle in fact ended on the 36th day when the American strength was still 52 500, and very few Japanese remained. The actual figures fit the model quite well.

(b)   The solution with no reinforcements

I am going to deal algebraically with the special case of no reinforcements, and I shall take

$$a = 0.04, \ b = 0.01$$

to make the algebra and arithmetic lighter. In this case the equations in Lanchester's model are

$$\begin{cases} x_{n+1} = x_n - 0.04y_n \\ y_{n+1} = y_n - 0.01x_n. \end{cases}$$

These can in fact be solved without too much difficulty. In Section 7.1 we found that the new variable

$$w_n = \alpha u_n + \beta v_n$$

had an easy equation associated with it. We shall use the same sort of idea here: we seek a new variable w_n that is a combination (in the same sort of way) of x_n and y_n. After a bit of trial and error you find that the right mixture is

$$w_n = 0.1x_n + 0.2y_n.$$

This is because if you take 0.1 times the first equation plus 0.2 times the second equation you get

$$w_{n+1} = 0.98w_n.$$

Now this equation has the solution

$$w_n = (0.98)^n w_0.$$

Similarly we can let

$$z_n = 0.1x_n - 0.2y_n.$$

which satisfies the equation

$$z_{n+1} = 1.02z_n,$$

with solution

$$z_n = (1.02)^n z_0.$$

Therefore we have

$$\begin{cases} 0.1x_n + 0.2y_n = (0.98)^n(0.1x_0 + 0.2y_0) \\ 0.1x_n - 0.2y_n = (1.02)^n(0.1x_0 - 0.2y_0), \end{cases}$$

and so

$$\begin{cases} x_n = \tfrac{1}{2}x_0\{(0.98)^n + (1.02)^n\} - y_0\{(1.02)^n - (0.98)^n\} \\ y_n = \tfrac{1}{2}y_0\{(0.98)^n + (1.02)^n\} - \tfrac{1}{4}x_0\{(1.02)^n - (0.98)^n\}. \end{cases}$$

These of course hold only for those n for which both x_n and y_n are positive (or zero).

So who wins the battle? Rewrite the solution as

$$\begin{cases} x_n = (\tfrac{1}{2}x_0 + y_0)(0.98)^n + (\tfrac{1}{2}x_0 - y_0)(1.02)^n \\ y_n = (\tfrac{1}{4}x_0 + \tfrac{1}{2}y_0)(0.98)^n - (\tfrac{1}{4}x_0 - \tfrac{1}{2}y_0)(1.02)^n. \end{cases}$$

The first term on the right in each equation is clearly positive, and decreases as n increases. The second terms depend on the size of

$$\tfrac{1}{2}x_0 - y_0.$$

If $\tfrac{1}{2}x_0 > y_0$, the second term in the solution for x_n is *increasing*, while the second term in the solution for y_n is *decreasing* because of the minus sign before it. Hence the x_n side will win the battle, with y_n reaching zero when

$$\left(\frac{0.98}{1.02}\right)^n = \frac{\tfrac{1}{4}x_0 - \tfrac{1}{2}y_0}{\tfrac{1}{4}x_0 + \tfrac{1}{2}y_0}.$$

But if $\tfrac{1}{2}x_0 < y_0$ the argument is reversed, and the y_n side wins.

If you solve the equations in general, using

$$\begin{cases} x_{n+1} = x_n - ay_n \\ y_{n+1} = y_n - bx_n, \end{cases}$$

the decision depends on the sign of

$$b^{1/2}x_0 - a^{1/2}y_0.$$

If

$$b^{1/2}x_0 > a^{1/2}y_0$$

the x_n side wins. This general result is known as

Lanchester's square law:

the side with larger value of efficiency times *square* of manpower wins the battle, because you can write it as

$$bx_0^2 > ay_0^2.$$

(c) Discussion

Lanchester's model has stood up to the classic test of a model very well: it has given good results for a situation unknown at the time the model was constructed; moreover it has a very small number of constants to be chosen, just a and b. But this does not mean that it will describe all battles well – it certainly makes no allowances for superior tactics or strategy by one side.

Exercise 7C

1   Refight the battle of Iwo Jima with the starting conditions (in thousands)
(i) $x_0 = 54$, $y_0 = 21.5$ (ii) $x_0 = 43$, $y_0 = 21.5$
(iii) $x_0 = 40$, $y_0 = 21.5$.
In each case use $a = 0.04$, $b = 0.01$ and assume no reinforcements are allowed; you should use both computer (or calculator) runs and the solution formulas.

2   Lanchester also made a model for a battle between an army and a guerilla force. If there are no reinforcements the equations are

$$\begin{cases} x_{n+1} = x_n - ax_ny_n \\ y_{n+1} = y_n - bx_n, \end{cases}$$

where x_n are the guerillas and y_n the army. The difference is due to the small number of guerillas, who have to be found before they can be killed. Do some calculations for the case $y_0 = 500$, and

$$a = 10^{-4} \quad \text{and} \quad b = 0.1,$$

using a variety of values of x_0. Plot your results as graphs.

3   Your graphs in the last exercise should be close to parabolas. Can you find out why?

7.4   LINEAR AND NON-LINEAR

The examples in this chapter have all been of the form

$$\begin{cases} u_{n+1} = f(u_n, v_n) \\ v_{n+1} = g(u_n, v_n), \end{cases}$$

with initial values u_0 and v_0 given. In these formulas $f(u_n, v_n)$ is the notation for a function of two variables; the examples were

$$\begin{cases} au_n/(u_n + v_n) - u_n & \text{for newspaper competition} \\ u_n - au_n + kv_n + g & \text{for arms races} \\ u_n - av_n & \text{for simple battles.} \end{cases}$$

In all cases these are expressions which require values for both u_n and v_n before they can be worked out (assuming that the constants are all known). That is, in essence, all that a function of two variables is. Formally, it is a mapping from a pair of real numbers (each in some suitable set) to a single real number. The two numbers u_n, v_n (in that order) are used to construct the value $f(u_n, v_n)$ of the function.

The mathematically serious differences between the models is that some have been *linear* – the u_n and the v_n occur as first powers only, with no products, quotients and so on (as for the arms race model and the simple battle model) – whereas others have been *non-linear* (as for the newspaper model and the guerilla battle in Exercise 7C). This is reflected in the ease with which you can get a solution formula; you can of course always compute solutions up to any required value of n. For the linear models you can always solve the problem completely by forming linear combinations of the variables, to form easier equations.

This method is related to matrix working. Take the case of the battle of Iwo Jima. The equations may be written as

$$\begin{pmatrix} x_{n+1} \\ y_{n+1} \end{pmatrix} = \begin{pmatrix} 1 & -a \\ -b & 1 \end{pmatrix} \begin{pmatrix} x_n \\ y_n \end{pmatrix} + \begin{pmatrix} f \\ g \end{pmatrix}.$$

The case we worked through in detail had no reinforcements, so that $f = g = 0$, and had values

$$a = 0.04, \ b = 0.01.$$

That is, we had

$$\mathbf{x}_{n+1} = \mathbf{A}\mathbf{x}_n$$

with

$$\mathbf{A} = \begin{pmatrix} 1 & -0.04 \\ -0.01 & 1 \end{pmatrix}.$$

Since the eigenvalues of $\mathbf{A}$ are 1.02 and 0.98, and its eigenvectors are given by equations

$$0.1x + 0.2y = 0 \quad \text{and} \quad 0.1x - 0.2y = 0$$

it is evident that the properties of the matrix $\mathbf{A}$ are deeply involved in the solution of the equation

$$\mathbf{x}_{n+1} = \mathbf{A}\mathbf{x}_n.$$

An outline of a formal matrix solution to these equations continues in Exercise 7D.

For non-linear models there are few, if any, standard solution methods. The cases in this chapter have been chosen so that some progress can be made with them, but often the best that you can do is carry out computer iterations.

Exercise 7D

1 The mathematician Volterra developed a classic predator–prey model in 1931, based on the observations of the biologist D'Ancona. If there are u_n prey and v_n predators, then the populations change according to the equations

$$\begin{cases} u_{n+1} = au_n - bu_nv_n \\ v_{n+1} = pv_n + qu_nv_n, \end{cases}$$

where a, b, p, q are constants. The constant $a > 1$ or else the prey rapidly dies out, and the constant $p < 1$ or else the predator survives very well without the prey. The populations were of fish, and the product terms represent predators meeting prey. Find the steady state solution which has both species present.

With $a = 1.5$, $b = 10^{-3}$, $p = \frac{1}{2}$, $q = 10^{-4}$ and $u_0 = 5000$, $v_0 = 490$, plot the changes of (u_n, v_n) up to $n = 30$.

2   Show that the difference equations

$$\mathbf{x}_{n+1} = \mathbf{A}\mathbf{x}_n,$$

where $\mathbf{A}$ is a matrix of constants (i.e. independent of n), have the solution

$$\mathbf{x}_n = \mathbf{A}^n \mathbf{x}_0.$$

3   Suppose that $\mathbf{A}$ is a 2×2 matrix with two different (real) eigenvalues. Then there is a matrix $\mathbf{U}$ such that

$$\mathbf{U}\mathbf{A}\mathbf{U}^{-1} = \mathbf{\Lambda}$$

where $\mathbf{\Lambda}$ is a diagonal matrix of eigenvalues (see for example *Linear Algebra and Geometry* in this series). Show that
(i) $\mathbf{U}\mathbf{A}^n\mathbf{U}^{-1} = \mathbf{\Lambda}^n$,
(ii) $\mathbf{U}\mathbf{x}_n = \mathbf{\Lambda}^n(\mathbf{U}\mathbf{x}_0)$
and hence that certain combinations of the original variables have very simple solutions.

7.5   SUMMARY

Much of this chapter has been concerned with mathematical models of particular aspects of reality. Models need to start simple, so that some progress can be made with understanding their consequences. Mathematical, rather than computer, solutions can lead to general principles emerging. However computer runs can suggest what mathematics to try.

One valuable technique is to look for linear combinations of variables which satisfy simpler equations. This will always work in *linear* systems, and may be useful in non-linear ones.

8

Least squares fitting

This chapter is concerned with a rather different kind of mathematical modelling. In the last chapter we tried to *understand* the real situation in order to produce equations which contained the main features, so as to predict behaviour in particular cases. In this chapter we shall be more concerned to *describe* the results of experiments or observations by particular mathematical formulas; we do not need to have any understanding of the processes, though it will help us to choose sensible formulas if we have.

We shall pick up ideas from Chapter 5 to use again here, on ill-conditioning and on residuals. The other contact point of the work of this chapter is with statistics, and a discussion of the important statistical aspects of the material can be found in *Statistics and Probability* in this series. The subject of least squares fitting is also closely connected to work on vector spaces and matrices.

8.1 FITTING A STRAIGHT LINE TO DATA

(a) The problem

Here is a set of observations, in which the *x* values are 'exact' and the *y* values are liable to contain errors.

x	1	2	3	5	10	20	25
y	132	291	452	778	1634	3444	4436

If you plot these points on graph paper, they look as though they can be quite well represented by a straight line (Fig. 1).

You could, of course, choose the straight line by eye; but would you choose the same line every time? Would I choose the same line as you? We need a more organised procedure than that.

If I suggest that we 'ought' to have the equation

$$y = ax + b$$

for some constants *a* and *b*, then by substitution of the given values I derive the set of equations,

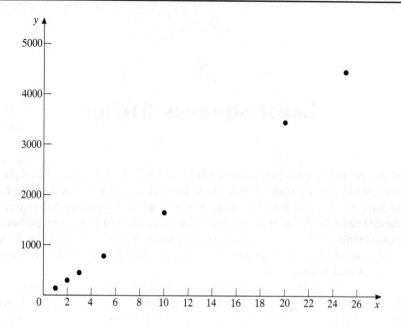

Figure 1. Experimental points

$$\begin{cases} 132 = \quad a+b \\ 291 = \quad 2a+b \\ 452 = \quad 3a+b. \\ \quad\quad \cdots \\ 4436 = 25a+b. \end{cases}$$

There are *seven* equations to determine the *two* unknowns a and b. What is more, they are inconsistent equations – the first two give

$$a = 159, \ b = -27$$

while the second and third give

$$a = 161, \ b = -31.$$

The best that I can do here is to say that $y \approx ax + b$; or I can introduce *residuals* r_1 to r_7 by

$$\begin{cases} 132 = \quad a+b+r_1 \\ 291 = \quad 2a+b+r_2 \\ \quad\quad \cdots \\ 4436 = 25a+b+r_7. \end{cases}$$

Here the residuals are defined as the difference between the actual value of y and the value predicted from the formula $ax+b$

$$r_i = y_i - (ax_i + b), \ i = 1, 2, ..., 7.$$

The problem is now certainly no better, because I have *nine* unknowns (a, b and 7 residuals).

What I have to do, to get a well-fitting line, is to make the vector $\mathbf{r}$ of residuals as small as possible in some sense. In Chapter 6 we saw three *norms* which could be used to describe the size of a vector

(i)   length, here $(r_1^2 + r_2^2 + r_3^2 + \ldots + r_7^2)^{1/2}$,
(ii) maximum modulus, here $\max |r_i|, \ i = 1, 2, ..., 7$,
(iii) sum of moduli, here $|r_1| + |r_2| + \ldots + |r_7|$.

The most familiar, and in many ways the easiest to use, is the length. So the guiding principle of this chapter is now decided:

> find the constants in the problem which give smallest length to the residual vector.

This is the *method of least squares*, because length is to do with a sum of squares.

Exercise 8A

A county cricketer opened his side's innings for 15 years. The number of his completed innings and the runs scored are tabulated for the years he played.

Year	'65	'66	'67	'68	'69	'70	'71
Innings	35	33	30	31	17	28	26
Runs	971	886	1701	1251	371	828	1044

Year	'72	'73	'74	'75	'76	'77	'78	'79
Innings	37	14	23	27	42	33	43	32
Runs	837	394	779	661	1141	1010	1357	719

Plot runs against innings and try drawing a line that best represents the data. Should you include 1967's results? Does your line pass through the 'average point', plotted as (average innings, average runs)?

(b)   The algebra of least squares

Before we try to find the a and b which minimise the square of the length of the residual vector, it is convenient to shift the origin to the average x value as origin for x and the average y value as origin for y. Later we can move back to the standard origin. So I now use x'_i and y'_i measured, respectively, from

$$X = \frac{1}{7}\sum_{i=1}^{7} x_i, \; Y = \frac{1}{7}\sum_{i=1}^{7} y_i.$$

The quantity I need to minimise is

$$\mathbf{r}^2 = r_1^2 + r_2^2 + \ldots + r_7^2$$
$$= (y'_1 - ax'_1 - b)^2 + \ldots + (y'_7 - ax'_7 - b)^2.$$

This can be expanded in the form

$$Aa^2 + 2Hab + Bb^2 - 2Ga - 2Fb + C$$

where

$$A = x_1'^2 + x_2'^2 + \ldots + x_7'^2 = \sum_{i=1}^{7} x_i'^2$$

$$H = x'_1 + x'_2 + \ldots + x'_7 = \sum_{i=1}^{7} x'_i$$

$$B = 1 + 1 + \ldots + 1 = 7$$

$$G = x'_1 y'_1 + x'_2 y'_2 + \ldots + x'_7 y'_7 = \sum_{i=1}^{7} x'_i y'_i$$

$$F = y'_1 + y'_2 + \ldots + y'_7 = \sum_{i=1}^{7} y'_i$$

$$C = y_1'^2 + y_2'^2 + \ldots + y_7'^2 = \sum_{i=1}^{7} y_i'^2.$$

But because I have chosen the origin at the average point, $H = F = 0$, and so

$$|\mathbf{r}|^2 = Aa^2 + Bb^2 - 2Ga + C$$
$$= A(a - G/A)^2 + Bb^2 + C - G^2/A.$$

This is made least when you choose

$$a = G/A \quad \text{and} \quad b = 0,$$

which confirms that the best line does indeed go through the average point. The relation of the two sets of axes and the best line is illustrated in Fig. 2.

We can now return to quantities measured from the 'real' origin by replacing

$$x' \text{ by } x - X$$
$$y' \text{ by } y - Y$$

in our formula for the slope of the best line: a point whose true coordinate is x is described from the average point as having coordinate $x' - X$.

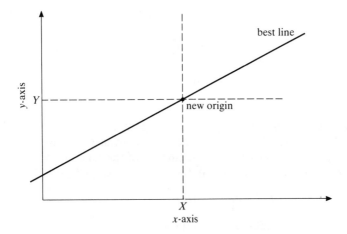

Figure 2. Axes at the average point, and the best line

That is

$$a = \frac{\sum\limits_{i=1}^{7} (x_i - X)(y_i - Y)}{\sum\limits_{i=1}^{7} (x_i - X)^2},$$

In these summations X and Y are independent of i, and so

$$\sum_{i=1}^{7} (x_i - X)(y_i - Y) = \sum_{i=1}^{7} (x_i y_i - X y_i - Y x_i + X Y)$$

$$= \sum_{i=1}^{7} x_i y_i - X \sum_{i=1}^{7} y_i - Y \sum_{i=1}^{7} x_i + 7 X Y$$

$$= \sum_{i=1}^{7} x_i y_i - 7 X Y,$$

because $\sum\limits_{i=1}^{7} y_i = 7Y$ and $\sum\limits_{i=1}^{7} x_i = 7X$.

Similarly $\sum\limits_{i=1}^{7} (x_i - X)^2 = \sum\limits_{i=1}^{7} x_i^2 - 7X^2$, giving the final formula for the slope of the best fitting line as

$$a = \frac{7 \sum\limits_{i=1}^{7} x_i y_i - \left(\sum\limits_{i=1}^{7} x_i \right)\left(\sum\limits_{i=1}^{7} y_i \right)}{7 \sum\limits_{i=1}^{7} x_i^2 - \left(\sum\limits_{i=1}^{7} x_i \right)^2} = \frac{BG - HF}{AB - H^2},$$

where A, B, C, F, G, H now refer to 'true' values, using x_i and y_i.

The intercept on the true y-axis is easily calculated from a, X, Y as

$$b = Y - aX = \left(\sum_{i=1}^{7} y_i - a \sum_{i=1}^{7} x_i \right) \Big/ 7$$

$$= -\frac{GH - AF}{AB - H^2}.$$

That was an unpleasantly long piece of algebra, with complicated looking answers. The work can be shortened enormously by using results in the calculus of two variables, to find where the minimum of the function of two variables occurs. The material can be well understood in its statistical setting, where

$$AB - H^2$$

is just the variance of the observations x_i multiplied by the number of observations squared. Similarly

$$BG - HF$$

is a covariance of x and y observations, again multiplied by the number of observations squared. The term

$$GH - AF$$

can also be interpreted, in a less obvious way.

Calculating a and b numerically is little trouble, and many calculators will do it automatically.

Exercise 8B

There are three observed points

$$(x_1, y_1), (x_2, y_2), (x_3, y_3)$$

and it is required to fit the best line *through the origin*

$$y = ax.$$

Carry out the determination of the best value of the coefficient a
(i) using calculus to minimise $|\mathbf{r}|^2$ with respect to changes in a,
(ii) using the algebraic method above.

(c)   The results of fitting the line

The figures in (a) above give

$$\begin{cases} n = 7, & \Sigma xy = 202\,800, \\ \Sigma x = 66, & \Sigma x^2 = 1164, \\ \Sigma y = 11\,167, & \Sigma y^2 = 35\,120\,881. \end{cases}$$

From these you may calculate

$$\begin{cases} X = \ \ 9.4286, & Y = \ 1595.3, \\ a = 180.00, & b = -101.85. \end{cases}$$

Using these values leads to the table

x_i	y_i	$ax_i + b$	r_i
1	132	78.15	53.85
2	291	258.15	32.85
3	452	438.15	13.85
5	778	798.15	−20.15
10	1634	1698.15	−64.15
20	3444	3498.15	−54.15
25	4436	4398.15	37.85

The final length squared of the residual vector is

$$|\mathbf{r}|^2 = r_1^2 + r_2^3 + \ldots + r_1^2 = 13\,056.9$$

and so an 'average error' is $\sqrt{(|\mathbf{r}|^2/7)} = 43.2$.

Though $|\mathbf{r}|^2$ has been minimised in this procedure the result is not a good one; look at r_1 and y_1 – the error is 40% of the value of y_1. We shall clearly have to come back later to consider whether this is an adequate description of the set of points we started with.

Exercise 8C

1   Fit a straight line $y = ax + b$ to the county cricketer's results
    (a) including 1967
    (b) excluding 1967.
    In each case you should calculate $|\mathbf{r}|^2$, and the *standard deviation* $\sqrt{(|\mathbf{r}|^2/n)}$.

2   In a practice examination 10 students were given the following marks.

Student	1	2	3	4	5	6	7	8	9	10
Paper 1	116	131	87	94	127	85	116	54	105	80
Paper 2	93	126	71	abs	93	66	108	44	96	67

Find a best fitting line to derive Paper 2 marks (y) from Paper 1 marks (x), so as to decide what overall result student 4 should be given. What is the likely range of error of the result that you give her?

8.2   ILL-CONDITIONING IN LEAST SQUARES LINES

Suppose you have the following observations y_i at given values x_i.

x	0.380	0.390	0.400	0.410	0.420
y	0.388	0.400	0.411	0.424	0.433

Plotting these points gives what appears to be a good straight line (Fig. 3), with slope about 1.1.

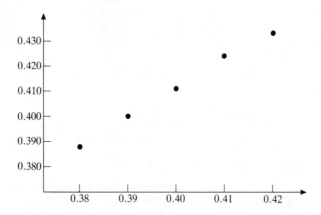

Figure 3. Five points with slope about 1.1

The values for both x and y are only given to 3 s.f. so it is perfectly reasonable to use three figure calculations. When we round the following results to three figures

$$\begin{cases} n=5 & \Sigma x_i y_i = 0.823\,54 \\ \Sigma x_i = 2.00 & \Sigma x_i^2 = 0.801 \\ \Sigma y_i = 2.056 & \Sigma y_i^2 = 0.846\,73 \end{cases}$$

we find $a=0$, $b=0.412$.

This does not seem a very sensible result, as the change in y is certainly as large as the change in x over the interval. What has happened here is that

$$AB - H^2 \quad \text{and} \quad BG - HF$$

or in detail

$$5\Sigma x_i^2 - (\Sigma x_i)^2 \quad \text{and} \quad 5\Sigma x_i y_i - (\Sigma x_i)(\Sigma y_i)$$

are both very small, due to the subtraction of nearly equal quantities. This is in fact a case of ill-conditioning, as you can see by changing one value slightly, to

$$x=0.410 \qquad y=0.423.$$

This changes the rounded value of $\Sigma x_i y_i$ to 0.823, and nothing else (except Σy_i^2 which does not affect a or b), and the values you now get are

$$a=-1.00 \qquad b=0.812.$$

Clearly this is now a useless result!

Working with full arithmetic on the original figures gives $a=1.14$, $b=-0.0448$, and using the modified value of y_4 gives

$$a=1.13 \qquad b=-0.041.$$

These are excessive changes in a and b for such a small change in only one of the observations; the ill-conditioning is really there, it is not just due to using shortened arithmetic. It has essentially been caused by having observation points close to each other (and far from the origin for x). You can, for example, evaluate

$$AB-H^2$$

when

$$x_i=p+iq, \ i=0,1,2,3,...,n-1$$

and get

$$n^2(n^2-1)q^2/12.$$

This will be very small (and far smaller than either AB or H^2 separately) if you have

$$n=5, \ q=0.01, \ p=0.38$$

as we did in the example.

The moral here is that least squares fitting, like all numerical work, is open to dangers, and you need to be alert to them. There are ways of mitigating this ill-conditioning, but they use matrix methods which are too advanced for this text.

Exercise 8D

1 Show that $AB-H^2=n^2(n^2-1)q^2/12$ when $x_i=p+iq, i=0,1,...,n-1$. Find the value of

$$BG-HF$$

if in addition

$$y_i=r+is, \ i=0,1,...,n-1.$$

2 Plot the points for the example in Section 8.2, using a scale of 1 cm = 0.1, and draw the two lines that were found using three figure arithmetic. Calculate the sum of squares of residuals in each case.

8.3   MATRIX FORMULATION

The equations

$$y_i = ax_i + b + r_i, \ i = 1, 2, \ldots, 7,$$

can be written in matrix form as

$$\mathbf{y} = \mathbf{A} \begin{pmatrix} a \\ b \end{pmatrix} + \mathbf{r}$$

where $\mathbf{y}$ and $\mathbf{r}$ are vectors, which in our initial example have 7 elements, and where $\mathbf{A}$ is a 7×2 matrix

$$\mathbf{A} = \begin{pmatrix} x_1 & 1 \\ x_2 & 1 \\ x_3 & 1 \\ x_4 & 1 \\ x_5 & 1 \\ x_6 & 1 \\ x_7 & 1 \end{pmatrix}.$$

A matrix formulation will allow generalisation later on, but it is not as easy to see what is going on.

I shall rewrite this equation as

$$\mathbf{y} = \mathbf{Ac} + \mathbf{r},$$

where $\mathbf{c}$ is the two-element vector of the variables of the problem, i.e. the slope and intercept of the straight line, which are to be found. The length squared of the vector $\mathbf{r}$ is then

$$\mathbf{r}^T\mathbf{r} = (\mathbf{y} - \mathbf{Ac})^T(\mathbf{y} - \mathbf{Ac}).$$

The rules for transposed matrices allow this to be rewritten as

$$\mathbf{r}^T\mathbf{r} = \mathbf{y}^T\mathbf{y} - \mathbf{y}^T\mathbf{Ac} - \mathbf{c}^T\mathbf{A}^T\mathbf{y} + \mathbf{c}^T\mathbf{A}^T\mathbf{Ac}.$$

Then, since each piece of this equation is just a number and so equal to its own transpose, we may put it as

$$\mathbf{r}^T\mathbf{r} = \mathbf{y}^T\mathbf{y} - 2\mathbf{c}^T\mathbf{A}^T\mathbf{y} + \mathbf{c}^T\mathbf{A}^T\mathbf{Ac}.$$

In this text we cannot do the formal minimisation of this expression; however, it is just like the minimisation of

$$r^2 = y^2 - 2A^Tyc + A^TAc^2,$$

where c is the variable, in ordinary calculus. In that case differentiation with respect to c shows that any local minimum can only occur when

$$A^TAc = A^Ty.$$

It clearly must be a local minimum, since c is unbounded in its range of values and you can get r^2 (the square of the error) as large as you like by stupid choices of c. This gives a good indication of why the correct equations for determining the constants in c turn out to be

$$\mathbf{A}^T\mathbf{A}\mathbf{c} = \mathbf{A}^T\mathbf{y}.$$

These are the *normal equations* of least squares fitting. Their advantage over the previous formulation (to which they are of course exactly equivalent) is that they generalise easily.

Let us repeat the previous example, using this formulation. The matrix A is 7×2 and is written above, and

$$\mathbf{A}^T = \begin{pmatrix} x_1 & x_2 & x_3 & x_4 & x_5 & x_6 & x_7 \\ 1 & 1 & 1 & 1 & 1 & 1 & 1 \end{pmatrix}.$$

Consequently

$$\mathbf{A}^T\mathbf{A} = \begin{pmatrix} \sum\limits_{i=1}^{7} x_i^2 & \sum\limits_{i=1}^{7} x_i \\ \sum\limits_{i=1}^{7} x_i & 7 \end{pmatrix},$$

and

$$\mathbf{A}^T\mathbf{y} = \begin{pmatrix} \sum\limits_{i=1}^{7} x_i y_i \\ \sum\limits_{i=1}^{7} y_i \end{pmatrix}.$$

Use the first of these matrices to multiply the vector

$$\mathbf{c} = \begin{pmatrix} a \\ b \end{pmatrix}$$

and you get the normal equations:

$$\begin{cases} (\Sigma x_i^2)a + (\Sigma x_i)b = \Sigma x_i y_i \\ (\Sigma x_i)a + 7b = \Sigma y_i. \end{cases}$$

These equations of course have the same solutions for a and b as were given in Section 8.2.

In particular, these equations are ill-conditioned if their determinant is very small, i.e. if

$$7 \sum_{i=1}^{7} x_i^2 - \left(\sum_{i=1}^{7} x_i \right)^2$$

is very small, as we found before.

Exercise 8E

1 Determine the normal equations for the data in
   (i) Exercise 8A,
   (ii) Exercise 8C, question 2.

2 When a best line *through the origin*

$$y = ax$$

is being fitted to a set of data pairs (x_i, y_i), the equations for the residuals can be put as

$$\mathbf{r} = \mathbf{y} - a\mathbf{x}.$$

Carry out the determination of the appropriate normal equation for this case, by differentiating

$$\mathbf{r}^T\mathbf{r} = (\mathbf{y}^T - a\mathbf{x}^T)(\mathbf{y} - a\mathbf{x})$$

with respect to a.

   (The number a can be regarded as a 1×1 matrix $\mathbf{a}$, so this work is closely parallel to the work omitted in Section 8.3.)

3 Show that, in the case of fitting a line

$$y = ax + b,$$

the matrix $\mathbf{A}^T\mathbf{A}$ is always a 2×2 matrix and $\mathbf{A}^T\mathbf{y}$ is always a vector with 2 elements, no matter how many data points are given.

8.4   MODELLING CONSIDERATIONS

(a)   What should we fit?

Take the case of the county cricketer in Exercise 8A. You can fit a reasonably satisfactory straight line to these data (if you exclude the information for 1967, clearly a freak year for him). My calculations gave values close to

$$y = 28x + 46$$

i.e. 'his score for the year is approximately 28 times the number of innings plus 46'.

   Any interested listener may now ask you

'What are the 46 runs for?'

This is a good question; presumably if, due to permanent rain for the whole season, he completed *no* innings, then he should have *no* runs scored in completed innings, not 46. The only conclusion can be that the model chosen for fitting,

$$y = ax + b,$$

was not a very intelligent one. Perhaps we should first have tried the model

$$y = ax,$$

for which no runs are scored in no innings (to see if a reasonable fit could be made with it).

Or, perhaps if he has *few* innings in a year he is likely to do badly for lack of match practice, so that runs per innings should *increase* with number of innings. You might feel that

$$y = ax^2$$

would be such a model. (I would have doubts about it being a good one – it increases very fast for large values of *x*.)

The point here is that blind application of any formula, without thought beforehand about its suitability, or reflection afterwards on the results it gives, is not good mathematical practice.

(b)   Organised residuals

One way of telling that you have made a bad choice of model is to look at the r_i that result from the values of *a* and *b* given by the calculation from the model. For example, the data in Section 8.1 were fitted by

$$y = 180x - 102 \text{ (to 3 s.f.)}$$

and gave residuals $y - ax - b$:

$$54, 33, 14, -20, -64, -54, 38.$$

This is not by any means a random scatter of experimental errors. It is a very *organised* set of residuals, starting positive, decreasing to a considerable negative value, and ending positive again. Of course some residuals must be positive and some must be negative – they must add to zero (within arithmetical errors), because the line has to go through the average point (the centroid, to give it its proper name).

This sort of organisation in the residuals is a good sign that the model was not well chosen; in this case we shall see why, and look for a better model directly.

(c)   Fitting a power law

I will now confess that the data I used in Section 8.1 were men's world records for running (at August 31 1988) with *x* in km and *y* in seconds. Two things follow from this:

(i)   0 km should take 0 seconds;
(ii)   speeds should decrease as distances increase.

That is

$$y = ax + b$$

is a singularly inept model to choose. What should I try instead? One choice would be

$$y = ax + bx^2$$

with *b* positive to make times increase rather more as distances increase; I shall leave this one to the Exercise, as it is only a small modification to what we have done already. Another choice would be

$$y = cx^s;$$

with s only a little greater than 1 the curve is little different from a straight line near $x=0$, but it gradually curves over longer ranges of x.

To process this new model it is easiest to use logarithms, because then

$$\ln y = \ln c + s \ln x.$$

This is just the model we have already studied, for if you put

$$\ln y = Y, \ln c = b, s = a, \ln x = X$$

you get

$$Y = aX + b$$

with a and b to be found for given values of X_i and Y_i.

I reprocessed the example, using the data

X	0	0.693	1.099	1.609	2.303	2.996	3.219
Y	4.883	5.673	6.114	6.657	7.399	8.144	8.398

which are the (natural) logarithms of the old data. These figures give

$$\begin{cases} n = 7 & \Sigma XY = 89.834 \\ \Sigma X = 11.919 & \Sigma X^2 = 28.919 \\ \Sigma Y = 47.268 & \Sigma Y^2 = 329.320. \end{cases}$$

Consequently

$$\text{average } X = 1.703 \qquad \text{average } Y = 6.753$$
$$a = 1.084 \qquad\qquad b = 4.907.$$

These give

$$c = 135.2 \qquad s = 1.084$$

and the fitted model is

$$y = 135.2 x^{1.084}.$$

From this the residuals can be calculated, and they are (from $y - rx^s$)

$$-3.2, 4.4, 7.2, 4.1, -6.5, -33.7, 6.6.$$

Are these acceptable residuals? They are certainly smaller than the previous ones, so this model is a better fit. The standard deviation of the errors is

$$\sqrt{(|\mathbf{r}|^2/7)} = 13.7,$$

but most of this is due to one very large error, derived from the 20 km distance.

My formula gives a time of 3477.7 seconds, while the record is actually 3444.2 seconds. Was this a fluke result, like the cricketer's year in 1967? Perhaps it was, because this record has stood since 1976.

(d)   Fitting straight lines

Any straight line can have its equation written in three equivalent forms:
(i) $y = ax + b$
(ii) $x = py + q$
(iii) $lx + my = 1$.
Corresponding to these there will be *three* ways of fitting data points by a straight line. They will *not* give the same answers, for a simple geometrical reason.

For the first straight line, the residuals are

$$y_i - ax_i - b,$$

which are projections parallel to the y-axis onto the line of best fit (Fig. 4).

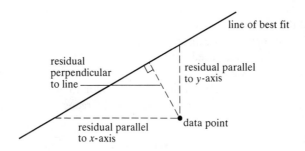

Figure 4. Residuals in three directions

But if you have used the second form of the line the residuals will be

$$x_i - py_i - q,$$

which are projections parallel to the x-axis. Minimising these residuals is not the same as minimising the previous ones, as we shall see in an example below.

Similarly, the third form of line gives the residuals

$$lx_i + my_i - 1,$$

which corresponds to minimising distances at right angles to the line.

To show this in action I shall use the data from Section 8.1 again, but with the roles of x and y interchanged. This will give the line of best fit which has the form

$$x = py + q$$

where

$$\begin{cases} p = \dfrac{7\Sigma x_i y_i - \Sigma x_i \Sigma y_i}{7\Sigma y_i^2 - (\Sigma y_i)^2}, \\ q = (\Sigma x_i - p\Sigma y_i)/7. \end{cases}$$

These give

$$p = 5.6344 \times 10^{-3}, \; q = 0.44001.$$

Is this the same line as before? No: the slope of the line is now

$$p^{-1} = 177.48 \neq 180.00$$

and the intercept on the y-axis is now

$$-q/p = -78.09 \neq -101.85.$$

This is again to do with the modelling of the data that you are considering. Which of the figures are reasonably exact, and which are subject to random influences? In the case of the athletics records the distances x_i are fixed (we hope that the distance raced over was very close to 20 km, though someone could have miscounted the number of laps run), but the record times y_i have many reasons for not fitting the formula (the distance is rarely attempted, the weather was good, excellent pacemakers were used, and so on). So in this case it is fair to measure residuals in y, i.e. as we did.

But if you had been seeking a line of best fit for weight and height of adult women of normal physique, you would need to recognise that neither of the variables

$$w = \text{weight in kg}$$

$$h = \text{height in m}$$

has priority over the other, and fitting a line

$$lw + mh = 1$$

might be more realistic.

Exercise 8F

1   The share price of an investment trust at the beginning of seven successive quarters was

quarter (x)	0	1	2	3	4	5	6
price (y)	710	756	825	830	820	970	1050

A market analyst fits the price by a model

$$y = ax + b.$$

What values for a and b does she get? Comment on the residuals and her choice of model.

2 (i) Fit a straight line through the origin
$$y = ax$$
to the data on the cricketer, and calculate residuals.
(ii) Fit a power law
$$y = px^s$$
to the data on the cricketer, and calculate residuals.
   Which do you think is the best model of the three that have been used on this data?

3 The normal equations for the model
$$y = ax + bx^2$$
for the data on athletics records, must be derived from the equations
$$\begin{cases} y_1 = ax_1 + bx_1^2 + r_1 \\ \quad\cdots \\ y_7 = ax_7 + bx_7^2 + r_7 \end{cases}$$
so that in this case
$$A = \begin{pmatrix} x_1 & x_1^2 \\ x_2 & x_2^2 \\ \cdots \\ x_7 & x_7^2 \end{pmatrix}.$$

Write down the matrix form of the normal equations and hence find a and b. Calculate and discuss the residuals. Which of the three models for this data do you think is most suitable?

4 In Exercise 8C question 2 it was appropriate to fit a line
$$y = ax + b$$
because we were trying to deduce a Paper 2 mark (y) from a *given* Paper 1 mark (x). But in reality both marks are subject to error. Fit a line
$$lx + my = 1$$
to the results of the nine students who completed both papers. In this case the matrix A is
$$A = \begin{pmatrix} x_1 & y_1 \\ x_2 & y_2 \\ \cdots \\ x_9 & y_9 \end{pmatrix}$$
and the total squared residual is
$$r^T r = (Al - e)^T (Al - e)$$
where l is the vector with entries l, m and e is a vector whose entries are nine 1's. You will need to use the fact that the normal equations are
$$A^T Al = A^T e.$$

5 Why do the residuals in Section 8.4(c) not add to zero?

8.5   FITTING QUADRATICS

Suppose you decide that the model

$$y = ax^2 + bx + c$$

is appropriate for some set of data points. It is easy to generalise the normal equations to fit this case as well. The residuals in this case will be (for n data points)

$$r_1 = y_1 - ax_1^2 - bx_1 - c$$

$$r_2 = y_2 - ax_2^2 - bx_2 - c$$

$$\dots$$

$$r_n = y_n - ax_n^2 - bx_n - c$$

and we write this as

$$\mathbf{r} = \mathbf{y} - \mathbf{Aa}$$

where $\mathbf{A}$ is now an $n \times 3$ matrix, and $\mathbf{a}$ is a vector with 3 entries a, b, c,

$$\mathbf{A} = \begin{pmatrix} x_1^2 & x_1 & 1 \\ x_1^2 & x_2 & 1 \\ x_3^2 & x_3 & 1 \\ & \dots & \\ x_n^2 & x_n & 1 \end{pmatrix}, \quad \mathbf{a} = \begin{pmatrix} a \\ b \\ c \end{pmatrix}.$$

The matrix work proceeds exactly as before to give normal equations

$$\mathbf{A}^\mathrm{T}\mathbf{Aa} = \mathbf{A}^\mathrm{T}\mathbf{y}.$$

These are now three equations in three unknowns, a, b and c.

Exercise 8G

1 Find the entries in the matrix $\mathbf{A}^\mathrm{T}\mathbf{A}$ and in the vector $\mathbf{A}^\mathrm{T}\mathbf{y}$.

2 Fit a model

$$y = ax^2 + bx + c$$

to the stockmarket data in Exercise 8F.

8.6   SUMMARY

To fit a straight line

$$y = ax + b$$

to data points (x_i, y_i), $i = 1, 2, \dots, n$ a good strategy is to minimise the sum of squares of residuals

$$|\mathbf{r}|^2 = r_1^2 + r_2^2 + \ldots + r_n^2$$
$$= (y_1 - ax_1 - b)^2 + \ldots + (y_n - ax_n - b)^2.$$

The values of a and b derived from this minimisation are

$$a = \frac{n\Sigma xy - (\Sigma x)(\Sigma y)}{n\Sigma x^2 - (\Sigma x)^2}$$

$$b = \frac{1}{n}(\Sigma y - a\Sigma x).$$

The line necessarily passes through the *centroid*

$$X = \frac{1}{n}\Sigma x, \quad Y = \frac{1}{n}\Sigma y,$$

and the sum of the residuals is zero. The standard deviation $\sqrt{(|\mathbf{r}|^2/n)}$ gives an estimate of how well the model fits.

The values of a and b can depend critically on the data when the problem is *ill-conditioned*, which occurs when $n\Sigma x_i^2 - (\Sigma x_i)^2$ is very small.

The values of a and b satisfy the *normal equations*

$$\mathbf{A}^T\mathbf{A}\mathbf{c} = \mathbf{A}^T\mathbf{y}$$

where $\mathbf{A}$, $\mathbf{c}$ and $\mathbf{y}$ are given for this problem as

$$\mathbf{A} = \begin{pmatrix} x_1 & 1 \\ x_2 & 1 \\ & \ldots \\ x_n & 1 \end{pmatrix}, \quad \mathbf{c} = \begin{pmatrix} a \\ b \end{pmatrix}, \quad \mathbf{y} = \begin{pmatrix} y_1 \\ y_2 \\ \ldots \\ y_n \end{pmatrix}.$$

For other models the normal equations will have different forms.

The model to fit must be chosen intelligently, and the residuals examined for organised structure. Among the simple models available are

$$\begin{cases} y = ax \\ y = ax + b \\ y = ax + bx^2 \\ y = cx^s, \end{cases}$$

and the last of these is dealt with by replacing it with

$$Y = \ln y = \ln c + s \ln x = b + aX.$$

Thought has to be given to a choice between

$$\begin{cases} y = ax + b \\ x = py + q \\ lx + my = 1 \end{cases}$$

as the equation to use for a straight line model.

General quadratics

$$y = ax^2 + bx + c$$

(and higher polynomial models) can be used as models by appropriate modifications of the normal equations.

9

Differences and interpolation

In my book of tables I find the following values for something called $J_0(x)$.

x	2.0	2.1	2.2	2.3	2.4	2.5
$J_0(x)$	0.2239	0.1666	0.1104	0.0555	0.0025	-0.0484

Several questions come to my mind.

(a) Plotting the points suggests that I might try to represent $J_0(x)$ over this range by a straight line. Is this likely to be a good idea?

(b) Suppose I need to know the value of

$$J_0(9/4).$$

How should I best calculate it from these values?

(c) Suppose I wish to know the (approximate) solution of

$$J_0(x) = 0.$$

What is the best I can get from the figures?

(d) Can I get a reasonable value of

$$J_0(2.6)$$

from the given values?

The first of these questions is best answered after looking at a *difference table* constructed from the table of values, because if the difference of the function from one point to the next is a constant, then you certainly have a straight line (exactly).

The second and third questions are about *interpolation*, how to get intermediate values from those given. The final question is about *extrapolation*, how to get outside the range of a table of values.

These topics in numerical work have been around since the time of Newton, and he derived many formulas in this area of work. Subsequently the subject has developed into a large one, and in this text we shall only have the time (and the need) to look at the easiest parts of it.

The development of computers has, moreover, introduced a new question into any discussion of interpolation and extrapolation: would it not be easier just to calculate

$$J_0(9/4) \text{ and } J_0(2.6)$$

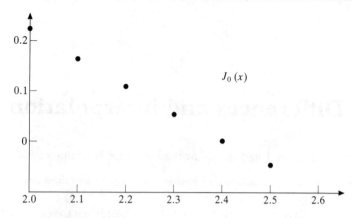

Figure 1. Values of $J_0(x)$

from the formula for $J_0(x)$ (whatever it is), and use iteration to solve $J_0(x)=0$? The answer is, unfortunately, not always; it depends on the cost (in time) of the two types of calculation. For example, using the standard definition of $J_0(x)$, you find that

$$J_0(9/4)=1-\left(\frac{9}{8}\right)^2+\frac{(9/8)^4}{1^2\times 2^2}-\frac{(9/8)^6}{1^2\times 2^2\times 3^2}+\cdots$$

This may be rather a trouble to compute, as many terms will be needed. And other functions are worse.

9.1   DIFFERENCE TABLES

If $J_0(x)$ were really a straight line (from 2.0 to 2.5) the differences of values would be constant. They are in fact given by

x	2.0	2.1	2.2	2.3	2.4	2.5
$J_0(x)$	0.2239	0.1666	0.1104	0.0555	0.0025	−0.0484
diff		−0.0573	−0.0562	−0.0549	−0.0530	−0.0509

What has been put in the row labelled 'diff' is

$$J_0(2.1)-J_0(2.0),\ J_0(2.2)-J_0(2.1),$$

and so on. These are called the

first (forward) differences

and are usually given the Greek letter Δ (capital delta), so that the entries are ΔJ_0 at

2.0   2.1   2.2   2.3   2.4.

In this case we have

$$\Delta J_0(2.0) = J_0(2.1) - J_0(2.0)$$

$$\Delta J_0(2.1) = J_0(2.2) - J_0(2.1)$$

and so on; the step forward in finding ΔJ_0 is of length 0.1, because the tabulation of J_0 is at intervals of 0.1. In other tables the step forward would be the interval of tabulation in that table.

Notice that the difference is written *between* the two values it is a difference of, as a useful reminder of its origin. As a final comment, it is common not to put in the decimal point or initial zeros in the differences. This leaves us finally with the table:

x	2.0	2.1	2.2	2.3	2.4	2.5
J_0	0.2239	0.1666	0.1104	0.0555	0.0025	−0.0484
ΔJ_0		−573	−562	−549	−530	−509

It is clear that ΔJ_0 is not a constant, and that it changes in an organised way. Perhaps the changes in ΔJ_0 are almost constant? To investigate this we need differences of differences, usually called *second differences* and defined here by

$$\Delta^2 J_0 = (\Delta J_0)_{\text{next point}} - (\Delta J_0)_{\text{present point}}.$$

The difference table is usually turned round when any higher differences are to be calculated, and written like this:

x	J_0	ΔJ_0	$\Delta^2 J_0$	$\Delta^3 J_0$	$\Delta^4 J_0$
1.5	0.5118				
		−564			
1.6	0.4554		−10		
		−574		4	
1.7	0.3980		−6		0
		−580		4	
1.8	0.3400		−2		+1
		−582		5	
1.9	0.2818		3		−2
		−579		3	
2.0	0.2239		6		+2
		−573		5	
2.1	0.1666		11		−3
		−562		2	
2.2	0.1104		13		+4
		−549		6	
2.3	0.0555		19		−4
		−530		2	
2.4	0.0025		21		
		−509			
2.5	−0.0484				

I have made the table rather longer here, to give a reasonable number of values of ΔJ_0. We can see here that:

(i) $\Delta^2 J_0$ is rather small, but is changing in an organised fashion,
(ii) $\Delta^3 J_0$ is also small, and has rather random changes around an average value near 4,
(iii) $\Delta^4 J_0$ seems to be quite disorganised.

Exercise 9A

1   The values given below are those for

$$1000 \times (2\pi)^{-1/2} e^{-x^2/2}$$

given to 3 figures – this function is of great importance in statistical theory. Complete the table.

x	$f(x)$	Δf	$\Delta^2 f$	$\Delta^3 f$	$\Delta^4 f$	$\Delta^5 f$	$\Delta^6 f$	$\Delta^7 f$	$\Delta^8 f$
0.5	352								
0.6	333	-19	-2						
0.7	312	-21	-1	1	-2				
0.8	290	-22	-2	-1	3	5			
0.9	266	-24	0	2					
1.0	242	-24							
1.1	218								
1.2	194								
1.3	171								
1.4	150								
1.5	130								
1.6	111								

2   Construct a difference table for the cubic function

$$f(x) = x^3 - 2x^2 + 1$$

for $x = -4, -3, -2, \ldots, 4$.
Find by experiment whether other cubics with integer coefficients give a difference table with $\Delta^4 f = 0$, for the same values of x.

3   Construct the difference table for $f(x)$ using the values $x = -\pi, -3\pi/4, -\pi/2, \ldots, \pi$, and working with 3 decimal places. Do you still find that $\Delta^4 f = 0$? Why?

4   Show (i) by arithmetical examples and (ii) algebraically that

$$\Delta^2 J_0 = J_0(x + 0.2) - 2J_0(x + 0.1) + J_0(x)$$

in the given table for J_0.

The values given for $J_0(x)$ in the tables in Section 9.1 are of course not exact, they are rounded values of (infinitely) long decimals. That is, each of the values of J_0 has a maximum error of $\pm 5 \times 10^{-5}$. What is the maximum error in the ΔJ_0 entries? It must be

$$\pm 1 \times 10^{-4},$$

since the two errors might reinforce each other if you were rather unlucky. Similarly for $\Delta^2 J_0$ the maximum error is $\pm 2 \times 10^{-4}$, and in general the maximum error in $\Delta^n J_0$ in this table is

$$\pm 2^{n-1} \times 10^{-4}.$$

At what stage does this increasing maximum error become larger than the 'real' differences you are calculating? In the J_0 table it is clear that

$$\Delta^3 J_0 \approx 4 \times 10^{-4}$$

with *maximum* errors due to rounding of entries

$$\pm 4 \times 10^{-4}.$$

Naturally the *likely* errors due to rounding will be smaller than this, as to get the maximum you need to have maximum error in each entry *and* the appropriate sign to give reinforcement. But errors as large as $\pm 3 \times 10^{-4}$ in $\Delta^3 J_0$ will indeed occur, with consequent errors of $\pm 4 \times 10^{-4}$ in $\Delta^4 J_0$ being quite likely. This is often described as the 'noise level' in the difference table, due to the rounding off errors in the function values.

This is another example of increasing relative errors by subtraction; you lose significant figures by subtraction of nearly equal quantities, and in this example $\Delta^3 J_0$ has scarcely one significant figure of accuracy in it, and $\Delta^4 J_0$ has none.

My conclusion here is that, for this selection of values of $J_0(x)$,

$$\Delta^4 J_0 \approx 0$$

to within the accuracy of the given values of J_0. But this suggests, from the examples you did in Exercise 9A question 2, that $J_0(x)$ is a cubic polynomial for the range

$$1.5 < x < 2.5,$$

to within the accuracy of the data. This is slightly surprising, considering the formula given in my book of tables for $J_0(x)$:

$$J_0(x) = 1 - \left(\frac{x}{2}\right)^2 + \frac{1}{(2!)^2}\left(\frac{x}{2}\right)^4 - \frac{1}{(3!)^2}\left(\frac{x}{2}\right)^6 + \cdots$$

There are no *odd* powers of x here at all, yet $J_0(x)$ is to be represented as a cubic between $x = 1.5$ and $x = 2.5$! The contradiction here is not a real one, as one formula is true for all x, the other only for a short range centred at $x = 2.0$.

A difference table has enabled us to see that $J_0(x)$ may be represented by a cubic polynomial in this interval to within the accuracy of the data values. What that cubic should be will be discussed in Section 9.2.

Exercise 9B

1   More accurate values of $J_0(x)$ at the values of x used above are:

0.511 83, 0.455 40, 0.397 98, 0.339 99, 0.281 82, 0.223 89,
0.166 61, 0.110 36, 0.055 54, 0.002 51, -0.048 38.

Recalculate the difference table for $J_0(x)$ as far as $\Delta^4 J_0$ to find better values for $\Delta^3 J_0$. Do you find better values of $\Delta^4 J_0$ also?

2   Suppose I had made a copying error in the original table for J_0, and had written

0.2329 at $x=2.0$.

Recalculate the difference table, and see how my error spreads out in a triangle from the point where it occurs.

3   Detect the error in this list of values by constructing a difference table and looking at the lack of regularity in $\Delta^3 r$:

n	1	2	3	4	5	6	7	8	9	10
$r(n)$	1414	1715	1918	2051	2124	2208	2256	2294	2324	2348

9.2   SIMPLE INTERPOLATION

(a)   General considerations

Interpolation, as described above, means looking for values between those which are given. To do this you have to make two assumptions:

(i)   that the function has a value to find;
(ii) that this value is related in some simple fashion to those round about it.

That is, you assume that the function is 'smooth' over the interval. But this need not be the case. Suppose you have the values

x	0	0.1	0.2	0.3	0.4
$f(x)$	0	0.2	0.4	0.6	0.8

What could be more natural than to *assume* that

$$f(x)=2x$$

and that 'therefore'

$$f(0.25)=0.5?$$

I can think of *hundreds* of functions which take the given values. Here are a few of them:

$$2x + \sin(10\pi x),$$

$$2x + 3\tan(10\pi x),$$

$$2x + 15x^{1/2}(x-0.1)(x-0.2)^2(x-0.3)^3(x-0.4)^4.$$

Moreover they give markedly different values for the value at 0.25:

$$1.5, \text{ no value}, 0.5 - 1.78 \times 10^{-10}.$$

Thus interpolation rests on faith that the function you are trying to model is an easy enough one, and not one invented by nature or me to trip you up. The same, of course, will be even more true for extrapolation, where you go outside the range of given values.

A second general point is that interpolation is a local process. We will not be trying to fit a cubic to *all* the values in the table; we already know how to do this, by using the method of least squares. What we shall be doing is to use the values *near*

$$x = 2.25$$

in order to fit a cubic; the obvious choice here would be to find the (only) cubic that goes through the four points

$$(2.1, 0.1666), (2.2, 0.1104), (2.3, 0.0555), (2.4, 0.0025)$$

and use it to find $J_0(2.25)$ (we hope) to a good approximation. But if I want to get a value for $x = 2.6$ from the information given, I should use the values at

$$x = 2.2, 2.3, 2.4, 2.5$$

to form my cubic, which may well be a slightly different one.

(b)   Simple interpolation

Let us look first at *linear* interpolation and extrapolation, where the arithmetic is easier. In the *SMP Formula Book* (2nd edition, 1989) I find on the χ^2-probability page the instruction

'for large values of v linear interpolation is adequate'.

(χ is the Greek letter 'chi'.) In this table v is a positive integer (the number of degrees of freedom). Suppose that I am interested in 33 degrees of freedom in a statistical problem (and a 5% significance level). How can I get the appropriate value to use from what is given?

v	20	30	40	50	60
$\chi^2_{v;0.05}$	31.41	43.77	55.76	67.50	79.08

Following the instruction, I calculate the line that passes through

$$(30, 43.77) \quad \text{and} \quad (40, 55.76),$$

which is

$$y = \{(55.76 - 43.77)/10\}v + 7.8$$
$$= 1.199v + 7.8.$$

This then gives the value I want when $v = 33$ as

$$1.199 \times 33 + 7.8 = 47.367.$$

This is the figure given by linear interpolation. The true value of $\chi^2_{33;0.05}$ will probably not be exactly this, there may be some error in the process because χ^2 is *not* exactly a linear function over this interval.

Note that in this example it would be pointless to calculate a value for $v = 32.5$, since χ^2 (as discussed here) only exists for positive integer values of v.

If you need the value of χ^2 for $v = 66$, then the instruction suggests that linear extrapolation is needed. That is, you find the line through

$$(50, 67.50) \quad \text{and} \quad (60, 79.08),$$

because these are the nearest two points to the point you need. The line is

$$y = 1.158v + 9.6,$$

which gives the extrapolated value 86.028 as an estimate of $\chi^2_{66;0.05}$.

You can see that it is *not* the same straight line that is being used in the two cases, but the line that is appropriate locally.

In this example, despite what the book of formulas says, linear interpolation will not give a *very* good answer, as you can see by looking at the difference table.

v	χ^2	$\Delta\chi^2$	$\Delta^2\chi^2$	$\Delta^3\chi^2$
20	31.41			
		12.36		
30	43.77		0.35	
		11.99		0.10
40	55.76		0.25	
		11.74		0.09
50	67.50		0.16	
		11.58		
60	79.08			

The entries in the Δ^2 column are *much* less than those in the Δ column, but they are *not* zero, and could easily cause some error in the answers we have found. The correct statements here would be

$$\chi^2_{33;0.05} \approx 47.4, \quad \chi^2_{66;0.05} \approx 86.0.$$

This, however, is a good enough level of accuracy for statistical work, so the statement in the formula book is not fundamentally misleading.

Let us now return to the cubic for $J_0(x)$. In order to estimate $J_0(2.25)$ I am going to find the cubic that passes exactly through the four points

$$(2.1, 0.1666), (2.2, 0.1104), (2.3, 0.0555), (2.4, 0.0025).$$

If I write the cubic as

$$y = ax^3 + bx^2 + cx + d,$$

I find that I have four equations to solve, by substituting values in the equation:

$$\begin{cases} 9.261a + 4.41b + 2.1c + d = 0.1666 \\ 10.648a + 4.84b + 2.2c + d = 0.1104 \\ 12.167a + 5.29b + 2.3c + d = 0.0555 \\ 13.824a + 5.76b + 2.4c + d = 0.0025. \end{cases}$$

These are best solved by Gauss elimination. They are somewhat ill-conditioned, with product of pivots 1.2×10^{-5}, which is much less than a product of typical elements (from each row and column). The ill-conditioning means that the results

$$\begin{cases} a = 0.10000 \\ b = -0.59500 \\ c = 0.60950 \\ d = 0.58450 \end{cases}$$

(to 5 s.f.) might be slightly inaccurate, and could be rather sensitive to the exact values of J_0 at the four values of x. But the residuals will be small even if a, b, c, d are not totally accurate. In fact the values derived from this cubic are correct at $x = 2.1, 2.2, 2.3$ and 2.4.

The prediction for the value of $J_0(2.25)$ from this interpolating cubic is

$$0.082\,750,$$

compared with the correct value (calculated from the series)

$$0.082\,749\,85.$$

What would I have found if I *had* fitted a straight line to the values at $x = 2.2$ and 2.3? Clearly the estimate of $J_0(2.25)$ would have been the average of the values of 2.2 and 2.3, i.e.

$$0.082\,95.$$

Fitting a cubic has indeed given a better result, though not much; after all, the values of $\Delta^2 J_0$ and $\Delta^3 J_0$ were really quite small compared to the values of ΔJ_0.

I shall leave questions (c) and (d) from the beginning of this chapter to the Exercise, as they raise no new ideas.

Exercise 9C

1 Use a linear interpolation based on the values of J_0 at $x = 2.4$ and 2.5 to estimate the value of x at which $J_0(x) = 0$. Find also the value of $J_0(2.6)$, by using the interpolation line to do the extrapolation.

2 The correct results for $J_0(x) = 0$ and $J_0(2.6)$ are

$$2.404\,826 \quad \text{and} \quad -0.096\,805.$$

Improve what you found in question 1 by using a cubic based on the values given at $x = 2.2$, 2.3, 2.4 and 2.5.

3 Here are some tabulated values of a function.

x	1	2	3	4	5	6
$f(x)$	0.2000	0.1000	0.0667	0.0500	0.0400	0.0333

Discuss whether you can interpolate with a polynomial to find $f(2.5)$.

4 A quadratic polynomial

$$ax^2 + bx + c$$

is to be fitted to the tabular values

x	$p-q$	p	$p+q$
$f(x)$	f	g	h

where q is very small. Show that the resulting equations are necessarily ill-conditioned. (You can solve for a by arranging for $f - 2g + h$ to occur; or else use Gauss elimination.)

9.3   INTERPOLATION FORMULAS

The linear interpolation formula that fits the values

$$\begin{cases} y_0 & \text{when} \quad x = x_0 \\ y_1 & \text{when} \quad x = x_1 \end{cases}$$

is easily found to be

$$y = \frac{y_1 - y_0}{x_1 - x_0} x + \frac{y_0 x_1 - y_1 x_0}{x_1 - x_0},$$

just by substituting values in $y = ax + b$. This can be rearranged as

$$y = \frac{x - x_1}{x_0 - x_1} y_0 + \frac{x - x_0}{x_1 - x_0} y_1.$$

This is *Lagrange's* form of interpolation formula for this linear case. You can easily check that the quadratic expression

$$y = \frac{(x-x_1)(x-x_2)}{(x_0-x_1)(x_0-x_2)}y_0 + \frac{(x-x_0)(x-x_2)}{(x_1-x_0)(x_1-x_2)}y_1$$

$$+ \frac{(x-x_0)(x-x_1)}{(x_2-x_0)(x_2-x_1)}y_2$$

has the values

$$\begin{cases} y_0 \text{ when } x=x_0 \\ y_1 \text{ when } x=x_1 \\ y_2 \text{ when } x=x_2. \end{cases}$$

There are further, very similar formulas, for cubic and higher interpolations. Their advantages are a clear structure, and an emphasis on how the values y_0, y_1, y_2 come into the answer. Moreover the x-values do not have to be equally spaced.

For example, a quadratic interpolation for the values

v	20	30	40
$\chi^2_{v;0.05}$	31.41	43.77	55.76

is

$$y = \frac{(x-30)(x-40)}{(20-30)(20-40)} \times 31.41 + \frac{(x-20)(x-40)}{(30-20)(30-40)} \times 43.77$$

$$+ \frac{(x-20)(x-30)}{(40-20)(40-30)} \times 55.76$$

$$= 0.15705(x^2 - 70x + 1200) - 0.4377(x^2 - 60x + 800)$$

$$+ 0.2788(x^2 - 50x + 600)$$

$$= -1.85 \times 10^{-3}x^2 + 1.3285x + 5.58.$$

But there is another way of organising these interpolation formulas which shows their connection with the difference tables. The linear formula can be rearranged as follows:

$$y = \frac{x-x_1}{x_0-x_1}y_0 + \frac{x-x_0}{x_1-x_0}y_1$$

$$= y_0 + \frac{x-x_0}{x_1-x_0}(y_1 - y_0)$$

$$= y_0 + \frac{x-x_0}{x_1-x_0}\Delta y_0.$$

Thus y is expressed in terms of the (forward) differences at x_0, and the fraction

$$\frac{x-x_0}{x_1-x_0}$$

that you need to predict forward from x_0.

Similarly the quadratic interpolation formula can be rewritten, when the distances x_1-x_0 and x_2-x_0 are *equal*, as

$$y=y_0+\left(\frac{x-x_0}{x_1-x_0}\right)\Delta y_0+\frac{1}{2}\left(\frac{x-x_0}{x_1-x_0}\right)\left(\frac{x-x_0}{x_1-x_0}-1\right)\Delta^2 y_0.$$

In this formula you could rewrite

$$\frac{x-x_0}{x_1-x_0}-1=\frac{x-x_1}{x_1-x_0},$$

but the general formula looks better if you don't. There is one slight change of notation here which is helpful. Let

$$\frac{x-x_0}{x_1-x_0}=r$$

for the fraction of an interval that you are predicting forward from x_0, to get the following formulas:

(i)   linear,

$$y=y_0+r\Delta y_0$$

(ii) quadratic,

$$y=y_0+r\Delta y_0+\tfrac{1}{2}r(r-1)\Delta^2 y_0$$

(iii) general,

$$y=y_0+r\Delta y_0+\tfrac{1}{2}r(r-1)\Delta^2 y_0+\dots$$
$$+\frac{1}{n!}r(r-1)(r-2)\dots(r-n+1)\Delta^n y_0.$$

These are the Newton–Gregory (or Gregory–Newton, or Newton – take your choice) forward difference interpolation formulas. There are corresponding *backward difference* formulas which start from the other end of the table of values, and further generalisations which we need not pursue here.

As an example of the Newton forward difference formula of degree three use the difference table for $y=\chi^2_{v;0.05}$ and take 20 as the 'x_0'. Then

$$\begin{cases} r=\tfrac{1}{10}(x-x_0)=\tfrac{1}{10}x-2 \\ r-1=\tfrac{1}{10}x-2-1=\tfrac{1}{10}x-3 \\ r-2=\tfrac{1}{10}x-4, \end{cases}$$

and also (working diagonally down and right)

$$\left\{ \begin{array}{l} y_0 = 31.41 \\ \Delta y_0 = 12.36 \\ \Delta^2 y_0 = 0.35 \\ \Delta^3 y_0 = 0.10 \end{array} \right.$$

from the table in Section 9.2(b). Putting these values in the Newton formula gives

$$y = 31.41 + (\tfrac{1}{10}x - 2) \times 12.36 + \tfrac{1}{2}(\tfrac{1}{10}x - 2)(\tfrac{1}{10}x - 3) \times 0.35$$
$$+ \tfrac{1}{6}(\tfrac{1}{10}x - 2)(\tfrac{1}{10}x - 3)(\tfrac{1}{10}x - 4) \times 0.10.$$

If you want to find the χ^2 value corresponding to $v = 33$, you put $x = 33$ in this formula and find

$$y = 47.5417$$

as the estimate using a cubic. Using this formula it is very easy to see how little the third difference affects the value:

$$\tfrac{1}{6} \times 1.3 \times 0.3 \times (-0.7) \times 0.10 = -0.004\,55.$$

Clearly a quadratic approximation would have been quite adequate for most purposes.

Exercise 9D

1   Plot the points

$$\left\{ \begin{array}{lllll} x & 1.1 & 1.7 & 2.3 & 2.9 \\ y & 0.812 & 2.031 & 2.966 & 2.694. \end{array} \right.$$

Use Newton forward difference interpolation formulas of degrees 1, 2 and 3 to estimate y when $x = 1.43$. Draw graphs of the three interpolation formulas between $x = 1.0$ and $x = 3.0$.

2   The quadratic formula for $\chi^2_{v;0.05}$ based on $v = 20, 30, 40$ has just been derived as

$$1.75 \times 10^{-3}x^2 + 1.3285x + 5.58.$$

Why does it give no better a result than the earlier linear approximation at $x = 33$?

9.4   SUMMARY

The use of a *difference table* shows whether a function is nearly a straight line (or a quadratic or cubic) over a tabulated interval. A *linear* function has *second* differences zero, a quadratic has third differences zero, and so on.

   Rounding errors in the function values grow in importance in higher differences; the maximum effect of rounding errors is

$$2^n \times \text{rounding error}$$

in the nth differences.

   Interpolation fits a simple function to a small number of points of a more complicated function. Interpolation is often done with polynomials of low degree. The results of interpolation should always be viewed with some suspicion, as many functions pass through any given set of points. *Extrapolation* uses the fitted polynomial (or other function) outside the points it was fitted to, and is always risky.

Interpolation may lead to ill-conditioned equations if it is done by simply substituting values into an assumed formula.

There are many systematic schemes for interpolation, among them *Lagrange's* interpolation formula, and *Newton's* interpolation formula (which requires equal intervals of tabulation).

Interlude and prospect

In general this book has avoided calculus and ideas associated with it up to this point. The iterations in Chapters 1, 2, 4, 6, 7 were all about processes which depended on an integer n; the discussion of computer arithmetic in Chapter 3 was concerned with decimals of finite length, i.e. points on a line which are *not* arbitrarily close together. Gauss elimination in Chapter 5 and least squares fitting in Chapter 8 were about sets of algebraic equations; least squares fitting, and interpolation in Chapter 9, were about functions given at a fixed set of points.

This restriction has been imposed partly to make the start of the book conceptually easier (and to leave time for you to learn the mechanisms of calculus concurrently if you need to), and partly because the main thrust of numerical methods is to reduce the continuous, the smooth and the infinitely subdivisible (which dominate calculus) to processes with finite sets of points. And if you are going to reduce the complicated to the 'easy', then it is as well to know how to do the easy first.

Why bother to learn calculus then, if it is going to be 'abolished' by the end of the book? There are several reasons.

(a) Many exact solutions can be found using calculus techniques; these can be valuable in themselves, and also provide checks on the inexact processes of numerical analysis.

(b) Calculus provides a valuable language with which to discuss reality and model it into mathematics; it would be harder to construct good models without this language.

(c) The methods and theorems of calculus suggest how numerical techniques should be devised.

From this point onwards in the book, you are expected to know the basic techniques of calculus; you should be able to differentiate and integrate simple functions, and know what those processes are about; you should also know the functions logarithm and exponential and their calculus properties. You are not (yet) expected to know how to solve differential equations by calculus; that comes into this book. My intention is that the demand for the techniques of calculus should not be large in the rest of the book, and most things will be shown to you as they are needed.

Revision exercise A

1   Given that two functions f and g have their values related by

$$f(n+1)-f(n)=g(n)$$

for integers $n \geqslant 1$, and that $f(1)=0$, show that

$$f(n)=\sum_{r=1}^{n-1} g(r), \quad \text{for } n \geqslant 2.$$

Hence solve the difference equation

$$\frac{u_{n+1}}{n+1}-\frac{u_n}{n}=n, \quad n \geqslant 1,$$

with initial value $u_1 = 1$.   [SMP 78]

2   Show that $u_n = n!$ satisfies the difference relation

$$u_{n+1}-nu_n=n!, \quad n \geqslant 1.$$

Hence find the solution of the difference equation

$$u_{n+1}-nu_n=n!$$

which satisfies the initial condition $u_1 = 0$.   [SMP 80]

3   (a) Derive the general solution

$$u_n = c\{(n-1)!\}^2$$

of

$$u_{n+1}=n^2 u_n, \quad n \geqslant 1.$$

(b) Solve

$$v_{n+2}=(n^2+n)v_n, \quad n \geqslant 1$$

with $v_1 = 0$ and $v_2 = 4$. (You may need different formulas for odd and even values
of n.)   [SMP 83]

4   In a 'repayment' mortgage, for an initial loan of £x_0 a Building Society charges $r\%$
interest at the start of each year, calculated on the amount still owed at that time.
During each year, a borrower repays £b to the Building Society, so that at the end of
the nth year he owes £x_n.

(a) Show that $x_{n+1}=x_n\left(1+\dfrac{r}{100}\right)-b.$

144

(b) Hence show that

$$x_n = \left(x_0 - \frac{100b}{r}\right)\left(1 + \frac{r}{100}\right)^n + \frac{100b}{r}.$$

(c) A young married couple with an initial loan of £30 000 at 12% interest repay £4000 per year. How long (to the nearest year) will they take to repay the mortgage? [AEB 89]

5 Equations of the form

$$x_{n+1} = ax_n(1 - x_n) \tag{I}$$

are of current interest in research (in bifurcation theory). We shall consider the case where $a > 1$.

(a) If x_n is small, the appropriate approximate equation is given to be

$$x_{n+1} = ax_n \tag{II}$$

Solve equation (II) with $x_0 = \alpha$ to show that solutions of (I) cannot remain near 0 except for the solution $x_0 = 0$.

(b) When x_n is near 1, put $x_n = 1 + y_n$: the appropriate approximate equation for y_n is then

$$y_{n+1} = -ay_n - 1. \tag{III}$$

Solve equation (III) with $y_0 = \beta$, and say what happens to solutions of (I) that start near the value 1.

(c) When x_n is much larger than 1 the appropriate approximate equation is

$$x_{n+1} = -ax_n^2. \tag{IV}$$

Show that

$$x_{n+1} = -a^3 x_{n-1}^4,$$

and solve (IV) for x_n in the case when $x_0 = A$. What are the implications for equation (I)?

(d) Consider now the special case $a = 4$. Show that, for real fixed θ,

$$x_n = \sin^2(2^n \theta)$$

satisfies (I). [SMP 84]

6 The cubic equation $x^3 + px^2 + qx + r = 0$, where p, q, r are real constants, has a root of the form $u + v$, where u and jv are real and $v \neq 0$. Show that u satisfies the equation

$$8u^3 + 8pu^2 + 2(p^2 + q)u + pq - r = 0.$$

The equation $x^3 - 3x^2 - 9x - 9 = 0$ is known to have a complex root of the form $u + jv$, where u and v are real and $v \neq 0$. Solve the equation completely, giving all numerical answers to 4 places of decimals. [UCLES 88]

7 (i) The quadratic equation $ax^2 + bx + c = 0$ has roots α and β, where $\alpha > \beta$. The quadratic equation $ax^2 + (b + \varepsilon)x + c = 0$ has roots $\alpha + \varepsilon_1$ and $\beta + \varepsilon_2$. Given that $\varepsilon, \varepsilon_1$ and ε_2 are small, prove that $\varepsilon_1 \approx \frac{\varepsilon}{a}\left(\frac{\alpha}{\beta - \alpha}\right)$, and obtain a similar expression for ε_2.

(ii) The roots of the equation

$$x^2 - 100x + 1 = 0$$

are α and β, where $\alpha > \beta$. Calculate α to five significant figures.

Hence obtain β to five significant figures, using a method which minimises the possible loss of significant figures.

Hence, using the results of (i) above, obtain estimates of the roots of

$$x^2 - (100 + k)x + 1 = 0,$$

where k is small.

[UCLES 88]

8 (a) (i)   Given that $z = p + q - r$, where $-P \leqslant p \leqslant P$, $-Q \leqslant q \leqslant Q$, and $-R \leqslant r \leqslant R$, write down, in terms of P, Q and R, limits within which z must lie.

(ii)   The acceleration a of a particle is calculated from the formula

$$a = 2\left(\frac{s - ut}{t^2}\right),$$

where s, u and t are measured experimentally. Given that the errors in s, u and t are δs, δu and δt respectively, show that δa, the error in a, is given by

$$\delta a \approx \frac{2}{t^2}\delta s - \frac{2}{t}\delta u + \left(-\frac{4s}{t^3} + \frac{2u}{t^2}\right)\delta t.$$

Given that $u = 2$, $|\delta u| < 0.01$, $s = 16$, $|\delta s| < 0.005$, $t = 4$ and $|\delta t| < 0.02$, obtain limits within which a may be taken to lie.

(b) Given that $w = \dfrac{xy}{\sqrt{z}}$, obtain an expression for the relative error in w in terms of the relative errors in x, y and z.

Given that each of x, y and z has been rounded to three significant figures, show that w may have a relative error as large as $1\frac{1}{4}\%$.

[UCLES 89]

9 (a) Show that the equation $2 \sin x - x = 0$ has a root in the interval $[1.6, 2.8]$.

This root is to be found by the interval bisection method. Taking x_1 as 2.2, obtain x_2, x_3 and x_4.

Without calculating further values of x_n, obtain the least value of n that will ensure that the root has been found to within 0.001 units.

(b) The equation $2 \cos x - x = 0$ has a root α in the interval $[1, 1.2]$. Iterations of the form $x_{n+1} = F(x_n)$ are based on each of the following rearrangements of the equation:

(i) $x = 2 \cos x$,
(ii) $x = \cos x + \frac{1}{2}x$,
(iii) $x = \frac{2}{3}(\cos x + x)$.

Apply an appropriate test to determine, for each rearrangement, whether or not the corresponding iteration converges to α, and illustrate your answer to (ii) by a 'staircase' or 'cobweb' diagram.

Using whichever of these iterations you consider most appropriate, and starting with $x_1 = 1$, find α to 4 significant figures.

[UCLES 88]

10 This question is concerned with the equation

$$u \sin u = 1, \tag{I}$$

where u is in radians. It is given that the equation has a root near 1.1 and another near 3.0.

(a) Calculate u_1 and u_2 using

$$u_{n+1} = 1/(\sin u_n), \quad u_0 = 1.1,$$

and giving your answers to five decimal places. Use Aitken's δ^2 process on these answers to find a better estimate of the root.

(b) The iteration method in (a) will not give the root of (I) near 3.0. Consider the iteration

$$v_{n+1} = -\sin^{-1}(1/v_n) + \pi,$$

and let the errors e_n be defined by

$$v_n = u + e_n$$

where u is the root near 3.0. Show that this root is between 2.5 and 3.0.
You are *given* that for small values of h

$$\sin^{-1}\left(\frac{1}{u+h}\right) \approx \pi - u + h/(u^2 \cos u);$$

deduce that (if e_n is small),

$$e_{n+1} \approx -\frac{1}{u^2 \cos u} e_n.$$

Deduce that, if e_1 is small, v_n tends to u as n becomes large.

[SMP 88]

11 Explain briefly what is meant by 'a set of ill-conditioned simultaneous linear equations'.
Solve the simultaneous equations

$$\begin{cases} ax + by = k, \\ cx + dy = l. \end{cases}$$

Deduce that a small change in k will produce a large change in the solution if $|c|$ or $|d|$ is large compared with $|ad - bc|$, and state a corresponding condition that ensures that a small change in l will produce a large change in the solution.
Find which of these conditions holds for the equations

$$\begin{cases} 2x - 7y = k, \\ 7x - 24y = l. \end{cases}$$

where k and l are constants.
Given that, in these equations, the coefficients of x and y are exact, but it is known only that k lies within 20 ± 0.5 and l within 69 ± 0.5, solve the equations, giving the greatest and least possible values for x, and the greatest and least possible values for y.

Show that the points in the x–y plane corresponding to possible solutions lie within a parallelogram, and give the coordinates of the vertices of this parallelogram.

12 This question concerns the solution of the equations

$$\begin{pmatrix} 1 & a & -2a \\ a & 1+2a & -\tfrac{3}{2}a \\ -2a & -\tfrac{3}{2}a & 1-2a \end{pmatrix}\begin{pmatrix} x \\ y \\ z \end{pmatrix} = \begin{pmatrix} 1 \\ 2 \\ 3 \end{pmatrix}$$ (I)

for various values of a.

(a) For the case $a=0.298$, show by using Gaussian elimination that the equations (I) are ill-conditioned. How do you recognise ill-conditioning in the computer solution of a set of equations? What briefly are the consequences for the accuracy of the resulting 'solution' given by the computer? Illustrate your answer by referring to your work on equations (I).

(b) Now take the case $a=0.1$. Show that the Jacobi and Gauss–Seidel iterative methods converge. Carry out two iterations using the Gauss–Seidel method in the form

$$\begin{pmatrix} 1 & 0 & 0 \\ 0.1 & 1.2 & 0 \\ -0.2 & -0.15 & 0.8 \end{pmatrix}\mathbf{x}_{n+1} + \begin{pmatrix} 0 & 0.1 & -0.2 \\ 0 & 0 & -0.15 \\ 0 & 0 & 0 \end{pmatrix}\mathbf{x}_n = \begin{pmatrix} 1 \\ 2 \\ 3 \end{pmatrix},$$

starting from

$$\mathbf{x}_0 = (1 \quad 2 \quad 3)^\mathrm{T}.$$

(c) The eigenvalues of the matrix

$$\begin{pmatrix} 0 & a & -2a \\ a & 2a & -\tfrac{3}{2}a \\ -2a & -\tfrac{3}{2}a & -2a \end{pmatrix}$$

are *given* to be 0 and $\pm a\sqrt{(45/4)}$. Could you use Jacobi iteration in the case $a=0.31$? Explain your answer.   [SMP 88]

13 A solution of the following system of equations is required

$$\begin{pmatrix} 0.60 & 0.80 & 0.10 \\ 1.10 & 0.40 & 0.30 \\ 1.71 & 1.20 & 0.41 \end{pmatrix}\begin{pmatrix} x \\ y \\ z \end{pmatrix} = \begin{pmatrix} 1.00 \\ 0.20 \\ 1.20 \end{pmatrix}.$$

Find the determinant of the matrix and comment upon the result with reference to the solution of the system of equations.

Explain why an iterative method of solution is not appropriate.

Solve the system of equations correct to two decimal places.   [MEI 87]

14 A sociological survey classified its sample into the four wealth classes: poor (P), comfortable (C), affluent (A), rich (R). From respondents' answers they found the following *changes* of class since the last census, expressed as a proportion of each group:

$$\text{P to C: } \tfrac{1}{20} \qquad \text{R to A: } \tfrac{1}{50}$$
$$\text{C to P: } \tfrac{1}{20} \qquad \text{C to A: } \tfrac{1}{10}$$
$$\text{A to C: } \tfrac{1}{20} \qquad \text{A to R: } \tfrac{1}{100}$$

There were no other changes. Set up a matrix to relate the present column vector $(p \quad c \quad a \quad r)^{\mathrm{T}}$ of numbers in the classes to the column vector $(w \quad x \quad y \quad z)^{\mathrm{T}}$ for numbers in the classes at the last census.

The present sample contains 200, 1000, 200, 50 in the four classes. Carry out one step of an iterative method (showing that it converges) to estimate the numbers in the classes at the last census, using the present sample as starting value. Write down (but do not solve) equations for a second step of your iteration. [SMP 89]

15 A cubic curve of best fit, in the least squares sense, having an equation of the form $y = ax^3 + bx + c$, is to be drawn for the set of points (x_i, y_i), $i = 1, 2, \ldots, n$, where the values of the x_i are exact, but the y_i are subject to error. Show that a, b and c are given by the equations

$$\begin{cases} \sum_{i=1}^{n} y_i = a \sum_{i=1}^{n} x_i^3 + b \sum_{i=1}^{n} x_i + nc, \\ \sum_{i=1}^{n} y_i x_i = a \sum_{i=1}^{n} x_i^4 + b \sum_{i=1}^{n} x_i^2 + c \sum_{i=1}^{n} x_i, \\ \sum_{i=1}^{n} y_i x_i^3 = a \sum_{i=1}^{n} x_i^6 + b \sum_{i=1}^{n} x_i^4 + c \sum_{i=1}^{n} x_i^3. \end{cases}$$

Find the cubic curve of best fit, as defined above, for the set of points given by:

x	-2	-1	0	1	2
y	4.0	3.5	2.0	0.2	0.2

[UCLES 88]

16 Show that the equation $f(x) = 1 - e^x \sin x = 0$ has a root at $x = a$ where $0 < a < 1$. Estimate a by linear interpolation between $x = 0$ and $x = 1$. Find the value of $f(0.5)$ and estimate another value of a by linear interpolation between $x = 0.5$ and $x = 1$. Repeat this process of halving the interval and estimating a by linear interpolation until two successive estimates of a differ by less than 0.01. Explain whether you consider you have now determined the value of a correct to 2 decimal places. [MEI 87]

17 The values of a function $f(x)$, truncated to 4 decimal places, are shown in the following table:

x	0	1	2	3	4	5
$f(x)$	1.0914	0.8086	0.5715	0.3511	0.2384	0.1448

x	6	7	8	9	10
$f(x)$	0.1015	0.1093	0.1691	0.2822	0.4497

Draw up a difference table for the function up to and including the third differences. Given that the table of values contains one error, show how to locate and correct the error on the assumption that the third differences are approximately constant.

The function $f(x)$ has a minimum value for some x in the range $0 \leqslant x \leqslant 10$. Use linear interpolation on the first differences to estimate the value of x at which the minimum occurs. Explain briefly how you would estimate the value of $f(x)$ at the minimum point.   [MEI 88]

18 You are given the polynomial $f(x) = ax^3 + bx^2 + cx + d$.
Find the polynomials

$$\begin{cases} g(x) = f(x+1) - f(x) \\ h(x) = g(x+1) - g(x) \\ k(x) = h(x+1) - h(x). \end{cases}$$

Find the relations between each of $g(x)$, $h(x)$ and $k(x)$ and one of the derivatives with respect to x of the functions $f(x)$, $f(x + \frac{1}{2})$ and $f(x+1)$.

If $f(0) = 1$, $g(0) = 5$, $h(0) = -2$, and $k(0) = 6$, show using a difference table that $f(4) = 33$.

Find the values of a, b, c and d in this case.   [MEI 89]

19 The following table is an incomplete difference table for y, which is a cubic polynomial in x.

x	y			
1	×			
		×		
2	0.6875		×	
		×		×
3	×		0.02	
		×		×
4	0.0525		×	×
		×		×
5	×		×	×
		−0.0425		
6	−0.2025			

Complete the table by finding all the entries which are marked with a cross. From your table, estimate the value of $y(2.6)$, using linear interpolation. By expressing y in the form

$$a+b(x-1)+c(x-1)(x-2)+d(x-1)(x-2)(x-3),$$

find the values of a, b, c and d.

Hence find the percentage error in the estimate of $y(2.6)$ obtained above.

[MEI 86]

Projects and investigations I

I.1 The logistic equation

$$x_{n+1} = rx_n(1 - x_n)$$

has surprising properties for values of r beyond 3. These can best be investigated using a computer to plot the points generated for

(i) different values of r
(ii) different values of x_0.

  As part of a mathematical investigation you should find the *fixed points* of the equation, for which $x_{n+1} = x_n$ for all n; and also the *points of period* 2, for which $x_{n+2} = x_n$. Are there any points of period 3?
  Show that there is an 'easy' solution for $r = 4$, $x_n = \sin^2(2^n\theta)$. Plot values of this chaotic solution. Can two values ever be equal?
  Suppose that US censuses had been taken every 40 years from 1790. What values of A and B would you have found in a logistic model $v_{n+1} = Av_n - Bv_n^2$? Use the values in Chapter 1.

I.2 Draw a divergent cobweb diagram, say with root x and first approximation x_0, and with the curve $y = F(x)$ having positive gradient. Then you can choose m such that the line with slope m through $(x_0, F(x_0))$ cuts $y = x$ at x_1, say, with x_1 between x and x_0. Set up a convergent iteration based on this idea. How do you choose m? Will it always converge? Try it out on some examples. How fast is the convergence?

I.3 From a graphics program, $x_0 = 4.11$ is close to a solution of $x = \frac{1}{10}e^x \sin^2 x$. However, iteration from there is divergent, giving $x_1 = 4.13798$, $x_2 = 4.41729$. Can you use Aitken's improvement technique backwards on this divergent iteration to find the root? Explain the theory behind this idea.
  Will a divergent iteration $x_{n+1} = F(x_n)$ always converge if it is run backwards as $x_n = F^{-1}(x_{n+1})$?
  Will the same be true for Jacobi iterations

$$\mathbf{x}_{n+1} = \mathbf{A}\mathbf{x}_n$$

which diverge?

I.4 Equations of the form $x = F(x)$ can sometimes be solved by the iteration $x_{n+1} = F(x_n)$. Can a similar iteration be done for the pair of equations

$$\begin{cases} x = F(x, y) \\ y = G(x, y) \end{cases}?$$

Try

(i) Jacobi iteration $\begin{cases} x_{n+1} = F(x_n, y_n) \\ y_{n+1} = G(x_n, y_n) \end{cases}$

152

(ii) Gauss–Seidel iteration $\begin{cases} x_{n+1} = F(x_n, y_n) \\ y_{n+1} = G(x_{n+1}, y_n) \end{cases}$

(iii) taking specially simple cases, such as

$$\begin{cases} x = ax + by \\ y = cx + dy \end{cases}$$

(iv) drawing cobweb diagrams (or staircases) for the surfaces $z = F(x, y)$ and so on. Can you find conditions for convergence?

I.5 Gauss elimination, without pivoting, on the $n \times n$ matrix

$$\begin{pmatrix} 1 & \dfrac{1}{2} & \dfrac{1}{3} & \cdots & \dfrac{1}{n} \\ \dfrac{1}{2} & \dfrac{1}{3} & \dfrac{1}{4} & \cdots & \dfrac{1}{n+1} \\ & \cdots & & & \\ \dfrac{1}{n} & \dfrac{1}{n+1} & \dfrac{1}{n+2} & \cdots & \dfrac{1}{2n-1} \end{pmatrix}$$

gives the pivots $1, \frac{1}{12}, \frac{1}{180}, \frac{1}{2800}, \ldots$ What is the general formula for these pivots? You may want to work some out by hand, and also a few more by computer. How large does n need to get, to give extremely ill-conditioned equations?

Are there any other matrices which will have similar properties?

I.6 Traffic flow round a large roundabout is modelled by the following assumptions.
  (i) At entry road i there are q_i cars per hour entering the roundabout, and Q_i cars per hour on the roundabout and crossing that road entry (so preventing access).
  (ii) Of the flow q_i, $\alpha_{1i}q_i$ wish to leave at entry point 1, $\alpha_{2i}q_i$ wish to leave at entry point 2, and so on.
  (iii) There are experimental constants A and B such that $q_i = A - BQ_i$; $A = 3000$ and $B = 1.5$ are reasonably good values, the units being cars per hour.
  (iv) The maximum flow rate through entry road i (the number of cars approaching along that road) is r_i.
Set up equations for a four-entry roundabout.

The preferred iterative scheme for solving this system is to
  (a) set $Q_1 = 0$
  (b) set $q_1 = r_1$
  (c) iterate round the roundabout by calculating Q_2 and then q_2, Q_3 and then q_3, and so on.
Choose some sensible numbers, and do this. How rapidly does it converge? Is this Jacobi iteration? Is it Gauss–Seidel iteration?

Could you use this kind of iteration on any set of linear equations?

I.7 The newspaper model in Chapter 7 left out many aspects of reality. For example, newspaper A might aim for the upper socio-economic groups by distributing in only the wealthier parts of the city, while B might aim for the mass market; both will no doubt aim at the middle ground also. Try the revised model

$$\begin{cases} u_{n+1} = \tfrac{1}{2}au_n/(u_n+v_n)+\tfrac{1}{4}a-u_n \\ v_{n+1} = \tfrac{1}{2}bv_n/(u_n+v_n)+\tfrac{1}{4}b-v_n, \end{cases}$$

which attempts to build in this new idea, to see what results you can derive. Use both computer runs and mathematics.

I.8 Suppose that you wished to fit a model

$$y = ae^{bx}$$

to a set of data points $(x_1, y_1), \ldots, (x_7, y_7)$. One way of doing it is to use least squares methods on

$$\ln y = \ln a + bx. \tag{A}$$

Another is to proceed directly by considering

$$S = \sum_{i=1}^{7} (y_i - ae^{bx_i})^2.$$

Then dS/da and dS/db can be calculated, and the two equations $dS/da = dS/db = 0$ can be solved for a and b; here the two equations can be reduced to a single equation for b, which can be solved iteratively.

Compare the results you get, using (say) the athletics data in Chapter 8, with the results of solving (A) by least squares. Which method gives the smaller sum of squares of residuals?

10

Slope and area

Calculus was invented to deal with two fundamental problems in geometry – the finding of the *slope* of a continuous curve at any point, and the calculation of the *area* under a curve. Both of these can be approached numerically on the basis of geometrically simple ideas.

10.1 THE SLOPE OF A GRAPH

If we have two points on a graph, say

$$(1, 3) \quad \text{and} \quad (2, 5),$$

then the slope of the line joining them is

$$\frac{5-3}{2-1} = 2.$$

This is just

$$\text{slope} = \frac{\text{change in } y}{\text{change in } x}$$

(see Fig. 1). We shall generally be interested in y-values derived from some function f:

$$y = f(x).$$

Thus if we call the x-values x_1 and x_2, we shall write either y_1 and y_2 or $f(x_1)$ and $f(x_2)$.

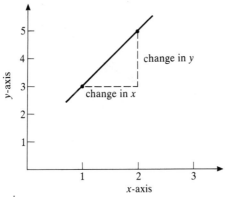

Figure 1. Slope $= \dfrac{\text{change in } y}{\text{change in } x}$

The slope will then be written either as

$$\frac{y_2 - y_1}{x_2 - x_1}$$

or as

$$\frac{f(x_2) - f(x_1)}{x_2 - x_1}.$$

You may notice here that the ideas from the last chapter are trying to intrude. If you have a table of values

x	x_1	x_2	x_3	...
y	y_1	y_2	y_3	...

then $y_2 - y_1$ is just Δy at x_1, and

$$\frac{y_2 - y_1}{x_2 - x_1}$$

is the slope of the interpolation line through (x_1, y_1) and (x_2, y_2).

How can we get the slope *at* a single point, rather than the slope *between* two points? The idea on which calculus is based is that we see what happens when x_2 gets very close to x_1, and use the *limiting value* of the ratio

$$\frac{y_2 - y_1}{x_2 - x_1}$$

as x_2 approaches x_1 (see Fig. 2).

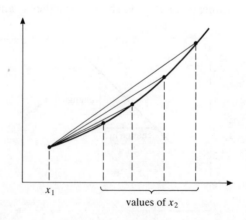

Figure 2. Slope at x_1 as a limit of slopes between x_2 and x_1

This is often expressed in the alternative form

| 'the slope at $x=a$ is given by the limit of $\{f(a+h)-f(a)\}/h$ as h becomes very small'

where the substitutions

$$\begin{cases} a+h \text{ for } x_2 \text{ and } a \text{ for } x_1 \\ f(a+h) \text{ for } y_2 \text{ and } f(a) \text{ for } y_1 \\ h \text{ for } x_2-x_1 \end{cases}$$

have been made (Fig. 3).

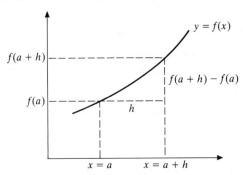

Figure 3. Slope $=\{f(a+h)-f(a)\}/h$

This suggests that the numerical estimate of the slope at $x=a$ should be achieved by taking a difference of very close function values and dividing by the distance apart. Let us try this. I used the function ln,

$$y=\ln x$$

with $a=3$. I calculated $\{\ln(3+h)-\ln 3\}/h$ for a variety of small values of h, and get

h	slope
$h=0.1$	0.327 898 228 3
$h=0.01$	0.332 779 009
$h=0.001$	0.333 277 79
$h=1 \times 10^{-4}$	0.333 327 8
$h=1 \times 10^{-5}$	0.333 334
$h=1 \times 10^{-6}$	0.333 34
$h=1 \times 10^{-7}$	0.333 4
$h=1 \times 10^{-8}$	0.334
$h=1 \times 10^{-9}$	0.34
$h=1 \times 10^{-10}$	0.4
$h=1 \times 10^{-11}$	0

The correct answer here is $\frac{1}{3}$, and my best answer came from $h = 1 \times 10^{-5}$, which is not very small. The problem is the one we have seen several times before: if you subtract very nearly equal numbers, you lose significant figures in the answer. Naturally we have to take h quite small, or we get a slope between two well separated points, but if you take h too small you start to lose accuracy again. We return to detailed analysis of the two sources of error later in the book.

Can we do any better than this? Think back to interpolation for a moment. If we wanted to find a value at some intermediate point, we used information from the nearest tabulated points to get it. In this case we want the slope at $x = a$: why not use information from *both* sides of $x = a$ to get it, rather than just from values to the right of $x = a$? Perhaps we can get a better estimate of the slope at a by using the *three* values

$$f(a-h), f(a), f(a+h)$$

instead of just the two we have used so far.

Since there are three values here, perhaps I should try the line of best fit by least squares. If you use the methods of Chapter 8, you find that the slope of this line is

$$\frac{f(a+h) - f(a-h)}{2h}.$$

You can easily confirm that this is a good idea by drawing a diagram (Fig. 4): the chord has very nearly the same slope as the graph has at $x = a$.

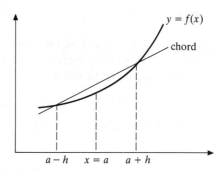

Figure 4. A chord whose slope is close to that of the graph at a

I recalculated the example of $f(x) = \ln x$ using this new formula, with the following results.

h	slope
0.1	0.333 456 872 5
0.01	0.333 334 567 5
0.001	0.333 333 345
1×10^{-4}	0.333 333 35
1×10^{-5}	0.333 334
1×10^{-6}	0.333 335
1×10^{-7}	0.333 35

The result is better; I can get 7 correct figures now, rather than the 5 I obtained before, and I only needed to go down to $h=0.001$ to do it.

From the point of view of calculus, each of these methods of obtaining the slope is equally good, because in the *limit* they are equal. But for numerical methods they are not the same, as limits right down towards $h=0$ cannot be taken because of restrictions imposed by the calculator or computer.

Exercise 10A

1 For the function $f(x)=2\sin x$ calculate
 (i) the slope at $x=1$ (radians, of course);
 (ii) $\{f(1+h)-f(1)\}/h$, for $h=10^{-n}$, $n=1,2,3,\ldots,7$;
 (iii) $\{f(1+h)-f(1-h)\}/(2h)$, for $h=10^{-n}$, $n=1,2,3,\ldots,7$.
 Discuss your results.

2 (i) For the function $f(x)=\ln x$ and the calculations done near $x=3$ above, calculate the errors in the slope for each formula, and investigate whether the size of the error is proportional to a power of h when h is not too small.
 (ii) Repeat the investigation for $f(x)=2\sin x$.

3 A quadratic $y=Ax^2+Bx+C$ can be fitted exactly to the three points
$$\begin{cases} x_1=a-h & y_1=f(a-h) \\ x_2=a & y_2=f(a) \\ x_3=a+h & y_3=f(a+h) \end{cases}$$
 by the methods of Chapter 9. Find its slope at $x=a$ in terms of function values and h.

4 Estimate the slope of the curve $y=J_0(x)$ at $x=2.25$ by
 (i) using the values of J_0 at $x=2.1$ and $x=2.4$,
 (ii) using the values of J_0 at $x=2.2$ and $x=2.3$,
 (iii) assuming that the errors have the form Ah^2 for some value of A.
 (Use values of $J_0(x)$ from Exercise 9B, question 1.)

10.2 THE SECOND DERIVATIVE

In calculus the slope of the graph of $y=f(x)$ at the point $x=a$ is usually abbreviated to

$$f'(a)$$

or to

$$\left(\frac{dy}{dx}\right)_{x=a}.$$

The operation of differentiation starts with one function $f(x)$ and gives you the derived function (or derivative) $f'(x)$ or dy/dx. Thus, for example

$$\begin{cases} x^3+3x^2+2 & \text{has derived function} & 3x^2+6x \\ \sin(3x) & \text{has derivative} & 3\cos(3x) \\ 3\cos(3x) & \text{has derivative} & -9\sin(3x). \end{cases}$$

The last of these is the derivative of the derivative of $\sin(3x)$, and is usually written as

$$\frac{d^2y}{dx^2} \quad \text{or} \quad f''(x)$$

depending on whether you prefer to write

$$y = \sin(3x) \quad \text{or} \quad f(x) = \sin(3x).$$

The question arises as to how we estimate second derivatives numerically.

There are two ways into this problem which look rather different, but give the same answer. I should like to start with a curve fitting idea, from question 3 in Exercise 10A and from Chapter 9. Suppose I fit a quadratic curve

$$y = Ax^2 + Bx + C$$

to the three points

$$\begin{cases} x = a-h, & y = f(a-h) \\ x = a, & y = f(a) \\ x = a+h, & y = f(a+h). \end{cases}$$

Then this quadratic will have second derivative

$$\frac{d^2y}{dx^2} = 2A$$

at $x = a$ (and indeed everywhere). Now you can solve for A from the information given (indeed you should have done so for question 3 above) and its value gives

$$2A = \frac{f(a+h) - 2f(a) + f(a-h)}{h^2}.$$

So it seems reasonable to estimate second derivatives numerically by this formula, with h taking small (but not too small) values. Let us try this process on the example done above, where we used

$$f(x) = \ln x, \ a = 3.$$

My calculations then gave the following values for

$$\frac{1}{h^2}\{\ln(3+h) - 2\ln 3 + \ln(3-h)\},$$

and its difference from $-\frac{1}{9}$, the correct second derivative.

h	expression	error
1	$-0.117\,783\,035\,6$	6.6719×10^{-3}
0.1	$-0.111\,172\,883$	6.1772×10^{-5}
0.01	$-0.111\,111\,7$	5.8889×10^{-7}
0.001	$-0.111\,11$	-1.1111×10^{-6}
1×10^{-4}	-0.111	-1.1111×10^{-4}
1×10^{-5}	0	

The best value is given near $h=0.006$ in fact, with error almost zero. This seems entirely satisfactory as a way of calculating a second derivative numerically.

The second approach is to work essentially from a difference table (starting at $x=a-h$).

x	y	Δy
$a-h$	$f(a-h)$	
		$f(a)-f(a-h)$
a	$f(a)$	
		$f(a+h)-f(a)$
$a+h$	$f(a+h)$	

Now $\{f(a+h)-f(a)\}/h$ is a good estimate of the derivative half way between $x=a$ and $x=a+h$ (and a less good estimate of the derivative at $x=a$, as we have seen), and $\{f(a)-f(a-h)\}/h$ is similarly a good estimate of the derivative half way between $x=a-h$ and $x=a$. That is,

$$f'(a+\tfrac{1}{2}h)\approx\{f(a+h)-f(a)\}/h$$

$$f'(a-\tfrac{1}{2}h)\approx\{f(a)-f(a-h)\}/h$$

and so the derivative of $f'(x)$ at $x=a$ will be well estimated by

$$\frac{f'(a+\tfrac{1}{2}h)-f'(a-\tfrac{1}{2}h)}{h}=\frac{f(a+h)-2f(a)+f(a-h)}{h^2}.$$

This is, of course, the same result as we found earlier, by another method.

Exercise 10B

1 For the function $f(x)=2\sin x$ calculate
   (i) the second derivative at $x=1$.
   (ii) $\{f(1+h)-2f(1)+f(1-h)\}/h^2$ for various values of h decreasing towards zero (the powers 10^{-n} may not be enough, try 3×10^{-n} also).
   (iii) the value of (error)/h^2 for each value of h.

2 Repeat question 1 (iii) for $f(x)=\ln x$ at $x=3$. Discuss your results.

3 Can you find a good estimate for the third derivative of $f(x)$ at $x=a$? (The good estimates for $f'(a)$ and $f''(a)$ are both *symmetric* about $x=a$, a change in the sign of h makes no difference to the formula.) Is there a pattern in the formulas for estimating derivatives?

4 Calculate estimates (using formulas in the text) of both first and second derivatives of

$$f(x)=x^{1/3}$$

   at $x=0$. What are the correct answers?

5 Show that $f''(a)\approx\Delta^2 f/h^2$.

10.3   SIMPLE CALCULATIONS OF AREA

(a)   Using rectangles

The easiest estimate of the area under the curve

$$y = e^{-x^2}$$

from $x=0$ to $x=1$ is found by chopping the area into ten strips, as shown in Fig. 5.

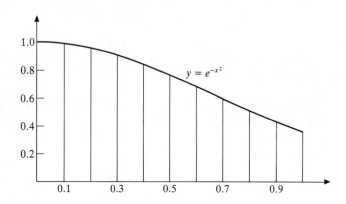

Figure 5. Strips for the area under $y = e^{-x^2}$

Then you can estimate the area of each strip by

width × height half way across.

This gives the total area estimate, by this method, to be

$$\tfrac{1}{10}(e^{-0.0025} + e^{-0.0225} + e^{-0.0625} + \ldots + e^{-0.9025}\} = 0.74713088.$$

This may be called the *rectangle method* or the *mid-point method*; it is rather like a histogram in statistics, as the whole content of a strip is represented by a rectangle sitting on that strip (Fig. 6).

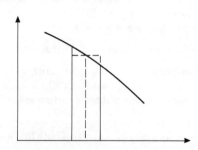

Figure 6. The area of a strip replaced by the area of a rectangle with height = function value at mid point

How accurate is this estimate of

$$A = \int_0^1 e^{-x^2}\, dx,$$

to give it the proper calculus notation? There are two ways of finding out; one is to try smaller and smaller strips (as in Exercise 10A question 2 and in Exercise 10B question 1 (iii), where we used smaller h to try to establish an error rule), the other is to ask if anyone has calculated it accurately. In fact this area is related to area for the normal distribution curve in statistics (see *Statistics and Probability* in this series), which is tabulated in most books of tables. The correct value for A is (by interpolation)

$$\sqrt{\pi}\{\Phi(\sqrt{2}) - \tfrac{1}{2}\} \approx 0.7468.$$

(This is the Greek capital phi.) However this has itself been calculated numerically, so we should be able to do better than this by using smaller strips.

I programmed my computer to do the summation, using strips of width h, and found the following estimates.

h	A	$|\text{error}| \times 10^8$
0.1	0.747 130 88	30 675
0.05	0.746 900 79	7666
0.02	0.746 836 40	1227
0.01	0.746 827 20	307
0.005	0.746 824 90	77
0.002	0.746 824 26	13
0.001	0.746 824 16	3
0.0005	0.746 824 14	1

I have put in the errors on the assumption that the correct answer is 0.746 824 13. Then $|\text{error}|/h^2$ is extremely close to a constant, 3.07×10^{-2}.

This method of working out areas numerically is perfectly sound, but it is not very efficient. To get an answer correct to 8 s.f. in the example will need a summation of about 5000 terms, which is time consuming.

(b)   Using trapezia

An alternative way of estimating the area A is by joining up points on the graph to form trapezia (Fig. 7). The area of the trapezium is

$$\text{average height} \times \text{base} = \tfrac{1}{2}(x_{i+1} - x_i)\{f(x_{i+1}) + f(x_i)\}$$
$$= \tfrac{1}{2}h\{f(x_{i+1}) + f(x_i)\}$$

if the strip width is h, as before. When you add up a whole set of trapezia you get

$$A \approx \tfrac{1}{2}h\{f(x_0) + 2f(x_1) + 2f(x_2) + \ldots + 2f(x_{n-1}) + f(x_n)\}.$$

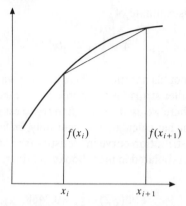

Figure 7. The area of a strip approximated by the area of a trapezium

This assumes that the whole area has been divided into n strips of width h; each intermediate height $f(x_i)$, $i=1,2,...,n-1$, comes into *two* trapezia, and so is counted twice. This result is called the *trapezium rule*; it corresponds closely to linear interpolation, because a line has been fitted between adjacent points

$$(x_i, f(x_i)),\ (x_{i+1}, f(x_{i+1}))$$

on the curve. The trapezium rule is also written as

$$A \approx \tfrac{1}{2}h\{y_0 + 2(y_1 + y_2 + \ ... \ + y_{n-1}) + y_n\},$$

by using the alternative notation

$$y_i = f(x_i).$$

If the end points of the integration are $x=a$ and $x=b$ you have the additional relations

$$\begin{cases} x_0 = a,\ x_n = b,\ b - a = nh, \\ x_i = a + ih,\ i = 0, 1, 2, ..., n. \end{cases}$$

Let us use the trapezium rule on the same example. We now have

$$y_i = e^{-x_i^2},$$

and the computer needs to be reprogrammed slightly. The results are as follows.

h	A	$|\text{error}| \times 10^8$
0.1	0.746 210 80	61 333
0.05	0.746 670 84	15 329
0.02	0.746 799 61	2 452
0.01	0.746 818 00	613
0.005	0.746 822 60	153
0.002	0.746 823 89	24
0.001	0.746 824 07	6
0.0005	0.746 824 12	1

These results show that the trapezium rule is of the same efficiency as the rectangle method, with error proportional to h^2 again. For most functions the two methods are almost exactly the same, as you can see from the results. But in Section 10.5 we shall see one case in which the rectangle method has a slight advantage.

Exercise 10C

1   Use the method of rectangles with 10 strips to estimate the area defined by

$$A = \int_1^2 e^{-x}\,dx.$$

What is the correct value?

2   Using the method of rectangles of width h to estimate

$$A = \int_1^2 e^{-x}\,dx$$

gives the sum

$$h\{e^{-(1+h/2)} + e^{-(1+3h/2)} + \ldots + e^{-(1+(2n-1)h/2)}\},$$

where $n = 1/h$. This is a geometric progression which can be summed in terms of h. Do this, to find a formula for the error in terms of h. Is it clear that it is approximately a constant times h^2 when h is small?

3   Use the trapezium rule to calculate

$$\int_{-1}^1 \frac{1}{1+x^2}\,dx$$

correct to 4 d.p.

4   Show geometrically that the trapezium rule is bound to give an underestimate for a graph which is convex upwards; and that the rectangle method will give an overestimate.

5   The error estimates in Section 10.3 were for an 'ordinary', 'smooth' function. Use
   (a) the rectangle method
   (b) the trapezium rule
   each with strips of width h, to estimate

$$\int_0^1 x^{1/3}\,dx,$$

for various h. Are the errors proportional to h^2? What is not smooth or ordinary about $x^{1/3}$?

10.4   SIMPSON'S RULE FOR AREA

The trapezium rule was based in essence on linear interpolation to join up the top corners of the strips into which we divided the area. It seems likely that a quadratic interpolation will do better (and, presumably, a cubic one even better still). We investigate this.

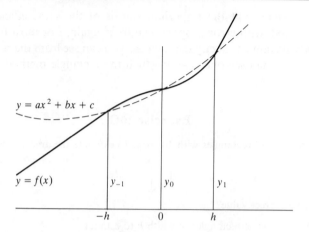

Figure 8. Curve $y=f(x)$ and the interpolating quadratic $y=ax^2+bx+c$

To make the curve fitting easier we shall start with the curve shown in Fig. 8, which passes through the three points

$$(-h, y_{-1}), (0, y_0), (h, y_1).$$

The quadratic curve of interpolation

$$y=ax^2+bx+c$$

also passes through these points.

Substitution in the quadratic shows that

$$\begin{cases} y_{-1}=ah^2-bh+c \\ y_1=ah^2+bh+c \end{cases}$$

and so

$$y_{-1}+y_1=2ah^2+2c.$$

Also

$$y_0=c.$$

Now the area under the quadratic in the two strips is the approximation to A, and so

$$A \approx \int_{-h}^{h} (ax^2+bx+c)dx$$

$$= \tfrac{2}{3}ah^3+2ch.$$

Converting this into an expression involving y_{-1}, y_0, y_1 from the relations above:

$$A \approx \tfrac{1}{3}h(y_{-1}+y_1-2y_0)+2hy_0$$

$$= \tfrac{1}{3}h(y_{-1}+4y_0+y_1).$$

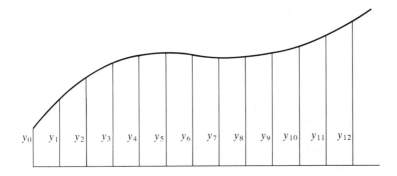

Figure 9. An area split into (double) strips ready for Simpson's rule

This is the basic Simpson formula for the approximate area under the curve $y = f(x)$ in the double strip from $-h$ to $+h$.

This formula does not involve the actual position of this double strip, just the width h and the heights y_{-1}, y_0, y_1. So in Fig. 9 (for example) the estimate of the whole area under the curve, from y_0 to y_{12}, is

$$A \approx \tfrac{1}{3}h(y_0 + 4y_1 + y_2) + \tfrac{1}{3}h(y_2 + 4y_3 + y_4)$$
$$+ \tfrac{1}{3}h(y_4 + 4y_5 + y_6) + \tfrac{1}{3}h(y_6 + 4y_7 + y_8)$$
$$+ \tfrac{1}{3}h(y_8 + 4y_9 + y_{10}) + \tfrac{1}{3}h(y_{10} + 4y_{11} + y_{12})$$
$$= \tfrac{1}{3}h\{(y_0 + y_{12}) + 4(y_1 + y_3 + y_5 + \ldots + y_{11})$$
$$+ 2(y_2 + y_4 + y_6 + \ldots + y_{10})\}.$$

This then is *Simpson's rule*. Split the area into $2n$ strips of width h. Add together:

the first and last heights and
4 times all the odd numbered heights and
twice the remaining even numbered heights,

then multiply by $\tfrac{1}{3}h$. In symbols:

$$A \approx \tfrac{1}{3}h\{(y_0 + y_{2n}) + 4(y_1 + y_3 + \ldots + y_{2n-1})$$
$$+ 2(y_2 + y_4 + \ldots + y_{2n-2})\}.$$

Let us apply this method to

$$\int_0^1 e^{-x^2}\, dx.$$

I programmed my computer with Simpson's rule and found the following results.

h	A	$|error| \times 10^8$
0.25	0.746 855 38	3125
0.1	0.746 824 95	82
0.05	0.746 824 18	5
0.02	0.746 824 13	0
0.01	0.746 824 13	0

The convergence to the correct answer is *far* faster with Simpson's rule than with the previous two methods; the program is a little more complicated, but not enough to discourage you from using this method. This is, in fact, the standard method of doing numerical integration. Faster methods can be invented, by using higher degree interpolating polynomials, but there is no real need for them now that computation is so easy.

As before, the error is proportional to a power of h. One way of determining what power k is correct in the equation

$$|error| \approx Ch^k$$

is to take logarithms, and plot

$$\ln |error| \text{ against } \ln h,$$

as in Fig. 10. The slope of the resulting line through the points is k, and it is clearly 4 here. You could, of course, use a least squares fit to determine k, but it seems hardly necessary here.

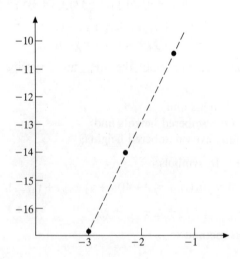

Figure 10. $\ln |error|$ against $\ln h$ for Simpson's rule errors

In general, for 'ordinary', 'smooth' curves the error in Simpson's rule is proportional to the fourth power of the interval. How to find the constant of proportionality will have to wait until later in the book.

Exercise 10D

1   Use Simpson's rule with $h = 0.1$ to estimate the area defined by

$$A = \int_1^2 e^{-x} \, dx.$$

Compare with your work in Exercise 10C, question 1.

2   Use Simpson's rule to calculate

$$A = \int_{-1}^1 \frac{1}{1+x^2} \, dx$$

correct to 8 d.p.

3   Use Simpson's rule with various values of h to evaluate

$$\int_0^1 x^{1/3} \, dx.$$

Determine the constant k in the relation

$$|\text{error}| \approx Ch^k.$$

Compare this with your work in Exercise 10C question 5. Explain why the result is *very* bad here by drawing a graph of $x^{1/3}$ and an approximating quadratic near $x = 0$.

10.5   PROBLEMS WITH SIMPSON'S RULE

You cannot leap in with Simpson's rule for every case of numerical integration. You should have seen that it is rather bad at dealing with an integral like

$$\int_0^1 x^{1/3} \, dx,$$

because $x^{1/3}$ has an infinite slope (a vertical tangent) at $x = 0$. There are other integrals for which it gives no answer at all, such as

$$\int_0^1 x^{-1/3} \, dx.$$

The value of this integral is, by calculus, just

$$[\tfrac{3}{2} x^{2/3}]_0^1 = 1.5.$$

But because Simpson's rule needs to use the value of the function at the left hand end point $x = 0$, we can get no answer at all, since

$$0^{-1/3}$$

is not defined (or 'is infinite').

Note here that the trapezium rule will not work either for these *improper* integrals which have an *infinite* value of the integral at an end point, but that the method of rectangles *will* work, as it does not use the end value.

Nobody would want to calculate

$$\int_0^1 x^{-1/3}\, dx$$

numerically, because it is so easily done exactly, but there are plenty of integrals which cannot be calculated exactly. I shall take as an example

$$A = \int_0^1 x^{-1/3}(1+x^3)^{1/2}\, dx$$

which I am convinced I cannot work out exactly. I shall offer you three methods for this type of example.

(a)   Avoid the end point

If I use the method of rectangles on this integral, I do not need to use $x = 0$, as my first function evaluation is at $x = \frac{1}{2}h$. The results I found for this, with various values of h, were as follows

h	A
0.1	1.567 326 127
0.05	1.587 680 848
0.02	1.603 428 474
0.01	1.610 333 735
0.005	1.614 680 977
0.002	1.618 063 09
0.001	1.619 549 269

You can see that the estimates of A are slowly converging to around

1.62.

The method works, but is very slow: you would need a tiny value of h to get a good answer. Or you could try to fit a curve to the given results, in the form

$$A = A_0 + Bh^k,$$

to get an extrapolated value for A_0.

(b)   Isolate the singularity

The unpleasantness of the integral is entirely due to the $x^{-1/3}$ factor, and I can integrate $x^{-1/3}$ exactly if it occurs by itself. So I shall rewrite the problem as

$$A = \int_0^1 x^{-1/3}\,dx + \int_0^1 x^{-1/3}\{(1+x^3)^{1/2}-1\}\,dx.$$

This is *exactly* the same as before. But the first integral can be calculated exactly, as

$$1.5,$$

and the second integral has no major difficulty at $x=0$. There is still the minor difficulty that you cannot calculate

$$x^{-1/3}\{(1+x^3)^{1/2}-1\}$$

when $x=0$, but for values of x approaching 0 this expression approaches 0 too. Thus all we have to do to evaluate the second integral is make sure that $y_0=0$ is fed into the Simpson's rule calculation. When I did this I found the following values.

h	A
0.1	$1.5+0.122\,075\,735\,4$
0.05	$1.5+0.122\,078\,995\,9$
0.02	$1.5+0.122\,079\,253\,5$
0.01	$1.5+0.122\,079\,261\,6$
0.005	$1.5+0.122\,079\,262\,3$

The correct value for A is clearly

$$1.622\,079\,26$$

and the process is converging rapidly. This is obviously a more successful method than a direct use of the rectangle method.

(c)   Substitutions

In many cases a preliminary substitution in the integral can remove the awkward aspects of the function. For example, if I let

$$t^3=x, \ t=x^{1/3}$$

in the integral

$$A = \int_0^1 x^{-1/3}(1+x^3)^{1/2}\,dx,$$

I find that

$$A = \int_0^1 3t(1+t^9)^{1/2}\,dt.$$

This will give an accurate answer very rapidly by Simpson's rule.

Exercise 10E

1 Evaluate

$$A = \int_0^1 x^{-1/3} \cos x \, dx$$

by the three methods of this section.

2 How fast is the Simpson's rule calculation converging for method (*b*) for

$$\int_0^1 x^{-1/3}(1+x^3)^{1/2} \, dx?$$

In other words, what is the value of k in

$$|\text{error}| = Ch^k?$$

How fast was the convergence in question 1 for the similar Simpson's rule calculation? Can you explain these results?

3 The integral

$$A = \int_0^\pi (\sin x)^{-1/2} \, dx$$

has a singularity at each end of the integral. This can be dealt with in two parts, from 0 to $\frac{1}{2}\pi$ and from $\frac{1}{2}\pi$ to π. Show that near $x=0$ you have $\sin x \approx x$ and so the singularity to subtract out is

$$x^{-1/2}.$$

Hence evaluate the integral.

4 Integrate by parts once, or more, in $\int_0^1 x^{-1/3} \cos x \, dx$ to get a 'better' integrand; you need to integrate $x^{-1/3}$ and differentiate $\cos x$.

5 Improve the speed of convergence of Simpson's rule for

$$A = \int_0^1 x^{1/2} \cos x \, dx$$

by subtracting out the unsmooth (but integrable) function $x^{1/2}$.

6 (*a*) Use a substitution to 'simplify' the integral in question 5.
(*b*) Can you use this method in question 3?

10.6   SUMMARY

(*a*) The value of the *derivative* $f'(a)$ can be estimated by

$$\frac{1}{h}\{f(a+h)-f(a)\}$$

for small values of h. If h is taken *too* small, accuracy is lost due to subtraction of almost equal quantities.

(b) A *better estimate* of $f'(a)$ is found to be

$$\frac{1}{2h}\{f(a+h)-f(a-h)\}.$$

This can be shown geometrically or by using a line of best fit.

(c) The *second derivative $f''(a)$* is estimated well by

$$\frac{1}{h^2}\{f(a+h)-2f(a)+f(a-h)\}.$$

This can be understood by fitting a quadratic to values of f, or by using a difference table.

(d) Simple calculations of area can be done with the *method of rectangles*:

area $\approx$ sum of (strip width $\times$ mid-point function value);

or with the *trapezium rule*:

area $\approx$ sum of (strip width $\times$ average function value).

The *error* in each of these is proportional to h^2 for *smooth* functions.

(e) The usual calculation method for areas is *Simpson's rule*:

$$A \approx \tfrac{1}{3}h\{(y_0+y_{2n})+4(y_1+y_3+\ldots+y_{2n-1})+2(y_2+y_4+\ldots+y_{2n-2})\}.$$

Its *error* for *smooth* functions is proportional to h^4.

(f) The method of *subtracting out the singularity* can allow the use of Simpson's rule when the integral has infinite values. A valuable alternative is to make a preliminary *substitution* before trying numerical work. When the function is finite but not smooth at an end point, these methods can reduce the errors for a given size of h. Another valuable method is to integrate by parts.

11

Elementary differential equations

11.1 DISCRETE AND CONTINUOUS MODELS

The population models for the USA in Chapter 1 were based on the numbers found at the censuses, and this suggested a 10 year time step for the iteration. This was a *discrete* model – the population was only considered at the censuses, and was (essentially) assumed not to be a quantity open to investigation in between the censuses. This is fair enough for years like 1827 or 1856 – there is no reasonable way of finding out the population at (say) midnight on the 4th/5th July.

But things have changed with the advent of computer networks. It is easy to envisage the day's births and deaths, and arrivals and departures into/from the country, being keyed in by keen registrars and airline companies (perhaps a week later), so that (almost) exact population figures would be known for each midnight. This of course is still discrete – there is no computation each *minute* of how many people there are in a country and the number of people is certainly an integer. However if you plotted the daily totals on a graph for a ten year span, between censuses, you would find yourself looking at an essentially continuous curve.

In other words, a continuous model may be a sensible choice for this case, when the interval between observations gets rather small.

What would the model be? If you accept Verhulst's ideas on how populations grow you would say, instead of the discrete model

$$u_{n+1} = au_n - bu_n^2,$$

that the change in population per day is equal to a constant times the population, minus another constant times the population squared. In symbols

$$\frac{dp}{dt} = \alpha p - \beta p^2.$$

As before α and β would have to be found by fitting a solution of this equation to the real census data.

This is a typical transition from a discrete to a continuous model. The change in some unit time interval

$$u_{n+1} - u_n$$

is replaced by a rate of change

$$dp/dt,$$

and the population u_n (a function defined for integers n) is replaced by a population p, defined for an interval of real numbers t.

The result of this change of attitude is to get a *differential equation* (i.e. an equation involving derivatives) to solve; the solutions of this differential equation will not usually agree with the values found by solving the difference equation.

The advantage is often with the continuous model, because many differential equations are easier to solve than the corresponding difference equations; and because you get values for p (or whatever other function is being discussed) between the observation points.

However, in each case a decision has to be made whether to use a discrete or a continuous model, and the decision may not be easy. Is it true that the solutions of

$$u_{n+1} = au_n - bu_n^2$$

are *always* similar in type to the solutions of

$$dp/dt = \alpha p - \beta p^2?$$

The answer appears to be no, as recent work on chaos theory has shown. Could you usefully rediscuss the battle of Iwo Jima using a continuous model based on casualties per minute? Possibly not, because there may be many minutes in a day with no casualties.

So whenever you use a continuous model hereafter, you should pause slightly to ask yourself whether a discrete model would not be more appropriate.

11.2   SIMPLE EQUATIONS

My electric kettle gives a constant source of heat to the water inside it. I do not think there is much heat loss during the heating, so I expect a reasonable model for the temperature T of the water in it to be

$$\frac{dT}{dt} = a,$$

where a is a constant related to the amount of water and the power of the kettle. The change in temperature in a second is a constant, because the heat input in a second is a constant. This very simple differential equation is solved by integrating, to get

$$T = at + b$$

where b is a constant of integration. If the temperature of the water is 15°C to start with, then

$$15 = a \times 0 + b$$

and so

$$b = 15$$
$$T = at + 15.$$

This extremely simple example says much about the solution of differential equations:

(i)   an integration has to be done,
(ii) a constant of integration is therefore introduced,
(iii) the value of this constant is found from an initial condition,
(iv) other constants must come from the modelling process.

Take another example. Suppose we have the differential equation

$$\frac{dy}{dx} = x.$$

This can be integrated as

$$y = \tfrac{1}{2}x^2 + c,$$

for any constant c. If you draw graphs of these solutions for different values of c you get a *family* of solutions (Fig. 1).

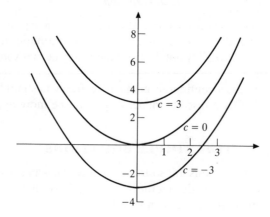

Figure 1. Some of the family of solutions $y = \tfrac{1}{2}x^2 + c$

Which member of the family is the correct one requires some further piece of information, such as the value of y when $x = 0$, or the value of y at some other value of x. This extra condition is often called a *boundary condition*, with *initial condition* being reserved for a value at a starting time t.

The general class of differential equations

$$\begin{cases} \dfrac{dy}{dx} = f(x) \\[2mm] y = y_0 \quad \text{when} \quad x = x_0 \end{cases}$$

can be solved directly by integration as

$$y = y_0 + \int_{x_0}^{x} f(s)\,ds.$$

Note that the variable over which the integration is done (or summation, if it is done numerically) is s, and that y depends on

$$\begin{cases} \text{where the integration starts, } x_0 \\ \text{what the value of } y \text{ is then, } y_0 \\ \text{where the integration finishes, } x. \end{cases}$$

This way of writing the solution shows you explicitly where the value y_0 (when $x = x_0$) comes into the solution.

Exercise 11A

1   Solve the following
   (i) $dy/dx = x^2$, given $y = 1$ when $x = 1$,
   (ii) $dx/dt = 2\sin t$, given $x(0) = 0$,
   (iii) $(x+2)\,dy/dx = x$,
   (iv) $dy/dx = e^{-x^2}$, with $y = \frac{1}{2}$ at $x = 0$; you cannot integrate this explicitly.

2   The acceleration of a freely falling object is $-g$. Determine its speed, and its position if it starts from rest at height h at time $t = 0$.

11.3   EQUATIONS WITH SEPARABLE VARIABLES

Suppose that I am slowly heating a quantity of water in an open pot on the cooker. I now expect that there will be some loss of heat, because the pot is open and because the time taken is long. It seems to me that the loss of heat will be higher when the water is hotter, and so I am led to the model

$$\frac{dT}{dt} = a - kT.$$

The term $-kT$ here is the *loss of heat* term, proportional to the temperature of the water.

One way of solving this equation is to rewrite it as

$$\frac{1}{a - kT}\frac{dT}{dt} = 1.$$

I can then integrate both sides, i.e. sum over values of the time during which the process is going on:

$$\int \frac{1}{a - kT}\frac{dT}{dt}\,dt = \int 1\,dt.$$

Both sides are easy to integrate. I rewrite the left hand side as

$$\int \frac{1}{a - kT}\,dT = -\frac{1}{k}\ln(a - kT)$$

by a change of variables to T in the integral; on the right I just get t; and I need a constant of integration. So finally

$$-\frac{1}{k}\ln(a-kT)=t+c,$$

which can be solved as

$$T=\frac{1}{k}(a-e^{-k(t+c)}).$$

Finally I shall put $e^{-kc}=B$, and arrive at

$$T=\frac{1}{k}(a-Be^{-kt}).$$

The process here has been to get one integral on the left of the equation with nothing but T (and constants) in it, and one on the right hand side with nothing but t in it. This is the *separation of variables*. If you can then work out both these integrals, you can write down a solution of the differential equation.

It is easy to verify that the result I have found for T satisfies the equation, since

$$\frac{dT}{dt}=Be^{-kt}$$

and so

$$\frac{dT}{dt}+kT=a-Be^{-kt}+Be^{-kt}=a.$$

You can fit any initial value, say $T=15$ at $t=0$; since, by substitution,

$$15=\frac{1}{k}(a-Be^{0})=\frac{1}{k}(a-B).$$

Hence $B=a-15k$ and the solution becomes

$$T=\frac{a}{k}-\frac{a-15k}{k}e^{-kt}.$$

I did not use the form

$$\ln|a-kT|$$

in the integration because I supposed that $a-kT$ would be positive in my solution, or else the pot would be actually cooling down as I tried to heat it.

The method of separation of variables is quite important, so I shall do two further examples, one involving modelling and one purely mathematical.

Consider the equation

$$dy/dx=(1+y^2)x.$$

Let us take all the y's to the left and the x's to the right, and then integrate. We get

$$\int \frac{1}{1+y^2}\frac{dy}{dx}\,dx = \int x\,dx,$$

or

$$\int \frac{1}{1+y^2}\,dy = \int x\,dx.$$

Each side can now be integrated, giving

$$\tan^{-1}y = \tfrac{1}{2}x^2 + c$$

or

$$y = \tan\left(\tfrac{1}{2}x^2 + c\right).$$

This is the solution, as can be verified by differentiation.

If I now give the condition

$$y = 1 \quad \text{when} \quad x = 0,$$

I can work out c, from $\tan c = 1$. The natural choice for c is $\tfrac{1}{4}\pi$, and other choices such as $\tfrac{5}{4}\pi$ or $-\tfrac{3}{4}\pi$ give the same values for y, so I may neglect them.

For what values of x have I found a solution of the equation and the boundary condition? In fact only for

$$-\sqrt{(\tfrac{1}{2}\pi)} < x < \sqrt{(\tfrac{1}{2}\pi)}.$$

The graph has asymptotes at $x = \pm\sqrt{(\tfrac{1}{2}\pi)}$, as in Fig. 2, and beyond those asymptotes there is no way of determining an appropriate value of c from the given condition at $x = 0$. The solution of the equation has a natural domain which is determined by where the asymptotes of

$$\tan\left(\tfrac{1}{2}x^2 + c\right)$$

are, and where the condition on y is given.

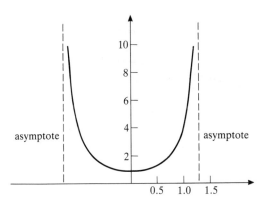

Figure 2. $y = \tan(\tfrac{1}{2}x^2 + \tfrac{1}{4}\pi),\ -\sqrt{(\tfrac{1}{2}\pi)} < x < \sqrt{(\tfrac{1}{2}\pi)}$

My other example will be Verhulst's population equation, from Section 11.1. To make the problem simple, I shall choose to solve

$$\begin{cases} \dfrac{dp}{dt} = \tfrac{1}{2}p - \tfrac{1}{10}p^2, \\[2mm] p = 3 \quad \text{when} \quad t = 0. \end{cases}$$

Separating the variables gives

$$\int \frac{1}{p(1 - \tfrac{1}{5}p)} \frac{dp}{dt} \, dt = \int \tfrac{1}{2} \, dt,$$

or

$$\int \left(\frac{1}{p} + \frac{\tfrac{1}{5}}{1 - \tfrac{1}{5}p} \right) dp = \int \tfrac{1}{2} \, dt.$$

This integrates as

$$\ln p - \ln(1 - \tfrac{1}{5}p) = \tfrac{1}{2}t + c,$$

and the constant c is found from the initial value, from

$$\ln 3 - \ln(1 - \tfrac{3}{5}) = c,$$

i.e.

$$c = \ln \tfrac{15}{2}.$$

Rearranging the solution gives us

$$\frac{1}{1 - \tfrac{1}{5}p} = e^{t/2 + c} = \tfrac{15}{2} e^{t/2}.$$

Finally, we may solve this for p in terms of t:

$$p = \frac{15e^{t/2}}{2 + 3e^{t/2}}, \quad \text{for } t \geqslant 0.$$

The graph of this population is shown in Fig. 3.

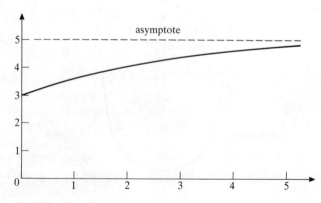

Figure 3. A solution of the logistic equation $\dfrac{dp}{dt} = \tfrac{1}{2}p - \tfrac{1}{10}p^2$, $p(0) = 3$

This graph too has an asymptote, at $p=5$. Because $0<p<5$ for all t, I did not need to use

$$\ln|p| \quad \text{or} \quad \ln|1-\tfrac{1}{5}p|$$

in the solution. But if the initial condition had been $p(0)=6$, I should have needed

$$\ln(\tfrac{1}{5}p-1)$$

in place of $\ln(1-\tfrac{1}{5}p)$, and I would have found a curve that descended to the asymptote.

Exercise 11B

1   Solve the following equations by separation of variables. In each case give an appropriate domain for the solution function.
   (i) $dy/dx=xy^2$, $y=1$ when $x=0$.
   (ii) $dy/dx=x^2y$, $y=1$ when $x=1$.
   (iii) $dv/dt=1-v^2$, $v(0)=10$.
   (iv) $dp/dt=\tfrac{1}{10}p-\tfrac{1}{1000}p^2$, $p=3$ at $t=0$.
   (v) $dy/dx=1+y^2$, $y(0)=a$.

2   Sketch the family of solution curves for
   (i) $dy/dx=-y/x$
   (ii) $dy/dx=x/y$.

3   Toricelli's law for water flow from a hole in the side of a barrel which has its top open to the air, is that the speed v of the water jet is proportional to the square root of the height of the water surface above the hole. Show that for an upright cylindrical barrel the equation

$$dh/dt=-kh^{1/2}$$

must be satisfied. Solve this equation, given that the hole was opened at $t=0$ and h was then 1 m.

4   Radioactive atoms in a lump of material decay as time progresses. The number decaying per second is proportional to the number present,

$$dp/dt=-rp.$$

Find the *half-life* of the atoms in terms of r, i.e. the time it takes for half the atoms to decay.

5   A sky diver in free fall is accelerated downwards at a constant rate by gravity, but this acceleration is reduced by kv^2, due to air resistance, where k is a constant and v is his speed. Show that

$$dv/dt=g-kv^2,$$

and solve this equation to find his greatest possible speed.

6   Determine a population equation

$$dp/dt=ap-bp^2, \quad p(0)=3.9$$

to fit the USA data from 1790 to 1910 in Chapter 1. Try values near $a=0.3$, $b=0.0015$.

11.4   SUMMARY

We are now moving on to continuous models of real processes; you should always ask yourself whether a continuous or a discrete model is more appropriate.

The differential equation

$$\begin{cases} dy/dx = f(x) \\ \quad\ y = y_0 \quad \text{when} \quad x = x_0 \end{cases}$$

has the solution

$$y = y_0 + \int_{x_0}^{x} f(s)\, ds.$$

For an equation without a *boundary condition* there is a *family* of solution curves, one for each value of a *constant of integration*.

If an equation can be put in the form

$$f(y)\, dy/dx = g(x)$$

for some functions f and g, then it is *separable*, and its solution is

$$\int f(y)\, dy = \int g(x)\, dx.$$

If there are *asymptotes* to a solution of a differential equation, then the solution is not known on the other side of the asymptotes from where the boundary condition is given.

12

First order linear differential equations

There are great similarities between the work here on differential equations and the work in Chapter 2 on difference equations. It is not that the solutions look similar in detail, but they have the same *structure*. This will save us some time here, and similar structures will recur later when we solve second order linear difference and differential equations.

For a differential equation, *linear* means that y and dy/dx occur as first powers (without any products of them either); *first order* means that no higher derivative of y is involved. These definitions are very similar to those for difference equations. The other variable, x, can occur in any way in a linear first order equation; for example

$$y \ln x + x^{17} \frac{dy}{dx} = \sin^3(x^2 - 1)$$

is linear, first order, and frightful. It is convenient to start with equations in which the coefficients of y and dy/dx are *constants* (though the right hand side above would still be allowed), as they are easiest.

12.1 EQUATIONS WITH CONSTANT COEFFICIENTS

The type of equation to be considered here is

$$\begin{cases} dy/dx + ay = f(x) \\ \qquad y = y_0 \quad \text{when} \quad x = x_0. \end{cases}$$

The first solution method, inspired by the work in Chapter 2, is to seek a solution in the form of

complementary function + particular solution.

The complementary function will be the solution of the homogeneous equation

$$dy/dx + ay = 0,$$

and the particular solution will be *any* solution of the full equation.
Start with the example

$$\begin{cases} \dfrac{dy}{dx} + 3y = 4 \\ \\ \qquad y = 1 \quad \text{when} \quad x = 0. \end{cases}$$

The solution of the homogeneous equation

$$\frac{dz}{dx} + 3z = 0$$

is found by the methods of the last section. The equation separates as

$$\int \frac{1}{z} \frac{dz}{dx} dx = -3 \int dx$$

and hence

$$\ln z = -3x + c$$

or

$$z = Ae^{-3x},$$

on putting

$$e^{-c} = A.$$

We now have the complementary function, Ae^{-3x}, for any constant A.

Next we need any particular solution of the full equation. We could again proceed by the methods of the last section, since the full equation is itself separable; but I would prefer you to remember the method of intelligent guesswork (since we shall need it again later). In Chapter 2, when we found a constant on the right hand side of a linear equation (with constant coefficients) we tried a constant as a particular solution. So try it again here: if $y = k$ is a solution of the equation, then

$$0 + 3k = 4$$

i.e.

$$k = \tfrac{4}{3}.$$

This provides our particular solution of the full equation, and so the general solution is

$$Ae^{-3x} + \tfrac{4}{3}.$$

Finally we fit the boundary condition, by putting in the value of y when $x = 0$:

$$1 = Ae^{0} + \tfrac{4}{3},$$

which gives

$$A = -\tfrac{1}{3}.$$

The solution is now completed:

$$y = -\tfrac{1}{3}e^{-3x} + \tfrac{4}{3}.$$

This method will work well for a range of examples like those in Chapter 2. I shall restrict the rest of the discussion here to the particular solutions of

$$\frac{dy}{dx} + ay = f(x)$$

when $f(x)$ is either

$$\begin{cases} \text{a polynomial, or} \\ \text{an exponential, or} \\ \text{a sine or cosine.} \end{cases}$$

All I shall do is state the results. You can explore the details in the Exercise.

(i) A particular solution of

$$dy/dx + ay = \text{polynomial}$$

is a polynomial of the same degree, if $a \neq 0$, with coefficients found by substitution.

(ii) A particular solution of

$$dy/dx + ay = e^{bx}$$

is ke^{bx} (with coefficient k found by substitution) *except* when $b = -a$, and then the solution is Kxe^{-ax} (with K found by substitution).

(iii) A particular solution of

$$dy/dx + ay = \text{sin or cos of } bx$$

is a combination of $\sin bx$ and $\cos bx$, with coefficients found by substitution.

Exercise 12A

1 Solve $dy/dx + 3y = 4$ with $y = 1$ when $x = 0$ by separation of variables.

2 Solve the following equations, by substituting guessed forms in the equations to get a particular solution.
  (i) $dy/dx - 3y = 4e^x$, $y = 2$ when $x = 0$.
  (ii) $dy/dx + \frac{1}{2}y = 6x + 4$, $y = 0$ when $x = 1$.
  (iii) $dx/dt + x = 3e^{2t}$, $x = 0$ when $t = 0$.
  (iv) $dx/dt + 4x = 2\sin t - 3\cos t$.
  (v) $dx/dt - x = 3e^{2t} - 2e^t$.
  (vi) $dy/dx + 3y = x^2 + \cos x$, $dy/dx = 0$ when $x = 0$.

3 Find a particular solution of

$$x\, dy/dx + 2y = 4x^2 + 2x + 2$$

by guesswork. Solve the equation, given that $y(1) = 0$.

An alternative way of attacking

$$\begin{cases} \dfrac{dy}{dx} + 3y = 4 \\ \\ y = 1 \quad \text{when} \quad x = 0 \end{cases}$$

is to try to write the left hand side of the equation as a derivative. If we can do that, then we only have to integrate both sides and we are finished.

How can I do this? I want something like

$$\frac{d}{dx}\{r(x)y\} = s(x)$$

to be the same equation as

$$\frac{dy}{dx} + 3y = 4.$$

Expand the new version of the equation:

$$r(x)\frac{dy}{dx} + \frac{dr}{dx}y = s(x).$$

Now divide by $r(x)$ and get

$$\frac{dy}{dx} + \left(\frac{1}{r}\frac{dr}{dx}\right)y = \frac{s}{r},$$

which must be identical to

$$\frac{dy}{dx} + 3y = 4.$$

Hence we must take

$$\frac{1}{r}\frac{dr}{dx} = 3 \quad \text{and} \quad \frac{s}{r} = 4.$$

The first of these integrates easily as

$$r(x) = Be^{3x}$$

for any constant B, and the second gives

$$s(x) = 4Be^{3x}.$$

We can therefore rewrite the equation as

$$\frac{d}{dx}(ye^{3x}) = 4e^{3x},$$

on removing a B from each side.

The function e^{3x} is generally known as an *integrating factor* since it enables you to prepare the equation for integration. The method of integrating factors is also useful for first order equations whose coefficients are not constant, as we shall see below.

Having put the equation in the form

$$\frac{d}{dx}\{ye^{3x}\} = 4e^{3x},$$

an integration gives

$$ye^{3x} = \tfrac{4}{3}e^{3x} + c,$$

so that

$$y = \tfrac{4}{3} + ce^{-3x}$$

as before. Fitting the value at $x=0$ gives the same solution as before,

$$y = \tfrac{4}{3} - \tfrac{1}{3}e^{-3x}.$$

Exercise 12B

1   Solve the equations of Exercise 12A, question 2, by using integrating factors.

2   Try intelligent guesswork *and* the integrating factor method on

$$\begin{cases} \dfrac{dy}{dx} + y = \dfrac{1}{1+e^x} \\ \quad y = 0 \quad \text{when} \quad x = 0. \end{cases}$$

(The substitution $t = e^x$ will help with the integral.)

12.2   NON-CONSTANT COEFFICIENTS

Any equation of the form

$$\frac{dy}{dx} + p(x)y = q(x)$$

can be reduced to a problem in integration by the integrating factor method. Of course if you choose horrible functions p and q, the integrals may be rather hard to do, so I shall start with an easy example.

Let us try the equation

$$\frac{dy}{dx} + \frac{3}{x}y = x.$$

As before, I am going to force this into the form

$$\frac{d}{dx}\{r(x)y\} = s(x),$$

because then I can integrate both sides to find y. In this case the differentiation of the product on the left, followed by a division by $r(x)$, gives

$$\frac{dy}{dx} + \frac{1}{r}\frac{dr}{dx}y = \frac{s}{r}$$

so that

$$\frac{1}{r}\frac{dr}{dx} = \frac{3}{x} \quad \text{and} \quad \frac{s}{r} = x.$$

The first of these integrates as

$$\int \frac{1}{r}\,dr = \int \frac{3}{x}\,dx$$

so that

$$r(x) = Bx^3.$$

Then

$$s(x) = Bx^4$$

from the other equation. We therefore have that

$$\frac{dy}{dx} + \frac{3}{x}y = x$$

is equivalent to

$$\frac{d}{dx}\{x^3 y\} = x^4,$$

on dropping an unnecessary B from each side. The integration now proceeds, to give

$$x^3 y = \tfrac{1}{5}x^5 + c$$

or

$$y = \tfrac{1}{5}x^2 + c/x^3.$$

It is easy to verify that what we have here is

(i)   a solution, by substituting it in the equation, and
(ii) composed of a particular solution $\tfrac{1}{5}x^2$ and a complementary function c/x^3.

Could we have reached this solution by means of the method of intelligent guesswork? Perhaps. Is it 'obvious' that the particular solution *must* have the form

$$kx^2$$

(because d/dx of this gives a term in x, so does $3/x$ times it, and we need a term in x only)? Well, not *very* obvious, which is why we usually prefer to try the integrating factor method.

If you work through with the general equation

$$\frac{dy}{dx} + p(x)y = q(x)$$

you find that you must take

$$\frac{1}{r}\frac{dr}{dx} = p(x) \quad \text{and} \quad \frac{s}{r} = q(x).$$

These give

$$\int \frac{1}{r}\,dr = \int p(x)\,dx$$

i.e.

$$\ln r = \int p(x)\,dx + c$$

or

$$r = Be^{\int p(x)\,dx};$$

and also

$$s = Bq(x)\,e^{\int p(x)\,dx}.$$

The equation is therefore reduced to

$$\frac{d}{dx}\{ye^{\int p(x)\,dx}\} = q(x)\,e^{\int p(x)\,dx}.$$

What if you can't integrate $p(x)$? Or what if you can't integrate

$$q(x)\,e^{\int p(x)\,dx}?$$

Well, the method does not help much in those cases, and we shall have to try something else. If nothing else, we can use numerical techniques

> *either* to work out the integrals
> *or* to solve the equations directly.

The latter may be the best course, especially if $\int p(x)\,dx$ proves impossible; we shall set off on numerical methods for differential equations like this in Chapter 14.

Exercise 12C

Use the method of integrating factors on the following equations

(i) $dy/dx + y/x = e^{-x}$, $y = 3$ at $x = 1$.
(ii) $dy/dx + 2xy = x$, $y = 1$ at $x = 0$.
(iii) $x\,dy/dx - (x+1)y = x^2 - x^3$, $y = 0$ at $x = 0$.
(iv) $\cos x\,dy/dx - 3y\sin x = \tan x$.
(v) $2(1 - x^2)dy/dx - (1 + x)y = 1$.

12.3   THREE REAL PROBLEMS

Differential equations can be viewed as a piece of pure mathematics; I write down a problem and then I (or you) try to solve it. But the origin of many differential equations is as models of some aspect of reality. When you think of them like that, there are several things to be done.

190 12 First order linear differential equations

(i) We must find a differential equation that is appropriate to model the piece of reality under discussion.

(ii) We must choose values for any constants that come into the equation, or choose the mathematical representation of any function that is needed.

(iii) We then solve the equation, with a formula if we can, or by the numerical methods described in Chapter 14 if necessary.

(iv) We next consider whether the answers are reasonable; if they are, then we have an acceptable solution to a reasonable model; if they are not, we may have to change the model and start again.

This process of modelling is often much harder than the pure mathematics of solving a given equation. Really the only way to learn it is by trying to do it, but you can at least make a start by seeing how I set up the models which follow.

(a) Trout fishing

A fishing club has a committee which is in charge of buying young trout to stock its lake. The problem is, how many trout to buy. Suppose that at time t there are $N(t)$ trout in the lake, and that they have a *natural* rate of increase a (births − deaths due to causes other than fishers). There is also a loss of trout in the lake due to fishing by club members; if the membership at time t is $n(t)$, then this loss rate is, we suppose,

$$bn(t)N(t),$$

because the more fish present, the more are caught, and also the more fishers, the more fish are caught.

Thus a reasonable equation for the situation may well be

$$\frac{dN}{dt} = aN - bn(t)N + r(t),$$

where $r(t)$ is the number of young fish put in. In reality they may be put in week by week (or even once a year) but let us assume a continuous model here. Thus the differential equation for $N(t)$ is assumed to be

$$\frac{dN}{dt} + (bn - a)N = r,$$

which is the kind considered in Section 12.2.

The real problem here for the committee is actually one of *control theory*; how do you choose the function $r(t)$ so as to get a desired number of trout, given that the number of members of the club is known? But we shall work the other way round here, and see what the consequences are of the choice of particular models of $n(t)$ and $r(t)$.

What sort of functions should we choose? Presumably there is a maximum number of fishers that the lake can accommodate, and so $n(t)$ should have the shape of the graph in Fig. 1, rising to a maximum value as t increases.

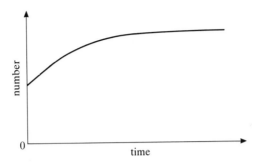

Figure 1. Number of fishing club members

Functions with this general shape include

(i) $2-e^{-t}$,
(ii) $(2t+1)/(t+1)$,
(iii) $(2/\pi)(\frac{1}{2}\pi+\tan^{-1}t)$,

all of which start with value 1 when $t=0$ and rise to value 2 as t gets large. Not all of these will be easy to work with, and you will have to put some constants in to match a real situation. For example

$$1000(2t+5)/(t+5),$$

with t in years, gives a membership rising from 1000 at $t=0$ to 1500 in 5 years, to 1700 in 12 years, and eventually to 2000.

Similarly you can choose sensible shaped functions for the restocking function $r(t)$. This could well have the same general shape as the membership function $n(t)$, or the committee could choose $r(t)=$ constant until falling catches persuaded them to make a change.

Notice that in the modelling you are certainly expecting to have

$$bnN > aN,$$

or else there is no need to stock the lake at all, as natural increase of fish numbers will be adequate to give $dN/dt>0$, i.e. an increasing number of trout.

The problem I shall use to check on the performance of the model is

$$\begin{cases} n=\text{constant} \\ r=\text{constant}. \end{cases}$$

Then I can solve

$$\begin{cases} \dfrac{dN}{dt}+(bn-a)N=r \\[2mm] \qquad\qquad N=N_0 \quad \text{at} \quad t=0 \end{cases}$$

rather easily. The integrating factor is

$$e^{\int (bn-a)\,dt}=e^{(bn-a)t},$$

so that

$$\frac{d}{dt}\{Ne^{(bn-a)t}\} = re^{(bn-a)t}.$$

This integrates as

$$Ne^{(bn-a)t} = \frac{r}{bn-a}e^{(bn-a)t} + c,$$

and so

$$N = \frac{r}{bn-a} + \left(N_0 - \frac{r}{bn-a}\right)e^{-(bn-a)t},$$

on fitting $N = N_0$ at $t = 0$. This seems to be a satisfactory result; the lake rapidly reaches an equilibrium stock of fish

$$r/(bn-a),$$

and the influence of the initial condition does not last long.

If you now go on to choose functions $n(t)$ and $r(t)$ without a great deal of care, you will have to integrate the resulting equations numerically. The investigations in the next Exercise are carefully chosen so that the mathematical behaviour of the differential equation can be investigated further.

Exercise 12D

1 The club committee decides to let the membership increase slowly, and to compensate for that by letting the restocking also increase. Solve the simplified problem

$$a = b = 1, \; n = 1 + t, \; r = t$$

to see what the possible consequences will be.

2 At the club annual general meeting it is suggested that the control problem can be solved by always choosing

$$r(t) = \{bn(t) - a\}N_1,$$

where N_1 is the desired fish stock. Is this true? Investigate by rewriting the equation in terms of $N - N_1$, and starting with $N = N_0$ at $t = 0$.

3 Investigate the policy
   (i) $n(t) = (2t + 1)/(t + 1)$, with
   (ii) $r(t) = (t + 1)^a$,
   by assuming that $a = b$, and that $N = 1$ at $t = 0$.

(b) Vertical rocket motion

Rockets rise by throwing out mass backwards at high speed. The mass of the rocket is therefore a quantity which changes with time, in some way organised by the designer of the rocket, say

$$\text{mass} = m(t).$$

If the ejected mass has a speed u (relative to the rocket) then the propulsive force is

$$-u\,dm/dt$$

(the negative sign is because dm/dt is itself negative, the mass of the rocket is decreasing). The equation of motion of the rocket is

$$m\frac{dv}{dt} = R - u\frac{dm}{dt} - mg,$$

where R is the air resistance force and mg is the weight of the rocket. (See *Mechanics and Vectors* in this series for a derivation of this type of equation.)

The modelling problems arise in the choice of the resistance R, and to a lesser extent in the choice of $m(t)$. If you are considering a firework rocket, then R is probably nearly proportional to v^2, and the equation needs numerical solution. If you are thinking of a space rocket, then R will be more nearly proportional to v (at *high* speeds, which are necessary to leave the Earth), but will also depend on the local atmospheric density.

For my model equation I shall choose

$$\begin{cases} m = m_0 - \alpha t \\ R = -kv, \end{cases}$$

with k a constant, so that

$$\frac{dv}{dt} + \frac{k}{m_0 - \alpha t}v = \frac{u\alpha}{m_0 - \alpha t} - g$$

is the equation for the rocket's vertical motion, during the time when the rocket motor is firing. I shall simplify this a bit more by giving values to most of the constants, to reduce the equation to

$$\frac{dv}{dt} + \frac{0.1}{1-t}v = \frac{u}{1-t} - g,$$

which is to be solved, for $0 \leqslant t \leqslant \frac{3}{4}$ (say), with $v = 0$ at $t = 0$. The solution will then give the appropriate type of solution for rocket ascent, even if not all the details (such as the actual values of α, m_0, k) are included.

This is another equation which can be solved using an integrating factor, and the solution is left to the Exercise.

Exercise 12E

1   Show that the integrating factor for

$$\frac{dv}{dt} + \frac{0.1}{1-t}v = \frac{u}{1-t} - g$$

is $(1-t)^{-0.1}$. Hence derive the solution

$$v = 10u\{1 - (1-t)^{0.1}\} - 10g\{(1-t)^{0.1} - (1-t)\}/9.$$

2   Use a graph plotter to draw graphs of v for various values of u, using $g = 9.8$. Why is $v < 0$ when $u < g$ and t is small?

3   Why does the solution have to be restricted to $t < 1$?

4   Solve the full equation

$$\frac{dv}{dt} + \frac{k}{m_0 - \alpha t} v = \frac{u\alpha}{m_0 - \alpha t} - g.$$

(c)   Growth of wheat plants

Wheat (and other) plants grow by taking carbon dioxide from the air and forcing it into more complicated molecules. The process is done by the leaves and so the growth of a wheat plant's dry mass is roughly proportional to its leaf area:

$$\frac{dM}{dt} = \text{constant} \times \text{effective leaf area},$$

where M is the mass of the plant.

Now the mass of the plant is partly root (of little mass), partly leaf, and partly stalk plus ear, which I shall write as

$$M = aL + S,$$

where L is leaf area, a is the density of the leaf and S is the mass of stalk plus ear. Wheat leaves start fully green, and all of their area is effective in taking in carbon dioxide; but later these leaves die off and are replaced by newer ones, and so the effective leaf area (contributing to growth) is not the same as the total leaf area (contributing to mass). Note that it is *dry* mass that is important, you don't grow wheat as a source of water. I shall put

$$\text{effective leaf area} = e(t)L,$$

where the 'drying of leaves function' $e(t)$ is to be found experimentally.

I can now construct a differential equation for M. Since

$$L = (M - S)/a,$$

it must be

$$\frac{dM}{dt} = ke(t)(M - S)/a$$

$$= \frac{k}{a} e(t)M - \frac{k}{a} e(t)S(t).$$

The function $S(t)$, representing the mass of stalk plus ear at time t, will have to be found from experiment, or else modelled in its turn.

Any model is an attempt to simplify a situation so as to be able to get some information mathematically from it. In this case *many* aspects of reality have been omitted, for example

(i) if the water supply is inadequate the absorption of carbon dioxide will be reduced,

(ii) stalk and ear contribute a small amount to carbon dioxide absorption,
(iii) energy input, typically from the sun, is also needed,
(iv) disease interferes with these processes.

The model equation above is another one for which an integrating factor solution is available, provided (preferably simple) functions $e(t)$ and $S(t)$ are assumed. What shapes should they have? Clearly $e(t)$ starts at 1 (all leaves green) and ends at 0 (all leaves dead at harvest). Reality will tell you that $e(t)$ has a shape roughly like the graph in Fig. 2, but if you want a solution formula (rather than a numerical solution) it would be as well to choose something simple, such as

$$e(t) = 1 - t \quad \text{or} \quad \frac{2}{1+t} - 1.$$

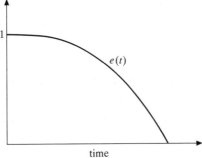

Figure 2. The ageing function $e(t)$ for green leaves

The stalk mass function $S(t)$ will start at zero and end with a maximum value near harvest time, when the ear is fully developed. Perhaps a function like

$$S(t) = \text{constant} \times (1 - \cos t/\pi)$$

sketched in Fig. 3, could be used as an approximation of an experimental shape.

In this example, as in the one on rocket flight, there is an interval of t for which the solution applies; you must not try to calculate M beyond harvest time, as the equations no longer apply.

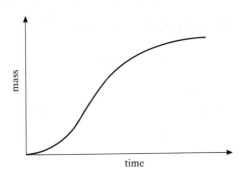

Figure 3. The mass of stalk plus ear

This particular model does not lead to a convenient formula for $M(t)$, if you use functions for $e(t)$ and $S(t)$ that are at all realistic. Its purpose here is not to show you a solution formula, but to give you another example of how modelling is done, and to lead on to the need for numerical solutions for differential equations. Real problems, even if greatly simplified, may need numerical treatment, and we start this process in Chapter 14.

Exercise 12F

1   Powdery mildew frequently attacks unsprayed wheat crops. It is a disease which covers the leaf surface and prevents the leaves functioning. The proportion of the leaf area covered starts at 0 and ends with over half the surface covered; infection starts later than the start of growth of the leaves. Revise the plant growth equation to allow for this disease, by varying the function $e(t)$ suitably.

2   Attempt to find functions $e(t)$ and $S(t)$ for which the (original) plant growth equation has solution formulas.

12.4   DIFFERENTIAL AND DIFFERENCE EQUATIONS

The methods used in Exercise 12A for differential equations with constant coefficients are closely similar to those used in Chapter 2 for difference equations with constant coefficients. In that chapter we had equations like

$$u_{n+1} + au_n = f(n),$$

where $f(n)$ was a polynomial, or a power c^n, or a combination of sines and cosines. In Exercise 12A we had equations like

$$dy/dx + by = g(x)$$

where $g(x)$ was a polynomial, or an exponential e^{kx}, or a combination of sines and cosines.

The similarity comes about because the derivative dy/dx is (the limit of) a difference of y-values divided by a difference of x-values

$$\frac{dy}{dx} = \lim_{h \to 0} \frac{y(x+h) - y(x)}{x+h-x}.$$

This is to be compared with the difference formula

$$\Delta u_n = \frac{u_{n+1} - u_n}{n+1-n},$$

where again you have a difference of u-values divided by a difference of n-values. Thus any difference equation (of the type we are considering) can be written as

$$\Delta u_n + (a+1)u_n = f(n).$$

The analogy with

$$\frac{dy}{dx} + by = g(x)$$

is now clear: Δ corresponds to d/dx, $a+1$ to b, f to g, and the solution u_n to the solution y.

The question now arises, what corresponds (for difference equations) to the method of integrating factors? Can we in fact solve equations like

$$u_{n+1}+p(n)u_n=q(n)$$

similarly to the way we solved

$$\frac{dy}{dx}+p(x)=q(x)?$$

Before we set off on such a method, we must ask what corresponds to integration, in the way that differences correspond to differentiation. This is not far to seek; integration (as we have seen in the numerical treatment of it) is just a form of summation. The correspondence is

$$\begin{cases} \Delta \text{ to } d/dx \\ \Sigma \text{ to } \displaystyle\int \ldots dx. \end{cases}$$

Therefore for

$$u_{n+1}+p(n)u_n=q(n)$$

we have to seek a *summation factor* $r(n)$ instead of an integrating factor $r(x)$, so that the equation becomes

$$\Delta\{r(n)u_n\}=s(n).$$

Its solution is then given by

$$r(n)u_n=\sum_{i=1}^{n-1} s(i)+\text{constant}$$

in the same way as we found a formula like

$$r(x)y(x)=\int s(x)\,dx$$

for the integrating factor method.

This is not often a very useful method, because it is usually very hard to find a formula for

$$\sum_{i=1}^{n-1} s(i),$$

and getting a reasonable formula for $r(n)$ is no trivial matter either. Some examples in the Exercise below show that this method will sometimes work.

Exercise 12G

1   Show that

$$\Delta\{r(n)u_n\}=r(n+1)u_{n+1}-r(n)u_n,$$

and hence that the equations for $r(n)$ and $s(n)$ are

$$\begin{cases} r(n+1) = -\dfrac{1}{p(n)}r(n) \\ \quad s(n) = q(n)r(n+1). \end{cases}$$

2   Show that the solution of

$$\Delta\{r(n)u_n\} = s(n) \quad \text{for } n = 0, 1, 2, \dots$$

is

$$u_n = \frac{1}{r(n)}\left\{\sum_{i=1}^{n-1} s(i) + \text{constant}\right\}.$$

3   The equation

$$u_{n+1} - \frac{n}{n+1}u_n = \frac{1}{n+1}$$

was solved in Section 2.4, Example 1. Show that for this equation

$$r(n) = An$$

for some constant A, and that

$$s(n) = A.$$

Hence solve the equation.

4   Solve Example 4 of Section 2.4 by finding a summation factor $r(n)$, if you can.

12.5   SUMMARY

Linear first order differential equations with *constant coefficients* can be solved by 'complementary function + particular solution' methods, using intelligent guesswork for the particular solution. The method of *integrating factors* can also be used.

If the coefficients are *not constant*, then the integrating factor method may give a solution, depending on how difficult the integrations are.

With problems *modelled* from *reality* the coefficient function and the right hand side of the equation will have to be taken from the real situation. With drastic simplification you can sometimes find solution formulas, but in some cases *numerical methods* will be needed.

There is a close *analogy* between difference and differential equations, with

$$\begin{cases} \Delta \text{ corresponding to } d/dx \\ \Sigma \text{ corresponding to } \displaystyle\int \dots dx. \end{cases}$$

This provides a method for solving first order difference equations with non-constant coefficients, but it is not often useful.

13

First order non-linear differential equations

13.1 SUBSTITUTION

Suppose we have the equation

$$\frac{dy}{dx} + 3y = y^{2/3}.$$

This is not linear, because of the $y^{2/3}$ term. The most basic method of dealing with numbers of non-linear equations is by substitution – this is related to intelligent guesswork, and also to substitution as a method of working out integrals.

If in this equation I choose to work, not with y, but with

$$z = y^{1/3}$$

as the function of x that is to be found, then the equation simplifies. Since

$$y = z^3$$

we have

$$\frac{dy}{dx} = 3z^2 \frac{dz}{dx}$$

and so the differential equation becomes

$$3z^2 \frac{dz}{dx} + 3z^3 = z^2.$$

Hence the equation for z simplifies to

$$\frac{dz}{dx} + z = \tfrac{1}{3}$$

if $z \neq 0$. This solves, using either of the methods in Section 12.2, as

$$z = Ae^{-x} + \tfrac{1}{3}$$

for some constant A. Putting this back in terms of y gives us

$$y = (Ae^{-x} + \tfrac{1}{3})^3$$

as the solution of the original equation.

This is all very splendid, except for one thing. How did I know that the particular substitution

$$z = y^{1/3}, \ y = z^3$$

was going to make it so much easier? This is where the intelligent guesswork came in. When you see the term

$$y^{2/3}$$

you guess that some substitution

$$z = y^a, \ y = z^{1/a}$$

might help. This gives

$$\frac{dy}{dx} = \frac{1}{a} z^{-1 + 1/a} \frac{dz}{dx},$$

and the equation becomes

$$\frac{1}{a} z^{-1 + 1/a} \frac{dz}{dx} + 3z^{1/a} = z^{2/3a}.$$

Multiply through by $az^{1 - 1/a}$ to get

$$\frac{dz}{dx} + 3az = az^{1 - 1/3a}.$$

Now choose a to make the right hand side easy: if you choose

$$1 - \frac{1}{3a} = 0$$

i.e.

$$a = \tfrac{1}{3}$$

you get the very easy equation

$$\frac{dz}{dx} + z = \tfrac{1}{3}.$$

Any other choice leaves a nasty equation.

Exercise 13A

1   Find the substitutions of the form

$$z = y^a, \ y = z^{1/a}$$

to simplify the equations

(i) $\dfrac{dy}{dx} + 2y = (x + 1)y^2,$

(ii) $\dfrac{dy}{dx} - 3xy = xy^3.$

2   Show that all *Bernoulli equations*

$$\frac{dy}{dx}+p(x)y=q(x)y^k$$

can be reduced to linear equations in z by the substitution

$$z=y^{1-k}.$$

3   Solve the equation

$$\frac{dy}{dx}=(x+y+1)^2-2$$

by the substitution

$$z=x+y+1.$$

Note that here

$$\frac{dz}{dx}=1+\frac{dy}{dx}.$$

4   Solve the equation

$$x\frac{dy}{dx}+y=(xy)^3$$

by using the substitution $xy=z$.

5   Find substitutions to solve the equations

(i) $dy/dx=e^{y-x}-1$,
(ii) $dy/dx+\sin^2(x+y)=0$,

13.2   INVERSION

Suppose you are offered the equation

$$\frac{dx}{dt}=-\frac{2tx}{t^2+x^2}$$

to solve. One way of doing it is to decide to find

$$t \text{ in terms of } x$$

rather than

$$x \text{ in terms of } t.$$

Now it is one of the standard rules of calculus that

$$dt/dx=\frac{1}{(dx/dt)},$$

giving the slope dt/dx of the inverse function $t(x)$ in terms of the slope dx/dt of the original function. So here we can rewrite the equation as

$$\frac{dt}{dx}=-\frac{t^2+x^2}{2tx}$$

or

$$t\frac{dt}{dx} + \frac{1}{2x}t^2 = -\tfrac{1}{2}x.$$

This now needs an intelligent substitution: since you have

$$t\,dt/dx \quad \text{and} \quad t^2$$

you might expect that

$$T = t^2$$

would help. If you make this substitution you find the equation

$$\frac{dT}{dx} + \frac{1}{x}T = -x.$$

We now have a linear equation for T, with solution (by integrating factor methods)

$$T = -\tfrac{1}{3}x^2 + c/x,$$

for some constant c. Therefore, the relation between t and x is

$$t^2 = \frac{c}{x} - \tfrac{1}{3}x^2.$$

You can solve this for t in terms of x, but not for x in terms of t (in any easy manner); this confirms that we tackled the equation the right way round in looking for $t(x)$.

If you wish to graph the solution it is convenient to rewrite it as

$$\left(\frac{t}{c^{1/3}}\right)^2 = \left(\frac{c^{1/3}}{x}\right) - \frac{1}{3}\left(\frac{x}{c^{1/3}}\right)^2,$$

or

$$Y^2 = \frac{1}{X} - \tfrac{1}{3}X^2.$$

Then you don't have to produce graphs for each value of c; one graph will do for $c > 0$, and another for $c < 0$.

This technique of *inversion*, solving for x in terms of y rather than y in terms of x, is only occasionally helpful. But you should be ready for the times when it does help.

Exercise 13B

1   Solve (using inversion and the substitution $z = \tfrac{1}{2}x^2$)

$$(x^2y^2 - 1)\frac{dy}{dx} + xy^3 = 0.$$

2   Solve

$$(x^2 - y^4)\frac{dy}{dx} = xy.$$

13.3   HOMOGENEOUS EQUATIONS

Consider the equation

$$\frac{dy}{dx} = \frac{x-y}{x+y}.$$

This may be rewritten as

$$\frac{dy}{dx} = \frac{1 - y/x}{1 + y/x}$$

$$= \frac{1-z}{1+z},$$

say, on putting $z = y/x$. This then solves easily in terms of z. We have

$$y = xz$$

and so

$$\frac{dy}{dx} = z + x\frac{dz}{dx}.$$

The equation becomes

$$z + x\frac{dz}{dx} = \frac{1-z}{1+z}$$

or

$$x\frac{dz}{dx} = \frac{1 - 2z - z^2}{1+z}.$$

We have reduced the original equation to one which is separable, with solution

$$\int \frac{1+z}{1 - 2z - z^2}\,dz = \int \frac{1}{x}\,dx.$$

Carrying out the integrations gives

$$-\tfrac{1}{2}\ln(1 - 2z - z^2) = \ln x + \text{constant},$$

which can be rearranged as

$$y^2 + 2xy - x^2 = c,$$

which is a family of rectangular hyperbolas (see *Linear Algebra and Geometry* in this series).

This is an example of the use of the particular substitution

$$z = y/x$$

when the differential equation is *homogeneous*. Homogeneous (in this context) means that if you make the transformation

$$\begin{cases} x \mapsto kx \\ y \mapsto ky \end{cases}$$

then you get the *same* equation back again. This is certainly true for the right hand side of the equation, as

$$\frac{kx - ky}{kx + ky} = \frac{x - y}{x + y}.$$

It is also true for the left hand side. If you put

$$kx = X \quad \text{and} \quad ky = Y$$

then

$$\frac{dY}{dX} = \frac{dx}{dX} \frac{dy}{dx} \frac{dY}{dy},$$

by the chain rule of calculus, so that

$$\frac{dY}{dX} = \frac{1}{k} \times \frac{dy}{dx} \times k = \frac{dy}{dx}.$$

On the whole, homogeneous equations merely provide an example of when the particular substitution

$$z = y/x$$

is helpful. But there is one circumstance in which homogeneous equations have more importance. We shall see examples later in the book of equations of the form

$$\frac{dy}{dx} = \frac{F(x, y)}{G(x, y)}$$

(see *Extensions of Calculus* in this series, for functions of two variables). Near a point at which both F and G vanish, the right hand side of this equation may be approximated to give

$$\frac{dy}{dx} = \frac{ax + by}{cx + dy}$$

(for constants a, b, c, d). The behaviour of the differential equation near this point can then be found explicitly in terms of the values of a, b, c, d, because the equation is homogeneous, and so can be fully solved.

Exercise 13C

1 Solve the homogeneous equations

(i) $\dfrac{dy}{dx} = \dfrac{y}{x + y}$,

(ii) $x\dfrac{dy}{dx} - y = x,$

(iii) $x\dfrac{dy}{dx} = xe^{y/x} + y,$

by using the substitution $z = y/x$.

2   The equation

$$\frac{dx}{dt} = -\frac{2tx}{t^2 + x^2},$$

solved in Section 13.2, is homogeneous; solve it by the substitution

$$z = x/t.$$

3   Reduce the equation

$$\frac{dy}{dx} = \frac{1 - xy^2}{2x^2 y}$$

to homogeneous form, by the substitution

$$x^{1/2} y = v,$$

and hence solve it.

13.4   SINGULAR SOLUTIONS

Equations involving powers of dy/dx behave differently to those we have looked at so far, and we should look at them briefly through an example.

Suppose that the solution family that you have for your equation is

$$y = mx + m^2.$$

This family of straight lines is shown in Fig. 1; the members pass through $(0, m^2)$ and have slope m.

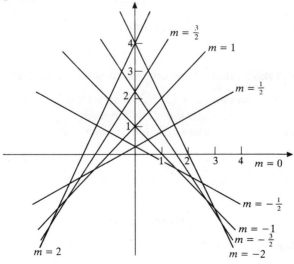

Figure 1. The family of lines $y = mx + m^2$

The differential equation for this family of lines is found by differentiating

$$y = mx + m^2$$

to get

$$dy/dx = m,$$

and so, on substituting this value of m into the equation,

$$y = x\frac{dy}{dx} + \left(\frac{dy}{dx}\right)^2$$

is the appropriate differential equation.

Now let us look at the problem the other way round. If we were given

$$y = x\frac{dy}{dx} + \left(\frac{dy}{dx}\right)^2,$$

how would we solve it? Surprisingly, the best move is to *differentiate* it:

$$\frac{dy}{dx} = \frac{dy}{dx} + x\frac{d^2y}{dx^2} + 2\frac{dy}{dx}\frac{d^2y}{dx^2},$$

or

$$\frac{d^2y}{dx^2}\left(2\frac{dy}{dx} + x\right) = 0.$$

This can only be true if

either $d^2y/dx^2 = 0$, when dy/dx is a constant, say m, and substitution in the original differential equation gives the family of lines

$$y = mx + m^2;$$

or $dy/dx = -\frac{1}{2}x$, which has solution

$$y = -\tfrac{1}{4}x^2 + c,$$

and substitution in the original equation shows that we need $c = 0$.

What is this new solution $y = -\frac{1}{4}x^2$? You can see it in Fig. 1: it is the *envelope* of all the lines $y = mx + m^2$, which are all its tangents.

This 'extra' solution is known as the *singular* solution of the differential equation.

Exercise 13D

1   Find the family of straight lines and the singular solution that satisfy

$$y = x\frac{dy}{dx} + 1 \bigg/ \left(\frac{dy}{dx}\right).$$

2   The *Clairaut equation* is

$$y = x\frac{dy}{dx} + f\left(\frac{dy}{dx}\right),$$

for some given function f (e.g. in Section 13.4, $f\left(\dfrac{dy}{dx}\right) = \left(\dfrac{dy}{dx}\right)^2$). Show that it is satisfied by the family of lines

$$y = mx + f(m)$$

and also by the envelope whose parametric equations are

$$\begin{cases} x = f'(m) \\ y = mf'(m) + f(m). \end{cases}$$

3   Solve the Clairaut equation

$$y = x\frac{dy}{dx} + \tfrac{1}{4}\left(\frac{dy}{dx}\right)^4.$$

4   Solve the equation

$$y = x + \left(\frac{dy}{dx}\right)^2 - \frac{2}{3}\left(\frac{dy}{dx}\right)^3$$

by differentiating it.

13.5   SUMMARY

Some differential equations can be simplified by using a *substitution*: which one to use is a matter of intelligent guesswork.

Others are easier if instead of trying to solve for y, you solve instead for x, by rewriting the equation in terms of dx/dy.

Homogeneous equations are *invariant* under

$$\begin{cases} x \mapsto kx \\ y \mapsto ky, \end{cases}$$

and can be solved by the particular substitution

$$z = y/x, \quad y = xz.$$

Equations involving *powers* of the derivative may have *singular* solutions as well as a family of solutions. Some equations of this type can be solved by differentiating them.

Revision exercise B

1 Show that $\int_0^1 x^2 e^x \, dx = e - 2$.

Show that use of the trapezium rule with 5 strips (6 ordinates) gives an estimate that is about 3.8% too high.

Explain why approximate evaluation of this integral using the trapezium rule will always result in an overestimate, however many strips are used. [MEI 86]

2 Using Simpson's rule with five ordinates, estimate the area under the curve $y = (\ln x)^2$ between $x = 1$ and $x = 2$, giving your answer to 2 decimal places. [MEI 87]

3 Evaluate, correct to 4 decimal places, the integral

$$\int_1^2 \frac{x+1}{x^2+x-1} \, dx.$$

[WJEC 87]

4 Briefly discuss why the following integrals might be difficult to evaluate numerically.

(i) $\int_0^1 \frac{e^x}{\sqrt{x}} \, dx$, (ii) $\int_1^\infty \frac{e^{-x}}{1+x^2} \, dx$.

Explain why, in the first integral, integration by parts might help and, in the second integral, why the substitution $x = \tan \theta$ might be of value.

Use Simpson's rule with four intervals and again with eight intervals to obtain two estimates of the second integral. Hence state, with reasons, the value of the second integral correct to an appropriate number of decimal places. Tabulate all figures used. [MEI 87]

5 You are given that $J = \int_0^1 \sqrt{(5-x^3)} \, dx$.

Working to 5 decimal places throughout,
(i) estimate the value of J using Simpson's rule with 4 strips, and
(ii) find a second estimate for J using Simpson's rule with 8 strips.

Using your estimates, write down an approximate value for J to an appropriate accuracy and comment on your answer. [MEI 89]

6 An experimental investigation resulted in the following table of values of a function $f(x)$:

x	1	2	3	4	5	6
$f(x)$	0.1409	0.2063	0.2808	0.3622	0.4477	0.5349

x	7	8	9	10	11	12
$f(x)$	0.6120	0.7034	0.7796	0.8473	0.9045	0.9489

Show that these data are consistent with a theory which suggests that $f(x)$ is *approximately* cubic in x, provided that one entry is amended. Using a difference table, deduce a value for the incorrect entry which best fits the theory.

Estimate a value for $\int_2^8 f(x)\,dx$ and comment on the accuracy of your answer.

[MEI 87]

7 A numerical value is to be found for a definite integral I. An estimate, I_1, of this value is found from the trapezium rule with 2 ordinates. A second estimate, I_2, is found from the trapezium rule with 3 ordinates, i.e. by halving the interval. Given that the errors in I_1 and I_2 are approximately proportional to h^2, where h is the distance between the ordinates in each case, show that

$$I \approx \frac{4I_2 - I_1}{3}.$$

Show also that this approximation is the same as that obtained by using Simpson's rule with 3 ordinates.

The value of

$$\int_0^{0.8} \frac{1}{\sqrt{(1+x^3)}}\,dx$$

is to be estimated by Romberg integration. $T_{0,m}$ is the estimate of the integral found by using the trapezium rule with $(2^m + 1)$ ordinates, for $m = 0, 1, 2, \ldots$, and further estimates can be obtained by using

$$T_{i,m} = \frac{T_{i-1,m+1} - (\tfrac{1}{4})^i T_{i-1,m}}{1 - (\tfrac{1}{4})^i}, \qquad i = 1, 2, \ldots$$

Show that $T_{0,0} \approx 0.725\,30$, and find $T_{0,1}$ to the same degree of accuracy.

Given that $T_{0,2} \approx 0.755\,79$, $T_{0,3} \approx 0.757\,09$ and $T_{1,0} \approx 0.758\,81$, obtain the best estimate you can of the value of the integral.   [UCLES 89]

8 The height of a particular tree at time t was h, where t is measured in years and h in metres. The growth of this tree is modelled by assuming that the sum of the rate of growth (in metres per year) and $\dfrac{h}{T}$ was k, where T and k are constants.

(a) Form a differential equation for h.
(b) Solve this equation, giving h explicitly as a function of t, k and T. You may assume that at time $t = 0$, the tree started to grow from seed.
(c) The maximum height to which the tree could grow is 40 m. Find how high (to the nearest metre) the tree was 15 years after it started growing, given that $T = 10$ years.
(d) Sketch a graph of h against t.   [AEB 89]

9 A biological population is of size P at time t. If the population continues to grow, the resources upon which it survives become more scarce and, as a consequence, the population has an upper bound, P_M, beyond which the local environment cannot support it. There is also a critical size, P_C, below which the population cannot sustain itself biologically and will eventually die out.

It is believed that for such a population the rate of change of the population is proportional to the product of the difference between the upper population bound and the actual population and the difference between the actual population and the critical size required for survival.

One such population is bounded by its local environment to a maximum size of 10 000 and has a self-sustaining critical size of 500. Initially the population was 600 and five years later had reached 1000. Find the constant of proportionality.

At this point an epidemic reduced the size of the population to 400. For how much longer will it survive? [MEI 87]

10 A body is cooling under conditions of forced convection and the temperature falls at a rate proportional to the difference between its own temperature T, and that of the coolant fluid, T_0, which is assumed to remain constant. The temperature of the body is initially $100\,^\circ\mathrm{C}$ and is cooled to $88\,^\circ\mathrm{C}$ after 10 minutes and to $78\,^\circ\mathrm{C}$ after a further 10 minutes.

Form a differential equation for T to describe the cooling process and find numerical values for the constant of proportionality and the coolant temperature T_0. Hence find an expression for T as a function of time. Determine how long the body takes to cool to $50\,^\circ\mathrm{C}$. [MEI 89]

11 The square horizontal cross-section of a container has side 2 m. Water is poured in at the constant rate of $0.08\,\mathrm{m^3\,s^{-1}}$ and, at the same time, leaks out of a hole in the base at the rate of $0.12x\,\mathrm{m^3\,s^{-1}}$, where x m is the depth of water in the container at time t s. Formulate a differential equation giving dx/dt in terms of x, and verify that the general solution of this equation is

$$x = \tfrac{2}{3} + Ce^{-3t/100},$$

where C is an arbitrary constant.

Determine to the nearest 0.1 s the time taken for the depth to rise from 0.1 m to 0.5 m. [MEI 85]

12 In a mathematical model of simple population growth the rate of increase of a population with respect to time t is proportional to the size P of the population at that time. The constant of proportionality is equal to the difference between the birth rate b and the mortality rate m. A population explosion can be derived from this model if it is assumed that the birth rate b, instead of being constant, is also proportional to the population size so that b is replaced by aP, where a is a constant.

A population which is initially of size P_0 is described by this explosion model. Find the size of the population as a function of time and hence the condition on P_0 for an explosion to take place. Find also the time at which, on this model, the population would become infinite. [MEI 89]

13 A body moves along a straight line. At time t its velocity v satisfies the differential equation

$$\frac{dv}{dt} + 4v = e^{-2t}.$$

Use the integrating factor method to find the general solution of this equation. [WJEC 88]

14 Show that an appropriate integrating factor for the differential equation

$$\frac{dy}{dx} + \frac{3y}{x} = x^3, \quad x > 0,$$

is x^3. Hence, or otherwise, find the solution for which $y = 1$ when $x = 1$. [WJEC 89]

15 Solve the equation

$$\frac{dy}{dx} - y \tan x = -4 \sin x$$

with the condition that $y = 2$ when $x = 0$. For what values of x is this solution appropriate?   [SMP 81]

16 Verify that an integrating factor of the differential equation

$$\frac{dy}{dx} + \left(x - \frac{3}{x}\right) y = -2e^{-x^2/2}$$

is $x^{-3} e^{x^2/2}$. Find the solution of the differential equation for which $y = 0$ when $x = 1$ and, in this case, find, correct to 3 decimal places, the value of y when $x = 2$.   [MEI 88]

17 Show that $\sec x$ is an integrating factor for the differential equation

$$\frac{dy}{dx} + y \tan x = 2 \sin x \cos^2 x.$$

Given that $y = 0$ when $x = \pi$, find y in terms of x. Show that there is one stationary point with $0 < x < \dfrac{\pi}{2}$ and find the value of y at this stationary point.   [MEI 89]

18 Show, by using an integrating factor or otherwise, that the solution of

$$dv/dt + kv = a + b \sin \omega t$$

which has $v(0) = 0$ is

$$v(t) = e^{-kt} \int_0^t (a + b \sin \omega s) e^{ks} \, ds.$$

A particle of unit mass and unit charge is moving vertically under gravity, with a resistance to motion equal to k times its velocity. At $t = 0$ an electric field $E \sin \omega t$ is switched on, and after half a cycle it is switched off; this applies an upward force $E \sin \omega t$ to the particle in this interval. At $t = 0$ the particle is instantaneously at rest. Find its speed when the field is switched off.

(Note: $\int e^{kz} \sin \omega z \, dz = e^{kz}(k \sin \omega z - \omega \cos \omega z)/(k^2 + \omega^2).$)   [SMP 77]

19 A rocket driven test vehicle moves along a straight horizontal track. The vehicle starts from rest at time $t = 0$. The velocity v of the vehicle satisfies the equation

$$m \, dv/dt = -F - c \, dm/dt,$$

where $m(t)$ is the total mass (of vehicle and remaining fuel) at time t. F is the force of resistance and c is a constant. The initial mass of fuel is m_0 and the mass of the rest of the vehicle can be neglected; fuel is burnt at a constant rate α. The resistance F is proportional to the speed of the vehicle. Show that the equation of motion can be rewritten as

$$\frac{dv}{dt} + \frac{kv}{m_0 - \alpha t} = \frac{\alpha c}{m_0 - \alpha t}$$

where k is a constant.

Solve this equation to find v in terms of t and the constants of the problem, giving the interval of t for which your solution is appropriate.   [SMP 86]

20 (i) An economic theory suggests that the relationship between the national debt £D and national income £I can be represented by the following differential equations:

$$\frac{dD}{dt} = aI \quad \text{and} \quad \frac{dI}{dt} = bI,$$

where a and b are positive constants. If I_0, D_0 are the initial values of I and D respectively, show that

$$D = \frac{aI_0}{b}(e^{bt} - 1) + D_0.$$

(ii) A body of mass 49 kg is released from rest at $t = 0$ and travels in a horizontal straight line in a medium which exerts a resistance of $5gv$ N, where v m s^{-1} is the velocity of the body. There is also a propulsive force of $196e^{-t/2}$ N acting on the body. Show that v satisfies the differential equation

$$\frac{dv}{dt} + v = 4e^{-t/2}.$$

Find v in terms of t and show that the acceleration vanishes just once during the motion. Sketch the graph of v against t $(t \geqslant 0)$.   [WJEC 87]

21 (i) Show that

$$u_n = rd^n/(d-c)$$

is a particular solution of the equation

$$u_{n+1} = cu_n + rd^n,$$

where r, c, d are constants and $c \neq d$. What is the general solution of this equation?

(ii) A man is considering retirement at age 55, when his savings are £100k (i.e. £100 000). He reckons that he can get a rate of return of $(a+s)\%$ on his savings where $s\%$ is the inflation rate and $a > 0$, and that he needs to derive an income of £b_nk from his savings to live in year n after retirement, where

$$b_n = b\left(1 + \frac{s}{100}\right)^n.$$

He uses the equation

$$u_{n+1} = \left(1 + \frac{a+s}{100}\right)u_n - b_n$$

to forecast the value of his savings n years after retirement. Write down the solution of this equation, and show that if

$$a = 5, \quad s = 3, \quad b = 8,$$

then his savings last for almost 21 years.

(iii) An alternative calculation uses the equation

$$\frac{du}{dt} = \frac{(a+s)u}{100} - b\exp\left(\frac{st}{100}\right)$$

to estimate the value of his savings after t years. Solve this equation and show that, for $b > a$, his savings run out after a time which is independent of the rate of inflation s.   [SMP 88]

22 An Eskimo in the Arctic builds an igloo to save himself from being frozen to death when a blizzard sets in. Heat is generated in the igloo by the Eskimo's body, and there is a consequent rate of increase of the temperature θ in the igloo equal to k times the excess of his (fixed) body temperature T_1 above θ. Heat is also lost from the igloo by conduction so that there is a rate of decrease of θ equal to $\frac{1}{6}k$ times the excess of θ above the outer temperature T. Write down a differential equation for θ.

At time $t=0$ the temperature in the igloo is $-T_0\,°C$, and the outer temperature T falls slowly according to the formula

$$T = -2T_0 + T_0 e^{-kt/6}.$$

Show that

$$\theta = A + B e^{-kt/6} + C e^{-7kt/6}$$

where A, B, C are constants. Express A in terms of T_0 and T_1.   [SMP 82]

23 Make the substitution $z = y^{\alpha}$ in the equation

$$2(1+x^2)\frac{dz}{dx} + 3xz = 3(x^3+x)z^{1/3}.$$

Choosing a particular value of α, reduce your equation to the form

$$\frac{dy}{dx} + f(x)y = g(x).$$

Hence find z as a function of x, given that $z=1$ when $x=0$.   [SMP 89]

24 Let y satisfy the differential equation

$$2x\,dy/dx = 1 - e^{2y-x}$$

and the condition that $y=0$ when $x=1$. Use the substitution

$$z = e^{-2y}$$

to find a linear differential equation for z.

Solve this equation and hence find y as a function of x, giving the domain of the function.   [SMP 87]

25 Use the substitution $u = 1/y$ to transform the equation

$$dy/dx + y/x = xy^2$$

into

$$du/dx - u/x = -x.$$

Hence solve for y, given that $y=1$ when $x=1$.
For what set of values of x is your solution valid? Sketch the graph of y.   [SMP 85]

26 Use the substitution $y = \ln u$ to reduce the equation

$$\frac{dy}{dx} = e^{-y} + x^{-1}, \quad x>0,$$

to the linear equation $x\,du/dx = u + x$. Hence solve for y, given that $y=1$ when $x=1$.
Show that this particular solution is valid only for $x > e^{-e}$.   [SMP 80]

27 Use the substitution $y = 1/z^{1/2}$ to reduce

$$x^3\,dy/dx = 2x^2y + y^3$$

to a linear equation for z, and solve this equation for $x \geqslant 0$ given that $y = \frac{1}{2}$ when $x = 1$. Sketch the graph of your solution.   [SMP 83]

28 (i) Solve the equation

$$\frac{dw}{dx} + \frac{3w}{x} = 0 \quad \text{for} \quad x > 0.$$

(ii) Solve the equation

$$\frac{dy}{dx} + y^2 = 1 \quad \text{for} \quad x > 0 \tag{A}$$

with the condition $y = 0$ when $x = 1$.
   Verify that the equation

$$\frac{dy}{dx} + y^2 = \frac{3}{4x^2} \quad \text{for} \quad x > 0 \tag{B}$$

has two solutions of the form $y = c/x$, neither of which satisfies $y = 0$ when $x = 1$.
   Make the substitution

$$y = \frac{1}{z}\frac{dz}{dx} + \frac{3}{2x}$$

in equation (B) to obtain an equation for z, and solve this equation. Hence find a solution of equation (B) which has $y = 0$ when $x = 1$.   [SMP 79]

29 The function $y(x)$ satisfies the integral equation

$$y(x) + 2x \int_0^x \frac{y(u)}{1+u^2}\,du = 3x^2 + 2x + 1.$$

Show that the substitution

$$z(x) = \int_0^x \frac{y(u)}{1+u^2}\,du$$

converts the integral equation into a first-order linear differential equation for $z(x)$. Hence solve the original integral equation for $y(x)$.   [MEI 88]

14

First order differential equations numerically

Many differential equations have no convenient solution formula, and for them we need numerical methods of finding the solution. We shall start with a rather inefficient solution method, because it is the easiest to understand, and then we shall derive a moderately efficient method. The very efficient methods that are normally used these days will not be considered in detail in this book, as they are quite complicated.

14.1   EULER'S METHOD

(a)   Geometrical background

In Fig. 1, (x_0, y_0) and (x_1, y_1) are two points on a curve $y = f(x)$ which is the solution to a differential equation of the form

$$\frac{dy}{dx} = P(x)y + Q(x).$$

Euler's method is based on the approximation

$$y_1 \approx y_0 + h \tan \alpha.$$

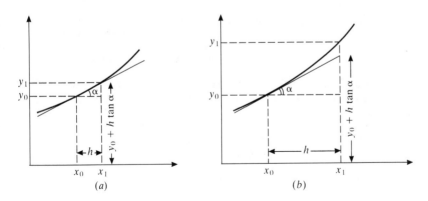

Figure 1. Going along the tangent to a curve as an approximation to going along the curve.
(a) h small   (b) h not small

You can see in the diagram that it *is* only an approximation, but that it is quite close to being true when h is very small. That is, when h is very small the tangent (at angle α) and the curve are extremely close together.

Now the slope of the tangent (and curve) is

$$\tan \alpha = \left(\frac{dy}{dx}\right)_{\text{at}(x_0,y_0)}$$

$$= P(x_0)y_0 + Q(x_0)$$

from the differential equation. Hence

$$y_1 \approx y_0 + h\{P(x_0)y_0 + Q(x_0)\}.$$

Thus if you know the point (x_0, y_0) on the curve, you can calculate a point (x_1, y_1) on the curve, which is further to the right, by the equations

$$\begin{cases} x_1 = x_0 + h \\ y_1 = y_0 + h\{P(x_0)y_0 + Q(x_0)\}, \end{cases}$$

and the calculation will be quite accurate if h is very small. More generally

$$\begin{cases} x_1 = x_0 + h \\ y_1 = y_0 + h\left(\dfrac{dy}{dx}\right)_{\text{at}(x_0,y_0)} \end{cases}$$

with $\left(\dfrac{dy}{dx}\right)_{\text{at}(x_0,y_0)}$ being found from the differential equation.

We need to start from an initial condition, and this is provided in the full statement of any differential equation problem. From this initial condition you can step to the right, a distance h at a time, calculating successive values of y.

(b)   A simple example, and the errors

Let us take a very simple example of this, with the differential equation problem

$$\begin{cases} \dfrac{dy}{dx} = 2y \\ y = 1 \quad \text{when } x = 0. \end{cases}$$

I shall start by using $h = 0.1$, and calculate as far as $x = 0.5$. My first step forward starts at $x = 0$, where $y = 1$; these are the values of (x_0, y_0) for the first step. The gradient is

$$\left(\frac{dy}{dx}\right)_{\text{at}(0,1)} = 2y = 2,$$

and so the next point in this approximation to the solution is

$$\begin{cases} x = 0 + 0.1 = 0.1 \\ y = 1 + 0.1 \times 2 = 1.2. \end{cases}$$

The next step starts from this point, and goes forward a step 0.1 along the x-axis. At this point the value of dy/dx is $2 \times 1.2 = 2.4$, i.e. the local value of $2y$ (using the differential equation). Hence the next point is

$$\begin{cases} x = 0.1 + 0.1 = 0.2 \\ y = 1.2 + 0.1 \times 2.4 = 1.44. \end{cases}$$

This sort of repetitive arithmetic is best done by computer of course; here, I shall set it out in a table:

Step	x_{start}	y_{start}	$y_{\text{new}} = y_{\text{start}} + h\left(\dfrac{dy}{dx}\right)_{\text{start}}$
0	0	1	1 $+0.1 \times 2$
1	0.1	1.2	1.2 $+0.1 \times 2.4$
2	0.2	1.44	1.44 $+0.1 \times 2.88$
3	0.3	1.728	1.728 $+0.1 \times 3.456$
4	0.4	2.0736	2.0736 $+0.1 \times 4.1472$
5	0.5	2.48832	

At each step, y_{new} from the previous step becomes y_{start}, and dy/dx is always calculated from the differential equation as $2y_{\text{start}}$.

The step length I have used, 0.1, is *not* very small, so I do not expect the answer to be very accurate. In fact the solution to

$$\begin{cases} dy/dx = 2y \\ \quad y = 1 \quad \text{when } x = 0 \end{cases}$$

is easy to work out (e.g. the equation is separable, or it is linear) as

$$y = e^{2x}.$$

The correct value at $x = 0.5$ is therefore just $e = 2.71828\ldots$

I programmed my computer to do this calculation for various step lengths h, and the results were as follows.

h	$y(0.5)$	Error	Number of steps
0.1	2.48832	0.2299618...	5
0.01	2.691588...	0.0266937...	50
0.001	2.715568...	0.0027133...	500
0.0001	2.718010...	0.0002717...	5000

It is clear that the error is approximately

$$2.7h$$

and that an intolerably large number of steps will be needed to get an accurate answer. It is useful to calculate $y(1.0)$ here, to see how the error depends on the number of steps for a given step size.

$$h=0.01 \qquad y(1)=7.244\,646\ldots \quad \text{Error}=0.144\,099\ldots$$

$$h=0.001 \quad y(1)=7.374\,312\ldots \quad \text{Error}=0.014\,743\ldots$$

An error formula that fits both these sets of experiments reasonably well is

$$\text{Error}\approx 2h^2 n\,y_{\text{end}},$$

where n is the number of steps taken and y_{end} is the final value of y. We will return to this in a later chapter. What it tells us at the moment is that Euler's method will not be good enough for accurate calculations where the distance nh to go forward is large.

(c)   The connection with difference equations

The Euler method can be interpreted as a difference equation. In the example we had

$$y_{n+1}=y_n+h(dy/dx)_{\text{at}\,y_n}$$
$$=y_n+2hy_n$$

for the given equation. That is, we have the difference equation

$$\begin{cases} y_{n+1}=(1+2h)y_n \\ \quad y_0=1. \end{cases}$$

The solution of this is, by the methods in Chapter 2,

$$y_n=(1+2h)^n,$$

exactly. This confirms the earlier tedious computer calculations; for example to find $y(1.0)$ with $h=0.001$, all we need to calculate is

$$(1.002)^{1000}=7.374\,312\ldots$$

Similarly

$$(1.0002)^{10\,000}=7.387\,578\ldots$$

gives the value of $y(1.0)$ with $h=0.0001$. Much easier! But for most differential equations the corresponding difference equation is very hard to solve, except by a step-by-step method, so it is *not* an advantage to try it.

(d)   The connection with integration

The equation

$$\begin{cases} dy/dx=2y \\ \quad y=1 \quad \text{when } x=0 \end{cases}$$

can be *integrated* on both sides to give an equivalent *integral equation*

$$\int_0^h \frac{dy}{dx}\, dx = \int_0^h 2y\, dx = 2\int_0^h y\, dx.$$

Now the left hand side can be integrated exactly as

$$y(h) - y(0) = y(h) - 1,$$

by using the condition at $x = 0$. For such an easy equation as this (for which we know the solution), we could integrate exactly on the right as well; but since in general we do not know how y changes with x – that is what we have to find out – we do an approximate integration.

In Fig. 2 you see the graph of y, and

$$\int_0^h y\, dx$$

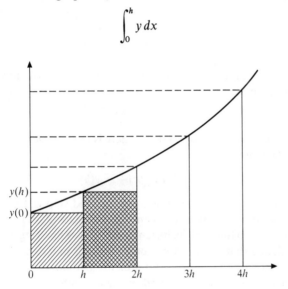

Figure 2. Approximate integrations for a differential equation

is the area under the curve between $x = 0$ and $x = h$. This area is (poorly) approximated by

$$h \times y(0),$$

the area of the shaded rectangle. That is $2\int_0^h y\, dx \approx 2hy(0)$, and using the previous evaluation of $\int_0^h \frac{dy}{dx}\, dx$ gives

$$y(h) - 1 \approx 2h\, y(0)$$

or

$$y(h) \approx 1 + 2h\, y(0) = 1 + 2h = 1.2.$$

This is *exactly* the first step that was made in Euler's method of integrating the differential equation:

$$y(0.1) \approx 1 + h \times \text{slope at } x = 0$$

$$= 1 + h \times 2y(0)$$

$$= 1.2.$$

Consider next the step from $x = h = 0.1$ to $x = 2h$. This can be achieved by a similar integration, from $x = h$ to $x = 2h$:

$$\int_h^{2h} \frac{dy}{dx} dx = \int_h^{2h} 2y \, dx$$

or

$$y(2h) = y(h) + 2 \int_h^{2h} y \, dx.$$

The area in this case is the area under the curve in Fig. 2 between $x = h$ and $x = 2h$, which is approximated by

$$h \times y(h).$$

Hence the corresponding approximation here is to use the cross-shaded area and in a similar fashion we get

$$y(2h) \approx y(h) + 2h \, y(h).$$

Once again, this is exactly the same as the second step in Euler's method.

Using this kind of argument you can show, in general, that Euler's method is exactly equivalent to this very inefficient method of estimating areas; it is such an inefficient scheme that we did not even *consider* it in Chapter 10.

This discussion shows clearly that Euler's method is not good enough for serious numerical work, as it is based on such a feeble estimate of area. It also shows us how to do better than Euler – we need to use one of the more efficient integration methods from Chapter 10.

(e)   A less obvious example, and the errors

This time I am going to choose an example where there is (as far as I know) no solution formula. Consider the differential equation

$$\begin{cases} \dfrac{dy}{dx} = x - y^3 \\ y = 0 \quad \text{when } x = 0. \end{cases}$$

There is no difficulty in programming a solution by Euler's method, for a variety of step lengths h. The results I found (to 4 decimal places) are set out in the table.

x	y			
	$h=0.1$	$h=0.05$	$h=0.02$	$h=0.01$
1	0.4419	0.4631	0.4753	0.4793
2	1.1862	1.1827	1.1809	1.1803
3	1.4141	1.4138	1.4136	1.4135
4	1.5690	1.5689	1.5688	1.5688
5	1.6965	1.6965	1.6965	1.6964
6	1.8067	1.8067	1.8066	1.8066
7	1.9045	1.9045	1.9045	1.9044
8	1.9930	1.9929	1.9929	1.9929
9	2.0741	2.0741	2.0741	2.0741
10	2.1492	2.1492	2.1492	2.1492

These figures were derived using the previous method. At each step

$$\begin{cases} x_{new} = x_{old} + h \\ y_{new} = y_{old} + h(x_{old} - y_{old}^3), \end{cases}$$

and the start was at $x_0=0$, $y_0=0$.
What should be noticed in these figures?

(i) The values for $x=1$ and $x=2$ progressively improve as h gets smaller, with limiting values (for h tending to zero) being about

$$0.4833 \quad \text{and} \quad 1.1797$$

(extrapolated by a straight line from the values at $h=0.02$ and $h=0.01$). I checked these figures by using $h=0.001$, and got

$$0.4828 \quad \text{and} \quad 1.1798.$$

Good: the errors are approximately proportional to h, as before.
(ii) The values for x beyond 5 scarcely change as h decreases; the solution found by using $h=0.1$ is *quite* accurate enough for many purposes.

Clearly when I estimated the errors in the earlier example I was not getting the whole story. The simple example showed how large the errors *could* be, this later example shows that sometimes they are *not* as big as that.

This is the normal state of affairs in numerical analysis. You can get an estimate of the largest size the error can possibly have, and that must guide your calculations; but in any actual case the errors could be much smaller, and it may be hard to know in advance.

How did I know that this example would produce this sort of result? After all, you wouldn't expect me to choose it by accident. Think of the sign of dy/dx: if $x>y^3$ it is positive, but if $x<y^3$ it is negative (Fig. 3).

The solution starts below the dividing curve $y=x^{1/3}$ (because it has $dy/dx=0$ at $x=y=0$). Thereafter it must always stay below $y=x^{1/3}$, and get closer to it as x

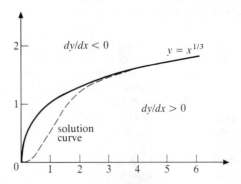

Figure 3. Sign of dy/dx in the equation, and the solution curve

increases. All the approximate solution curves for different values of h converge onto the curve $y = x^{1/3}$ as x gets large, and so the errors are *all* small for large values of x.

This sort of discussion of the general shape of the solution curve can be very valuable before the solution is computed, but the discussion can also be hard to do.

Exercise 14A

1   Use Euler's method and a step length $h = 0.1$ to solve the equation

$$\begin{cases} \dfrac{dy}{dx} = x - y \\ y = 1 \quad \text{when } x = 0 \end{cases}$$

approximately. Do the calculations with a calculator, and go as far as $x = 1.2$.

2   Plot your results from question 1 and the exact solution of the equation. Why must the approximate solution always lie below the exact solution?

3   Show that the difference equation representing Euler's method for

$$\begin{cases} dy/dx = x - y \\ y = 1 \quad \text{when } x = 0 \end{cases}$$

is

$$\begin{cases} y_{n+1} = (1 - h)y_n + h^2 n \\ y_0 = 1. \end{cases}$$

Solve this difference equation, and compare it with the exact solution of the differential equation.

4   The exact solution at $x = 1$ for the differential equation in question 3 is

$$y(1) = 2e^{-1}.$$

The solution of the difference equation at that point is (if h^{-1} is an integer)

$$y(1) = 2(1 - h)^{1/h}.$$

From these two results, make a table of how the error in Euler's method (at $x=1$) varies with h. Carry out similar calculations for $x=2$.

5   Use a computer to calculate values for $y(1)$, using Euler's method with $h=0.1, h=0.05,$ $h=0.02, h=0.01$ and $h=0.001$, for the differential equation

$$\begin{cases} \dfrac{dy}{dx} = \dfrac{x}{y} - x^2 \\[2mm] y=1 \quad \text{at } x=0. \end{cases}$$

6   For the equation

$$\begin{cases} \dfrac{dy}{dx} = \dfrac{x}{y} - x^2 \\[2mm] y(0)=1 \end{cases}$$

find the curve where $dy/dx=0$, and state in what regions dy/dx is positive and dy/dx is negative. Hence sketch the solution curve.

Calculate values for $y(3)$ using Euler's method for $h=0.1, 0.05, 0.02, 0.01, 0.001.$ Discuss your answers.

7   If in question 6 you integrate on beyond $x=3$, to $x=10$ say, you will get some very odd results. They will be explained in Chapter 15, but see what you can make of them now.

14.2   USING SIMPSON'S RULE

If you look at the differential equation

$$\begin{cases} \dfrac{dy}{dx} + y\sin x = x^2 \\[2mm] y=1 \quad \text{at } x=0, \end{cases}$$

you will see that it is linear, and has an integrating factor. This allows us to rewrite it as

$$\begin{cases} \dfrac{d}{dx}\{y e^{-\cos x}\} = x^2 e^{-\cos x} \\[2mm] y=1 \quad \text{at } x=0. \end{cases}$$

You can now formally integrate it as

$$y e^{-\cos x} = e^{-1} + \int_0^x s^2 e^{-\cos s}\, ds,$$

using the fact that $y e^{-\cos x}$ is e^{-1} when $x=0$, and introducing the *summing variable s*. That is, the solution of the differential equation is

$$y = e^{\cos x}\{e^{-1} + \int_0^x s^2 e^{-\cos s}\, ds\}.$$

You can now use Simpson's rule to calculate the integral, and you have a numerical solution for the equation. It ought to be a better solution than Euler's method would give, because Simpson's rule is a good integration rule, whereas Euler's method is equivalent to a very poor integration rule.

The table of values below shows the results I got from my computer. Simpson's method with $h=0.05$ is accurate to 5 decimal places (as I checked for a few values by using $h=0.01$). Euler's method with $h=0.002$ is still inaccurate.

	Simpson		Euler	
x	$h=0.05$	$h=0.01$	$h=0.005$	$h=0.002$
0.5	0.924 49	0.925 36	0.924 93	0.924 66
1.0	0.912 66	0.911 45	0.912 05	0.912 42
1.5	1.217 93	1.213 93	1.215 93	1.217 13
2.0	2.001 81	1.994 73	1.998 27	2.000 40
2.5	3.529 66	3.516 45	3.523 05	3.527 01
3.0	6.464 24	6.434 82	6.449 51	6.458 35

This method is useful occasionally; of course you can only use it when the solution of the equation can be expressed as an integral which gives y explicitly. And remember that Simpson's rule is not always so accurate: there were cases in Chapter 10 where the errors in using Simpson's rule were of size proportional to h, approximately, and this is no better than the usual error in Euler's method.

Exercise 14B

1 Solve the differential equation

$$\begin{cases} \dfrac{dy}{dx} - y \tan x = e^{-x} \\ \quad y(0)=1 \end{cases}$$

to evaluate y at $x=1, 2, 3, 4$

(i) by using Euler's method with various values of h,
(ii) by using Simpson's rule with a well chosen value of h,
(iii) exactly.

2 Repeat question 1 with the right hand side replaced by $x^{1/2} \sin x$, and omitting (iii).

14.3   THE MODIFIED EULER METHOD

(a) A simple example

We saw in Section 14.1 that Euler's method was poor because it used a very crude approximation to an integral. It seems natural to try to improve Euler's method by using a better approximation to the integral.

Let us go back to the example

$$\begin{cases} \dfrac{dy}{dx} = 2y \\ y = 1 \quad \text{at } x = 0. \end{cases}$$

We rewrote this, by integrating both sides of the equation, as

$$y(h) = 1 + 2\int_0^h y\,dx.$$

The area represented by the integral is shown in Fig. 4. We can use the trapezium rule to estimate the area represented by $\int_0^h y\,dx$ as

$$\tfrac{1}{2}\{y(0) + y(h)\} \times h.$$

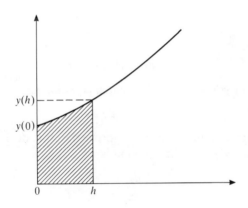

Figure 4. The area $\int_0^h y\,dx$

Hence our equation for $y(h)$ is

$$y(h) \approx 1 + h\{y(0) + y(h)\}$$
$$= 1 + h\{1 + y(h)\}.$$

That is,

$$y(h) \approx (1 + h)/(1 - h).$$

Proceeding strip by strip you find that

$$y(nh) \approx \left(\frac{1 + h}{1 - h}\right)^n$$

for this equation. For example, and to compare with the results in Section 14.1, here are values for $y(0.5)$ for various values of h.

h	$y(0.5)$	Error
0.1	2.727 412 8	-9.131×10^{-3}
0.01	2.718 372 4	$-9.06 \ \times 10^{-5}$
0.001	2.718 282 7	$-9 \quad \times 10^{-7}$

As you can see, the accuracy is greatly improved, the error being apparently proportional to h^2.

This example has been rather too simple, because the equation we found for $y(h)$ by using the trapezium rule could be solved exactly, and this is not usually the case. But it did show us that the idea was a good one, as errors were much reduced.

(b)   General discussion

Euler's estimate of $y(h)$ from the differential equation is

$$y(h) \approx y(0) + h(dy/dx)_{\text{at } x=0}.$$

This can be used in a simple manner to improve the estimate of the area for more general equations. Suppose the equation is

$$\frac{dy}{dx} = E$$

where E is an expression involving x and y. Then integrating this from 0 to h gives

$$y(h) - y(0) = \int_0^h E \, dx,$$

and the trapezium rule estimate for the integral is

$$\tfrac{1}{2}h\{E_{\text{at } x=0} + E_{\text{at } x=h}\}.$$

But in this estimate we do not know $y(h)$, and so cannot calculate $E_{\text{at } x=h}$. And we will only rarely be able to *solve*

$$y(h) - y(0) = \tfrac{1}{2}h\{E_{\text{at } x=0} + E_{\text{at } x=h}\}$$

for $y(h)$, as we did in the example in (a). What we can do is evaluate

$$E_{\text{at } x=h}$$

approximately, by using

$$y(h) \approx y(0) + hE_{\text{at } x=0}.$$

We shall then have an adequate approximation for $y(h)$, in the form

$$y(h) \approx y(0) + \tfrac{1}{2}h\{E_{\text{at } x=0} + (E_{\text{at } x=h})_{\text{approx}}\}.$$

Why is this an adequate approximation? Because Euler's estimate

$$y(h) \approx y(0) + hE_{\text{at } x=0}$$

is in error by about a constant times h^2, but this error introduced into $E_{\text{at } x=h}$ is then being multiplied by $\tfrac{1}{2}h$, which reduces its effect to a constant times h^3; which is the size of the error in the trapezium rule anyway. Thus this estimate of $y(h)$ should be in error by a constant times h^3; and when you take n steps (with $n = 1/h$ to go unit distance forward) the total error must be about a constant times h^2.

The method for stepping forward from $x = 0$, $y = y(0)$ to $x = h$ is therefore as follows.

(i)   Calculate the intermediate or trial value

$$y_{\text{inter}} = y(0) + hE_0,$$

where E_0 is calculated using $x = 0$ and $y = y(0)$.

(ii) Calculate

$$E_{\text{inter}}$$

by using $x = h$ and $y = y_{\text{inter}}$.

(iii) Make the step forward by

$$y(h) \approx y(0) + \tfrac{1}{2}h\{E_0 + E_{\text{inter}}\}.$$

This method is known variously as the

modified Euler, or improved Euler, or trapezium, or Heun

method and it is adequately effective for many problems, as its error is about a constant times h^2.

(c) Example

Let us solve the equation

$$\begin{cases} \dfrac{dy}{dx} = e^{-xy} + x \sin y \\[2mm] y = 1 \quad \text{when } x = 0, \end{cases}$$

using this modified Euler method. I shall do one step by hand, and then use my computer. Start from $x = 0$, $y = 1$, and take $h = 0.1$.

(i) $y_{\text{inter}} = 1 + 0.1E_0$, where E_0 is the right hand side of the equation evaluated using $x = 0$ and $y = 1$. That is

$$E_0 = e^0 + 0 = 1,$$

and so

$$y_{inter} = 1.01.$$

(ii) Next calculate E_{inter}, using $x = 0.1$ and $y = y_{inter} = 1.01$. In this case

$$E_{inter} = e^{-0.101} + 0.1 \sin 1.01$$

$$= 0.988\,616$$

to six decimal places.

(iii) The average of the two E values is

$$0.994\,308$$

and so the step forward gives

$$y = 1 + 0.1 \times 0.994\,308$$

$$= 1.099\,431.$$

I programmed my computer to solve this equation, and my results are in the table.

x	$h = 0.1$	$h = 0.05$	$h = 0.02$	$h = 0.01$
1	1.993 730	1.993 573	1.993 531	1.993 525
2	2.867 914	2.869 110	2.869 424	2.869 468
3	3.118 380	3.119 060	3.119 228	3.119 251
4	3.140 825	3.140 901	3.140 918	3.140 920
5	3.141 582	3.141 585	3.141 585	3.141 585

After this y reached, and remained at, π. It is in fact clear that $y \to \pi$ as $x \to \infty$, for then $e^{-xy} \to 0$ and $x \sin y = 0$ also, so the equation is satisfied. This provides a useful check on my programming, and shows why all the approximate solutions come together as x increases.

Are the errors varying like h^2, as expected? More accurate values are

$$y(1) = 1.993\,523$$

$$y(2) = 2.869\,482$$

so that you can calculate errors/h^2 for the top two lines of the table and find

x	$h = 0.1$	$h = 0.05$	$h = 0.02$	$h = 0.01$
1	−2.07	−2.04	−2.00	−2.00
2	15.68	14.88	14.50	14.00

This confirms experimentally that errors in this method are proportional to h^2, to a good approximation. Hence this is definitely a better method than Euler's method, and we should no longer use the Euler version.

(d)   A geometrical view

We started Section 14.1 with a diagram of a curve, with a tangent as a local approximation to the curve. Let us reconsider that diagram (Fig. 5). To get from the point (x_0, y_0) to (x_1, y_1) you need to go along the chord. Now the chord is steeper than the tangent at (x_0, y_0), which has slope $\tan \alpha$ in the diagram; and it is less steep than the tangent at (x_1, y_1), which has slope $\tan \beta$. It seems a reasonable guess that

$$\tfrac{1}{2}(\tan \alpha + \tan \beta)$$

is a good approximation to the slope of the chord.

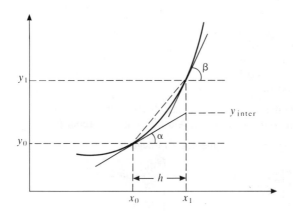

Figure 5. Tangents at x_0 and x_1 and the chord from x_0 to x_1 (on the curve)

Now

$$\begin{cases} \tan \alpha = (dy/dx)_{\text{at}(x_0, y_0)} \\ \tan \beta = (dy/dx)_{\text{at}(x_1, y_1)} \end{cases}$$

and while we know the first of these from the differential equation, we don't know the second if y_1 is needed for it. What we can do is use

$$\tan \gamma = (dy/dx)_{\text{at}(x_1, y_{\text{inter}})}.$$

This is the slope of another member of the family of solutions, the one passing through

$$(x_1, y_{\text{inter}}),$$

where

$$y_{\text{inter}} = y_0 + h(dy/dx)_{(x_0, y_0)}.$$

This will not be correct, but will not be too far wrong, especially when h is much smaller than it appears to be in Fig. 5.

This is an alternative explanation of why the modified Euler scheme has the form given in (*b*) above.

Exercise 14C

1   Repeat question 1 of Exercise 14A using the modified Euler method and $h=0.1$. Use the exact solution to calculate the errors, and compare them with the errors from Euler's method.

2   Repeat question 5 of Exercise 14A using the modified Euler method and the same values of h.

3   For the *exact* solution of

$$\begin{cases} \dfrac{dy}{dx} = x - y \\[2mm] y = 1 \quad \text{when } x = 0 \end{cases}$$

calculate

(i) dy/dx at $x=0.3$
(ii) dy/dx at $x=0.4$
(iii) y at $x=0.3$
(iv) $y_{\text{inter}} = y(0.3) + 0.1(dy/dx)_{0.3}$.

Now use the *equation* to calculate dy/dx when $x=0.4$ and $y=y_{\text{inter}}$. Compare your result with your answer in (ii). Do they differ by about h^2?

4   Use the improved Euler method to integrate

$$\begin{cases} \dfrac{dy}{dx} = \dfrac{x}{y} - x^2 \\[2mm] y(0) = 1 \end{cases}$$

out to $x=10$ with $h=0.1, 0.05, 0.02, 0.01$.

5   If you use Euler's method on

$$\frac{dy}{dx} = 2y, \; y(0) = 1$$

the answers are all too small. If you use the improved Euler method the answers are also too small. Can you explain this geometrically? What would you expect for $\dfrac{dy}{dx} = \dfrac{y^{1/2}}{x}$, using the improved Euler method, and starting from $y=0$ at $x=1$?

14.4   IMPROVED METHODS

There are two obvious ways forward. One is to use a still better integration formula for

$$\int_0^h E \, dx,$$

in place of the trapezium rule of Section 14.3(a) and (b). The other is to use a better estimate than

$$y_{\text{inter}} = y(0) + hE_0$$

in Section 14.3(b). I shall outline both these approaches, as they use ideas developed earlier in the book; but I shall not give a full treatment, which can be found in more advanced texts.

(a)   Runge–Kutta formulas

As before we work from

$$\int_0^h \frac{dy}{dx}\,dx = \int_0^h E\,dx,$$

where E is the expression involving x and y which gives the value of dy/dx. If we use Simpson's rule to evaluate the right hand integral, we need to introduce *two* strips, so we must divide the area by the line $x = \frac{1}{2}h$, as in Fig. 6.

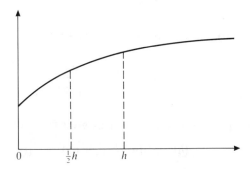

Figure 6. The double strip for Simpson's rule

We then have

$$\int_0^h E\,dx = \tfrac{1}{6}h\{E_0 + 4E_{1/2} + E_1\},$$

where

$$\begin{cases} E_0 & \text{is the value at } x=0,\ y=y(0) \\ E_{1/2} & \text{is the value at } x=\tfrac{1}{2}h,\ y=y(\tfrac{1}{2}h) \\ E_1 & \text{is the value at } x=h,\ y=(h). \end{cases}$$

As before, we do not actually know the values of $E_{1/2}$ and E_1 yet, but we can estimate them, just as we had to estimate $y(h)$ in the improved Euler method, by y_{inter}.

It turns out that the best way of estimating is in terms of *four* values of the slope expression E:

$$\begin{cases} E_0, \text{ as above} \\ E_a = E \text{ evaluated at } x_0 + \tfrac{1}{2}h, \; y_0 + \tfrac{1}{2}h E_0 \\ E_b = E \text{ evaluated at } x_0 + \tfrac{1}{2}h, \; y_0 + \tfrac{1}{2}h E_a \\ E_c = E \text{ evaluated at } x_0 + h, \; y_0 + h E_b. \end{cases}$$

Then

$$y(h) \approx y_0 + \tfrac{1}{6}h(E_0 + 2E_a + 2E_b + E_c)$$

gives total errors proportional to h^4 when it is used as an integration method.

This fourth order Runge/Kutta method is one of the commonly used integration schemes. Because its error is around h^4 in size you do not need to have h very small to get an accurate answer; the cost is that you have to evaluate all the E's at each step.

(b)   **Predictor–corrector methods**

Start again from

$$\int_0^h \frac{dy}{dx} dx = \int_0^h E \, dx$$

and use the trapezium rule on the right. This gives

$$y(h) \approx y(0) + \tfrac{1}{2}h\{E_0 + E_1\},$$

where

$$\begin{cases} E_0 = E \text{ evaluated at } x=0, \; y=y(0) \\ E_1 = E \text{ evaluated at } x=h, \; y=y(h). \end{cases}$$

This is, in effect, an equation for $y(h)$; and we can solve equations by iteration. The iteration we set up is

$$\begin{cases} y_{n+1}(h) = y(0) + \tfrac{1}{2}h\{E_0 + E_1^{(n)}\} \\ E_1^{(0)} = E \text{ evaluated at } y_{\text{inter}} \end{cases}$$

and where $E_1^{(n)}$ means E evaluated at

$$x=h, \; y=y_n(h).$$

This iteration will converge when h is small in all usual cases, and will remove the inaccuracy due to using y_{inter} in place of $y(h)$ in the modified Euler method.

This is just one example of the use of an iteration to improve an estimated value, but it will be enough for us here.

14.5   SUMMARY

Euler's method uses the equations

$$\begin{cases} x_{\text{new}} = x_{\text{old}} + h \\ y_{\text{new}} = y_{\text{old}} + h(dy/dx)_{\text{old}} \end{cases}$$

to step forward a distance h from known values

$$x_{\text{old}}, \; y_{\text{old}}$$

to new values. Solutions derived by this means will have errors up to a *constant times h* in size.

Euler's method is equivalent to estimating integrals by using rectangles based on a left hand function value.

Some differential equations can be converted to integrals, which may then be evaluated by Simpson's rule. This is usually a very accurate method.

The *modified Euler* or *improved Euler* or *trapezium* or *Heun* method uses the equations

$$\begin{cases} y_{\text{inter}} = y_{\text{old}} + h(dy/dx)_{\text{old}} \\ x_{\text{new}} = x_{\text{old}} + h \\ y_{\text{new}} = y_{\text{old}} + \tfrac{1}{2} h\{(dy/dx)_{\text{old}} + (dy/dx)_{\text{inter}}\} \end{cases}$$

where $(dy/dx)_{\text{inter}}$ is evaluated at x_{new} and y_{inter}. The errors will often be as much as a *constant times h^2* in solving a differential equation. This method is equivalent to estimating an integral by the trapezium rule, together with Euler's method to estimate $(dy/dx)_{\text{new}}$.

Better methods either replace the trapezium rule with Simpson's rule (to get Runge–Kutta methods), or improve the estimate of $(dy/dx)_{\text{new}}$ by iteration (to get predictor–corrector methods).

15

Instability and other difficulties

Numerical integration of differential equations is a reasonably simple process to carry out on a computer, apparently to any required accuracy, just by taking h small enough. Unfortunately it is *not* always certain that the numbers you get out of the computer in fact represent the solution you are looking for. In this chapter we look at some awkward cases, for some of which we can produce exact solutions so that we can find why they have gone wrong.

15.1 INSTABILITY OF THE SOLUTION

We saw cases of instability in Chapters 1 and 2, when numerical solutions of difference equations veered sharply away from the expected (correct) solutions: see Section 1.4, Exercise 1E and Exercise 2C for examples. The reason for these instabilities was the inaccurate arithmetic carried out by a computer (numbers are either chopped or rounded to a finite length, whereas some numbers such as $\sqrt{2}, \pi, \frac{1}{3}$ need decimals of infinite length), amplified by solutions like

$$a \times 4^n$$

which can grow without bound, however small a is.

Since there is a close analogy between difference equations and differential equations, you must expect instability in differential equations too, and it will now be shown in two examples.

(a) First example of instability

I took the equation

$$\begin{cases} \dfrac{dy}{dx} = 7y - x \\ y(0) = \frac{1}{49} \end{cases}$$

and solved it numerically on my computer. The figures I found using first Euler's method and then the improved Euler method, both with $h = 0.01$, are shown in the table.

234

x	y (Euler)	Error	y (improved)	Error
1	0.163 265 306 5	-3.28×10^{-10}	0.163 265 306 5	-3.28×10^{-10}
2	0.306 122 731 8	-2.83×10^{-7}	0.306 122 791 6	-3.43×10^{-7}
3	0.449 224 977 0	-2.45×10^{-4}	0.449 353 251 5	-3.74×10^{-4}
4	0.804 761 479 1	-0.2129	0.999 387 386 6	$-0.407 6$
5	185.492	-184.76	445.250	-444.52

The correct answer here, from which the errors were derived, is

$$y = \tfrac{1}{7}x + \tfrac{1}{49}.$$

The trouble here is that the complementary function of the equation is

$$Ae^{7x},$$

and A *should* be exactly zero to match the general solution

$$y = Ae^{7x} + \tfrac{1}{7}x + \tfrac{1}{49}$$

to the condition $y = \tfrac{1}{49}$ at $x = 0$. But there are two possible reasons why A in the numerical solution turns out not to be exactly zero. You can see that the errors are indeed growing roughly like Ae^{7x} for some constant A, because

$$e^7 = 1096.63 \ldots$$

which is roughly the ratio of the errors at successive values of x. One reason is that the Euler and improved Euler methods *introduce* errors into the numbers held in the computer at each step; the Euler error is at most about h^2 in size, the improved Euler error about h^3, at each step. The errors are equivalent to starting with a slightly different value of A at each step, and if $A \neq 0$, the factor e^{7x} soon amplifies the error. The other possible error is that of finite length computer arithmetic: perhaps $\tfrac{1}{7}$ and $\tfrac{1}{49}$, which are infinite decimals, are not used accurately enough in the computer.

In this example the errors are arising through the inadequacies of the numerical methods. I found this out by taking $h = 0.001$ in the improved Euler method; the errors in the numerical solution did not build up, never exceeding 3×10^{-11} in size in a calculation out as far as $x = 15$. In Section 1.4 the error was in the arithmetic done by the computer in calculating fractions as finite decimals, so this sort of error can easily arise also.

This example is unstable according to the kind of definition we had in Chapter 1: if you start with slightly different initial conditions, you get widely different solutions. When I ran the improved Euler method (with $h = 0.001$) for the equation starting from

$$y = \tfrac{1}{49} + 10^{-11},$$

I found that by $x = 5$ I had the solution

$$y = 18\,477.807\,22$$

which is very different from the value

$$y = 0.734\,693\,877\,5$$

found by starting at $y = \frac{1}{49}$.

The effects of the inaccurate method for solving the differential equation can be seen in Fig. 1.

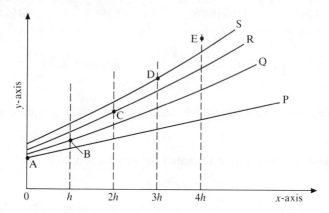

Figure 1. Solution curves through various points

Suppose the correct solution curve through the initial point at A is the curve AP. There will be solution curves (members of the family of solutions) through all points near A also, and some of them are drawn on the figure. Now the Euler or improved Euler method gives you a new point, at $x = h$ and some slightly inaccurate value of y; say this point is B. This is a new starting value, and you ought to follow BQ from here. But again the method is inaccurate, and when $x = 2h$ you find yourself at C, on yet another solution curve CR. So the process goes on, to D and to E. If the solution curves near A are diverging from each other, as in Fig. 1, the values found by the solution method leave the correct curve AP more and more rapidly. This is an unstable case, and it is compounded of two elements:

(i) an inaccurate method of solving the differential equation,
(ii) solution curves which diverge from the correct curve.

If the solution curves are (approximately) parallel to the correct curve AP in the whole region of interest (Fig. 2(a)), then the small inaccuracies in the solution method will not be serious. But if the solution curves diverge far from the correct curve, then small inaccuracies get much amplified (Fig. 2(b)), and the computed results can be badly wrong.

The most serious instabilities are *exponential* ones, where errors grow like

$$ce^{kx}.$$

Even if c is very small, then by the time that $kx = 30$ you have errors of serious size. This was the kind of error in the example above.

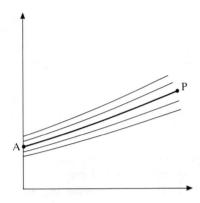

Figure 2(a). An almost parallel family of solution curves

Figure 2(b). A rapidly diverging family of solution curves

(b) A non-linear example

It is too difficult to find a solution formula for the equation

$$\begin{cases} \dfrac{dy}{dx} - 3y = -6\left(\dfrac{x}{\pi}\right)^{1/2} y^{2/3} \\ \quad y(0) = 1. \end{cases}$$

I solved it numerically with the improved Euler method, first with $h=0.1$ then with $h=0.001$.

x	$h=0.1$	$h=0.001$
1	3.867 989	3.767 159 548
2	7.631 592	7.211 725 41
3	12.834 556	11.267 990 40
4	21.526 602	15.861 452 51
5	42.355 900	20.945 353 81
6	121.667 897	26.503 270 02
7	619.660 453	32.577 737 17

This looks like an instability. To check on whether it is, I solved again with $h=0.001$ but with the initial value $y=1+10^{-9}$ at $x=0$.

x	y
1	3.767 159 558
2	7.211 725 449
3	11.267 990 54
4	15.861 452 99
5	20.945 355 40
6	26.503 275 07

I cannot now say much about the errors, because I have no correct solution to calculate the errors from. But you can see the two (approximate) solutions slowly diverging from each other, after starting very close together. This is the easiest way of looking for an instability in such cases – by doing numerical experiments.

The trouble with numerical experiments is the time they take. You may also be left with a feeling that some other numerical experiment might have given a quite different result. There *are* mathematical techniques for discussing the stability of such an equation as this, which may reasonably be started here and left to the Exercise to finish.

The first technique is to ask yourself if you can solve any equations which are 'close' to the one given. In fact there are two equations which you *can* solve, which are in some sense 'a little bigger' and 'a little smaller' than the given one. You *can* solve the equation

$$\begin{cases} \dfrac{dy}{dx} - 3y = -6y^{2/3} \\ \quad y = 1 \quad \text{when } x = 0. \end{cases}$$

This is very close to the equation solved in Section 13.1, and its general solution is

$$y = (Ae^x + 2)^3.$$

The solution satisfying the initial condition is given by

$$A = -1,$$

and after a slow start the solution clearly increases rapidly in size, because of the exponential in it.

The other equation you can try is

$$\frac{dy}{dx} - 3y = -6\left(\frac{x}{\pi}\right)y^{2/3}.$$

The same method of solution will work here. Since $(x/\pi)^{1/2}$ lies between 1 and x/π you can expect the real solution to lie between these two that you *can* find. Since each of them has terms in e^x, you can expect the solution of

$$\frac{dy}{dx} - 3y = -6\left(\frac{x}{\pi}\right)^{1/2} y^{2/3}$$

to have exponentials in it, unless the initial condition is chosen very carefully.

The other technique for examining two solutions which start near each other is to call one of them $y_0(x)$, and the other $y_0(x) + \delta(x)$, where $\delta(x)$ should at least start very small. $y_0(x)$ satisfies (say) the equation

$$\frac{dy}{dx} - 3y = -6\left(\frac{x}{\pi}\right)^{1/2} y^{2/3}, \quad y(0) = 1,$$

and $y_0(x) + \delta(x)$ satisfies the same equation, but the initial condition $y(0) = 1 + \varepsilon$ (with ε very small).

You can then substitute into the equation, and neglect terms such as $\{\delta(x)\}^2$, which will be (at least to start with) extremely small. This gives a linear equation for δ, which can be used to find if it grows from its very small initial value.

Exercise 15A

1   The linear equation

$$\frac{dy}{dx} - xy = -x, \quad y = 1 \quad \text{when } x = 0$$

has exact solution $y = 1$. Determine

(i) by solving the equation
(ii) by numerical experiment

whether this solution is stable.

2   Solve the linear equation

$$\begin{cases} \dfrac{dy}{dx} + 9y \sin x = \sin x \cos x \\ \\ \qquad\qquad y = \tfrac{10}{81} \quad \text{at } x = 0 \end{cases}$$

numerically. Determine whether your solution is stable or unstable by calculating and drawing solution curves through

$$\begin{cases} y = 0.12 \text{ at } x = 0, \\ y = 0.13 \text{ at } x = 0. \end{cases}$$

3   For the non-linear example in Section 15.1(b) there are two numerical solutions using $h = 0.001$

(i) with $y = 1$ at $x = 0$, say $y_0(x)$,
(ii) with $y = 1 + 10^{-9}$ at $x = 0$, say $y_1(x)$.

Calculate the differences

$$|y_0(x) - y_1(x)|$$

for $x = 1, 2, \ldots, 7$, and show that they are growing roughly exponentially.

4   Find the general solution of

$$\frac{dy}{dx} - 3y = -6\left(\frac{x}{\pi}\right) y^{2/3}$$

by the method in Section 13.1.

5   Show that the solution in Section 15.1(b) for $y(0) = 1$ is *not* growing exponentially, by forming a difference table and showing that second differences are approximately constant.

6   Show that $\delta(x)$ in Section 15.1(b) satisfies

$$\frac{d\delta}{dx} \approx \left\{ 3 - 4\left(\frac{x}{\pi}\right)^{1/2} y_0^{-1/3} \right\} \delta.$$

By examining values of the bracketed term (use the computed solution for y_0) show that $\delta(x) \approx A e^{kx}$, with k between 1 and 2.

15.2   INSTABILITY OF THE METHOD

In Chapter 14, in Exercises A and C, you were offered the equation

$$\begin{cases} \dfrac{dy}{dx} = \dfrac{x}{y} - x^2 \\[2mm] y = 1 \quad \text{at } x = 0 \end{cases}$$

to solve. It is quite easy to draw a diagram of the signs of dy/dx in various regions of the x, y plane. I have sketched the result you should have found already in Fig. 3(a), where $dy/dx = 0$ on the curve $y = 1/x$, and where dy/dx is undefined ('infinite') on $y = 0$. The solution curve must have the shape shown in Fig. 3(b), because

(i) $dy/dx = 0$ when $x = 0$ and $y = 1$,
(ii) $dy/dx > 0$ until $y = 1/x$ is reached,
(iii) $dy/dx = 0$ at $y = 1/x$,
(iv) $dy/dx < 0$ thereafter (you cannot cross $y = 1/x$ again, as you would need *both* $dy/dx < 0$ and $dy/dx = 0$ at such a point.

I integrated the equation numerically using the improved Euler method and $h = 0.01$; this is usually quite a good method, and a suitably small value of h for a first attempt at the calculation. My results were very surprising.

x	y
1	1.122 344 302
2	0.584 083 338 9
3	0.337 807 348 4
4	0.251 001 710 4
5	0.200 324 210 2
6	0.166 833 340 4
7	0.402 580 112 1
8	$-46.663\ 624\ 61$

You can see that the solution behaves correctly as far as $x = 5$. It is approaching the curve $y = 1/x$, as it seems reasonable that it should. But between $x = 6$ and $x = 7$ we have dy/dx *positive*, despite Fig. 3(a), and after $x = 7$ the solution jumps across the curve $y = 1/x$ (where it should have $dy/dx = 0$), and thereafter zooms off towards $-\infty$.

This needs explanation. To find out what was happening I collected some more figures, of which the following are a sample.

x_{old}	6.15
y_{old}	0.164 114 461
$(dy/dx)_{\text{old}}$	$-0.261\ 007\ 573$ (from the equation)

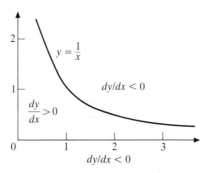

Figure 3(a). Regions of positive and negative slope

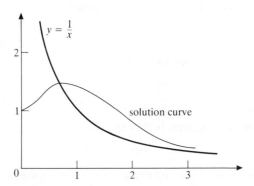

Figure 3(b). The shape of the solution curve

y_{inter}	$0.161\,504\,385\,3$ $(=y_{old}+h\times(dy/dx)_{old})$
$(dy/dx)_{inter}$	$0.283\,521\,320\,6$ (using x_{new} and y_{inter})
y_{new}	$0.164\,390\,678\,3$
x_{new}	6.16

The point

$$(x_{old}, y_{old}) = (6.15, 0.164\,11\ldots)$$

is *above* the curve $y = 1/x$, as it should be. But unfortunately the prediction along the tangent

$$y_{inter} = y_{old} + h(dy/dx)_{old}$$

takes you to

$$(x_{new}, y_{inter}) = (6.16, 0.161\,50\ldots)$$

which is *below* the curve $y = 1/x$, into the region where dy/dx is positive, as in Fig. 4.

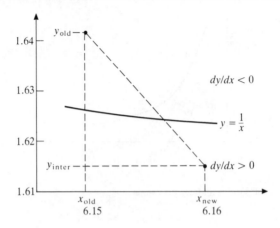

Figure 4. Prediction of y_{inter} from y_{old} and the differential equation

Notice that $(dy/dx)_{old} < 0$ here; but the values of y at $x = 6.14$ and 6.15 are

$$x = 6.14 \qquad y = 0.164\,001\,892\,2$$

$$x = 6.15 \qquad y = 0.164\,114\,461$$

so that the computed 'solution curve' is sloping upwards!

What has gone wrong here is that the point

$$(x_{new}, y_{inter})$$

is nowhere near the true solution curve, and using it causes an increasingly large difference in the values of $(dy/dx)_{old}$ and $(dy/dx)_{inter}$, with the consequence that y_{new} has no relation to the correct solution curve. It is a fault of the method: if you are near a curve where dy/dx changes sign, the Euler prediction along the tangent can give you y_{inter} on the wrong side of that curve.

Reducing h will give some improvement, because you do not then predict so far forward. But eventually the solution curve will get so close to $y = 1/x$ (where dy/dx must be zero) that the problem will reappear. This instability due to the method can only be cured by using a different method, and we shall not attempt that here. Just be warned that any method can go wrong for a suitably chosen equation.

Exercise 15B

1   Compare the three solutions of

$$\frac{dy}{dx} = \frac{x}{y} - x^2$$

(i)   starting at $y = 1.01$,
(ii) starting at $y = 1$,
(iii) starting at $y = 0.99$,

all at $x = 0$. Hence show that the *solution* is not unstable.

2   Use a step length $h=0.001$ to compute the true solution to

$$\frac{dy}{dx} = \frac{x}{y} - x^2, \quad y(0)=1$$

as far as you can.

15.3   CROSSING AN ASYMPTOTE

In Section 11.3 we saw the solution

$$y=\tan(\tfrac{1}{2}x^2+c)$$

to the equation

$$\frac{dy}{dx} = (1+y^2)x.$$

The solution that passed through

$$y=1 \text{ at } x=0$$

had asymptotes at $x=\pm\sqrt{(\tfrac{1}{2}\pi)}$, and there was no solution beyond them.

What happens when we try a numerical solution of this equation? There is nothing in the equation to make you aware that

$$x=\pm 1.253\,314\,1\ldots$$

is a barrier to the computation: you can calculate a value for dy/dx at *any* value of x and y, and step forward to new values for x and y. And this is just what I found when I ran an improved Euler calculation with $h=0.01$.

x	y	Error
1.0	3.407 452 279	$-7.711\,633\times 10^{-4}$
1.1	5.477 909 85	0.005 120 246 1
1.2	15.098 836 16	0.170 307 522 6
1.25	115.081 654 6	125.987 504 9
1.26	694.053 661	—
1.27	294 219.33	—
1.28	7.7394×10^{15}	—
1.29	3.7914×10^{57}	—

The values for y get large as you approach the asymptote, and the slope

$$dy/dx=(1+y^2)x$$

is also very large, but the calculation goes forward perfectly well. Yet the numbers we obtain for $x>\sqrt{(\tfrac{1}{2}\pi)}$ have no relation to the exact solution of the equation, which does not exist in that region.

Two questions arise:

(i)   how can we deduce that the correct solution has an asymptote?
(ii) how can we find the position of the asymptote?

The first question is apparently quite easy to answer: the calculation goes off towards infinity before $x = 1.30$ (my calculator reported an overflow here), so you might well say that there is an asymptote before here. But is it so easy? What about

$$y = e^{x^2}?$$

My computer tells me that at

$$\begin{cases} x = 230 & y = 7.7220 \times 10^{99} \\ x = 231 & \text{overflow.} \end{cases}$$

Yet this function has no asymptote near $x = 230$, or indeed anywhere.
   It is less easy in another way also. The equation

$$\frac{dy}{dx} = \frac{-4xy}{(x^2 - 2)}, \quad y = 1 \quad \text{at } x = 0$$

looks as though it may have an asymptote at $x = \sqrt{2}$; the exact solution (found by separation of the equation) shows that it does. But numerical solution gives the following results (with $h = 0.01$):

x	y	Error
1.40	2 206.279 049	293.721
1.41	16 298.654 72	11 947.938
1.42	− 107 072.039 6	—
1.43	− 89 663.890 6	—
1.44	− 42 162.085 09	—
1.45	− 23 070.663 74	—

There is no overflow here, y gets large, but not outstandingly so.
   As you can see from these examples it is *not* going to be easy to tell from a computed solution that you have passed over an asymptote. But at least you should think that you might have when y becomes enormous, or when dy/dx becomes huge.

Exercise 15C

1   Solve the equation

$$\begin{cases} \dfrac{dy}{dx} = (1 + y^2)x \\ y = 1 \quad \text{at } x = 0 \end{cases}$$

using $h=0.001$ and the improved Euler method, to find at what value of x the computer reports overflow.

2   Solve the equation

$$\begin{cases} \dfrac{dy}{dx} = x + y^2 \\[2mm] y = 1 \quad \text{at } x = 0 \end{cases}$$

as in question 1. By comparing the equation with

(i) $dy/dx = 1 + y^2$,
(ii) $dy/dx = (1 + y^2)x$,

can you prove that there is certainly an asymptote in this case?

3   Explain (by calculating y_{inter} and $(dy/dx)_{inter}$) why y jumps from large positive to large negative in the solution of

$$\frac{dy}{dx} = \frac{-4xy}{(x^2 - 2)}, \quad y(0) = 1.$$

15.4   NON-ASYMPTOTES

The equation

$$\frac{dy}{dx} - \frac{1}{x}y = \frac{x^2}{\sqrt{|1 - x^2|}}$$

looks as though it will give trouble if you integrate it numerically. How can you deal with the point $x = 0$, where the coefficient $\dfrac{1}{x}$ cannot be done numerically? How can you deal with the point $x = 1$, where the right hand side becomes infinite? Are there going to be asymptotes at $x = 0$ and $x = 1$?

In fact this equation can be solved by means of an integrating factor. Deal first with $-1 < x < 1$ by rewriting it as

$$\frac{d}{dx}\left(\frac{1}{x}y\right) = \frac{x}{\sqrt{(1 - x^2)}},$$

and then integrate both sides to get

$$\frac{y}{x} = \tfrac{1}{2}\sqrt{(1 - x^2)} + c.$$

The solution is therefore

$$y = -\tfrac{1}{2}x\sqrt{(1 - x^2)} + cx$$

for $-1 \leqslant x \leqslant 1$, and there is apparently no trouble either at $x = 0$ or $x = \pm 1$. A similar integration can be done for $x > 1$ or $x < 1$ on the equation

$$\frac{d}{dx}\left(\frac{1}{x}y\right) = \frac{x}{\sqrt{(x^2 - 1)}}.$$

to get

$$y = \tfrac{1}{2}x\sqrt{(x^2 - 1)} + cx$$

for $x \geqslant 1$ or $x \leqslant 1$ (I have matched up the values of y at $x = \pm 1$ which is why I have the same value of c everywhere).

A graph of the function y helps to show what we have found, and also one of the numerical problems (Fig. 5).

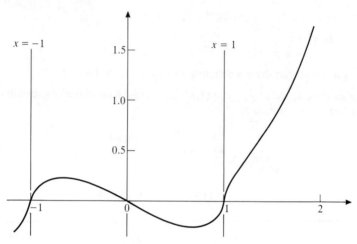

Figure 5. Solution of the equation

The problem is that dy/dx is infinite at $x = \pm 1$, that is, the graph is vertical there. This is likely to cause trouble in any numerical integration which tries to pass through this point.

The resolution of the sort of problem raised here is not easy; in Chapter 16 we shall see a method for dealing with some cases of this sort.

15.5   SUMMARY

The numerical solution of differential equations is *not* always easy. Among the problems that can be encountered are the following.

(i)   *Instability* of the *solution* when small errors grow as you compute to larger values of x. This can be detected by numerical experiment or by analysis of the equation.

(ii) *Instability* of the *method*, when the prediction step in the solution method does not give an appropriate value for the derivative $(dy/dx)_{inter}$. This can be detected by comparing $(dy/dx)_{old}$ and $(dy/dx)_{inter}$.

(iii) *Asymptotes* of the solution curve, leading to very large values of y and dy/dx.

(iv) Points where terms in the equation become *infinite*, so that they cannot be used in computations.

When computing solutions you need to be always alert to the possibility that the numbers generated by your program have nothing to do with the solution of the problem.

16

Taylor and mean value theorems

The last five chapters have been concerned with techniques for doing things. These are all valuable and necessary, but there has to come a time for reviewing the general principles on which these techniques rest. In particular, the likely error in a numerical process has been treated up till now by numerical experiment, and it is time to confirm and explain the results we found experimentally.

Until now we have been concerned mainly with particular functions and particular differential equations. You can compare this with an earlier stage in mathematics: in arithmetic you deal with *particular* numbers, but eventually you move on to doing algebra, when whole *classes* of numbers can be talked about at once. We now have to make the same sort of step in calculus, and move on from individual functions to whole classes of functions.

I can exemplify these two types of approach for you.

Example 1

$$\text{Arithmetic: } 3 \times (5+7) = 15 + 21.$$

$$\text{Algebra: } a \times (b+c) = a \times b + a \times c \text{ for } all \text{ real numbers } a, b, c.$$

Example 2

Number based: the solutions of

$$x^2 - 10x + 9 = 0$$

are

$$x = 9 \quad \text{and} \quad x = 1.$$

Class-of-number based: the solutions of

$$x^2 - 2bx + c = 0$$

are

$$x = b \pm \sqrt{(b^2 - c)}.$$

for all real numbers b and c, and they are real if $b^2 > c$.

Example 3

Particular function based:

$$\frac{d}{dx}(x + \sin 3x) = 1 + 3\cos 3x.$$

Class-of-function based:

$$\frac{d}{dx}(f(x)+g(x))=\frac{df}{dx}+\frac{dg}{dx},$$

for all differentiable functions f and g.

The step we are going to take in this chapter is from *calculus* (about particular functions) to *analysis* (about classes of functions). It is a change of level of abstraction such as has to happen at certain stages in mathematics, and it can be difficult to make. When you find the argument hard to follow, allow yourself to go *back* a stage, and put in some (easy) particular function instead of an anonymous f or g. This can often give you the confidence to go on successfully; it is one of the techniques used by *everyone* in learning new mathematics, so you need not feel that it is a form of cheating, or only necessary for the stupid.

You may also take comfort from the fact that the dose of analysis is not very long, and that the third section of this book is largely a matter of technique again.

16.1   THE MEAN VALUE THEOREM

(a)   A theorem for integrals

Let us start with integration, as it is easy to draw convincing diagrams for it. If I want the area of the strip in Fig. 1, then clearly $hf(a)$ is too little, and $hf(a+h)$ is too much. One gives a rectangle entirely below the curve, and one gives a rectangle with a large part above the curve. That is,

$$hf(a) < A < hf(a+h)$$

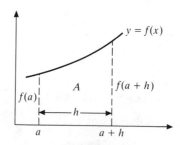

Figure 1. Area of a strip

for an *increasing* function f. Rearrange this as

$$f(a) < A/h < f(a+h).$$

Now if A is the required area, A/h is the height of a rectangle with this area. This height (since it lies between the height at a and the height at $a+h$) must be the height at some point c (say), as in Fig. 2.

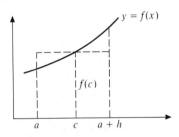

Figure 2. The rectangle of the same area

We now have a 'mean value theorem' for integrals:

$$A = \int_a^{a+h} f(x)\,dx = hf(c)$$

where c lies between a and $a+h$, for smooth increasing functions f.

The argument for a *decreasing* function is of course similar; the argument for a general smooth function f is more complicated, involving the largest and smallest values of f. But the result holds for all such functions:

$$\int_a^{a+h} f(x)\,dx = hf(c)$$

where c is some value between a and $a+h$, for all smooth functions f.

This theorem is of the general kind I described earlier, and it does not tell you the *value* of c, just that it exists. Let us do an example.

$$\int_1^{1.5} \sin x\,dx = \cos 1 - \cos 1.5,$$

and the theorem asserts that there is a value of c such that

$$0.5 \times \sin c = \cos 1 - \cos 1.5.$$

It is easy enough, for this particular function, to find the value of c (approximately), since

$$\sin c = 2(\cos 1 - \cos 1.5)$$

$$\approx 0.939\,130\,208\,4$$

so that

$$c \approx 1.220\,089\,79.$$

This is indeed between 1 and 1.5, and not very surprisingly is close to half-way between.

There are advantages for later work in rewriting the theorem in a slightly different form:

$$\int_a^{a+h} f(x)\,dx = hf(a+\theta h)$$

where $0 < \theta < 1$, for all smooth functions f. (θ is the Greek letter 'theta'.) This says nothing different, it just replaces

$$c \text{ by } a + \theta h$$

and since c lay between a and $a + h$, θ has to have value between 0 and 1.

You may note at this stage that the *method of rectangles* for the approximate evaluation of integrals in Section 10.3 assumed this result, with $\theta \approx \frac{1}{2}$ when h is small. The theorem however, makes no assumption about h being small, and so θ does not have to be nearly equal to $\frac{1}{2}$ in applications of the theorem.

Exercise 16A

1   Find the values of c such that

(i) $\displaystyle\int_0^h x^3\, dx = hc^3$,

(ii) $\displaystyle\int_1^2 e^x\, dx = e^c$.

2   Find the values of θ such that

(i) $\displaystyle\int_1^{1.2} \cos x\, dx = 0.2\cos(1 + 0.2\theta)$,

(ii) $\displaystyle\int_1^{1+h} e^{-x}\, dx = he^{-(1+\theta h)}$.

3   Show, by integrating $\cos x$ suitably, that

$$\frac{\sin(a+h) - \sin a}{h} = \cos(a + \theta h)$$

for some value of θ between 0 and 1. Use the approximation

$$\sin x \approx x$$

for small values of x, and also the formula for

$$\sin A - \sin B,$$

to show that $\theta \approx \frac{1}{2}$ when h is small.

(b)   The geometry of curves

When we were trying to solve differential equations approximately with Euler's method, we predicted forward along the tangent at $x = a$, as in Fig. 3(a). This gives too low a result, in the case illustrated, for the value of the function at $x = a + h$. On the other hand, if we could have used the slope of the tangent at $x = a + h$ for our prediction here, we would have got too high a result for our estimate of $f(a+h)$, as in Fig. 3(b). There must be some slope in between those of the two tangents which will get you to the correct value at $x = a + h$, and moreover this must be the slope of the curve at some point (Fig. 4), say at $x = c$.

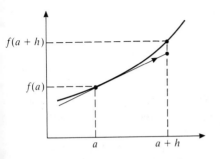

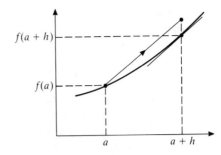

Figure 3(a). Prediction using the slope of the tangent at $x=a$

Figure 3(b). Prediction using the slope of the tangent at $x=a+h$

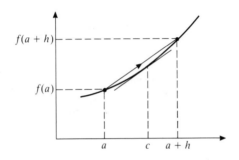

Figure 4. Correct prediction using an intermediate slope

When we translate this statement into symbols we get

$$f(a+h)=f(a)+hf'(c)$$

for smooth increasing functions f and for some c between a and $a+h$. In words again: to predict correctly from a to $a+h$ we need to use the slope of the curve at some intermediate point c. This is a 'mean value theorem', but not quite in the final form that you should remember.

As before, the argument for a *decreasing* smooth function is similar and the argument for a more general smooth function is more complicated. I shall show you an example of how an argument can be constructed for more general cases. Consider Fig. 5, and suppose I want a formula

$$f(a+h)=f(a)+hm,$$

where m is the slope of the *chord* between the points on the curve at $x=a$ and $x=a+h$.

You can see in Fig. 5 that there are *two* values c_1 and c_2 for which

$$f(a+h)=f(a)+hf'(c).$$

The general argument, which does not rely on a particular diagram, must be along these lines.

(i)   There is a greatest slope, say S, for the (graph of the) function between a and $a+h$. Similarly there is a least slope, say s. This depends on the function f being smooth.
(ii)   To get from a to $a+h$ on the curve you need some slope in between s and S. With s you would certainly finish too low, as some parts of the curve have greater slope than s; and with S you would similarly end too high.
(iii) The slope of the curve takes all values between s and S, if the function f is properly smooth (technically, having continuous derivative f').
(iv)   Hence m is the value of $f'(x)$ at some point c between a and $a+h$ (and perhaps at more than one point, as in Fig. 5).

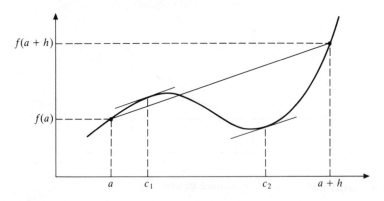

Figure 5. A case with two tangents parallel to the chord from $x=a$ to $x=a+h$

This completes an outline of the proof of the Mean Value Theorem:

$$f(a+h)=f(a)+hf'(c)$$

for any smooth function f and for at least one point c between a and $a+h$. As before, the theorem will sometimes be written as

$$f(a+h)=f(a)+hf'(a+\theta h)$$

for some θ between 0 and 1 and for smooth functions f.

I should point out that this does not count as a *proper* proof in Pure Mathematics, because the word 'smooth' has not been thoroughly defined, and because there has been a reliance on diagrams (which must always be particular) to discuss general statements.

When you take most examples, the result of the theorem becomes rather trivial. Let us take a slightly complicated one,

$$\begin{cases} f(x)=x\sin 4x, \\ a=\dfrac{\pi}{12},\ h=\dfrac{2\pi}{3}. \end{cases}$$

In this case

$$f'(x) = \sin 4x + 4x \cos 4x$$

and the theorem asserts that the equation

$$\frac{3\pi}{4} \sin 3\pi = \frac{\pi}{12} \sin \frac{\pi}{3} + \frac{2\pi}{3} \{\sin 4c + 4c \cos 4c\}$$

has at least one solution for c. That is, the equation

$$\sin 4c + 4c \cos 4c + \tfrac{1}{16}\sqrt{3} = 0$$

has at least one solution for c. I confirmed that this was the case by using my graphics calculator to find roots of the equation at

$$c \approx 0.5, \; c \approx 1.2, \; c \approx 2.0,$$

all of which are between

$$a = \frac{\pi}{12} \quad \text{and} \quad a + h = \frac{3\pi}{4}.$$

Alternatively, I could have plotted

$$y = x \sin 4x$$

and looked for tangents parallel to the chord joining

$$x = \frac{\pi}{12} \quad \text{and} \quad x = \frac{3\pi}{4}.$$

on the curve (Fig. 6), to confirm the figures.

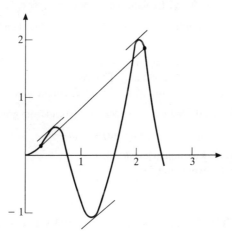

Figure 6. A chord on $y = x \sin 4x$ and three tangents parallel to it

Most of the particular results that you can derive from the Mean Value Theorem, such as the existence of a solution to the equation above, can be found much more easily in other ways, for example by using graphics or computer solutions. However, we shall need the Mean Value Theorem for theoretical results, which apply to all smooth functions.

Exercise 16B

1   (i) Take $f(x) = x^2$. Show that

$$f(a+h) = f(a) + hf'(a + \tfrac{1}{2}h)$$

for any values of a and h.
(ii) Repeat (i) for $f(x) = px^2 + qx + r$.

2   Find the values of c such that

(i) $e^2 - e = e^c$,
(ii) $\tan\tfrac{1}{3}\pi - \tan\tfrac{1}{4}\pi = \tfrac{1}{12}\pi\sec^2 c$.

Relate your answers to Mean Value Theorem statements.

3   Show that

$$e^{a+\theta h} = \frac{e^{a+h} - e^a}{h}$$

for some θ between 0 and 1.
Use the standard approximation

$$e^x \approx 1 + x + \tfrac{1}{2}x^2$$

when x is small to show that $\theta \approx \tfrac{1}{2}$ when h is small.

4   Show that the Mean Value Theorem does *not* give a true statement if it is applied to $f(x) = |x|$ with $a = -\tfrac{1}{2}$, $h = \tfrac{3}{4}$. Explain why it does not.

5   Rolle's theorem states that if f is smooth and if $f(a) = f(b)$, then for some c between a and b, $f'(c) = 0$.

(i) Draw a diagram illustrating this theorem.
(ii) Prove it by using the Mean Value Theorem.
(iii) Prove it in the way that the Mean Value Theorem was proved.

6   Take $g(x) = \sqrt{x}$ for $x \geqslant 0$. Deduce from question 1(i) and from graphs of x^2 and $\sqrt{x}$ that

$$g(a+h) = g(a) + hg'(a + \theta h)$$

where $\theta < \tfrac{1}{2}$. You may assume $a \geqslant 0$, $h > 0$.
Find an algebraic expression for θ.

(c)   The Mean Value Theorem by integration

When the functions involved are smooth it is easy and useful to relate the two mean value theorems, one for integration and one involving differentiation.
   Take a function F, and suppose that

$$F(x) = df/dx.$$

Then we may integrate to get

$$\int_a^{a+h} F(x)\,dx = \int_a^{a+h} \frac{df}{dx}\,dx$$

$$= f(a+h) - f(a).$$

But the mean value theorem for integrals gives

$$\int_a^{a+h} F(x)\,dx = F(a+\theta h), \quad 0<\theta<1,$$

and the equation $F(x) = f'(x)$ allows us to write

$$F(a+\theta h) = f'(a+\theta h).$$

So finally we have

$$f'(a+\theta h) = f(a+h) - f(a), \quad 0<\theta<1,$$

which is the Mean Value Theorem for f.

This looks like an easier proof of the Mean Value Theorem, but it has two disadvantages.

(i) It hides the geometrical meaning of the Mean Value Theorem.

(ii) The technical conditions on the function f are slightly more restrictive.

However, its advantage is that we shall find it much easier to generalize the Mean Value Theorem by a method involving integration, in Section 16.3.

16.2   NEWTON–RAPHSON ITERATION

Newton–Raphson iteration is usually derived from a diagram (Fig. 7).

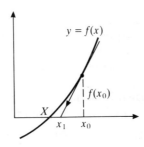

Figure 7. Improvement of an approximate root by using the tangent

If you have the equation $f(x) = 0$ to solve, and x_0 is a starting approximation, then an improved approximation is (usually) found by going backwards along the tangent at x_0:

$$x_1 = x_0 - f(x_0)/f'(x_0),$$

from the geometry of the triangle in Fig. 7. This is converted into an iteration by writing

$$x_{n+1} = x_n - \frac{f(x_n)}{f'(x_n)}, \quad n = 0, 1, 2, \ldots$$

This is a very commonly used and efficient iteration, usually giving rapid convergence to the root X. Take as example the solution of the equation

$$x^4 = e^x.$$

Rewrite it as

$$x^4 - e^x = 0$$

so that here

$$\begin{cases} f(x) = x^4 - e^x \\ f'(x) = 4x^3 - e^x \end{cases}$$

and the iteration formula becomes

$$x_{n+1} = x_n - \frac{x_n^4 - e^{x_n}}{4x_n^3 - e^{x_n}}.$$

I decided to start with $x_0 = 2$ (rather a poor guess), and a short computer program gave me the following:

n	x_n	Error ε_n
0	2.0	0.570 388 175
1	1.650 117 284	−0.220 505 459
2	1.477 256 490	−0.047 644 644 92
3	1.432 453 483	−0.002 841 658 27
4	1.429 622 711	−1.008 605 × 10^{-5}
5	1.429 611 825	−1.6 × 10^{-10}
6	1.429 611 825	1 × 10^{-11}
7	1.429 611 825	0

The errors here are calculated from the computer value for x_7.

If you calculate $|\varepsilon_{n+1}/\varepsilon_n^2|$, $n = 0, 1, 2, 3, 4$ you find the sequence of values

$$0.678, \ 0.980, \ 1.252, \ 1.348, \ 1.350$$

(all to four decimal places). This sequence appears to be tending to some value near 1.35. That is

$$|\varepsilon_{n+1}/\varepsilon_n^2| \to K,$$

so that this is not the *linear* convergence we observed in earlier iterations (in section 4.4). There we had

$$|\varepsilon_{n+1}/\varepsilon_n| \to K,$$

and here we have

$$|\varepsilon_{n+1}/\varepsilon_n^2| \to K,$$

so we call this *quadratic* (or second order) convergence.

Notice that you must not use Aitken's acceleration technique on this iteration, because it is not a linear convergence. But then there is no need to anyway, because it is converging so fast.

In the next chapter we shall analyse the Newton–Raphson process in detail. For that it will be useful to see a derivation of this iteration from the Mean Value Theorem.

Suppose we want to find the value X that makes $f(X)=0$. Suppose that we guess that x_0 is near to the correct value. Since it is not correct we have

$$x_0 = X + h$$

where $-h$ is the error. Now use the Mean Value Theorem:

$$f(x_0) = f(X+h)$$
$$= f(X) + hf'(X + \theta h)$$

with $0 < \theta < 1$. But $f(X)=0$ since X is the actual solution, and so

$$h = \frac{f(x_0)}{f'(X + \theta h)}$$

(provided the derivative is not zero). Now

$$X + \theta h$$

lies between X and x_0, so that we can *estimate* $f'(x + \theta h)$ by $f'(x_0)$. This gives

$$h \approx \frac{f(x_0)}{f'(x_0)}$$

which leads to the Newton–Raphson estimate

$$X \approx x_0 - \frac{f(x_0)}{f'(x_0)}.$$

In the next chapter we shall see how to convert these estimates to more exact statements.

Exercise 16C

1   Apply Newton–Raphson iteration to the solution of

$$x^4 + x^3 - 1 = 0$$

using $x_0 = 0.8$. Compare the number of iterations to the number used for this equation in Section 4.2.

Is the convergence of the Newton–Raphson iteration quadratic in this case?

2   Use the Newton–Raphson technique on the equation

$$x^5 + 3x^4 - 4x^3 - 12x^2 + 4x + 12 = 0$$

starting with

(i) $x_0 = 2$ (ii) $x_0 = 1$ (iii) $x_0 = 0$
(iv) $x_0 = -2.55$ (v) $x_0 = -2.65$.

Do you get quadratic convergence? Relate your answers to the graph of the function.

3   Use the Newton–Raphson iteration on the equation

$$\sqrt{(1 + \cos x)} = 0$$

starting with $x_0 = 0.5$. Is the iteration quadratically convergent? Explain your answer.

4   Repeat question 3 on the equation

$$(1 + \cos x)^{1/4} = 0.$$

5   Consider the following two iteration schemes on

$$x^4 + x^3 - 1 = 0, \quad x_0 = 0.8:$$

(i)   Newton–Raphson.
(ii) Two iterations of $x_{n+1} = (x_n + 1)^{-1/3}$ followed by one Aitken acceleration, all done twice.
Which is more efficient?

16.3   TAYLOR'S THEOREM

(a)   A theorem for integrals

I am going to work in much the same way as in Section 16.1(a) to produce a 'higher mean value theorem' for integrals. Then I can use the method of Section 16.1(c) to produce a similar theorem involving differentiation.

In Fig. 8, instead of using a rectangle, I shall use a trapezium which has the

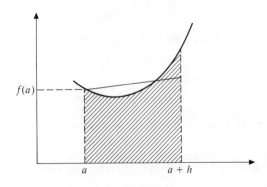

Figure 8. Area under a curve and a trapezium of the same area

same area as the strip under the curve. The trapezium I have chosen to use has one corner at the point

$$(a, f(a))$$

on the curve, and its upper line slopes at such an angle that it has the required area. I now assert that the slope of this line lies between the smallest slope of the curve between a and $a+h$, and the largest slope of the curve in that interval. If the slope of the curve changes smoothly we must have

$$\text{slope of line} = f'(c),$$

which is the slope of the curve at some point c between a and $a+h$. This now gives me

$$A = hf(a) + \tfrac{1}{2}h^2 f'(c)$$

for the area of the trapezium (the height at its right end is $f(a) + hf'(c)$). Since this is also the area of the strip, I have shown that

$$\int_a^{a+h} f(x)\,dx = hf(a) + \tfrac{1}{2}h^2 f'(c)$$

for some value of c between a and $a+h$, and for all smooth functions f. This is my higher mean value theorem for integrals. Of course it may also be written as

$$\int_a^{a+h} f(x)\,dx = hf(a) + \tfrac{1}{2}h^2 f'(a+\theta h)$$

for some θ between 0 and 1.

(b)   The corresponding theorem for derivatives

Rewrite the previous theorem for the smooth function F:

$$\int_a^{a+h} F(x)\,dx = hF(a) + \tfrac{1}{2}h^2 F'(a+\theta h)$$

with $0 < \theta < 1$, and take F so that

$$F(x) = df/dx.$$

The left hand side then integrates as

$$f(a+h) - f(a)$$

and the right hand side is

$$hf'(a) + \tfrac{1}{2}h^2 f''(a+\theta h).$$

Thus we have shown that

$$f(a+h) = f(a) + hf'(a) + \tfrac{1}{2}h^2 f''(a+\theta h)$$

for some θ between 0 and 1 and for functions which are smooth (technically, the second derivative of f must be continuous for all the arguments to work).

Exercise 16D

1 Let $f(x)=x^3$. Find the appropriate values of θ in

(i) $\displaystyle\int_0^1 f(x)\,dx = f(0) + \tfrac{1}{2}f'(\theta)$,

(ii) $f(1+x) = f(1) + xf'(1) + \tfrac{1}{2}x^2 f''(1+\theta x)$.

2 Use the Second Mean Value Theorem (for integrals) on

$$\int_1^{1+x} \frac{1}{t}\,dt$$

to write down a formula for $\ln(1+x)$. If $|x| < 10^{-3}$, find the maximum possible error in the approximation

$$\ln(1+x) \approx x.$$

3 Use the Second Mean Value Theorem (for derivatives) on

$$f(X+h)$$

to estimate the error in x_1, after a single Newton–Raphson iteration from $x_0 = X+h$.

4 Use a mean value theorem on $\displaystyle\int_a^{a+h} \cos x\,dx$ to show that

$$\frac{\sin(a+h) - \sin a}{h^2} - \frac{\cos a}{h} = -\frac{1}{2}\sin(a+\theta h),$$

for some θ between 0 and 1. Use the approximation $\sin x \approx x$ and trigonometric formulas to find the value of θ in this formula when h is very small.

5 Derive the Mean Value Theorem:

$$\int_a^{a+h} f(x)\,dx = hf(a) + \frac{1}{2}h^2 f'(a) + \frac{1}{6}h^3 f''(a+\theta h),$$

with $0 < \theta < 1$, by arguing about a quadratic curve with slope $f'(a)$ through the point $(a,f(a))$ on an area diagram. Show also that

$$f(a+h) = f(a) + hf'(a) + \tfrac{1}{2}h^2 f''(a) + \tfrac{1}{6}h^3 f'''(a+\theta h).$$

(c)   The full Taylor theorem

The theorems found in Sections 16.1 and 16.3, and the extension in question 5 of Exercise 16D, suggest that there ought to be a generalisation. There is, and it is *Taylor's theorem*:

$$f(a+h) = f(a) + hf'(a) + \ldots + \frac{1}{n!}h^n f^{(n)}(a) + \frac{1}{(n+1)!}h^{n+1} f^{(n+1)}(a+\theta h).$$

In this theorem θ is some number between 0 and 1 (whose value we shall usually not know, and which will depend on what function f is being used, what value a, and what order or degree n is in question). The function f has to be very smooth – having a continuous $(n+1)$th derivative will do. The notation

$$f^{(n)}(a)=\left(\frac{d^n f}{dx^n}\right)_{x=a}$$

is used for the nth derivative of the function f at $x=a$.

A proof of Taylor's theorem can be constructed along the lines used for the earlier special cases $n=0$ (the Mean Value Theorem), $n=1$ (in Section 16.3) and $n=2$ (in Exercise 16D); but it will not be as intuitively appealing as those special cases. The two standard proofs of Taylor's theorem, one using polynomials and the other using integration by parts, are outlined in Section 16.5; read and work through them if you wish.

Taylor's theorem gets written, and used, in various different forms; it is such a widely used theorem that you should be used to common variants. For example, the following are often seen.

(i) $$f(x+a)=f(a)+xf'(a)+ \ldots +\frac{x^n}{n!}f^{(n)}(a)+R_{n+1}$$

where R_{n+1} is the remainder after $n+1$ terms,

$$R_{n+1}=\frac{x^{n+1}}{(n+1)!}f^{(n+1)}(a+\theta x).$$

This formulation emphasises that $f(x+a)$ is in some sense rather like a polynomial.

(ii)   There is an alternative form

$$R_{n+1}=\int_a^{a+x}\frac{(a+x-t)^n}{n!}f^{(n+1)}(t)\,dt$$

for the remainder which is sometimes useful.

(iii) $$f(x)=f(a)+(x-a)f'(a)+ \ldots +\frac{(x-a)^n}{n!}f^{(n)}(a)+S_{n+1}$$

where

$$S_{n+1}=\frac{(x-a)^{n+1}}{(n+1)!}f^{(n+1)}(a+\theta x-\theta a).$$

This is just a rearrangement of the formula in (i).

(iv) $$f(x)=f(0)+xf'(0)+ \ldots +\frac{x^n}{n!}f^{(n)}(0)+T_{n+1}$$

with

$$T_{n+1}=\frac{x^{n+1}}{(n+1)!}f^{(n+1)}(\theta x).$$

This is often called Taylor's theorem, of which it is a special case; it is equally often called Maclaurin's theorem.

(v)   Remainder terms are often written differently, for example as

$$R_{n+1} = \frac{x^{n+1}}{(n+1)!}f^{(n+1)}(\xi)$$

where ξ is a number between a and $a+x$. (This is the Greek letter 'xi'.)

(d)   Theorem, approximation, series

Taylor's theorem is an exact statement (for smooth enough functions) in which we do not know the value of θ. Taylor's name also gets applied to

Taylor's (polynomial) approximation

which is

$$f(a+h) \approx f(a) + hf'(a) + \ldots + \frac{1}{n!}h^n f^{(n)}(a).$$

This is a useful approximation if the remainder term

$$\frac{1}{(n+1)!}h^{n+1}f^{(n+1)}(a+\theta h)$$

is very small in size. In numerical calculations where h may typically have size 10^{-2} or 10^{-3} this will clearly be true if n is as small as 3 or 4, unless f has very large values for its higher derivatives.

You will also meet

Taylor series,

of the form

$$f(a+h) = f(a) + hf'(a) + \tfrac{1}{2}h^2 f''(a) + \ldots$$

This is an *infinite* series, and the two sides are equal, once you have decided what this means in the context of adding up an infinite set of numbers. Taylor series are a most important part of Pure Mathematics, and you should read (for example) *Extensions of Calculus* in this series, for more information.

For the purposes of this book we shall usually need Taylor's approximation, with an estimate of the largest possible size of the remainder term.

Exercise 16E

1   Find the general Taylor theorems for

(i) $\ln(1+x)$,
(ii) e^x,
(iii) $(1+x)^k$.

2   Estimate the largest error in using a Taylor approximation of degree 4 for

(i) $\ln(1+x)$,
(ii) e^x,
(iii) $(1+x)^k$,

when $|x| < 0.1$.

3 Show that

$$f(a+h)-f(a-h)\approx 2hf'(a)+\tfrac{1}{3}h^3f'''(a),$$

and that

$$f(a+h)-2f(a)+f(a-h)\approx h^2f''(a)+\tfrac{1}{12}h^4f^{(4)}(a).$$

4 For the function $f(x)=x^{11/3}$ use Taylor's theorem to show that

$$x^{11/3}=\frac{1}{3!}x^3\frac{440}{27}(\theta x)^{2/3}.$$

Deduce the value of θ in this case.

Does $x^{11/3}$ have any higher order Taylor theorem forms? Explain your answer.

5 In question 1 find the values of x for which the remainder terms become vanishingly small as n increases.

16.4 TAYLOR'S THEOREM AND DIFFERENTIAL EQUATIONS

(a) Polynomial approximations

Taylor's approximation essentially says that any smooth function can be approximated by a polynomial, whose coefficients happen to be derivatives of the function at some chosen point; for example

$$f(x)\approx f(a)+(x-a)f'(a)+\tfrac{1}{2}(x-a)^2f''(a),$$

or

$$f(x)\approx f(0)+xf'(0)+\tfrac{1}{2}x^2f''(0)+\tfrac{1}{6}x^3f'''(0).$$

A method of investigating the *local* behaviour of a differential equation can be based on this idea.

For example, consider the equation

$$\frac{dy}{dx}=\frac{y^2}{x^2}-x,\quad\text{with }y=0\text{ when }x=0,$$

which I cannot solve numerically because of the $1/x^2$ term at $x=0$. Assume that there is a reasonable solution, and use as its Taylor approximation

$$y\approx a+bx+cx^2+dx^3.$$

Here b, c, d are the (unknown) derivatives of y at $x=0$, divided by an appropriate factorial:

$$\begin{cases} b=(dy/dx)_{x=0} \\ c=\tfrac{1}{2}(d^2y/dx^2)_{x=0} \\ d=\tfrac{1}{6}(d^3y/dx^3)_{x=0}. \end{cases}$$

The constant a is just the value of y at $x=0$, which is given to be zero in this case.

What we do here is substitute the polynomial approximation

$$bx + cx^2 + dx^3$$

into the equation, and get

$$b + 2cx + 3dx^2 \approx (b + cx + dx^2)^2 - x.$$

This can be rewritten as

$$(b - b^2) + (2c - 2bc + 1)x + (3d - 2bd - c^2)x^2 \approx 0.$$

I cannot go on and include terms in x^3, because some of them would come from terms I have missed out in my original approximation (see Exercise 16F, where a longer approximation is used). Now this has to be true for lots of values of x – we are not trying to find one or two values of x for which the left hand side is zero, we seek instead values of b, c, d for which the left hand side is zero for *all* values of x in some interval. So the method is now to solve

$$\begin{cases} b - b^2 = 0 \\ 2c - 2bc + 1 = 0 \\ 3d - 2bd - c^2 = 0. \end{cases}$$

This gives

$$b = 0, \quad c = -\tfrac{1}{2}, \quad d = \tfrac{1}{12}.$$

So I have an approximation

$$y \approx -\tfrac{1}{2}x^2 + \tfrac{1}{12}x^3,$$

which ought to be useful for small values of $|x|$, where the original Taylor approximation should be satisfactory. For example, if

$$|x| \leqslant 10^{-3}$$

then terms in $x^4/4!$ should be quite small enough to neglect. Thus this approximate solution gives you the value

$$y = -4.999\,166 \times 10^{-7} \quad \text{at} \quad x = 1 \times 10^{-3},$$

as a *new* initial condition. Thereafter I can find a numerical solution by standard methods.

This method provides a possible way round some of the problems raised in an example in Section 15.4. However, it assumes that y is a smooth function, so it cannot deal with the problems in that example at $x = \pm 1$, because there y was *not* smooth, its derivative was infinite.

Let us look at another example, for which both a numerical solution and a solution formula are available to check the working. Consider the equation

$$\frac{dy}{dx} - xy^2 - y = 0, \quad y = 1 \text{ at } x = 0.$$

Attempt a solution near $x=0$ with

$$y=a+bx+cx^2+dx^3.$$

Substitute into the equation, after observing that $a=1$ is needed to give $y=1$ at $x=0$:

$$b+2cx+3dx^2-x(1+bx+cx^2+dx^3)^2-(1+bx+cx^2+dx^3)\approx0.$$

Rewrite this as

$$(b-1)+(2c-1-b)x+(3d-2b-c)x^2\approx0,$$

keeping no higher terms because the highest power that is common to all of dy/dx, xy^2 and y is the second power. Make this true by taking

$$b=1,\ c=1,\ d=1.$$

Thus the approximate solution near $x=0$ is

$$y\approx1+x+x^2+x^3.$$

The exact solution can be found by using the substitution

$$y=\frac{1}{z},\ \frac{dy}{dx}=-\frac{1}{z^2}\frac{dz}{dx},$$

which gives the linear equation

$$\frac{dz}{dx}+z=-x.$$

The solution of this is $z=Ae^{-x}-x+1$, and using the initial condition gives

$$y=\frac{1}{1-x}.$$

This gives 10 significant figure agreement with the approximate solution at $x=0.01$.

(b)   Improved prediction formulas

Euler's method for solving a differential equation numerically in effect used

$$f(a+h)\approx f(a)+hf'(a);$$

that is, it used

$$y_{new}=y_{old}+h(dy/dx)_{old}.$$

Thus it is based on the first order Taylor approximation. Could we not do better by using a second order Taylor approximation? This would be

$$f(a+h)\approx f(a)+hf'(a)+\tfrac{1}{2}h^2f''(a),$$

and would lead to the method

$$y_{\text{new}} = y_{\text{old}} + h(dy/dx)_{\text{old}} + \tfrac{1}{2}h^2(d^2y/dx^2)_{\text{old}}.$$

This certainly *ought* to be better, because the second derivative makes allowance for the curvature of the solution.

In order to implement this method we need to have a formula for d^2y/dx^2, and this can often be derived by differentiating the differential equation.

Take as example the equation

$$\frac{dy}{dx} = x - y^3 \text{ with } y = 0 \text{ when } x = 0,$$

which was solved numerically by Euler's method in Section 14.1(e). The formula I shall use for d^2y/dx^2 is

$$\frac{d^2y}{dx^2} = 1 - 3y^2\frac{dy}{dx}$$

$$= 1 - 3y^2(x - y^3)$$

from the differential equation. This allows me to calculate d^2y/dx^2 at each step. The results from using this *second order* Euler method are as follows:

x	y	
	$h=0.1$	$h=0.01$
1	0.484 068	0.483 196
2	1.179 669	1.179 734
3	1.413 408	1.413 473
4	1.568 787	1.568 793
5	1.696 437	1.696 439
6	1.806 623	1.806 624

The results are given to 6 decimal places. You can see by comparing them with the earlier values that the figures derived here using $h=0.1$ are better than the figures from the simple Euler method with $h=0.01$. And the values from the second order method and $h=0.01$ can be compared with a set of figures from the modified Euler (or trapezoidal) method using $h=0.01$:

x	1	2	3	4	5	6
y	0.483 184	1.179 719	1.413 471	1.568 792	1.696 439	1.806 624

This second order Euler method appears to be giving errors of size around h^2, the same as the modified Euler (or trapezoidal) method. So why not use it all the time? The main reason is that the formula for d^2y/dx^2 can be rather involved, which makes the computer take longer to run the program.

Now if you wished, you could construct a third order Euler solution method, using values of d^3y/dx^3 calculated using the differential equation. You might even consider constructing a second order improved Euler method. Most people do not in fact go along this route to seek more accuracy, but use Runge–Kutta methods (or ones similar to them), as described in Section 14.4

Exercise 16F

1   Solve the equation

$$\frac{dy}{dx} = x - \frac{y^3}{x}, \quad y = 0 \text{ at } x = 0$$

for small values of x by using a cubic polynomial.

2   Use the polynomial approximation

$$y \approx bx + cx^2 + dx^3 + ex^4$$

in the equation

$$\frac{dy}{dx} = \frac{y^2}{x^2} - x, \quad y(0) = 0$$

to find a solution valid for small values of x. How many correct decimal places do you expect to get at $x = \frac{1}{4}$?

3   Start a numerical solution of

$$\begin{cases} \dfrac{dy}{dx} = \dfrac{y^2}{x} + 1 \\ y = 0 \quad \text{at } x = 0 \end{cases}$$

by using a Taylor approximation based on $x = 0$.

4   Does the second order Euler method improve the solution found in Section 15.2 for

$$\frac{dy}{dx} = \frac{x}{y} - x^2, \quad y(0) = 1?$$

16.5   PROOF OF TAYLOR'S THEOREM

(a)   Proof using integrals

(i) We start with a general result on integrals. The change of variables

$$t = 2a + h - X$$

shows that

$$\int_a^{a+h} F(t) \, dt = \int_a^{a+h} F(2a + h - X) \, dX.$$

You can easily verify the meaning of this for particular functions such as

$$\begin{cases} F(t) = \sin t, \\ F(t) = e^t. \end{cases}$$

(ii) Start from the simple statement that

$$\int_a^{a+h} \frac{df}{dt}\, dt = f(a+h) - f(a),$$

and rewrite it as

$$f(a+h) = f(a) + \int_a^{a+h} f'(t)\, dt.$$

Now use the result from (1) above, with F put equal to f':

$$f(a+h) = f(a) + \int_a^{a+h} f'(2a+h-X)\, dX.$$

In this integral it is convenient to make the change of variables

$$x = X - a,$$

which gives us

$$f(a+h) = f(a) + \int_0^h f'(a+h-x)\, dx.$$

From now on we shall proceed by integrating by parts repeatedly, with the parts for the initial move being 1 and $f'(a+h-x)$. Thus

$$f(a+h) = f(a) + [xf'(a+h-x)]_0^h + \int_0^h xf''(a+h-x)\, dx$$

$$= f(a) + hf'(a) + [\tfrac{1}{2}x^2 f''(a+h-x)]_0^h$$

$$+ \int_0^h \tfrac{1}{2}x^2 f'''(a+h-x)\, dx$$

$$= \dots \text{ (carry on integrating by parts)}$$

$$= f(a) + hf'(a) + \dots + \frac{1}{n!}h^n f^{(n)}(a) + R_n,$$

where $R_n = \int_0^h \frac{x^n}{n!} f^{(n+1)}(a+h-x)\, dx.$

This is Taylor's theorem, with the remainder expressed in an integral form.

(iii) The integral form of the remainder can be converted to a derivative form without too much trouble. Suppose that $f^{(n+1)}$ is a continuous (and positive, for simplicity), with values between (say) m and M in the interval $[0, h]$. Then

$$m \int_0^h \frac{x^n}{n!}\, dx < \int_0^h \frac{x^n}{n!} f^{(n+1)}(a+h-x)\, dx < M \int_0^h \frac{x^n}{n!}\, dx.$$

That is

$$m < \frac{\displaystyle\int_0^h \frac{x^n}{n!} f^{(n+1)}(a+h-x)\,dx}{h^{n+1}/(n+1)!} < M.$$

Now *any* value between m and M is the value of $f^{(n+1)}(a+h-x)$ for *some* x, say $x = \alpha h$ with $0 < \alpha < 1$. Thus

$$\int_0^h \frac{x^n}{n!} f^{(n+1)}(a+h-x)\,dx = \frac{h^{n+1}}{(n+1)!} f^{(n+1)}(a+h-\alpha h)$$

$$= \frac{h^{n+1}}{(n+1)!} f^{(n+1)}(a+\theta h)$$

with $0 < \theta < 1$, by putting $\theta = 1 - \alpha$.

(b)   Proof using polynomials

(i) Consider the function

$$g(x) = f(x) - f(a) - \frac{x-a}{h}\{f(a+h) - f(a)\}.$$

Then it is easy to check that

$$g(a) = 0 \quad \text{and} \quad g(a+h) = 0.$$

Hence by Rolle's theorem (which can be proved from first principles) there is a value of x between a and $a+h$, say $a + \theta h$, such that

$$g'(a+\theta h) = 0.$$

Now

$$g'(x) = f'(x) - \frac{1}{h}\{f(a+h) - f(a)\}$$

and so we have that

$$0 = f'(a+\theta h) - \frac{1}{h}\{f(a+h) - f(a)\}.$$

This is the Mean Value Theorem.

(ii) You can proceed along a similar route with

$$G(x) = f(x) - f(a) - (x-a)f'(a)$$

$$- \frac{(x-a)^2}{h^2}\{f(a+h) - f(a) - hf'(a)\}$$

for which

$$G(a) = 0, \ G(a+h) = 0, \ G'(a) = 0.$$

The first two of these show that there is a θ_1 such that (by Rolle's theorem)

$$G'(a+\theta_1 h)=0.$$

Then take this with $G'(a)=0$ and use Rolle's theorem again to find

$$G''(a+\theta_2 h)=0,$$

where $0<\theta_2<\theta_1<1$. But, working as before,

$$G'(x)=f'(x)-f'(a)-\frac{2(x-a)}{h^2}\{f(a+h)-f(a)-hf'(a)\},$$

and so

$$G''(x)=f''(x)-\frac{2}{h^2}\{f(a+h)-f(a)-hf'(a)\}.$$

Now put $x=a+\theta_2 h$ to obtain

$$f(a+h)=f(a)+hf'(a)+\tfrac{1}{2}h^2 f''(a+\theta h),$$

on replacing θ_2 by θ. This is the Second Mean Value Theorem.

(iii) Proceeding one step at a time leads finally to Taylor's theorem, with the remainder in the form

$$\frac{h^{n+1}}{(n+1)!}f^{(n+1)}(a+\theta h).$$

Exercise 16G

1   Verify the result

$$\int_a^{a+h} F(t)\,dt = \int_a^{a+h} F(2a+h-X)\,dX$$

for the cases (i) $F(t)=\sin t$, (ii) $F(t)=e^t$.

2   By using the change of variables

$$x=X-a$$

show that

$$R_n = \int_a^{a+h} \frac{(X-a)^n}{n!} f^{(n+1)}(2a+h-X)\,dX.$$

3   Derive the integral formula

$$\int_a^{a+h} f(x)\,dx = hf(a)+\frac{1}{2}h^2 f'(a)+\ldots+\frac{1}{n!}h^n f^{(n-1)}(a+\theta h).$$

16.6   SUMMARY

The Mean Value Theorem is

$$f(a+h) = f(a) + hf'(a+\theta h),$$

where θ is a (generally) unknown number between 0 and 1. The theorem applies to *smooth* function f (having a continuous derivative).

It may be proved from evaluation of the area of a strip by a rectangle of intermediate height, or from an argument on chords and tangents.

Rolle's theorem is that if $f(a) = f(b)$ and f is smooth, then there is a value c between a and b for which $f'(c) = 0$. It is equivalent to the Mean Value Theorem.

Newton–Raphson iteration replaces the approximation x_0 to the solution X of $f(x) = 0$, by the approximation

$$x_1 = x_0 - \frac{f(x_0)}{f'(x_0)},$$

which is usually better. In many cases this iteration is *quadratically convergent*. The Newton–Raphson formula is easily constructed from a diagram or from the Mean Value Theorem.

Taylor's theorem is

$$f(a+h) = f(a) + hf'(a) + \ldots + \frac{h^n}{n!}f^{(n)}(a) + \frac{h^{n+1}}{(n+1)!}f^{(n+1)}(a+\theta h),$$

where θ is some number between 0 and 1 and where $f^{(n+1)}$, the $(n+1)$th derivative of f, is continuous.

The *remainder term* may be written as

$$\frac{h^{n+1}}{(n+1)!}f^{(n+1)}(a+\theta h)$$

or as

$$\int_a^{a+h} \frac{t^n}{n!}f^{(n+1)}(t)\,dt.$$

Taylor's approximation of degree n is

$$f(a+h) \approx f(a) + hf'(a) + \ldots + \frac{1}{n!}h^n f^{(n)}(a).$$

If the remainder term tends to 0 as n tends to infinity, then there is a *Taylor series*

$$f(a+h) = f(a) + hf'(a) + \tfrac{1}{2}h^2 f''(a) + \ldots$$

which is an infinite sum.

Polynomials, i.e. Taylor approximations, may be used to solve differential equations locally; for example near $x = 0$, when a coefficient in the equation is infinite there.

The Euler numerical solution method for differential equations is equivalent to a first order Taylor approximation. A *second order Euler* method can be constructed by using a second order Taylor approximation.

17
Errors in numerical formulas

In this chapter we shall be considering the errors that are introduced into numerical work by the use of approximate formulas. As an example

$$f(a+h) \approx f(a) + hf'(a)$$

is not exact; the exact formula is

$$f(a+h) = f(a) + hf'(a) + \tfrac{1}{2}h^2 f''(a+\theta h),$$

from Taylor's theorem, and so the error introduced by using the approximation is

$$e = \tfrac{1}{2}h^2 f''(a+\theta h).$$

The purpose of the study is to *control* the errors. In this example we can keep e very small by making our step length h extremely small (assuming that the second derivative is not large near the point a).

We shall say less in this chapter about the sort of errors discussed in Chapter 3, those due to the finite length of the numbers stored in a computer. But of course when you reduce the step length h, you necessarily increase the number of steps to cover a given interval, and this allows the computer arithmetic error more opportunity to build up. This again is a reason for analysing formula errors: if you can get great accuracy in few steps, computer arithmetic error has little time to grow.

Equally, we shall not spend much time here on instability, which allows apparently trivial errors to grow enormously in relatively few steps. That too has been discussed before (in Chapters 3 and 15); though in any real and unknown situation you have to keep in mind formula error *and* computer arithmetic error *and* stability.

17.1 CONVERGENCE IN SIMPLE ITERATIONS

I should like to start with the simple iterations, such as

$$x_{n+1} = F(x_n)$$

to find a root of $x = F(x)$; or

$$x_{n+1} = x_n - f(x_n)/f'(x_n),$$

the Newton–Raphson iteration for a root of $f(x) = 0$. The iterations used in solving differential or matrix equations need separate treatment.

Many of the results here are a support to, and an explanation of, the experimental results that we found in Chapters 4 and 16. The theoretical results will, in particular, tell you when the usual is not going to happen.

(a)   Simple root iteration

Let us start with the iteration

$$x_{n+1} = F(x_n)$$

for which the actual solution will be called X, so that

$$X = F(X).$$

Each iterate x_n has an error e_n associated with it:

$$\begin{cases} X - x_n = e_n \\ X - x_{n+1} = e_{n+1}. \end{cases}$$

Thus the iteration equation may be written as

$$X - e_{n+1} = F(X - e_n).$$

Now apply the Mean Value Theorem:

$$X - e_{n+1} = F(X) - e_n F'(X - \theta_n e_n).$$

But $X = F(X)$, because X is the solution of the equation, so we can rewrite this as

$$\frac{e_{n+1}}{e_n} = F'(X - \theta_n e_n)$$

with each θ_n being some number between 0 and 1.

This is an *exact* equation for how the errors change as n increases. If $F'(X - \theta_n e_n)$ lies between 0 and 1 the errors decrease and have the same sign; if $-1 < F'(X - \theta_n e_n) < 0$ the errors still decrease in size, but alternate in sign.

Now suppose we have

$$|F'(X)| < 1$$

and also

$$|F'(x)| < 1$$

all the way from $X - e_0$ to $X + e_0$. Then certainly

$$|F'(X - \theta_0 e_0)| < 1$$

and so

$$|e_1| < |e_0|.$$

Hence we shall also have

$$|F'(X - \theta_1 e_1)| < 1,$$

because $X - \theta_1 e_1$ is *inside* the interval where the gradient $F'(x)$ has size less than 1.

Carrying on like this shows that the errors decrease in size continually.
In fact, if

$$|F'(x)| \leqslant K < 1$$

in this interval, you have

$$|e_{n+1}| \leqslant K|e_n|$$

$$\leqslant K^2|e_{n-1}|$$

$$\leqslant \dots \leqslant K^{n+1}|e_0|$$

so that e_n inevitably tends to 0 as n increases.
Let us look at an example. The iteration

$$x_{n+1} = \tfrac{1}{10} x_n^2 + 1$$

was suggested in Exercise 4B to solve the equation

$$x^2 - 10x + 10 = 0.$$

In this case

$$F(x) = \tfrac{1}{10} x^2 + 1, \quad \text{and} \quad F'(x) = \tfrac{1}{5} x.$$

Hence the interval for which $|F'(x)|$ is less than 1 in size is $-5 < x < 5$. If you start
with x_0 in this interval you are bound to get convergence to the solution point
$X = 1.1270 \dots$

Note that this theorem does *not* say what happens if you start outside this
interval. You can find by trial that for x between about

$$-8.87 \quad \text{and} \quad 8.87$$

you still get convergence to the same solution. How does this happen? It must be
because

$$|F'(X - \theta_0 e_0)| < 1$$

even though

$$|F'(X - e_0)| > 1$$

which would certainly happen in this case if θ_0 had a value near $\tfrac{1}{2}$. In most
practical cases we do not need to carry out a detailed analysis like this of how the
errors behave. Usually we have quite a close estimate x_0 of the root X (e.g. from a
graphics program), and hence e_0 is usually quite small. Hence all we do is look at
the size of $F'(x_0)$, which will tell us whether iteration from x_0 will converge to the
root near x_0.

For example, a graphic display for the equation

$$x^2 - 10x + 10 = 0$$

shows that the roots are near $x = 1.1$ and $x = 8.9$. For the iteration described
above

$$F'(1.1) = 0.22, \quad F'(8.9) = 1.78.$$

Hence the iteration starting at $x_0 = 1.1$ will converge to the root near 1.1; and iteration from $x_0 = 8.9$ will either diverge away to infinity or eventually converge on the other root. In fact in this case experiment shows that the iteration diverges to infinity.

Exercise 17A

1   For the iteration

$$x_{n+1} = \tfrac{1}{10}x_n^2 + 1$$

the function $F(x) = \tfrac{1}{10}x^2 + 1$, $F'(x) = \tfrac{1}{5}x$. Find the value of θ in

$$F(x-t) = F(x) - tF'(x - \theta t)$$

and hence show for what values x_0 the iteration converges to the root near 1.1.

2   A graphics display suggests that the roots of

$$x^4 + x^3 - 1 = 0$$

are near -1.40 and 0.82. Determine which root can be found by using the iteration

$$x_{n+1} = (x_n + 1)^{-1/3}$$

by calculating suitable values of $F'(x)$.

3   The equation

$$x^3 - x^2 - 2x + 2 = 0$$

clearly has a root at $x = 1$, and its other roots are near -1.4 and 1.4. One iteration for the roots is

$$x_{n+1} = x_n^3 - x_n^2 - x_n + 2.$$

Show that $F'(1) = 0$ for this iteration, and use a longer form of Taylor's theorem to discuss the convergence of the iteration to this root.
   Will this iteration converge at the other roots?
   Confirm all your deductions by numerical experiments.

(b)   Newton–Raphson iteration

In this iteration we are seeking to find the root X such that

$$f(X) = 0.$$

If x_n is near the root, then we have

$$0 = f(X) = f(x_n + e_n)$$

where e_n is a small error term. Now use Taylor's theorem on this:

$$0 = f(x_n) + e_n f'(x_n) + \tfrac{1}{2}e_n^2 f''(x_n + \theta e_n),$$

where $0 < \theta < 1$, and assuming that f is a smooth function. If the last term is small, then

$$e_n \approx -f(x_n)/f'(x_n)$$

which should give a better estimate

$$x_{n+1} = x_n - f(x_n)/f'(x_n)$$

of the root X (assuming that $f'(x_n) \neq 0$), by using $x_n + e_n$ as the new estimate. This discussion also gives an estimate of the error in this approximation, because (exactly)

$$e_n = \frac{f(x_n)}{f'(x_n)} - \frac{1}{2}e_n^2\frac{f''(x_n + \theta e_n)}{f'(x_n)}.$$

Thus the error in making the correction

$$-\frac{f(x_n)}{f'(x_n)}$$

is exactly

$$-\frac{1}{2}e_n^2\frac{f''(x_n + \theta e_n)}{f'(x_n)}$$

and approximately

$$-\frac{1}{2}\left(\frac{f(x_n)}{f'(x_n)}\right)^2\frac{f''(x_n)}{f'(x_n)}$$

on replacing e_n by its estimate, and $x_n + \theta e_n$ by x_n.

This shows that a more accurate, but considerably more involved, form of Newton–Raphson iteration would use

$$x_{n+1} = x_n - \frac{f(x_n)}{f'(x_n)} - \frac{\{f(x_n)\}^2 f''(x_n)}{2\{f'(x_n)\}^3}.$$

Since the Newton–Raphson method is normally rapidly convergent, there is little purpose in using such an improvement in usual cases.

The speed of convergence of standard Newton–Raphson iteration can be deduced similarly. If

$$x_{n+1} = x_n - \frac{f(x_n)}{f'(x_n)}$$

then (subtracting both sides from X)

$$e_{n+1} = e_n + \frac{f(X - e_n)}{f'(X - e_n)}.$$

Now use Taylor approximations on each of $f(X - e_n)$ and $f'(X - e_n)$:

$$\begin{cases} f(X - e_n) \approx f(X) - e_n f'(X) + \frac{1}{2}e_n^2 f''(X) \\ f'(X - e_n) \approx f'(X) - e_n f''(X), \end{cases}$$

so that

$$e_{n+1} \approx e_n - e_n\frac{f'(X) - \frac{1}{2}e_n f''(X)}{f'(X) - e_n f''(X)}$$

having used $f(X)=0$ once. This can be rewritten as

$$\frac{e_{n+1}}{e_n} \approx 1 - \frac{1 - \frac{1}{2}\{e_n f''(X)/f'(X)\}}{1 - \{e_n f''(X)/f'(X)\}}.$$

If we assume that e_n is small enough so that the bracketed term, B say, is very small, we can use the standard approximation

$$\frac{1}{1-B} \approx 1 + B \quad \text{for small } B$$

to approximate again:

$$\frac{e_{n+1}}{e_n} \approx 1 - (1 - \tfrac{1}{2}B)(1+B) \approx -\tfrac{1}{2}B,$$

on neglecting B^2. That is, we have shown that

$$\frac{e_{n+1}}{e_n} \approx -\tfrac{1}{2}e_n \frac{f''(X)}{f'(X)}$$

or

$$e_{n+1} \approx -\tfrac{1}{2}e_n^2 \frac{f''(X)}{f'(X)}.$$

This confirms earlier numerical experiments which suggested that the convergence was *quadratic*, and tells us that the constant in the quadratic relationship is

$$\frac{1}{2}\frac{f''(X)}{f'(X)}$$

when e_n is small enough.

Exercise 17B

1   Carry out a Newton–Raphson iteration on

$$10x^4 + 10x^3 + 1 = 0$$

starting at $x_0 = -1$.
  Determine the errors e_n at each step, and evaluate also

$$e_{n+1}/e_n^2, \quad n = 0, 1, \ldots, 4.$$

Compare your values with

$$-\frac{1}{2}\frac{f''(X)}{f'(X)}.$$

2   Carry out the improved iterative scheme

$$x_{n+1} = x_n - \frac{f(x_n)}{f'(x_n)} - \frac{\{f(x_n)\}^2 f''(x_n)}{2\{f'(x_n)\}^3}$$

for the equation of question 1, starting again at $x_0 = -1$.

3   In the case when $f'(X)=0$ show that $e_{n+1}\approx\frac{1}{2}e_n$ follows from

$$x_{n+1}=x_n-\frac{f(x_n)}{f'(x_n)}$$

(assuming still that $f'(x_n)\neq0$), provided that $f''(X)\neq0$.

4   Use Taylor's theorem in the case $f'(X)=0$ to suggest a more rapid iteration formula than the Newton–Raphson iteration. Apply it to $x^5+x^4-4x^3-4x^2+4x+4=0$ starting from $x_0=2$.

(c)   Newton–Raphson iteration with non-smooth functions

All of the discussion in (b) above has assumed that the function f is smooth. What happens if it isn't?

Take as example the function

$$f(x)=x^{2/3},$$

which is sketched in Fig. 1.

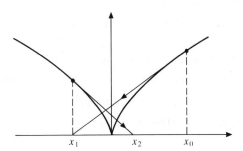

Figure 1. Newton–Raphson iteration on $x^{2/3}$

The iteration is easily carried out exactly:

$$x_{n+1}=x_n-\frac{x_n^{2/3}}{\frac{2}{3}x_n^{-1/3}}=-\tfrac{1}{2}x_n,$$

so that each step is just halving the size of the error.

You cannot do any Taylor theorem analysis here, because the function is *not* smooth at the root $x=0$. Here

$$f'(x)=\tfrac{2}{3}x^{-1/3}$$

so that

$$f'(0) \text{ is infinite.}$$

Consequently, analysis involving $f'(0)$ will be useless, and there is no reason to expect quadratic convergence.

If instead you try the function

$$f(x) = x^{2/5},$$

which has a very similar graph, the iteration is

$$x_{n+1} = x_n - \frac{x_n^{2/5}}{\frac{2}{5}x_n^{-3/5}} = -\frac{3}{2}x_n.$$

In this case the iteration diverges away from the solution $x = 0$. Again you cannot use Taylor's theorem, because $f'(0)$ does not exist.

The results here depend markedly on how 'smooth' the function is at the solution point X, and it is best to investigate each case individually, either by numerical experiment, or using some mathematics.

Exercise 17C

1   Investigate Newton–Raphson iteration for $f(x) = \sqrt{|x|}$, both numerically and mathematically.

2   Let $f(x) = x^{5/3}$. Show that the equation

$$f(x) = f(0) + xf'(0) + \tfrac{1}{2}x^2 f''(\theta x)$$

is valid for $x \neq 0$, provided that θ is properly chosen. Hence justify a Newton–Raphson iteration of this function. Is the convergence quadratic?

3   The function $1 + \cos x$ is zero when $x = 3\pi$. Put $3\pi - x = y$ to show that

$$1 + \cos x \approx \tfrac{1}{2}y^2$$

when x is nearly equal to 3π. Hence discuss questions 3 and 4 of Exercise 16C again, if necessary.

17.2   ERRORS IN DIFFERENTIATION

In Section 10.1 we saw the two approximations for the derivative of a function f:

(i) $f'(a) \approx \dfrac{f(a+h) - f(a)}{h}$

(ii) $f'(a) \approx \dfrac{f(a+h) - f(a-h)}{2h}$.

We then did numerical experiments on the accuracy of these approximations. We can now support these with calculations using Taylor's theorem, for we have

$$\begin{cases} f(a+h) = f(a) + hf'(a) + \tfrac{1}{2}h^2 f''(a + \lambda h) \\ f(a+h) = f(a) + hf'(a) + \tfrac{1}{2}h^2 f''(a) + \tfrac{1}{6}h^3 f'''(a + \theta h) \\ f(a-h) = f(a) - hf'(a) + \tfrac{1}{2}h^2 f''(a) - \tfrac{1}{6}h^3 f'''(a - \phi h), \end{cases}$$

where each of λ, θ, ϕ (this is the Greek letter 'phi') is a number between 0 and 1 (they are unlikely to be equal). This lets us calculate

(i) $\dfrac{1}{h}\{f(a+h) - f(a)\} = f'(a) + \tfrac{1}{2}hf''(a + \lambda h)$,

(ii) $\dfrac{1}{2h}\{f(a+h)-f(a-h)\}=\frac{1}{12}h^2\{f'''(a+\theta h)+f'''(a-\phi h)\}.$

Hence the errors in these two derivative approximations are, for *small* values of h, approximately

(i) $-\frac{1}{2}hf''(a)$
(ii) $-\frac{1}{6}h^2f'''(a),$

assuming in all cases that f is a smooth enough function. This confirms what we found numerically, that the second formula is much superior to the first.

Could we construct an even better formula? Yes, without too much trouble. Try to improve on (ii) by taking

$$f'(a)\approx\frac{1}{h}\{\alpha f(a+2h)+\beta f(a+h)-\beta f(a-h)-\alpha f(a-2h)\},$$

where symmetry has been used in guessing at a good formula. We need to choose α and β here so that the right hand side gives us

$$f'(a)-\text{error terms in } h^3 \text{ or less,}$$

i.e. the coefficients of $f'(a)$ when we do Taylor expansions must sum to 1, and the coefficients of $f(a),f''(a),f'''(a)$ must all sum to zero. We now need longer Taylor theorem expressions, and it turns out that with

$$\alpha=-\tfrac{1}{12},\ \beta=\tfrac{2}{3}$$

you find that the right hand side sums to

$$f'(a)+\frac{h^4}{180}\{f^{(5)}(a+\lambda h)+f^{(5)}(a+\mu h)\}$$

$$-\frac{h^4}{45}\{f^{(5)}(a+\theta h)+f^{(5)}(a+\phi h)\}.$$

Thus this better formula has an error which, when h is small, is approximately

$$\tfrac{1}{30}h^4f^{(5)}(a).$$

This is an extremely small error; as long as $f^{(5)}(a)$ is not large, even with $h=10^{-2}$ you get an error around 10^{-9} in size, and other errors in any calculation process may be larger than this.

The second derivative approximation from Section 10.2 is

$$f''(a)\approx\frac{1}{h^2}\{f(a+h)-2f(a)+f(a-h)\}.$$

This can be analysed in exactly the same way, using the Taylor theorems for $f(a+h)$ and $f(a-h)$ to show that the error is approximately

$$-\tfrac{1}{12}h^2f^{(4)}(a)$$

when h is small. Once again, we have assumed that f is a smooth enough function. Can you find a better formula for $f''(a)$? Yes – see Exercise 17D.

Exercise 17D

1   For the function x^3 show directly that the error in

$$f'(a) \approx \frac{f(a+h)-f(a)}{h}$$

is approximately $\frac{1}{2}hf''(a)$, and the error in

$$f'(a) \approx \frac{1}{2h}\{f(a+h)-f(a-h)\}$$

is approximately $\frac{1}{6}h^2f'''(a)$.

2   Use Taylor's theorem to establish the error in the approximation

$$f'(a) \approx \frac{1}{h}\{f(a)-f(a-h)\}.$$

3   Use Taylor theorems including remainder terms in fifth derivatives to confirm the error term in

$$f'(a) \approx \frac{1}{12h}\{-f(a+2h)+8f(a+h)-8f(a-h)+f(a-2h)\}.$$

4   Show that

$$f(a+h)-2f(a)+f(a-h) \approx h^2f''(a)+\tfrac{1}{12}h^4f^{(4)}(a).$$

Deduce a corresponding expression for

$$f(a+2h)-2f(a)+f(a-2h),$$

and hence construct an approximation for $f''(a)$ whose error term is proportional to h^4.

5   Show that

$$f(a+h) \approx -\tfrac{1}{2}f(a-2h)+3f(a-h)-\tfrac{3}{2}f(a)+3hf'(a)$$

and find the error term, by using Taylor theorem expansions of a suitable length. Could this approximation be used as the basis of a method for solving differential equations?

17.3   ERRORS IN INTEGRATION FORMULAS

(a)   The area of a strip

To assess the error in any of the integration formulas in Chapter 10 we need a correct value of the area to compare them with. You can either do this by using functions that you can integrate by calculus to get exact answers (as we did in Chapter 10), or you can look at what happens when the strip width h gets extremely small (we did this also in Chapter 10), or you can use Taylor's theorem. The advantage of using Taylor's theorem is its generality – you can do the process for *all* smooth functions at once; the other methods only work for one function at a time.

To calculate

$$I = \int_a^{a+h} f(t)\,dt$$

I am going to make the preliminary substitution

$$t = a + \tfrac{1}{2}h + x.$$

This moves the origin to the mid point of the base of the strip, and shortens the algebra. This gives us

$$I = \int_{-h/2}^{h/2} f(a + \tfrac{1}{2}h + x)\,dx$$

to calculate. We can now use Taylor's theorem on the integrand, expanding about the point $a + \tfrac{1}{2}h$ (the mid point). I shall do two such expansions out of the many available.

First, then, consider

$$f(a + \tfrac{1}{2}h + x) = f(a + \tfrac{1}{2}h) + xf'(a + \tfrac{1}{2}h) + \tfrac{1}{2}x^2 f''(a + \tfrac{1}{2}h + \theta x)$$

as a short version of Taylor's theorem. This gives us

$$I = hf(a + \tfrac{1}{2}h) + 0 + \int_{-h/2}^{h/2} \tfrac{1}{2}x^2 f''(a + \tfrac{1}{2}h + \theta x)\,dx.$$

Now the integral here cannot be done exactly (or else you would not need approximate methods to do the original integral); but we have already processed an integral like this in Section 16.5(a), where we dealt with

$$\int_0^h \frac{x^n}{n!} f^{(n+1)}(a + h - x)\,dx.$$

Using the same type of argument on the present integral shows that

$$\int_{-h/2}^{h/2} \tfrac{1}{2}x^2 f''(a + \tfrac{1}{2}h + \theta x)\,dx = \tfrac{1}{24}h^3 f''(a + \phi h)$$

where ϕ is some number between 0 and 1, i.e. $a + \phi h$ lies between a and $a + h$, which is the interval of integration we started with.

This gives us three results

(i) $I \approx hf(a + \tfrac{1}{2}h)$,
(ii) $I - hf(a + \tfrac{1}{2}h) = \tfrac{1}{24}h^3 f''(a + \phi h)$,
(iii) the error in using the approximation

$$I \approx hf(a + \tfrac{1}{2}h)$$

is certainly no bigger than $\tfrac{1}{24}h^3$ times the largest size (L, say) of f'' in the interval $(a, a + h)$.

If you wanted a better estimate of the integral, you could take a longer Taylor expansion. For example, using

$$f(a+\tfrac{1}{2}h+x)=f(a+\tfrac{1}{2}h)+ \ldots +\tfrac{1}{24}x^4f^{(4)}(a+\tfrac{1}{2}h+\theta x)$$

leads to

$$I-hf(a+\tfrac{1}{2}h)-\tfrac{1}{24}h^3f''(a+\tfrac{1}{2}h)=\frac{h^5}{1920}f^{(4)}(a+\phi h),$$

for some number ϕ between 0 and 1.

(b)   The rectangle method of integration

In Section 10.3 we saw the rectangle method of numerical integration

$$I= \int_a^b f(x)\,dx \approx h\{f(a+\tfrac{1}{2}h)+f(a+\tfrac{3}{2}h)+ \ldots +f(b-\tfrac{1}{2}h)\}$$

where the total interval from a to b was divided into (say) n strips of width h. From the results in (a) we can see that

$$I-h\sum_{i=1}^{n} f(a-\tfrac{1}{2}h+ih)$$

$$=\tfrac{1}{24}h^3\{f''(a+\phi_1 h)+f''(a+h+\phi_2 h)+ \ldots +f''(b-\phi_n h)\},$$

where each of the numbers ϕ_i lies between 0 and 1. The long sum on the right of this equation can be reduced to a single term by using the following line of argument:

(i)   the average of n terms lies between the largest and the smallest;
(ii) f'', if continuous, takes all values between the largest and the smallest of the $f''(a+\phi_i h)$;
(iii) hence the terms on the right must have value

$$\tfrac{1}{24}nh^3f''(\xi)$$

where ξ is some number between a and b.

We now have an exact result:

$$\int_a^b f(x)\,dx=h\sum_{i=1}^{n} f(a-\tfrac{1}{2}h+ih)+\tfrac{1}{24}(b-a)h^2f''(\xi),$$

on using $nh=b-a$, for smooth functions f. The most useful form of this is to say that the error in the rectangle method has size no bigger than

$$\tfrac{1}{24}(b-a)h^2M,$$

where M is the maximum of $|f''(x)|$ in $a\leqslant x\leqslant b$.

Let us try an easy example,

$$\int_0^{\pi/4} \sin 2x\,dx.$$

The exact value here is $\frac{1}{2}$. I next calculated it using the rectangle method with n strips, so that $h=\pi/(4n)$. The second derivative here is

$$f''(x)= -4\sin 2x$$

which has largest size 4 (for its modulus) in the interval of integration from 0 to $\frac{1}{4}\pi$. My results were:

n	Value	Error	$|\text{Error}|/(\frac{1}{24}(b-a)h^2)$
10	0.500 514 412 1	-5.1441×10^{-4}	2.5483
20	0.500 128 533 6	-1.2853×10^{-4}	2.5469
50	0.500 020 562 3	-2.0562×10^{-5}	2.5466
100	0.500 005 140 5	-5.1405×10^{-6}	2.5465
200	0.500 001 285 1	-1.2851×10^{-6}	2.5465

By the theory, the last column should be at most 4, the largest value of $|f''(x)|$ in the interval from $a=0$ to $b=\frac{1}{4}\pi$. You can see that the result, not very surprisingly, is less than 4. In the early intervals the value of

$$f'' = -4\sin 2x$$

is rather small, and it is only when x gets near $\frac{1}{4}\pi$ that the size of f'' approaches 4. The actual entry in the last column is some sort of average value of $|f''|$ over the interval.

Exercise 17E

1 Find the largest size of f'' in the interval $0 \leqslant x \leqslant 4$ for $f(x)=e^{-x}$. Hence estimate the largest size of the error in a rectangle method estimation of

$$\int_0^4 e^{-x}\,dx.$$

Confirm your estimate by numerical experiments.

2 Reconsider the figures in Section 10.3(a) in the light of the error estimates in this section.

(c) The trapezium method

The trapezium method estimates the area of the strip by using the average height,

$$\text{area} \approx \tfrac{1}{2}h\{f(a+h)+f(a)\}.$$

Since this is not very much like the area estimate

$$hf(a+\tfrac{1}{2}h)$$

in (a) above, I will do some more Taylor expansions on $f(a+h)$ and $f(a)$. This time I want to *force* $a+\frac{1}{2}h$ to come into the answer, so I shall put

$$\begin{cases} f(a+h)=f(a+\frac{1}{2}h+\frac{1}{2}h) \\ f(a)=f(a+\frac{1}{2}h-\frac{1}{2}h) \end{cases}$$

and then use the *second* $\frac{1}{2}h$ in each bracket as the expansion variable. This gives me

(i) $f(a+h)=f(a+\frac{1}{2}h+\frac{1}{2}h)$

$\qquad =f(a+\frac{1}{2}h)+\frac{1}{2}hf'(a+\frac{1}{2}h)+\frac{1}{8}h^2f''(a+\lambda h)$

with $\frac{1}{2}<\lambda<1$,

(ii) $f(a)=f(a+\frac{1}{2}h-\frac{1}{2}h)$

$\qquad =f(a+\frac{1}{2}h)-\frac{1}{2}hf'(a+\frac{1}{2}h)+\frac{1}{8}h^2f''(a+\phi h)$

with $-\frac{1}{2}<\phi<0$.

Thus the trapezium rule estimate for the area of a single strip is *exactly*

$$hf(a+\tfrac{1}{2}h)+\tfrac{1}{16}h^3\{f''(a+\lambda h)+f''(a+\phi h)\},$$

and from (a) above the *exact* area of the strip is

$$hf(a+\tfrac{1}{2}h)+\int_{-h/2}^{h/2}\tfrac{1}{2}x^2f''(a+h+\theta x)\,dx.$$

So the exact area minus the trapezium rule estimate (the error in the method of integration) is

$$\int_{-h/2}^{h/2}\tfrac{1}{2}x^2f''(a+h+\theta x)\,dx-\tfrac{1}{16}h^3\{f''(a+\lambda h)+f''(a+\phi h)\}.$$

The first term in this error can be processed as before (in (b) above) to get

$$\tfrac{1}{24}h^3f''(a+\mu h)$$

for some number μ between 0 and 1, and the second term reduces to

$$-\tfrac{1}{8}h^3f''(a+vh).$$

(These are the Greek letters 'mu' (μ) and 'nu' (v).) A theorem which you can find in more advanced books, but which we cannot prove here, states that these two expressions can be combined as

$$-\tfrac{1}{12}h^3f''(a+\psi h)$$

for some number ψ (the Greek letter 'psi') between 0 and 1. Consequently the error in the trapezium rule calculation (adding up over n strips) is

$$-\tfrac{1}{12}h^2(b-a)f''(\xi)$$

for some number ξ between a and b. The largest size of this error cannot exceed

$$\tfrac{1}{12}h^2(b-a)M,$$

where M is the maximum of $|f''(x)|$ in $a\leqslant x\leqslant b$.

Notice that the error here is of the same form as that in the rectangle method, but twice as large and of the opposite sign. You can see the doubling of the size of the error in the figures in Section 10.3 for

$$\int_0^1 e^{-x^2}\,dx,$$

estimated by the two methods.

Exercise 17F

1   Verify the error estimate in the trapezium rule by using $f(x)=x^2$ and an integral from 0 to 1.

2   Try the following estimate for an integral:

$$\int_a^b f(x)\,dx \approx \tfrac{2}{3} \text{ of rectangle estimate } + \tfrac{1}{3} \text{ of trapezium estimate,}$$

on

(i) $\displaystyle\int_0^{\pi/4} \sin 2x\,dx$ (ii) $\displaystyle\int_0^1 e^{-x^2}\,dx.$

Is this method as good as Simpson's rule?

(d)   Simpson's rule

No new ideas come in for Simpson's rule; we must use longer Taylor expansions, up to the fourth derivative; and it will be better to start again, as the strip is a double one in Simpson's rule. Because the ideas are those used earlier, much of the detail is left to the Exercise.

Take the basic (double) strip to be centred on the origin, as in Fig. 2.

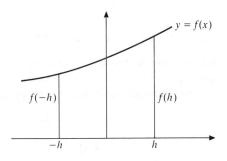

Figure 2. The basic (double) strip for Simpson's rule

(i)   From a Taylor expansion we find that the area of the double strip is *exactly*

$$I = \int_{-h}^{h} f(x)\,dx = 2hf(0) + \tfrac{1}{3}h^3 f''(0) + \int_{-h}^{h} \tfrac{1}{24}x^4 f^{(4)}(\theta x)\,dx$$

for some value of θ between 0 and 1.

(ii)   The Simpson estimate of this area is

$$S = \tfrac{1}{3}h\{f(-h)+4f(0)+f(h)\}.$$

Again using Taylor expansions you find that

$$S = 2hf(0) + \tfrac{1}{3}h^3 f''(0) + \tfrac{1}{72}h^5\{f^{(4)}(-\lambda h)+f^{(4)}(\phi h)\}$$

where λ and ϕ are some numbers between 0 and 1. This again is exact.

(iii)   Hence the error in the Simpson estimate is exactly

$$I - S = \int_{-h}^{h} \tfrac{1}{24}x^4 f^{(4)}(\theta x)\,dx - \tfrac{1}{72}h^5\{f^{(4)}(-\lambda h)+f^{(4)}(\phi h)\}.$$

(iv)   The integral can be expressed as

$$\tfrac{1}{60}h^5 f^{(4)}(\mu h)$$

with μ between -1 and $+1$, and the other terms as

$$-\tfrac{1}{36}h^5 f^{(4)}(\psi h)$$

with ψ between -1 and $+1$.

(v)   The proof that these can be equated to

$$-\tfrac{1}{90}h^5 f^{(4)}(\xi)$$

with ξ between $-h$ and h, can be found in more advanced books.

(vi)   For an integral from a to b the error is

$$-\tfrac{1}{180}(b-a)h^4 f^{(4)}(\eta)$$

with η (the Greek letter 'eta') between a and b. The maximum size of the error is then

$$\tfrac{1}{180}(b-a)h^4 M,$$

where M is the maximum of $|f^{(4)}(x)|$ in $a \leqslant x \leqslant b$.

This confirms what we saw in numerical experiments, that the error in Simpson's rule is proportional to h^4 for smooth functions f. The calculation of M, so as to estimate the error without experiments, can often be a trouble. For example, take

$$f(x) = \frac{1}{1+x^2}$$

as in Exercise 10D, question 2. It takes a lot of effort to derive

$$f^{(4)}(x) = \frac{24 - 240x^2 + 120x^4}{(1+x^2)^5}$$

(and to be sure it is correct), while to find the largest value of this in the interval from -1 to $+1$ would be a great deal more effort if I did not have a graphics calculator (Fig. 3).

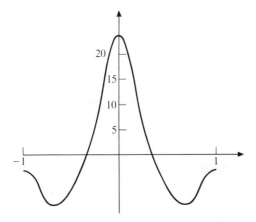

Figure 3. Fourth derivative of $(1+x^2)^{-1}$

This shows me that M for the Simpson's rule calculation of

$$I = \int_{-1}^{1} \frac{1}{1+x^2} \, dx$$

is 24, and hence that the largest possible error is

$$\tfrac{24}{180} \times 2 \times h^4 = \tfrac{4}{15} h^4.$$

Thus if you require the value of I with an error no larger than (say) 5×10^{-8}, you need to have h no larger than

$$(\tfrac{75}{4} \times 10^{-8})^{1/4} = 2.08 \times 10^{-2}.$$

In fact calculation with $h = 0.1$ gives the error to be just

$$1.98 \times 10^{-8}.$$

Why is the error so small here, when I might expect it to be reasonably close to

$$\tfrac{48}{180} \times (0.1)^4 = 2.67 \times 10^{-5}?$$

The answer lies in the shape of the curve of $f^{(4)}(x)$. There is a region where $f^{(4)}(x)$ is positive, from about $x = -0.32$ to $x = +0.32$, and the rest of the range of integration has $f^{(4)}(x)$ negative. Thus there is a lot of cancellation of positive and negative errors, and the total error is much reduced. I checked on this explanation by calculating

$$\int_{0}^{0.25} \frac{1}{1+x^2} \quad \text{with } h = 0.025;$$

my estimate for the largest size of the error is

$$\tfrac{24}{180} \times \tfrac{1}{4} \times (0.025)^4 = 1.30 \times 10^{-8}.$$

The size of error I actually found was

$$9.60 \times 10^{-9}$$

which is satisfactory agreement.

Exercise 17G

1   Find the largest size of $f^{(4)}(x)$ for

$$f(x) = e^{-x^2}$$

in the interval $0 \leqslant x \leqslant 1$. Hence discuss the largest size of error you could get in finding

$$\int_0^1 e^{-x^2}\, dx$$

using Simpson's rule. Compare your answer with the figures in Section 10.4.

2   Fill in the missing calculations in (i), (ii) and (iv) above.

3   Investigate

$$I = \int_0^6 e^{-\cos x}\, dx$$

as follows. Find the fourth derivative of $e^{-\cos x}$, and so find a largest error size for given h. Would you expect a much smaller error? Find the actual errors by evaluating I (by Simpson's rule) with $h = 0.01, 0.05, 0.10$.

(e)   Functions that are not smooth

The estimation of the error in Simpson's rule is based on Taylor expansions, which require the function to have very smooth behaviour in the interval of integration: the fourth derivative of f needs to be continuous for our estimation to be correct. What if it is not as smooth as that? Can we still estimate the error, or do we need to rely on the sort of numerical experiments we did in Exercise 10D, question 3?

If you notice that you have a non-smooth function, the best method of proceeding (if you can find a way of doing it), is to make a substitution in the integral to get a smoother function to integrate. For example

$$I = \int_0^8 \cos(x^{2/3})\, dx$$

has $f(x) = \cos(x^{2/3})$ so that

$$\begin{cases} f'(x) = -\tfrac{2}{3}x^{-1/3}\sin(x^{2/3}) \\ f''(x) = \tfrac{2}{9}x^{-4/3}\sin(x^{2/3}) - \tfrac{2}{9}x^{-2/3}\cos(x^{2/3}). \end{cases}$$

In this case

$$f(0) = 1, f'(0) = 0$$

because $\sin(x^{2/3}) \approx x^{2/3}$ for small x, but

$$f''(0) \text{ is infinite.}$$

In this integral you can make the substitution

$$x = t^3$$

to get

$$I = \int_0^2 3t^2 \cos(t^2)\, dt,$$

which can be evaluated by Simpson's rule with no problem.

If you did not notice the unsmoothness of the function at $x = 0$, you could integrate

$$\int_0^8 \cos(x^{2/3})\, dx$$

by Simpson's rule without trouble. I did, and found errors that varied like

$$\text{constant} \times h^{7/3}.$$

It is possible to explain this behaviour by using a shorter version of Taylor's theorem

$$f(x) = f(0) + xf'(0) + \tfrac{1}{2}x^2 f''(\theta x)$$

with

$$\begin{cases} f'(0) = 0 \\ f''(\theta x) \approx \tfrac{2}{9}(\theta x)^{-2/3} \text{ for } x \text{ small but not zero.} \end{cases}$$

However, the analysis is more complicated than seems appropriate in this book.

Unfortunately, it is not always easy to make a substitution to improve the integral. What substitution would help with

$$I = \int_0^1 \frac{\sin x}{x^{1/2}}\, dx?$$

The obvious one is $\dfrac{1}{x^{1/2}} = t$, to remove the $1/x^{1/2}$ term; but this leaves you with

$$I = \int_1^\infty \frac{2}{t^2} \sin\left(\frac{1}{t^2}\right) dt,$$

which is unpleasant because you have to integrate over a very large interval.

In this case, the only alternative to a not very accurate Simpson's rule calculation, is the other remedy suggested in Section 10.5. Since

$$\sin x \approx x - \tfrac{1}{6}x^3 + \tfrac{1}{120}x^5$$

(from Taylor's theorem), you could rewrite the integral as

$$I = \int_0^1 \left\{ \frac{\sin x}{x^{1/2}} - x^{1/2} + \tfrac{1}{6}x^{5/2} \right\} dx + \int_0^1 \{ x^{1/2} - \tfrac{1}{6}x^{5/2} \}\, dx.$$

The second integral can be calculated exactly, and the first has an integrand with continuous fourth derivative, for which Simpson's rule will give an accurate result for moderately small values of h.

17.4   DIFFERENTIAL EQUATIONS

The analysis of the errors in solving a differential equation numerically is rather difficult, and only a little can be done here, mostly by example.

(a)   Local error

The Euler method for differential equations makes the step

$$\begin{cases} y_{\text{new}} = y_{\text{old}} + h\left(\dfrac{dy}{dx}\right)_{\text{old}} \\ x_{\text{new}} = x_{\text{old}} + h, \end{cases}$$

or

$$y(x_{\text{old}} + h) = y(x_{\text{old}}) + h\left(\frac{dy}{dx}\right)_{x_{\text{old}}}.$$

This is clearly related to the Taylor theorem

$$f(x + h) = f(x) + hf'(x) + \tfrac{1}{2}h^2 f''(x + \theta h),$$

and it shows that at each step in a Euler solution the *local error*

$$\tfrac{1}{2}h^2 f''(x_{\text{old}} + \theta h)$$

is being made, where $y = f(x)$ is the 'solution' found by Euler's method. Assuming that f is smooth enough (f'' continuous is needed), you may therefore estimate the error at each step as

$$\tfrac{1}{2}h^2 \frac{d^2 y}{dx^2}$$

approximately. For example, in the equation

$$\frac{dy}{dx} = x + y^3$$

we have

$$\frac{d^2 y}{dx^2} = 1 + 3y^2 \frac{dy}{dx}$$

$$= 1 + 3xy^2 + 3y^5;$$

in this case the local (formula) error will become rather large if y becomes large on the solution curve, unless h is very small.

If you use the Taylor approximation method, for example using

$$\begin{cases} y_{\text{new}} = y_{\text{old}} + h\left(\dfrac{dy}{dx}\right)_{\text{old}} + \tfrac{1}{2}h^2\left(\dfrac{d^2y}{dx^2}\right)_{\text{old}} \\ x_{\text{new}} = x_{\text{old}} + h, \end{cases}$$

it is not hard to see from a Taylor expansion that the local error is approximately

$$\tfrac{1}{6}h^3\frac{d^3y}{dx^3}.$$

In the example above it is straightforward to calculate d^3y/dx^3, using the differential equation; and again if y becomes large the error is likely to become very large.

There is, unfortunately, no such simple analysis for the improved Euler method. However, as we have seen in Chapter 14, the improved Euler method is in essence based on the trapezium rule for area, which has an error of size

$$\tfrac{1}{12}h^3y'''$$

for each strip. So it is fair to expect that the local formula error in the improved Euler method will have about this size, and in particular be proportional to h^3. The reason why it is not exactly this size is that the point $(x_{\text{new}}, y_{\text{inter}})$ is used in the integration instead of $(x_{\text{new}}, y_{\text{new}})$, and y_{inter} is only a Euler estimate for y_{new}, which introduces a further error of size proportional to h^3.

When we were estimating errors in integration formulas in the last section, all we had to do was add up lots of local errors to get a total error estimate. Unfortunately that will not do now; each local error changes you onto a new member of the family of solution curves of the differential equation, and so the overall behaviour of the solution curves also comes into the final error.

(b)   Global error

It can be proved (but will not be proved here because the mathematics is too complicated), that the *global error* in Euler's method is proportional to h. That is, that if $y(x)$ is the true solution of the differential equation and $y_n(x)$ is what you derive from Euler's method, then

$$|y(x) - y_n(x)| < Ah.$$

In this error formula A depends on what the equation is and how far you have gone along the x-axis from the initial point, but it does *not* depend on h. Hence if you make h small enough you ought to get the correct answer to any desired accuracy. Unfortunately, rounding errors in the arithmetic will prevent unlimited accuracy, but at least this result shows that Euler's method is in essence a good one. Its only bad point is that you need to take h rather small, and thousands of steps, to achieve any useful accuracy.

The best we can do here is to illustrate this result with an example. Take the equation

$$\frac{dy}{dx} = ay + x, \quad y = 0 \quad \text{when } x = 0.$$

The exact solution of this is found to be

$$y = \frac{1}{a^2}\{e^{ax} - ax - 1\}$$

(assuming $a \neq 0$). When you use Euler's method on it you replace the x by nh (i.e. n steps to get there) and the y by y_n; the equation is replaced by

$$y_{n+1} = y_n + h(dy/dx)$$
$$= y_n + h(ay_n + nh),$$

i.e. by the difference equation

$$\begin{cases} y_{n+1} = (1 + ah)y_n + nh^2 \\ \quad y_0 = 0. \end{cases}$$

This equation has the solution

$$y_n = \frac{1}{a^2}\{(1 + ah)^n - anh - 1\}.$$

Hence for this example the global error is of size

$$\frac{1}{a^2}|e^{anh} - (1 + ah)^n|$$

since $nh = x$. Now we use the standard approximations

$$e^{anh} \approx 1 + anh + \tfrac{1}{2}(anh)^2$$
$$(1 + ah)^n \approx 1 + anh + \tfrac{1}{2}n(n-1)(ah)^2,$$

(valid when anh is small) to approximate the global error as $\tfrac{1}{2}nh^2 = \tfrac{1}{2}xh$. So certainly when you don't go too far ($ax \ll 1$), the global error is proportional to h. For larger values of anh the best we can do here is numerical experiment. Take $a = 3$ and you get the table of values shown, for the size of the global error.

			h	
x	0.1	0.01	0.001	1×10^{-4}
1	0.7000	0.0963	0.0100	0.0010
2	23.709	3.7859	0.4008	0.0403
3	609.23	111.62	12.049	1.2144

You can see that Euler's method is *very* inaccurate except when h is extremely small, but you can also see on the right of the table that the global error is approximately proportional to h when h is small.

(c) Solution instability

This discussion of local and global error is of no value at all if the solution is unstable. Take a modified form of the last equation:

$$\frac{dy}{dx} = ay + x, \quad y = -\frac{1}{a^2} \quad \text{when } x = 0.$$

The exact solution of this differential equation is

$$y = -\frac{x}{a} - \frac{1}{a^2}.$$

The corresponding difference equation has solution

$$y_n = -\frac{nh}{a} - \frac{1}{a^2},$$

and the global error is apparently exactly zero. But take the example

$$a = 2\pi$$

and you find numerically that the error reaches 0.1607 by $x = 5$, 2.105 by $x = 6$, 275.9 by $x = 7$.

The exact solution is unstable because of the term Ae^{ax} in the complementary function of the equation. Any rounding error in the computer (such as in evaluating $1/(4\pi^2)$) will put you onto a solution curve with $A \neq 0$, and thereafter there is exponential growth of errors.

(d) Method instability

Similarly if a bad method is employed, it is no use relying on a small local error to save you. Here is an example of the application of a bad method (which has a smaller local error than Euler's method) to an equation whose solution is stable.

Start from the standard formula

$$\frac{f(a+h) - f(a-h)}{2h} \approx f'(a).$$

You can rewrite this as

$$f(a+h) \approx f(a-h) + 2hf'(a),$$

which estimates $f(a+h)$ when you already know the values of $f'(a)$ and $f(a-h)$. This can be tried as a differential equation solver, in the form

$$y_{n+1} = y_{n-1} + 2h\left(\frac{dy}{dx}\right)_n,$$

so that providing you have the *two* starting values y_0 and y_1 you can go on to calculate the rest. The *local* error, from the derivative approximation, is about $\frac{1}{6}h^3 f'''(a)$ (using the results in Section 17.2), so you might hope for a *global* error of size a constant times h^2, at least for an equation with a stable solution.

How do we get the second starting value y_1? Use Taylor's theorem again, preferably a form with error of size h^3 to match the other local errors:

$$y_1 \approx y_0 + h\left(\frac{dy}{dx}\right)_0 + \frac{1}{2}h^2\left(\frac{d^2 y}{dx^2}\right)_0.$$

I programmed this method, and ran it on my computer for the equation

$$\frac{dy}{dx} = -\pi y + x, \quad y = \frac{1}{\pi^2} \quad \text{at } x = 0.$$

The exact solution is

$$y = \frac{x}{\pi} - \frac{1}{\pi^2},$$

and this is stable because the complementary function of the equation is $Ae^{-\pi x}$, so that small errors *decrease* as x increases. In the table below you see the results from this 'leapfrog' method, and the errors; you also see the results and errors for the improved Euler method. I used $h = 0.1$ for both methods.

		Leapfrog		Improved Euler	
x	y	error		y	error
1	0.2170	1 $\times 10^{-12}$		0.2170	1×10^{-12}
2	0.5353	3.4 $\times 10^{-11}$		0.5353	1×10^{-12}
3	0.8536	8.45 $\times 10^{-10}$		0.8536	-1×10^{-12}
4	1.1719	1.871 $\times 10^{-8}$		1.1719	-1×10^{-11}
5	1.4902	4.123 $\times 10^{-7}$		1.4902	2×10^{-11}
6	1.8085	9.080 $\times 10^{-6}$		1.8085	-1×10^{-11}
7	2.1266	2.000 $\times 10^{-4}$		2.1268	-1×10^{-11}
8	2.4408	0.004404		2.4452	-1×10^{-11}
9	2.6665	0.096985		2.7635	0
10	0.9459	2.135895		3.0818	-4×10^{-11}

The leapfrog method as applied to this equation (and to many others) is fundamentally unstable, whereas the improved Euler method is usually stable. We can start the analysis of the leapfrog method's poor performance here; the completion must wait until Chapter 19.

The difference equation corresponding to the leapfrog method is

$$y_{n+1} = y_{n-1} + 2h\left(\frac{dy}{dx}\right)_n.$$

In the example we have just considered this is

$$y_{n+1} + 2h\pi y_n - y_{n-1} = 2nh^2.$$

This is a *second* order linear difference equation, for which as yet we have no solution method. However since it is *linear*, the solution will undoubtedly arrive in the form of

'complementary function + particular solution'.

What in fact happens is that there is a term

$$Ac^n$$

in the complementary function, with $|c| > 1$, so that any error in the arithmetic (giving rise to a non-zero value of A) may get amplified as n increases.

17.5   SUMMARY

The discussion of errors in numerical processes is largely based on *Taylor's theorem*, together with an estimation of the largest possible size of the remainder term. The use of Taylor's theorem requires the function under discussion to be smooth.

The iteration

$$x_{n+1} = F(x_n)$$

will *converge* to X if $|F'(x)| < 1$ in an interval containing the root X, which includes the starting point x_0. It may converge to X in a wider interval.

Newton–Raphson iteration is normally *quadratically* convergent, with K in

$$e_{n+1} \approx Ke_n^2$$

being given for *smooth* functions with $f'(X) \neq 0$ and $f''(X) \neq 0$, by

$$K = \frac{1}{2}\frac{f''(X)}{f'(X)}.$$

The error at each iteration is approximately

$$-\frac{\{f(x_n)\}^2 f''(x_n)}{2\{f'(x_n)\}^3}.$$

For functions which are *not* smooth at the root X, Newton–Raphson iteration will show a variety of other behaviours, depending on the function chosen.

The standard *derivative approximations* are in error by approximately the amounts shown, for small h:

$$\frac{1}{h}\{f(a+h) - f(a)\} \approx f'(a) + \tfrac{1}{2}hf''(a),$$

$$\frac{1}{2h}\{f(a+h) - f(a-h)\} \approx f'(a) + \tfrac{1}{6}h^2 f''(a).$$

The usual *second derivative* approximation has approximate error given by

$$\frac{1}{h^2}\{f(a+h)-2f(a)+f(a-h)\} \approx f''(a)+\tfrac{1}{12}h^2f^{(4)}(a),$$

for small values of h. All these results require an appropriate degree of smoothness of the function f.

The *rectangle* method of numerical integration has, for strip width h, an error

$$\tfrac{1}{24}(b-a)h^2f''(\xi).$$

The *trapezium* and *Simpson* rules similarly have errors

$$-\tfrac{1}{12}(b-a)h^2f''(\xi)$$

and

$$-\tfrac{1}{180}(b-a)h^4f^{(4)}(\xi).$$

These can be *estimated* in advance by finding the maximum value of the appropriate derivative of f. *Cancellation* of positive and negative values of the derivative can reduce the error. If the functions are *not* smooth, errors can often be larger; *substitution* or *subtraction* of an easier non-smooth function can give a smooth function to integrate numerically.

The *local error* in a numerical method for a differential equation can sometimes be found by a Taylor expansion; for *Euler's* method it is proportional to h, for the *improved Euler* method to h^2, for the *Taylor expansion* method to a power of h depending on the length of the expansion.

The *global error* is the difference between the true solution and that provided by the method used. For *Euler's* method it is proportional to h, the constant depending on the length of the interval and the properties of the family of solutions.

Errors due to *solution instability* may far outweigh errors due to inaccuracies in the method; in linear equations they are associated with a rapidly growing term in the complementary function.

Some apparently attractive solution *methods* are in themselves *unstable*; this is due to increasing terms in the complementary function of the associated difference equation.

18

Pairs of differential equations

Before we start on the purely mathematical problems in dealing with pairs of differential equations, we should look back to some previous discussions. In Chapter 7 we worked through some examples where there were linked pairs of difference equations. Since difference and differential equations have many properties in common, we may need to refer to results from that chapter. In Section 11.1 we discussed whether a discrete or continuous model was more appropriate for a description of a population. It is often desirable to think before you start building a mathematical model whether it should be a discrete one (giving results only at $n = 0, 1, 2, \ldots$) or a continuous one (giving results for any value of some variable x or t). In Chapters 12 and 13 we saw some mathematical methods for solving single differential equations; we may need some of these techniques here. In Chapter 14, methods were described for numerical solution of a single differential equation, and we shall doubtless need to extend these methods to deal with pairs of equations.

18.1   EXAMPLES OF LINKED EQUATIONS

To qualify under this heading an example will need to have

(i)   two observable functions (e.g. of time),
(ii)   some link between them in the modelling,
(iii)   reasonably continuous behaviour.

The restriction to only *two* observable functions is only for simplicity; real situations will arise with more than two functions to model, but we shall avoid them here. The demand for a link between them is there to give us a new problem to deal with; two unlinked equations can be dealt with one at a time. The requirement of continuous behaviour is often hard to be sure about. The population of the USA must be *almost* continuous (barring some huge disaster) when viewed week by week, yet on the smallest scale, of each individual, it must be discontinuous, as the population can only be an integer. Whether we choose to regard a problem as discrete or continuous is often a matter of mathematical convenience, and any resulting error will often be ignored as 'small'.

The models I shall work with in this chapter will be drawn from the general areas of population numbers, as they are easy to understand, but similar pairs of equations can come up in many contexts. The general methods to use will of course be similar for all contexts.

(a)   The battle of Iwo Jima

In Section 7.3 we looked at the battle of Iwo Jima, using one day as the unit of time and using the difference equations

$$\begin{cases} x_{n+1} = x_n - ay_n \\ y_{n+1} = y_n - bx_n \end{cases}$$

to represent Lanchester's ideas on how the battle would progress. In these equations x_n and y_n are the strengths of the opposing forces on day n, and the constants a and b are the efficiencies of the two sides at destroying the other side. The choice of a day as the unit of time for the calculation is quite sensible, as the battle had to calm down with nightfall; but you could also make out a good case for using a smaller time step such as an hour, as then the change in each side's strength would not be so large at each step forward in time, which would make the model equations more reasonable. Would it be sensible to reduce the time step to a minute or a second? Not really, because then the process becomes random rather that deterministic, and a different sort of model should be used. However, the results from Lanchester's model do look very like a smooth curve if you plot them as a graph, so it is tempting to see whether

(i)   a continuous model is easier to deal with, and
(ii) it gives essentially the same results.

The change in the strength of the first fighting force in one day is

$$x_{n+1} - x_n,$$

and if you use the day as the unit of time the approximate rate of change of the strength is

$$\frac{x_{n+1} - x_n}{1} \text{ men per day.}$$

It is reasonable (and fits well with our work on doing calculus numerically in Chapter 10) to replace this by dx/dt in a continuous version. This leads to the two equations

$$\begin{cases} \dfrac{dx}{dt} = -ay \\ \dfrac{dy}{dt} = -bx \end{cases}$$

as the continuous version for Lanchester's model of battles.

What we have here is a pair of differential equations for the two functions x and y, which show how x and y change as the variable t increases. Naturally we must also have some starting values

$$x(0), \ y(0)$$

to set off from. The equations are first order, because only first derivatives of x

and y come into them; they are linear, because each term in the equations has at most one of the functions (or their derivatives) in it; and they are linked, because x and y occur in both equations. Notice that two initial values are needed for two first order equations.

The equations will sometimes be written as

$$\begin{cases} \dot{x} = -ay \\ \dot{y} = -bx, \end{cases}$$

replacing the derivative d/dt with a dot over the function; we may then write $\dot{x}(2)$, for example, to mean the derivative of the function x when the time t has the value 2 (days).

A similar change can be made to the guerilla conflict problem described in Exercise 7C, question 2; this gives a linked pair of non-linear equations

$$\begin{cases} \dfrac{dx}{dt} = -axy \\ \dfrac{dy}{dt} = -bx, \end{cases}$$

where x is the strength of the guerilla force, and y is that of the opposing army.

(b)   A model of infection

Consider a non-fatal disease to which you are immune after you have recovered from it. Think of a population of N members, of which a few are infected with the disease at $t = 0$. Does an epidemic start, or does the infection die out?

Set up the functions:

(i) $I(t)$, the number who are infected at time t;
(ii) $S(t)$, those who are susceptible (i.e. who could catch the disease) at time t;
(iii) $R(t)$, those who have recovered at time t.

We do not really need all three functions, because

$$N = I + S + R;$$

that is, everybody fits into *one* of categories (i) to (iii), so that, for example

$$R = N - I - S,$$

and R (say) could always be replaced if it came in.

The number infected *increases* due to interactions between those already infected and those who are susceptible; but it *decreases* as people naturally recover from the disease. Thus the equation for $I(t)$ is (in this model)

$$\frac{dI}{dt} = -aI + bIS.$$

The number who are susceptible decreases every time that someone catches the disease, and so

$$\frac{dS}{dt} = -bIS.$$

Finally

$$\frac{dR}{dt} = cI$$

represents the recovery of the infected, at rate c.

Notice that there are *three* linked non-linear equations here, but that any one can be removed by using the total population constraint

$$N = I + S + R.$$

Because epidemics are very important (think of rabies, or AIDS, or smallpox) a great deal of work has gone into constructing model equations for various diseases, and solving them. The equations above give a very simple example, of limited validity.

(c)   Predator and prey equations

In Exercise 7D, question 1, the classic model of a fish population interacting with a predator population was given as a pair of difference equations. The corresponding differential equations are quite likely to be a better model if there is no dependence of fish (or predator) behaviour that is closely related to the season of the year. They are firstly

$$\frac{du}{dt} = (a-1)u - buv$$

for the natural increase of the prey fish as they reproduce (provided that $a > 1$), and the eating of prey fish by the predators at a rate

$$buv$$

(they have to meet, and so this term is proportional to both the number u of prey and also the number v of predators). Secondly

$$\frac{dv}{dt} = (p-1)v + quv,$$

where the natural dying out of predators if they get no food is represented by the term

$$(p-1)v$$

with $p < 1$; and the maintenance of the predators by eating prey gives the term

$$quv.$$

Both b and q need to be positive, and you would expect $b > q$, as many prey fish are needed to keep one predator going.

This simple model of the interaction of a prey species and a predator gives a pair of linked non-linear equations. The model is again too simple, as real populations in the sea are bound to have far more complicated interactions than just one prey species and one predator species.

Exercise 18A

1 What would be the differential equations for the newspaper model in Section 7.1? Would you expect to get similar behaviour from the differential equations to what was found for the difference equations?

2 Foxes eat rabbits (and other things); rabbits eat grass (and flowers and vegetables). Set up equations for the fox population $f(t)$ and the rabbit population $r(t)$ which
(i)   ignore all other fox food,
(ii) give a finite rabbit population in the absence of foxes,
(iii) are reasonably simple.

3 Guerilla forces can have discipline and communication problems, so that some may leave the fight if the opposing army is rather large. Modify the equations in Section 18.1(a) suitably to allow for this.

4 Suppose that you decide to take the unit of time in the battle equations in Section 18.1(a) to be one hour instead of one day, and that you decide to take the length of the day to be 12 hours (fighting time). What changes do you have to make in
(i) the difference equations?
(ii) the differential equations?

5 What has been left out of the infection model? Can you modify the equations easily?

18.2 COMBINATIONS OF THE EQUATIONS

When we refought the battle of Iwo Jima (with our model equations) in Section 7.3, we found that taking combinations of the two equations gave single equations that could be solved. This was also useful for the newspaper and arms race models in Chapter 7. So we may hope, since differential and difference equations are in many ways similar, to advance this way here too.

Using the numbers from Section 7.3, the differential equations for Iwo Jima are

$$\begin{cases} \dfrac{dx}{dt} = -0.04y \\[2mm] \dfrac{dy}{dt} = -0.01x; \end{cases}$$

there must also be initial values, say

$$x = X \quad \text{and} \quad y = Y \quad \text{at } t = 0.$$

If we take

$$w = 0.1x + 0.2y$$

(as in Section 7.3) we find that the equation for w is

$$\frac{dw}{dt} = -0.004y - 0.002x$$

$$= -0.02w.$$

The solution of this first order linear (separable) equation is

$$w = Ae^{-0.02t}.$$

The constant A needs to be chosen to fit the value at $t = 0$, and so

$$A = 0.1X + 0.2Y.$$

Similarly the combination

$$z = 0.1x - 0.2y$$

satisfies

$$\frac{dz}{dt} = 0.02z$$

with solution

$$z = Be^{0.02t}$$

where

$$B = 0.1X - 0.2Y.$$

Consequently the full solution of the pair of equations is given by

$$\begin{cases} x = 5(w + z) \\ y = 2.5(w - z). \end{cases}$$

In terms of the initial values these are

$$\begin{cases} x = \frac{1}{2}X(e^{0.02t} + e^{-0.02t}) - Y(e^{0.02t} - e^{-0.02t}) \\ y = \frac{1}{2}Y(e^{0.02t} + e^{-0.02t}) - \frac{1}{4}X(e^{0.02t} - e^{-0.02t}). \end{cases}$$

The change from a discrete model in Chapter 7 to a continuous model here is really rather small; in place of

$$\begin{cases} 1.02^n \text{ put } e^{0.02t} \\ 0.98^n \text{ put } e^{-0.02t}. \end{cases}$$

The occurrence of terms like

$$\begin{cases} e^{0.02t} + e^{-0.02t} \\ e^{0.02t} - e^{-0.02t} \end{cases}$$

is common enough for them to be given special names (and special ways of calculating them on 'scientific' calculators). The new names are

$$\cosh \quad \text{and} \quad \sinh,$$

where

$$\begin{cases} \cosh t = \frac{1}{2}(e^t + e^{-t}) \\ \sinh t = \frac{1}{2}(e^t - e^{-t}). \end{cases}$$

Thus the solutions for the Iwo Jima differential equations are

$$\begin{cases} x = X \cosh(0.02t) - 2Y \sinh(0.02t) \\ y = Y \cosh(0.02t) - \frac{1}{2}X \sinh(0.02t). \end{cases}$$

The use of the *hyperbolic functions* cosh and sinh can always be regarded as an optional extra, because their definition in terms of the exponential e^t is quite easy. But they are part of the common language of mathematics by now, arising in many contexts, so it is more sensible to get used to them. Their basic properties are in some ways very similar to those of the *circular functions*

$$\cos \quad \text{and} \quad \sin$$

of trigonometry; this similarity is the reason for their names. A brief description of their properties is given in Section 18.6.

This method of combinations will always solve a pair of linear equations; the reason for this was outlined in Section 7.4 and will be explored more fully in Chapter 20, where the relation to matrices is considered. But it can also help in some non-linear cases too; see for example the newspaper competition equations in Section 7.1.

Exercise 18B

1   Compare in detail the solutions of the difference equations

$$\begin{cases} x_{n+1} = x_n - 0.04y_n \\ y_{n+1} = y_n - 0.01x_n \end{cases}$$

with $x_0 = 60\,000$ and $y_0 = 20\,000$, and the differential equations

$$\begin{cases} dx/dt = -0.04y \\ dy/dt = -0.01x \end{cases}$$

with $x = 60\,000$ and $y = 20\,000$ at $t = 0$. Which model is easier to use?

2   Solve the equations

$$\begin{cases} dx/dt = -ay \\ dy/dt = -bx \end{cases}$$

with $x = X$ and $y = Y$ at $t = 0$, to find Lanchester's square law again, i.e. that the army whose number is x wins if

$$bX^2 > aY^2.$$

3 Find the combinations which simplify the following pairs of equations. Hence solve equations (i) and (ii).

(i) $\dfrac{dx}{dt} = 3x + 2y$, $\dfrac{dy}{dt} = 2x + 3y$

(ii) $\dfrac{dx}{dt} = 5x + 4y$, $\dfrac{dy}{dt} = x + 5y$

(iii) $\dfrac{dy}{dx} = y + az$, $\dfrac{dz}{dx} = by + z$, $a > 0$ and $b > 0$.

4 An agricultural scientist is conducting experiments on the growth of wheat plant roots in pots with different water treatments. For her first experiment she expects that the rate of loss of water from the pot will be proportional to the root weight $R(t)$ in the pot, and the rate of increase of root weight will be proportional to the weight $W(t)$ of water present. Initially the root weight is very small. Set up the equations she needs to describe her experiments, and find solutions in terms of sine and cosine functions.

5 For the guerilla battle equations in Section 18.1(a)
(i) $dx/dt = -axy$
(ii) $dy/dt = -bx$
consider the combination of a constant times the first equation and a constant times y times the second equation. Hence show that

$$bx - \tfrac{1}{2}ay^2$$

is a constant. What corresponds to Lanchester's square law here?

6 Show, by taking a combination of the equations, that in the infection model

$$c = a.$$

7 Prove that

(i) $\dfrac{d}{dt}\cosh t = \sinh t$, $\dfrac{d}{dt}\sinh t = \cosh t$;

(ii) $\cosh^2 t - \sinh^2 t = 1$;
(iii) $\cosh 2t = \cosh^2 t + \sinh^2 t$.

18.3 ELIMINATION AND REDUCTION

The method of taking combinations of the given equations to give easier resulting equations is very useful when you can find what combinations to choose; but there are other methods too, and we shall look here at one alternative procedure, that of eliminating one of the functions.

Start again with the equations for the battle, in general form,

$$\dot{x} = -ay, \quad \dot{y} = -bx.$$

If you differentiate the first of these you get

$$\ddot{x} = -a\dot{y},$$

where $\ddot{x}$ means the second derivative of x, or d^2x/dt^2. You can now use the second equation to find

$$\ddot{x} = (ab)x.$$

This is a second order linear differential equation (i.e. it has a second derivative in it). At the moment we do not know how to solve such equations in general, though we know from previous work what the solution of this particular equation is like: it comes out in terms of exponentials of

$$\pm (ab)^{1/2}t.$$

Notice that the solution for $x(t)$, given in the previous section, needs two initial values, for $x(0)$ and $y(0)$. It is more helpful for later work if I restate this in a slightly different form: the solution for $x(t)$ needs two initial values, for $x(0)$ and $\dot{x}(0)$ – which is equal to $-y(0)/b$.

This process of elimination can always be done for linear equations (and sometimes for non-linear ones as well). For example, start with

$$\dot{x} = x - y, \quad \dot{y} = y - x.$$

Differentiation of the first gives you

$$\ddot{x} = \dot{x} - \dot{y} = \dot{x} - (y - x),$$
$$= \dot{x} + x - y.$$

But from the first equation

$$y = x - \dot{x},$$

so that we finish with

$$\ddot{x} = 2\dot{x}.$$

This is just

$$\frac{d^2x}{dt^2} = 2\frac{dx}{dt}$$

and you can integrate it once to find

$$\frac{dx}{dt} = 2x + C;$$

the solution is therefore

$$x = Ke^{2x} - \tfrac{1}{2}C$$

for some constants K and C. Check that you would have got this by the method of combinations too.

Let us do a non-linear example. Take the equations derived from the battle between an army and guerilla forces, (see question 5 in Exercise 18B)

$$\dot{x} = -axy, \quad \dot{y} = -bx.$$

Differentiating the second gives

$$\ddot{y} = -b\dot{x} = abxy = -ay\dot{y}.$$

This is a second order, non-linear differential equation.

There is a special trick available for reducing a wide class of second order differential equations to corresponding first order ones, which may then be soluble by the methods of Chapters 11 to 13. Take as example the equation derived above

$$\ddot{y} = -ay\dot{y}.$$

Let us put $p = \dot{y}$. Then

$$p\frac{dp}{dy} = \frac{dy}{dt}\frac{dp}{dy}$$

and by the chain rule this is equal to dp/dt, which is itself equal to d^2y/dt^2. This gives the useful result that

$$\frac{d^2y}{dt^2} = p\frac{dp}{dy}.$$

The equation for y can therefore be rewritten as

$$p\frac{dp}{dy} = -ayp.$$

Assuming that $p \neq 0$ we find the rather simple linear equation

$$dp/dy = -ay.$$

We have *reduced* the order of the equation from second order to first order by this trick of a change from using t as variable to using y as variable. We have to pay for it by integrating two first order equations instead of one second order one. The last equation can be solved by separation of variables as

$$p = C - \tfrac{1}{2}ay^2$$

where C is a constant; the value of C comes from the initial values, as follows. When $t = 0$, y has value $y(0)$, and p (which is equal to $\dot{y}$) has value $-bx(0)$, from the second of the original equations. Hence

$$-bx(0) = C - \tfrac{1}{2}a\{y(0)\}^2,$$

which shows that

$$C = \tfrac{1}{2}a\{y(0)\}^2 - bx(0).$$

All we have to do now is solve the first order equation

$$dy/dt = C - \tfrac{1}{2}ay^2,$$

and this is another separable equation, whose solution is given by integrating

$$\int \frac{1}{C - \tfrac{1}{2}ay^2}\,dy = \int dt.$$

To finish off the problem it is slightly easier to rearrange a bit, as

$$\int \frac{1}{y^2 - 2C/a}\,dy = -\tfrac{1}{2}a\int dt.$$

If you put $2Ca = r^2$ the integral on the left is easily done by partial fractions, giving

$$\ln\frac{y+r}{y-r} = art + D,$$

where D is a constant of integration. After a little more pushing you can find y in terms of t, and $x(t) = -b^{-1}\,dy/dt$ gives x.

The trick that has just been described is particularly useful in problems in the dynamics of a particle. If the particle has mass m and is moving along the x-axis under the influence of a force which depends only on x, say having value $F(x)$, then the equation of motion is

$$m\ddot{x} = F(x).$$

Replacing $\dot{x}$ by v (for velocity) we find, as above, that the equation of motion becomes

$$mv\,dv/dx = F(x).$$

This is again a separable equation which has solution

$$\tfrac{1}{2}mv^2 = \int F(x)\,dx.$$

In the language of mechanics this equation is relating a change in kinetic energy to an amount of work done, but in the present context it is just an intermediate equation on the way to finding x in terms of t. Let us suppose that we can integrate F to get W (for work); the equation becomes

$$\tfrac{1}{2}mv^2 = W(x) - W_0,$$

where W_0 is a constant of integration. You can rearrange this as

$$dx/dt = \{2(W(x) - W_0)/m\}^{1/2},$$

which is again a separable equation whose solution requires the evaluation of the (unpleasant looking) integral

$$\int \frac{1}{\{2(W(x) - W_0)/m\}^{1/2}}\,dx = \int dt.$$

Only in very special cases of $F(x)$ will it be possible to calculate these integrals other than numerically, but the method of solving equations in dynamics by considering energy and work is of wide importance. See, for example, *Mechanics and Vectors* in this series.

Exercise 18C

1 Solve the equations

$$\begin{cases} \dot{x} = x - y, & x = 1 \quad \text{at } t = 0 \\ \dot{y} = y - x, & y = 2 \quad \text{at } t = 0 \end{cases}$$

(i) by the method of combinations,

(ii) by elimination to get a second order equation for y, and then integrating it directly once,

(iii) by elimination to get a second order equation for x and then using $\ddot{x} = v\,dv/dx$.

2 Solve the equations

$$\begin{cases} \dot{x} = -2 \times 10^{-5} xy \\ \dot{y} = -0.2x \end{cases}$$

with $y = 10^3$ at $t = 0$, in the two cases

(i) $x = 32$ at $t = 0$,

(ii) $x = 50$ at $t = 0$.

3 Solve the 'simple harmonic motion' equation

$$\ddot{x} + n^2 x = 0$$

in the cases

(i) $x = a$ and $\dot{x} = 0$ at $t = 0$,

(ii) $x = 0$ and $\dot{x} = U$ at $t = 0$.

4 Consider the disease equations

$$\begin{cases} \dfrac{dI}{dt} = -aI + bIS \\[2mm] \dfrac{dS}{dt} = -bIS. \end{cases}$$

Show that

$$\begin{cases} \ddot{S} = abIS - b^2 IS^2 - bI\dot{S} \\ I = -\dot{S}/(bS). \end{cases}$$

Hence find a second order equation for S, and a corresponding equation for $\dot{S} = T$ (say). Is it easily solved?

18.4   DIVISION OF EQUATIONS

There is another ingenious method for dealing with pairs of equations that also relies on a theorem of calculus. If x and y are both functions of t then

$$\frac{dy}{dx} = \frac{dy/dt}{dx/dt},$$

provided of course that you are not dividing by zero.

Applying this to the guerilla war model

$$\begin{cases} dx/dt = -axy \\ dy/dt = -bx. \end{cases}$$

You obtain

$$dy/dx = b/ay$$

for x and y not zero. This is a separable equation with solution

$$\tfrac{1}{2}y^2 = bx/a + A,$$

where A is a constant; if the two forces start off with strengths x_0 and y_0 the value of A is $\tfrac{1}{2}y_0^2 - bx_0/a$. You should compare this result with the equation derived by a combination method in Exercise 18B, question 5.

The solution to the guerilla war model is

$$y^2 - y_0^2 = \frac{2b}{a}(x - x_0),$$

which is the equation of a family of parabolas, drawn in Fig. 1.

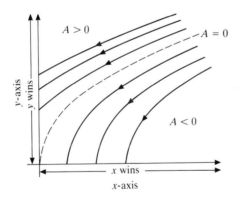

Figure 1. The family of solutions of the guerilla war equations

The solution point (x, y) moves along a particular parabola, in the direction shown, because both $\dot{x}$ and $\dot{y}$ are negative. This (partial) solution of the equations doesn't tell you how fast the solution point moves along the solution curve, or how long it takes to get to whichever axis it ends at. For that you need to solve to find x in terms of t and y in terms of t, as described in Section 18.3.

This method only works when the expression you get for dy/dx comes out with no t in it; although even in this case it may not help you because you may find a first order equation that you cannot solve.

In the example we have used here we *could* continue the solution by putting

$$dy/dt = -bx = aA - \tfrac{1}{2}ay^2.$$

This is the same equation as we had before for y in terms of t, and so we will find the same solution.

The advantage of this rather simple method is that you get some useful information about the solution (the shape of the solution curves in the x, y plane) without having to work out the solution completely.

Let us see this method at work on a mechanics problem. Suppose a particle of unit mass is moving along the x-axis and the force on it is

$$F(x) = 1 - x^3.$$

This means that the particle can remain at rest at $x = 1$ (it is a point of equilibrium), and that the force is towards that point. The corresponding pair of equations is

$$\begin{cases} dv/dt = 1 - x^3 \\ dx/dt = v. \end{cases}$$

When you divide them, you obtain

$$v\, dv/dx = 1 - x^3,$$

which is just what you would have found by the method of the previous section.

In this example we can integrate to get

$$\tfrac{1}{2}v^2 = x - \tfrac{1}{4}x^4 + E,$$

where E is a constant, usually called the total energy. Here it is the curves of v against x that tell you how the solution behaves. The way to find out what they look like is first to draw curves for v^2 against x (Fig. 2(a)), which are rather like parabolas. Then you take the square root of each value to get the curves of v against x (not forgetting the $\pm$) in Fig. 2(b).

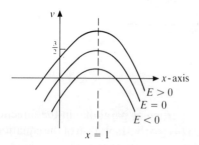

Figure 2(a). Curves of v^2 against x
for $v\, dv/dx = 1 - x^3$

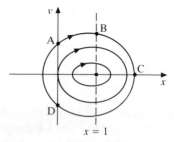

Figure 2(b). Corresponding curves
of v against x

The plane with axes labelled x and v is often called the *phase plane*. The curves in the phase plane tell you how the speed v must vary with the position x in such a problem; but, as before, how x varies with t is not clear at this stage.

In this example all the curves in the phase plane cut the x-axis at right angles, because

$$\frac{dv}{dx} = \frac{1-x^3}{v},$$

which is infinite when $v=0$. All the curves are closed loops, and the solution point moves in the direction shown because dx/dt has (of course) the sign of v.

In this example there is no way of finding a formula for x in terms of t; if you need to know this information, you must find it numerically. But you can get a very good idea of how x varies with t by following round one of the curves of v against x. I shall use the outermost curve in Fig. 2(b), and I shall start at the point I have labelled A. At that point $x=0$ and $\dot{x}>0$ (because $v>0$); as you move on towards B the slope $\dot{x}$ increases and x also increases. Between B and C the slope decreases but x continues to increase as v is still positive. At C, x reaches its largest value, where $v=dx/dt=0$. From C to D the slope is negative and x is getting smaller, and at D, x passes through zero. Finally from D to A we have $x<0$. Then the whole cycle starts again at A, but from a larger value of t (Fig. 3). The motion is periodic, with a periodic time which would have to be found by numerical means if we needed to know it.

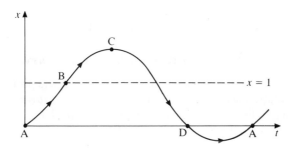

Figure 3. Diagram of x in terms of t for $vdv/dx = 1-x^3$

Exercise 18D

1   Find the curves of y against x for Lanchester's battle equations

$$\dot{x} = -ay, \quad \dot{y} = -bx.$$

Sketch the curves, and hence derive the Lanchester square law.

2   Guerilla forces can have discipline and communication problems, so that some leave the fight if the opposing army is rather large. Modify the equations to

$$\dot{x} = -axy - cy, \quad \dot{y} = -bx;$$

find the curves for y in terms of x and determine a criterion for the winning army (in terms of a, b, c, x_0, y_0).

3 The agricultural scientist of Exercise 18B modifies her experiment by adding water at a constant rate to each pot, so that

$$dW/dt = -aR + c, \quad dR/dt = bW.$$

Sketch curves for W in terms of R, and for R against t.

4 Check what you have done in the previous exercise by solving for R in terms of t.

5 For the infectious disease in Section 18.1 find the equation for dS/dR and hence show that

$$S = S_0 e^{-bR/a}.$$

Deduce from the equation

$$\frac{dI}{dt} = -aI + bIS$$

a formula for I in terms of R. Hence find the first order (separable) equation for R in terms of t

$$\frac{dR}{dt} = a\{N - R - S_0 e^{-bR/a}\}.$$

6 After the infectious disease in question 5 has run its course, has everyone been infected? (Use the equation for dR/dt in question 5.)

18.5 NUMERICAL SOLUTIONS

(a) The general shape of solution curves

If the equations describing a situation are at all involved, you probably have to do a numerical solution. This introduces few new ideas, but it is often useful to do some mathematics first to see what it is that is to be calculated. I shall discuss the subject in terms of the prey–predator model equations from Section 18.1(c), which were

$$\begin{cases} \dfrac{du}{dt} = (a-1)u - buv \\[2mm] \dfrac{dv}{dt} = (p-1)v + quv, \end{cases}$$

where $a > 1, p < 1, b > 0, q > 0$. When I come to do numerical work I shall use the values

$$\begin{cases} a = 2 \text{ so that the prey reproduces quite fast,} \\ p = 0.9 \text{ so that the predator dies out slowly,} \\ b = 10^{-3}, q = 10^{-5}, \text{ not a strong interaction.} \end{cases}$$

These are merely chosen as easy values to work with; you need to find a specialist if you want realistic values.

One way of proceeding would be to divide the equations:

$$\frac{du}{dv} = \frac{(a-1)u - buv}{(p-1)v + quv}.$$

This is a separable equation, giving as solution

$$\int \frac{p-1+qu}{u} \, qu = \int \frac{a-1-bv}{v} \, dv.$$

The resulting solution curves are not simple, and their shape would have to be plotted by computer. So start again from the equations.

It is easy to find the steady state (or equilibrium) solutions of the equations, for if $du/dt = dv/dt = 0$ we have the equations

$$\begin{cases} (a-1)u - buv = 0 \\ (p-1)v + quv = 0. \end{cases}$$

The solutions of these are

$$u = v = 0$$

which is the trivial solution with no fish at all, or

$$u = (1-p)/q, \quad v = (a-1)/b.$$

The latter solution is the relevant one, unless a massive dose of pollution wipes out both populations. These two solution points are rather special points of the u, v plane, as at them the slope du/dv takes the unpleasant form $0/0$, which is indeterminate. Except at these *critical* points the sign of the slope can be easily determined. To the right of the line

$$u = (1-p)/q,$$

$\dot{v} > 0$; similarly above the line $v = (a-1)/b$, $\dot{u} < 0$. The plane divides up as in Fig. 4, and du/dv has the sign given by dividing $\dot{u}$ by $\dot{v}$. Hence, for example, in the top right part of the plane you find that $du/dv < 0$, which means that any solution curves of u with v must slope downwards to the right or upwards to the left.

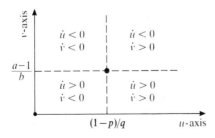

Figure 4. Signs of $\dot{u}$ and $\dot{v}$

Similarly, near the origin the curves slope in the same way. This enables us to sketch the curves shown in Fig. 5(a), (b) and (c) for the relations between

(i)   prey numbers u and predator numbers v,
(ii) prey numbers u and time,
(iii) predator numbers v and time.

These are *not* accurate graphs, only sketches to indicate the kind of shape.

You can see in Fig. 5(a) that this system is repeating itself. When you get back to A again after going once round you have the *same* values of u and v, and hence the same values of $\dot{u}$ and $\dot{v}$ as when you set off (from the equations) the cycle ABCDA repeats endlessly. Not all systems behave in this way; the curve ABCD need never have cut itself again, but could have spiralled in (or out). How can we be sure that this is the correct behaviour in this case? Not easily, but the exact solution for u in terms of v can provide a route to this result.

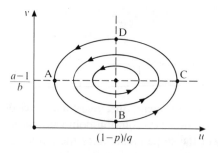

Figure 5(a). Sketch graph of v against u

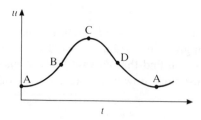

Figure 5(b). Prey numbers u against time

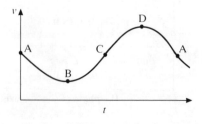

Figure 5(c). Predator numbers v against time

Exercise 18E

1   If u and v are both small then the equations are approximately

$$du/dt = (a-1)u, \quad dv/dt = (p-1)v.$$

Solve these to find the shape of the curve for u against v near the origin.

2   Set up and solve approximate equations for u and v both large.

3   An agricultural scientist is conducting experiments on the leaves of wheat plants, when they are subject to attacks of the disease powdery mildew. In the early stages of growth of the wheat plant she expects the total leaf area L of the plant to follow the equation

$$dL/dt = a(L-M)$$

where M is the area of mildewed leaf, and she expects also that

$$dM/dt = b(1 - M/L)M,$$

because mildew spread must be slower when much of the leaf is already infected. Determine for her the curves of M against L; you should sketch the curves, together with the important line $M = L$. Explain why the model requires $b \geqslant a$. Sketch curves for $M(t)$ and $L(t)$. Check your answers by solving the special case $b = 2a$.

4   The shape of the u, v curves near the critical point

$$u = \frac{1-p}{q}, \quad v = \frac{a-1}{b}$$

can be found by putting

$$u = \frac{1-p}{q} + x, \quad v = \frac{a-1}{b} + y$$

where x and y are both *small*. Then you can find the corresponding equations for x and y, in which non-linear terms in x and y may be neglected. Do this, to show that the curves near the critical point are ellipses, and that $x(t)$ and $y(t)$ are in terms of sines and cosines.

(b)   The numerical procedure

We now know what we have to compute: closed curves round the critical point. Which equations shall we solve? We could solve

(i)   the original equations for u and v,
(ii)   the single equation for du/dv,
(iii)   the integrated form of equation (ii).

I intend to solve (i), because this also gives me information on the *time* at which the various values of u and v occur. I used Euler's method, which in this case becomes

$$\begin{cases} t_{\text{new}} = t_{\text{old}} + h \\ u_{\text{new}} = u_{\text{old}} + h\{(a-1)u_{\text{old}} - bu_{\text{old}}v_{\text{old}}\} \\ v_{\text{new}} = v_{\text{old}} + h\{(p-1)v_{\text{old}} + qu_{\text{old}}v_{\text{old}}\}. \end{cases}$$

The program for this calculation is easy enough to write, and I decided to use the values suggested above,

$$a=2, \quad b=10^{-3}, \quad p=0.9, \quad q=10^{-5};$$

these give the equilibrium population to be

$$u=10^4 \quad \text{and} \quad v=10^3.$$

I started with a run near the equilibrium point by using the values

$$u=10^4 \quad \text{and} \quad v=900.$$

Then I tried a run not quite so close to equilibrium, starting from

$$u=10^4 \quad \text{and} \quad v=700.$$

In each case I used a step length $h=10^{-2}$, and printed results at integer values of t. I found the periodic time for the first run to be almost 20: at $t=20$ the values were $u=10\,030$, $v=899$. For the second run the periodic time was about 20.7. The curves generated by these runs are shown in Fig. 6.

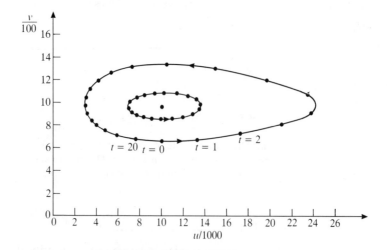

Figure 6. Numerical solution curves for the relation between u and v

Curves of u against t show clearly how long the prey population takes to recover from a large fall in numbers caused by an increase in the number of predators (Fig. 7). The curves are periodic. The one near the equilibrium point is quite like a sine curve, but the one further from equilibrium is much flatter in the trough of the wave and steeper near the crest. Curves for v against t are of generally similar shape, but displaced along the t-axis so that v has its minimum at $t=0$, and its maximum near $t=9$.

The calculations above have been done using Euler's method. We have seen in earlier chapters that the improved Euler method is quite a good all-purpose

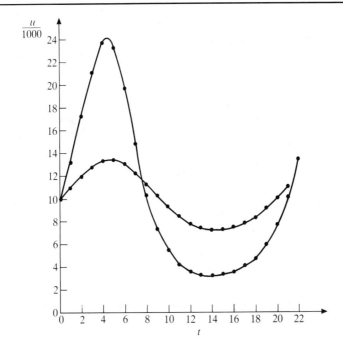

Figure 7. Numerical solutions for u against t

differential equation solver. In the present context it has the following form

$$\begin{cases} t_{new} = t_{old} + h \\ u_{inter} = u_{old} + h(du/dt)_{old} \\ v_{inter} = v_{old} + h(dy/dt)_{old} \\ u_{new} = u_{old} + \tfrac{1}{2}h\{(du/dt)_{old} + (du/dt)_{inter}\} \\ v_{new} = v_{old} + \tfrac{1}{2}h\{(dv/dt)_{old} + (dv/dt)_{inter}\} \end{cases}$$

where $(du/dt)_{inter}$ and $(dv/dt)_{inter}$ are calculated using u_{inter} and v_{inter} (and t_{new} if necessary, which it isn't in the present example).

Exercise 18F

1   Use the improved Euler method to solve

$$\begin{cases} \dfrac{du}{dt} = u - 10^{-3}uv \\[2mm] \dfrac{dv}{dt} = -0.1v + 10^{-5}uv \end{cases}$$

with starting values $u = 10^4, v = 500, t = 0$. What period has the solution? Plot graphs of

(i) u and v (ii) u and t (iii) v and t.

2 Set up a program to solve the equations of Exercise 18E, question 3 (on leaf area). Greenhouse experiments with disease-free wheat suggest that $a = 0.04$. Carry out runs for various values of b, all starting from $L = 100 \, \text{cm}^2$ and $M = 1 \, \text{cm}^2$, and measuring time in days. Do not take $t > 60$, because leaves cease to grow at about that time.

3 A cruise ship with 100 people on board arrives at a small island with 900 inhabitants. Some of those on the ship have been suffering from a new strain of 'flu to which the islanders have no immunity. On arrival, 40 of those on the ship are infectious, and 50 have recovered. Follow the course of the infection by solving the equations

$$\begin{cases} \dfrac{dI}{dt} = -0.2I + bIS \\[2em] \dfrac{dS}{dt} = -bIS \end{cases}$$

numerically in the cases $b = 10^{-4}, b = 3 \times 10^{-4}, b = 10^{-3}$. How many people eventually have an attack of 'flu? How long does the outbreak last, if t in the equations is measured in days?

4 If the authorities on the island in question 3 decided to quarantine the ship to prevent 'flu attacking any islanders, for how long should they do it?

18.6 HYPERBOLIC FUNCTIONS

(a) Definitions and graphs

The two basic definitions are

$$\begin{cases} \cosh x = \tfrac{1}{2}(e^x + e^{-x}) \\ \sinh x = \tfrac{1}{2}(e^x - e^{-x}). \end{cases}$$

Subsidiary definitions are just like those in trigonometry:

$$\tanh x = \frac{\sinh x}{\cosh x} \qquad \coth x = \frac{\cosh x}{\sinh x}$$

$$\operatorname{sech} x = \frac{1}{\cosh x} \qquad \operatorname{cosech} x = \frac{1}{\sinh x}$$

Graphs for $\cosh x, \sinh x, \tanh x$ are sketched in Fig. 8. Cosh is an even function, sinh and tanh are both odd functions.

(b) Calculus properties

From the definitions you can quickly derive

$$\frac{d}{dx} \cosh x = \sinh x, \qquad \frac{d}{dx} \sinh x = \cosh x.$$

Hence for each function, its second derivative is itself. It follows that the differential equation

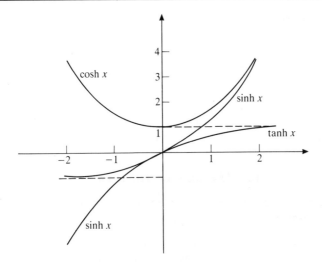

Figure 8. Graphs of hyperbolic functions

$$\frac{d^2y}{dx^2} = n^2 y$$

is solved by

$$y = A \cosh nx + B \sinh nx,$$

for any constants A and B. Compare with

$$\frac{d^2y}{dx^2} = -n^2 y$$

which is solved by $C \cos nx + D \sin nx$.

Taylor approximations to $\cosh x$ and $\sinh x$ are

$$\cosh x \approx 1 + \tfrac{1}{2}x^2 + \ldots + \frac{1}{(2n)!}x^{2n}$$

$$\sinh x \approx x + \tfrac{1}{6}x^3 + \ldots + \frac{1}{(2n+1)!}x^{2n+1}$$

for any n. Compare with the approximations for $\cos x$ and $\sin x$, which have the same terms but alternating signs.

The integrals

$$\begin{cases} \displaystyle\int \frac{1}{\sqrt{(1+x^2)}} \, dx = \sinh^{-1}x \\[2mm] \displaystyle\int \frac{1}{1-x^2} \, dx = \tanh^{-1}x, \ |x| < 1 \end{cases}$$

should be compared with

$$\begin{cases} \int \dfrac{1}{\sqrt{(1-x^2)}} dx = \sin^{-1}x, \ |x| < 1 \\ \qquad \int \dfrac{1}{1+x^2} dx = \tan^{-1}x \end{cases}$$

(c) 'Trigonometric' formulas

All the trigonometric formulas for sines and cosines have analogues for sinh and cosh. For example

(i) $\cosh^2 x - \sinh^2 x = 1, \quad \cos^2\theta + \sin^2\theta = 1;$
(ii) $\cosh 2x = \cosh^2 x + \sinh^2 x, \quad \cos 2\theta = \cos^2\theta - \sin^2\theta;$
(iii) $\sinh 2x = 2 \sinh x \cosh x, \quad \sin 2\theta = 2 \sin\theta \cos\theta;$
(iv) $\cosh(x+y) = \cosh x \cosh y + \sinh x \sinh y,$
       $\cos(\theta + \phi) = \cos\theta \cos\phi - \sin\theta \sin\phi;$
(v) $\cosh x + \cosh y = 2 \cosh\frac{1}{2}(x+y)\cosh\frac{1}{2}(x-y),$
       $\cos\theta + \cos\phi = 2 \cos\frac{1}{2}(\theta+\phi)\cos\frac{1}{2}(\theta-\phi).$

There are many other similar formulas. The general conversion rule is that when two sines occur in a product, there is a change of sign between circular and hyperbolic formulas.

(d) Complex number relations

Many of the above formulas may best be understood in terms of the following:

$$\begin{cases} \cosh x = \cos(jx), \quad \cos x = \cosh(jx) \\ \sinh x = -j\sin(jx), \quad \sin x = -j\sinh(jx) \end{cases}$$

where $j = \sqrt{(-1)}$.
   For these to make full sense you need general definitions of cosh, sinh, cos, sin which allow them to be used on complex numbers.

18.7   SUMMARY

Forming a *combination* of two equations can sometimes lead to unlinked equations to solve; this method can always be used for *linear* equations.
   Elimination of one variable from a pair of first order differential equations will give a single second order equation. *Reduction* of the order by

$$p = \frac{dy}{dx}, \quad \frac{d^2y}{dx^2} = p\frac{dp}{dy}$$

will often give a first order equation to solve for p in terms of y; then y in terms of x comes from solving

$$p = \frac{dy}{dx}.$$

This technique in mechanics involves the ideas of *energy* and *work*.

Division of equations for $\dot{y}$ and $\dot{x}$ gives an equation for dy/dx; this may sometimes be solved to give the solution for y in terms of x.

Numerical solution can be done for the pair of equations by adjusting either Euler's method or the improved Euler method slightly. Alternatively, numerical methods can be applied to equations derived in any of the earlier ways.

Hyperbolic functions can come into the solutions for a pair of linear equations. They have definitions in terms of exponentials, and many properties very similar to those of the usual trigonometric functions.

Revision exercise C

1 Consider the equation

$$\frac{dp}{dt} = p - 5\ln p \qquad (1)$$

with $p=1$ when $t=0$, one of a class of equations considered in early work on population growth.

(i) Sketch the graph of $5\ln p$ and show that there is just one solution, p_s, of the equation

$$p - 5\ln p = 0$$

in the range $0 < p \leqslant 2$. Why will the iterative process

$$p_{n+1} = 5\ln p_n$$

never converge to p_s, whatever the starting value? Use another direct iterative process on an equivalent equation, with Aitken's δ^2 acceleration technique, to find p_s correct to 3 d.p.

(ii) Using the modified Euler (Heun) method applied to equation (1), carry out a single step to calculate a value for p when $t=0.1$. Work to 4 d.p. and show your working clearly.

(iii) Equation (1) was integrated numerically by Heun's method in order to find the value of t at which $p = p_s$. The following table gives the values of t at which p first exceeded p_s, using various values of the step length h.

h	0.2	0.1	0.05	0.02
t	3.40	3.10	3.00	2.96

Use the method of least squares to fit the formula

$$t = A + Bh^2$$

and hence find an estimate of the value of t as h becomes vanishingly small. (*Note*: In the method of least squares the coefficients of an approximating line $y = a + bx$ are given by

$$a = \frac{1}{D}\{\Sigma x^2 \Sigma y - \Sigma x \Sigma xy\}, \quad b = \frac{1}{D}\{n\Sigma xy - \Sigma x \Sigma y\},$$

where

$$D = n\Sigma x^2 - (\Sigma x)^2. \qquad \text{[SMP 89]}$$

2 A numerical solution is required of the differential equation

$$\frac{dy}{dx} = f(x, y) = \sin(xy),$$

with the initial condition $y = 1$ when $x = 0$. The value of $y = y_i$ at the point $x = x_i$ is found using the following method:

(i)   put $i = 0$, $h = 0.1$, $x_0 = 0$, $y_0 = 1$
(ii) calculate $k_1 = hf(x_i, y_i)$
(iii) calculate $k_2 = hf(x_i + h, y_i + k_1)$
(iv) calculate $k = \frac{1}{2}(k_1 + k_2)$
(v)   calculate $y_{i+1} = y_i + k$, and $x_{i+1} = x_i + h$
(vi) replace i by $i + 1$ and repeat steps (ii) to (vi).

Use this method to estimate y_5 working to 5 decimal places throughout.
   On a rough sketch of the solution y against x, show how the method may be interpreted graphically.   [MEI 89]

3 It is given that $\frac{dy}{dx} = f(x, y)$, where y is itself a function of x. Given also that h is a positive constant, and denoting $x_0 + nh$ by x_n and the value of y when $x = x_n$ by y_n, use the trapezium rule to prove that

$$y_1 \approx y_0 + \tfrac{1}{2}h(f(x_0, y_0) + f(x_1, y_1)) \quad \text{(the modified Euler formula)}.$$

A differential equation of the form $\frac{dy}{dx} = yP(x) + Q(x)$, with $y = y_0$ when $x = x_0$, is to be solved numerically. Use the modified Euler formula to obtain an approximation for y_1 in terms of y_0, $P(x_0)$, $P(x_1)$, $Q(x_0)$, $Q(x_1)$ and h.

Given that $\frac{dy}{dx} = y \sin x$, show that

$$y_{n+1} \approx \frac{y_n(2 + h \sin x_n) + 2hx_n + h^2}{2 - h \sin x_{n+1}}.$$

Given also that $y = 1$ when $x = 1$, obtain values for y when $x = 1.1$ and $x = 1.2$.
                                                                [UCLES 88]

4 (i) It is given that $\frac{dy}{dx} = f(x, y)$. Denoting $x_0 + nh$ by x_n, where h is a positive constant, and denoting the value of y when $x = x_n$ by y_n, use Simpson's rule to show that

$$y_2 \approx y_0 + \tfrac{1}{3}h\{f(x_0, y_0) + 4f(x_1, y_1) + f(x_2, y_2)\}.$$

(ii) Given that $\frac{dy}{dx} = \frac{1}{2} - xy$, and that $h = 0.1$, deduce that

$$y_2 \approx \frac{(30 - x_0)y_0 - 4x_1y_1 + 3}{30 + x_2}.$$

(iii) A numerical solution is required for the differential equation $\frac{dy}{dx} = \frac{1}{2} - xy$ for which $y = 1$ when $x = 0$. Obtain the Taylor series expansion of y up to and including the term in x^4. Show that, to 5 decimal places, the value of y given by this series when $x = 0.1$ is 1.04485.

(iv) Use the results of (ii) and (iii) to obtain values for y when $x = 0.2$ and 0.3.
                                                                [UCLES 89]

5 Show that the second derivative of $\sec^k x$ with respect to x may be written
$k(k+1)\sec^{k+2}x - k^2\sec^k x$.

Given that $f(x) = \sec x$, deduce that, for all n, $f^{(2n)}(x)$ may be expressed as a polynomial in $\sec x$.

Show also that, for all n, $f^{(2n+1)}(0) = 0$.

Prove that $f^{(5)}(x) = (120\sec^4 x - 60\sec^2 x + 1)\sec x \tan x$.

Obtain the power series expansion of $\sec x$ up to and including the term in x^4.

This series is to be used to obtain approximate values of $\sec x$ for $-0.3 < x < 0.3$. By considering the remainder term R_5 in the form

$$R_5 = \frac{x^5}{5!}f^{(5)}(\xi), \text{ where } -0.3 \leqslant \xi \leqslant 0.3,$$

and assuming that $f^{(5)}(x)$ increases throughout $(-0.3, 0.3)$, find an absolute error bound for the values so obtained.   [UCLES 88]

6 Plans put forward for the replacement of A-level envisage a three-part final test of a candidate's ability, denoted by $f(x)$, which is assumed to depend on the candidate's age x in years. The candidate would gain marks A in July of the examination year, B in April, and C in January. It is assumed that the marks measure the candidate's ability, so that
(i) $A = f(x)$, if his age is x in July,
(ii) $B = f(x - \frac{1}{4})$, because his age was $x - \frac{1}{4}$ in April,
(iii) $C = f(x - \frac{1}{2})$, because his age was $x - \frac{1}{2}$ in January.
The final assessment mark is to be given by a formula

$$F = \alpha A + \beta B + \gamma C.$$

Write down Taylor expansions for

$$f(x - \tfrac{1}{4}) \quad \text{and} \quad f(x - \tfrac{1}{2})$$

up to terms in $f''(x)$. Hence show that

$$F \approx (\alpha + \beta + \gamma)f(x) - (\tfrac{1}{4}\beta + \tfrac{1}{2}\gamma)f'(x) + \tfrac{1}{8}(\tfrac{1}{4}\beta + \gamma)f''(x),$$

assuming that remainder terms are small.

Determine α, β, γ to satisfy the requirements of 'natural justice', which are

(a) $\alpha + \beta + \gamma = 1$,
(b) F depends only on $f(x)$ and $f'(x)$, with the coefficient of each being positive,
(c) equal weight is to be given to the candidate's ability $f(x)$ and his rate of increase of ability $f'(x)$.   [SMP 88]

7 Write down the first two terms of the Taylor expansion of $y(x+h)$. Hence, or otherwise, show that

$$y'_r \approx \frac{1}{h}(y_{r+1} - y_r).$$

Use this approximation to estimate $y(1.1)$ and $y(1.2)$ if

$$y' = x^2 - \frac{y}{x} \quad \text{and} \quad y(1) = 1.$$

Explain why, in general, the use of the approximation

$$y'_r \approx \frac{1}{2h}(y_{r+1} - y_{r+1})$$

is to be preferred. Use this second approximation to solve

$$y' = x^2 - \frac{y}{x}$$

for $x = 1(0.2)2$ where $y(1) = 1$ and the estimate of $y(1.2)$ is taken from the first approximation. (This means: find y at $x = 1.2$, 1.4, 1.6, 1.8, 2.0.)

Compare the value of $y(2)$ with that obtained from an exact solution of the differential equation.   [MEI 86]

8 Derive the numerical approximation to the second derivative

$$y_0'' \approx \frac{1}{h^2}(y_1 - 2y_0 + y_{-1}).$$

Derive also expressions for
(i)   the leading term of the truncation error in terms of h and a derivative of y at $x = 0$,
(ii) the rounding error in terms of h and E where E is the maximum of $|e_1|$, $|e_0|$ and $|e_{-1}|$, and e_i is the (unknown) error in y_i.
A table of values of x in steps of 0.05 and the corresponding values of a function $f(x)$, correct to nine decimal places, is given below.

x	$f(x)$
0.90	0.673 326 909
0.95	0.703 415 504
1.00	0.731 470 984
1.05	0.757 423 225
1.10	0.781 207 360

Using these data, obtain two estimates for $f''(1.00)$, one based upon $h = 0.10$, the other upon $h = 0.05$. By considering the relative magnitudes of the truncation errors of these two estimates, obtain an improved value for $f''(1.00)$.

Repeat the process described in the previous paragraph but using, this time, data rounded to five decimal places. Discuss the results in terms of both the truncation error and the rounding error.   [MEI 87]

9 Use a form of Taylor's theorem to show that the error in the approximation

$$f'(x) \approx \frac{1}{h}\{f(x+h) - f(x)\}$$

does not exceed $\frac{1}{2}h$ times the maximum value of $|f''(\xi)|$, where ξ is between x and $x+h$.
Determine the coefficients, α, β, γ so that the approximation

$$f'(x) \approx \alpha f(x) + \beta f(x+h) + \gamma f(x+2h)$$

has a maximum error similar to that above, but involving h^2 and a third derivative of f.

Use this formula and the values (correct to 7 decimal places)

$$\log_{10} 2 = 0.301\,030\,0$$

$$\log_{10} 2.01 = 0.303\,196\,1$$

$$\log_{10} 2.02 = 0.305\,351\,4$$

to estimate the derivative of $\log_{10} x$ for $x=2$. What is the largest possible error in your answer caused by the rounding errors in the above values?   [SMP 89]

10   The differential equation $y' = x^2 - y^2$ is to be solved in the interval $x=0$ to $x=0.5$ by an approximate step-by-step method with a step length of $h=0.1$. The value of y when $x=0$ is given to be 1. Use a Maclaurin series to estimate $y(0.1)$ to 4 decimal places. Hence, using the formula $y(x+h) - y(x-h) \approx 2hy'(x)$, find the values of $y(0.2)$, $y(0.3)$, $y(0.4)$ and $y(0.5)$.

Explain what further steps you would take to obtain the solution to a specified degree of accuracy.   [MEI 88]

11   The variables x and y are related by the equation

$$y = 1 - ke^{x+y},$$

where k is a constant.
Find the first three terms in the expansion of x for small y.

Let λ be the value of y when $x=0$ so that $\lambda = 1 - ke^{\lambda}$. Show that $y'(0) = \dfrac{\lambda - 1}{2 - \lambda}$ and find $y''(0)$ in terms of λ. Hence write down the first three terms in the expansion of y for small x in terms of x and the constant λ.

State in each case any restrictions on k for the expansions to exist.   [MEI 87]

12   The variable y satisfies the differential equation

$$\frac{dy}{dx} = 1 - y\sqrt{x},$$

and $y=2$ when $x=1$. In order to obtain approximate values of y when $x=1.1$, $x=1.2$ and $x=1.3$, a second-order Taylor approximation

$$y_{n+1} \approx y_n + hy'_n + \frac{h^2}{2!} y''_n$$

is used, where y_n denotes the value of y when $x = 1 + nh$. Find y'' when $x=1$, and show that, when $x=1.1$, $y \approx 1.900$.

Repeat this process, continuing to use $h=0.1$, to obtain approximate values of y when $x=1.2$ and 1.3. Give your answers to 3 places of decimals.

Show that $y_{n+2} \approx y_n + 2hy'_{n+1}$, and use this approximation to verify the values you have obtained for y when $x=1.2$ and 1.3.   [UCLES 89]

13   The solution of the differential equation

$$\frac{dy}{dx} = x^2 - \cos y$$

for which $y=0$ when $x=1$ is to be found numerically. Use a Taylor series method with $h=0.2$, and keeping terms up to and including h^3, to find the values of y for $x=1.2$ and $x=1.4$, giving your answers to three places of decimals.   [UCLES 88]

14   Derive the trapezium rule for finding the approximate integral of $y = f(x)$ for $a \leqslant x \leqslant b$ using n strips with a fixed step interval of h.

By considering the integral over a single interval $x_r \leqslant x \leqslant x_{r+1}$ show that

$$\int_{x_r}^{x_{r+1}} f(x)\,dx = hf(x_r) + \tfrac{1}{2}h^2 f'(x_r) + \tfrac{1}{6}h^3 f''(x_r) + \dots$$

Deduce that the modulus of the truncation error, which occurs by approximating to this integral by using the trapezium rule with a single strip, is approximately

$$\tfrac{1}{12}h^3|f''(x_r)|.$$

Show that an approximate upper bound to the modulus of the truncation error over $a \leqslant x \leqslant b$ is given by

$$\tfrac{1}{12}(b-a)h^2 M$$

where M is the maximum value of $|f''(x)|$ for $a \leqslant x \leqslant b$.   [MEI 88]

15   To solve the first-order differential equation

$$y' = f(x, y)$$

a predictor–corrector method may be used. This involves using a predictor formula to find an initial approximation to y_{k+1} from y_k. This initial approximation is then used in a corrector formula to improve the approximation. Application of the corrector formula may be repeated.

A simple predictor–corrector pair consists of the Euler formula

$$y_{k+1} = y_k + hy_k'$$

as the predictor and the modified Euler formula

$$y_{k+1} = y_k + \tfrac{1}{2}h(y_k' + y_{k+1}')$$

as the corrector.

Derive these two formulas and indicate why the second is likely to be the more accurate.

Use the method with two applications of the corrector formula to solve

$$y' = x^3 + \frac{y}{x}, \quad y(1) = 1,$$

for $x = 1.00(0.05)1.25$. All working and tabulations should be performed correct to five decimal places.   [MEI 89]

16   Throughout this question, y_r denotes the value of y at $x = rh$, where $h = 0.1$.

The differential equation $y' = x^2 + y^2$ is to be solved numerically using a step-by-step method with a starting condition $y(0) = 1$.

Find the Maclaurin expansion of y for small values of x up to the term in x^4 and hence find an approximation to $y(0.1)$.

Using the approximation

$$y_{r+1} = y_{r-1} + 2hy_r'$$

and $h = 0.1$, estimate a value for y_5, working to 4 decimal places.

Each time this approximate formula is used, an error is introduced into the calculated value of y. The effect of the accumulation of these errors can be investigated by using a modified approximation

$$y_{r+1} = y_{r-1} + 2hy_r' + \varepsilon,$$

where ε is an error introduced for the purpose of this investigation. Taking $\varepsilon = 0.01$, show that the previous estimate of y_5 is increased by approximately 0.044.   [MEI 86]

17 (i) Using Simpson's rule with three ordinates, obtain a value for $\int_{x_0-h}^{x_0+h} p(x)\,dx$, where $p(x)=kx^4$, and show that the value you obtain is in error by

$$\tfrac{1}{90}h^5 p^{(4)}(x).$$

Deduce that, when Simpson's rule with $(2n+1)$ ordinates is applied to $\int_a^b kx^4\,dx$ (so that $b-a=2nh$), the error is $\dfrac{(b-a)h^4}{180}p^{(4)}(x)$.

(ii) When $\int_a^b f(x)\,dx$ is evaluated by Simpson's rule with $(2n+1)$ ordinates, the error is known to be $\dfrac{(b-a)h^4}{180}f^{(4)}(\xi)$, where $a\leqslant\xi\leqslant b$, and $b-a=2nh$.

A value for $\int_0^{\pi/2} \sin x\,dx$ is to be found using Simpson's rule. Using the above expression for the error, calculate a value for h that will ensure that the integral is found to within $0.000\,05$ units, and deduce that Simpson's rule with 7 ordinates should be used.

Perform the integration in this way and verify that the required accuracy is obtained. [UCLES 88]

18 A scientist needs to evaluate

$$\int_1^5 \{\ln x\}^2\,dx$$

and intends to use Simpson's rule (because he doesn't notice that the integral can be evaluated). He wishes to choose a width h for the interval so that the truncation error will be less than 5×10^{-9} in magnitude; the truncation error in using Simpson's rule to evaluate

$$\int_a^b f(x)\,dx$$

using many intervals of width h is

$$-(b-a)h^4 f^{(4)}(\xi)/180,$$

where $f^{(4)}$ denotes the fourth derivative of f and for some number ξ in the interval (a,b). Show that, when

$$f(x)=\{\ln x\}^2,$$
$$f^{(4)}(x)=(22-12\ln x)/x^4,$$

and hence find the largest value of $f^{(4)}(x)$ in the interval $1\leqslant x\leqslant5$. Hence determine a suitable value of h for him.

The scientist decides to use $h=10^{-2}$, and his calculating device gives a maximum error of 10^{-10} in each evaluation of $\ln x$. Estimate the maximum possible total rounding error due to incorrect function evaluation in his use of Simpson's rule. [SMP 88]

19 (i) Given that $f(x)=px^2+qx+r$, and that $I=\int_a^b f(x)\,dx$, prove that

$$I\approx(b-a)f\!\left(\frac{a+b}{2}\right)$$

and that the error ε_1 in this approximation (the mid-ordinate rule) is given by $\varepsilon_1 = -\frac{1}{12}p(b-a)^3$.

(ii) The interval $[a, b]$ is divided into n equal sub-intervals, each of length $\left(\dfrac{b-a}{n}\right)$. A value I_n for I is found by applying the mid-ordinate rule to each sub-interval and summing the results. Deduce that the error ε_n in this process is given by

$$\varepsilon_n = -\frac{p(b-a)^3}{12n^2},$$

and state a relationship between ε_{kn} and ε_n, where k is an integer.

(iii) The value of J, where $J = \displaystyle\int_0^{0.9} \frac{\sin x}{x}\,dx$ is to be found numerically. Using notation corresponding to that in (ii), apply the mid-ordinate rule to obtain an approximation J_1, giving your result to six decimal places.

(iv) Calculate J_3, and, assuming that for this integral the relationship between the errors ε_3 and ε_1 is approximately that obtained in (ii), obtain an estimate for J to six decimal places.

(v) Given also that $J_9 = 0.860586$, and making an appropriate assumption concerning the relationship between ε_9 and ε_3, obtain a better estimate for J.
[UCLES 88]

20 Draw the graph of $y = 2x^3 - 3x^2 - 2x + 1$ over an appropriate range of x to find approximate solutions to the equation

$$2x^3 - 3x^2 - 2x + 1 = 0.$$

By rewriting this equation in two different ways, find two convergent iterative formulas of the form $x_{n+1} = F(x_n)$ to find the middle solution. Use the formula with the faster convergence to find this middle solution correct to four decimal places. How might this iterative method be adapted to improve the rate of convergence?

Use the Newton–Raphson formula to find the remaining solutions correct to four decimal places.
[MEI 89]

21 Show that the equation $2x^3 + 3x^2 - 4 = 0$ has only one real root and that this root lies between $x = 0$ and $x = 1$. Using the Newton–Raphson method and a starting value of 1, find the value of the root correct to 3 decimal places. Explain why you are confident that you have achieved the required accuracy.

An alternative iterative process

$$x_{n+1} = \frac{1}{2}\left[x_n + \sqrt{\left(\frac{4 - 2x_n^3}{3}\right)}\right], \quad n \geqslant 0,$$

is proposed. Show algebraically that, if this converges, it does so to the real root of $2x^3 + 3x^2 - 4 = 0$.

Investigate whether this process converges with starting values of

(i) 1,

(ii) 2.
[MEI 88]

22 (i) By writing $a^x = e^{x \ln a}$ (where $a > 0$), show that

$$\frac{d}{dx}(a^x) = a^x \ln a.$$

(ii) Sketch the curve $y = 2^x$. Given that the area of the region enclosed between the curve, the two co-ordinate axes and the line $x = b$ $(b > 0)$ is equal to unity, obtain an expression for b in terms of natural logarithms. Evaluate b correct to two decimal places.

(iii) Show that the equation

$$2^x = 3 + x^2$$

has a root between 4 and 5. By drawing another curve on your sketch, show that this is the only real root. Taking 4.5 as the initial approximation, use the Newton–Raphson method to find the value of this root correct to two decimal places.   [WJEC 89]

23 (a) Show by applying the Newton–Raphson method to the equation

$$x^m - a = 0$$

that the positive mth root of the positive number a may be found using the iterative process

$$x_{n+1} = \frac{(m-1)x_n^m + a}{mx_n^{m-1}}.$$

Hence calculate $\sqrt[5]{16}$ correct to 2 decimal places.

(b) Show that the equation

$$1 - x^4 = \tan x - \sin x$$

has a root lying between 0.8 and 0.9.

Rewrite the equation in the form

$$x = F(x)$$

and use the iterative sequence

$$x_{n+1} = F(x_n)$$

to find the value of the root correct to 2 decimal places.

Illustrate graphically the convergence of the sequence.   [WJEC 88]

24 By completing the square, show that $x^2 + 3x + 3$ is always positive.

By considering $\dfrac{dy}{dx}$, show that the graph of the equation

$$y = 2x^3 + 9x^2 + 18x - 10$$

crosses the x-axis once only.

Show that the graph does cross the x-axis between $x = 0$ and $x = 1$, and use linear interpolation once to find an approximation to the value of x at this point. Illustrate your results by a sketch. Use the Newton–Raphson method of iteration to find the value of x when $y = 0$ correct to 2 decimal places.   [AEB 89]

25 (a) The iteration formula

$$x_{n+1} = f(x_n), \quad n \geqslant 0,$$

is being used to calculate a root X of the equation $x = f(x)$. Draw two diagrams, one to illustrate the case of a convergent iteration to X, and one to show an iteration which does not converge.

Let $x_n = X + \varepsilon_n$ define the error ε_n in the approximate solution x_n. By using the Mean Value Theorem, find a sufficient condition on $|f'(x)|$ and ε_0 for the iteration to converge.

(b) Draw a diagram to illustrate a case in which the Newton–Raphson iteration converges. How fast is the convergence in Newton–Raphson iteration in the usual cases?

The equation

$$1 + \cos x = 0$$

has a root at $x = \pi$. Carry out four steps of the Newton–Raphson iteration with

$$f(x) = 1 + \cos x, \quad x_0 = 3.14.$$

Tabulate the errors $\varepsilon_n = x_n - \pi$ $(n = 0, 1, 2, 3)$ in your calculation. Explain why

$$\varepsilon_{n+1} \approx \tfrac{1}{2}\varepsilon_n.$$

Repeat the iteration using

$$f(x) = (1 + \cos x)^{1/4}, \quad x_0 = 3.14$$

and again tabulate the errors ε_n. Explain the results you find, using a sketch graph of $f(x)$.   [SMP 89]

26 The Newton–Raphson iterative formula for the solution of the equation $f(x) = 0$ may be written

$$x_{r+1} = \phi(x_r),$$

where

$$\phi(x) = x - \frac{f(x)}{f'(x)}.$$

Show that if X is a root of $f(x) = 0$ then $\phi'(X) = 0$. Show further that, in general, $\phi''(X) \neq 0$.

Hence show that the errors e_r and e_{r+1} in the iterates x_r and x_{r+1} are such that

$$e_{r+1} \approx k e_r^2$$

for some constant k. Explain briefly what this relationship indicates about the convergence of the Newton–Raphson process.   [MEI 88]

19

Second order difference equations

In Section 18.3 we saw that it is possible to convert two first order differential equations into one second order differential equation. The same manoeuvre is possible for difference equations. For example, take the simple pair of equations

$$x_{n+1} = -ay_n, \quad y_{n+1} = -bx_n,$$

with given values x_0, y_0 to start the iteration. Increase n by one in the first equation to get

$$x_{n+2} = -ay_{n+1}, \quad y_{n+1} = -bx_n.$$

It is clear that you can now eliminate y_{n+1} to find

$$x_{n+2} = abx_n.$$

This second order equation (second order because the largest difference between suffices is 2) comes with two initial conditions: x_0 is given, but so is x_1, because $x_1 = -ay_0$, from the first equation with $n=0$.

The general second order difference equation is far too hard for us to solve, except numerically, so we shall restrict our attention during most of this chapter to *linear* equations with *constant* coefficients and *easy* right hand sides. That is, we have equations like

$$u_{n+2} + pu_{n+1} + qu_n = f(n),$$

where p and q are constants and $f(n)$ is some simple function of n. Now the easiest function to start with is the zero function, so in the next section we attack the equation

$$u_{n+2} + pu_{n+1} + qu_n = 0.$$

19.1   THE EQUATION $u_{n+2} + pu_{n+1} + qu_n = 0$

(a)   Real distinct roots of the auxiliary equation

In Section 7.3 we solved a pair of equations by forming combinations, and we can certainly do the same for

$$\begin{cases} x_{n+1} = -ay_n, \\ y_{n+1} = -bx_n. \end{cases}$$

If you form the combinations

$$\begin{cases} z_n = b^{1/2}x_n + a^{1/2}y_n \\ w_n = b^{1/2}x_n - a^{1/2}y_n \end{cases}$$

you can reduce the equations to the two unlinked equations

$$\begin{cases} z_{n+1} = -(ab)^{1/2}z_n, \\ w_{n+1} = (ab)^{1/2}w_n. \end{cases}$$

These have easy solutions

$$\begin{cases} z_n = A\{-(ab)^{1/2}\}^n \\ w_n = B\{(ab)^{1/2}\}^n \end{cases}$$

for some constants A and B, which can be found in terms of the initial values x_0 and y_0.

Thus the original variables x_n and y_n have solutions of the form

$$\begin{cases} x_n = C\{-(ab)^{1/2}\}^n + D\{(ab)^{1/2}\}^n \\ y_n = E\{-(ab)^{1/2}\}^n + F\{(ab)^{1/2}\}^n \end{cases}$$

where C, D, E, F are constants related to the initial values.

But we have just seen that the corresponding *second* order equation is

$$x_{n+2} = (ab)x_n.$$

Thus we have shown that this second order equation has the solution

$$x_n = C\{-(ab)^{1/2}\}^n + D\{(ab)^{1/2}\}^n.$$

That is, the solution comes out in terms of *powers* of the solutions of the quadratic equation

$$c^2 = ab.$$

This encourages us to find out whether our more general equation has any solutions of the same general shape. Substitute

$$u_n = Ac^n$$

into the general equation to see if it provides a solution.

This gives us

$$Ac^{n+2} + pAc^{n+1} + qAc^n = 0.$$

Divide through by Ac^n and we get the quadratic equation

$$c^2 + pc + q = 0.$$

Suppose for the moment that this has two real roots – we shall look at the other possibilities later. Then we have found that for any constants A and B we have two solutions of the second order equation

$$Ac_1^n \quad \text{and} \quad Bc_2^n,$$

where c_1 and c_2 are the roots of the quadratic derived from the original equation. This quadratic equation clearly has an important place in the solution, so it is usually given a special name, the *auxiliary equation*.

It is quickly seen that the sum of the two solutions that we have just found is also a solution. Moreover, it has two as yet unfixed constants in it, which we can choose to give specified values to the two initial values u_0 and u_1. For if

$$u_n = Ac_1^n + Bc_2^n$$

then we can solve

$$\begin{cases} u_0 = A + B \\ u_1 = Ac_1 + Bc_2 \end{cases}$$

to find

$$\begin{cases} A = (u_0c_2 - u_1)/(c_2 - c_1) \\ B = (u_0c_1 - u_1)/(c_1 - c_2). \end{cases}$$

We now have a solution of the difference equation which gives the correct values for the first two terms, u_0 and u_1. Is that good enough? Yes, because the first two terms determine the next one, by using the difference equation with $n = 0$ to get u_2. And then u_1 and u_2 fix u_3 through the difference equation with $n = 1$; and so on for all the higher values of n. We have therefore found the one and only solution of

$$\begin{cases} u_{n+2} + pu_{n+1} + qu_n = 0 \\ u_0 \text{ and } u_1 \text{ given,} \end{cases}$$

in the case where the auxiliary equation

$$c^2 + pc + q = 0$$

has two (distinct) real roots.

Exercise 19A

1 Solve, with $u_0 = 1$ and $u_1 = 2$, the equations
   (i) $u_{n+2} + 3u_{n+1} + 2u_n = 0$
   (ii) $u_{n+2} - 3u_{n+1} + 2u_n = 0$
   (iii) $u_{n+2} - \frac{1}{2}u_{n+1} - \frac{1}{2}u_n = 0$.
   In each case find what the form of the solution is (approximately) when n is large.

2 The equation

$$u_{n+2} - 4u_{n+1} + 0u_n = 0$$

can be solved by the methods just introduced, *or* by putting

$$v_n = u_{n+1}$$

and solving

$$v_{n+1} = 4v_n.$$

Show that both solutions give the same result.

3   Reduce the Iwo Jima equations

$$\begin{cases} x_{n+1} = x_n - 0.04y_n \\ y_{n+1} = y_n - 0.01x_n \end{cases}$$

to a second order equation for x_n, and hence show (as in Section 7.3) that

$$x_n = A(0.98)^n + B(1.02)^n.$$

Determine A and B in terms of x_0 and y_0.

(b)   Complex roots for the auxiliary equation

In question 4 of Exercise 18B, an agricultural experiment is described in terms of a pair of differential equations. It was implicitly assumed there that the root weight R depended only on the weight of water W in the pot, whereas in reality plants behave differently by day and by night. It might therefore be more sensible to use difference equations to model the situation, with time steps of one day. Thus we might prefer the model

$$\begin{cases} R_{n+1} = R_n + aW_n \\ W_{n+1} = W_n - bR_n \end{cases}$$

to describe how root weight and water weight change from day to day. You can eliminate W_n from these equations to get a second order equation for R_n as before. It turns out that

$$R_{n+2} - 2R_{n+1} + (1+ab)R_n = 0.$$

The auxiliary equation is then

$$c^2 - 2c + (1+ab) = 0,$$

which has the solutions

$$c = 1 \pm (ab)^{1/2}j$$

where j is the square root of -1. It may not seem promising to get complex numbers coming into a perfectly real problem about root growth, but all will be well in the end; we will just follow the example of the mathematicians who first met complex numbers, and get on with the calculations to see what comes out as the final answer.

Following our previous work, the solution of the problem ought to be of the form

$$R_n = A\{1 + (ab)^{1/2}j\}^n + B\{1 - (ab)^{1/2}j\}^n,$$

where A and B are constants (which could be complex, so as to give a real value for the root weight R_n).

Now any complex number $x + yj$ can also be written in the form

$$r(\cos\theta + j\sin\theta),$$

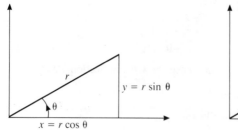
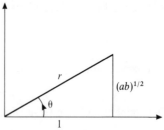

Figure 1(*a*). The relation of *r* and θ to *x* and *y*   Figure 1(*b*). Values of *r* and θ for the example

where x, y, r, θ are related as in Fig. 1(*a*). In the present case I shall need Fig. 1(*b*) to give the specific values needed for r and θ in this example:

$$\begin{cases} r = (1 + ab)^{1/2} \\ \theta = \tan^{-1}\{(ab)^{1/2}\}. \end{cases}$$

Note that $ab > 0$ so that θ is inevitably in the *first* quadrant. In general you need to take care to get a correct value of θ; do *not* rely on a formula, but draw a sketch.

It is a standard theorem for complex numbers (De Moivre's theorem) that

$$(\cos \theta + j \sin \theta)^n = \cos n\theta + j \sin n\theta$$

(see *Extensions of Calculus* in this series). Hence the solution for R_n can be reorganised into

$$R_n = Ar^n(\cos n\theta + j \sin n\theta) + Br^n(\cos n\theta - j \sin n\theta).$$

This can be rewritten as

$$R_n = (A + B)r^n \cos n\theta + j(A - B)r^n \sin n\theta$$
$$= Cr^n \cos n\theta + Dr^n \sin n\theta,$$

on writing C for $A + B$ and D for $j(A - B)$.

The solution is now free from the square root of -1 provided we take C and D to be real constants, and we will have to do this to get R_0 and R_1 having the correct initial values. Let us complete the problem, having got this far with it. Let us measure n as days from germination, so that $R_0 = 0$. Then, putting $n = 0$ in the solution for R_n gives us $C = 0$. From the original equations we have that

$$aW_0 = R_1 = Dr \sin \theta,$$

but we know that

$$r \sin \theta = (ab)^{1/2}$$

from Fig. 1(*b*), so that $D = W_0(a/b)^{1/2}$, and the solution is

$$\begin{cases} R_n = W_0(a/b)^{1/2}(1 + ab)^{n/2} \sin n\theta \\ \theta = \tan^{-1}\{(ab)^{1/2}\}. \end{cases}$$

This solution clearly cannot apply for $n\theta > \frac{1}{2}\pi$, because it would predict a decreasing weight of roots; if you investigate the solution for W_n you will find that W_n becomes negative at that stage: the model fails to reflect what happens to a plant when there is no water left.

Notice that we have found a solution here in terms of $\sin n\theta$, and that in question 4 of Exercise 18B the solution came out in terms of a sine function also. There is often a close resemblance between the solutions of difference and differential equations; this is only to be expected when, as here, they are alternative models for the same real situation.

What this example suggests is that when the auxiliary equation has a pair of complex conjugate roots (a *real* quadratic always gives a conjugate pair) you should express them as

$$r(\cos\theta \pm j\sin\theta)$$

for appropriate values of r and θ. The solution of the second order difference equation then is

$$u_n = Cr^n\cos n\theta + Dr^n\sin n\theta.$$

This is in fact correct, though checking it without the use of complex numbers would be an unpleasant exercise in trigonometrical formulas.

Exercise 19B

1 Solve the following equations with $u_0 = 0$ and $u_1 = 2$.
  (i) $u_{n+2} + 2u_{n+1} + 5u_n = 0$,
  (ii) $u_{n+2} - 2u_{n+1} + 5u_n = 0$,
  (iii) $u_{n+2} + \frac{1}{2}u_{n+1} + \frac{1}{2}u_n = 0$,
  (iv) $u_{n+2} + 4u_n \quad\quad = 0$.
  In each case determine how u_n behaves when n gets large.

2 Verify by using trigonometrical formulas that $u_n = \cos n\theta$ is a solution of $u_{n+2} - 2pu_{n+1} + u_n = 0$, provided that $p = \cos\theta$. Solve the equation with $u_0 = a$ and $u_1 = b$ and with p any number between 0 and 1.

3 For the example of plant growth show that

$$W_{n+2} - 2W_{n+1} + (1 + ab)W_n = 0.$$

Show that the corresponding solution for the weight of water left in the pot on day n is

$$W_n = W_0(1 + ab)^{n/2}\cos n\theta,$$

where $\theta = \tan^{-1}\{(ab)^{1/2}\}$.

4 The solution of

$$\begin{cases} u_{n+2} + 9u_n = 0 \\ \quad\quad u_0 = 0, \; u_1 = 1 \end{cases}$$

comes out in terms of $\sin n\theta$ for a certain value of θ. Can the solution of

$$\begin{cases} u_{n+2} - 9u_n = 0 \\ \quad\quad u_0 = 0, \; u_1 = 1 \end{cases}$$

be put in terms of $\sinh n\phi$ for some value of ϕ?

(c)   Equal roots for the auxiliary equation

The remaining case for equations of the type we are considering and with zero right hand sides, has equal roots for the auxiliary equation. This happens when the equation is

$$u_{n+2} - 2pu_{n+1} + p^2 u_n = 0.$$

We can in this case rewrite the equation as

$$(u_{n+2} - pu_{n+1}) - p(u_{n+1} - pu_n) = 0.$$

If we now put

$$u_{n+1} - pu_n = v_n$$

the equation reduces to

$$v_{n+1} - pv_n = 0,$$

which is first order, and which was solved in Section 2.2. The solution is

$$v_n = v_0 p^n.$$

This leaves us with the equation

$$u_{n+1} - pu_n = v_0 p^n$$

to solve. An equation of this kind came into question 3(ii) of Exercise 2D, and you find its solution:

either by writing down some terms till you see a pattern emerging:

$$u_1 = pu_0 + v_0$$

$$u_2 = pu_1 + pv_0$$
$$= p^2 u_0 + 2pv_0$$

$$u_3 = pu_2 + p^2 v_0$$
$$= p^3 u_0 + 3p^2 v_0;$$

or   by intelligent guesswork, i.e. by assuming that the answer is like the right hand side, perhaps with an extra n.

Either way leads you to the solution

$$u_n = Ap^n + nBp^n,$$

for some constants A and B, related to the initial values.

So in the case where the auxiliary equation has the repeated root p you need the special form

$$u_n = Ap^n + nBp^n$$

for the solution. The method of producing this result, by splitting the equation's left hand side into two closely related terms

$$(u_{n+2} - pu_{n+1}) - p(u_{n+1} - pu_n)$$

is one that will recur for other awkward equations. But it is usually easier just to remember the result rather than go through the working in any example.

Exercise 19C

1 Solve the equation $u_{n+2}+4u_{n+1}+4u_n=0$ with $u_0=1$ and $u_1=a$
 (i) by using the solution formula
 (ii) by deriving a first order equation for a suitable v_n.

2 Split the equation $u_{n+2}-3u_{n+1}+2u_n=0$ into two equations of the form

$$u_{n+1}-au_n=v_n, \quad v_{n+1}-bv_n=0,$$

and hence solve it.

3 The equation $u_{n+2}-2au_{n+1}+u_n=0$ with $u_0=0$ and $u_1=2$ has three different types of solution depending on the value of a. Find them.

19.2   THE PARTICULAR SOLUTION FOR RIGHT HAND SIDE $an+b$

(a)   The special case $a=0$

We must now try to solve some of the equations

$$u_{n+2}+pu_{n+1}+qu_n=f(n).$$

There is no prospect of getting a simple formula as an answer except for a few simple cases, such as

(i) $f(n)=an+b$
(ii) $f(n)=r^n$
(iii) $f(n)=\cos n\theta,$

or functions like these, or combinations of such functions.
 These are just the cases for which we found methods of solving first order equations, in Section 2.5.
 Let us start off then with the case

$$u_{n+2}+pu_{n+1}+qu_n=b,$$

where b is a constant. By the method of intelligent guesswork, and in view of our experience from Section 2.5, we may guess that a likely particular solution of the equation is

$$u_n=\text{constant, say } s.$$

This is indeed a solution if it satisfies the equation, which it does if

$$s+ps+qs=b.$$

Thus we have found that the solution is

$$u_n=b/(1+p+q),$$

except in the case when $1+p+q=0$.

Now the auxiliary equation is

$$c^2 + pc + q = 0,$$

and so the special case when $1 + p + q = 0$ is the case when the auxiliary equation has $c = 1$ as one of its solutions; and hence when a constant $A \times 1^n$ is part of the complementary function (the solution with zero right hand side). In this special case, since $1 + p + q = 0$, we may replace q by $-1 - p$; the equation to be solved is therefore

$$u_{n+2} + pu_{n+1} - (1 + p)u_n = b.$$

The complementary function is derived from the auxiliary equation

$$c^2 + pc - (1 + p) = 0,$$

which has solutions $c = 1$ and $c = -1 - p$; so the complementary function is

$$A + B(-1 - p)^n.$$

To find the particular solution in this case we split the equation into two, as in the last section; write it first as

$$(u_{n+2} - u_{n+1}) + (1 + p)(u_{n+1} - u_n) = b,$$

and then we see that we need

$$\begin{cases} u_{n+1} - u_n = v_n \\ v_{n+1} + (1 + p)v_n = b. \end{cases}$$

The solution of the second equation, by the methods of Section 2.5, is

$$v_n = b/(2 + p),$$

for $p \neq -2$. Next we must solve

$$u_{n+1} - u_n = b/(2 + p),$$

which was also done in Section 2.5. The solution is rather simple, being just

$$u_n = bn/(2 + p),$$

as you can check by substitution, provided (of course) $2 + p$ is not zero.

The first result in this section is therefore as follows. If the right hand side of a linear second order equation with constant coefficients is a *constant*, then a particular solution is

(i) a constant, if this is not already part of the complementary function;

(ii) a constant times n if the auxiliary equation has $c = 1$ as a solution, but not as a repeated root.

(iii) a constant times n^2 if the auxiliary equation has $c = 1$ as a repeated root – this is proved in exactly the same way as above and is left to the Exercise.

Exercise 19D

1   Solve the following equations, with $u_0 = 0$ and $u_1 = 3$,

(i) $3u_{n+2} + 4u_{n+1} + u_n = 16$,

(ii) $3u_{n+2} - 2u_{n+1} - u_n = 16$,

(iii) $5u_{n+2} + 4u_{n+1} - u_n = 20$,

(iv) $u_{n+2} + 2u_{n+1} + u_n = 1$.

2   Verify by substitution that $u_n = \tfrac{1}{6} n^2$ is a particular solution of

$$3u_{n+2} - 6u_{n+1} + 3u_n = 1.$$

Find u_n given that $u_0 = -1$ and $u_1 = 2$.

3   Solve the equation

$$u_{n+2} - 2u_{n+1} + u_n = 4,$$

by using the intermediate variable

$$v_n = u_{n+1} - u_n.$$

(b)   The case when $a \neq 0$

What do we expect to get for

$$u_{n+2} + pu_{n+1} + qu_n = an + b$$

in the way of a particular solution? From our experience above we might think that usually the solution would be something of the form

$$u_n = An + B,$$

perhaps with some special cases to consider. Let us try this assumed solution.

$$\{A(n+2) + B\} + \{Ap(n+1) + Bp\} + \{Aqn + Bq\} = an + b$$

is what we get on substitution; this can only be true for *all* n if

$$\begin{cases} A(1 + p + q) = a \\ A(2 + p) + B(1 + p + q) = b, \end{cases}$$

on looking at the coefficients of n and 1.

In general, then, the particular solution is $u_n = An + B$, with

$$\begin{cases} A = a/(1 + p + q) \\ B = b/(1 + p + q) - a(p + 2)/(1 + p + q)^2. \end{cases}$$

As before, this does not apply when $1 + p + q = 0$; that is, when the complementary function has one part which is just a constant.

For the special case when $1 + p + q = 0$ we can either split the equation into two (as we did above) to get

$$\begin{cases} u_{n+1} - u_n = v_n \\ v_{n+1} + (1 + p)v_n = an + b; \end{cases}$$

or we can use intelligent guesswork. I intend to use the latter method here and leave the former method to the Exercise.

On the basis of previous experience, I shall try

$$An + Cn^2$$

as particular solution in the case $1 + p + q = 0$, because each time we had a special case before, a higher power of n came into the particular solution. When we substitute this for u_n into the equation with $q = -1 - p$, we get

$$\{A(n+2) + C(n+2)^2\} + \{pA(n+1) + pC(n+1)^2\}$$
$$- \{(1+p)(An + Cn^2)\} = an + b.$$

This equation is to hold for all n, so take the coefficients of powers of n.
(i) n^2: $C + pC - C - pC = 0$, which does not fix C,
(ii) n: $A + 4C + pA + 2pC - A - pA = a$,
(iii) 1: $2A + 4C + pA + pC = b$.

Solving these equations for A and C gives

$$\begin{cases} C = \tfrac{1}{2}a/(p+2), \\ A = b/(p+2) - \tfrac{1}{2}a(p+4)/(p+2)^2. \end{cases}$$

This guess has given us the solution, except in the very special case when $p + 2 = 0$, when the equation becomes

$$u_{n+2} - 2u_{n+1} + u_n = an + b.$$

Why did I not try $An + B + Cn^2$ in the last calculation? You can start from that assumed form of solution if you like, but all the terms involving B are bound to cancel out, because any constant, such as B, is part of the complementary function for the special equation

$$u_{n+2} + pu_{n+1} - (1+p)u_n = an + b.$$

This helps us to see what to do in the *very* special case

$$u_{n+2} - 2u_{n+1} + u_n = an + b.$$

The complementary function now includes both a constant and a term in n, so it is no good including either of these in an assumed solution, because they will just give terms which cancel out. Since we want an assumed form that has two constants in it, which will be determined by the values of a and b, we must try

$$u_n = Cn^2 + Dn^3.$$

To summarise then, the equation

$$u_{n+2} + pu_{n+1} + qu_n = an + b$$

has the following particular solutions.

(i) $An + B$, except when $q = -1 - p$, i.e. when a constant is already part of the complementary function;
(ii) $An + Cn^2$ when $q = -1 - p$ and $p \neq -2$, i.e. in those cases when a constant is the complementary function but a constant times n is not;

(iii) $Cn^2 + Dn^3$ in the remaining case, when the complementary function is linear in n, i.e. $An + B$.

Exercise 19E

1   Solve $u_{n+2} + u_{n+1} - 2u_n = n + 1$ completely,
   (i)   by using the guesswork method,
   (ii) by using the results given above,
   (iii) by splitting the equation into two first order equations.

2   Verify that $u_{n+2} - 2u_{n+1} + u_n = an + b$ has the particular solution $Cn^2 + Dn^3$ by determining C and D in terms of a and b.

3   Solve completely $4u_{n+2} - 3u_{n+1} - u_n = 4n + 12$ with $u_0 = 2$ and $u_1 = -1$. What is the form of the solution when n becomes large?

4   Use intelligent guesswork, based on the work of this section, to find the particular solutions for

   (i) $u_{n+2} + 2u_{n+1} + 3u_n = 3n^2 + 5$,
   (ii) $u_{n+2} + 2u_{n+1} - 3u_n = 3n^2 + 5$.

19.3   THE PARTICULAR SOLUTION FOR OTHER RIGHT HAND SIDES

You may feel by now that you have followed the methods in the last section, and so can perfectly well deal with other right hand sides by yourself. If so, jump to the Exercise to check; if not, read on.

Section 19.2 has shown us that the particular solution of

$$u_{n+2} + pu_{n+1} + qu_n = f(n)$$

seems to be closely related to the form of $f(n)$, with a little modification being needed when $f(n)$ contains something which is already part of the complementary function of the equation. Let us apply these ideas to right hand sides other than polynomials in n.

Start with the equation

$$u_{n+2} + pu_{n+1} + qu_n = ar^n,$$

where r is *not* a solution of the auxiliary equation, so that

$$r^2 + pr + q \neq 0,$$

and so that the complementary function does *not* include a term in r^n. Then we will try Ar^n as a particular solution. Substitute it in:

$$Ar^{n+2} + pAr^{n+1} + qAr^n = ar^n.$$

You find that

$$A = a/(r^2 + pr + q),$$

so that the solution has indeed been determined for this case.

What happens when $r^2 + pr + q = 0$? It seems reasonable to assume that in this case, as well as in every case in the previous section, the thing to do is try a particular solution with an extra n in it every time we find a problem case. So we will try Bnr^n as particular solution for the equation

$$u_{n+2} + pu_{n+1} - (pr + r^2)u_n = ar^n,$$

which is the appropriate equation. Substitution gives us

$$(n+2)Br^{n+2} + p(n+1)Br^{n+1} - (pr + r^2)nBr^n = ar^n.$$

Again this equation has to hold for all values of n, and this requires us either to look at the coefficients of r^n and nr^n, or (equivalently) to take two particular values of n (e.g. $n=0$ and $n=1$). Using the former method (the latter is in the Exercise) gives us

$$\begin{cases} r^n: & 2Br^2 + pBr = a \\ nr^n: & Br^2 + pBr - (pr + r^2)B = 0. \end{cases}$$

The second equation is automatically satisfied (it wouldn't have been if we had guessed a non-solution), and the first gives the value of B as

$$B = a/(2r^2 + pr),$$

unless $p = -2r$.

The exceptional case $p = -2r$, $q = r^2$ need not delay us for long; in this case both r^n and nr^n are part of the complementary function of the equation, and so both give zero when operated on by the left hand side of the equation. The intelligent guess is that we need Cn^2r^n, and confirmation that this is correct is left to the Exercise.

The last form of right hand side that was suggested at the start of Section 19.2 was a trigonometric one, $f(n) = \cos n\theta$, where θ is some given constant angle. This case is not quite as easy as the previous ones. Remember the formula

$$\cos(n+1)\theta = \cos n\theta \cos \theta - \sin n\theta \sin \theta.$$

This shows that if you guess that the particular solution will have a term in $\cos n\theta$, then any term u_{n+1} in the equation (and equally a term in u_{n+2}) will bring in $\sin n\theta$ as well. Since we cannot avoid a term in $\sin n\theta$, we had better try

$$A \cos n\theta + B \sin n\theta$$

as the particular solution for the equation

$$u_{n+2} + pu_{n+1} + qu_n = a \cos n\theta.$$

Substitution gives rather a mess, which reduces after a little work to

$$\cos n\theta(A \cos 2\theta + Ap \cos \theta + Aq + B \sin 2\theta + Bp \sin \theta)$$

$$+ \sin n\theta(-A \sin 2\theta - Ap \sin \theta + B \cos 2\theta + Bp \cos \theta + Bq)$$

$$= a \cos n\theta.$$

In this case we look at the coefficients of $\cos n\theta$ and $\sin n\theta$, or take two special values of n, say $n=0$ and $n=1$. Either way gives

$$\begin{cases} A\cos 2\theta + Ap\cos\theta + Aq + B\sin 2\theta + Bp\sin\theta = a \\ -A\sin 2\theta - Ap\sin\theta + Bq + B\cos 2\theta + Bp\cos\theta = 0. \end{cases}$$

These two equations determine A and B, except in the special case when *both* $\cos n\theta$ and $\sin n\theta$ are part of the complementary function of the equation. In terms of p, q, θ the condition for this to happen is

$$\cos 2\theta + p\cos\theta + q = 0 = \sin 2\theta + p\sin\theta,$$

as you may find by

(i) solving the above two equations for A and B,
(ii) substituting $\cos n\theta$ and $\sin n\theta$ into $u_{n+2} + pu_{n+1} + qu_n = 0$, and doing some work.

So usually the particular solution has the form

$$A\cos n\theta + B\sin n\theta;$$

but when these terms are already part of the complementary function we must have a different particular solution, which (if past experience is a good guide) will be

$$Cn\cos n\theta + Dn\sin n\theta,$$

with C and D being found by substitution into the equation.

The case of a right hand side $b\sin n\theta$ will of course be treated in an exactly similar fashion, and is left to the Exercise.

Exercise 19F

1 Solve the following equations:
(i) $u_{n+2} + 2u_{n+1} - 8u_n = 3^n$, $u_0 = 0$, $u_1 = 1$.
(ii) $u_{n+2} - 4u_{n+1} - 5u_n = 2\sin\frac{1}{2}n\pi$, $u_0 = 0$, $u_1 = 0$.
(iii) $u_{n+2} + 2u_{n+1} - 3u_n = 3^{n+1}$, $u_0 = 1$, $u_1 = 0$.
(iv) $u_{n+2} + u_n = \cos\frac{1}{2}n\pi$, $u_0 = 1$, $u_1 = 1$.
(v) $u_{n+2} - 2u_{n+1} - 3u_n = 3^{n-1}$, $u_0 = 1$, $u_1 = 0$.
(vi) $u_{n+2} - 6u_{n+1} + 9u_n = 3^n$, $u_0 = u_1 = 0$.

2 Check that using the special values $n=0$ and $n=1$ in the equation

$$(n+2)Br^{n+2} + p(n+1)Br^{n+1} - (pr+r^2)nBr^n = ar^n$$

gives the same value for B in terms of a, p, r as the method shown above does.

3 We have seen above (Exercise 19B, question 2) that $\cos n\theta$ and $\sin n\theta$ both satisfy the equation

$$u_{n+2} - 2cu_{n+1} + u_n = 0$$

where $-1 \leqslant c \leqslant 1$ and the value of θ is related to the value of c. Solve the equation (using that value of c)

$$u_{n+2} - 2cu_{n+1} + u_n = 2\sin n\theta.$$

4 Verify that Cn^2r^n satisfies the equation

$$u_{n+2} - 2ru_{n+1} + r^2u_n = ar^n$$

for a suitable value of C.

5 The agricultural experiment described in Section 19.1(b) had no addition of water during the course of the experiment. This is possible, but rather unlikely, so let us modify the equations to allow for various watering schemes. Let the water addition on day n be written as z_n, so that the equations are now

$$\begin{cases} R_{n+1} = R_n + aW_n \\ W_{n+1} = W_n - bR_n + z_n. \end{cases}$$

Solve the equations in the cases

(i) $z_n = p$, constant,   (ii) $z_n = qs^n$, where q and s are constants (with s chosen greater than 1 to allow for increasing use of water as the plant grows).

6 Solve the equation

$$\begin{cases} u_{n+2} - 4u_{n+1} + ku_n = 1 + 2^n \\ u_0 = 0, \quad u_1 = 1. \end{cases}$$

(Watch out for special values of k, there are four different cases here.)

19.4   STABILITY AND INSTABILITY

(a)   Three examples

There will still be many equations that we cannot find a solution formula for. Two examples are

(i) $u_{n+2} - u_{n+1} + \frac{1}{2}u_n = 1/(n^2 + 1)$, $u_1 = 0$, $u_2 = 0$,
(ii) $u_{n+2} + (4/n)u_{n+1} - \frac{1}{4}u_n = 1$, $u_1 = 2$, $u_2 = -1$.

In cases like these we can always compute the solutions, by rearranging the equations as

(i) $u_{n+2} = u_{n+1} - \frac{1}{2}u_n + 1/(n^2 + 1)$,
(ii) $u_{n+2} = 1 - (4/n)u_{n+1} + \frac{1}{4}u_n$.

If you now take $n = 1$, each equation gives you u_3 from the known values of u_1 and u_2; then with $n = 2$ you find u_4, and so on. This looks like a very easy piece of programming to get a value of u_n for any desired value of n.

Unfortunately, the problem is not quite as simple as that. Go back to Section 1.4 and you will find an example which went badly wrong after quite a small number of computational steps. Will these two examples do the same, or will the calculated values be close to the correct values?

There are two methods of investigation open to us here. One is to do more computing: take starting values very near the ones given, and see whether the new computed values come out close to the previous ones. If they do, then small errors in computer arithmetic will (probably) cause no trouble either. That is, the solution is *stable*.

As an example of this approach, I worked out values for equation (ii), starting both at the given values for u_1 and u_2, and also with $u_1 = 2 + 10^{-3}$, $u_2 = -1 - 10^{-3}$ (which I call the modified results).

n	10	20	30	40	50
u_n, original	-10.528	0.809	1.116	1.167	1.19867
u_n, modified	-10.537	0.809	1.116	1.167	1.19867

The two computations start off slightly differently, because of the changed initial conditions, but they are much less than 10^{-3} apart by $n = 50$.

I could use the same approach for equation (i) as well, but it is rather easier to note that the homogeneous equation

$$u_{n+2} - u_{n+1} + \tfrac{1}{2}u_n = 0$$

can be solved easily. Using standard methods the solution is just

$$Ac_1^n + Bc_2^n$$

for some constants A and B, where c_1 and c_2 are the solutions of the auxiliary equation

$$c^2 - c + \tfrac{1}{2} = 0.$$

That is, c_1 and c_2 are just $\tfrac{1}{2} \pm \tfrac{1}{2}j$. These complex numbers can also be written as $2^{-1/2}e^{\pm j\pi/4}$, which have modulus less than 1. Consequently the nth powers of c_1 and c_2 both become smaller and smaller as n increases. Now any small error in computing the solution of the full equation, including its right hand side, will give a small change in the coefficients of c_1^n and c_2^n; but since these powers decrease as n increases, the effect of the small error will be removed after a dozen or so terms, and in particular the error will not get larger as n increases. So this example is also stable.

When I solved the example

$$\begin{cases} u_{n+2} - 2u_n = 3 + \dfrac{3n+1}{n^2-1}, & n = 2, 3, \ldots \\ u_2 = 2, \quad u_3 = 1.5 \end{cases}$$

numerically (and there is not any other way of doing it that seems obvious), I found the values

$$\begin{cases} u_{99} = 3.910\,49\ldots \\ u_{100} = -686.436\ldots \end{cases}$$

Now this example actually has an easy solution

$$u_n = n/(n-1)$$

(because I constructed it to have this solution). The complementary function here is

$$2^{n/2}\{A\cos(\tfrac{1}{2}n\pi)+B\sin(\tfrac{1}{2}n\pi)\},$$

and the values of A and B turn out to be exactly 0, because of the initial values. However, small errors in computer arithmetic pick up a solution of the equation (but not the exact initial conditions) that has A and B non-zero; thereafter the power $2^{n/2}$ amplifies the error until by $n=100$ it has swamped the true solution. This example is *unstable* because the complementary function has increasing powers in it which amplify errors.

(b)   The leapfrog method for differential equations

In Section 17.5(d) we saw the 'leapfrog' differential equation solver, which used the good formula

$$\frac{f(a+h)-f(a-h)}{2h}\approx f'(a)$$

to give the prediction formula

$$f(a+h)\approx f(a-h)+2hf'(a).$$

This was found to work very badly on the equation

$$\begin{cases} \dfrac{dy}{dx}=-\pi y+x \\ y=-\dfrac{1}{\pi^2}\text{ at } x+0. \end{cases}$$

If you look at the underlying difference equation you can find out why. Write y_n for the value of $y=f(x)$ at $x=nh$ to replace the method by

$$y_{n+1}=y_{n-1}+2h\left(\frac{dy}{dx}\right)_n$$

and use the differential equation to get

$$\left(\frac{dy}{dx}\right)_n=-\pi y_n+nh.$$

The difference equation to be solved is then

$$y_{n+1}+2\pi h y_n-y_{n-1}=2nh^2,\quad n=1,2,\ldots$$

with some initial values for y_0 and y_1.
  The complementary function here comes from

$$c^2+2\pi hc-1=0,$$

whose roots are

$$c=-\pi h\pm\sqrt{(\pi^2h^2+1)}.$$

However small h is, one of these values is less than -1, and so the complementary function

$$Ac_1^n + Bc_2^n$$

is found to increase in size as n increases, unless A and B are exactly zero. But even if A and B start at exactly zero, small errors in computer arithmetic inevitably lead to non-zero values for A and B, and consequent growth of errors in the computed values.

The calculations in Section 17.5(d) used $h = 0.1$, so that

$$c_1 = 0.7340, \quad c_2 = -1.3623.$$

If you need $n = 100$ (to reach $x = 10$), you have

$$c_2^{100} = 2.7 \times 10^{13},$$

so that even if B is only of size 10^{-12}, Bc_2^{100} could give an error of up to 27 in the computed solution.

This discussion of the stability of the leapfrog method for a simple differential equation shows why the method is not used: it is likely to be unstable for almost all equations.

Exercise 19G

1 Investigate the following equations for stability:

  (i) $u_{n+2} + 3u_{n+1} - 4u_n = (5n+3)/n(n^2-1)$, $\quad u_2 = -1$, $\quad u_3 = -\frac{1}{2}$.
  (ii) $nu_{n+2} - u_n = n$, $\quad u_1 = 1$, $\quad u_2 = 0$.

  Numerical work with equation (i) may suggest an exact solution for it.

2 The equation $u_{n+2} + (4/n)u_{n+1} - \frac{1}{4}u_n = 1$ becomes close to

$$u_{n+2} + 0 - \tfrac{1}{4}u_n = 1$$

  when n is large. Solve the latter equation with $u_1 = 2$, $u_2 = -1$ as another way of investigating the former equation.

3 Show that Euler's method on the equation

$$\frac{dy}{dx} = -\pi y + x$$

  is equivalent to using the difference equation

$$y_{n+1} - (1 - h\pi)y_n = h^2 n.$$

  Show that the method is stable for small values of h.

4 Investigate for stability the equation

$$u_{n+2} - u_{n+1} - \tfrac{1}{2}u_n = \frac{1}{n^2+1}, \quad u_1 = 0, \quad u_2 = 0.$$

19.5   SUMMARY

(a) The *auxiliary equation* for

$$u_{n+2} + pu_{n+1} + qu_n = 0,$$

where p and q are *constants* is

$$c^2 + pc + q = 0.$$

(i)   If its roots are *real* and *distinct*, then the solution is

$$u_n = Ac_1^n + Bc_2^n$$

where A and B are constants.

(ii)   If its roots are *complex conjugates*

$$r(\cos\theta \pm j\sin\theta),$$

then the solution is

$$r^n(A\cos n\theta + B\sin n\theta).$$

(iii)   If it has *only one* root c_1, then the solution is

$$(A + Bn)c_1^n.$$

(b) The *complementary function* for

$$u_{n+2} + pn_{n+1} + qu_n = f(n)$$

is the solution of the *homogeneous equation*

$$u_{n+2} + pu_{n+1} + qu_n = 0.$$

The *general solution* of

$$u_{n+2} + pu_{n+1} + qu_n = f(n)$$

is the sum of any *particular solution* and the complementary function. The *constants* in the general solution are found by using *initial values*, e.g. given values of u_0 and u_1.

(c) Particular solutions are found by guessing (intelligently) the correct form, and determining constants by substitution in the equation.

(i) The particular solution for

$$f(n) = b$$

is *in general* a constant; but if $c = 1$ is one of two distinct roots of the auxiliary equation, the required particular solution is a constant times n; and if $c = 1$ is the only root of the auxiliary equation, the particular solution is a constant times n^2.

(ii) For

$$f(n) = ar^n$$

three cases similarly arise. *In general* you need a constant times r^n, if $c=r$ is a *single root* you need a constant times nr^n; if $c=r$ is a *double root* you need a constant times n^2r^n.

(iii) For

$$f(n)=an+b$$

the particular solution is in general of the form $An+B$, but in special cases (when $c=1$ is a root or the only root of the auxiliary equation) the required form is $An+Cn^2$ or Cn^2+Dn^3.

(iv) For

$$f(n)=a\cos n\theta + b\sin n\theta$$

you generally need a particular solution of the form

$$C\cos n\theta + D\sin n\theta;$$

but if this is part of the complementary function you need the form

$$Cn\cos n\theta + Dn\sin n\theta.$$

(*d*) *Numerical solutions* of second order equations with either non-constant coefficients or awkward right hand sides may be necessary. They are *unstable* if there is a rapidly increasing term in the complementary function.

Solution methods for differential equations should be chosen which have stable associated difference equations.

20

Matrix methods for linear systems

The root–water interaction equations of Section 19.1(b) were written initially as a pair of equations:

$$\begin{cases} R_{n+1} = R_n + aW_n \\ W_{n+1} = W_n - bR_n. \end{cases}$$

They could equally well be written as a matrix equation

$$\begin{pmatrix} R \\ W \end{pmatrix}_{n+1} = \begin{pmatrix} 1 & a \\ -b & 1 \end{pmatrix} \begin{pmatrix} R \\ W \end{pmatrix}_n,$$

giving the $(n+1)$th vector in terms of the nth vector. They were also reduced to a single second order equation in that section:

$$R_{n+2} - 2R_{n+1} + (1+ab)R_n = 0.$$

So it is evident that there are three equivalent forms here, any of which must give the same solution.

There is in fact also an alternative matrix form which is often more convenient. Start from the second order equation and put

$$S_n = R_{n+1}$$

in it. Then you get the pair of equations

$$\begin{cases} R_{n+1} = S_n \\ S_{n+1} = 2S_n - (1+ab)R_n; \end{cases}$$

these have the matrix form

$$\begin{pmatrix} R \\ S \end{pmatrix}_{n+1} = \begin{pmatrix} 0 & 1 \\ -(1+ab) & 2 \end{pmatrix} \begin{pmatrix} R \\ S \end{pmatrix}_n.$$

The advantage here is that it is easy to derive this from the second order equation; the disadvantage is that this pair of equations has less obvious meaning.

In this chapter I shall concentrate on the matrix version of linear equations, and often on the alternative form. The equations will have constant coefficients, so that the matrix is composed of constants, and the matrices will usually be 2×2 or 3×3, even though they may in practice be much larger.

Note that complex numbers may arise during the course of the solution of *real* problems, as we saw in Chapter 19.

354

20.1   EIGENVALUES AND EIGENVECTORS

(a)   The second order case, 2×2 matrices

The kind of solution that the equation

$$u_{n+2} + pu_{n+1} + qu_n = 0,$$

has, is determined by the auxiliary equation

$$c^2 + pc + q = 0,$$

as we saw in Chapter 19. How does this show up in any matrix forms of the equation? Introduce the extra variable v_n defined by

$$u_{n+1} = v_n$$

and the equation can be put in the matrix form

$$\begin{pmatrix} u \\ v \end{pmatrix}_{n+1} = \begin{pmatrix} 0 & 1 \\ -q & -p \end{pmatrix} \begin{pmatrix} u \\ v \end{pmatrix}_n.$$

I shall also write this as

$$\mathbf{z}_{n+1} = \mathbf{M}\mathbf{z}_n.$$

The matrix $\mathbf{M}$ has its eigenvalues given by the equation

$$\lambda^2 + p\lambda + q = 0$$

(see *Linear Algebra and Geometry* in this series).

Thus the eigenvalues of $\mathbf{M}$ are just the roots of the auxiliary equation for the second order version. And if you use some other matrix version (as we had in the root–water interaction example) you still get the same eigenvalues.

The matrix $\mathbf{M}$ will certainly have two eigenvectors if the eigenvalues are distinct, i.e. if the roots of the auxiliary equation are distinct. What if they are not? In that case the auxiliary (or eigenvalue) equation is

$$c^2 + pc + \tfrac{1}{4}p^2 = 0$$

and the matrix $\mathbf{M}$ is

$$\mathbf{M} = \begin{pmatrix} 0 & 1 \\ -\tfrac{1}{4}p^2 & -p \end{pmatrix}.$$

The eigenvalue in this case is $\lambda = -\tfrac{1}{2}p$, and the equation for the eigenvector is

$$\begin{pmatrix} -\tfrac{1}{2}p & 1 \\ -\tfrac{1}{4}p^2 & \tfrac{1}{2}p \end{pmatrix} \begin{pmatrix} u \\ v \end{pmatrix} = 0$$

which has the *single* solution vector

$$\begin{pmatrix} 1 \\ \tfrac{1}{2}p \end{pmatrix}$$

(or any constant multiple of it). So in this case there is only *one* eigenvector for the matrix. This corresponds to the special case in Section 19.1(c), when the auxiliary equation had only one solution.

(b)   The third order case, 3×3 matrices

In Section 6.6 we discussed a set of three equations for the Ruritanian population, which had a matrix form

$$\begin{pmatrix} s \\ w \\ p \end{pmatrix}_{n+1} = \begin{pmatrix} \frac{19}{20} & \frac{1}{30} & 0 \\ \frac{1}{20} & \frac{29}{30} & 0 \\ 0 & \frac{1}{30} & \frac{19}{20} \end{pmatrix} \begin{pmatrix} s \\ w \\ p \end{pmatrix}_{n}.$$

You can (with some trouble) produce a single, third order equation for p_n, by eliminating s_n and w_n. It is

$$240p_{n+3} - 688p_{n+2} + 239p_{n+1} - 209p_n = 0.$$

The substitutions

$$p_{n+1} = u_n, \quad p_{n+2} = v_n = u_{n+1}$$

give the alternative matrix form

$$\begin{pmatrix} p \\ u \\ v \end{pmatrix}_{n+1} = \begin{pmatrix} 0 & 1 & 0 \\ 0 & 0 & 1 \\ \frac{209}{240} & -\frac{239}{240} & \frac{688}{240} \end{pmatrix} \begin{pmatrix} p \\ u \\ v \end{pmatrix}_{n}.$$

The eigenvalues of either matrix (and the roots of the auxiliary cubic equation for the third order equation for p_n) are

$$\lambda_1 = 1, \quad \lambda_2 = \tfrac{19}{20}, \quad \lambda_3 = \tfrac{11}{12}.$$

As stated in Section 6.6, the matrix

$$\mathbf{M} = \begin{pmatrix} \frac{19}{20} & \frac{1}{30} & 0 \\ \frac{1}{20} & \frac{29}{30} & 0 \\ 0 & \frac{1}{30} & \frac{19}{20} \end{pmatrix}$$

has the three (independent) eigenvectors

$$\mathbf{e} = \begin{pmatrix} 2 \\ 3 \\ 2 \end{pmatrix}, \ \mathbf{e}_2 = \begin{pmatrix} 0 \\ 0 \\ 1 \end{pmatrix}, \ \mathbf{e}_3 = \begin{pmatrix} 2 \\ -2 \\ 1 \end{pmatrix}.$$

What about the matrix

$$\mathbf{N} = \begin{pmatrix} 0 & 1 & 0 \\ 0 & 0 & 1 \\ \frac{209}{240} & -\frac{239}{240} & \frac{688}{240} \end{pmatrix},$$

which represents the same situation, though from a different point of view? Its eigenvectors are

$$\mathbf{f}_1 = \begin{pmatrix} 1 \\ 1 \\ 1 \end{pmatrix}, \ \mathbf{f}_2 = \begin{pmatrix} 400 \\ 380 \\ 361 \end{pmatrix}, \ \mathbf{f}_3 = \begin{pmatrix} 144 \\ 132 \\ 121 \end{pmatrix}.$$

They are not the same, simply because we are taking a different point of view (technically, we are using a different *basis* for the three dimensional space). But they are still independent of each other.

This kind of example could easily be developed to give larger matrices $\mathbf{M}$ or $\mathbf{N}$, just by taking a finer subdivision of the population. The normal result is that, whatever the size of $\mathbf{M}$ and $\mathbf{N}$, there will be as many eigenvalues (real *or* complex) as there are *dimensions* in $\mathbf{M}$, and the same number of essentially different eigenvectors. By 'essentially different' I wish to exclude

$$\begin{pmatrix} 4 \\ 6 \\ 4 \end{pmatrix}$$

which, though an eigenvector of $\mathbf{M}$, is not *really* different from

$$\begin{pmatrix} 2 \\ 3 \\ 2 \end{pmatrix}.$$

it gives the same direction. Similarly, if $\mathbf{g}_1$ and $\mathbf{g}_2$ were eigenvalues of a matrix $\mathbf{P}$, both with eigenvalue λ, $3\mathbf{g}_1 + 4\mathbf{g}_2$ would not be an essentially different eigenvector.

Exercise 20A

1   Consider the equations

$$\begin{cases} R_{n+1} = R_n + \tfrac{1}{10} W_n \\ W_{n+1} = W_n - \tfrac{1}{10} R_n. \end{cases}$$

Show that they can be rewritten in terms of

$$U_n = R_n + W_n, \quad V_n = R_n - W_n$$

as

$$\begin{cases} U_{n+1} = U_n - \tfrac{1}{10} V_n \\ V_{n+1} = \tfrac{1}{10} U_n + V_n. \end{cases}$$

Calculate the eigenvalues and eigenvectors for the matrix appropriate to the R_n, W_n equations, and for the matrix of the U_n, V_n equations.

2   Calculate eigenvalues and eigenvectors for the matrix of

$$\begin{cases} R_{n+1} = R_n + a W_n \\ W_{n+1} = W_n - b R_n. \end{cases}$$

3   The captive population of Burmese beetles in Exercise 6G question 3 obeyed the equations

$$\begin{pmatrix} f \\ s \\ t \end{pmatrix}_{n+1} = \begin{pmatrix} 0 & 1 & 3 \\ \frac{1}{2} & 0 & 0 \\ 0 & \frac{1}{3} & 0 \end{pmatrix} \begin{pmatrix} f \\ s \\ t \end{pmatrix}_n.$$

where f_n, s_n, t_n are the populations of first year, second year and third year beetles. Derive a third order equation for f_n, and calculate the roots of the auxiliary equation; check that they equal the eigenvalues of the matrix.

4   Use the third order equation for f_n to rewrite the (captive) beetle equations in terms of

$$f_n, \quad u_n = f_{n+1}, \quad v_n = f_{n+2}.$$

Hence find three essentially different eigenvectors of the matrix for this form of the equations.

Find also the eigenvectors for the matrix in question 3.

(c)   General results using eigenvalues and eigenvectors

Take $\mathbf{M}$ to be any square matrix with a full set of essentially different (independent) eigenvectors. Define $\mathbf{U}$ to be the matrix made up of the eigenvectors of $\mathbf{M}$ as columns. Then it is a theorem in matrix theory that

$$\mathbf{U}^{-1}\mathbf{M}\mathbf{U} = \Lambda$$

where Λ (Greek capital lambda) is a diagonal matrix with entries equal to the eigenvalues of $\mathbf{M}$.

For example, consider

$$\mathbf{M} = \begin{pmatrix} \frac{19}{20} & \frac{1}{30} & 0 \\ \frac{1}{20} & \frac{29}{30} & 0 \\ 0 & \frac{1}{30} & \frac{19}{20} \end{pmatrix}.$$

Then the matrix of eigenvectors is

$$\mathbf{U} = \begin{pmatrix} 2 & 0 & 2 \\ 3 & 0 & -2 \\ 2 & 1 & 1 \end{pmatrix},$$

and it is easy to check that

$$\mathbf{U}^{-1} = \frac{1}{10} \begin{pmatrix} 2 & 2 & 0 \\ -7 & -2 & 10 \\ 3 & -2 & 0 \end{pmatrix}.$$

Doing the multiplications gives

$$\mathbf{M}\mathbf{U} = \begin{pmatrix} 2 & 0 & \frac{22}{12} \\ 3 & \frac{29}{30} & -\frac{22}{12} \\ 2 & \frac{19}{20} & \frac{11}{12} \end{pmatrix} = (\mathbf{e}_1, \tfrac{19}{20}\mathbf{e}_2, \tfrac{11}{12}\mathbf{e}_3),$$

and

$$U^{-1}MU = \begin{pmatrix} 1 & 0 & 0 \\ 0 & \frac{19}{20} & 0 \\ 0 & 0 & \frac{11}{12} \end{pmatrix}.$$

This example also indicates the line the proof would take (if we wanted to construct one): because U is made of eigenvectors, MU is composed of eigenvalues times eigenvectors.

The way we can use this theorem on

$$u_{n+1} = Mu_n$$

is by multiplying by U^{-1}, and noting that

$$UU^{-1} = I,$$

the identity matrix:

$$U^{-1}u_{n+1} = U^{-1}MUU^{-1}u_n.$$

Now let

$$U^{-1}u_n = z_n$$

(say), and you have

$$z_{n+1} = \Lambda z_n.$$

Each component of z_n is a *combination* of the components of u_n. And each component of z_n occurs in an equation with no other component, with the appropriate eigenvalue on the right hand side.

In the Ruritanian population example we have

$$U^{-1}u_n = \frac{1}{10} \begin{pmatrix} 2 & 2 & 0 \\ -7 & -2 & 10 \\ 3 & -2 & 0 \end{pmatrix} \begin{pmatrix} s_n \\ w_n \\ p_n \end{pmatrix}$$

so that

$$z_n = \begin{pmatrix} 0.2s_n + 0.2w_n \\ -0.7s_n - 0.2w_n + p_n \\ 0.3s_n - 0.2w_n \end{pmatrix}.$$

The equations for the components of z_n are

$$\begin{cases} 0.2s_{n+1} + 0.2w_{n+1} = 1 \times (0.2s_n + 0.2w_n) \\ -0.7s_{n+1} - 0.2w_{n+1} + p_{n+1} = \frac{19}{20} \times (-0.7s_n - 0.2w_n + p_n) \\ 0.3s_{n+1} - 0.2w_{n+1} = \frac{11}{12} \times (0.3s_n - 0.2w_n), \end{cases}$$

where the multipliers on the right hand side are the eigenvalues.

The third equation solves as

$$0.3s_n - 0.2w_n = (\tfrac{11}{12})^n (0.3s_0 - 0.2w_0),$$

and the first is similarly solved as

$$0.2s_n + 0.2w_n = (1)^n (0.2s_0 + 0.2w_0).$$

Clearly you can then solve for s_n, w_n and p_n; for example

$$s_n = \{0.6(\tfrac{11}{12})^n + 0.4(1)^n\}s_0 + 0.4\{1 - (\tfrac{11}{12})^n\}w_0.$$

In general terms this can be put as

$$\mathbf{z}_n = \Lambda^n \mathbf{z}_0$$

where Λ^n is a diagonal matrix whose entries are the eigenvalues raised to the nth power. Then

$$\mathbf{u}_n = \mathbf{U}\mathbf{z}_n = \mathbf{U}\Lambda^n \mathbf{z}_0$$
$$= (\mathbf{U}\Lambda^n \mathbf{U}^{-1})\mathbf{U}\mathbf{z}_0$$
$$= (\mathbf{U}\Lambda^n \mathbf{U}^{-1})\mathbf{u}_0.$$

This gives the solution for $\mathbf{u}$ in terms of the eigenvalues and eigenvectors of the matrix $\mathbf{M}$ of the system. It shows what combination of the original equations is needed to give a very simple set of separated equations, justifying the work using the method of combinations in earlier chapters.

The only drawback to this method, and it is a large one, is that you have to find the eigenvalues and eigenvectors of $\mathbf{M}$, which can be a difficult numerical process for a large matrix.

Exercise 20B

1   In Section 7.2 we had the pair of equations

$$\begin{cases} x_{n+1} = 0.8x_n + 1.4y_n \\ y_{n+1} = 1.4x_n + 0.8y_n. \end{cases}$$

Determine the matrices $\mathbf{M}$, $\mathbf{U}$, $\mathbf{U}^{-1}$ for this situation, and verify that

$$\mathbf{U}^{-1}\mathbf{M}\mathbf{U}$$

is a diagonal matrix composed of eigenvalues.

Calculate $\mathbf{U}\Lambda^n\mathbf{U}^{-1}$, and hence determine the solutions x_n, y_n in terms of x_0 and y_0.

2   Question 3 in Exercise 20A uses the matrix

$$\mathbf{M} = \begin{pmatrix} 0 & 1 & 3 \\ \tfrac{1}{2} & 0 & 0 \\ 0 & \tfrac{1}{3} & 0 \end{pmatrix}.$$

Find the matrices $\mathbf{U}$ and $\mathbf{U}^{-1}$ for it, and verify that

$$\mathbf{U}^{-1}\mathbf{M}\mathbf{U}$$

is a diagonal matrix composed of eigenvalues.

3 Solve the system given by

$$\mathbf{u}_{n+1} = \mathbf{Mu}_n + \mathbf{k},$$

where $\mathbf{k}$ is a vector of constants, by using the eigenvector matrix $\mathbf{U}$ and the eigenvalue matrix $\mathbf{A}$. Note any special cases you are excluding.

4 Solve the system of equations

$$\begin{cases} u_{n+1} = u_n + v_n \\ v_{n+1} = v_n + w_n \\ w_{n+1} = w_n \end{cases}$$

by elementary methods (start with the last equation). Why can you *not* solve this set by using the matrix methods described above?

20.2   SETS OF DIFFERENTIAL EQUATIONS

As before, we shall consider *linear* equations, with *constant* coefficients, and we shall write them in vector and matrix form. For example, the set of three equations

$$\begin{cases} \dfrac{du}{dt} = \quad\ Av \\[2mm] \dfrac{dv}{dt} = -Au \quad\quad -Bw \\[2mm] \dfrac{dw}{dt} = \quad\quad Bv \quad\quad -g \end{cases}$$

gives approximately the velocity components

$$u,\ v,\ w$$

in the directions

$$\text{south, east, up}$$

for a particle falling under gravity, allowing for the rotation of the Earth (see *Mechanics and Vectors* in this series). The constants A and B are concerned with the latitude where the particle's motion takes place, the mass of the particle, and the rotation rate of the Earth.

These equations have the matrix form

$$\frac{d}{dt}\begin{pmatrix} u \\ v \\ w \end{pmatrix} = \begin{pmatrix} 0 & A & 0 \\ -A & 0 & -B \\ 0 & B & 0 \end{pmatrix}\begin{pmatrix} u \\ v \\ w \end{pmatrix} + \begin{pmatrix} 0 \\ 0 \\ -g \end{pmatrix},$$

or

$$\frac{d}{dt}\mathbf{x} = \mathbf{Mx} + \mathbf{k}.$$

In general the matrix equation

$$\frac{d\mathbf{x}}{dt} = \mathbf{M}\mathbf{x}$$

can be solved by the methods in the last section. Construct the matrix of eigenvectors $\mathbf{U}$, and then consider

$$\mathbf{U}^{-1}\frac{d\mathbf{x}}{dt} = \mathbf{U}^{-1}\mathbf{M}\mathbf{U}\mathbf{U}^{-1}\mathbf{x}.$$

This reduces to

$$\frac{d\mathbf{z}}{dt} = \mathbf{\Lambda}\mathbf{z}$$

where $\mathbf{z} = \mathbf{U}^{-1}\mathbf{x}$, and the solution of each component equation is then very simple. For example, for the system

$$\begin{cases} \dfrac{dx}{dt} = 2x + y \\[2mm] \dfrac{dy}{dt} = x + 2y \end{cases}$$

you will find that $\lambda_1 = 3$, $\lambda_2 = 1$, and that

$$\mathbf{e}_1 = \begin{pmatrix} 1 \\ 1 \end{pmatrix}, \quad \mathbf{e}_2 = \begin{pmatrix} -1 \\ 1 \end{pmatrix}.$$

So here

$$\mathbf{U} = \begin{pmatrix} 1 & -1 \\ 1 & 1 \end{pmatrix}, \quad \mathbf{U}^{-1} = \frac{1}{2}\begin{pmatrix} 1 & 1 \\ -1 & 1 \end{pmatrix}.$$

Thus

$$\mathbf{z} = \mathbf{U}^{-1}\mathbf{x} = \begin{pmatrix} \frac{1}{2}x + \frac{1}{2}y \\ -\frac{1}{2}x + \frac{1}{2}y \end{pmatrix}$$

and the separated equations are

$$\begin{cases} \dfrac{d}{dt}(\tfrac{1}{2}x + \tfrac{1}{2}y) = 3(\tfrac{1}{2}x + \tfrac{1}{2}y) \\[2mm] \dfrac{d}{dt}(-\tfrac{1}{2}x + \tfrac{1}{2}y) = 1(-\tfrac{1}{2}x + \tfrac{1}{2}y), \end{cases}$$

where the multipliers on the right are the eigenvalues. The solutions of these equations are

$$\begin{cases} \tfrac{1}{2}x + \tfrac{1}{2}y = e^{3t}(\tfrac{1}{2}x_0 + \tfrac{1}{2}y_0) \\ -\tfrac{1}{2}x + \tfrac{1}{2}y = e^{t}(-\tfrac{1}{2}x_0 + \tfrac{1}{2}y_0). \end{cases}$$

or

$$\begin{cases} x = e^{3t}(\tfrac{1}{2}x_0 + \tfrac{1}{2}y_0) - e^t(-\tfrac{1}{2}x_0 + \tfrac{1}{2}y_0) \\ y = e^{3t}(\tfrac{1}{2}x_0 + \tfrac{1}{2}y_0) + e^t(-\tfrac{1}{2}x_0 + \tfrac{1}{2}y_0). \end{cases}$$

The last steps of this method are easy to explain, but harder to prove. You need another diagonal matrix $\mathbf{E}$, whose entries are the exponential of eigenvalues times time. In the example above

$$\mathbf{E} = \begin{pmatrix} e^{3t} & 0 \\ 0 & e^t \end{pmatrix}.$$

Then

$$\mathbf{z} = \mathbf{E}\mathbf{z}_0,$$

and

$$\mathbf{x} = \mathbf{U}\mathbf{x} = \mathbf{U}\mathbf{E}\mathbf{z}_0$$
$$= \mathbf{U}\mathbf{E}\mathbf{U}^{-1}\mathbf{x}_0.$$

You can see this structure very clearly in the solution for x and y in terms of x_0 and y_0 in the example, for which

$$\mathbf{U}^{-1}\mathbf{x}_0 = \frac{1}{2}\begin{pmatrix} 1 & 1 \\ -1 & 1 \end{pmatrix}\begin{pmatrix} x_0 \\ y_0 \end{pmatrix}$$
$$= \begin{pmatrix} \tfrac{1}{2}x_0 + \tfrac{1}{2}y_0 \\ -\tfrac{1}{2}x_0 + \tfrac{1}{2}y_0 \end{pmatrix}.$$

You only get this sort of solution when the matrix $\mathbf{M}$ has the full number of independent eigenvectors, because it is only in this case that you can get a matrix $\mathbf{U}$. Try an example of the case when there are too few eigenvectors.

Take (for example)

$$\mathbf{M} = \begin{pmatrix} 1 & -1 \\ 1 & 3 \end{pmatrix}$$

corresponding to the equations

$$\begin{cases} \dot{x} = x - y \\ \dot{y} = x + 3y. \end{cases}$$

There is only one eigenvalue, $\lambda = 2$, for $\mathbf{M}$; and the *only* eigenvector is (any constant times)

$$\begin{pmatrix} -1 \\ 1 \end{pmatrix}.$$

In this case the corresponding second order equation, found by elimination of y, is

$$\ddot{x} - 4\dot{x} + 4x = 0.$$

We shall see in Chapter 23 that the solution is

$$x = Ae^{2t} + Bte^{2t}$$

(compare with the extra n that comes in when a second order *difference* equation has an auxiliary equation with equal roots). Thus in such cases there are two reasons why you cannot get such an easy solution as

$$\mathbf{x} = \mathbf{UEU}^{-1}\mathbf{x}_0,$$

first $\mathbf{U}$ is not available, and second, $\mathbf{E}$ should not just involve exponentials.

In this last discussion, the reduction of two first order equations to one of second order was used. The transformation in the other direction, from one second order to two first order, is usually made by putting

$$\dot{x} = z$$

as a new variable. For example

$$\ddot{x} - 4\dot{x} + 4x = 0$$

is usually replaced by the pair of equations

$$\begin{cases} \dot{x} = z \\ \dot{z} = 4z - 4x, \end{cases}$$

and the matrix form is then

$$\begin{pmatrix} \dot{x} \\ \dot{z} \end{pmatrix} = \begin{pmatrix} 0 & 1 \\ -4 & 4 \end{pmatrix} \begin{pmatrix} x \\ z \end{pmatrix}.$$

This is a different matrix, corresponding to a different pair of equations, but both are equivalent to the single second order equation

$$\ddot{x} - 4\dot{x} + 4x = 0.$$

Both matrices have the single eigenvalue $\lambda = 2$; each matrix has only one eigenvector.

The resolution of the difficulties with systems with too few eigenvectors is too hard for us to complete here. However, the outline of the route that is used is interesting.

First, consider

$$\frac{dx}{dt} = ax;$$

it has solution

$$x = e^{at}x_0.$$

Why not look for a solution of

$$\frac{d\mathbf{x}}{dt} = \mathbf{Ax}$$

along the same lines, with

$$\mathbf{x} = e^{\mathbf{A}t}\mathbf{x}_0?$$

In order to attempt this you first need the definition of the exponential of a matrix, which is through the Taylor series for the exponential function:

$$e^{\mathbf{A}t} = \mathbf{I} + \mathbf{A}t + \frac{1}{2}\mathbf{A}^2 t^2 + \frac{1}{3!}\mathbf{A}^3 t^3 + \cdots$$

This can be shown to be both a sensible idea, and also a solution of the differential equation.

Secondly, we have to do something with this infinite sum of matrices to make it useful. This is done using the Cayley–Hamilton theorem (see *Linear Algebra and Geometry* in this series), which states that any matrix satisfies the same polynomial equation as its eigenvalues. For example

$$\mathbf{M} = \begin{pmatrix} 1 & -1 \\ 1 & 3 \end{pmatrix}$$

satisfies

$$\mathbf{M}^2 - 4\mathbf{M} + 4\mathbf{I} = 0,$$

so that $\mathbf{M}^2$ can be replaced by $4\mathbf{M} - 4\mathbf{I}$. Similarly

$$\mathbf{M}^3 = \mathbf{M}\mathbf{M}^2 = 4\mathbf{M}^2 - 4\mathbf{M}$$

$$= 4(4\mathbf{M} - 4\mathbf{I}) - 4\mathbf{M}$$

$$= 12\mathbf{M} - 16\mathbf{I}.$$

In this way *all* powers of $\mathbf{M}$ can be reduced to the form

$$k\mathbf{M} + l\mathbf{I},$$

and

$$e^{\mathbf{M}t} = f(t)\mathbf{M} + g(t)\mathbf{I}$$

for some functions f and g.

The actual execution of this method to find f and g is more than we can do here: see more advanced books for the details.

Exercise 20C

1   Show that the system of equations

$$\begin{cases} \dot{x} = 2x + y \\ \dot{y} = 2x + 3y \end{cases}$$

has the eigenvector matrix

$$\mathbf{U} = \begin{pmatrix} 1 & 1 \\ 2 & -1 \end{pmatrix}.$$

Hence solve the system with $x = x_0$ and $y = y_0$ at $t = 0$.

2   For the system in question 1, find the second order equation for x and show it has matrix

$$\mathbf{M} = \begin{pmatrix} 0 & 1 \\ -4 & 5 \end{pmatrix},$$

when the variables x and $z \, (= \dot{x})$ are used. Find the corresponding eigenvector matrix.

3   Show that

$$-\mathbf{M}^{-1}\mathbf{k}$$

is a particular solution of the system

$$\frac{d\mathbf{x}}{dt} = \mathbf{M}\mathbf{x} + \mathbf{k},$$

provided that $\mathbf{M}$ has an inverse. Hence write down the general solution of the system in this case, assuming that $\mathbf{M}$ has distinct eigenvalues.

4   The matrix for the example of a particle falling near the rotating Earth, has *no* inverse. Find a particular solution of

$$\frac{d\mathbf{x}}{dt} = \mathbf{M}\mathbf{x} + \mathbf{k}$$

for that example, by assuming a particular solution

$$\mathbf{x} = tp\mathbf{e}_1 + q\mathbf{e}_2 + r\mathbf{e}_3,$$

where

$$\begin{cases} \mathbf{e}_1 \text{ is the eigenvector with eigenvalue } 0, \\ \mathbf{e}_2 \text{ and } \mathbf{e}_3 \text{ are the other eigenvectors}, \\ p, q, r \text{ are constants}. \end{cases}$$

(Hint: write $\mathbf{k}$ as $\alpha\mathbf{e}_1 + \beta\mathbf{e}_2 + \gamma\mathbf{e}_3$.)

20.3   SUMMARY

(a)   A set of linear first order *difference* equations is directly equivalent to a matrix difference equation; an alternative matrix form can be found via the equivalent higher order difference equation for one unknown function.

(b)   If the matrix has a *full set* of eigenvectors, then

$$\mathbf{u}_{n+1} = \mathbf{M}\mathbf{u}_n$$

can be solved by using the *eigenvector matrix* $\mathbf{U}$, giving

$$\mathbf{u}_n = (\mathbf{U}\boldsymbol{\Lambda}\mathbf{U}^{-1})\mathbf{u}_0.$$

Here $\boldsymbol{\Lambda}$ is a diagonal matrix consisting of the eigenvalues of $\mathbf{M}$ and $\mathbf{u}_0$ is a vector of initial values.

(c)   A set of linear first order *differential* equations is also directly equivalent to a differential equation for a vector of functions. An alternative form can be found via the equivalent higher order equation for one of the functions.

(*d*) If the matrix has a *full set* of eigenvectors, then

$$\frac{d\mathbf{x}}{dt} = \mathbf{Mx}$$

can be solved as

$$\mathbf{x} = (\mathbf{UEU}^{-1})\mathbf{x}_0.$$

Here **E** is a diagonal matrix consisting of terms

$$e^{\lambda_1 t}, e^{\lambda_2 t}, \ldots$$

where $\lambda_1, \lambda_2, \ldots$ are the eigenvalues of **M**.

Second interlude

The first two sections of this book have been concerned mainly with:

(a) numerical calculation,
(b) applying numerical calculation to the concerns of calculus,
(c) applying calculus to the methods of numerical calculation.

We have not, of course, said everything there is to be said on the subjects treated so far. The area of study is large and still growing, and also quite difficult; but we have done enough to get a good flavour of its methods and results.

The focus of interest will now shift a little, to the *use* of the kind of techniques we have studied on rather more real problems. We have, of course, seen some real applications in the first two sections; but they have been a bit restricted by the mathematical and numerical techniques available up till now. We shall also spend more time on deriving suitable equations to represent the reality we wish to discuss, i.e. on the process called modelling.

Now very many useful mathematical models turn out to need sets of two or more difference or differential equations, or to need second order equations. So the concern with modelling forces us to return to calculus to learn how to deal with:

(i) pairs and sets of first order equations,
(ii) second order differential equations;

and also to go back to numerical ideas for ways of calculating solutions when formulas are not available.

You will see that second order equations lead to a wide range of new techniques, both for finding solution formulas and for numerical work. Should we go on again, and look at third order and fourth order equations? Fortunately there is little need to, as they have essentially the same properties as second order equations. Thus this book can come to a decent conclusion after one further section.

Projects and investigations II

II.1   (a)   Dufton's rule for integration is based on

$$\int_0^{10h} f(x)\,dx \approx \tfrac{5}{2}h\{f(h)+f(4h)+f(6h)+f(9h)\}.$$

        (i)   Investigate its accuracy by calculating $\int_0^1 e^{-x^2}\,dx$ using $h=0.1$ and $h=0.05$.

        (ii)   Is the formula exact for any polynomials?

        (iii)   What is the error term for smooth functions f?

   (b)   Investigate similarly Gauss' three-point formula

$$\int_{-h}^{h} f(x)\,dx \approx \tfrac{1}{9}h\{5f(-\xi)+8f(0)+5f(\xi)\}$$

        where $\xi = h\sqrt{\tfrac{3}{5}}$.

   (c)   Find a Gauss two-point formula which is exact for all cubics.

II.2   The improved Euler method for differential equations is equivalent to the trapezium rule for integrals. The rectangle method for integrals is slightly better than the trapezium rule, so it is sensible to ask if it gives a good integrator for differential equations. Show that it gives

$$f(a+h)=f(a)+hf'(a+\tfrac{1}{2}h);$$

estimate $f'(a+\tfrac{1}{2}h)$ here by using $x_{\text{inter}}=a+\tfrac{1}{2}h$ and $y_{\text{inter}}=f(a)+\tfrac{1}{2}hf'(a)$, i.e. by using Euler's method as a predictor.

   (a)   Use this method on some of the examples in the text, and compare its results with those from Euler's method and the improved Euler method.

   (b)   What size of error does it give?

   (c)   This appears to be very like the leapfrog method discussed in Section 17.5. Is this new method unstable? Try examples and a mathematical investigation.

II.3   The differential equations corresponding to the newspaper competition model of Chapter 7 are

$$\begin{cases} du/dt = au/(u+v)-2u \\ dv/dt = bv/(u+v)-2v. \end{cases}$$

Investigate their properties, along the following lines.

   (i)   Look for simple combinations of the equations which can be integrated mathematically – it may help to notice that the equations are invariant when you interchange (a,u) and (b,v).

   (ii)   Try computer solutions.

   (iii)   Division gives an equation for du/dv which can be solved numerically.

     The revised equations of Project I.7, and other similar equations, can also be investigated. Do they provide any steady solutions, i.e. solutions independent of t?

II.4   The roots of

$$x^7 - 28x^6 + 322x^5 - 1960x^4 + 6769x^3 - 13\,132x^2 + 13\,068x - 5040 = 0$$

are exactly 1, 2, 3, 4, 5, 6, 7.
(a)   What do you get from Newton–Raphson iterations, starting at $x = 0.9, 1.9, \ldots, 6.9$? Explain your results.
(b)   What do you get if you change 13 132 to

(i) 13 131   (ii) 13 133?

Explain what has happened by using graphs.
(c)   Analyse this ill-conditioned system by discussing how the roots of $x^2 + ax + b = 0$ depend on a, b. Try the same analysis on other simple polynomial equations.

II.5   It can be a nuisance calculating $f'(x_n)$ in the Newton–Raphson method, and it may be useful to replace it by the approximation

$$f'(x_n) \approx \frac{f(x_n) - f(x_{n-1})}{x_n - x_{n-1}}, \quad n \geqslant 1.$$

Try this method, and compare its rate of convergence with the standard method. Can you analyse the convergence by using Taylor's theorem?
Another way of avoiding the calculation of $f'(x_n)$ is always to use $f'(x_0)$. Discuss this method similarly.

II.6   The error for each strip of the trapezium rule is $-h^3 f''(\theta)/12$, where θ lies in the appropriate strip. Hence the total error for integration from a to b is

$$E = -\frac{h^2}{12}\{hf''(\theta_1) + hf''(\theta_2) + \ldots + hf''(\theta_n)\}$$

where θ_i lies in the ith strip. Thus $E \approx -\dfrac{1}{12}\displaystyle\int_a^b f''(x)\,dx$, i.e. the trapezium rule can be improved by taking account of $E \approx -\frac{1}{12}\{f'(b) - f'(a)\}$.
(a)   Try this revised trapezium rule on some examples. Is it as good as Simpson's rule?
(b)   Can you 'correct' Simpson's rule similarly?
(c)   The improved Euler method for differential equations is based on the trapezium rule. Can you construct a better differential equation solver by using this improved trapezium rule?

II.7   Let M_n and T_n be the tridiagonal $(n \times n)$ matrices

$$M_n = \begin{pmatrix} 1 & 1 & 0 & 0 & 0 & \cdots \\ 1 & 1 & 1 & 0 & 0 & \cdots \\ 0 & 1 & 1 & 1 & 0 & \cdots \\ 0 & 0 & 1 & 1 & 1 & \cdots \\ & & \cdots & & \end{pmatrix}, \quad T_n = \begin{pmatrix} -2 & 1 & 0 & 0 & 0 & \cdots \\ 1 & -2 & 1 & 0 & 0 & \cdots \\ 0 & 1 & -2 & 1 & 0 & \cdots \\ 0 & 0 & 1 & -2 & 1 & \cdots \\ & & \cdots & & \end{pmatrix}$$

Also let $m_n = \det M_n$ and $t_n = \det T_n$. The matrices have such simple structures that m_n and t_n ought to be rather simple.
(i)   Evaluate m_3, m_4, m_5 by Gauss elimination (or otherwise), and verify that $m_5 = m_4 - m_3$, and $m_4 = m_3 - m_2$. Show that $m_n = m_{n-1} - m_{n-2}$.

(ii)   Solve the difference equation with $m_1 = 1$, $m_2 = 0$ to find m_n.

(iii) Carry out a similar programme for t_n.

(iv)   Try the general case of the tridiagonal matrix where each entry in the 'subdiagonal' is a, in the diagonal is b, and in the 'superdiagonal' is c.

II.8   In matrix calculations it can be hard to compute $\mathbf{A}^{-1}$ accurately, especially for ill-conditioned matrices; but $\mathbf{A}k$ is easy to compute exactly. Here is an analogous calculation, based on simple arithmetic.

We solve $ax = b$ by iteration, when a^{-1} can only be found to 3 s.f. Work with the example $\frac{13}{17}x = 273$, which has exact solution 357. Here a^{-1}, to 3 s.f., is 1.31. Then $1.31 \times 2.73 = 357.63$ (this can be computed exactly, it is only inverses that cannot); take this as x_0, the first approximate solution.

Then the first residual r_1 is $273 - \frac{13}{17} \times 357.63 = -0.4818$, in which I have kept only 4 s.f., though as it is only multiplication, it can be done accurately. Now solve $\frac{13}{17}e_1 = -0.4818$, to get $e_1 = -1.31 \times 0.4818 = -0.6312$; this gives you

$$x_1 = 357.63 - 0.6312 = 357.0012.$$

You may go on to calculate $r_2 = -9.176 \times 10^{-4}$, $e_2 = -1.202 \times 10^{-3}$ and $x_2 = 357 + 2 \times 10^{-6}$, and so on, to any desired accuracy.

Apply this method to

(a) the equations

$$\begin{cases} 2.28101x + 1.61514y = 2.76255, \\ 1.61514x + 1.14365y = 1.95611. \end{cases}$$

(b) the equations in Exercise 5C question 5, for $n = 5$;

(c) the equations

$$\mathbf{Ax} = \mathbf{k},$$

where $\mathbf{A}^{-1}$ can only be found approximately.

Can you show that this procedure gives a convergent sequence $x_0, x_1, x_2, \ldots$? What determines how fast it converges?

II.9   Integrals over an infinite range such as

$$I = \int_1^\infty \frac{1}{\sqrt{(1+x^3)}}\,dx, \quad J = \int_0^\infty \frac{\sin x}{x}\,dx$$

come into advanced mathematics. Their numerical evaluation may be necessary.

(a) In I, put $x = 1/u$ to get an integral in terms of u. Is the new integrand smooth? Can you use Simpson's rule here, after some preliminary treatment as in Section 10.5?

(b) In J, split the range of integration to $[0, 1] + [1, \infty)$, and use the method in (a). What problems are there with Simpson's rule in this case?

(c) Is there any simple change of variables that deals with the whole range $[0, \infty)$ in one go?

(d) For what functions $f(x)$ do you get errors of size h^4 when you use $x = 1/u$ in $\int_1^\infty f(x)\,dx$?

(e) Find an accurate value of $\int_1^\infty x^{-1/2}\sin x\,dx$.

21

Three numerical solutions for a model equation

In this chapter I shall use material from earlier chapters to try to get solutions to a (rather unpleasant) differential equation which is a mathematical model of a real situation. You may need to refer back to:

(i) Chapter 18 for the relation between one second order equation and two first order equations,
(ii) Chapters 13 and 18 for the improved Euler method and its application to a pair of equations,
(iii) Chapter 10 for approximations to derivatives, and also for Simpson's method of numerical integration,
(iv) Chapter 17 for the errors inherent in all these methods.

21.1 THE MODEL EQUATION

The physical idea which gives rise to the mathematical problem is as follows. A vertical pipe full of water has a tap at the bottom, through which the water can escape. How long does the pipe take to empty, in terms of the sizes of pipe, tap and so on? In Fig. 1 the pipe has a uniform cross-sectional area A_1, and the exit hole in the tap has cross-sectional area A_0. The surface level of the water is at height $X(t)$ above the bottom of the pipe at time t.

The flow is taken to be smooth and frictionless – both these assumptions are open to doubt, but if the values chosen for A_1 and A_0 are not extreme, they are probably quite nearly true. The water in the pipe is assumed to be moving vertically downwards – this certainly will not be true when $X(t)$ is almost zero, but otherwise it will be almost true for most of the water. For this reason, the model equation given below will probably fail to apply when $X(t)$ is very small. The motion of the small amount of water in the tap is neglected, and this too should not make much difference, except when $X(t)$ is very small.

The appropriate differential equation for this model is provided by textbooks on Fluid Dynamics, and is

$$\tfrac{1}{2}(1 - A_1^2/A_0^2)(dX/dt)^2 + gX + (A_1/A_0)X d^2X/dt^2 = 0.$$

There is no need here to understand how it is derived, except to note that it is based on the ideas of Newtonian mechanics.

This equation is second order, because the highest derivative in it is a second derivative; it is non-linear because there is a term involving the square of dX/dt

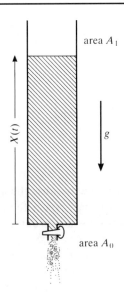

area A_1

$X(t)$

g

area A_0

Figure 1. Flow out of a pipe through a tap

and also because there is a product term $X\, d^2X/dt^2$. It is very common for non-linear equations to need numerical methods for their solution, so I shall start on the solution that way.

It will be easier if there are numbers in the problem rather than letters, so I shall take SI units with the values

$$\begin{cases} A_1/A_0 = 9,\ g = 10 \\ X = 1 \text{ and } dX/dt = 0 \text{ when } t = 0. \end{cases}$$

That is, I am starting with a one metre depth of water which is at rest. Putting these numbers in and rearranging the equation, I have the problem

$$\begin{cases} d^2X/dt^2 = 40(dX/dt)^2/(9X) - 10/9 \\ X(0) = 1,\ \dot{X}(0) = 0. \end{cases}$$

This rearrangement of the equation shows again that there will be problems when $X = 0$, because then the acceleration will be very large, unless the speed $\dot{X}$ is also very small; anyway, division by the small value of X may lead to inaccuracy.

I will ask the following questions about the mathematical model that I have set up.

(i) How does $X(t)$ vary with t?
(ii) When is X zero?

It will help in the numerical work if I make a preliminary estimate of the answer to the second question, because I can then consider how many steps I shall need in the numerical work. The time for a metre of water to fall freely through its own length is approximately $1/\sqrt{5} = 0.45$ seconds, so I might expect that the pipe will

Figure 2. A smoother exit for the water

empty in about nine times this time, because the area ratio is nine: this gives a time of about 4.0 seconds. So I may expect that, if I choose a step length of $h = 0.01$, I will need about 400 steps in the computation.

The model we have set up is *not* one of the highest quality. It would clearly be better to have a smoother change from area A_1 to area A_0, say as in Fig. 2. The mathematics for this can be done, but the increased complication just hides the underlying ideas, which are more important here.

21.2 THE EQUIVALENT FIRST ORDER EQUATIONS

The first method that I shall use involves splitting the second order equation into two first order ones, by writing the velocity as a new variable:

$$\begin{cases} \dot{X} = V \\ \dot{V} = 40V^2/(9X) - 10/9 \\ X = 1, \text{ and } V = 0, \text{ when } t = 0. \end{cases}$$

This is a very natural move in a problem based on dynamics, where the velocity is an easily understood variable, and where its values may be wanted anyway. It is an equally good move in other second order equations, even if the first derivative is not an obvious variable, because we have numerical methods available for first order equations. I shall use the improved Euler method to solve the pair of first order equations numerically, as I know that this gives reasonably good accuracy in not too many steps. It is also quite easy to write a program for.

For a preliminary run I used a step length of $h = 0.1$, and ran into trouble near $t = 3.7$, as the table of computed values shows.

t	3.3	3.4	3.5	3.6	3.7	3.8
X	0.044	0.034	0.025	0.0165	0.0091	0.0321
V	-0.109	-0.092	-0.072	-0.0347	0.0896	1.87

The velocity becomes positive at $t = 3.7$, which means that the pipe is filling up again! The problem here is to do with the rather large step length, which has given inaccurate results, together with the trouble which is bound to arise near $X = 0$.

My next run was with a step length of $h = 0.01$, with results printed every 25 iterations. The calculation failed after $t = 4.12$, where the reported values were $X = 1.83 \times 10^{-43}$, $V = -3.18 \times 10^{-53}$.

t	3.00	3.25	3.50	3.75	4.00
X	0.084	0.050	0.024	0.008	6×10^{-4}
V	-0.153	-0.118	-0.083	-0.047	-0.012

Note that the apparently awkward term in

$$V^2/X$$

is becoming extremely small as X gets very near 0. This is comforting: there is no reason to expect (in reality) any strange behaviour as the pipe empties, and we are finding that the numerical mathematics is also predicting no disasters. The graph in Fig. 3 shows the smooth behaviour of X with t, with V becoming zero when X does.

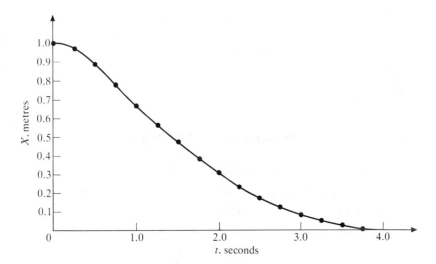

Figure 3. X in terms of t for the pipe flow

A final run with $h = 0.005$ gave only very slightly different figures, so I may now reasonably conclude that I have a sufficiently accurate set of results for $X(t)$ and $V(t)$, and that the time to empty the pipe is probably very close to 4.1 seconds.

Exercise 21A

A hot air balloon rises because the density of the air in the balloon is sufficiently less than the density of the surrounding air to carry the basket and passengers and also to give a net upward force. There will also be a resistance to upward motion, and because the balloon is so large this will be proportional to the square of the upward speed. Finally, the surrounding air density decreases as you go upwards. The model equation I therefore suggest is

$$d^2Z/dt^2 + c(dZ/dt)|dZ/dt| - b(1-aZ) = 0,$$

with Z and dZ/dt both zero at $t=0$.

This does not make any allowance for cooling or loss of hot air: the pilot may keep the air in the balloon at constant density by operating the burner. The product of dZ/dt and $|dZ/dt|$ gives the force in the correct direction, whether the balloon is going up or down, so that you can follow the motion after it reaches its highest point.

Suitable values of the constants a, b, c can be guessed as follows. The balloon can remain at rest at $Z = a^{-1}$, so choose $a = 0.004 \, \mathrm{m}^{-1}$, to give a rest height of 250 m. The initial acceleration is b, so choose $b = 1 \, \mathrm{ms}^{-2}$ as a moderate value. The maximum upward speed at ground level is $(b/c)^{1/2}$, and taking the value $3 \, \mathrm{ms}^{-1}$ for this gives the value of c to be $0.1 \, \mathrm{m}^{-1}$, approximately.

1 Show that the appropriate first order equations for this problem are

$$\begin{cases} \dot{Z} = V \\ \dot{V} = b(1-aZ) - cV|V| \\ Z = V = 0 \text{ at } t = 0. \end{cases}$$

Set up a program to solve them, using the improved Euler method.

2 Hence find the maximum height of the balloon, the time to reach that height, and the next minimum height of the balloon.

3 Discuss the modelling of the real situation into the given set of differential equations and values for the constants.

21.3   DISCRETISING THE PROBLEM

(a)   Discretising the equation

An alternative way of attacking a differential equation is to convert it to a difference equation by using standard approximations to derivatives. The approximations

$$\left(\frac{d^2f}{dx^2}\right)_{\text{at } x=a} \approx \frac{f(a+h) - 2f(a) + f(a-h)}{h^2}$$

$$\left(\frac{df}{dx}\right)_{\text{at } x=a} \approx \frac{f(a+h) - f(a-h)}{2h}$$

were found in Chapter 10. Their errors were shown in Chapter 17 to be each of size h^2 (for smooth functions f).

In the pipe flow example we shall consider the times

$$t = 0, h, 2h, 3h, \ldots, (r-1)h, rh, (r+1)h, \ldots$$

which I shall write as

$$t_0, t_1, t_2, \ldots, t_{r-1}, t_r, t_{r+1}, \ldots$$

and the values of the height of water at these times I shall write as

$$X_0, X_1, X_2, ..., X_{r-1}, X_r, X_{r+1}, ...$$

This means that I shall be writing approximations for the derivatives as

$$(d^2X/dt^2)_{\text{at } t=t_r} \approx (X_{r+1}-2X_r+X_{r-1})/h^2$$

$$(dX/dt)_{\text{at } t=t_r} \approx (X_{r+1}-X_{r-1})/(2h).$$

Substituting into the model equation in Section 21.1 we find

$$X_r(X_{r+1}-2X_r+X_{r-1})/h^2=40(X_{r+1}-X_{r-1})^2/(36h^2)-10X_r/9,$$

which may be rearranged as

$$9X_r(X_{r+1}-2X_r+X_{r-1})-10(X_{r+1}-X_{r-1})^2+10h^2X_r=0.$$

This is a difference equation, because if the values of X_{r-1} and X_r are given, then the value of X_{r+1} can be found. The difference equation must hold for

$$r=1,2,3,...$$

because the differential equation holds for values of t from 0 onwards, and the difference equation uses X_{r-1}. That is, the differential equation has been discretised to give a second order and non-linear difference equation, which can be solved numerically.

(b)   Errors, and initial values

As I said above, there were errors of size h^2 in the approximations to the derivatives. Thus in the discretised equation there are errors of size h^4, because a multiplication by h^2 was used in deriving it. This has two consequences.

(i) The total error (due to inaccurate formulas) after $1/h$ steps forward will be of size about h^3.
(ii) We need a value of X_1 which has errors of size h^4 so as to maintain the accuracy.

The initial conditions we were given were

$$X=1, \dot{X}=0 \text{ at } t=0.$$

To find a good approximation for $X_1=X(h)$ we use Taylor's approximation

$$X(h) \approx X(0)+h\dot{X}(0)+\tfrac{1}{2}h^2\ddot{X}(0)+\tfrac{1}{6}h^3\dddot{X}(0).$$

which has error of size h^4. Now we can find $\ddot{X}(0)$ from the differential equation:

$$\frac{d^2X}{dt^2}=\frac{40}{9X}\left(\frac{dX}{dt}\right)^2-\frac{10}{9};$$

putting $t=0$ here (and using known values of X and $\dot{X}$ at $t=0$) gives

$$\ddot{X}(0)=0-10/9.$$

And if we differentiate the differential equation we find

$$\frac{d^3X}{dt^3} = \frac{80}{9X}\frac{dX}{dt}\frac{d^2X}{dt^2} - \frac{40}{9X^2}\left(\frac{dX}{dt}\right)^3.$$

so that (similarly) $\ddot{X}(0)=0$.

Thus an approximation for X_1 which is of accuracy *consistent* with that used in the differential equation is

$$X_1 \approx 1 - 5h^2/9.$$

(c) Solving the discretised equation

The equation to be solved is

$$X_{r+1}^2 - (0.9X_r + 2X_{r-1})X_{r+1} + (1.8X_r^2 + X_{r-1}^2 - 0.9X_rX_{r-1} - h^2X_r) = 0$$

with $X_0 = 1$ and $X_1 = 1 - 5h^2/9$. Write the equation, for simplicity, as

$$X_{r+1}^2 - BX_{r+1} + C = 0.$$

This has the *two* solutions

$$X_{r+1} = \tfrac{1}{2}\{B \pm (B^2 - 4C)^{1/2}\}.$$

Which do we need? Clearly we must have

$$X_2 < X_1$$

because the water is moving *down* the pipe, and a trial calculation soon shows that the negative sign gives this and the positive does not.

There is one further problem before we can start the calculation. If we use the formula

$$X_{r+1} = \tfrac{1}{2}\{B - (B^2 - 4C)^{1/2}\}$$

we shall be subtracting nearly equal quantities from each other, because C eventually becomes very small, and this (as we have seen in Section 3.4) is a sure way of losing accuracy. So we must use the fact that the product of the roots of the quadratic equation is C, and divide this by the larger root to find the smaller root. Finally, therefore, we find the appropriate formula for X_{r+1}:

$$X_{r+1} = 2C/\{B + (B^2 - 4C)^{1/2}\},$$

with B and C given by

$$\begin{cases} B = 0.9X_r + 2X_{r-1} \\ C = 1.8X_r^2 + X_{r-1}^2 - 0.9X_rX_{r-1} - h^2X_r. \end{cases}$$

I carried out this calculation on my computer, using $h=0.02$ and $h=0.01$, and found the following values for X.

	$h=0.02$	$h=0.01$
t	X	X
4.00	5.626×10^{-4}	5.642×10^{-4}
4.02	3.390×10^{-4}	3.402×10^{-4}
4.04	1.717×10^{-4}	1.726×10^{-4}
4.06	6.081×10^{-5}	6.130×10^{-5}
4.08	6.202×10^{-6}	6.362×10^{-6}
4.10	7.936×10^{-6}	4.981×10^{-6}

This shows that when X is very nearly equal to 0, the program ceases to behave as expected: X ceases to decrease rapidly, and in one case even increases. What has gone wrong?

There seem to be several possible sources of error.

(i) B and C are both approaching zero, and so $X_{r+1} \approx 0/0$, which is a dangerous calculation. By the end of the calculation with $h=0.02$

$$B \approx 10^{-3} \quad \text{and} \quad C \approx 10^{-8},$$

so this should not be the case, since

$$C/B$$

will be calculated quite accurately.

(ii) Rounding errors have built up in the arithmetic. This is not very likely as it only takes 200 steps to reach $t=4.0$, and each step only uses some 20 arithmetical operations, so that the total rounding error cannot have reached as much as 10^{-8}.

(iii) The solution could be unstable. This seems very unlikely on physical grounds: a small perturbation of the water in the tube is unlikely to cause a great change to the flow.

(iv) The method could be unstable. This is not easy to analyse for a non-linear equation like the one we have here.

(v) The errors in the derivative formulas are becoming large. As we saw, the errors are of general size h^4, and here this has value 1.6×10^{-7}, which is larger than the value of C. It therefore seems inevitable that when X_r gets very near zero this source of error will corrupt the equation for X_{r+1}. The use of a smaller value of h will postpone the difficulty, but not totally overcome it.

Once again the conclusion is that the time at which X reaches zero is close to

$$t=4.1 \text{ seconds.}$$

Exercise 21B

1   During the *rise* of the balloon in Exercise 21A the height Z satisfies

$$\begin{cases} \dfrac{d^2Z}{dt^2} = b(1-aZ) - c\left(\dfrac{dZ}{dt}\right)^2. \\ Z = 0 \quad \text{and} \quad \dot{Z} = 0 \quad \text{at } t = 0. \end{cases}$$

(i)   Discretise the differential equation.
(ii) Determine the initial values to use for Z_0 and Z_1.

2   For question 1, find the quadratic equation for Z_{r+1}, in the form

$$Z_{r+1}^2 + PZ_{r+1} + Q = 0.$$

Solve this difference equation, using your values for Z_0 and Z_1, to find the time at which Z reaches its maximum value.

3   Does anything go wrong with your solution in question 2 as Z approaches its maximum value? Give reasons, if you can.

4   In the pipe emptying problem the following values were obtained with $h = 0.005$.

t	X	B	C
4.07	2.687×10^{-5}	1.610×10^{-3}	3.605×10^{-8}
4.08	6.402×10^{-6}	6.714×10^{-4}	3.888×10^{-9}
4.09	1.525×10^{-8}	1.411×10^{-4}	2.149×10^{-12}
4.095	8.064×10^{-7}	7.563×10^{-6}	-1.900×10^{-10}

Discuss these figures.

21.4   DIRECT INTEGRATION

In the last two sections I have described direct attacks on the differential equation that is the mathematical model of water flow out of a pipe. In many cases a direct attack on the differential equation is all that can be usefully done, because there is no way of solving the equation otherwise. But in some cases, including this one, it is possible to do some mathematical manipulation before starting on the necessary numerical work.

The mathematics is only of the sort that we have seen before when discussing differential equations, but we need to use several techniques that have been discussed earlier, so it will be quite a lengthy process.

This method will not be available for all differential equations, and you may feel that the extra accuracy achieved at the end is not worth the effort involved. You may however find that reading through the next few pages is useful, to remind you of many earlier pieces of work.

In Section 18.3, we saw that you could use the chain rule for differentiating to show that

$$d^2X/dt^2 = V\,dV/dX,$$

where $V = dX/dt$, which in this case is the velocity of the water surface. Making this change reduces the equation to a first order equation for V in terms of X: this is because the original equation did not have any mention of t *except* in so far as X and V depended on t. The new equation is

$$SXV\,dV/dX + \tfrac{1}{2}(1 - S^2)V^2 + gX = 0,$$

where I have written the area ratio $A_1/A_0 = S$.

The next move is to notice that $V\,dV/dX = \dfrac{1}{2}\dfrac{d}{dX}(V^2)$, so that the substitution $V^2 = W$ may be a good idea. Doing this, and at the same time dividing by X, gives us

$$S\,dW/dX - (S^2 - 1)W/X = -2g.$$

Tidy up a bit more, and the equation looks like

$$dW/dX - KW/X = -L,$$

where $K = (S^2 - 1)/S$ and $L = 2g/S$.

This can now be seen to be a linear equation, of the type solved in Section 12.2 by using an integrating factor. In the present case the integrating factor is

$$\exp\left\{\int (-K/X)\,dX\right\} = X^{-K} \quad \text{(provided } K \neq 1\text{)},$$

so that the equation may be written as

$$\frac{d}{dX}(WX^{-K}) = -LX^{-K}.$$

Both sides can now be integrated, and we obtain

$$WX^{-K} = -LX^{-K+1}/(-K+1) + C,$$

where C is a constant of integration.

The next step is to determine the constant C. This is done by using the initial conditions of the problem, that $X = 1$ and $V = 0$ when the flow starts at $t = 0$. Since $W = V^2$, W is also zero at the start, and consequently

$$0 = -L/(-K+1) + C.$$

Take the value of C so found, and we get as final result for W that

$$W = \{L/(K-1)\}(X - X^K),$$

where values for K and L are given above in terms of the area ratio S.

The velocity V follows at once,

$$V = -\{L/(K-1)\}^{1/2}(X - X^K)^{1/2},$$

where the negative sign is necessary because the water moves downwards in the pipe. There is not far to go after finding V, which can be replaced at once by dX/dt:

$$dX/dt = -\{L/(K-1)\}^{1/2}(X - X^K)^{1/2}.$$

In this differential equation the variables are separable, as described in Section 11.3 of this book. You can therefore write the solution as

$$\{L/(K-1)\}^{1/2}t = -\int_1^X (x-x^K)^{-1/2}\,dx,$$

where the lower limit of integration comes from the condition that $X=1$ when $t=0$.

This lengthy process of mathematical trickery has led to the 'solution' of the original equation, as long as you are happy to accept that t in terms of an unpleasant integral involving X is a solution. Let me say at once that the integral cannot be 'worked out', except in very special cases such as $K=2$. However, what we may be able to do with it is a numerical evaluation, so that we can find the time t which is needed to achieve a specified value of X. For example, we can ask how long it takes for the water level to fall from the initial one metre to half a metre; the answer is

$$\{(K-1)/L\}^{1/2}\int_{1/2}^1 (x-x^K)^{-1/2}\,dx$$

seconds, where the integral can be found numerically, using Simpson's rule perhaps.

The reason I write 'perhaps' here is that there are still some difficulties left in the problem, even though we 'only' have an integral left to evaluate. The two remaining difficulties are that you may not put $x=1$ in the function to be integrated, because you get 'infinity' if you do, and the same thing happens at $x=0$. You can of course run a numerical integration from $x=10^{-5}$ up to $x=1-10^{-5}$: when I did this with 1000 division points in the Simpson's formula, and with the area ratio $S=9$, I found that the time t was 4.256. This answer is *most* unlikely to be correct, for several reasons.

(i)   It disagrees with our previous answers.
(ii) The computer cannot deal with $x-x^K$ when x is so small and with $K=80/9$: all you get is just the value of x, because x^K is so much smaller.
(iii) The computer also loses a little accuracy in calculating $x-x^K$ when x is extremely near to 1.
(iv) Simpson's rule requires a bounded integrand, and here the function becomes very large at both ends of the range of integration.
(v)   The error in Simpson's rule depends on the fourth derivative of the function, and the fourth derivative becomes infinite at both $x=0$ and $x=1$.

There is a way round these difficulties, though it requires some more work. What I shall do is calculate the integral using Simpsons' rule, over a slightly reduced range at each end; then I shall do separate pieces of mathematics for the two pieces that have been left out.

My computation of the integral from $x=0.01$ to $x=0.99$, using 600 division points and $S=9$, was 3.57755 seconds.

Now I start on the piece near $x = 0$, which is

$$\{(K-1)/L\}^{1/2} \int_0^{0.01} (x - x^K)^{-1/2} \, dx.$$

The integrand can be rewritten as

$$x^{-1/2}(1 - x^{K-1})^{-1/2},$$

and the (general) binomial theorem can be used on the term in brackets, giving

$$x^{-1/2}(1 + \tfrac{1}{2}x^{K-1} + \tfrac{3}{8}x^{2K-2} + \ldots).$$

Since x is no larger than 0.01, this can be well approximated by

$$x^{-1/2} + \tfrac{1}{2}x^{K-3/2}.$$

Making this approximation, this piece of the integral is replaced by

$$\{(K-1)/L\}^{1/2} \int_0^{0.01} (x^{-1/2} + \tfrac{1}{2}x^{K-3/2}) \, dx,$$

which can be worked out exactly, and has value 0.37683 in the present case.

The piece near $x = 1$ can be done with the same sort of technique, expanding the integrand after putting $x = 1 - y$. This produces a very tedious calculation if a high degree of accuracy is wanted. I propose instead to use another method, which was introduced in Section 16.4, which is to use a Taylor approximation. That is, I put

$$X(t) \approx 1 + at + bt^2 + ct^3 + dt^4,$$

where the first term is 1 since $X = 1$ when $t = 0$. Further, I can see straight away that a must be zero, since dX/dt is given to be zero when $t = 0$. Substituting what is left in the original equation gives

$$\tfrac{1}{2}(1 - S^2)(2bt + 3ct^2 + 4dt^3)^2 + g(1 + bt^2 + ct^3 + dt^4)$$
$$+ S(1 + bt^2 + ct^3 + dt^4)(2b + 6ct + 12dt^2) = 0.$$

I need to make the coefficients of the powers of t in this equal to zero, at least as far as the coefficient of t^2: I cannot go further because I have omitted terms in the series which would be needed after this.

$$\begin{cases} t^0: g + 2bS = 0 \quad \text{and so} \quad b = -\tfrac{1}{2}g/S. \\ t^1: 6cS \quad = 0 \quad \text{and so} \quad c = 0. \\ t^2: 2b^2(1 - S^2) + gb + 2b^2S + 12dS = 0 \quad \text{so} \quad d = g^2(S^2 - 1)/(24S^3). \end{cases}$$

Thus a good approximation to $X(t)$ near $t = 0$ is given by

$$X(t) = 1 - \tfrac{1}{2}gt^2/S + g^2t^4(S^2 - 1)/(24S^3).$$

The first term omitted is in fact one in t^6, because you can show that X is an even function of t.

From this polynomial approximation to $X(t)$ I can determine when $X(t) = 0.99$, just by solving a quadratic equation in t^2:

$$g^2 t^4 (S^2 - 1)/(24S^3) - \tfrac{1}{2} g t^2 / S + 0.01 = 0.$$

Using the values $S = 9$ and $g = 10$ gives the time to be 0.13518 seconds.

This completes the third calculation of the time to empty the pipe. The total time comes from a sum of the three partial times: it is 4.0896 seconds. This has been the most accurate method, because it has confronted the difficulty of the calculation near $X = 0$, rather than just hoping for the best. However we have had to pay for this extra accuracy with a lot of extra mathematical work on the way.

Exercise 21C

1   Sketch the graph of V against X for the case $S = 9$ and using $g = 10$.

2   Calculate or estimate the fourth derivative of $(x - x^K)^{-1/2}$ at $x = 0.99$ and $x = 0.01$ for the case $S = 9$. Hence discuss the size of h needed in the evaluation of the integral using Simpson's rule. Is it easier to use a different size of h and check whether or not the value given for the integral is the same?

3   Do the balloon problem by the method of this section, to determine the time to reach maximum height, as follows.

(i)   Show that the equation of motion can be rewritten as

$$dW/dZ + 2cW = 2b(1 - aZ).$$

(ii)   Determine the integrating factor for this linear equation, and hence integrate it, with $W = 0$ at $Z = 0$.

(iii) Integrate it instead by regarding it as a linear equation with constant coefficients.

(iv)   Determine the value of Z at which $W = V = 0$, say M.

(v)   Show that the time required to reach maximum height is

$$\int_0^M \{R(1 - e^{-2cZ}) - abZ/c\}^{-1/2}\, dZ, \text{ for some } R.$$

(vi)   Calculate the integral in three pieces.

Which method of calculating this time seems easiest?

21.5   SUMMARY AND DISCUSSION

The whole of this section has been devoted to the solution of a particular differential equation, using a variety of numerical methods. In fact the accuracy with which we have done the mathematics is certainly excessive, since the model that we have used is most unlikely to represent the physical situation to such a high degree of accuracy. I should be surprised if more than 2 significant figures could be justified in the calculation, because aspects of physical reality missed out of the mathematical model are bound to have an effect; the missing reality could be taken into a better model, which would then have to be solved numerically, or else accurate experiments could be done. We shall pursue neither of these methods here, since the main aim was to show methods for solving a second order equation numerically.

(a)   Two first order equations solved numerically

The first method that was described, in Section 21.2, is easy to apply to any equation which you can express as

$$d^2X/dt^2 = F(\dot{X}, X, t),$$

where the right hand side means any combination of the first derivative, the function itself, and the variable that everything depends on. This is because the pair of first order equations that then have to be solved are just

$$dX/dt = V, \quad dV/dt = F(V, X, t),$$

together with some initial values of X and V.

As an example of this you could consider a modified version of the balloon model from Exercise 21A. The buoyancy of the balloon in the original model is represented by the term $b(1 - aZ)$, which was the excess of lift over weight at height Z. Replace this with the term

$$k\{e^{-aZ} - f(t)\} - g$$

as a more realistic model of how atmospheric density varies and how the pilot can change the lift. The new equation for the height of the balloon is

$$d^2Z/dt^2 + c(dZ/dt)|dZ/dt| - k\{e^{-aZ} - f(t)\} + g = 0.$$

The equivalent first order equations are now

$$dZ/dt = V, \quad dV/dt = k\{e^{-aZ} - f(t)\} - g.$$

These are only slightly more complicated to solve, using the modified Euler method, than the previous ones were, for any given function $f(t)$.

(b)   The discretised equation

The second method for second order differential equations, described in Section 21.3, replaced d^2X/dt^2 by $(X_{r+1} - 2X_r + X_{r-1})/h^2$, and dX/dt by $(X_{r+1} - X_{r+1})/(2h)$. This will always reduce the differential equation to an algebraic equation, and for the examples considered above it is a quadratic equation, which is easily solved.

Consider now another modification to the balloon flight example, in which the air resistance term $cV|V|$, which is certainly not exactly correct, is replaced by some more accurate formula, such as $cV|V|^{1.2}$. With this resistance term the equation for X_{r+1} is quite unpleasant, and will have to be solved at each step of the computer program by a Newton–Raphson (or other similar) procedure. This increases the running time for the solution of the differential equation, and makes this method less useful.

(c)   Mathematics first, calculate afterwards

The third method by which we found a numerical solution of the pipe flow equation, was to do some preliminary mathematical work to reduce the problem to that of calculating an integral. This can rarely be done, as it requires an equation which does not contain t explicitly, so that an equation involving only V and X can be found. Moreover this latter equation has to be one that can be integrated by some sort of formula. Despite these drawbacks, it is always worth thinking before you start on a numerical solution of a differential equation, whether it might be useful to do a little preliminary mathematics on the equation to get it into a more easily treated form. For example, some of the problems with the pipe flow equation near the time when both X and V are zero, could have been avoided by making the substitution $X = Y^2$. When this is done, the equation is transformed to

$$2(1+S-S^2)(dY/dt)^2 + g + 2SY\,d^2Y/dt^2 = 0.$$

Consequently, when $Y=0$, dY/dt has the non-zero value

$$-\{\tfrac{1}{2}g/(S^2-S-1)\}^{1/2},$$

and the integration has no difficulty at $Y=0$, where $d^2Y/dt^2=0$ also. I wrote a program (using Euler's method) for this new equation and found that dY/dt indeed reached the given constant value, soon after $t=2$. With $h=0.01$ I found that Y was zero at $t=4.0916$; with $h=0.005$ the corresponding time was $t=4.0906$. Since the error in the method I used is approximately proportional to h, I therefore expect that the time for h very close to 0 would be $t=4.0896$, which is what I found before.

(d)   Conclusions

The general conclusions to be drawn here are:

(i)   the method of reduction to first order equations is almost always available and useful;
(ii)   reduction to a second order difference equation is always possible, but may sometimes give a longer program;
(iii) preliminary mathematical work can often help, but it may not be easy to see what the appropriate manoeuvre is.
(iv)   it may be necessary to estimate errors carefully.

22

Models leading to second order differential equations

In this chapter we shall look at some of the modelling situations in which second order differential equations arise. There is no hope of being exhaustive here; the possibilities are almost endless.

22.1 DYNAMICS OF A PARTICLE

The fundamental equation in the dynamics of particle motion is

$$m\mathbf{a} = \mathbf{F},$$

where $\mathbf{a}$ is the acceleration of the particle whose (fixed) mass is m, and where $\mathbf{F}$ is the total force acting on it. The acceleration has to be measured with respect to a proper frame of reference, one that is not itself accelerating or rotating. When the motion is confined to a straight line the equation reduces to

$$m d^2 x/dt^2 = F,$$

where x is the distance along the line, and F is the force component along the line. The force F may arise from various causes, and its value may depend on the position x, the velocity dx/dt and the time t.

It is clear that problems in particle dynamics, once they have been formulated as far as stating the force F in terms of the position, velocity and time, are just problems in solving second order differential equations. An example of this was seen in Exercise 21A, where the balloon was the (rather large) particle, and the forces on it were due to air resistance and to the buoyancy of the balloon.

The process of modelling, by which you go (for example) from a very large object like a hot air balloon to a particle (which is usually thought of as having no size at all), is not always obvious. What is being done in this case is to say that the major things to do with the balloon's size are put into the forces; the air resistance force includes the fact that the balloon has a large cross-sectional area which makes the air flow round it and causes a drag force, and the buoyancy force includes the balloon's large volume containing a huge amount of hot and therefore light air. The very simple differential equation does not represent all aspects of the balloon and its motion, but it includes enough of the reality to give a start on the discussion of the vertical motion of hot air balloons. How do we find out what the forces are in such a situation? For this we have to go to those who are experts in the subject we are proposing to model; one of the hard things about mathematical modelling is that its practitioners have to get well acquainted with the reality of the subject that they wish to model, and this can be a time consuming business.

One of the standard models of particle dynamics concerns the vertical oscillation of a particle hanging from a light elastic string. This model illustrates so well much of the work on differential equations that is to follow, that it is worth spending some time on deriving it.

I took a piece of elastic about 20 cm long and tied it to an empty torch of mass about 300 g. The elastic stretched to 50 cm under this load; when it was displaced slightly, the load moved up and down with a period of about one second.

The model of this real situation is shown in Fig. 1, where the torch, represented as a particle, is at height $x(t)$ above the floor. My hand (not entirely steady) is at height $h(t)$ above the floor, and the length of the elastic at any time is $l(t) = h(t) - x(t)$. I know, from books on the subject, that the force required to stretch a piece of elastic is proportional to the extension, as long as this is not too large, so that the (elastic) force E in the diagram is equal to $k(l - L) = k(h - x - L)$, where L is the original length of the piece of elastic. So if I suppose that there are any other forces mF also acting on the torch (or particle), I will get the equation for its motion to be

$$m\, d^2x/dt^2 = k(h - x - L) + mF - mg,$$

the last term representing the particle's weight.

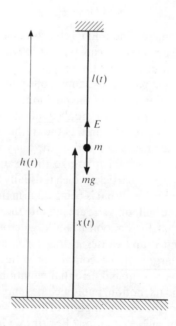

Figure 1. A particle on an elastic string

The value of k turns out to be $10\,\mathrm{kg\,s^{-2}}$ (because the elastic stretches $30\,\mathrm{cm}$ to hold up $300\,\mathrm{g}$ against gravity). Putting in the values, and rearranging a bit, gives the equation

$$d^2x/dt^2 + 33\tfrac{1}{3}x = F + 33\tfrac{1}{3}h(t) - 16\tfrac{2}{3}.$$

What can be said about the force F? Three reasonable choices are:

(i)   put it equal to zero and see what the model then predicts;
(ii) assume that it is due to air resistance and proportional to the product of dx/dt and $|dx/dt|$, as in the balloon model;
(iii) assume that various reasons for loss of energy can all be taken into a term proportional to dx/dt.

Whichever of these seems most appropriate, we end up with a second order differential equation to solve. Given the function for h, and some initial conditions on x and dx/dt, we have to find x in terms of t.

Other areas of dynamics also lead to second order differential equations, and I shall give you two out of the many which are available.

The motion of a planet (or a comet) round the sun obeys the equations

$$\begin{cases} d^2r/dt^2 - h^2/r^3 = F(r) \\ d\theta/dt = h/r^2, \end{cases}$$

where r and θ are shown in Fig. 2, and where h is a constant. The force $F(r)$ is closely equal to $-GM/r^2$, where M is the mass of the sun and G is the gravitational constant, with direction along the line separating sun and planet. This gives a second order equation for r in terms of t, one which has been studied for over three hundred years.

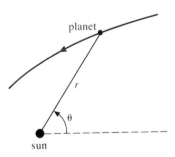

Figure 2. Diagram for planetary motion

As far as we are concerned here, planetary motion is just an example of a model that leads to a second order (non-linear) differential equation. The details of the solution formulas that can be found are contained (for example) in *Mechanics and Vectors* in this series.

The motion of a space probe as it passes through the solar system is considerably more complicated, because at certain parts of its journey it will be moving under the influence of more than one body (for example, the Sun and

Jupiter, or Saturn and its moons), and so the force on the probe will not have such a simple form. But there will still be some set of differential equations to solve, and this must be done numerically if you want to control the probe through a series of meetings with planets and their moons.

The rotational motion of rigid bodies also leads to second order equations. The model I shall discuss here is a very rough version of how a ship rolls under the influence of long waves. First, there is an 'angular mass-acceleration' term to put in the equation; this is usually described as moment of inertia times rate of change of angular velocity. Secondly, there is a tendency for the ship to right itself. Thirdly, the waves cause the ship to heel over. Finally, the relative motion of ship and water is opposed by forces between them, perhaps due to stabilising fins. The equation which I suggest to represent all these effects is

$$I\, d^2\theta/dt^2 + A \sin \theta = B \sin \omega t - C(d\theta/dt)^2,$$

where you need to consult a naval architect to obtain values for the constants I, A, B, C, and where ω (the Greek letter 'omega') is related to the length of the waves causing the motion. Once again, the equation is a second order differential equation.

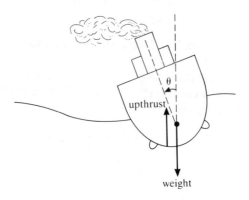

Figure 3. A ship rolling in waves

Exercise 22A

1   For the elastic and torch model find the solution $x(t)$ when $F = 0$ is assumed, together with $h = 1$. Take as initial conditions that

$$x = 0.4, \quad \dot{x} = 0, \quad \text{when } t = 0.$$

You will need a solution like one of those to question 3 in Exercise 18C.

2   Verify that the period of oscillation in question 1 is approximately one second.

3   A comet is first observed at a distance from the Sun

$$r = 5\,\text{AU}$$

(i.e. 5 astronomical units, or 5 times the distance from Earth to Sun). Measurements show that at that time

$$\begin{cases} d\theta/dt = 0.24 \text{ radians/year}, \\ d^2\theta/dt^2 = 0.096 \text{ radians/year}^2. \end{cases}$$

Determine the values of h and of dr/dt at the time of observation.

4 It is known that the value of GM for the Sun is $41\,\text{AU}^3/\text{yr}^2$. Integrate the comet's equation of motion numerically to find
(i) the minimum value of r,
(ii) the time spent inside the Earth's orbit.

5 Set up an equation to describe the vertical motion of a buoy in response to long sea waves.

22.2 ENERGY AND FLOW

There are several important situations where a difference of some form of energy causes a flow to take place, and where the total amount of flowing substance is conserved.

One of the most studied examples is electric circuit theory, for reasons that will become apparent later. In this case the energy is electrical, and is measured in volts above a standard zero level; the substance flowing in this case is electrically charged particles (electrons), and the flow takes place in wires. The energy is supplied by generators or batteries.

Flow of water in pipes has many similarities, and is to some extent easier to understand, so we shall start the discussion with this example. In this case the energy is expressed either as a pressure (above a standard level, often atmospheric), or as a height (a 'head') to which the water would rise in a vertical pipe from that point. Energy sources here are pumps, or reservoirs (tanks, cisterns) which keep water at a height above the reference level. Note that blood flow has many similarities with water flow in pipes, with the heart as energy source for the flow.

Other examples of flows driven by energy differences include the flow of water in plants, where the energy is more complicated, as it includes chemical energy of solution and surface energy; and the flow of heat by conduction, where the energy is temperature.

Consider a junction of pipes, as shown in Fig. 4. It is rather obvious that the flows are related by

$$Q = q_1 + q_2 + q_3.$$

In this case the flows Q, q_1, q_2, q_3 would be measured in (e.g.) cm^3 per second. The equation may be rewritten as

$$q_1 + q_2 + q_3 - Q = 0,$$

or the total outflow from the junction is zero. In electric circuit theory this would be called

Kirchhoff's first law,

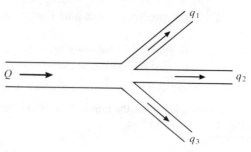

Figure 4. Flow rates at a junction of pipes

where the outflows would be electric currents. It depends, of course, on leaks being either prevented, or allowed for as flows or currents.

The second law for flows depends on the fact that the energy has a definite value at each point of the flow – you could put in a pressure measuring device there, if it was a water flow. Consequently, if you consider going round some complete circuit in the flow, you must get back to the same value for the pressure at the end of the circuit. If the circuit contains some energy losing sections (energy will be lost against friction as water flows along a pipe), then it must have some source of energy in it also to replace the loss. This may be put as

Total loss of energy round a circuit = 0,

when you make allowance for any gain at a pump or other generator. In electric circuit theory this would be called

Kirchhoff's second law,

where the energy losses would be voltage differences or potential differences.

As an example, consider the garden cascade in Fig. 5. The top pond is at a height of 2.5 metres above the pump, the others at 1.5 and 0.5 metres. The energies at the ponds are 2.5, 1.5, 0.5, if the unit of energy is the 'metre height of water'. The pump causes a difference of energy of 3 m of water, and the resistances in the two pipes cause losses of 0.5 m of water in each. Between the ponds the water trickles down over stones, and loses 1 m of energy in each of these cascades. Thus as you follow once round the circuit there is an energy loss of 3 m in pipes

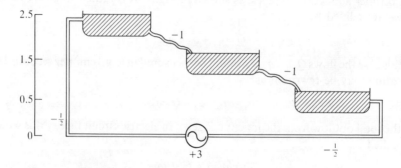

Figure 5. Water flowing round a garden cascade

and cascades, with an energy gain of 3 m at the pump, a total for the circuit of zero loss.

After this discussion to introduce Kirchhoff's two laws, we shall not discuss water flow in pipes much more. The reason for this is that the relation between pressure difference and flow rate in pipes is not very simple, whereas for many electrical components the relation between potential difference (voltage loss) and current flowing is reasonably straightforward. Moreover, there are more applications of electric circuits than there are of water pipe networks.

Exercise 22B

Draw a circuit diagram to represent a central heating circuit in a two-storey house. You should include a pump, at least two branches with several resistances, and a reservoir in the roof (or some other high point) to keep the circuit full. Mark on some sample pressures, stating the units you use.

22.3   ELECTRIC CIRCUITS

The first important law of the flow of electric currents in wires is *Ohm's Law*, which is that the current is proportional to the drop in electric potential (or voltage) across any resistance in a circuit. That is,

$$V = IR,$$

where V is the drop in potential measured in volts, I is the current in the direction of the fall in potential, measured in amperes, and R is the constant of proportionality (called the resistance), measured in ohms. The extent to which this is an exact truth, and the reasons for its truth or for deviations from it, are matters for Physics to discuss. Here we take it as an adequate mathematical model for currents through resistances.

What are these resistances? The light bulb of a cycle torch which I took apart informed me that it operated at 2.5 V (where the V is the abbreviation for volts) and 0.3 A (the A standing for amperes). This means that its resistance is found from

$$2.5 = 0.3R;$$

That is, the resistance is 25/3 Ω (where the Greek letter capital omega Ω stands for ohms). Similarly, my car handbook tells me that the rear fog lamp has a 5 A fuse; at that current, and with a 12 V car battery, I would deduce a resistance of 12/5 Ω as the least that the bulb can have.

In mechanics, the product of a force and a velocity in the same direction gives the rate of working or power of the force. The same concept translates directly to all subjects where an energy difference causes a flow. For steady water flow in pipes, the product of pressure drop and volume flow rate gives the rate of working against friction in that section. For current electricity similarly, the rate of working or power is given by

$$\text{power} = \text{voltage drop} \times \text{current},$$

with a value given in watts.

For example, my rear fog lamp is stated to have a power of 21 W (where the W stands for watts). From this I deduce that the normal current in it is 21/12 A, because the battery provides a potential drop of 12 V across the bulb. I can now recalculate the resistance of the bulb to be 48/7 Ω, considerably higher than the estimate I found from the evidence of the fuse. As a second example, my calculator has a 3 V battery (or, rather, two 1.5 V batteries) and is said to have a power consumption of 0.8 W. Combining the formulas

$$V = IR \quad \text{and} \quad W = VI$$

gives $W = V^2/R$, so that I can find the resistance of my calculator circuits as $9/0.8 = 11\frac{1}{4}\,\Omega$.

The discussion above has introduced the ideas of resistance and power, but only in the context of electrical devices which use batteries, and in which the current is always flowing in one direction. These are *direct current* or DC situations. However, very many electrical machines, and also domestic lighting, use a source of energy which oscillates in time, and we go on to discuss the equations that are then appropriate.

The source of energy is now the voltage difference $V(t)$; this could have any sort of behaviour with varying t, but only two need concern us here, for the reason that only two have wide application. The first is

$$V(t) = V_0 \cos(\omega t + \delta),$$

which is known as *alternating current*, or AC, and where V_0, ω, δ are constants known as the amplitude, the (radian) frequency, and the phase. It is important to notice that the number of cycles per second is $\omega/2\pi$, and that you may find the energy source given in alternative forms, such as

$$V(t) = V_0 \cos(2\pi f t - \beta),$$

where now the frequency is f cycles per second, or f hertz (symbol Hz). The period of the oscillation is $2\pi/\omega$ or $1/f$ seconds. Usually I shall put

$$V(t) = V_0 \cos \omega t,$$

to represent an oscillating source of electric energy that is maintained for a long time.

The other main possibility is that the source is switched on at some instant. For that case the energy source is

$$\begin{cases} V(t) = 0 & \text{for } t < 0, \\ V(t) = V_0 \cos \omega t & \text{for } t \geqslant 0. \end{cases}$$

There are three major components with which electric circuits can be built up. The first is the resistor, which has the conventional symbol shown in Fig. 6(a); the earlier version of the resistor symbol is shown in Fig. 6(b).

The resistance of the resistor is given in ohms, and it is still assumed that an appropriate model is that the voltage drop across a resistor of resistance $R\,\Omega$ is $RI(t)$, when $I(t)$ is the current flowing through it, in amperes.

The second component is the capacitor, with a conventional symbol which

Figure 6(*a*). The modern symbol for a resistor    Figure 6(*b*). The former symbol for a resistor

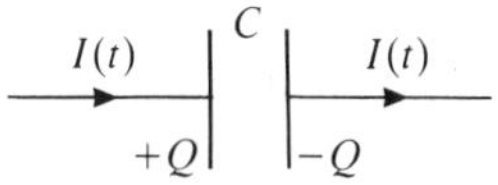

$$I(t) \quad \overset{C}{\dashv\vdash} \quad I(t)$$
$$+Q \qquad -Q$$

Figure 7. A capacitor of capacitance C with charges and currents

shows that capacitors used to be made out of parallel plates. A capacitor stores up charge in the same way as a reservoir stores up water, and the voltage drop across it is Q/C, where Q is the charge on one side of it (and $-Q$ on the other) and C is its capacitance, measured in farads (with symbol F) (see Fig. 7). The former name for a capacitor was a condenser. The charge Q on the capacitor is measured in coulombs (symbol C), and is related to the current which is flowing in the wire leading to the capacitor, by

$$dQ/dt = I.$$

This is just the same as saying that the rate of change of the volume of water in a reservoir is equal to the flow rate in the pipe leading into the reservoir.

The third major component used in simple electric circuits is the inductor, whose symbol (shown in Fig. 8) again reflects its origin, this time as a wire coiled round a cylindrical support. The voltage drop across an inductor is

$$L \, dI/dt,$$

where $I(t)$ is the current in the wire leading to it, and L is the inductance, measured in henries (symbol H).

Figure 8. The symbol for an inductor

We may now consider a complete circuit using all of these components.

In Fig. 9 a source, of voltage $V(t)$, is connected in series to a resistor, a capacitor and an inductor; the values of the components are also shown on the diagram. Using Kirchhoff's second law round the complete circuit gives the equation

$$RI + Q/C + L \, dI/dt = V(t).$$

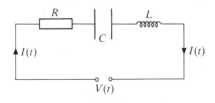

Figure 9. A circuit with three components and a voltage generator

If you differentiate this with respect to t, and use $dQ/dt = I$, you get

$$L\,d^2I/dt^2 + R\,dI/dt + I/C = dV/dt,$$

which is a second order differential equation for $I(t)$ when $V(t)$ is given.

Alternatively, you could put $I = dQ/dt$ in the first equation to obtain

$$L\frac{d^2Q}{dt^2} + R\frac{dQ}{dt} + \frac{Q}{C} = V(t),$$

a second order differential equation for $Q(t)$.

It is worth looking at a second example, in which the capacitor and inductor are connected in parallel, while the resistor is in series with the voltage source. The currents I, J and $I - J$ in Fig. 10 ensure that Kirchhoff's first law is satisfied at the junction points of the wires.

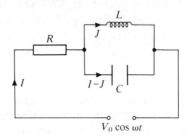

Figure 10. Another circuit with three components and generator

Next consider Kirchhoff's second law on voltage drop round a circuit. Since the potentials at the junction points are the same whichever way you get to them, you must have

$$L\,dJ/dt = Q/C.$$

And using Kirchhoff's second law through the upper branch and via the generator, gives

$$RI + L\,dJ/dt = V_0 \cos \omega t.$$

Combine these two equations with $dQ/dt = I - J$ and you find

$$RCL\,d^2J/dt^2 + RJ + L\,dJ/dt = V_0 \cos \omega t,$$

which is another second order differential equation, this time for J.

Notice that the wires between the components in the circuit are assumed to have no resistance (or inductance or capacitance). This kind of model, where (for example) *all* the resistance is put into the resistors and none elsewhere, is called a *lumped parameter* model.

The numerical values of the constants R, C, L, V_0, Q, ω, depend very much on the kind of application under discussion. I looked at the circuit diagram for a cassette recorder, and found

(i)   resistances from $180\,\Omega$ to $1\,M\Omega$ (i.e. $10^6\,\Omega$);

(ii) capacitances from $1\,nF$ (i.e. $10^{-9}\,F$) to $33\,\mu F$ ($33 \times 10^{-6}\,F$).

A local electronics shop sells a slightly wider range of these components, and also inductors from $100\,\mu H$ to $1.2\,mH$. The voltages suitable for the recorder were $7.5\,V$ DC or 200 to $240\,V$ AC at 50 to $60\,Hz$ (which is $\omega = 100\pi$ to 120π). The charge on a capacitor of $1\,mF$ at $7.5\,V$ is $Q = 7.5\,mC$. In this application you can see that resistances are high, but capacitances and inductances are small.

On the other hand, for power station applications where voltages will be measured in kV, you need to have low resistances, otherwise the high currents needed to transmit large amounts of power will generate too much heat.

The three types of components that have been described in this section have been assumed to be *linear*, that is, doubling of the source of electricity in the circuit would just double all currents. This is not true for other components such as transistors and valves, and so equations for circuits containing them will be more complicated to deal with; you must look elsewhere for such a treatment.

Exercise 22C

1 My programmable calculator uses a 6 V battery, and has a consumption of 0.02 W. What current is flowing through what resistance? If its life will be 300 hours, how much charge has flowed out of the battery?

2 Determine what single resistance S would give the same current I
   (i)   in the circuit of Fig. 11(a),
   (ii) in the circuit of Fig. 11(b).
   (These are important results for combining resistances (i) in series and (ii) in parallel.)

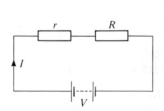

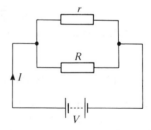

Figure 11(a). Resistors in series   Figure 11(b). Resistors in parallel

3 (i) Use the circuit in Fig. 12(a) to show that the three inductances in series are equivalent to a single inductance L given by

$$L = L_1 + L_2 + L_3.$$

(ii) Use the circuit in Fig. 12(b) to show that the three capacitances in series are equivalent to a single capacitance C given by

$$\frac{1}{C} = \frac{1}{C_1} + \frac{1}{C_2} + \frac{1}{C_3}.$$

You will need to show first that the charges on the three capacitors are equal.
(iii) Find a similar formula for three inductors, and another for three capacitors, connected in parallel.

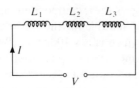

Figure 12(a). Three inductors connected in series

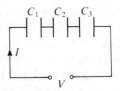

Figure 12(b). Three capacitors connected in series

4 In the circuit shown in Fig. 13, Q is the charge on the capacitor and the currents are marked in two of the wires. What is the current in the resistor? Show that the equation for Q is

$$LRC\frac{d^2Q}{dt^2} + L\frac{dQ}{dt} + RQ = V_0 RC \cos \omega t.$$

5 Find the equation for I in Fig. 13.

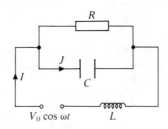

Figure 13. A three element circuit.

22.4   PAIRS OF FIRST ORDER EQUATIONS

Second order differential equations also arise frequently from the combination of two first order equations, as we have already seen in Section 18.3. These can bring in entirely different sorts of models from those seen in Sections 22.1 and 22.3, so we will look at three examples.

(a)   Interacting species

In Section 18.1 it was suggested that the interaction of a predator species of fish with a prey species could be modelled by two first order differential equations. This assumed that the numbers of fish involved were large enough, so that you could round any answers to the nearest whole number without any serious loss of accuracy; and also that the time intervals between interactions were small compared with the total length of time, so that the whole process could be assumed to run continuously. With these assumptions, the equations for the interaction of the species were of the form

$$\begin{cases} du/dt = pu - quv \\ dv/dt = rv + suv, \end{cases}$$

where $u(t)$ is the number of prey fish and $v(t)$ the number of predators. The constants p and r give the rates of increase of each population in the absence of the other, so that p is positive and r is negative (the predators die out if they have nothing to eat). The constants q and s show the interaction, which reduces the number of prey and increases the number of predators.

Suppose I wish to have a single differential equation for $u(t)$. I can rearrange the first equation as

$$v = (pu - \dot{u})/qu,$$

and also differentiate the first equation to get

$$\ddot{u} = p\dot{u} - q\dot{u}v - qu\dot{v}.$$

The equation for dv/dt and the equation for v can now be used to express d^2u/dt^2 entirely in terms of du/dt and u. The resulting equation is

$$u\, d^2u/dt^2 = (du/dt)^2 + (du/dt)(ru - su^2) - spu^3 - rpu^2,$$

which does not look very helpful. In fact you would almost certainly want to solve it numerically by going back to two first order equations. But it does show one surprising thing that you would not have noticed from the original equation, which is that the value of q does not come into the equation for u. It does however affect the initial value of du/dt. The equation also shows that the equilibrium value of u is $-r/s$ (when $\ddot{u} = \dot{u} = 0$), which is entirely determined by the lifestyle of the predator.

This example shows that there may be very little advantage in taking two first order equations and forcing them to become one second order equation.

(b) Heat flow

One way of warming a room is to have a deep freeze cabinet in it, because the operation is never 100% efficient, so that more heat is created than cold. Moreover, the smaller the room you put your deep freeze into, the warmer it will get, and so the deep freeze will have to work harder as some of this warmth leaks in through its insulation, which is also not 100% efficient. I made a crude model of the processes involved here to find out if it was possible or likely that the room would go on getting hotter and hotter.

Assume that the air outside the room has fixed temperature T_0 and that the thermostat in the deep freeze is set at the fixed temperature θ_0. Denote the room temperature by T and the temperature inside the deep freeze by θ. Now model the heat flow out of the room to the outside air, and into the room from the working of the deep freeze motor, by the equation

$$dT/dt = -a(T - T_0) + b(\theta - \theta_0),$$

where a and b are positive constants. This has assumed that the heat flow out of the room is proportional to the temperature difference, and that the deep freeze motor is running continuously. A better model at this stage would give a very complicated equation, so let us accept this for the moment.

The heat flow into the deep freeze through its insulated walls, and the heat extraction from the deep freeze due to the action of the motor, will be modelled by the equation

$$d\theta/dt = c(T-\theta) - k(\theta-\theta_0),$$

using the same assumptions as before.

It is now possible to eliminate T, and you will find that the result is a reasonably simple equation for $\theta - \theta_0$:

$$\frac{d^2}{dt^2}(\theta-\theta_0) + A\frac{d}{dt}(\theta-\theta_0) + B(\theta-\theta_0) = C,$$

where the constants A, B, C are given by

$$\begin{cases} A = a+c+k \\ B = ac+ak-bc \\ C = ac(T_0-\theta_0). \end{cases}$$

As we will find later, the sign of B determines what happens. A negative value of B will cause a disaster, and this will occur if the room is well insulated (small a) and the deep freeze is very inefficient (b and c large), as you might expect.

It is equally possible to eliminate θ from the first order equations to get a second order equation for T; this is left to an exercise – the conclusions cannot be different.

In this case, elimination of one variable to get a second order equation is a help, because the resulting equation (as we shall see later) can be solved quite easily with a formula, and does not require numerical work.

(c)   Radioactive decay

For a radioactive element, the number of atoms decaying into some other element per second is a constant times the number of atoms present, provided that you have a large number of the atoms and do not mind rounding numbers to integers. Consider a chain of elements, in which A decays at rate a into element B, which in its turn decays at rate b to element C, which is stable and so does not decay any further. The equation for the number of atoms x of element A is therefore

$$dx/dt = -ax.$$

Similarly for B and C you get

$$\begin{cases} dy/dt = ax-by \\ dz/dt = by, \end{cases}$$

when there are y atoms of B and z of C. One way of finding out how many atoms of B are present at any time, is to eliminate x from the first two equations to find a second order equation for y. It is

$$d^2y/dt^2 + (a+b)dy/dt + aby = 0,$$

which we shall later discover to be quite easy to solve.

In this case there are alternative methods available which are easier. You can solve the first of the three equations at once to find

$$x(t) = Ne^{-at},$$

where N is the initial number of atoms of element A. If you then put this result into the second equation, the equation becomes

$$dy/dt + by = aNe^{-at},$$

which is a first order equation whose solution can be found by using an integrating factor (or by other methods).

It is also useful to note here that $x+y+z$ is a constant, because its derivative is zero, so that it is not necessary to integrate the third equation.

This example shows that even when the equations can easily be reduced to a simple second order equation, this may not be the simplest method of finding the solution.

Exercise 22D

1   Find a second order equation for
   (i) $x(t)$ in question 2 of Exercise 18D;
   (ii) $L(t)$ in question 3 of Exercise 18E.
   Show that the second of these can be 'solved' quite easily by putting

$$d^2L/dt^2 = V\,dV/dL \text{ where } V = dL/dt.$$

   What about the first?

2   Find the second order equation for T in the deep freeze model.

3   Set up a matrix equation for the three equations of the radioactive decay model, and solve the problem by the methods of Section 20.2.

22.5 SUMMARY

Second order differential equations arise frequently in the models of dynamics and electric circuit theory. They also arise from pairs of linked equations, when one of the variables is eliminated.

Kirchhoff's two laws for electric circuit theory (and for other similar models) are:

(i) that no current is lost at a junction,
(ii) that for a complete circuit the total of energy (potential) differences is zero, when allowance is made for gains of energy at sources (such as batteries, generators, pumps).

For the three standard electrical components, the energy decreases, in the direction of the current I, are

$$\begin{cases} IR \text{ for a resistance } R \text{ (Ohm's law),} \\ L\,dI/dt \text{ for an inductance } L, \\ Q/C \text{ for a capacitance } C, \end{cases}$$

where Q is the charge on the capacitance, related to I by

$$I = dQ/dt.$$

The electrical SI units are:

> volts, V, for energy or potential
> amperes, A, for current
> ohms, Ω, for resistance
> henries, H, for inductance
> farads, F, for capacitance
> coulombs, C, for charge.

The unit of frequency is the hertz, Hz.

23

Solving second order differential equations

Rather few second order differential equations can be solved exactly in terms of the usual elementary functions. Most non-linear equations have to be solved numerically; most linear equations with non-constant coefficients also need numerical solutions. In fact the only large class of differential equations that have solution formulas is those which are linear and have constant coefficients, and reasonably simple right hand sides. So this chapter deals with equations of the form

$$\frac{d^2y}{dx^2} + p\frac{dy}{dx} + qy = f(x),$$

where p and q are constants and $f(x)$ is a reasonably simple function. There will often be two conditions which the solution will be required to satisfy, which will usually be in one of two forms:

(i) two conditions given at the same point (often called *initial* conditions), such as

$$y(a) = c \quad \text{and} \quad (dy/dx)_{x=a} = c;$$

(ii) two conditions given at different points, such as

$$y(a) = c \quad \text{and} \quad y(b) = d.$$

In either case these conditions will be referred to as boundary conditions on the equation.

We shall not need to use a computer in this section; the methods are all analytic, that is they involve formulas and work with pen and paper. This is one of the reasons why we concentrate on these equations for a while, because exact solutions can be found for them. There are other reasons as well. They occur frequently in applications, either as the proper or approximate equations for some situation. And they reveal the structure and shape of solution that will be appropriate for more complicated equations.

Much of the work in this section has a close resemblance to work done on second order difference equations in Chapter 19 above, and you should look back to that work from time to time to see the similarities, and the occasional differences.

The underlying theory for these equations has two parts:

(a) the first order linear equation

$$dz/dx + rz = f(x)$$

can be solved rather easily by the methods in Section 12.1.

(b) the equation that we wish to solve can be *factorised* as

$$\left(\frac{d}{dx} + r\right)\left(\frac{dy}{dx} + sy\right) = f(x).$$

However this theory does not play a large part in the rest of the section because, after a few examples showing the theory in action, it is much easier to work (using intelligent guesswork) from experience of the *kind* of solution that is suitable for these equations.

23.1   SOLUTION BY FACTORISATION

First we should verify that the second order equation

$$\frac{d^2y}{dx^2} + p\frac{dy}{dx} + qy = 0$$

can be factorised. That is, that it can be expressed as

$$\left(\frac{d}{dx} + r\right)\left(\frac{dy}{dx} + sy\right) = 0$$

for some choice of constants r and s. The only meaning we can easily give to this factorised form is

$$\frac{d}{dx}\left(\frac{dy}{dx} + sy\right) + r\left(\frac{dy}{dx} + sy\right) = 0;$$

that is,

$$\frac{d^2y}{dx^2} + (r+s)\frac{dy}{dx} + rsy = 0.$$

Hence the factorisation is possible if we can find r, s such that

$$r + s = p, \quad rs = q.$$

This is indeed easily done, by choosing r and s to be the solutions of the quadratic equation

$$m^2 - pm + q = 0.$$

Hence we shall always be able to factorise the equation we are dealing with, should we want to. Note here that if p and q are *not* constants the factorisation may be difficult or impossible.

I shall start with the equation

$$d^2y/dx^2 - dy/dx - 12y = 6x,$$

with the boundary conditions $y(0)=0$ and $y(1)=0$; this is a not quite random choice of example, to show the method and the results.

The equation can be factorised as

$$(d/dx+3)(dy/dx-4y)=6x,$$

as you can check by solving the appropriate quadratic. I shall now define the new variable z to be $dy/dx-4y$, which means that the equation can be rewritten as

$$(d/dx+3)z=6x,$$

which is just

$$dz/dx+3z=6x.$$

First order linear equations can be dealt with by integrating factors, and in this case the integrating factor is e^{3x}, giving

$$\frac{d}{dx}(ze^{3x})=6x\,e^{3x}.$$

You now integrate both sides, not forgetting the constant of integration, and find

$$ze^{3x}=A+2xe^{3x}-\tfrac{2}{3}e^{3x}.$$

So we have found z:

$$z=Ae^{-3x}+2x-\tfrac{2}{3}.$$

But from the definition of z we know that

$$dy/dx-4y=z=Ae^{-3x}+2x-\tfrac{2}{3},$$

and this is another first order linear equation to solve, this time to find y in terms of x. Here the integrating factor is e^{-4x}, so that

$$\frac{d}{dx}(ye^{-4x})=(Ae^{-3x}+2x-\tfrac{2}{3})e^{-4x}.$$

This in its turn can be integrated, and I found

$$y=Be^{4x}-(A/7)e^{-3x}-\tfrac{1}{2}x+1/24,$$

where A and B are as yet unknown constants of integration. These constants are to be found from the boundary conditions, which have not been used so far. Taking first $y=0$ and then $y=1$ gives us

$$\begin{cases}0=B-A/7+1/24\\0=Be^4-(A/7)e^{-3}-11/24,\end{cases}$$

which can be solved to find A and B. I found

$$A=\frac{7(e^4+11)}{24(e^4-e^{-3})}\quad\text{and}\quad B=A/7-1/24.$$

There are several things to be pointed out about the solution which we have achieved by this method.

(i)   Two constants came in because there were two integrations to do, and that was because it was a second order equation, which needed two factors.

(ii)   The exponentials came in because of the integrating factors of the first order equations, and the -3 and 4 in the exponentials came from the factorisation of the original equation.

(iii) The shape of the solution is

'constants times exponentials plus an extra bit'.

The extra bit was derived from the right hand side of the original equation.

(iv)   The values of the constants were found right at the end from the boundary conditions.

In the questions in Exercise 23A you should find exactly the same structure to your solutions, though the details will vary from case to case.

Exercise 23A

1   Solve the equation $d^2y/dx^2 + 4dy/dx - 12y = f(x)$ in the following cases, using the factorisation method:

(i) $f(x) = 0$
(ii) $f(x) = 6$
(iii) $f(x) = 6$, $y(0) = 0$ and $(dy/dx)_{x=0} = 1$
(iv) $f(x) = 6$, $y(0) = 0$ and $(dy/dx)_{x=1} = 1$.

2   Solve the equation $d^2y/dx^2 + dy/dx - 2y = e^x$ with $y(0) = 0$ and $(dy/dx)_{x=0} = 0$. The solution of this problem and the next will be discussed further below.

3   Solve the equation $d^2y/dx^2 + 2dy/dx + y = e^{-x}$. Your solution here should not have quite the shape suggested in (iii) above: one of the exponential terms will have an extra factor in it.

4   The equation

$$\frac{d^2y}{dx^2} - \frac{dy}{dx} - 12y = 6x$$

can also be factorised as

$$\left(\frac{d}{dx} - 4\right)\left(\frac{dy}{dx} + 3y\right) = 6x.$$

Check that you get the same answer from this factorisation.

5   (i) The following equation can be solved by factorisation.

$$d^2y/dx^2 - (1 + 1/x)dy/dx + y/x = x.$$

(ii) You can also make some progress with

$$d^2y/dx^2 + (1 - \tan x)dy/dx - (\tan x)y = \sin x.$$

23.2   HOMOGENEOUS EQUATION, COMPLEMENTARY FUNCTION

We concentrate first on the equation

$$d^2y/dx^2 + p\,dy/dx + qy = 0$$

which is called the *homogeneous* equation, and which is found by putting the right hand side of our previous equation equal to 0. The solution of this equation is called the

complementary function

– or CF for short – just as in Chapters 2, 12 and 19.

Now the part of the solution in the examples above that was independent of the right hand side of the equation was (usually) a pair of exponential terms. So the method that we normally use to find solutions of the homogeneous equation is to look for solutions of the form Ae^{mx}. Substitute this into the homogeneous equation and find the *auxiliary equation* (much as in Section 19.1):

$$A(m^2 + pm + q)e^{mx} = 0$$

or, in general, since A need not be zero, and e^{mx} certainly is not zero,

$$m^2 + pm + q = 0.$$

Three cases arise here, because a quadratic equation can have three rather different sorts of solution; again this is just as in Section 19.1.

(i) Two real roots, say k and l. Then

$$y = Ae^{kx} + Be^{lx}$$

is the solution. Compare this with the result in Section 19.1(a):

$$u_n = Ac_1^n + Bc_2^n.$$

These are actually very similar in form, because you can write

$$c^n = e^{n\ln c},$$

so both solutions are 'really' exponentials (or 'really' powers).

(ii) One (repeated) real root, say k. Then

$$y = Ae^{kx} + Bxe^{kx}$$

is the solution, as you can quite easily check by substitution. You had an example like this in Exercise 23A (question 3), and you can confirm that this is indeed the correct solution when the quadratic has a repeated root by working through the method of factorisation. Compare again with what happened in Section 19.1(c), where a repeated root of the auxiliary equation led to a solution

$$u_n = Ac^n + nBc^n,$$

i.e. a solution with an extra n in the second term. In the differential equation version of the theory it is an extra x that comes into the solution.

(iii) Two conjugate complex roots. Start with an example:

$$d^2y/dx^2 + y = 0.$$

It is easily checked that this equation has auxiliary equation

$$m^2 + 1 = 0,$$

with roots the conjugate pair

$$m = \pm j.$$

It is also easily checked that the solution is

$$y = A \cos x + B \sin x.$$

The relation of these two facts is through the equation

$$e^{jx} = \cos x + j \sin x,$$

as we shall see in detail below. You should again look back to Section 19.1(b), where cos and sin functions came into the solution of difference equations when the auxiliary equation had a pair of conjugate complex roots.

More generally, let us suppose that the roots of the auxiliary equation

$$m^2 + pm + q = 0$$

are

$$k + js \quad \text{and} \quad k - js,$$

a conjugate pair. Then

$$y = Ae^{(k + js)x} + Be^{(k - js)x}$$

is a solution, as you can verify by substitution. This solution can be rearranged as follows:

$$y = e^{kx}(Ae^{jsx} + Be^{-jsx})$$

$$= e^{kx}\{A(\cos sx + j \sin sx) + B(\cos sx - j \sin sx)\}$$

$$= e^{kx}\{(A + B)\cos sx + j(A - B)\sin sx\}.$$

Let us rewrite this as

$$y = e^{kx}(C \cos sx + D \sin sx)$$

by defining $C = A + B$ and $D = j(A - B)$. Note that there is no promise anywhere that any of A, B, C, D is a *real* number; but if y is to be a function that represents something with real values then it is C and D that need to have real values, and A and B must therefore be complex numbers.

Let us have a summary of this important work. For this equation

the auxiliary equation is $m^2 + pm + q = 0$;
roots k, l give a solution $Ae^{kx} + Be^{lx}$;
root k only gives a solution $Ae^{kx} + Bxe^{kx}$;
roots $k \pm js$ give a solution $e^{kx}(C \cos sx + D \sin sx)$.

The constants A, B (or *C, D*) correspond to the constants of integration in the factorisation method, and will eventually be found from the boundary conditions.

Warning: *p* and *q* must be constants in this work.

Exercise 23B

1 Verify the solutions given in (i), (ii), (iii) by substituting them into appropriate differential equations, i.e. with values of *p* and *q* chosen to give quadratic equations with the right roots.

2 For (i) to (vi) write down the auxiliary equation and determine the solution.
  (i) $d^2y/dx^2 + dy/dx - 6y = 0$.
  (ii) $d^2y/dx^2 - 4 dy/dx + 4y = 0$.
  (iii) $d^2y/dx^2 + 6 dy/dx + 9y = 0$.
  (iv) $d^2y/dx^2 \qquad + 4y = 0$.
  (v) $d^2y/dx^2 + 4 dy/dx + 5y = 0$.
  (vi) $d^2y/dx^2 + 2 dy/dx + 5y = 0$.

3 Consider the equation $d^4y/dx^4 - 5 d^2y/dx^2 + 4y = 0$. If you were to try the factorisation method how many factors, how many integrations and how many constants of integration would there be? (Please don't work through the whole method, just think what it would have to be like.) Now write down and solve the auxiliary equation, and see if you can guess the solution of the differential equation.

4 The same as question 3, but with $d^4y/dx^4 - y = 0$.

5 Write down the homogeneous equation and solve it to find the complementary function for the following equations:
  (i) $y'' - 2y' - 3y = \ln(1 + x^2)$,
  (ii) $y'' - 4y = x^3 + 3$,
  (iii) $4y'' + 20y' + 25y = \tan^{-1}x$,
  (iv) $y'' - 2y' + 3y = e^{x^2}$.

6 Find the complementary functions for these equations with non-constant coefficients (use factorisation):
  (i) $d^2y/dx^2 - (1 + 1/x)dy/dx + y/x = x$.
  (ii) $\dfrac{d^2y}{dx^2} + \dfrac{a}{x}\dfrac{dy}{dx} + \dfrac{b}{x^2}y = x$.

23.3 THE PARTICULAR INTEGRAL FOR A POLYNOMIAL

Most people prefer to avoid the method of factorisation because it is rather a long way of solving equations. It is easier to use the

'method of intelligent guesswork',

which is what we got round to in earlier chapters when we were solving differential or difference equations. As in those chapters, we shall proceed largely by example, to build up the background of experience on which the guessing must be based. What we are aiming at here is *any* solution of the full equation (i.e.

including a non-zero right hand side), and this is what will be called a *particular integral* of the equation (or PI for short). Notice that it was called a 'particular solution' earlier, but the tradition in differential equations is actually to call it a particular integral.

(i)   Start with the equation

$$d^2y/dx^2 - 4y = K, \text{ a constant,}$$

and ask

'what sort of y, when you do the left hand side to it,
could just give you a constant?'

It doesn't take too long to see that some constant will do this, so intelligent guesswork says 'try $y=c$' as a solution. You substitute this into the equation and find

$$0 - 4c = K, \quad c = -\tfrac{1}{4}K.$$

The particular integral we have found is thus $-\tfrac{1}{4}K$.

(ii)   Now try the equation

$$d^2y/dx^2 - 4y = Kx,$$

and ask yourself a similar question. Intelligent guesswork suggests that you should try $y=cx$, and not $y=cx+d$ (try it, to see that it will not work). Put this into the equation and you find

$$0 - 4cx = Kx,$$

giving you $c = -\tfrac{1}{4}K$, as before. The particular integral this time is therefore $-\tfrac{1}{4}Kx$.

(iii) Try a slightly more complicated equation

$$d^2y/dx^2 + 3\,dy/dx - 4y = Kx.$$

It is no good guessing $y=cx$ this time, because if you do you find (on substituting)

$$0 + 3c - 4cx = Kx,$$

which certainly cannot be true for all values of x (try $x=0$ and $x=1$) as it must be to be a solution. So the guessing this time must be a little more intelligent. Try $y=cx+d$: this gives

$$0 + 3c - 4(cx+d) = Kx,$$

which can only hold for *all* x if

$$3c - 4d = 0, \quad -4c = K.$$

I would say this to myself as

'coefficients of the powers of x must be zero'

and the coefficient of x^0 is $3c - 4d$, while the coefficient of x^1 is $-4c - K$; but you may prefer to understand it as what follows if you take some special values of x.

The particular integral in this case has turned out to be

$$-\tfrac{1}{4}Kx - 3K/16,$$

on solving the equations for c and d.

(iv)   Complicate the right hand side a little more:

$$d^2y/dx^2 + 3\,dy/dx - 4y = rx^2 + sx + t.$$

Does it seem sensible to try a polynomial for y? Is there any obvious reason for having it more difficult than a quadratic? Try

$$cx^2 + dx + e$$

as a particular integral. After substitution and collecting up similar powers of x I found

$$\begin{cases} x^0: 2c + 3d - 4e = t \\ x^1: 6c - 4d \qquad = s \\ x^2: -4c \qquad\qquad = r. \end{cases}$$

These are easily solved for c, d, e in turn (no need for Gauss elimination here, they automatically come out in triangular form).

Should we now guess a rule, that a polynomial right hand side will always lead to a polynomial particular integral of the same degree? Well, no; wait for the next example.

(v)   Try next

$$d^2y/dx^2 + 4\,dy/dx + 0y = 1.$$

The particular integral cannot be $y = c$, because substitution would give you $0 = 1$! Two things have gone wrong here. The obvious one is that there is a zero coefficient for y in the equation. The one that is not obvious is that because $m = 0$ is a solution of the auxiliary equation, you already have

$$Ae^{0x} = A$$

as part of the complementary function for any value of A. So a constant put into the left hand side can *only* give zero, and not 1. You have to guess again (perhaps using what was found in similar circumstances in Section 19.2), and after a few guesses you find that $\tfrac{1}{4}x$ is a particular integral of this equation.

Similarly for

$$d^2y/dx^2 + 4\,dy/dx = rx^2 + sx + t:$$

to get a term in x^2 on the left hand side you need to have something in x^3 in y, because all the terms in y are differentiated at least once; so the particular integral has to be cubic in x.

We are still not quite ready for a rule, as another simple example shows.

(vi)   Consider $d^2y/dx^2 = 1$. A particular integral here is evidently $\frac{1}{2}x^2$, which is two degrees higher than the right hand side. In this case the complementary function (from the auxiliary equation $m^2 = 0$) is $Ax + B$, so that anything of degree less than 2 must give zero when substituted into the left hand side, whatever the values of A and B.

We are at last ready to state a *rule* for polynomial right hand sides for second order equations.

> A polynomial right hand side gives a polynomial particular integral: the degrees are the same if the CF does not include Ae^{0x}, the PI has one higher degree if Ae^{0x} *is* included, but *not* Bxe^{0x}, and the PI has degree two higher if *both* of these terms are included in the CF.

I have put the rule in this slightly awkward form involving e^{0x} to remind you that you have to look at the auxiliary equation and complementary function before you make a guess at what the particular integral will be.

Exercise 23C

1   Find particular integrals for equations (i) to (iii).
(i) $d^2y/dx^2 + 4\,dy/dx + y = x^2 + 2x + 1$.
(ii) $d^2y/dx^2 + 4\,dy/dx\ \ \ \ = x^2 + 2x + 1$.
(iii) $d^2y/dx^2\ \ \ \ \ \ \ \ \ \ \ \ \ = x^2 + 2x + 1$.

2   Guess what the rule would be for a fourth order equation

$$d^4y/dx^4 + \ldots + ky = rx^2 + sx + t.$$

23.4   THE PARTICULAR INTEGRAL FOR OTHER RIGHT HAND SIDES

The solution of

$$\frac{d^2y}{dx^2} + p\frac{dy}{dx} + qy = f(x)$$

can be done quite easily by intelligent guesswork for several other right hand sides $f(x)$.

(a)   Exponential right hand sides

We can get through this piece of work rather more quickly, by building on the experience of the last section on polynomial right hand sides, and also on similar work in Sections 12.1 and 19.3.

(i)   Start with the example

$$d^2y/dx^2 - 4y = 10e^{3x}.$$

Once again you ask yourself the question

'what sort of y, when you do the left hand side to it, could give you a term in e^{3x} on the right hand side?'

A little thought leads to the suggestion that a constant times e^{3x} should do this for you; substitute $y = ce^{3x}$ and find

$$(9c - 4c)e^{3x} = 10e^{3x},$$

and so $2e^{3x}$ is a particular integral for this equation. Note that the CF here is $Ae^{2x} + Be^{-2x}$, because the auxiliary equation is $m^2 - 4 = 0$, and so the CF does not contain any multiple of e^{3x}.

(ii)   Next try

$$d^2y/dx^2 - 4y = 8e^{2x}.$$

Here the CF contains Ae^{2x} and the right hand side has the same form; the PI *cannot* have the form ce^{2x}, as this must give zero when put into the left hand side (being part of the CF). You must either go back to the factorisation method, or think about Section 19.3. What is needed is an extra x: the PI needs to have the form cxe^{2x}. Substitute it in and you get

$$(4c + 4cx - 4cx)e^{2x} = 8e^{2x},$$

which shows that we need $c = 2$, and the particular integral is $2xe^{2x}$ in this example.

To judge from experience here (and in Section 19.3) there seems to be an informal rule working:

'when in doubt, put in an extra x'.

(iii)   Finally, let us find a PI for

$$d^2y/dx^2 - 4\,dy/dx + 4y = 8e^{2x}.$$

The CF here is

$$Ae^{2x} + Bxe^{2x},$$

so neither of these terms can give us a PI. Follow the informal rule and try cx^2e^{2x} as a possible form for the PI: it gives

$$(2c + 8cx + 4cx^2)e^{2x} - 4(2cx + 2cx^2)e^{2x} + 4cx^2 = 8e^{2x},$$

so that $c = 4$ and the PI is $4x^2e^{2x}$ for this example.

We can now state the rule for *exponential* right hand sides for these second order equations.

Find the CF of the equation: if the right hand side is not contained in the CF, then the PI is a constant times the right hand side; if the right hand side *is* contained in the CF (but x times the right hand side is not), then the PI is a constant times x times the right hand side; if both of these are contained in the CF, then the PI is a constant times x^2 times the right hand side. The constants in each case are found by substitution.

Exercise 23D

1 Find particular integrals for the following equations.
   (i) $d^2y/dx^2 + 2\,dy/dx - 3y = 4e^{-x}$,
   (ii) $d^2y/dx^2 + 2\,dy/dx - 3y = 2e^x$,
   (iii) $d^2y/dx^2 - 6\,dy/dx + 8y = 12e^{-2x}$,
   (iv) $d^2y/dx^2 - 6\,dy/dx + 8y = 4e^{4x}$,
   (v) $d^2y/dx^2 - 8\,dy/dx + 16y = e^{-x}$,
   (vi) $d^2y/dx^2 - 8\,dy/dx + 16y = 12e^{4x}$,
   (vii) $d^2y/dx^2 - 4\,dy/dx + 4y = (x+1)e^x$,
   (viii) $d^2y/dx^2 - 4\,dy/dx + 4y = 8xe^{2x}$.
   (The last two of these requires a little more intelligent guesswork.) Could you generalise these last two examples?

2 (i) Use intelligent guesswork to find a particular integral for

$$\frac{d^2y}{dx^2} + \frac{dy}{dx} + y = e^x + 2e^{2x} + 3e^{3x}.$$

(ii) Generalise the result in (i) as follows. Let $U(x)$ be a particular integral of $y'' + py' + qy = u$, and let $V(x)$ and $W(x)$ similarly be PIs for $y'' + py' + qy = v$ and w. Show that

$$\alpha U + \beta V + \gamma W$$

is a PI for

$$y'' + py' + qy = \alpha u + \beta v + \gamma w,$$

when α, β, γ (as well as p, q) are constants.

(b)   Sines and cosines

We should be able to jump straight to the rule in this case, after the experience we have gained here and also in Section 19.3. The rule is as follows.

If the right hand side of the equation is a sine or a cosine of rx, the solution you want has the form $c\cos rx + d\sin rx$, unless these terms are already in the CF of the equation, when you need to 'put in an extra x' and the PI has the form $cx\cos rx + dx\sin rx$. As usual, the constants c and d are found by substituting the given form into the equation.

For example, try $d^2y/dx^2 + 4y = 2\cos x$. Here the CF is $A\cos 2x + B\sin 2x$, which does not include the term $2\cos x$ for any choice of the constants A and B. Hence we try the form

$$c\cos x + d\sin x$$

as a particular solution. Put it into the equation and you find

$$(-c+4c)\cos x + (-d+4d)\sin x = 2\cos x.$$

In this case we take all the $\cos x$ terms together, and all the $\sin x$ terms together, and put the coefficient of each equal to 0:

$$3c - 2 = 0 \quad \text{and} \quad 3d = 0.$$

This is again justified by taking special values of x (e.g. 0 and $\frac{1}{2}\pi$). The PI has thus been found to be $\frac{2}{3}\cos x$.

As the next example take

$$d^2y/dx^2 + 4y = 4\sin 2x.$$

This time the right hand side *is* included in the CF of the equation, as the special case $A=0$, $B=4$, and so the PI must have the form

$$cx\cos 2x + dx\sin 2x.$$

Substitution gives

$$(-4cx + 4d + 4cx)\cos 2x + (-4c - 4dx + 4dx)\sin 2x = 4\sin 2x$$

which shows that we need $c=-1$ and $d=0$ to get a solution. That is, the PI is $-\cos 2x$.

For a last example consider

$$d^2y/dx^2 + 2\,dy/dx + 10y = \cos 3x + 2\sin 3x.$$

The auxiliary equation is $m^2 + 2m + 10 = 0$, with roots

$$-1 \pm 3j,$$

and the CF is therefore $e^{-x}(C\cos 3x + D\sin 3x)$. There are no values of C and D for which this is the same as the right hand side of the equation (because of the e^{-x} term), and so the PI must be

$$c\cos 3x + d\sin 3x.$$

Once again you find c and d by substitution in the equation. The results are that

$$c = -\tfrac{11}{37}, \quad d = \tfrac{8}{37}.$$

Exercise 23E

1   Find a particular integral for each of the following equations.
   (i) $d^2y/dx^2 + 2\,dy/dx + 2y = 3\sin 2x$,
   (ii) $d^2y/dx^2 + 2\,dy/dx + 2y = 3\sin x$,
   (iii) $d^2y/dx^2 + y = 3\sin x + 4\cos x$,
   (iv) $d^2y/dx^2 + 4y = r\sin(x+s)$, where r and s are constants,
   (v) $d^2y/dx^2 + 4y = r\cos(2x+s)$.

2   Use trigonometric formulas and then find particular integrals for
   (i) $d^2y/dx^2 + 9y = \cos^3 x$,
   (ii) $d^2y/dx^2 + y = \cos x \sin 2x$.

(c)   Products on the right hand side

As a first example consider

$$d^2y/dx^2 + 2\,dy/dx + 5y = e^x \sin 2x.$$

Start by finding the CF; the auxiliary equation is $m^2+2m+5=0$, with roots $-1\pm2j$, and so the CF is

$$e^{-x}(A\cos 2x+B\sin 2x).$$

The right hand side of the differential equation is not of this form, so no problem arises here. Does intelligent guesswork suggest the form of the PI in this case? It does to me, because I know that when I differentiate $e^x\sin 2x$ or $e^x\cos 2x$ I get the same sort of thing back again. I shall therefore try

$$ce^x\cos 2x+de^x\sin 2x$$

as the particular integral for the right hand side of this equation. When I substitute this form into the equation I find, after quite a deal of algebra, that

$$(4c+8d)\cos 2x+(-8c+4d)\sin 2x=0.$$

Each bracket must be zero to make the last equation true for all x, so $c=-\frac{1}{10}$, $d=\frac{1}{20}$ and the PI is indeed of the form given,

$$-\tfrac{1}{10}e^x\cos 2x+\tfrac{1}{20}e^x\sin 2x.$$

For a second example take

$$d^2y/dx^2+2\,dy/dx+5y=e^{-x}\sin 2x.$$

This time the right hand side *is* part of the CF and so the previous guess will not do. Our experience suggests that the thing to do is put an extra x into what we had in the last example, and try

$$cxe^{-x}\cos 2x+dxe^{-x}\sin 2x$$

as particular integral. I shall leave the detail of this example as an exercise: the result is that the form assumed is correct, and the values of c and d are $-\frac{1}{4}$ and 0 respectively.

As a final example of a product let us look at

$$d^2y/dx^2+2\,dy/dx+5y=x^2\sin 2x.$$

In this case the right hand side is not part of the CF of the equation, and we are left with the problem of making an intelligent guess. If you do the operations of the left hand side of the equation to $x^2\sin 2x$ you get lower powers of x coming in as well as x^2, and you also get terms in $\cos 2x$ appearing. So the intelligent guess looks like

$$(ax^2+bx+c)\cos 2x+(px^2+qx+r)\sin 2x.$$

The working out of the detail can again be left as an exercise.

Exercise 23F

1   Show that $-\frac{1}{4}xe^{-x}\cos 2x$ is a PI of

$$\frac{d^2y}{dx^2}+2\frac{dy}{dx}+5y=e^{-x}\sin 2x.$$

2 Determine the constants a, b, c, p, q, r so that $(ax^2+bx+c)\cos 2x + (px^2+qx+r)\sin 2x$ is a PI of

$$\frac{d^2y}{dx^2}+2\frac{dy}{dx}+5y=x^2\sin 2x.$$

3 Find particular integrals for
   (i) $d^2y/dx^2-4\,dy/dx+5y=3e^{-2x}\cos x$,
   (ii) $d^2y/dx^2+2\,dy/dx+5y=e^{-x}\sin^2x$.

We have done enough on finding the particular integral and on the method of intelligent guesswork. There will always be equations whose right hand sides look so unlikely that no amount of intelligence will suffice, in which case you can fall back on the factorisation method. But do remember that the factorisation process is equivalent to doing two integrals, and there are plenty of functions which have no formula to express their integrals; so there will also be plenty of differential equations for which you cannot find a particular integral as a formula.

Exercise 23G

Find particular integrals, if you can, for
(i) $d^2y/dx^2+dy/dx+y=x^2\ln x$,
(ii) $d^2y/dx^2+dy/dx+y=\tan x$.

23.5 SOLVING EQUATIONS WITH BOUNDARY CONDITIONS

We are now (at last) ready to solve the problem that was posed at the start of this chapter, which was to find the solution of

$$d^2y/dx^2+p\,dy/dx+qy=f(x)$$

with two boundary conditions. The method of factorisation has told us what we need, which is a part with two constants in it depending on the left hand side of the equation, together with a part depending on the right hand side of the equation. We now know how to find these one at a time as complementary function and particular integral. Together these make what is called the *general solution*; in brief

$$\text{GS}=\text{CF}+\text{PI}.$$

Finally we determine (or attempt to do so) the constants in this general solution, by using the boundary conditions.

This is most easily understood in terms of an example. Let us solve

$$\begin{cases} d^2y/dx^2+6\,dy/dx+5y=3e^{-2x} \\ y(0)=0, \quad (dy/dx)_{x=0}=6. \end{cases}$$

The method of doing any problem like this follows a set pattern.

(i)   Determine the complementary function.
       The auxiliary equation is $m^2+6m+5=0$, whose roots are -5 and -1.

Hence the CF is $Ae^{-5x} + Be^{-x}$. Note that it is not the *solution* of the problem which has this form, but only the CF, which is just a *part* of the solution (except of course when the right hand side of the equation is zero).

(ii)   Find a particular integral.

Intelligent guesswork (or experience) suggests ce^{-2x}, which is not contained in the CF. Substitute into the equation and get

$$(4 - 12 + 5)ce^{-2x} = 3e^{-2x}.$$

This has to hold for all x (in some domain in which the equation is to hold, strictly), and so $c = -1$. Hence a PI is $-e^{-2x}$.

(iii)   The general solution can be written down.

The general solution is the sum of what has been found in (i) and (ii):

$$GS = CF + PI$$

$$= Ae^{-5x} + Be^{-x} - e^{-2x}.$$

Note that this is not yet y, which also has to satisfy the two boundary conditions.

(iv)   Use the boundary conditions.

For the GS to have value 0 when $x = 0$, we must have $A + B - 1 = 0$.

Moreover for the GS to have its derivative equal to 6 when $x = 0$, we must have

$$-5A - B + 3 = 6.$$

These two equations for A and B can be solved, and they give

$$A = -1, \quad B = 2.$$

(v)   The solution of the given problem is therefore

$$y = -e^{-5x} + 2e^{-x} - e^{-2x}.$$

Notice that the boundary conditions must not be used *until* you have found the general solution; if you try to use them earlier you are quite likely to get the wrong answer, as the following example shows.

Example

Solve $\dfrac{d^2y}{dx^2} + y = 1$ with both y and $\dfrac{dy}{dx}$ equal to 0 when $x = 0$.

The *correct solution* is:

(i)   CF is $A \cos x + B \sin x$.

(ii)   PI is 1.

(iii)   GS is $1 + A \cos x + B \sin x$.

(iv)   boundary conditions require

$$1 + A = 0 \quad \text{and} \quad B = 0.$$

(v)   the solution is $y = 1 - \cos x$, which can be easily verified.

The *non-solution* is:

(i)   CF is $y = A\cos x + B\sin x$
(ii) but we need $y(0) = 0$ and $y'(0) = 0$, so $A = B = 0$, CF is $y = 0$.
(iii) PI is $y = 1$.
(iv) hence the solution is CF + PI, which gives the solution $y = 1$.

You can easily verify here that $y = 1$ *does* satisfy the equation, but *not* the boundary conditions. Part of the mistake here has been to write '$y =$' in the CF; the complementary function is *not* y, it is only a part of what eventually turns into y, and it is dangerously bad practice to use '$y =$' at this stage.

Exercise 23H

Solve the following differential equation problems.

(i) $\dfrac{d^2y}{dx^2} - 6\dfrac{dy}{dx} + 5y = e^x$

with $y = 3$ and $\dfrac{dy}{dx} = 4$ when $x = 1$.

(ii) $\dfrac{d^2y}{dx^2} - y = 2x^2$

with $y = 0$ and $\dfrac{dy}{dx} = 1$ when $x = 1$.

(iii) $\dfrac{d^2y}{dx^2} + 2\dfrac{dy}{dx} + 10y = 3\sin x$

with $y = 0$ when $x = 0$ and when $x = 1$.

(iv) $\dfrac{d^2y}{dx^2} + 4\dfrac{dy}{dx} - 5y = 10$

with $y = 3$ when $x = 0$ and y bounded as x approaches $+\infty$.

(v) $\dfrac{d^2y}{dx^2} + y = x\cos x$

with $y = 0$ when $x = 0$ and $\dfrac{d^2y}{dx^2} = 2$ when $x = 2$.

Uniqueness of solutions

At the end of solving

$$\frac{d^2y}{dx^2} + y = 1 \text{ with } y \text{ and } \frac{dy}{dx} \text{ zero at } x = 0,$$

it is no great matter to check that the function that has been found satisfies the differential equation and the boundary conditions. It is certainly, therefore, *one* solution of the problem. But is it the only solution? Or could someone else, working in another fashion, come up with another solution of the problem that is different from the one above, and yet is still correct?

The resolution of these questions is contained in the following theorem on the existence and uniqueness of the solution of initial value problems.

Theorem

An initial value problem (i.e. one in which the two boundary values are given at the same point, with y and dy/dx having specified values there) for the equation

$$d^2y/dx^2 + p\,dy/dx + qy = f(x)$$

has one and only one solution, for continuous functions f.

If you look back to Section 19.1 you will see that the corresponding theorem for difference equations was quite easy to prove, because the two starting values u_0 and u_1 and the equation immediately gave the value for u_2, and so on. The idea must be the same here – that the starting position and slope on the graph of y, together with the equation, give all the later values of y. The proof is much too hard to attempt here.

The theorem says nothing about problems which have boundary values given at *two* points, and they can indeed cause difficulties: it is easy to find examples which have *no* solutions, and even examples which have infinitely many solutions.

An example of the first of these behaviours is provided by the case

$$\begin{cases} d^2y/dx^2 + y = x \\ y(0) = 0,\ y(\pi) = 1. \end{cases}$$

We attempt to follow the general method given above.

(i) The auxiliary equation is $m^2 + 1 = 0$, roots $\pm j$. Hence the complementary function is $A\cos x + B\sin x$.
(ii) A particular integral is easily seen to be x.
(iii) The general solution is therefore $A\cos x + B\sin x + x$.
(iv) The boundary conditions would be satisfied if we could find A and B which satisfied

$$\begin{cases} A + 0 + 0 = 0 \\ -A + 0 + \pi = 1, \end{cases}$$

which is clearly impossible. The conclusion is therefore:
(v) the stated problem has *no* solution.

Note that the method of working has still come up with the correct answer, which is that the problem is no good.

A slight modification to the example shows the other possible and unpleasant behaviour. Consider

$$\begin{cases} d^2y/dx^2 + y = x \\ y(0) = 0,\ y(\pi) = \pi. \end{cases}$$

The work follows the same steps (i), (ii) and (iii), but then

(iv) the boundary conditions are satisfied by any A and B such that

$$\begin{cases} A+0+0=0 \\ -A+0+\pi=\pi. \end{cases}$$

These equations are satisfied by $A=0$ for *any* value of B. The conclusion is therefore:

(v) the stated problem has solution $B\sin x+x$ for any B.

Once again the method of working has produced a correct answer.

Exercise 23I

1 Determine whether the following have solutions; if they have, find them.
  (i) $d^2y/dx^2+y=x^2$, $y(0)=0$, $y(2\pi)=0$.
  (ii) $d^2y/dx^2+y=x$, $y(0)=0$, $(dy/dx)_{x=\pi}=1$.
  (iii) $d^2y/dx^2+y=x$, $y(0)=0$, $(dy/dx)_{x=\pi/2}=1$.

2 For what value of k does the following problem have a solution?

$$d^2y/dx^2+2\,dy/dx+2y=1, \ y(0)=0, \ y(\pi)=k.$$

Find it.

3 Solve the equations $x+y=1$, $x+ay=b$, for any values of the constants a and b. Relate these solutions to the work above.

23.6 MODELLING EXAMPLES

Many second order linear differential equations with constant coefficients have their origins in real (modelled) situations, and it may be necessary to use information from the situation either in setting up the equation or in finding the appropriate boundary conditions. A few examples of this process follow.

(a) A model of motorway driving in fog

Can we model the extraordinary way that some people drive on motorways when fog has drastically reduced visibility? Their strategy seems to be to do two things: first to try to keep a fixed distance behind the vehicle in front (so that they can just see its fog lights), and to change their speed if that distance appears to be changing; and second to change speed if the driver ahead changes from the steady speed that the traffic appears to be running at.

Let us say that the driver in front has distance y along the motorway (from some fixed origin), and the following vehicle is at distance x along the motorway (from the same origin), both varying with the time t. Model the first piece of behaviour by an acceleration (they have only a brake pedal or an accelerator

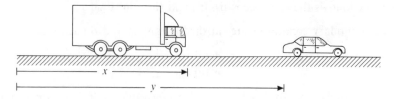

Figure 1. Positions on the motorway

pedal to operate) which is proportional to the difference between $y-x$ and the range of good visibility, say X. Express this relation as

$$d^2x/dt^2 = a(y-x-X),$$

giving positive acceleration when $y-x$ gets bigger than X.

Now if the following driver sees $y-x$ equal to zero he will presumably brake sharply, so I shall suggest that we take $a = \frac{1}{4}g/X$ as a fair estimate of how rapidly he may slow down. Now add on a term for the second piece of behaviour. Taking the steady state to be V, I am going to add an extra acceleration $b(dy/dt - V)$, and I shall use $b = \frac{1}{4}g/V$. This means that if both terms are at crisis level then his deceleration is $\frac{1}{2}g$, which is quite severe, but not unreasonably so. The equation with both terms included is then

$$d^2x/dt^2 = \tfrac{1}{4}g(y-x-X)/X + \tfrac{1}{4}g(dy/dt - V)/V.$$

This is a differential equation for x, assuming that y is some given function of time.

As a first test of the modelling, check that there is a solution which has $dx/dt = dy/dt = V$, i.e. both vehicles travelling at the steady speed V. When you substitute this information into the equation you find that there is indeed a solution provided that the separation of the vehicles is X, that is $y-x=X$.

Now suppose that both vehicles are travelling at speed V, and are at separation X, when the leading one crashes into a pile of wrecked cars and lorries, and stops dead. Will the following driver also crash into the wreckage? I intend to use the values $g = 10$ and $V = 20$ (in SI units) to give me an estimate of what is a safe value for X. I need to solve the differential equation, but what are the initial conditions? Let us suppose that the leading driver crashes at time $t = 0$, and that her position is then $y = Y$; thereafter her speed is zero. At that time the following driver must have position $x = Y - X$, because the separation is X, and speed V. The initial conditions are therefore

$$\text{at } t=0, \; x = Y - X, \text{ and } dx/dt = V,$$

and the equation is

$$d^2x/dt^2 + \tfrac{1}{4}gx/X = \tfrac{1}{4}gY/X - \tfrac{1}{2}g,$$

using $y = Y$ and $dy/dt = 0$.

The method of solution is exactly as described in Section 23.5 above.

(i) The auxiliary equation is $m^2 + \frac{1}{4}g/X = 0$, roots $\pm j\,(\frac{1}{4}g/X)^{1/2}$. This gives a CF of

$$C \cos(\tfrac{1}{4}g/X)^{1/2}t + D \sin(\tfrac{1}{4}g/X)^{1/2}t.$$

(ii) The right hand side is a constant, and so a PI is also a constant,

$$Y - 2X.$$

(iii) The GS is therefore

$$C \cos(\tfrac{1}{4}g/X)^{1/2}t + D \sin(\tfrac{1}{4}g/X)^{1/2}t + Y - 2X.$$

(iv) This satisfies the initial values (boundary values) if

$$\begin{cases} Y - X = C + 0 + Y - 2X \\ \quad V = 0 + (\tfrac{1}{4}g/X)^{1/2}D + 0. \end{cases}$$

(v) Therefore the required solution is

$$x = X\cos(\tfrac{1}{4}g/X)^{1/2}t + V(4X/g)^{1/2}\sin(\tfrac{1}{4}g/X)^{1/2}t + Y - 2X.$$

The question I still need to answer is whether the following vehicle stops before it reaches the wreckage at $x = Y$. So I need to know when $dx/dt = 0$; for this I must solve

$$0 = -X\sin(\tfrac{1}{4}g/X)^{1/2}t + V(4X/g)^{1/2}\cos(\tfrac{1}{4}g/X)^{1/2}t,$$

which has solution

$$t = (4X/g)^{1/2}\tan^{-1}(4V^2/gX).$$

At this stage it seems easier to go into numbers, so I have written a program to calculate the time at which the following car stops for various values of X, and the distance it would then be behind the crashed vehicle. What I find is that $X = 50$ is not quite enough to prevent a crash. The conclusion of this piece of modelling and differential equation solving is that if the model of driver behaviour is right, then drivers should aim to stay more than 50 metres apart.

Do I believe this result? I have certainly tried to put realistic numbers into the model, and the answer of 50 metres looks hopeful. But I cannot be sure without considerable research whether the model of driver behaviour is any good. However, the general approach, via a differential equation as a model, looks far better than mere guesswork.

(b)   The buckling of an elastic strut

A vertical strut made of elastic material (and all materials are elastic to some extent) cannot support an indefinitely large load on its upper end without buckling. A simple theory can be found for this, as follows.

Suppose that the top end of the strut has moved sideways a distance d under the influence of a weight W on top of it, as in Fig. 2. Then the elementary theory of elasticity (which we need not discuss here) shows that the equation for the shape of the strut is

$$B\,d^2y/dx^2 + Wy = Wd,$$

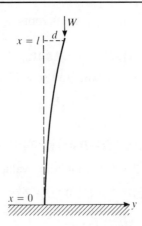

Figure 2. An elastic strut deflecting in response to a load W at its upper end

where B is related to the stiffness of the material of the strut. If the strut is fixed rigidly at the ground, then you must have the conditions

$$y=0, \quad dy/dx=0$$

when $x=0$.

Solving the equation with these two conditions, the usual method gives the following.

(i) Auxiliary equation $Bm^2+W=0$ with roots $\pm j(W/B)^{1/2}$, and so the CF is $C\cos(W/B)^{1/2}x+D\sin(W/B)^{1/2}x$.

(ii) The constant PI is just d.

(iii) The GS is $C\cos(W/B)^{1/2}x+D\sin(W/B)^{1/2}x+d$.

(iv) The conditions at $x=0$ are satisfied if

$$0=C+d, \quad 0=(W/B)^{1/2}D.$$

(v) Hence the required solution is

$$y=d-d\cos\{(W/B)^{1/2}x\}.$$

This is by no means the end of the matter, because we still have *another* condition to impose on the solution. After all, the deflection at the top of the strut was assumed to be d; so putting $y=d$ at $x=l$ you find

$$d=d-d\cos\{W/B)^{1/2}l\}.$$

There are two possibilities here: either $d=0$ and the strut is undeflected, i.e. has not buckled, or the load W has a value that makes $\cos\{(W/B)^{1/2}l\}=0$. Now the first value of W which satisfies this is $W=\frac{1}{4}\pi^2B/l^2$. The theory has therefore predicted that buckling takes place at this critical load. Note that the theory does not predict a value for d when buckling has occurred; a fuller version of the theory would be needed.

(c) 'Transient' and 'steady state' for an electric circuit

Set up the circuit in Fig. 3 with an input voltage

$$V_0 \cos \omega t,$$

and switch it on at $t=0$. What current flows?

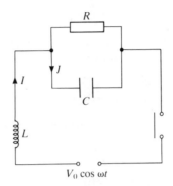

Figure 3. An electric circuit which rejects an oscillation

This question requires a differential equation to be set up before we can start on finding an answer.

If the currents I, J flow in the wires shown, then the current in the resistor must be $I-J$, by Kirchhoff's first law (using SI units as usual). Then Kirchhoff's second law round the small loop of resistor and capacitor gives

$$(I-J)R = Q/C,$$

where Q is the charge on the capacitor, which is related to the current J by

$$dQ/dt = J.$$

Kirchhoff's second law round the loop which includes the input and the resistor is

$$L\,dI/dt + (I-J)R = V_0 \cos \omega t.$$

These three equations can be reduced to a single equation for Q by using the first equation to replace I by $J+Q/RC$, and then using the second to replace J. The result is

$$L\,d^2Q/dt^2 + (L/RC)\,dQ/dt + Q/C = V_0 \cos \omega t.$$

It will be assumed that Q and I are both zero before the switch is closed. Since $J=I-Q/RC$, the two conditions for the differential equation are $Q=0$ and $dQ/dt=0$ at $t=0$.

The values that I shall take for the electrical components are

$$L=10^{-3}\,\text{H},\ R=5\,\Omega,\ C=10^{-5}\,\text{F},$$

which are all of a sensible size for a small circuit. With these values the circuit equation is

$$d^2Q/dt^2 + 2 \times 10^4 \, dQ/dt + 10^8 Q = 10^3 V_0 \cos \omega t,$$

and we go into the standard solution routine.

(i)   The auxiliary equation is $m^2 + 2 \times 10^4 m + 10^8 = 0$, which has root $m = -10^4$ only. The CF is therefore

$$(A + Bt)e^{-10^4 t}.$$

(ii) The PI will be of the form $c \cos \omega t + d \sin \omega t$, where substitution in the equation will (eventually) lead to values for c and d. These are

$$c = \frac{(10^8 - \omega^2)10^3 V_0}{(10^8 + \omega^2)^2}, \quad d = \frac{2 \times 10^7 \omega V_0}{(10^8 + \omega^2)^2}.$$

(iii) The GS is thus $(A + Bt)e^{-10^4 t} + c \cos \omega t + d \sin \omega t$.

(iv) The initial conditions will be satisfied if

$$\begin{cases} 0 = A + c \\ 0 = -10^4 A + B + \omega d, \end{cases}$$

which give the values of A and B to be

$$A = -c, \quad B = -\omega d - 10^4 c.$$

(v)   The general solution with these values of the constants is the required solution of the problem, giving Q in terms of t. Since I originally asked for the current rather than the charge, I must use the equations

$$J = dQ/dt, \quad I = J + Q/RC$$

to find the two currents in the circuit.

It should be noted that in this solution the part derived from the complementary function very rapidly becomes zero; with t as small as 10^{-3} seconds the CF has a factor of $e^{-10} = 5 \times 10^{-5}$ in it. Because it decays rapidly to zero, this part of the solution is called a 'transient'. After a short time only the particular integral part of the solution remains, and it is an unchanging oscillation, which is often called the 'steady state response' of the circuit.

If $\omega = 100\pi$ radians per second, corresponding to a frequency of 50 Hz, then $c \approx 10^{-5} V_0$ and $d \approx 2 \times 10^{-7} V_0$, showing that this circuit has rather small charges and currents in it when the input voltage is of reasonable size. The circuit is rejecting the oscillation.

(d)   A model for particle motion in the Dead Sea

The Dead Sea is extremely salty, and is more salty the deeper you go; that is, the density is a function of depth (because, of course, the saltier the water, the heavier it is). But the density of the upper levels also varies as energy is taken from sunlight penetrating through the water, and this changes throughout the day.

Taking both these effects together, assume that the density of the water in the Dead Sea has the value

$$\rho = \rho_0(1 - n^2 y + a \cos \omega t),$$

where n, a are small constants, and $y = 0$ is taken at some convenient level in the sea. (ρ is the Greek letter 'rho'.)

Now consider a small clay particle of volume V and mass $\rho_0 V$, suspended in the water. According to Archimedes' theorem it will have a hydrostatic force upwards on it of size $\rho V g$. If it moves relative to the water there will also be a force on it due to the viscosity of the water; this resistance force is proportional to the velocity (for small particles and slow speeds), say $-2k\, dy/dt$.

The equation governing the motion of the particle is therefore

$$\rho_0 V\, d^2 y/dt^2 = \rho_0 V g(1 - n^2 y + a \cos \omega t) - \rho_0 V g - 2k\, dy/dt,$$

the terms on the right being upthrust, weight and resistance.

How does the particle move? We have to solve the differential equation with some assumed initial conditions. Start off by rewriting it:

$$d^2 y/dt^2 + 2K\, dy/dt + N^2 y = b \cos \omega t,$$

where the new constants are

$$K = k/\rho_0 V, \quad N^2 = n^2 g, \quad b = ag.$$

The solution procedure works as usual.

(i)   The auxiliary equation is $n^2 + 2Km + N^2 = 0$. The roots now depend on the relative sizes of K and N; for if $N > K$, the roots are

$$-K \pm j(N^2 - K^2)^{1/2},$$

but if $N < K$ the roots are

$$-K \pm (K^2 - N^2)^{1/2},$$

and if $N = K$ there is only the one root $-K$. However in all three cases there are negative exponentials here, which become very small rapidly as t increases. As in the last example, this part of the solution is a 'transient', which rapidly becomes an unimportant part of the solution.

(ii)   The PI must have the form $c \cos \omega t + d \sin \omega t$. When you substitute this into the equation, collect together terms in $\cos \omega t$ and terms in $\sin \omega t$, and take each collection to be zero, you get the equations

$$\begin{cases} (N^2 - \omega^2)c + 2K\omega d = b \\ -2K\omega c + (N^2 - \omega^2)d = 0. \end{cases}$$

These solve to give you

$$\begin{cases} c = \dfrac{N^2 - \omega^2}{(N^2 - \omega^2)^2 + 4K^2\omega^2}b \\[2mm] d = \dfrac{2K\omega}{(N^2 - \omega^2)^2 + 4K^2\omega^2}b. \end{cases}$$

Note that the form of the solution here is much easier than the method of finding it; this suggests that there might be a better way of finding it, and we return to this later.

(iii), (iv), (v) Since we don't need the CF the later parts of the process are not needed; the only part of the solution that is of interest here is the PI, which represents an oscillation of the particle in response to the change of density of the water with time. Now (when the transient has died away) the oscillation has the formula

$$y = c \cos \omega t + d \sin \omega t,$$

and it is well known that this can be rewritten instead as

$$y = R \cos (\omega t - \delta)$$

where

$$R = (c^2 + d^2)^{1/2}, \quad \cos \delta = c/R, \quad \sin \delta = d/R.$$

The constant R is the *amplitude* of the resulting oscillation, and in the present case it has the value $\{(N^2 - \omega^2)^2 + 4K^2 \omega^2\}^{-1/2} b$ which is again a very simple formula (compared to the means of finding it). The constant δ is known as the *phase lag*, because it gives the delay in the time at which the response reaches its maximum value after the forcing term $b \cos \omega t$ reaches its maximum value: this is best seen on the graphs (in Fig. 4) of

$$b \cos \omega t \quad \text{and} \quad R \cos (\omega t - \delta)$$

against t. In the example we are discussing the phase lag is

$$\begin{cases} \delta = \tan^{-1}\{2K\omega/(N^2 - \omega^2)\} & \text{if } N > \omega, \\ \delta = \pi + \tan^{-1}\{2K\omega/(N^2 - \omega^2)\} & \text{if } N < \omega. \end{cases}$$

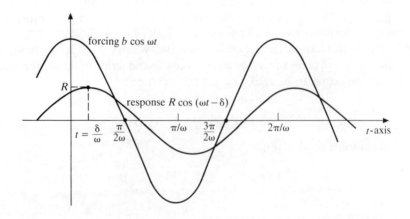

Figure 4. The 'forcing' $b \cos \omega t$ and the 'response' $R \cos (\omega t - \delta)$ for the clay particles

In this model the term $b \cos \omega t$ on the right hand side of the equation is what causes the motion to happen: it is called the *forcing* term in the equation. The steady state solution

$$y = R \cos(\omega t - \delta)$$

is often called the *response* function. The amplitude R of the response depends in particular on how close N and ω are to each other; the case when they are very close (or equal) is discussed in more detail in the next chapter under the heading of 'resonance'.

The forcing term has frequency ω, which in this model is just once every 24 hours, because the heating is due to the incidence of sunshine. The constant N is an example of a *Brunt–Vaisala* frequency, and all problems with density stratification involve such a frequency, provided that the stratification is *stable*, i.e. lighter material above heavier.

Exercise 23J

1   Using material from Sections 7.3 and 18.1, calculate the progress of the battle of Iwo Jima by setting up and solving a second order differential equation for the size of the Japanese force after the last reinforcements had arrived.

2   Set up a second order differential equation for the root weight R in question 3 of Exercise 18D, and solve it with the conditions $R=0$ and $W=W_0$ at $t=0$. For what values of t will the solution be sensible?

3   In Section 22.3 the equation for the circuit in Fig. 5 is shown to be

$$RCL \, d^2J/dt^2 + L \, dJ/dt + RJ = V_0 \cos \omega t.$$

Find the steady state solution in the case $CL = \omega^{-2}$, $RC = \omega^{-1}$, and $LCR = V_0/J_0$. What is the phase lag?

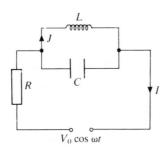

$V_0 \cos \omega t$

Figure 5. A three element circuit

4   Solve the second order temperature equation in Section 22.4(b), and verify that if B is negative, $\theta - \theta_0$ becomes very large as t increases, for almost any choice of initial conditions in the room.

5   Solve the second order equation in Section 22.4(c) for y in terms of t, and verify that you get the same answer from the first order equation for y. Take as initial condition that there are only atoms of type A present at $t=0$.

6 For the Dead Sea model above show that in the three cases

$$\text{(i) } N = 3K \qquad \text{(ii) } N = K \qquad \text{(iii) } N = K/3$$

the CF will become small rapidly as t increases.

23.7 SUMMARY

(a) Linear second order equations

$$\frac{d^2y}{dx^2} + p\frac{dy}{dx} + qy = f(x) \qquad (A)$$

with constant coefficients p and q can be solved by *factorisation*, as the pair of first order equations

$$\begin{cases} \dfrac{dz}{dx} + rz = f(x) \\[2mm] \dfrac{dy}{dx} + sy = z. \end{cases}$$

This is usually unnecessarily lengthy.

(b) The *homogeneous equation* corresponding to (A) is

$$\frac{d^2y}{dx^2} + p\frac{dy}{dx} + qy = 0 \qquad (B)$$

and the general solution of (B) is called the *complementary function* or CF of equation (A).

(c) The CF is found by considering the *auxiliary equation*

$$m^2 + pm + q = 0 \qquad (C)$$

There are three cases:

(i) two real roots for equation (C), say k and l, when the CF is

$$Ae^{kx} + Be^{lx};$$

(ii) a single root for (C), say k, when the CF is

$$Ae^{kx} + Bxe^{kx};$$

(iii) conjugate complex roots for (C), say $k \pm js$, when the CF is (in real terms)

$$e^{kx}(C\cos sx + D\sin sx).$$

(d) The *general solution* or GS of equation (A) is composed of any *particular solution*, or particular integral (PI) together with the complementary function:

$$GS = CF + PI.$$

(e) An easy way of finding the PI is to use intelligent guesswork, which is a blend of experience and using functions related to the right hand side $f(x)$ of equation (A). Where the right hand side is

(i) a polynomial, (ii) an exponential, or (iii) a sine or cosine

the guess is *usually*

(i)   a polynomial of the same degree with arbitrary coefficients
(ii) the same exponential with an unknown coefficient
(iii) a combination of sine *and* cosine with unknown coefficients.

In each case the coefficients are found by substituting the guess into equation (A).

(f) If the normal guess is already part of the CF of the equation, you need to use an extra factor of x in the guess; or even of x^2 if the modified guess is still part of the CF.

(g) Some more complicated right hand sides can also be dealt with by intelligent guesswork.

(h) Often a differential equation problem consists of the equation (A) together with two *boundary conditions*. These boundary conditions are used on the *general solution* to determine the constants in the CF part of the solution.

(i) If the boundary conditions are *both at one value* of x, and if f is continuous, then the solution of the problem exists and is unique. If the boundary conditions are to be imposed at *two different points*, then there may be no solution, or a non-unique solution, to the problem.

(j) The right hand side $f(x)$ of equation (A) is often called the *forcing term* in applications of differential equations. When the forcing term is sinusoidal (in time) and the CF contains a negative exponential (in time), the CF is often called a transient; the PI is then also sinusoidal and is called a *steady state* oscillation.

Revision exercise D

1 Solve the equation

$$u_{n+2} - 6u_{n+1} + 9u_n = 2, \quad n \geq 0,$$

with the conditions

$$u_0 = 1, \quad u_1 = \alpha.$$

For what values of α does u_n become large and positive as n becomes large?

[SMP 81]

2 Find the solution of the difference equation

$$u_{n+2} + 4u_{n+1} + u_n = c, \quad n \geq 0,$$

(where c is a constant) which satisfies the condition $u_0 = 0$ and does not become infinitely large as $n \to \infty$. What value is approached by u_n as n becomes very large?

[SMP 85]

3 Show that

$$\cos(n+2)\theta - 2\cos\theta\cos(n+1)\theta + \cos n\theta = 0.$$

Solve the difference equation

$$u_{n+2} - 2cu_{n+1} + u_n = 0, \quad n \geq 0,$$

for $c > 1$ and with the conditions

$$u_0 = 1, \quad u_1 = c.$$

Can your solution be expressed as $\cos n\theta$ for some value of θ?

[SMP 82]

4 The first four terms of a sequence u_n, $(n = 0, 1, 2, \ldots)$ are $0, 1, -6, 27$. Assuming that the general terms of the sequence satisfy a recurrence relation

$$u_{n+2} + au_{n+1} + bu_n = 8n - 2,$$

find the values of a and b.
Determine u_n as a function of n.

[SMP 86]

5 An insect population has size u_n in year n, where u_n is related to the populations of the two previous years by

$$u_n = au_{n-1} + bu_{n-2}.$$

Solve this equation for u_n, assuming that a and b are positive constants.
Show that in the case $a + b = 1$ the population tends to a non-zero value.

[SMP 79]

6 (i) Find the difference equation satisfied by

$$u_r = (Ar + B)3^r.$$

(ii) Find the general solution of the difference equation

$$u_{n+2} - 6u_{n+1} + 8u_n = 0$$

and hence solve the difference equation

$$(n+2)v_{n+2} - 6(n+1)v_{n+1} + 8nv_n = 0,$$

given that $v_1 = 2$, $v_2 = -2$.   [O&C 84]

7   Solve the difference equation

$$u_{n+2} - 3u_{n+1} + 2u_n = 0 \quad (n = 1, 2, \ldots),\tag{1}$$

given that $u_1 = 1$, $u_2 = 5$.

It is required to solve the difference equation

$$(n+1)(n+2)v_{n+2} - 3(n+1)v_{n+1} + 2v_n = 0 \quad (n = 1, 2, \ldots),\tag{2}$$

subject to the condition $v_1 = 1$, $v_2 = 2\frac{1}{2}$. Show how (2) may be reduced to (1) and hence solve (2) completely.   [O&C 89]

8   An afforestation programme plants young trees, each with 4 small branches, in plots which have 12 (large) weeds per plot. The trees are expected to grow (on average) in accordance with the equation

$$B_{n+1} = 2B_n - \tfrac{1}{4}W_n$$

for $n \geq 0$. Here B_n is the number of branches on the tree in year n and W_n is the number of weeds in the plot in that year (tree growth is restricted because the weeds use up water and nutrients). Weed growth is discouraged by the shading caused by the trees, and so weed numbers in later years are given by

$$W_{n+1} = W_n - 9B_n/16$$

if $W_n > 9B_n/16$, and

$$W_{n+1} = 0 \text{ otherwise.}$$

Show that

$$B_{n+2} = 3B_{n+1} - 119B_n/64$$

for $n \geq 0$ and while weeds are still present. Solve this equation for B_n.

                                                                          [SMP 88]

9   (i)   Solve the equation

$$\frac{dy}{dx} = y + x,$$

given that $y = -1$ when $x = 0$.

(ii) A corresponding difference equation is *given* to be

$$\frac{y_{n+1} - y_{n+1}}{2h} = y_n + nh, \quad n \geq 1,$$

with $y_0 = -1$ and $y_1 = -1 - h$. Solve this difference equation, and verify that your solution here corresponds to the solution in (i).   [SMP 89]

10 A deep-freeze cabinet stands in a small room; the deep-freeze compressor cools the interior of the cabinet, but warms the room; some of the heat in the room escapes to

the outside air, and some penetrates into the cabinet. Let the various temperatures be as follows:

Room	Outside air	Cabinet	Thermostat
T	T_0	θ	θ_0
variable	fixed	variable	fixed

The relations between the temperatures are modelled as follows, with a, b, c, k all constants:

(i) T tends to decrease at rate $a(T-T_0)$ due to loss to the outside air;

(ii) T tends to increase at rate $b(\theta-\theta_0)$ due to the action of the compressor;

(iii) θ tends to decrease at rate $k(\theta-\theta_0)$ due to the action of the compressor;

(iv) θ tends to increase at rate $c(T-\theta)$ due to heat flow into the cabinet.

Set up a pair of differential equations for T and θ and reduce them to

$$\frac{d^2}{dt^2}(\theta-\theta_0)+(a+c+k)\frac{d}{dt}(\theta-\theta_0)+(ac+ak-bc)(\theta-\theta_0)=ac(T_0-\theta_0).$$

If $ac+ak>bc$, find the temperature in the freezer after a long time.

[SMP 80]

11   The atoms of a radioactive substance A decay into atoms of a substance B at a rate λ times the number of atoms of A present. The atoms of B are themselves unstable, and decay into atoms of a third substance C at a rate μ times the number of atoms of B present. C is a stable substance and does not decay further. In a given sample there are initially N atoms of A (where N is a very large number), and no atoms of B and C. If x, y, z denote the numbers of atoms of A, B, C present at time t, assuming that they may be represented as smooth functions of the time explain why

$$\begin{cases} \dot{x}=-\lambda x \\ \dot{y}=\lambda x-\mu y, \end{cases}$$

and write down a similar equation for z. Solve these equations in the case $\lambda\neq\mu$ to find the values of x, y and z at time t. Show that y has a maximum value at time $t=\dfrac{1}{\mu-\lambda}\ln\mu/\lambda$. Sketch your solutions for x, y and z, showing the limiting values as $t\to\infty$.

[SMP 85]

12   Find the general solution of the differential equation

$$\frac{d^2y}{dx^2}+4\frac{dy}{dx}+3y=9x.$$

[WJEC 87]

13   Solve the second order linear differential equation

$$y''+4y'+4y=e^{-2x}$$

where $y(0)=1$ and $y'(0)=0$.

[MEI 87]

14   Find the solution of the differential equation

$$y''+3y'-4y=5e^x+8$$

which satisfies the conditions $y(0)=2$, $y'(0)=0$.

[MEI 86]

15 Solve the equation

$$\frac{d^2y}{dx^2} + 2\frac{dy}{dx} + cy = x$$

for the cases (a) $0 < c < 1$, (b) $c = 1$.   [SMP 79]

16 Find the solution of

$$\frac{d^2y}{dx^2} + 2\frac{dy}{dx} + 2y = \cos 2x$$

which satisfies the conditions

$$y = \frac{dy}{dx} = 0 \quad \text{when } x = 0.$$

Determine d^2y/dx^2 when $x = 0$.
Give a simpler (approximate) expression for y when x is large.   [SMP 86]

17 Given that g and n are positive constants, find the solution of the differential equation

$$\frac{d^2x}{dt^2} + n^2x = g$$

that satisfies $x = (3g/n^2)$ and $dx/dt = 0$. (You may quote without proof the form of the complementary function.)
Sketch a graph showing how x varies with nt for $nt \geqslant 0$.
Describe a mechanical system in which a particle's motion is governed by the above equation, explaining the significance of each of the three terms.
                                                                                          [MEI 85]

18 The motion of a damped freely-oscillating system is governed by a differential equation of the form

$$\ddot{x} + 2k\dot{x} + 9x = 0,$$

where k is a positive constant and initially $x = 0$ and $\dot{x} = 1$.
Discuss and sketch the various solution forms which occur for different values of k.
                                                                                          [MEI 89]

19 Find the solution of the differential equation

$$y'' - 3y' + 2y = e^{ax}$$

where a is a constant $(a \neq 1, a \neq 2)$, and where y satisfies the conditions $y(0) = y'(0) = 0$.
By putting $a = 1 + \varepsilon$ and expanding all terms in the solution involving ε in powers of ε, show that as $\varepsilon \to 0$ the solution obtained becomes

$$y = e^{2x} - xe^x - e^x.$$ [MEI 87]

20 (a) Find the general solution of the differential equation

$$\frac{d^2y}{dx^2} - 4y = -12.$$

(b) Find the general solution of the difference equation

$$u_{n+2} - 4u_n = -12.$$ [SMP 77]

21 (a) Find the solution of the differential equation

$$(1+x^2)\frac{dy}{dx}+xy=1,$$

such that $y=1$ when $x=0$.

(b) Find the general solution of

$$\frac{d^2y}{dx^2}+(1+a)\frac{dy}{dx}+ay=(2-a)e^{-2x},$$

where the real constant a is such that $a\neq 1$ and $a\neq 2$.

Find the solution for which $y=1$ and $\dfrac{dy}{dx}=-1$ when $x=0$.

[UCLES 89]

22 Find general solutions of

(a) $\dfrac{dy}{dx}-\dfrac{(x+1)y}{x}=2x$ for $x>0$,

(b) $d^2y/dx^2+4y=\cos x$.   [SMP 84]

23 (a) Given that $y=Ae^{2x}+Be^{-2x}+3$ is the general solution of the differential equation

$$\frac{d^2y}{dx^2}+ky=n,$$

find the values of the constants k and n.

(b) Solve the differential equation $y^2+x^2\dfrac{dy}{dx}=0$, given that $y=-1$ when $x=1$.

[O&C 87]

24 (a) Find the solution of the differential equation

$$x\frac{dy}{dx}-y=x^3$$

such that $y=1$ when $x=1$.

(b) Find the general solution of the differential equation

$$\frac{d^2y}{dx^2}+\frac{dy}{dx}+y=\sin x+3\cos x.$$ [UCLES 88]

25 Solve the equations

(a) $du/dt+2ut/(1+t^2)=t$,
    if $u=1$ when $t=0$;
(b) $d^2y/dx^2+4dy/dx+4y=4$,
    if $y=0$ and $dy/dx=1$ when $x=0$.   [SMP 88]

26 (a) Find two solution curves satisfying the differential equation

$$\left(\frac{dy}{dx}\right)^2=xy$$

and passing through the point P $(1,\frac{1}{9})$. At what angle (to the nearest degree) do the two curves meet at P?

(b) Find the general solution to the differential equation

$$\frac{d^2y}{dx^2} - 4\frac{dy}{dx} + 4y = e^{kx},$$

(i) when $k=1$,
(ii) when $k=2$.   [O&C 89]

27 (i) Obtain the solution of the differential equation

$$\frac{dy}{dx} + (\tanh x)y = 1$$

such that $y=1$ when $x=0$.

(ii) Show, by means of the substitution $z=y^3$, that the differential equation

$$3y^2\frac{d^2y}{dx^2} + 9y^2\frac{dy}{dx} + 6y\left(\frac{dy}{dx}\right)^2 + 2y^3 = 0$$

can be reduced to the form

$$\frac{d^2z}{dx^2} + a\frac{dz}{dx} + bz = 0,$$

where a and b are numbers which are to be determined.

Hence, or otherwise, find the general solution of the given differential equation, expressing y in terms of x.   [UCLES 88]

28 (a) The functions x and y satisfy the simultaneous differential equations

$$\begin{cases} \dot{x} = y - 4x \\ \dot{y} = -4x, \end{cases}$$

and the boundary conditions $x=0$ and $y=1$ when $t=0$. Show, by differentiating the first equation, that

$$\ddot{x} + 4\dot{x} + 4x = 0.$$

Hence solve for both x and y in terms of t.

(b) The functions u and v satisfy the simultaneous differential equations

$$\begin{cases} \dot{u} = -u^2 - uv - \frac{1}{2}v^2 \\ \dot{v} = -\frac{1}{2}v^2 - uv \end{cases}$$

for $t \geqslant 0$, and the boundary conditions $u=0$ and $v=1$ when $t=0$. Let $w=u+v$. Find a differential equation for w and show that

$$w = (1+t)^{-1}.$$

Hence show that

$$\dot{v} + (1+t)^{-1}v = \frac{1}{2}v^2.$$

By making the substitution $v = \dfrac{1}{z}$, find a linear equation for z, and solve it so as to find v and u in terms of t for $t < e^2 - 1$.   [SMP 82]

29 A weather balloon of mass M kg floats in still air at a height of z_0 m and, if displaced from this level to a height z m, experiences a force tending to restore it to the

equilibrium height, of amount $n^2(z-z_0)$ N. During any vertical motion there is assumed to be a resistance to relative motion of air and balloon equal to λMn N s m^{-1} times the relative vertical speed. In disturbed air there is a vertical air velocity $a \sin pt$ ms^{-1}, where $p = n/\sqrt{M}$. Set up an equation for the vertical motion of the balloon and calculate this vertical motion for times well after the time of arrival at height z_0 m.   [SMP 78]

30 Find the solution of

$$\frac{d^2x}{dt^2} = 16x$$

with $x = a$ and $\dfrac{dx}{dt} = -b$ at $t = 0$, where a and b are positive constants.

Verify that, if $a > \dfrac{b}{4}$ then x will never become zero and $\dfrac{dx}{dt}$ will be zero for a positive value of t.

It is assumed, in a simple war game, that there are two military forces, the 'A-force' and the 'B-force', engaged in combat. The numbers in the A-force and B-force at time t are denoted by x and y respectively. It is also assumed that the rate at which the number in the A-force is decreasing is equal to twice the number in the B-force at that time and that the number in the B-force is decreasing at a rate equal to eight times the number in the A-force. Show that x satisfies the above differential equation.

The game is won when one of the forces is annihilated and the other is not. Given that x_0 and y_0 denote the numbers in the A-force and B-force respectively at time $t = 0$, find a condition on x_0 and y_0 which will ensure that the A-force wins the game.
                                                                          [WJEC 89]

31 A particle moves in a straight line so that, at time t, it is at a distance x from the point O of the line and it is moving according to one of the following two possible rules:

(i)   its velocity (i.e. the rate of change of x with respect to t) is proportional to the amount by which x is less than a fixed distance A,

(ii) its rate of change of velocity is proportional to the amount by which its velocity is less than a fixed velocity $U > 0$, where $U \neq kA$. In each case, the constant of proportionality is $k > 0$.

In each case, find the differential equation satisfied by x as a function of t and, given that the particle is initially at O, having velocity kA, solve each of the two equations.

Show that in only one of the two cases is the particle able to travel an unlimited distance from O.   [O&C 88]

32 A freewheeling fan in a window is driven by the difference of air pressure between the room and the outside air; this difference δp is given by

$$\delta p = \tfrac{1}{2}\rho U^2$$

where ρ is air density and U is the wind speed past the window. The couple exerted on the fan is $ca^3 \delta p$, where a is the radius of the fan and c is a constant. The moment of inertia of the fan about its axis is $\frac{1}{10}ma^2$ where m is its mass. There is a resistance to the motion of the fan equal to $k\omega$, where ω is the angular velocity of the fan and k is a constant. Write down an equation for ω, and show that the steady running speed ω_0 corresponding to a steady wind speed U_0 is given by

$$\omega_0 = \tfrac{1}{2}c\rho a^3 U_0^2/k.$$

In gusty conditions U is not constant, but may be modelled as

$$U = U_0 + u \cos nt$$

where u and n are constants. Show that the corresponding ω has the form

$$\omega_1 + \omega_2 + \omega_3$$

where ω_1 decreases to zero, ω_2 is composed of oscillating terms with average zero, and ω_3 is a constant greater than ω_0. You need not determine the exact form of ω_2, but you should find equations sufficient to determine any constant coefficients in it.

[SMP 79]

33   (a)   A body of mass 4 kg is moving along the Ox axis. The motion is subject to a resisting force of $(28v + 24x)$ N, where $v \,\mathrm{m\,s^{-1}}$ is the velocity of the body and x m is its displacement from O. Show that the displacement x satisfies

$$\frac{d^2 x}{dt^2} + 7\frac{dx}{dt} + 6x = 0, \text{ where } t \text{ denotes time.}$$

Given that $x = 4$, $v = 1$ when $t = 0$, find x in terms of t. Show that the body passes through O at time $\frac{1}{5}\ln\frac{1}{3}$ s.

(b)   A manufacturer estimates that the rate at which the value of machinery at time t depreciates is proportional to the value of the machinery at that time. Write down a differential equation for P, the value of the machinery at time t. Find the general solution of this equation.

A machine which costs £8000 new is only worth £4000 in 3 years time. Find the value of the machine after 8 years, correct to the nearest pound.

[WJEC 88]

34   (i)   A particle of mass m is projected vertically upwards with speed U, and when it is at a height x above its starting point, and moving upwards, its speed is v. There is air resistance of magnitude $(mg/W^2)v^2$, where W is constant. Show that the acceleration of the particle is $v(dv/dx)$, and deduce that

$$\frac{d}{dx}(v^2) + \left(\frac{2g}{W^2}\right)v^2 = -2g.$$

(ii)   Given that

$$y = \left(\frac{b}{a}\right) + \left(c - \frac{b}{a}\right)c^{-ax},$$

where a, b, c are constants, verify that y is a solution of the differential equation $(dy/dx) + ay = b$ and that y also satisfies the condition $y = c$ when $x = 0$.

(iii)   Use the result in (ii) with $y = v^2$ (and appropriate values of a, b, c) to find v^2 in (i) as a function of x. Hence show that the maximum height H of the particle above its starting point is given by

$$H = \frac{W^2}{2g}\ln\left(1 + \frac{U^2}{W^2}\right). \qquad \text{[MEI 88]}$$

35   In one kind of car compass in common use, the rotation of the north marker is governed by the equation

$$I\ddot{\theta} = -n^2 \sin\theta - 2\mu(\dot{\theta} - \dot{\phi}),$$

where θ and ϕ denote the angles that the north marker and the car are currently pointing east of north, and n, I and μ are physical constants. Show that when θ is small, the equation for θ is approximately

$$\ddot{\theta} + 2\lambda\dot{\theta} + k^2\theta = 2\lambda\dot{\phi}, \tag{1}$$

where λ and k are constants which you should express in terms of μ, n and I. You are given that the design of the compass is such that $\mu = (n^2 I)^{1/2}$. Show that $\lambda = k$.

The car is travelling steadily north along a straight road, and the compass is locked with the north marker pointing θ_0 east of north. If the compass is then unlocked, solve the above equation for θ in terms of t, the time from the instant of unlocking.

Some time later, after the compass has reached equilibrium, the car negotiates a right-angle bend in which the car's angle of travel east of north is

$$\phi(t) = \begin{cases} 0 & \text{for } t < 0 \\ \dfrac{\pi t}{2T} & \text{for } 0 \leqslant t \leqslant T \\ \tfrac{1}{2}\pi & \text{for } t > T \end{cases}$$

(where t now denotes the time after reaching the bend). Find a solution of equation (1) which applies for $0 \leqslant t \leqslant T$. Verify that $\dot{\theta} \geqslant 0$ and hence show that $0 \leqslant \theta \leqslant \dfrac{\pi}{kT}$ (for $0 \leqslant t \leqslant T$). Hence explain why this solution will be a good approximation to the true angle θ of the north marker if $kT > 10\pi$. [SMP 89]

36

An automatic control of a car is being tested on a motorway. The front of the controlled car is a distance x from O along the motorway, and the back of the vehicle in front is a distance y from O (as in the diagram). The control on an earlier model set the relation between the acceleration $\ddot{x}$ and the gap $y - x$ so that

$$\ddot{x} = \alpha(y - x - L)/L,$$

where α and L are constants. If the version now being tested also makes an allowance for the speed $\dot{y}$ of the vehicle in front and further increases the acceleration by a term which is proportional to the excess of $\dot{y}$ over a standard speed V, show that its motion satisfies the equation

$$\ddot{x} + \alpha\frac{x}{L} = \alpha\frac{y}{L} + \beta\frac{\dot{y}}{V} - (\alpha + \beta),$$

where β is a constant. Verify that this equation has a steady-state solution in which both vehicles move with a constant speed V separated by a constant gap L.

(a)   In a safety test both vehicles are moving at a steady speed V with gap L when the leading vehicle stops dead. Taking $\alpha = \beta$, find an expression for the separation of the vehicles at a time t later. Deduce that a crash is avoided only if $\alpha > \dfrac{V^2}{3L}$.

(b)   In another test the leading vehicle moves with a speed which fluctuates about the steady-state value, so that

$$y = L + Vt + b\cos\omega t,$$

where b is a small constant length. Simplify the equation for x to the form

$$\ddot{x} + \frac{\alpha x}{L} = f(t).$$

What value of ω is likely to cause problems with the control? Give reasons for your answer.   [SMP 83]

37 The output potential V volts of a circuit is governed by the differential equation

$$\ddot{V} + 6\dot{V} + 25V = F(t)$$

where $F(t)$ is the input potential and t is the time in seconds. Initially $V = \dot{V} = 0$ when a potential

$$F(t) = V_0(1 - e^{-t})$$

is applied, where V_0 is a constant.

Find the subsequent output potential V as a function of time t and make a rough sketch of V against t.   [MEI 88]

38 A toy diver moves vertically in a plastic jar of height $2L$ which is filled with water, and which has a flexible watertight lid. The pressure p at a depth x below the lid is given to be

$$p = P + \rho g x,$$

where P is the pressure at the lid, ρ is the density of water and g the gravitational acceleration. The pressure P can be varied by pressing on the lid.

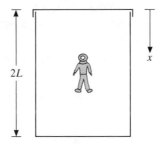

The material of the diver has mass M, and its weight in water (gravitational force less the upthrust due to water pressure) is λMg. Inside the diver is an air bubble whose volume V is assumed to respond to the local pressure according to the law

$$pV = c,$$

where c is a constant; this air bubble gives an upward force ρVg on the diver. Show that the diver can remain at rest at $x = L$ if the pressure P has the value

$$P_1 = \frac{\rho c}{\lambda M} - \rho g L.$$

When the diver moves, there is a resistance to motion equal in magnitude to a constant k times the diver's speed. Derive the differential equation for the diver's depth x in the form

$$\ddot{x} + 2\alpha\dot{x} + f(x) = \beta,$$

giving values for α, β, $f(x)$.

With P fixed at $P_1, f(x)$ may be reasonably approximated by the first two terms of its Taylor approximation in powers of $x - L$. Show that the differential equation then reduces to a linear equation

$$\ddot{x} + 2\alpha\dot{x} - \gamma^2(x - L) = 0,$$

and give the value for γ. Write down the solution to this equation, given that $x = L$ when $t = 0$. Hence, or otherwise, show that if the diver starts at $x = L$ but is not exactly at rest then it will move away to one end or the other.   [SMP 81]

39 A man floats vertically in a swimming pool, with only a small portion of his head above the water. His breathing, by changing his volume, causes him to oscillate vertically. The pool surface is at rest apart from the slight disturbance caused by the man.

   The man's breathing is described as follows. He has basic volume $A_0 \, \text{m}^3$, and his breathing changes this to

$$A = A_0 + a \sin \omega t.$$

His head, near the waterline, is modelled by a cylinder of cross-sectional area $\frac{1}{36} \, \text{m}^2$. He has mass 80 kg and his centre of mass does not move relative to his body as he breathes. Holding his breath, at volume $A_0 \, \text{m}^3$, he would float in equilibrium with $3.6 \times 10^{-2} \, \text{m}$ of his cylindrical head out of the water. The water has density $10^3 \, \text{kg m}^{-3}$ and air has negligible density. Take $g = 10 \, (\text{m s}^{-2})$.

   The water exerts three forces:
(i)   an upthrust equal to the weight of water displaced;
(ii) a resistance equal to 20 kg times the man's acceleration;
(iii) a resistance equal to $200 \, \text{kg s}^{-1}$ times his velocity.
Using as coordinate the height x (in metres) of the man's head which is above the water, show that the upthrust is

$$10^4(A - x/36) \text{ newtons},$$

and that $A_0 = 8.1 \times 10^{-2}$.

   Set up the vertical equation of motion of the man, and find the general solution of this equation.   [SMP 77]

40

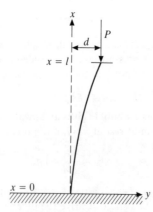

A uniform vertical column of length l is clamped at its base $x = 0$ and is free to deflect laterally at the end $x = l$. At the free end there is a small horizontal platform of radius a, placed symmetrically. When the column supports a vertical load P at the centre of this platform (see diagram), the small lateral deflection y at a distance x above the base satisfies the differential equation

$$By'' + Py = Pd,$$

where d is the lateral deflection of the free end $x = l$, and B is a positive constant. Vertical displacements are assumed negligible. Given that y satisfies the boundary conditions

$$y = 0, \quad y' = 0 \quad \text{at} \quad x = 0,$$

show that

$$y = d(1 - \cos \alpha x),$$

where $\alpha^2 = P/B$. By considering the value of y when $x = l$ deduce that when $P = \dfrac{\pi^2 B}{9l^2}$ the deflection of the column is zero. Show that non-zero deflections are possible when P has the critical value

$$P_c = \frac{\pi^2 B}{4l^2}.$$

If the load P is instead applied at the edge of the platform (at a small horizontal distance a from the axis of the column) the equation governing the lateral deflection is given to be

$$By'' + Py = P(d + a).$$

Show that the solution in this case is

$$y = \frac{a(1 - \cos \alpha x)}{\cos \alpha l} \quad \text{if } \cos \alpha l \neq 0. \qquad \text{[SMP 87]}$$

24

Further methods for differential equations

24.1 COMPLEX NUMBER METHODS

(a) Equations with sinusoidal forcing

Consider the equation

$$d^2x/dt^2 + 2p\,dx/dt + qx = f(t)$$

with both p and q positive. The roots of the auxiliary equation must be one of

$$
\begin{cases}
-p \pm j(q-p^2)^{1/2} & \text{if } q > p \\
-p & \text{if } q = p \\
-p \pm (p^2-q)^{1/2} & \text{if } q < p.
\end{cases}
$$

In all three cases there is a negative exponential involved – in the third case $p^2 - q$ is *less* than p^2, so both roots are negative. In all three cases therefore, the CF must decrease rapidly as t increases. Many real situations force p and q to be positive; for example, resistances always act *against* a motion or current, and elastic behaviour always acts *against* a displacement, so that positive signs on the left hand side of the equation inevitably follow.

With p and q positive then, the CF is a transient of the system, and unless we are concerned with the initial reaction of the system we can omit further discussion of the CF and of the initial conditions which determine the constants in it.

We have seen several examples in the last two chapters of equations of this type, in which $f(t)$ was (or could have been) a sinusoidal function:

(i) in Sections 22.3 and 23.6(c) where x was either a charge or a current, with a forcing term due to an electric generator;
(ii) in Section 22.6(d) where x was a vertical displacement of a clay particle, with a forcing term due to solar heating;
(iii) in Section 22.1 where x was vertical motion of a suspended mass, if $h(t)$ was taken to be sinusoidal, and F was chosen suitably;
(iv) in Section 23.6(a) if the car in front moved with oscillating velocity,

$$y = Vt + k \sin \omega t.$$

There is indeed a considerable number of problems related to real situations for which a reasonable model is

$$\begin{cases} d^2x/dt^2 + 2p\,dx/dt + qx = F_0 \cos \omega t \\ p > 0,\ q > 0 \end{cases}$$

and for which we want to know only the amplitude R and the phase lag δ of the steady state response

$$R \cos(\omega t - \delta).$$

A method which has been developed to simplify the calculations for such systems starts by *complicating* the mathematics, by setting up a new problem for the complex function $z = x + jy$. The equation for z is taken to be

$$d^2z/dt^2 + 2p\,dz/dt + qz = F_0 e^{j\omega t},$$

because if you take the real part of this equation you get back to the one we started with, since the real part of $e^{j\omega t}$ is $\cos \omega t$.

In this formulation each of x and y is just an ordinary real function of time t. We have used the linearity of the equations to combine

$$\begin{cases} \dfrac{d^2x}{dt^2} + 2p\dfrac{dx}{dt} + qx = F_0 \cos \omega t \\[2mm] \dfrac{d^2y}{dt^2} + 2p\dfrac{dy}{dt} + qy = F_0 \sin \omega t \end{cases}$$

into a single equation for the complex number z, which varies with time.

The particular integral for z is found, as usual, by intelligent guesswork. Since

$$\frac{d}{dt} e^{j\omega t} = j\omega e^{j\omega t}$$

it seems reasonable to suppose that the solution for z is $Ae^{j\omega t}$ for some (complex) constant A. When we substitute the assumed solution into the equation we find

$$(-\omega^2 + 2j\omega p + q)Ae^{j\omega t} = F_0 e^{j\omega t}.$$

The term in the bracket came from the left hand side of the equation, i.e. from the forces (or other constituents) that describe the system. So the complex number

$$-\omega^2 + 2j\omega p + q$$

is an important descriptive parameter of the system as a whole. It is usually given the name *impedance*, because it shows how much the system *impedes* the forcing term on the right hand side from causing a response. When this term is large (i.e. has large magnitude), the response amplitude A, which multiplies it to give the forcing amplitude F_0, must be small.

Let us use the symbol Z for the impedance:

$$Z = -\omega^2 + 2j\omega p + q.$$

We can write this complex number in modulus–argument form as

$$Z = Z_0 e^{j\delta},$$

where Z_0 and δ are real. Substituting this into the equation for A we find

$$Z_0 e^{j\delta} A e^{j\omega t} = F_0 e^{j\omega t}$$

so that

$$A = (F_0/Z_0) e^{-j\delta}.$$

We have discovered that the steady state response of the equation for the complex function z is

$$(F_0/Z_0) e^{j(\omega t - \delta)}.$$

But since x is the real part of z we only have to take the real part of this steady state response for z to get the corresponding steady state response for x, which will therefore be

$$(F_0/Z_0) \cos(\omega t - \delta).$$

The method of using complex impedances can now be summarised.

(i) The differential equation is linear with constant coefficients and forcing term $F_0 \cos \omega t$, and with CF which tends to 0 as t increases.
(ii) Calculate the impedance Z of the left hand side by replacing each d/dt by $j\omega$.
(iii) Set Z into modulus–argument form: $Z = Z_0 e^{j\delta}$.
(iv) The response of the system is $(F_0/Z_0) \cos(\omega t - \delta)$, with amplitude F_0/Z_0 and phase lag δ.

Exercise 24A

1   Can you use the complex impedance method on the equation

$$\frac{dx}{dt} + ax = F_0 \cos \omega t$$

(i) if $a=2$, (ii) if $a=0$, (iii) if $a=-2$?

2   Find the steady state response for the equation

$$\frac{dx}{dt} + 3x = 2\cos 4t$$

(i) by using the complex impedance method;
(ii) by using intelligent guesswork to find the PI;
(iii) by using an integrating factor.
Which is the easiest method?

3   Find the steady state response (using the complex impedance method) for

$$\frac{d^2 y}{dt^2} + 2\frac{dy}{dt} + 10y = \cos 3t + 2\sin 3t$$

by writing $\sin 3t = \cos(3t - \tfrac{1}{2}\pi)$.

4 Find the steady state responses, by using the complex impedance method, for any of the following for which it is appropriate.
(i)   Exercise 23E question 1, (i) to (v).
(ii) The equation derived in Section 23.6(c).
(iii) The equation derived in Section 23.6(d).

5 Is there a complex impedance theory for difference equations of the form
(i) $u_{n+1} + au_n = F_0 \cos kn$,
(ii) $u_{n+2} + 2pu_{n+1} + qu_n = F_0 \cos kn$?

(b) Impedance methods for electric circuits

The impedance method can be applied directly to the circuit diagrams of electric circuit theory, without the bother of deriving the differential equation first.

To start this process we need to know the impedances associated with the standard (linear) circuit elements. The terms that come into the differential equation for the circuit in Fig. 1 are (as in Section 22.3)

$$L\frac{dI}{dt}, \quad RI, \quad \frac{Q}{C}.$$

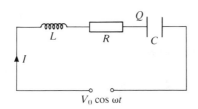

Figure 1. The standard electric circuit elements

The differential equation for the current is

$$L\frac{dI}{dt} + RI + \frac{Q}{C} = V_0 \cos \omega t,$$

where the charge Q on the capacitor is related to the current I by

$$I = dQ/dt$$

or

$$Q = \int I(t)dt.$$

If you now put

$$I = I_0 e^{j\omega t}$$

in the complex version of the differential equation, you get terms

(i) $j\omega L I_0 e^{j\omega t}$ for the inductor
(ii) $R I_0 e^{j\omega t}$ for the resistor

(iii) $\{1/(j\omega C)\}I_0 e^{j\omega t}$ for the capacitor, by using the equation

$$Q = \int I(t)dt$$

for the charge Q.

That is, the impedances of the separate circuit elements are

$$\begin{cases} j\omega L & \text{for the inductance } L, \\ R & \text{for the resistance } R, \\ 1/(j\omega C) & \text{for the capacitance } C. \end{cases}$$

The next thing that is needed is how to combine impedances. What are the equivalent single impedances for the two in series in Fig. 2(a), and for the two in parallel in Fig. 2(b)?

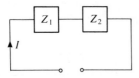

Figure 2(a). Two impedances in series

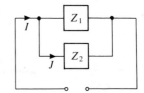

Figure 2(b). Two impedances in parallel

For the impedances in series, the (complex) voltage drops are

$$Z_1 I_0 e^{j\omega t} \quad \text{and} \quad Z_2 I_0 e^{j\omega t}.$$

Thus in total

$$(Z_1 + Z_2)I_0 e^{j\omega t} = V_0 e^{j\omega t},$$

and the total impedance is given by

$$Z = Z_1 + Z_2$$

for two impedances in series.

For the impedances in parallel we have both

$$Z_1(I_0 - J_0)e^{j\omega t} = V_0 e^{j\omega t}$$

and

$$Z_2 J_0 e^{j\omega t} = V_0 e^{j\omega t}$$

as the voltage drop across each impedance is $V_0 e^{j\omega t}$. Now these have to be the same as

$$Z I_0 e^{j\omega t} = V_0 e^{j\omega t},$$

where Z is the equivalent single impedance. These quickly give

$$\frac{V_0}{Z} = I_0 = I_0 - J_0 + J_0 = \frac{V_0}{Z_1} + \frac{V_0}{Z_2},$$

so that the rule for combining impedances in parallel is

$$\frac{1}{Z} = \frac{1}{Z_1} + \frac{1}{Z_2}.$$

Let us now reconsider the circuit in Fig. 3 (from Section 22.3, where it was Fig. 10), which has differential equations

$$\begin{cases} L\,dJ/dt = Q/C, \; dQ/dt = I - J, \\ RI + L\,dJ/dt = V_0 \cos \omega t, \end{cases}$$

from which you can deduce the differential equation for I (with some trouble).

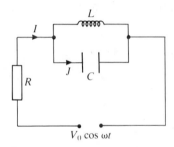

Figure 3. A three element circuit

Set up instead the corresponding diagram of impedances (Fig. 4). The total impedance for the capacitor and inductor in parallel is

$$\frac{1}{\dfrac{1}{j\omega L} + j\omega C}$$

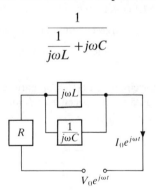

Figure 4. The corresponding impedance diagram

from the results above. This can be simplified to

$$\frac{j\omega L}{1 - \omega^2 LC}.$$

But this is in series with the resistor, so that the impedance for the whole circuit is

$$Z = R + \frac{j\omega L}{1 - \omega^2 LC}.$$

The complex number calculation in this case has been rather easier than the manipulation of three differential equations into a single one for I. This method of impedances is used in electric circuit theory (and other places with similar differential equations) to avoid the construction of differential equations, and replace them with some complex number calculations.

Exercise 24B

1 Find the impedance for the circuit in

(i) Fig. 5(a)   (ii) Fig. 5(b),

given that $R = 1\,\Omega$, $L = 10^{-3}$ H, $C = 10^{-6}$F, $\omega = 100\pi$ rads/s.

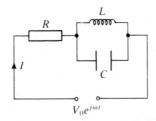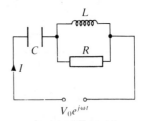

Figure 5(a), (b). Series and parallel circuits

2 Find the series and parallel circuits (i.e. like those in Figs. 5(a) and (b)) which give

(i) the largest,   and   (ii) the smallest

modulus to the impedance, using the values from question 1. What are the two phase shifts?

3 Find the impedance for the circuit in Fig. 6. Compare your result with what you found for Exercise 22C, question 5 in the special case $L = 0$.

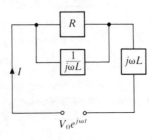

Figure 6. A three impedance circuit

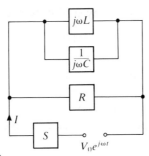

Figure 7. Circuit for question 4

4 Outline how to find the steady state response for the circuit of Fig. 7
(i) by using impedances,
(ii) by setting up a differential equation.

(c)   Resonance

In Section 22.1 a model was set up for the vertical motion of a particle (an empty torch case) on a piece of elastic when the upper end of the elastic was moved vertically. The equation that resulted had the form

$$d^2x/dt^2 + n^2x = n^2h + F - \tfrac{1}{2}n^2,$$

and the substitution $y = x - \tfrac{1}{2}$ reduces the equation to

$$d^2y/dt^2 + n^2y = n^2h + F.$$

One of the options discussed in that section was to use $F = 0$ as a model, and I shall start with that choice. I shall also choose to take

$$h(t) = a \cos \omega t,$$

i.e. the top of the elastic is moved vertically with (radian) frequency ω and amplitude a.

The general solution of the differential equation is, by methods which should now be familiar,
$$C \cos nt + D \sin nt + \{a/(n^2 - \omega^2)\} \cos \omega t,$$

provided that $\omega \neq n$; the constants C and D will come from any initial values that are given, but I do not want to discuss that part of the solution. What I want to concentrate on is the part of the solution due to the forcing term $a \cos \omega t$, which is

$$\{n^2a/(n^2 - \omega^2)\} \cos \omega t.$$

For any choice of ω, other than $\omega = n$, this has a finite and fixed amplitude; it may be very large when ω is nearly equal to n, but it is fixed, and this part of the response represents a sinusoidal oscillation.

Now consider the case $\omega = n$. The particular integral of the differential equation no longer has the same form because $\cos nt$ and $\sin nt$ are already part of the complementary function; using the methods developed in Section 23.4 we find that the PI has to be of the form

$$ct \cos nt + dt \sin nt.$$

The constants c and d are found by substitution as usual, and the PI is in fact

$$\tfrac{1}{2}nat \sin nt.$$

This PI has a completely different character from the previous one. It is indeed oscillatory, but the amplitude *increases* with time, apparently without limit. This growing response from a fixed sinusoidal input is one of two situations which are given the name of resonance. This one cannot be very realistic for long, as the model is very unlikely to be valid if the velocities and displacements become very large. In particular

(i) the response of the elastic will cease to be linear,
(ii) air resistance cannot be neglected at high speeds.

In an application such as this in Mechanics, resonance is usually an undesirable phenomenon, often leading to mechanical failure of some components, and mechanical systems will usually be carefully designed to avoid it. Some years ago now a new higher voltage electricity supply line was slung across the mile-wide Severn crossing near Bristol, and at certain wind speeds oscillatory forces from the interaction of wind and wire matched a natural frequency of wire oscillation. The result was resonance and a very large (though not infinite) motion of the wire, and sparks between adjoining wires when they met. This was destructive, and the configuration of the wires was redesigned. The most impressive example of mechanical resonance is to be seen in the film of the Tacoma Bridge disaster, when a similar wind-induced resonance led to huge motions of the bridge carriageway and the eventual destruction of the bridge. In both of these examples the oscillation became large due to a matching of frequencies, but in neither did the oscillation become indefinitely large, as other forces which opposed the motion came into (noticeable) effect when the amplitude became large.

The other meaning of resonance is that appropriate to these two examples, which is a response that is much larger than you might expect, at one particular value of the frequency.

Resonance may be designed *into* electric circuits, as amplification of a small input signal to give a much larger response is a desirable effect in many applications. However, until cheap superconductors become available, a circuit with no resistance in it is impossible to achieve: any inductor must have *some* resistance associated with it, so the simplest resonant circuit is that in Fig. 8,

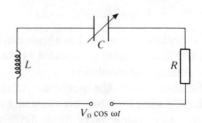

Figure 8. A resonant circuit, tuned by a variable capacitance

where the variable capacitance C will be adjusted so as to get a very large amplitude of current for a modest input V_0. The impedance of this circuit is

$$Z = j\omega L + \frac{1}{j\omega C} + R,$$

and the steady state response has amplitude

$$V_0/|Z|.$$

This has the value

$$\frac{V_0}{\left\{ R^2 + \left(\omega L - \frac{1}{\omega C} \right)^2 \right\}^{1/2}}.$$

Clearly the largest value of this occurs when

$$\omega L = \frac{1}{\omega C}$$

or

$$C = \frac{1}{\omega^2 L},$$

giving the resonant amplitude to be V_0/R, which can be very large if the circuit has only a small resistance.

A graph of the steady state response for different values of C shows how accurately the circuit has to be tuned to get the very high resonant amplitude. I used the values

$$V_0 = 10^{-2}\,\text{V},\ L = 10^{-3}\,\text{H},\ R = 10^{-2}\,\Omega,$$

with $\omega^2 = 10^5\,\text{rad}^2/\text{s}^2$ (to match closely to the usual 50 Hz supply). With these figures resonance occurs at $C = 10^{-2}\,\text{F}$ and the current amplitude is 1 A. If you take R smaller you get a sharper and higher resonance peak. The curve in Fig. 9 shows well enough that you have to tune the value of C quite closely to $10^{-2}\,\text{F}$ in order to get close to the maximum response of 1 A.

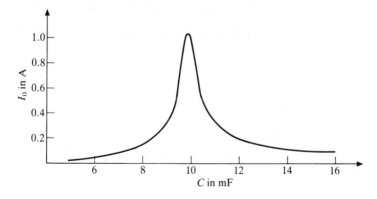

Figure 9. Resonance curve for the circuit of Fig. 8

Exercise 24C

1 Find the steady state solution for

$$\frac{d^2y}{dt^2} + 36y = 0.36 \cos \omega t - 10^{-1}\frac{dy}{dt}.$$

Relate your answer to the model in Section 22.1 of the vertical motion of a particle on a piece of elastic, with a resistance force proportional to speed.

2 Plot the magnitude of the steady state response in question 1 against the forcing frequency ω.

3 Consider the model in Section 23.6(d). The viscous resistance force for a particle of radius r moving in water of viscosity μ at speed dy/dt is $6\pi\mu r \, dy/dt$. Will this system exhibit resonance if the stratification parameter N has value near ω? You will need to choose a value for r; μ has a value around 10^{-3} SI units.

4 The electric circuit in Section 23.6(c) has equation

$$\frac{d^2Q}{dt^2} + 2 \times 10^{-4}\frac{dQ}{dt} + 10^8 Q = 10^3 V_0 \cos \omega t.$$

Is there a resonant response at some value of ω? Explain your answer.

24.2 EQUATIONS WITH NON-CONSTANT COEFFICIENTS

For most equations

$$\frac{d^2y}{dx^2} + p(x)\frac{dy}{dx} + q(x) = f(x)$$

the best we can do is one of:

(i) a numerical solution for particular initial values;
(ii) an approximate solution near some particular value of x;
(iii) a very involved formula using advanced methods.

But there are a few easy equations like this, and it can be useful to see that some of the previous ideas carry over.

(a) Euler equations

Consider the equation

$$d^2y/dx^2 + (a/x)\,dy/dx + (b/x^2)y = 0,$$

where a and b are constants. This is known as an Euler equation, and it has some straightforward solutions.

The corresponding first order equation is

$$dy/dx + (a/x)y = 0,$$

which is separable and has the solution

$$y = Ax^{-a},$$

for any constants a and A. This should encourage you to try a similar solution for the second order equation. Try $y = Ax^m$, and you find

$$\{m(m-1)+am+b\}Ax^{m-2}=0$$

as the condition for it to be a solution. Since A and x are not necessarily zero, the condition for Ax^m to be a solution is

$$m^2+(a-1)m+b=0,$$

which corresponds to the auxiliary equation we had before.

The easy case here is when this quadratic has two real roots, say m_1 and m_2. Then each of Ax^{m_1} and Bx^{m_2} is a solution, and so is their sum because the equation is linear. We have found the complementary function of this equation, which is

$$Ax^{m_1}+Bx^{m_2}.$$

For example

$$d^2y/dx^2-(6/x^2)y=0$$

has the auxiliary equation

$$m^2-m-6=0$$

with roots $m=3$ and $m=-2$, leading to solutions

$$y=Ax^3+Bx^{-2};$$

it is easily checked that this is a solution of the equation.

What happens when there is a conjugate pair of complex numbers as solution to the auxiliary equation, say $m=k\pm js$? The solution appears to be

$$y=x^k(Ax^{js}+Bx^{-js}).$$

In this unpleasant looking equation we put

$$x^{js}=e^{js\ln x}$$
$$=\cos(s\ln x)+j\sin(s\ln x).$$

Then defining C and D in the same way as in Section 23.2 we can rewrite the solution as

$$y=x^k\{C\cos(s\ln x)+D\sin(s\ln x)\}:$$

nasty, but at least an explicit formula.

The final case is when there is only one root of the auxiliary equation, say $m=k$. The solution in this case turns out to be

$$y=Ax^k+Bx^k\ln x;$$

one derivation of this answer can be seen in (c) below, and another is included in the Exercise.

We could go on and look for functions $f(x)$ (easy ones preferably) for which the particular integrals of

$$\frac{d^2y}{dx^2}+\frac{a}{x}\frac{dy}{dx}+\frac{b}{x^2}y=f(x)$$

could be found by intelligent guesswork. This kind of equation rarely arises, and so it can be left to the Exercise.

Exercise 24D

1   Solve the Euler equations

   (i) $d^2y/dx^2-(4/x)\,dy/dx+(6/x^2)y=0,\ y(0)=y(1)=0;$
   (ii) $d^2y/dx^2+6x^{-1}\,dy/dx+6x^{-2}y=0,\ y(1)=0,\ y'(1)=1;$
   (iii) $d^2y/dx^2-x^{-1}\,dy/dx+5x^{-2}y=0,\ y(1)=0,\ y'(1)=1;$
   (iv) $d^2y/dx^2-x^{-1}\,dy/dx+x^{-2}y=0,\ y(1)=0,\ y(e)=0.$

2   Make the change of variable

$$t=\ln x \quad\text{or}\quad x=e^t$$

and show that dy/dx must be replaced by $e^{-t}\,dy/dt$. What must you use to replace d^2y/dx^2? Verify that this substitution converts any Euler equation into an equation with constant coefficients.

3   Use the result of question 2 to prove that the equation

$$d^2y/dx^2+(2a+1)x^{-1}\,dy/dx+a^2x^{-2}y=0$$

has the general solution

$$y=Ax^{-a}+Bx^{-a}\ln x.$$

4   Show that the Euler equation

$$\frac{d^2y}{dx^2}+\frac{a}{x}\frac{dy}{dx}+\frac{b}{x^2}y=f(x)$$

can be factorised as

$$\left(\frac{d}{dx}+\frac{\alpha}{x}\right)\left(\frac{dy}{dx}+\frac{\beta y}{x}\right)=f(x)$$

for suitable choice of α and β.
Hence solve the equation when

$$a=6,\,b=6,\,f(x)=x^2+2.$$

5   By using

   (i)   the method of question 2,
   (ii) the method of question 4,
   (iii) intelligent guesswork,

find the particular integral of

$$\frac{d^2y}{dx^2}+\frac{6}{x}\frac{dy}{dx}+\frac{6}{x^2}y=x^k.$$

(b) Bessel equations

Bessel's equation is

$$d^2y/dx^2 + x^{-1}\,dy/dx + (1 - k^2/x^2)y = 0,$$

which doesn't look any harder than Euler's equation, since it has an x^{-1} with the dy/dx and a term including x^{-2} with the y. In fact *most* cases of Bessel's equation have no simple solution formula – the equation is used to define *new* functions that cannot be expressed in terms of simpler things than a differential equation. Why bother to define new functions like this? Bessel first needed them in an astronomical context in 1824, though there they arose as complicated integrals and not through a differential equation. Since then they have come into a host of applications.

The case $k^2 = \frac{1}{4}$ is in fact easy, and shows the character of the solutions of Bessel's equation quite adequately. Direct substitution shows that in this case two solutions are

$$x^{-1/2}\sin x \quad \text{and} \quad x^{-1/2}\cos x$$

so that the general solution for Bessel's equation 'of order $\frac{1}{2}$' is

$$x^{-1/2}(A\cos x + B\sin x).$$

It is common to write the two halves of this solution as the 'Bessel functions'

$$\begin{cases} J_{1/2}(x) = (2/\pi x)^{1/2}\sin x \\ J_{-1/2}(x) = (2/\pi x)^{1/2}\cos x, \end{cases}$$

by choosing special values for the constants. But for most values of k it is impossible to write the Bessel functions in an easy way.

How do you find the values of the solutions of other Bessel equations? You do it numerically, there is no other way (except in the few very special cases); the values for $J_0(x)$ – one of the Bessel functions of order zero – in Chapter 9 were found numerically.

Exercise 24E

1   Verify that $x^{-1/2}\cos x$ and $x^{-1/2}\sin x$ satisfy Bessel's equation with $k = \pm\frac{1}{2}$.

2   When k is half an odd integer Bessel's equation has a 'simple' solution. Try to find these solutions when $k = \frac{3}{2}$, using $\sin x$ and $\cos x$ combined with x^{-1} and 1 in some fashion, and then the combination multiplied by $x^{-1/2}$.

(c) Reduction of order

If you sit and stare at the equation

$$(1 + 2x)\,d^2y/dx^2 - 4\,dy/dx + 4x^{-1}y = 0$$

for long enough you will either get depressed or you will see that one solution of the equation is just

$$y = Ax,$$

because the terms on the left are then 0, $-4A$, $4A$.

There is a cunning way of using this easy solution to find another solution of the equation, by the method known as *reduction of order*. The method goes like this. Replace the constant A in the solution you have found by a function of x, say $F(x)$, and find out what equation F satisfies by substituting

$$y = F(x)x$$

into the equation. When I did this I found the equation for F to be

$$(1 + 2x)x \, d^2F/dx^2 + 2(1 + 2x) \, dF/dx - 4x \, dF/dx = 0$$

or

$$(1 + 2x)x \, dG/dx + 2G = 0$$

where

$$G = dF/dx.$$

This is where the 'reduction of order' comes in: I now have a *first* order equation for G instead of a second order one for F. This looks like a cheat; I must have chosen a very special equation to start with so that the reduction would work. In fact this is not so: you always get a reduction like this *provided* you start with a solution of the original equation for y. We shall prove this below, after finishing this example, and another one.

The equation for G is separable, giving

$$\int \frac{dG}{G} = -\int \frac{2dx}{x(1 + 2x)},$$

so that (after using partial fractions to do the integration)

$$G(x) = 4 + 4x^{-1} + x^{-2}.$$

This can now be integrated in its turn to give $F(x)$,

$$F(x) = 4x + 4\ln x - x^{-1}.$$

Finally the second solution of the equation for y is

$$xF = 4x^2 + 4x\ln x - 1.$$

You may check by substitution that this is a solution as claimed. The general solution of the equation has thus been found as

$$y = Ax + B(4x^2 + 4x\ln x - 1).$$

As a second example I shall do the Euler equation with only one root to its auxiliary equation. The equation is

$$d^2y/dx^2 - (2k - 1) \, dy/dx + k^2y = 0,$$

with auxiliary equation (as described above, on substituting x^m)

$$m^2 - 2km + k^2 = 0,$$

which has root $m = k$. One solution of the equation is therefore

$$Ax^k,$$

and so I try to find another solution of the form

$$F(x)x^k.$$

When you put this into the equation you find

$$d^2F/dx^2 + x^{-1}dF/dx = 0.$$

Reduce the order by writing $dF/dx = G$, which gives the easy equation

$$dG/dx + x^{-1}G = 0.$$

Separate and integrate this equation to find that

$$G(x) = 1/x,$$

which means that F, the integral of G, is $\ln x$. The second solution of the Euler equation has thus been proved to be

$$x^k \ln x,$$

as required.

Finally I shall show why this method always reduces the order of the differential equation from second to first order. Take the equation

$$d^2y/dx^2 + p(x)\,dy/dx + q(x)y = 0,$$

and assume that inspiration of some sort has led you to notice that $u(x)$ is a solution, which means that

$$d^2u/dx^2 + p(x)\,du/dx + q(x)u = 0.$$

Look for another solution which has the form $F(x)u(x)$. If you substitute and rearrange you will find the equation for F to be

$$u\,d^2F/dx^2 + (2\,du/dx + up)\,dF/dx$$
$$+ (d^2u/dx^2 + p\,du/dx + qu) = 0.$$

But the last bracket here is zero because u is a solution of the original equation, and putting $dF/dx = G$ you get

$$u\,dG/dx + (2\,du/dx + up)G = 0,$$

which is a first order equation for G. Since you can always solve a first order linear equation by means of an integrating factor (or, here, by separation), you can find G; it may sometimes be impossible to find an easy formula for F by integrating G.

Exercise 24F

1                    $$x(x+1)\,d^2y/dx^2 - dy/dx - 2y = 0$$

has the 'easy' solution Ax^2. Find the other solution by reduction of order.

2                    $$x(x+1)\,d^2y/dx^2 + (3x+2)\,dy/dx + y = 0$$

has the solution $1/x$. Find a second solution.

3                    $$x\,d^2y/dx^2 + x\,dy/dx + y = 0$$

has one solution xe^{-x}. Try to find a second solution by reduction of order.

4   Find a cubic polynomial which satisfies

$$(1+x^2)\,d^2y/dx^2 - 6y = 0,$$

and hence find a second solution.

5   Solve, if you can,

$$x^2\,d^2y/dx^2 + x(x-1)\,dy/dx - 2xy = 0.$$

24.3 SUMMARY

(a) The *impedance* of the differential equation

$$\frac{d^2z}{dt^2} + 2p\frac{dz}{dt} + qz = F_0 e^{j\omega t}$$

is

$$Z = -\omega^2 + 2j\omega p + q.$$

The steady state response for the differential equation

$$\frac{d^2x}{dt^2} + 2p\frac{dx}{dt} + qx = F_0 \cos \omega t$$

(where p and q are positive) taking $Z = Z_0 e^{j\delta}$, is

$$\frac{F_0}{Z_0} \cos(\omega t - \delta).$$

(b) The impedance of an AC circuit can be found directly by using the following rules:

(i)   replace inductances L by impedances $j\omega L$
      replace resistances R by impedances R
      replace capacitances C by impedances $1/(j\omega C)$;

(ii) combine impedances in series by

$$Z_{\text{total}} = Z_1 + Z_2 + \ldots + Z_n;$$

(iii) combine impedances in parallel by

$$\frac{1}{Z_{\text{total}}} = \frac{1}{Z_1} + \frac{1}{Z_2} + \ldots + \frac{1}{Z_n}.$$

(c) The differential equation

$$\frac{d^2x}{dt^2} + n^2x = F_0 \cos nt$$

has the particular integral

$$\tfrac{1}{2}(F_0/n)t \sin nt;$$

this increasing response is sometimes called *resonance*. When this response is found, the model underlying the equation will usually need to be revised.

The other meaning of resonance is to describe a steady state response much larger than the forcing which causes it. This is found, for example, in the equation

$$\frac{d^2x}{dt^2} + 2k\frac{dx}{dt} + n^2x = F_0 \cos \omega t$$

when (i) k is small (and positive) and (ii) ω is close to n.

(d) *Euler's equation* is

$$\frac{d^2y}{dx^2} + \frac{a}{x}\frac{dy}{dx} + \frac{b}{x^2}y = 0.$$

Its auxiliary equation, found from trying $y = Ax^m$ as solution, is

$$m^2 + (a-1)m + b = 0.$$

Its complementary function is

(i) $Ax^{m_1} + Bx^{m_2}$ if the auxiliary equation has distinct real roots m_1 and m_2;
(ii) $Ax^k + Bx^k \ln x$ if the auxiliary equation has only the one root k;
(iii) $x^k\{C \cos(s \ln x) + D \sin(s \ln x)\}$ if the auxiliary equation has the complex roots $k \pm js$.

(e) If the differential equation

$$\frac{d^2y}{dx^2} + p(x)\frac{dy}{dx} + q(x)y = 0$$

has *one* solution $u(x)$, then a second solution may be found by *reduction of order*: you substitute

$$y = F(x)u(x)$$

and find a first order equation for

$$G = dF/dx.$$

(f) Most second order differential equations with non-constant coefficients have *no* easy solution by formula, and need to be solved numerically.

25

Boundary conditions at two points: shooting

In Chapter 21 we discussed numerical methods for solving second order differential equations which had both boundary conditions given at some starting value of the coordinate. In the problem of water flow out of a pipe the given conditions were

(i) height of water $= 1$ m at time $= 0$,
(ii) water at rest at time $= 0$.

In the problem of the rise of a hot air balloon the corresponding conditions were that the balloon started at ground level and at rest. This kind of pair of conditions gives an

initial value problem

and the solution methods stepped forward from one value of time to the next by using the differential equations.

Another major kind of differential equation problem arises when the two conditions (which determine the two constants in the general solution) are given at different places or at different times. These are called

boundary value problems

or, more explicitly

two point boundary value problems.

They require rather different numerical solution methods, which will be described in this chapter and the next.

It is worth remembering at this point the statements in Chapter 23 on these two different kinds of differential equation problem:

(*a*) a linear initial value problem (with constant coefficients and continuous right hand side $f(x)$) always has a solution, which is unique;
(*b*) a two point boundary value problem may have *no* solution, or a *non*-unique solution.

25.1 MODELLING A REAL PROBLEM

In 1986 an airliner was hijacked to Pakistan, and an army sniper attempted to shoot the leader of the hijacking (according to newspaper reports) through the

462

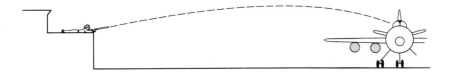

Figure 1. Shooting a hijacker

cockpit window from the airport terminal building. What was the angle above the line of sight at which he needed to fire? What was the speed of the bullet on impact with the window? What was its angle of travel at that moment? (Fig. 1.)

The first answer is known (to armies and snipers); the rifle sight is graduated so that if you know the distance to the target, then the correct angle of elevation can be automatically set up. But the other two questions, whose answers are vital for determining whether the shooting will be successful (it wasn't), do not have such an easy solution.

What I shall do is to model the problem with some differential equations, and then solve the model equations

(i)   numerically;

(ii) exactly, after approximating them a little.

I shall describe the situation in terms of the horizontal and vertical distances x and y from the end of the rifle, and the corresponding velocity components u and v. I shall also use θ as the angle the bullet's track is making with the horizontal, so that $v/u = \tan\theta$.

The forces that act on the bullet during its flight are gravity and a drag force due to its motion through the air, and this drag force is assumed to be proportional to the square of the speed and to act backwards along the path of the bullet (these are reasonably good approximations). See Fig. 2.

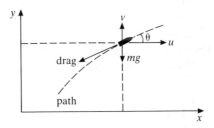

Figure 2. The variables in the problem

With these assumptions the horizontal and vertical components of the equation of motion are (if I take the constant of proportionality in the drag force to be mk, where m is the mass of the bullet)

$$\text{horizontally}: m\,du/dt = -mk(u^2+v^2)\cos\theta$$
$$\text{vertically}: m\,dv/dt = -mk(u^2+v^2)\sin\theta - mg.$$

The conditions that a solution has to satisfy are

$$
\begin{cases}
\text{the moment of firing is taken as } t=0, \\
\text{the speed of the bullet at } t=0 \text{ is known, say } W, \\
\text{the initial position is } x=y=0, \\
\text{the bullet passes through the target at } x=X \text{ and } y=Y.
\end{cases}
$$

When the problem has been solved, we shall expect to know

$$
\begin{cases}
\text{the initial angle, say } \theta = \alpha, \\
\text{the time to reach the target, say } T, \\
\text{the speed of the bullet when it hits its target,} \\
\text{the angle at which it is then travelling.}
\end{cases}
$$

The equations of motion above can be put entirely in terms of u and v by noting that

$$
\begin{cases}
\cos \theta = u/(u^2 + v^2)^{1/2} \\
\sin \theta = v/(u^2 + v^2)^{1/2};
\end{cases}
$$

this gives

$$
\begin{cases}
du/dt = -ku(u^2+v^2)^{1/2} \\
dv/dt = -kv(u^2+v^2)^{1/2} - g.
\end{cases}
$$

Fortunately the newspaper that I read gave me enough information to find the values of k and W and X, and I shall take $Y=0$ just to make the problem look nicer. In fact they told me that the bullet slowed from 1772 to 1210 miles an hour over a distance of 400 yards, and that it weighed 0.022 pounds. These figures look unconvincingly accurate, but thay gave me $k=1.04 \times 10^{-3}$; in what follows I shall assume the value $k = 10^{-3}$ (in SI units, of course). I shall also take the initial speed to be 792 m/s and the range to be 366 m.

You should note for future reference that all the values of θ will be small; the vertical component v of the velocity will be very much less than the horizontal component u; and the height y and the time t will not have large values (when measured in metres and seconds).

The mathematical problem which results from this modelling is thus the pair of non-linear first order differential equations for u and v

$$
\begin{cases}
\dfrac{du}{dt} = -10^{-3}u(u^2+v^2)^{1/2} \\[2mm]
\dfrac{dv}{dt} = -10^{-3}v(u^2+v^2)^{1/2} - 9.8
\end{cases}
$$

(where of course $u = dx/dt$ and $v = dy/dt$), together with the two point boundary values

$$
\begin{cases}
(u^2+v^2)^{1/2} = 792 & \text{at } t=0 \\
x=y=0 & \text{at } t=0
\end{cases}
$$

and
$$x = 366, \quad y = 0 \quad \text{at } t = T$$

for some as yet unknown value of T.

It is unlikely that we can solve these equations exactly (an approximate solution will be found in Section 25.3), so we should look for a numerical method.

Exercise 25A

1   A mass of 0.022 pounds is just 10 grams converted from the old 'imperial' system. I would be surprised if bullets were made to have such a 'tidy' mass, and I expect that this is a rounded figure, representing a true mass of perhaps 9.9 g or 10.2 g. Estimate errors in the other values given in the newspaper report.

2   What equations would you get to solve if you made an alternative statement about the air resistance force, that its magnitude is proportional to the speed of the bullet?

Solve your equations exactly to find u and v in terms of t. What value of k should you use for this model?

3   The modelling has assumed that there was no wind at the time of the shooting. Modify the model in the text by adding a wind
(i) of velocity $-10\mathbf{i}$ (metres per second, parallel to the x-axis),
(ii) of velocity $10\mathbf{k}$ (i.e. perpendicular to the x, y coordinate plane).

4   Since v is always small, the equation of motion parallel to the ground is very close to

$$\frac{du}{dt} = -ku^2.$$

Solve this with $u = 792$ at $x = 0$ and $u = 541$ at $x = 366$ to show that $k \approx 1.04 \times 10^{-3}$.

5   Is the solution to the shooting problem unique? If it is not, how could it be made unique?

25.2   THE SHOOTING METHOD OF NUMERICAL SOLUTION

The most obvious numerical method for solving a problem like the one I have set up is to guess an initial angle α, and then do a step-by-step integration of the equations, using the modified Euler method. This of course will not give a bullet path that passes through the target; if it is too high, guess a smaller value of α and try again, and so on (see Fig. 3). After a dozen 'shots' you should get a hit! This is

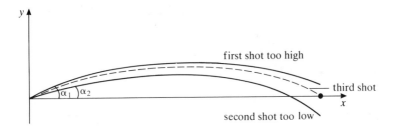

Figure 3. Three shots in the shooting method

known as the 'shooting' method of solving a problem like this one, which has conditions on the solution given at *both* ends of the interval of integration.

I set up such a method on my computer to solve for u and v, and also to solve the equations

$$dx/dt = u, \quad dy/dt = v.$$

Taking $g = 9.8 \, \mathrm{m \, s^{-2}}$ and with $\alpha = 0.004$ radians, my program stopped at the values

t	x	y	u	v
0.559	366.5	0.105	549.0	-2.44

My shot had been about 10 cm too high, so I tried again with $\alpha = 0.0039$. This gave

t	x	y	u	v
0.559	366.5	0.069	549.0	-2.50

Still too high! From these two failures I deduced from linear extrapolation that $\alpha = 0.0037$ would be almost correct

t	x	y	u	v
0.558	366.0	-0.002	549.3	-2.60

A perfect shot (well, 2 millimetres too low will do). The impact speed on the cockpit window is $(u^2 + v^2)^{1/2} = 549.3 \, \mathrm{m/s}$ at an angle $\tan^{-1} v/u = 0.00473$ radians $= 0.271$ degrees downwards. The path of the bullet has not been a symmetrical one, it comes down at a steeper angle than it went up.

The lack of symmetry of the path is more obvious over a longer range. With a range of 1000 m and an initial angle of 0.983° I found an angle at impact which was almost twice as large, at 1.876°. Figure 4 shows the lack of symmetry, with

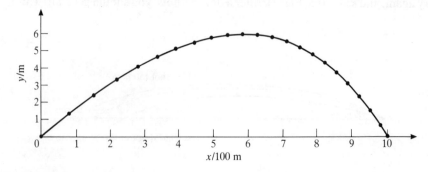

Figure 4. Bullet flight over 1000 m, using an integration time step of $h = 0.005 \, \mathrm{s}$

the maximum height just before $t = 1.00$ s when $x = 583.3$ m. The points on the graph are plotted at time steps of 0.1 s, except for the last point which is at $t = 2.17$ s. The speed on impact was only 291.5 m/s, quite a reduction.

<h3 style="text-align:center">Exercise 25B</h3>

1 Carry out a numerical solution of the problem

$$d^2y/dx^2 + kxy = 0, \quad y(2) = 0, \quad y(3) = 0,$$

to find the smallest value of k that gives a solution. Do it by introducing the variable $z = dy/dx$ so as to get two first order equations, and then use the improved Euler method starting with $z = 1$. (This is Airy's equation, and you cannot solve it other than by numerical methods.)

2 Solve the following problems analytically, if they have any solutions:
   (i) $d^2y/dx^2 + \pi^2 y = 0$, $y(0) = 0$, $y(1) = 0$.
   (ii) $d^2y/dx^2 + \pi^2 y = 0$, $y(0) = 0$, $y(1) = 1$.

3 Try solving the problems in question 2 numerically. Suppose that you had a problem of the same kind, that is either with an infinity of solutions or no solution, but where there was no exact solution to tell you what was going wrong. How would you be able to tell from the computer output?

4 The flight of a golf ball, if it has *no spin*, is rather similar mathematically to the flight of a bullet, except that the angles are much larger. My (ancient) golf balls each have mass 41 g and diameter 4.1 cm. A text on fluid dynamics assures me that the resistance force due to the motion through the air is about

$$0.22 \times \tfrac{1}{4}\pi d^2 \times \rho(u^2 + v^2),$$

where ρ, the air density, is about 1.2 kg/m^3. The distance to the far side of a lake is 130 m. Find two initial angles for the initial speed 75 m/s for which the ball lands 10 m beyond the water.

5 If the golf ball of question 4 has spin (about a horizontal axis perpendicular to the plane of the trajectory) there is an extra 'lift' force on the ball (if the spin is such as to make the top of the ball go backwards relative to the bottom) of size proportional to the spin ω and the speed $(u^2 + v^2)^{1/2}$. This force is perpendicular to the path. Naturally ω is not a constant, decreasing due to air friction at a rate proportional to ω (approximately). Set up three equations for u, v, ω.

25.3   AN APPROXIMATE ANALYTICAL SOLUTION

The equations given in Section 25.2 for the flight of a bullet cannot be solved exactly, which is why a numerical solution seemed a good idea. But as you saw, the angle of flight in the examples given was extremely small, and this will allow us to get a very good approximate solution without too much trouble.

Since the vertical velocity component v is always *very* much smaller in size than the horizontal component u, the equations can be approximated as follows. First we rewrite $(u^2 + v^2)^{1/2}$ as

$$(u^2 + v^2) = u(1 + v^2/u^2)^{1/2};$$

this is useful because $v^2/u^2 \ll 1$, and we can use a binomial approximation

$$u(1+v^2/u^2)^{1/2} \approx u(1+\tfrac{1}{2}v^2/u^2)$$

$$\approx u$$

since v^2/u^2 is extremely small, never exceeding 1.08×10^{-3} in the flight over 1 km. Thus the equations in Section 25.1 can be approximated as

$$\begin{cases} du/dt + ku^2 = 0 \\ dv/dt + kuv = -g. \end{cases}$$

The first of these is a separable equation for $u(t)$, which you can solve by the methods seen in Section 11.2. Once $u(t)$ has been found, the second equation is a linear equation for $v(t)$ with a simple integrating factor. Finally you can integrate u and v to find x and y in terms of t. This is all straightforward, so I shall leave it to the Exercise.

I intend to do something a little less obvious, though still not difficult. Notice that in the original problem of shooting at a target it is not really necessary to know the values of t at which the bullet reaches various points on its path. What I shall therefore do is to use x as parameter on the path rather than t. At the end of the calculation I shall expect to get the path as $y(x)$, rather than the pair of functions $y(t)$ and $x(t)$.

The method of doing this is to use the Chain Rule of calculus,

$$\frac{df}{dt} = \frac{dx}{dt}\frac{df}{dx}$$

taking first u and then v as f. This gives us

$$\begin{cases} \dfrac{du}{dt} = \dfrac{dx}{dt}\dfrac{du}{dx} = u\dfrac{du}{dx} \\ \dfrac{dv}{dt} = \dfrac{dx}{dt}\dfrac{dv}{dx} = u\dfrac{dv}{dx}. \end{cases}$$

The first of these equations has been seen a number of times before; the second is unfamiliar, but of exactly the same type. Now take these two forms for du/dt and dv/dt and substitute them into the two approximate equations of motion. You get (after division by u)

$$\begin{cases} du/dx + ku = 0 \\ dv/dx + kv = -g/u. \end{cases}$$

The first of these has the easy solution $u = u_0 e^{-kx}$, which leaves a linear equation to solve for v as a function of x. I shall leave this to the Exercise, and instead use the Chain Rule again:

$$v = \frac{dy}{dt} = \frac{dy}{dx}\frac{dx}{dt} = u\frac{dy}{dx}.$$

The equation for $v(x)$ can now be replaced by the following equation for $y(x)$

$$\frac{dv}{dx} = \frac{d}{dx}\left(u\frac{dy}{dx}\right) = -ku\frac{dy}{dx} - \frac{g}{u},$$

or

$$u\frac{d^2y}{dx^2} + \left(\frac{du}{dx} + ku\right)\frac{dy}{dx} = -\frac{g}{u}.$$

But we already know that the term in the brackets is zero, so we end up with the splendidly simple equation

$$d^2y/dx^2 = -g/u^2,$$

in which $u(x)$ is the easy function $u_0 e^{-kx}$. Consequently y can be found by two integrations to be

$$y = \left\{\frac{v_0}{u_0} + \frac{g}{2ku_0^2}\right\}x - \frac{g}{4k^2u_0^2}\{e^{2kx} - 1\},$$

where v_0/u_0 is the value of dy/dx when $x=0$.

I used this explicit equation for the path of the bullet to find the value of the initial angle needed to hit a target at $X = 1$ km and $Y=0$, where the initial speed is 792 m/s. In doing the calculation I replaced u_0^2 by 792^2 because this is what I had already done in approximating the equations; I found the initial angle to be $0.982°$, which is very close to the computed value of $0.983°$. That is, approximation here is as effective as numerical solution.

Exercise 25C

1   Solve the approximate equations

$$\begin{cases} \dfrac{du}{dt} + ku^2 = 0 \\[2mm] \dfrac{dv}{dt} + kuv = -g \end{cases}$$

to find first $u(t)$ and then $v(t)$.

2   Use your results from question 1 to show that

$$x(t) = k^{-1}\ln(1 + u_0 kt).$$

Check this answer by showing that for small values of t

$$x(t) \approx u_0 t - \tfrac{1}{2}u_0^2 kt^2,$$

and comparing this with the solution of

$$du/dt = -ku_0^2.$$

3   Find $y(t)$ from your result in question 1, and check it using the methods of question 2.

4   Use $x(t)$ and $y(t)$ to determine $y(x)$, by eliminating t.

5 Solve

$$\frac{dv}{dx} + kv = -(g/u_0)e^{kx}$$

to find $v(x)$. Then find the path $y(x)$ by solving

$$\frac{dy}{dx} = \frac{v(x)}{u(x)}.$$

6 Put $w = (u^2 + v^2)^{1/2}$, $\tan\theta = v/u$. By differentiation show (using the equations in the text) that

$$\frac{d\theta}{dx} = -\frac{g}{w^2};$$

show also that

$$\frac{1}{w}\frac{dw}{dx} = \tan\theta\frac{d\theta}{dx} - k.$$

Integrate this equation to find $\tan\theta$ and w in terms of x.

25.4 SUMMARY

A second order differential equation, or a pair of first order equations with boundary conditions at two points, can be solved numerically by the *shooting* method. In this method you *guess* a second boundary condition at one of the points, solve by a step-by-step method, and adjust the guess if you do not reach the correct value at the other point.

This method will not necessarily work if the conditions that are given lead to either *no* solution or a *non-unique* solution for the equation.

For the problem discussed in this chapter an adequate solution can be found by approximating the equations, rather than by solving them numerically. This may involve less work, and anyway is a check on the numerical work.

26

Boundary conditions at two points: discretisation

26.1 AN EXAMPLE

When the problem to be solved is linear in y, then it is often quite easy to convert it into a set of simultaneous equations, and solve them. The way that we achieve this is as follows.

We have seen earlier in the book that a good approximation to d^2y/dx^2 is given by

$$d^2y/dx^2 \approx \{y(x+h)-2y(x)+y(x-h)\}/h^2,$$

with error of size h^2. Similarly, the approximation

$$dy/dx \approx \{y(x+h)-y(x-h)\}/2h$$

also had error of size h^2. We shall use these two approximations to replace the derivatives in a differential equation, after having cut up the range of integration into equal parts (in much the same way as for Simpson's rule).

It will be easier to see what we are doing if we have a particular problem in mind, so I shall conduct the explanations in terms of the example

$$\begin{cases} d^2y/dx^2 + 2x\,dy/dx + 4y = 0, \\ y(0)=0, \quad y(1)=1. \end{cases}$$

In order to keep the number of equations not too large I shall take $h=0.2$: this will not give very accurate results, but we can always reduce the size of h when we have found out what is going on. With $h=0.2$ then, I am using the division points

$$x_0=0, \quad x_1=0.2, \quad x_2=0.4, \quad x_3=0.6, \quad x_4=0.8, \quad x_5=1.0.$$

The values of y at these points will be called

$$y_0, y_1, y_2, y_3, y_4, y_5.$$

I already know from the boundary conditions that

$$y_0=0, \quad y_5=1.$$

The derivative approximations are, for example,

$$\left(\frac{dy}{dx}\right)_{\text{at }x_2} \approx \frac{y_3-y_1}{2h};$$

and similarly

$$\left(\frac{d^2y}{dx^2}\right)_{\text{at }x_2} \approx \frac{y_3 - 2y_2 + y_1}{h^2}.$$

In general the approximations are

$$\left(\frac{dy}{dx}\right)_{x_r} \approx \frac{y_{r+1} - y_{r-1}}{2h}$$

and

$$\left(\frac{d^2y}{dx^2}\right)_{x_r} \approx \frac{y_{r+1} - 2y_r + y_{r-1}}{h^2},$$

for $r = 1, 2, 3$ and 4.

When these approximations are put into the differential equation, you get four equations (one each for $r = 1$ to 4), which can be summarised as

$$\frac{y_{r+1} - 2y_r + y_{r-1}}{h^2} + 2rh\frac{y_{r+1} - y_{r-1}}{2h} + 4y_r = 0.$$

In these equations you also need to use the boundary conditions

$$y_0 = 0, \quad y_5 = 1,$$

and $h = 0.2$ will be put in later.

Written out in detail, the equations are

$$\begin{cases} -2y_1 + y_2 + h^2(4y_1 + y_2) & = 0 \\ y_1 - 2y_2 + y_3 + h^2(-2y_1 + 4y_2 + 2y_3) = & 0 \\ y_2 - 2y_3 + y_4 + h^2(-3y_2 + 4y_3 + 3y_4) = & 0 \\ y_3 - 2y_4 + h^2(-4y_3 + 4y_4) & = -1 - 4h^2. \end{cases}$$

The term on the right of the last equation comes from $y_5 = 1$. These are the equations that we now have to solve for y_1, y_2, y_3, y_4.

I have not yet put $h = 0.2$ in them because later I shall need to refer to the smallness of the terms involving h.

Exercise 26A

1   Discretise the equations

(i) $\dfrac{d^2y}{dx^2} + xy = 0, \quad y(0) = 0, \quad y(1) = 1, \quad h = 0.2;$

(ii) $\dfrac{d^2y}{dx^2} + 2\dfrac{dy}{dx} + y = 1, \quad y(0) = 1, \quad y(1) = 0, \quad h = 0.2.$

2   Find the exact solution of the equation in (ii) above. Find also the solution of the difference equation you have found as its discretised approximation, by using the methods of Chapter 19. Find the values of the errors at the four intermediate points.

3   Discretise the equation

$$\frac{d^2y}{dx^2}+2x\frac{dy}{dx}=1,\quad y(0)=1,\quad y(1)=0,\quad h=0.1.$$

26.2   FIRST SOLUTION METHOD: GAUSS ELIMINATION

The equations in the last section were reduced to four linear equations in four unknowns, so Gauss elimination can be used. Taking the value of h^2 as 0.04 the equations are

$$\begin{pmatrix} -1.84 & 1.04 & 0 & 0 \\ 0.92 & -1.84 & 1.08 & 0 \\ 0 & 0.88 & -1.84 & 1.12 \\ 0 & 0 & 0.84 & -1.84 \end{pmatrix}\begin{pmatrix} y_1 \\ y_2 \\ y_3 \\ y_4 \end{pmatrix}=\begin{pmatrix} 0 \\ 0 \\ 0 \\ -1.16 \end{pmatrix}.$$

The elimination process is very simple, and doesn't really need a computer. I found that the equations reduced to

$$\begin{pmatrix} -1.84 & 1.04 & 0 & 0 \\ 0 & -1.32 & 1.08 & 0 \\ 0 & 0 & -1.12 & 1.12 \\ 0 & 0 & 0 & -1.00 \end{pmatrix}\begin{pmatrix} y_1 \\ y_2 \\ y_3 \\ y_4 \end{pmatrix}=\begin{pmatrix} 0 \\ 0 \\ 0 \\ -1.16 \end{pmatrix},$$

Consequently the (approximate) solution is given by

$$y_4=1.160,\quad y_3=1.160,\quad y_2=0.949,\quad y_1=0.536.$$

As you might expect, I chose an example where I knew the exact solution: it is

$$y=x\exp(1-x^2),$$

as you can check by substituting into the original equation. Thus the exact solution has the values (to three decimal places)

$$y_4=1.147,\quad y_3=1.138,\quad y_2=0.927,\quad y_1=0.504.$$

The errors are no bigger in magnitude than $h^2=0.04$, which is reasonable, as the errors in each equation were of this size at most, and there is no reason to suspect that the equations are ill-conditioned.

As a check on how the error varied with the size of h, I did the calculation again with $h=0.1$, which gave me nine equations to solve. I did it using a calculator, because the shape of the matrix of coefficients for the equations is so simple that very little work is involved (though you do have to be careful not to make slips). The largest error in my results, when compared with the true solution, was 0.0057 at $x=0.5$. This again is an error a little less than h^2.

Exercise 26B

1   Solve the two sets of equations you found in question 1 of Exercise 26A, using Gauss elimination.

2   Solve the equations for question 3 of Exercise 26A, using Gauss elimination.

26.3   TRIDIAGONAL GAUSS ELIMINATION

When you have done Exercise 26B you will appreciate how little work there is in the Gauss elimination scheme for the equations that arise for these two-point problems. This is because the matrix of coefficients is *tridiagonal*, i.e. the only non-zero entries occur along three lines from the top left hand corner of the matrix to the bottom right hand corner.

$$
\begin{pmatrix}
d_1 & u_1 & 0 & 0 & 0 & \dots & 0 & 0 \\
l_1 & d_2 & u_2 & 0 & 0 & \dots & 0 & 0 \\
0 & l_2 & d_3 & u_3 & 0 & \dots & 0 & 0 \\
0 & 0 & l_3 & d_4 & u_4 & \dots & 0 & 0 \\
& & & \dots & & & & \\
0 & 0 & 0 & 0 & 0 & \dots & d_{n-1} & u_{n-1} \\
0 & 0 & 0 & 0 & 0 & \dots & l_{n-1} & d_n
\end{pmatrix}
\begin{pmatrix}
y_1 \\ y_2 \\ y_3 \\ y_4 \\ \dots \\ y_{n-1} \\ y_n
\end{pmatrix}
=
\begin{pmatrix}
k_1 \\ k_2 \\ k_3 \\ k_4 \\ \dots \\ k_{n-1} \\ k_n
\end{pmatrix}.
$$

I have set out the equations in matrix form here, with the diagonal entries labelled as $d_1, d_2, \dots, d_n$. The non-zero entries above the diagonal ('upper') are called $u_1, u_2, \dots, u_{n-1}$, and the ones below the diagonal ('lower') are $l_1, l_2, \dots, l_{n-1}$. On the right hand side of the equation I have put constants k_1 to k_n; in the previous example only k_n was non-zero, but in general they will all be needed.

The first step of Gauss elimination uses a multiplier

$$m_1 = l_1/d_1.$$

Replacing row$_2$ by row$_2 - m_1 \times$ row$_1$ gives the new row$_2$ as

$$0 \quad d_2' \quad u_2 \quad 0 \quad 0 \quad \dots \quad 0 \quad k_2'$$

where

$$d_2' = d_2 - u_1 l_1/d_1, \quad k_2' = k_2 - k_1 l_1/d_1.$$

Continue this process, one row at a time, until all the lower elements have been replaced with zeros, and all the diagonal and constant elements have been replaced with dashed values in a similar fashion. This process is much shorter than the usual one for Gauss elimination, because there are so many zeros in the original matrix; it is therefore worth writing a new computer program for tridiagonal elimination.

In this program it is better not to interchange rows to get the largest possible pivots, because this spoils the simple structure of the matrix, and also small pivots do not often arise. Let us see why.

Suppose the equation is

$$d^2y/dx^2 + f(x)\,dy/dx + g(x)y = K(x),$$

where the functions f, g, K are given. Then if division points

$$x_0, x_1, x_2, \ldots, x_n$$

are used, with spacing h, the approximate form of the equation is

$$y_{r+1} - 2y_r + y_{r-1} + \tfrac{1}{2}hf_r(y_{r+1} - y_{r-1}) + h^2g_ry_r = h^2K_r.$$

In this I have put f_r for $f(x_r)$ and so on. Rearrange this to get

$$(1 - \tfrac{1}{2}hf_r)y_{r-1} + (-2 + h^2g_r)y_r + (1 + \tfrac{1}{2}hf_r)y_{r+1} = h^2K_r.$$

As long as the terms $\tfrac{1}{2}hf_r$, h^2g_r are small, the matrix of coefficients will be tridiagonal with entries approximately equal to -2 on the diagonal and 1 above and below it, and no small pivots look likely.

We shall return to whether there can be small pivots in awkward cases below: in fact there can, as we shall show from simple examples.

At the end of the reduction process the equations reach the following form.

$$
\begin{pmatrix}
d_1 & u_1 & 0 & 0 & 0 & \ldots & 0 & 0 \\
0 & d_2' & u_2 & 0 & 0 & \ldots & 0 & 0 \\
0 & 0 & d_3' & u_3 & 0 & \ldots & 0 & 0 \\
0 & 0 & 0 & d_4' & u_4 & \ldots & 0 & 0 \\
 & & & \ldots & & & & \\
0 & 0 & 0 & 0 & 0 & \ldots & d_{n-1}' & u_{n-1} \\
0 & 0 & 0 & 0 & 0 & \ldots & 0 & d_n'
\end{pmatrix}
\begin{pmatrix}
y_1 \\ y_2 \\ y_3 \\ y_4 \\ \ldots \\ y_{n-1} \\ y_n
\end{pmatrix}
=
\begin{pmatrix}
k_1 \\ k_2' \\ k_3' \\ k_4' \\ \ldots \\ k_{n-1}' \\ k_n'
\end{pmatrix}.
$$

After this the solution starts to appear; working from the bottom you find

$$\begin{cases} y_n = k_n'/d_n' \\ y_{n-1} = (k_{n-1}' - u_{n-1}y_n)/d_{n-1}' \end{cases}$$

and so on. Once again the process is made much shorter than in standard Gauss elimination because there are so many zeros in the matrix.

26.4   AN AWKWARD EXAMPLE

In the last section it was stated that the pivots are not usually small; it is as well to see from an example the sort of case in which you can get very small pivots, and therefore possibly inaccurate solutions from these sub-division methods.

Consider the equation

$$\begin{cases} d^2y/dx^2 + y &= 1 \\ y(0)=1, \quad y(\pi)=2. \end{cases}$$

The equation has constant coefficients and the right hand side is an easy function, so we can solve the equation by the methods described in Section 23.3. The auxiliary equation is

$$m^2 + 1 = 0$$

with solutions

$$m = \pm j.$$

Hence the complementary function is

$$A \sin x + B \cos x.$$

Since the right hand side is a constant, so is the particular solution, and substitution shows that a particular solution is $y = 1$. This gives us the general solution

$$y = A \sin x + B \cos x + 1.$$

Fitting $y(0) = 1$ shows that $B = 0$. The second condition is then

$$y(\pi) = 2 = A \sin \pi + 1 = 1.$$

There is no value of A which can make $2 = 1$, so this equation has *no* solution.
    What would happen if you tried to do it by the sub-division method? I used $h = \pi/8$ and seven equations, which reduced to

$$\begin{pmatrix} -1.8458 & 1 & 0 & 0 & 0 & 0 & 0 \\ 0 & -1.3040 & 1 & 0 & 0 & 0 & 0 \\ 0 & 0 & -1.0789 & 1 & 0 & 0 & 0 \\ 0 & 0 & -0 & -0.9189 & 1 & 0 & 0 \\ 0 & 0 & 0 & 0 & -0.7576 & 1 & 0 \\ 0 & 0 & 0 & 0 & 0 & -0.5258 & 1 \\ 0 & 0 & 0 & 0 & 0 & 0 & 0.0561 \end{pmatrix}$$

$$\times \begin{pmatrix} y_1 \\ y_2 \\ y_3 \\ y_4 \\ y_5 \\ y_6 \\ y_7 \end{pmatrix} = \begin{pmatrix} -0.8458 \\ -0.3040 \\ -0.0789 \\ 0.0811 \\ 0.2424 \\ 0.4742 \\ -0.9439 \end{pmatrix}.$$

Notice the small pivot in the last equation, leading to

$$y_7 = -16.83.$$

As before, small pivots and large solutions indicate that something is wrong in the problem. The numerical solution is 'trying' to give $0 \times y_7 = $ non-zero as the last equation, which would show that there is *no* solution to the equation. Errors (of size h^2) in the discretisation have prevented this from happening.

Let us try a geometrical explanation of why awkward examples like this arise. The underlying differential equation in this case was

$$d^2y/dx^2 + y = 0,$$

and I shall ask you to consider the solution with

$$y(a) = 0 \quad \text{and} \quad (dy/dx)_{x=a} > 0.$$

The differential equation can be rewritten as

$$\frac{d}{dx}\left(\frac{dy}{dx}\right) = -y,$$

so that when y is positive the slope dy/dx must be decreasing: this is illustrated in Fig. 1.

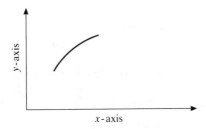

Figure 1. $\dfrac{d}{dx}\left(\dfrac{dy}{dx}\right) < 0$ for $y > 0$

Now since $dy/dx > 0$ at $x = a$ it follows that y is indeed positive just to the right of $x = a$, so that the solution curve has to start to bend back towards the x-axis. This will continue as long as y exceeds 0, and the solution curve will continue to bend round, and will finally cut the axis again, as in Fig. 2.

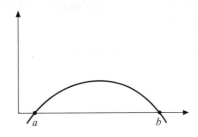

Figure 2. Positive curvature causes the solution to cut the x-axis at b

For the particular equation in question you can confirm all this by actually solving the equation and plotting the resulting function. But the line of argument still applies even if you cannot solve the equation, so long as you can show that the curvature is such as to make the curve recross the axis. Let the point where it recrosses be called $x=b$; then the equation with $y(b) \neq 0$ cannot have any solution, because we have just defined b so that $y(b)=0$. So there are many of these nasty examples around, and it may not be easy to spot whether you have one to deal with. One sort of test is to look at the size of the pivots. Another sort of test is to try and sketch the shape of the solution curve by discussing the curvature; a full discussion of methods like this is too difficult for us to cover here.

Exercise 26C

1   What happens if you try to solve

$$\begin{cases} \dfrac{d^2y}{dx^2} + y = 0 \\[2mm] y(0) = 1, \quad y(\pi) = 1 \end{cases}$$

by using a tridiagonal solution scheme? Use $h = \frac{1}{8}\pi$, for example.

2   Show that small pivots cannot arise in solving

$$\begin{cases} \dfrac{d^2y}{dx^2} = K(x) \\[2mm] y(0) = 0, \ y(1) = A \end{cases}$$

(i) by showing that the solution exists and is unique (if $K(x)$ is any reasonable given function);

(ii) by using a tridiagonal solution method.

3   What shape is the solution curve of

$$\begin{cases} d^2y/dx^2 - xy = 0 \\ y(1) = 0, \quad y(2) = 10? \end{cases}$$

Try (i) discussing curvature, (ii) the shooting method, (iii) a subdivision method.

26.5   THE INVERSE OF A TRIDIAGONAL MATRIX

The sequence of row operations in Gauss elimination can be written down in matrix form to give a reduction to *upper triangular* form. I intend to do this to the tridiagonal matrix with -2 on the main diagonal and 1 above and below the main diagonal, which I shall call the matrix $\mathbf{T}$. It does not take long to discover that

$$\begin{pmatrix} 1 & 0 & 0 & 0 \\ \frac{1}{2} & 1 & 0 & 0 \\ \frac{1}{3} & \frac{2}{3} & 1 & 0 \\ \frac{1}{4} & \frac{1}{2} & \frac{3}{4} & 1 \end{pmatrix} \begin{pmatrix} -2 & 1 & 0 & 0 \\ 1 & -2 & 1 & 0 \\ 0 & 1 & -2 & 1 \\ 0 & 0 & 1 & -2 \end{pmatrix} = \begin{pmatrix} -2 & 1 & 0 & 0 \\ 0 & -\frac{3}{2} & 1 & 0 \\ 0 & 0 & -\frac{4}{3} & 1 \\ 0 & 0 & 0 & -\frac{5}{4} \end{pmatrix}.$$

I shall write this matrix equation as

$$\mathbf{LT} = \mathbf{B}.$$

Gauss elimination is about row operations; you can do column operations in much the same way to reduce a matrix to *lower triangular* form, and I intend to do this to the *bidiagonal* matrix **B**. Again it does not take much trial and error to find that

$$
\begin{pmatrix}
-\frac{1}{2} & -\frac{1}{3} & -\frac{1}{4} & -\frac{1}{5} \\
0 & -\frac{2}{3} & -\frac{1}{2} & -\frac{2}{5} \\
0 & 0 & -\frac{3}{4} & -\frac{3}{5} \\
0 & 0 & 0 & -\frac{4}{5}
\end{pmatrix}
\begin{pmatrix}
-2 & 1 & 0 & 0 \\
0 & -\frac{3}{2} & 1 & 0 \\
0 & 0 & -\frac{4}{3} & 1 \\
0 & 0 & 0 & -\frac{5}{4}
\end{pmatrix}
=
\begin{pmatrix}
1 & 0 & 0 & 0 \\
0 & 1 & 0 & 0 \\
0 & 0 & 1 & 0 \\
0 & 0 & 0 & 1
\end{pmatrix},
$$

which I shall write in matrix form as

$$\mathbf{UB} = \mathbf{I}.$$

This piece of work has shown that

$$\mathbf{ULT} = \mathbf{I},$$

so that the inverse matrix for **T** must be just **UL**. That is, on multiplying the matrices together,

$$
\mathbf{T}^{-1} = \mathbf{UL} = -\frac{1}{5}
\begin{pmatrix}
4 & 3 & 2 & 1 \\
3 & 6 & 4 & 2 \\
2 & 4 & 6 & 3 \\
1 & 2 & 3 & 4
\end{pmatrix}.
$$

Notice that the inverse matrix has the same symmetries as **T** has, and check by multiplying that this inverse is correct, i.e. that $\mathbf{T}^{-1}\mathbf{T} = \mathbf{I}$.

What we have found here is that the tridiagonal matrix **T** can be *inverted* (i.e. have its inverse $\mathbf{T}^{-1}$ found) at no great cost in computer time, because it has so many zeros in it. This provides an alternative way of solving the tridiagonal set of equations resulting from a second order linear differential equation.

Let us now go back to the example in Section 26.1, and write the equations there in matrix form as

$$
\begin{pmatrix}
-2 & 1 & 0 & 0 \\
1 & -2 & 1 & 0 \\
0 & 1 & -2 & 1 \\
0 & 0 & 1 & -2
\end{pmatrix}
\begin{pmatrix}
y_1 \\ y_2 \\ y_3 \\ y_4
\end{pmatrix}
+ h^2
\begin{pmatrix}
4 & 1 & 0 & 0 \\
-2 & 4 & 2 & 0 \\
0 & -3 & 4 & 3 \\
0 & 0 & -4 & 4
\end{pmatrix}
\begin{pmatrix}
y_1 \\ y_2 \\ y_3 \\ y_4
\end{pmatrix}
=
\begin{pmatrix}
0 \\ 0 \\ 0 \\ -1-4h^2
\end{pmatrix}
$$

In abbreviated form these will be written as

$$\mathbf{Ty} + h^2\mathbf{Ay} = k.$$

Multiply this equation by the inverse matrix $\mathbf{T}^{-1}$:

$$\mathbf{y} + h^2\mathbf{T}^{-1}\mathbf{Ay} = \mathbf{T}^{-1}k,$$

which may be written as

$$\mathbf{y} = -h^2\mathbf{T}^{-1}\mathbf{A}\mathbf{y} + \mathbf{T}^{-1}\mathbf{k}.$$

In this equation the matrix product $\mathbf{T}^{-1}\mathbf{A}$ can be worked out, and it is

$$-\begin{pmatrix} 2 & 2 & 2 & 2 \\ 0 & 3 & 4 & 4 \\ 0 & 0 & 4 & 6 \\ 0 & 0 & 0 & 5 \end{pmatrix}.$$

Similarly

$$\mathbf{T}^{-1}\mathbf{k} = \frac{1+4h^2}{5}\begin{pmatrix} 1 \\ 2 \\ 3 \\ 4 \end{pmatrix}.$$

The equations are now in a form suitable for iterative solution (or indeed for direct solution as $\mathbf{T}^{-1}\mathbf{A}$ in this case is in upper triangular form) because the terms represented by $-h^2\mathbf{T}^{-1}\mathbf{A}$ will all be small provided h^2 is small. In the case we are discussing $h^2 = 0.04$, and the row-sum and column-sum tests show that an iterative solution will certainly converge. In fact the largest eigenvalue of $-h^2\mathbf{T}^{-1}\mathbf{A}$ is 0.2, so convergence is fairly rapid.

I wrote a short program to run the iteration and started from the initial vector $(0.2 \quad 0.4 \quad 0.6 \quad 0.8)^{\mathrm{T}}$, which seemed a fair guess, as the boundary conditions on the equation are $y(0) = 0$ and $y(1) = 1$. After six iterations the previous solution reappeared:

$$y_1 = 0.536, \quad y_2 = 0.949, \quad y_3 = 1.160, \quad y_4 = 1.160.$$

Exercise 26D

1 Guess the matrices $\mathbf{L}$ and $\mathbf{U}$ for the 9×9 tridiagonal matrix $\mathbf{T}$ with -2 on the diagonal and 1 above and below the diagonal. Check that your guesses are correct.

2 Calculate $\mathbf{T}^{-1}$ in the 9×9 case as the product of $\mathbf{U}$ and $\mathbf{L}$. Check your calculation
   (i)   by working out $\mathbf{T}^{-1}\mathbf{T}$,
   (ii) by comparing it with the 4×4 version,
   (iii) by looking at its symmetries.

3 Use your 9×9 version of $\mathbf{T}^{-1}$ to set up an iterative solution of the equation from Section 26.1. Determine whether it will converge, and if it will, use it to calculate the solution at $x = 0.1, 0.2, \dots, 0.9$.

26.6   COMPARISON OF METHODS

(a)   The shooting method

This works for non-linear as well as linear equations. The trouble with it is that you have to solve the same equation a number of times before you actually hit the target at the far end, and this can make it rather a long method, especially if the distance you have to integrate over is large.

(b) Sub-division methods

(i) Gauss elimination.
This method is wasteful of time and computer space.

(ii) Tridiagonal elimination.
This is an efficient method which does not use much storage space in the computer, but it can only be used on linear problems.

(iii) Inverse matrix and iteration.
Apparently not as good as (ii), but it can be used on equations with slightly non-linear terms in dy/dx and y, for which a reasonably good initial vector can be guessed – you will have to go to other books to find out about this. The method is not as slow as it looks, because $\mathbf{T}^{-1}$ does not need to be recalculated each time.

In conclusion, the method to use depends on the equation you have to solve.

Conclusion

Applied mathematics, in its wider sense, involves the creation of mathematical models of aspects of reality; and then the solution of these mathematical models by whatever means are most convenient. In this sense this book has been squarely about the area of applied mathematics that uses deterministic (i.e. non-random) models.

What I hope to have provided you with is the following.

(*a*) Some experience of how models are created, and tested by looking at what their solutions are like.

(*b*) Some experience of some of the standard models, for example those involved in mechanics, electric circuit theory, in population studies and in competition more generally.

(*c*) The easier methods of finding solution formulas for differential and difference equations, and the general structure of the solutions to linear problems.

(*d*) Some reasonably effective numerical methods for iteration, for integration, for solving differential equations, and for solving sets of (linear) algebraic equations.

(*e*) Some ideas on when, and why, numerical methods of solution may go badly wrong.

(*f*) An interesting context in which to do some mathematics, and feel the power that discussion of marks on a piece of paper can give in relation to real problems.

The application of mathematics has no end that I can see; new areas of interest will arise which will respond to mathematical modelling, and new mathematical methods will be created. On a smaller scale, the subjects discussed in this book are carried forward in textbooks and courses at the next level to extend the ideas in (*a*) to (*e*) above, as follows.

(i) Models of better quality, and models of other situations, can be formed when more advanced mathematics has been learned.

(ii) More involved solutions of more difficult differential equations can be found, for example by expressing solutions in terms of integrals or sums of functions.

(iii) Numerical methods of a better quality are available for differential equations.

(iv) Numerical methods can be found for the mathematics arising in (i).

(v) A more thorough analysis of the errors involved in numerical processes is available.

(vi) There are general theories of iteration, which apply to the various special cases we have seen.

Finally, there is a lot more enjoyment to be had in struggling with, and finally understanding, the higher levels of models and their mathematics.

Revision exercise E

1 Show that the finite difference approximation

$$y''(x) \approx \frac{1}{h^2}[y(x+h) - 2y(x) + y(x-h)]$$

is exact when $y(x)$ is a cubic polynomial in x.

The function $V(x)$ satisfies the differential equation $V'' = xV$ and the conditions $V(0) = 1$, $V(0.4) = 3$. Using the above approximation and a step length of $h = 0.1$, estimate the value of $V(0.2)$. [MEI 87]

2 Show that the two first-order equations

$$\frac{dz}{dx} = -\frac{2yz}{x}, \quad \frac{dy}{dx} = z$$

are equivalent to the second order equation

$$\frac{d^2y}{dx^2} + 2x^{-1}y\frac{dy}{dx} = 0.$$

The two given first order equations, with the conditions

$$z = 2, \quad y = 0, \quad \text{when} \quad x = 1$$

are solved numerically by the modified Euler (Heun) method, and the following results are found with a step length $h = 0.1$:

x	y	z
1.6	1.0185	1.2384

Calculate, using the same method and showing your working, the corresponding value for y when $x = 1.7$.

Three values of y were found at $x = 1.6$ by using three different step lengths h:

h	y
0.20	1.0277
0.15	1.0222
0.10	1.0185

Assuming that the error in the method is proportional to the *square* of the step length, use the method of least squares to determine a more accurate value of y at $x = 1.6$. [SMP 88]

3 (a) Find the general solution of the differential equation

$$x^4 \frac{d^2 y}{dx^2} + (2x^3 - x^2)\frac{dy}{dx} - 6y = 10,$$

by making the substitution $u = 1/x$.

(b) Find the general solution of the differential equation

$$1 + \left(\frac{dy}{dx}\right)^2 = y\frac{d^2 y}{dx^2}$$

by making the substitution $p = \dfrac{dy}{dx}$ and transforming it into an equation

involving y and p only.   [O&C 88]

4 Write down the general solution of the differential equation

$$\frac{d^2 y}{dt^2} + a\frac{dy}{dt} + by = 0$$

(a, b real) for each of the various cases which may arise.

(i) Show that, if for each solution $y = f(t)$ one can find a fixed k such that $|y| \leqslant k$ for all $t \geqslant 0$, then neither a nor b can be negative.

(ii) Prove that the equation

$$x^2 \frac{d^2 y}{dx^2} + 2x\frac{dy}{dx} - 6y = 0$$

(where $x > 0$) can be reduced to the above type by the substitution $x = e^t$ and hence solve the equation completely, given that $y = 2, \dfrac{dy}{dx} = 9$ when $x = 1$.

                                                                       [O&C 84]

5 (a) Solve the differential equation

$$\frac{d^2 y}{dx^2} = x,$$

given that $y = 0, \dfrac{dy}{dx} = 1$ when $x = 2$.

(b) Use the substitution $z = \dfrac{dy}{dx} + 2y$ to solve the differential equation

$$x\frac{d^2 y}{dx^2} + 2(x-1)\frac{dy}{dx} - 4y = 0,$$

subject to the boundary conditions $y = 1, \dfrac{dy}{dx} = -1$ when $x = 1$.

                                                                       [O&C 86]

6 The function f satisfies the equation

$$f(x)f'''(x) = f'(x)f''(x)$$

and also $f(0) = 1, f'(0) = 0$. Show that $f(x) = \cos 2x$ is *one* solution. Show that

$$d/dx\{f''(x)/f(x)\} = 0$$

for any solution (where $f(x)$ is not 0). Deduce a second order differential equation for $y = f(x)$. [SMP 84]

7 Show that the differential equation

$$y'' + p(x)y' + q(x)y = 0$$

can be transformed into

$$u'' + f(x)u = 0$$

by letting $y(x) = u(x)v(x)$ and making an appropriate choice of the function $v(x)$. Hence solve

$$y'' + 4xy' + (3 + 4x^2)y = 0,$$

where $y = 1$ and $y' = 2$ at $x = 0$. [MEI 86]

8 Find the differential equation having the general solution

$$y = Ax + Be^{2x},$$

where A, B are arbitrary constants. Show that this differential equation is of the form

$$(1 - 2x)\frac{d}{dx}\left(\frac{dy}{dx} + ly\right) + k\left(\frac{dy}{dx} + ly\right) = 0,$$

where k, l are constants to be determined.
  For these values of k, l, solve the differential equation

$$(1 - 2x)\frac{d}{dx}\left(\frac{dy}{dx} + ly\right) + k\left(\frac{dy}{dx} + ly\right) = (1 - 2x)^2,$$

given that $y = \dfrac{dy}{dx} = 1$ when $x = 0$. [O&C 89]

9 The function f is the solution of the equation

$$f''(x) - f(x) = 2e^x$$

with boundary values $f(0) = f'(0) = 0$. Find $f(x)$.
  In a numerical solution of this equation, the second derivative $f''(x)$ is replaced by

$$h^{-2}\{f(x) - 2f(x - h) + f(x - 2h)\},$$

where h is small, and the boundary values by $f(0) = f(h) = 0$. Moreover, only the points $x = rh$ are considered, for $r = 0, 1, 2, \ldots, n$, and n, h are chosen so that $nh = 1$; also $f(rh)$ is denoted by f_r. Show that the difference equation that results is

$$(1 - h^2)f_r - 2f_{r-1} + f_{r-2} = 2h^2 e^{rh}, \quad 2 \leqslant r \leqslant n.$$

  Find a particular solution of this equation in the form ke^{rh}, giving an expression for the constant k. Show that the general solution has the form

$$ke^{rh} + \frac{a}{(1 + h)^r} + \frac{b}{(1 - h)^r},$$

and write down two equations for the constants a and b (you need not solve these equations). [SMP 78]

10   When the two-point boundary value problem

$$\begin{cases} \dfrac{d^2 y}{dx^2} + 9y = 1 \\ y = 0 \quad \text{at } x = 0 \text{ and at } x = 1 \end{cases}$$

is discretised with step length $h = 0.2$, the resulting equations are

$$\begin{cases} y_0 = y_5 = 0 \\ \dfrac{y_{r-1} - 2y_r + y_{r+1}}{0.04} + 9y_r = 1, \quad 1 \leqslant r \leqslant 4. \end{cases}$$

However, since the problem is symmetric about $x = \frac{1}{2}$, it is clear that $y_1 = y_4$ and $y_2 = y_3$. Derive two equations for y_1 and y_2, and solve them, working to 4 d.p.

Solve the differential equation directly, and hence estimate the maximum possible error in the approximation used for $d^2 y/dx^2$.   [SMP 89]

11   Solve the differential equation

$$f''(x) + 4f'(x) + 4f(x) = x$$

with the conditions $f(1) = f'(1) = 0$.

Using the formulae

$$f'(x) \approx \frac{1}{2h}(f(x+h) - f(x-h))$$

$$f''(x) \approx \frac{1}{h^2}(f(x+h) - 2f(x) + f(x-h))$$

with $h = 1$ (even though it is *not* small), show that the above differential equation may be converted to the difference equation

$$3y_{n+1} + 2y_n - y_{n-1} = n, \quad n \geqslant 1,$$

where y_n denotes $f(n)$. Show that this difference equation has the solution

$$y_n = A(-1)^n + B(\tfrac{1}{3})^n + \tfrac{1}{4}(n-1).$$

Hence show that y_n is a good approximation to $f(n)$ for *large* values of n, in the sense that $y_n/f(n)$ is very close to 1.   [SMP 80]

Revision exercise F

1 ABCD and EFGH are two faces of a cube, as shown in the diagram. Each of the twelve edges is a wire of resistance $1\,\Omega$ and a voltage V is applied across AC. Draw a topologically equivalent *plane* network.

From the symmetries of the network show that there are only three different currents in the wires of the cube, and use Kirchhoff's laws to construct a 4×4 matrix **M** such that

$$\mathbf{M}\begin{pmatrix} i_1 \\ i_2 \\ i_3 \\ I \end{pmatrix} = \mathbf{E}$$

where i_3 is a current and **E** is a vector, both of which you must specify.

Calculate the resistance of the network.

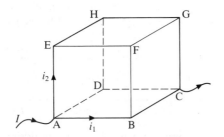

[SMP 82]

2 An emergency lighting system for a hotel uses a set of batteries of voltage E (volts) and resistance R (ohms). A total of N lights each of resistance $r\,\Omega$ is to be connected to it, in n parallel circuits each with N/n lights in series along it. The diagram illustrates the case $n = 3$, $N = 15$.

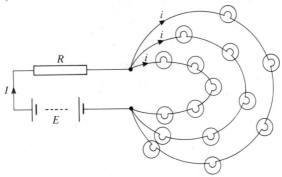

487

Determine the resistance of the whole system and hence show that the current through each light is (in amperes)

$$i = E/(nR + Nr/n).$$

The lighting system will be most efficient when the total power used in the lights is largest. Find the most efficient choice for n in the case

$$N = 60, \quad R = 2, \quad r = 3.$$ [SMP 88]

3

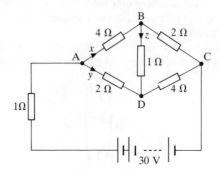

A battery of e.m.f. 30 V is connected through resistors as shown in the diagram, and the currents in branches AB, AD, BD are (respectively) x, y, z A. Obtain simultaneous equations for x, y, z and hence find the currents in *all* branches.

Calculate the rate at which energy is expended by the battery. [SMP 86]

4

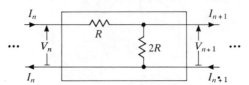

A long row of four terminal networks, each comprising a resistance R and a resistance $2R$ as shown in the diagram, are connected together. Show that the matrix relating

$$\begin{pmatrix} V_{n+1} \\ I_{n+1} \end{pmatrix} \quad \text{to} \quad \begin{pmatrix} V_n \\ I_n \end{pmatrix}$$

is

$$\begin{pmatrix} 1 & -R \\ -\frac{1}{2}R^{-1} & \frac{3}{2} \end{pmatrix}.$$

You are *given* that manipulation of the equations implied by this matrix leads to

$$V_{n+2} - \tfrac{5}{2}V_{n+1} + V_n = 0.$$

Find two independent solutions of this equation, and state which you expect to be relevant if the far end of the row (where n is large) is short circuited (so that the final voltage drop is 0). [SMP 84]

5

A d.c. electric circuit contains a sequence of N resistances R, connected in series, and a sequence of $N-1$ earthed wires each of resistance S, as shown in the diagram. A voltage V_0 is applied (at A_0) to the first resistance, and the Nth resistance is earthed (at A_N) as shown. Denote the currents through the resistances R by $I_1, I_2, ..., I_N$, and the voltages at the junctions $A_1, A_2, ..., A_{N-1}$ by $V_1, V_2, ..., V_{N-1}$. Write down two equations relating $V_n, V_{n+1}, I_n, I_{n+1}$ (for $n = 1, 2, ...$). Deduce that the voltages in the circuit satisfy the difference equation

$$V_{n+1} - 2\left(1 + \frac{R}{2S}\right)V_n + V_{n-1} = 0.$$

Writing

$$1 + \frac{R}{2S} = \tfrac{1}{2}(e^\lambda + e^{-\lambda}),$$

show that the roots of the auxiliary quadratic equation are e^λ, $e^{-\lambda}$. Deduce that the general solution of this difference equation can be written

$$V_n = A \cosh \lambda n + B \sinh \lambda n.$$

Hence show that the voltages are

$$V_n = V_0 \frac{\sinh \lambda(N-n)}{\sinh \lambda N}. \qquad \text{[SMP 86]}$$

6   The constants in the circuit in the diagram are $L = 0.2\,\mathrm{H}$, $R = 1\,\Omega$, $E_0 = 10\,\mathrm{V}$, and the frequency of the oscillating voltage is $50\,\mathrm{Hz}$. The switch is closed at time $t = 0$. Write down the impedance of the circuit. Calculate the current for $t > 0$.

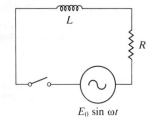

$E_0 \sin \omega t$ [SMP 81]

7

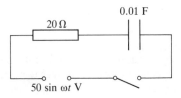

50 sin ωt V

A circuit driven by an applied e.m.f. $50 \sin \omega t$ V contains a resistor of $20\,\Omega$ and a capacitor of $0.01\,\mathrm{F}$. The capacitor is initially uncharged, and the switch (see the diagram) is then closed at time $t = 0$. Write down a differential equation for the charge Q on the capacitor and solve it for Q.   [SMP 87]

8

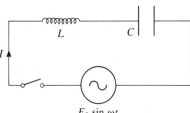

$E_0 \sin \omega t$

The circuit shown in the diagram is driven by an applied e.m.f. $E_0 \sin \omega t$, where $E_0 = 0.25$ V. It has an inductance $L = 0.25$ H in series with a capacitance $C = 1$ F. At time $t = 0$ the switch is closed and the capacitance is uncharged and no current is flowing. Write down a differential equation for the current I in the circuit and solve it for the cases

$$\text{(i) } \omega = 1 \, \text{s}^{-1}, \quad \text{(ii) } \omega = 2 \, \text{s}^{-1}.$$

[SMP 85]

9

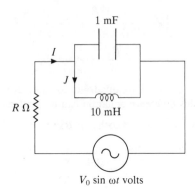

$$V_0 \sin \omega t \text{ volts}$$

Show that for the circuit in the diagram

$$\dot{J} = 10^5 (I - J),$$

where currents are in amperes, and set up a differential equation for J.

The frequency of the a.c. voltage is 50 Hz. Show that the amplitude of the steady state current through the inductance is approximatelty V_0/π provided R is not large, say $R < 1$.

[SMP 82]

10

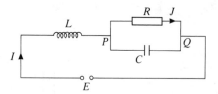

A fluctuating voltage E is applied to a circuit containing a load of resistance R and a coil of inductance L. A condensor of capacitance C is connected across the load. If V is the voltage across PQ explain why

$$\dot{V} = (I - J)/C,$$

where I is the current taken from the supply and J is the current supplied to the load (see diagram). Write down two further first order differential equations relating I, J and V. Deduce that

$$\ddot{J} + \frac{1}{RC}\dot{J} + \frac{1}{LC}J = E/RLC.$$

Solve this equation for J when $E = E_0 + \varepsilon \sin \omega t$ and $L = 0.1$ H, $C = 2.5$ F, $R = 0.1 \, \Omega$, $\omega = 2 \, \text{rad s}^{-1}$, given that $I = J = 0$ at time $t = 0$, and that E_0 and ε are constants.

[SMP 86]

11

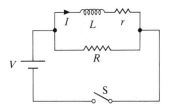

The switch S in the circuit shown is closed at time $t = 0$ when no currents are flowing. Calculate the current I through the inductance at later times.

You are given that $L = 2\,\text{H}$, $r = 20\,\Omega$ and $V = 10\,\text{V}$. The switch is opened again at $t = 0.23\,\text{s}$. Calculate I at this time, and sketch the graph of I for $0 < t < 1$.

[SMP 83]

12

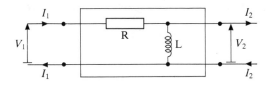

(a) If the complex voltages and currents in the circuit shown are

$$V_1 e^{j\omega t},\ V_2 e^{j\omega t},\ I_1 e^{j\omega t},\ I_2 e^{j\omega t},$$

use the Kirchhoff laws to derive the complex matrix $\mathbf{M}$ such that

$$\begin{pmatrix} V_2 \\ I_2 \end{pmatrix} = \mathbf{M} \begin{pmatrix} V_1 \\ I_1 \end{pmatrix}.$$

(b) If a long cable has resistance $r\,\Omega$ per unit length and inductance $l\,\text{H}$ per unit length between its two wires, it may be shown that (when an a.c. voltage is applied) the complex voltage $V e^{j\omega t}$ at any point of the cable satisfies

$$d^2 V / dx^2 = (jr/\omega l)V.$$

Show that an appropriate solution of this equation with amplitude V_0 at $x = 0$, and no voltage applied at the other end, is

$$V = V_0 \exp \left\{ -\left(\frac{1+j}{\sqrt{2}} \right) \left(\frac{r}{\omega l} \right)^{1/2} x \right\}.$$

[SMP 88]

13 Calculate, in the form $R + Sj$, the impedance between A and B when an e.m.f. of frequency $f\,\text{Hz}$ is applied across AB.

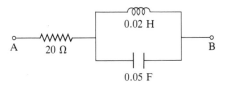

The frequency f may be varied. Calculate the frequency which gives the smallest amplitude of the current through AB.

[SMP 79]

14

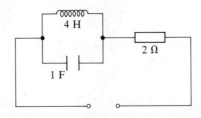

The a.c. circuit in the diagram is powered by a generator with frequency $\frac{1}{2}\omega/\pi$ Hz. The resistor has value $2\,\Omega$, the inductor is of $4\,\text{H}$ and the capacitor of $1\,\text{F}$. Write down the complex impedances of the three circuit elements and determine the total impedance of the circuit in the form $a+jb$.

The parameter ω can be varied from 0 to large values (although the amplitude of the voltage of the generator is fixed at V_0). Find the magnitude of the current I from the generator when $\omega=\frac{1}{2}$. Sketch a graph which shows how I varies with ω.

[SMP 86]

Projects and investigations III

III.1 Consider the example of water flow out of a pipe in Chapter 21. Results for the time to empty the pipe, using $g = 10$ and finding the numerical solution of two first order equations, were as follows for various area ratios S.

S	1	2	3	4	9
t	0.445	0.900	1.370	1.835	4.12

These are very close to S times the time to fall 1 metre freely under gravity, i.e. $S/\sqrt{5}$. Why?
  (a) Show that the answer should be exactly $1/\sqrt{5}$ when $S=1$, both from the equations and from direct argument.
  (b) Approximate the governing second order equation when S is large, by replacing $1-S^2$ by $-S^2$; then note from the computer runs that d^2X/dt^2 is rather smaller than other terms, so that this term too can reasonably be neglected. Solve the resulting simplified equation.
  (c) Try to explain the cases between $S=1$ and $S=9$.
  (d) Are there any circumstances in which the term in d^2X/dt^2 is important in the equation?

III.2 The pipe flow equation, either for X in Section 21.1 or for Y in Section 21.5(c), is invariant under change from t to $-t$. Make the transformation $T=\frac{1}{2}t^2$ in those equations and investigate whether the resulting equations are easier to deal with.
   Is there any advantage in putting $X=Z^2$ or $T=\frac{1}{2}t^2$ in the balloon flight equations?

III.3 The flight patterns of paper darts are well known, and can be modelled reasonably well.
  (a) If the resistance is proportional to speed (and along the path) and if the lift is also proportional to speed (and perpendicular to the path), then the equations ought to be

$$\begin{cases} du/dt = -au - bv \\ dv/dt = -av + bu - g. \end{cases}$$

  (b) Determine possible paths by putting $w=u+jv$, adding j times the second equation to the first, and integrating the resulting (complex) second order equation for $z=x+jy$.
  (c) Find some of the constants experimentally by observing straight line flight at steady speed.
  (d) Can you get loop-the-loop paths from these equations? Can you discuss stalling, and what happens thereafter?

(e) By adjusting the dart you can get flight which is not in the x, y-plane. How can you model this? Solve the equations that you produce, if possible, to show whether a flight returning to its starting place is possible.

III.4 There are a number of ways of modelling a child's swing.

(a) Let the speed at the lowest point on the forward down swing be u_n on the nth oscillation. Assume you would get a reduction to αu_n on the $(n+1)$th oscillation (with $0 < \alpha < 1$), due to friction; and assume a helper adds on an extra velocity β, by pushing.

(b) Much as in (a), but with some extra assumption to prevent u_n from becoming unbounded.

(c) Assume an equation of motion

$$ml\ddot{\theta} = -mg\sin\theta - mk\dot{\theta} + F(t),$$

the terms representing mass-acceleration, gravity acting along the path, resistance, and some external push. Try to solve this (by any means)

(i)   for $F(t)=0$, for use in models (a) or (b);
(ii) with $F(t)=F_0\cos\omega t$, for various ω;
(iii) for some more realistic model.

(d) Are there any modelling assumptions that ought to be changed to get realistic answers?

III.5 The zeros of $J_{1/2}(x)$ are easy to find, they are just at $x=n\pi$. Where are the zeros of $J_0(x)$ or $J_1(x)$? Solve Bessel's equation numerically. For $J_0(x)$ you should start from $J_0(0)=1$, and use a Taylor expansion to find a value to put in for $\left(\dfrac{1}{x}\dfrac{dy}{dx}\right)_{x=0}$. For $J_1(x)$ you should calculate $J_1(0.1)$ from a Taylor series, using $J_1(0)=0$ and $J_1'(0)=\tfrac{1}{2}$, and start the numerical solution from 0.1. You will need to go out as far as $x=20$ to see a pattern in the zeros.

Use your results also to calculate $x^{1/2}J_0(x)$ and $x^{1/2}J_1(x)$. Comment on what you find.

An alternative approach to numerical values for Bessel functions is to use

$$J_n(x) = \frac{1}{\pi}\int_0^\pi \cos(n\theta - x\sin\theta)\,d\theta,$$

and work with Simpson's rule.

III.6 The exact solution of the integral equation

$$y(x) = \int_0^1 y(t)e^{x+t}dt + x$$

must be $y(x)=Ae^x+x$, where $A=\displaystyle\int_0^1 y(t)e^t\,dt$. Substitute this form for y in the equation and you find $A=2$. Most integral equations have no exact solution, and many are solved numerically by discretising. Divide $[0,1]$ into strips of width 0.25, and write y_i for $y(0.25i)$, to get (by Simpson's rule)

$$\begin{cases} y_0 = \tfrac{1}{3}\times0.25\{y_0 + 4y_1e^{0.25} + 2y_2e^{0.5} + 4y_3e^{0.75} + y_4e\} + 0 \\ y_1 = \tfrac{1}{3}\times0.25\{y_0e^{0.25} + 4y_1e^{0.5} + 2y_2e^{0.75} + 4y_3e + y_4e^{1.25}\} + 0.25 \\ \ \vdots \\ y_4 = \tfrac{1}{3}\times0.25\{y_0e + 4y_1e^{1.25} + 2y_2e^{1.5} + 4y_3e^{1.75} + y_4e^2\} + 1. \end{cases}$$

These equations can then be solved to give $y_0, \ldots, y_4$. Carry out this procedure, and note the size of the errors.

There is no exact solution for

$$y(x) = \int_0^1 y(t) \cos(xt)\, dt + x.$$

Use the above method to find a numerical solution.

An alternative method is to use a Taylor approximation

$$\cos(xt) \approx 1 - \tfrac{1}{2}(xt)^2 + \tfrac{1}{24}(xt)^4 - \tfrac{1}{120}(xt^6),$$

and then find an exact solution of the resulting approximate equation. Compare the two methods.

III.7 Equations like $d^2x/dt^2 + 2k\, dx/dt + n^2 x = F_0 \cos \omega t$ show simple bounded oscillations in response to the (externally imposed) forcing term $F_0 \cos \omega t$. There are non-linear equations that give bounded non-zero motion without any external forcing.

One is the Van der Pol equation

$$d^2y/dt^2 - k(1 - y^2)\, dy/dt + y = 0.$$

It is hard to investigate this analytically, so try numerical solution, for various positive values of k (including large ones) and various starting values of y and dy/dt.

Another is the Lorenz set of equations

$$\begin{cases} dx/dt = 10(y - x) \\ dy/dt = xz + 28x - y \\ dz/dt = xy - \tfrac{8}{3}z. \end{cases}$$

These have the added problem of visualising the three dimensional solution. Again, try numerical solutions.

Both these equation sets arose from applications of mathematics – the Van der Pol equation from work on valves for electronic circuits, and the Lorenz equations in modelling weather systems.

Outline solutions to exercises in the text

Warning: It is unlikely that all the answers are correct. Numerical answers depend on the calculating device and method of calculation used.

Exercise 1A

1 $2^{30} \approx 1000$ million (not all distinct). Thirty generations ago is around 900 years; world population was probably less than this.

2 Paper $\approx 10^{-4}$ m thick, and $2^{50} \times 10^{-4} \approx 10^{11}$, so it would reach to about 10^8 km, well beyond the Moon (if you could do it).

3 3^{10} layers, each about 1.7×10^{-5} mm thick. Causes of inaccuracy include uneven rolling, effects at corners, and squeezing of fat into the dough; but roughly right for the first few rollings.

4 (i) $a_n = 2^{10-n}$. (ii) $u_n = 3$ for n odd, -3 for n even (which you could write as $3 \times (-1)^{n+1}$, or as $-3\cos(n\pi)$, or in other forms). (iii) $v_n = Ak^n$. (iv) $a_n = 2$ for n even, 0 for n odd (which can be written as $1 + (-1)^n$ or as $2\cos^2(\frac{1}{2}n\pi)$ or otherwise).

Exercise 1B

1 $\left(1 + \dfrac{1}{10 \times 365}\right)^{365} = 1.105\,16$, so 10.52%.

2 $(1 + 0.02)^{12} = 1.268\,24$, so 26.8%.

3 For a loan of £A you pay interest of $\frac{12}{100}A$. Suppose the APR is $100r\%$. In the first month you owe A, and the interest due is $rA/12$. In the second month you only owe $11A/12$, and interest at the constant rate r is $11rA/144$. Proceeding similarly you pay, in total, $78rA/144$. Hence $r = 22.15\%$ for the one year loan. Similarly for the five year loan it is 28.24%.

4 The value is £$10^{-2}(1 + 10^{-4})^{10^6} = £2.675 \times 10^{41}$.

Exercise 1C

1 (i) $u_{15} = 2.154\,49$, $10^{1/3} = 2.154\,434\,7$.
   (ii) $u_{15} = 1.618\,033\,912$, $\frac{1}{2} + \sqrt{(\frac{5}{4})} = 1.618\,033\,988$.
   (iii) An apparently random sequence is produced.

2 $a_{20} = 112\,700.55$. For $n \geqslant 32$, $1000 + n^2 > 2000$ and so a_n decreases, eventually passing near 2.

Exercise 1D

1   5.3, 7.1, 9.5, 12.7, 16.9, 22.4, 29.5, 38.4.

2   For example $a = 1.78, b = 1.1 \times 10^{-3}$. The steady level is given by $u_{n+1} = u_n$, so that here it is 709. There is no reason why the model should be a good predictor; it is merely descriptive.

3   The equation is $u_{n+1} = (1 - c)u_n + 1.8$ (measuring in millions).

4 $c = 0.075$ gives a reasonable fit.

Exercise 1E

1   (i) $u_{10} = 1.000\,000\,102$, $u_{20} = 1.000\,104\,858$, $u_{30} = 1.107\,374\,182$, $u_{40} = 110.951\,162\,8$, for all $u_0 = 1 + 10^{-10}$.
(ii) $u_{10} = 0.999\,999\,897\,6$, $u_{20} = 0.998\,895\,142\,4$, $u_{30} = 0.892\,625\,817\,6$, $u_{40} = -108.951\,162\,8$, all for $u_0 = 1 - 10^{-10}$.
Notice that the pairs of terms add almost exactly to 2.

2 $u_5 = 0.200\,000\,002\,4$, $u_{10} = 0.100\,036\,288$, $u_{13} = 0.124\,823\,236\,9$, $u_{15} = 8.784\,495\,787$. There is a large change in u_{15} from its previous value (for $u_0 = 1$) of $0.066\,666\,666\,67$.

3   (i)   The solution for $u_0 = 2$ is $u_n = 2$ for all n; with $u_0 = 2 + 10^{-10}$ you also find $u_n = 2$ for all n, so it is stable.
(ii)   You get the same values for $v_0 = 1$ and $v_0 = 1 + 10^{-10}$: stable.
(iii)   The exact solution is $w_n = 1/n$. If you start with $w_1 = 1 + 10^{-10}$ you find $w_9 = 0.273\,229\,767\,1$, $w_{10} = 13.231\,611\,14$, so it is unstable.

Exercise 2A

1 $a_{n+1} = a_{n-1}$

2 $u_{n+1} = au_n - bu_n^2$, first order.

Exercise 2B

3 $u_n = 0$ when $1.1^n = 6$; $n = 19$ (by trial) gives $u_n < 0$ for the first time. Using logarithms gives $n = 18.8$, so after 18 years and 10 months I have paid my debt, and a little extra.

4   The corresponding debt equation is

$$u_{n+1} = \left(1 + \frac{r}{100}\right)u_n - 12c, \quad u_0 = P.$$

Its solution is $u_n = \dfrac{1200c}{r} + \left(p - \dfrac{1200c}{r}\right)\left(1 + \dfrac{r}{100}\right)^n$, and so $c = \dfrac{rP}{1200}\left(\dfrac{R}{R-1}\right)$ where $R = \left(1 + \dfrac{r}{100}\right)^{20}$.

5 $(\frac{1}{15})^3 \approx 3 \times 10^{-4}$, so the term in k^n in the solution is negligible for $n \geqslant 3$ (unless d is large). This leaves

$$u_n \approx \frac{c}{1-k} = \frac{15c}{14}.$$

6 (i) First dose $2c$ reduces to $\frac{3}{2}c$; second dose raises this to $\frac{7}{2}c$, which reduces to $\frac{21}{8}c$, which is greater than $2.5c$; thereafter the concentration remains above $2.5c$.

(ii) First dose $3c$ reduces to $\frac{9}{4}c$; second dose raises this to $\frac{13}{4}c$, which reduces to $\frac{39}{16}c$; third dose raises this to $\frac{55}{16}c$, which reduces to $\frac{165}{64}c$, which is greater than $2.5c$. The first system gets to $2.5c$ more quickly.

Exercise 2C

1 (a) The equation is $u_{n+1} = 1.15u_n - 6$, $u_0 = 38$. The solution is $u_n = 40 - 2(1.15)^n$, giving $u_n = 0$ when $n = 21.4$ years.

(b) The equation is $u_{n+1} = 1.15u_n - 12c$, $u_0 = 38$. The solution is

$$u_n = 80c + (38 - 80c)(1.15)^n$$

and using $u_{15} = 0$ gives $c = £541.55$.

2 (a) Your fund builds up according to $u_{n+1} = \left(1 + \dfrac{r}{100}\right)u_n + 12c$, with $u_0 = 0$. The solution, at $n = 40$, gives the retirement fund as

$$\frac{1200c}{r}\left\{\left(1 + \frac{r}{100}\right)^{40} - 1\right\}.$$

(b) The fund now decreases according to

$$v_{n+1} = \left(1 + \frac{r}{100}\right)(v_n - 12A), \qquad v_0 = u_{40}.$$

The value of v_{15} must be zero and so

$$0 = \frac{(100 + r)12A}{r} + \left\{v_0 - \frac{(100 + r)12A}{r}\right\}\left(1 + \frac{r}{100}\right)^{15}.$$

This gives the relation between A and c as

$$A = \frac{100c}{100 + r} \times \frac{R^{15}(R^{40} - 1)}{R^{15} - 1}, \qquad R = 1 + \frac{r}{100}.$$

(c) Use $r = 3$, $A = 1000$ in this formula.

3 The complementary function is $C/n!$ and so the general solution is $u_n = n + 1 + C/n!$. Using $u_1 = 1$ gives $u_n = n + 1 - 1/n!$.

4 GS is $u_n = C(n-1)! + 1/n$. Use the value of u_9 to get $u_n = \dfrac{1}{n} - \dfrac{10^{-13}}{8!}(n-1)!$. The difference exceeds 1 when $(n-1)! > 8! \times 10^{13}$, which occurs for $n = 21$.

5 (a) CF is $C(-1)^n$; PS is $\frac{1}{2}$; GS is $u_n = \frac{1}{2} + C(-1)^n$.

(b) CF is $Dn!$; PS is $(n+1)!$; GS is $u_n = (n+1)! + Dn!$

Using $u_0 = 1$ gives $C = \frac{1}{2}$ and $D = 0$. Hence the values for u_{10} are (a) 1 and (b) 11!

6 $U_0 = 0 \Rightarrow U_1 = 0$ (using the equation) $\Rightarrow U_2 = 0$ and so on. Hence $V_n = W_n$ for all n.

Exercise 2D

1 (i) Try $an^2 + bn + c$ as PS. Substitution gives

$$n^2(a - 3a - 1) + n(2a + b - 3b) + (a + b + c - 3c) = 0.$$

Putting each coefficient equal to zero gives

$$a=-\tfrac{1}{2}, \quad b=-\tfrac{1}{2}, \quad c=-\tfrac{1}{2}.$$

(ii) Try pn^3+qn^2+rn as PS. Substitution and equating coefficients to zero leads to $p=\tfrac{1}{3}, q=-\tfrac{1}{2}, r=-\tfrac{5}{6}$.

2 (i) $u_0=1, u_1=3, u_2=10, u_3=34, u_4=111$, using the equation. The CF is $A\times 3^n$, so the GS is $A\times 3^n-\tfrac{1}{2}n^2-\tfrac{1}{2}n-\tfrac{1}{2}$, and fitting $u_0=1$ gives

$$u_n=\tfrac{1}{2}\{3^{n+1}-n^2-n-1\}.$$

This gives the same values.

(ii) $u_0=1, u_1=0, u_2=0, u_3=3, u_4=11$ using the equation. The CF is $A\times 1^n$, so the GS is $A+\tfrac{1}{3}n^3-\tfrac{1}{2}n^2-\tfrac{5}{6}n$, and fitting $u_0=1$ gives

$$u_n=\tfrac{1}{6}\{2n^3-3n^2-5n+6\}.$$

This gives the same values.

3 (i) Try ka^n; substitution gives

$$ka^{n+1}=-2ka^n+a^n$$

i.e. $(ka+2k)a^n=a^n$, for all n.

Since $a\neq-2$ this gives $k=\dfrac{1}{a+2}$, and the PS is

$$\frac{1}{a+2}a^n.$$

(ii) In this case $k2^n$ does not give a PS, and you need to try $Kn2^n$. Substitution gives $K=\tfrac{1}{2}$, so the PS is $n2^{n-1}$.

4 (i) CF is $A4^n$. For PS try $a\cos(\tfrac{1}{2}n\pi)+b\sin(\tfrac{1}{2}n\pi)$; substitution gives

$$(4a-b)\cos(\tfrac{1}{2}n\pi)+(a+4b+1)\sin(\tfrac{1}{2}n\pi)=0, \text{ for all } n,$$

and so $b=4a$ and $a+16a+1=0$, i.e. $a=-\tfrac{1}{17}, b=-\tfrac{4}{17}$; the PS is $-\{\cos(\tfrac{1}{2}n\pi)+4\sin(\tfrac{1}{2}n\pi)\}/17$. Hence the GS is

$$A4^n-\{\cos(\tfrac{1}{2}n\pi)+4\sin(\tfrac{1}{2}n\pi)\}/17,$$

and fitting $u_0=1$ gives $A=\tfrac{16}{17}$.

(ii) CF is $B1^n$. A similar PS calculation gives

$$-\tfrac{1}{2}\cos(\tfrac{1}{2}n\pi)+\tfrac{1}{2}\sin(\tfrac{1}{2}n\pi).$$

This gives the GS as $B-\tfrac{1}{2}\cos(\tfrac{1}{2}n\pi)+\tfrac{1}{2}\sin(\tfrac{1}{2}n\pi)$, and fitting $u_0=0$ leads to $B=\tfrac{1}{2}$.

5 (i) CF is $A\times 10^n$. PS is of form $an+b$, where

$$a(n+1)+b=10(an+b)-n,$$

so that $a=\tfrac{1}{9}, b=\tfrac{1}{81}$. That is, the GS is

$$A\times 10^n+\tfrac{1}{9}n+\tfrac{1}{81},$$

and fitting $u_0=\tfrac{1}{81}$ gives $A=0$.

(ii) Computer iteration gives $u_5=0.567\,901\,23, u_{10}=1.123, u_{15}=-44$. Calculator gives $u_5=0.567\,901, u_{10}=1.1, u_{12}=-22$.

(iii) This iteration is unstable; starting at $u_0=\tfrac{1}{81}+10^{-10}$ gives $u_{10}=2.123$, which is a large change.

The exact result $A=0$ only follows if u_0 is exactly $\frac{1}{81}$. No computer can hold $\frac{1}{81}$ exactly in decimal form, as it is an infinite (recurring) decimal. With $A\neq0$, $A\times10^n$ eventually becomes very large.

6   (i) The equation is $u_{n+1}=(1-c)u_n+1.2+0.05n$. Its CF is $A(1-c)^n$. Its PS has the form $an+b$ and substitution shows that $a=0.05/c$, $b=1.2/c-0.05/c^2$. Hence the GS is

$$u_n=A(1-c)^n+0.05n/c+1.2/c-0.05/c^2.$$

Fitting $u_0=13.95$ gives $A=13.95-1.2/c+0.05/c^2$.

(ii) The solution is $u_n=B2^n+1$, and in the two cases the required solutions are

$$u_n=10^{-10}\times2^n+1 \quad\text{and}\quad u_n=-10^{-10}\times2^n+1,$$

which sum to 2.

Exercise 3B

1   $\{(12\times255)/9\}/340=1$.

2   0.0003162, because $\sqrt{10}=3.16227\ldots$

3   $(0.0003\times0.0003)\times2=0$, $0.0003\times(0.0003\times2)=0.0000001$.

Exercise 3C

1   (i) 5.623×10^6, 5.624×10^6.   (ii) 9.513×10^5, 9.514×10^5.   (iii) 1.576×10^2, 1.576×10^2. (iv) -5.937×10^0, -5.938×10^0.   (v) -3.258×10^{-4}, -3.259×10^{-4}.

2   (i)   (a) Bracket chops to 41.31, division gives 6.425 on chopping.
          (b) Bracket rounds to 41.32, division gives 6.427 on rounding. Correct result is 6.4264299 …
    (ii) (a) Bracket gives 1.023, result is 6.422, using chopping.
          (b) Bracket gives 1.024, result is 6.429, using rounding.
    (iii) (a) 28.97   (b) 29.02 (5.7295 rounds to 5.730). 29.01380 … is the correct answer.

Exercise 3D

1   You should get the correct value $x=9$. But note that my computer gave different values for $(1.61514)^2$ and 1.61514×1.61514, even though it is supposed to work with 12 figures.

2   The equation for y reduces to $-1.33\times10^{-7}y=1.464\times10^{-6}$, giving y as quoted. This leads to $x=9.005323909$, by using the first of the two equations.

3   Taking largest and smallest values for the coefficients gives 64 possible lines, which will bound a solution region. It is easier to consider largest and smallest intercepts on the axes.

4   This is similar to question 3, except that the region is very large despite such small changes in the coefficients. For example taking the equations to be

$$\begin{cases} 2.281005x+1.615135y=2.76255 \\ 1.615145x+1.143655y=1.95611 \end{cases}$$

gives a (computer) solution $x=4.0325$, $y=-3.9846$.

5 Roots given are 10^6 and 0, because '$b^2 - 4ac$' $= 10^{12} - 4$, which is recorded as 10^{12}.

6 For Example 2 we have $P + Q = -100\,345$, $PQ = 1$. The first estimate of P is the machine result $p = -100\,345$. Using $PQ = 1$ gives the estimate $q = 1/p = -9.965\,618\,6 \times 10^{-6}$. Now use $P + Q = 100\,345$ to get a better estimate of P as

$$-100\,345 + 9.9656\ldots \times 10^{-6} = -100\,344.999\,990\ldots$$

Exercise 3E

1 (i) $\alpha = 193 - 191 = 2$, $\beta = 216 - 217 = -1$. (ii) absolute errors 2, 1. (iii) $|\alpha/A| = 0.0104$, $|\beta/B| = 0.004\,63$. (iv) For $a + b$: 1, 1, 2.445×10^{-3}. For $a - b$: 3, 3, 0.1304. For ab: 241, 241, 5.781×10^{-3}. For a/b: 0.013 33, 0.013 33, 0.014 92.

2 The errors I calculated were, multiplied by 10^7: 0.615, 1.04, 1.28, 1.33, 1.57, 1.97, 1.71, 1.66, 1.69, 1.89, 3.66, 7.01. The value for $r = 3000$ was calculated by addition as 144.770 081, and by the formula as 144.770 081 701.

3 $\alpha/A \geqslant \beta/B \Rightarrow \alpha B \geqslant \beta A$ for positive numbers. Add αA on each side to get (i). Divide by A to get (ii). Add instead βB on each side of $\alpha B \geqslant \beta A$ to get (iii). Then (ii) and (iii) together give (iv) from the definitions of r_a, r_{a+b}, r_b.

4 (ii) $(1 + \beta/B)(1 - \beta/B) = 1 - \beta^2/B^2 \approx 1$ if β/B is small; divide by $1 - \beta/B$ on both sides to get the result.

(iii) From (i) and (ii) you have

$$a/b \approx (A/B)(1 - \alpha/A)(1 + \beta/B)$$
$$\approx (A/B)(1 - \alpha/A + \beta/B)$$

if the product $r_a r_b = \alpha\beta/AB$ is very small.

Thus $\dfrac{A/B - a/b}{A/B} \approx \dfrac{\alpha}{A} - \dfrac{\beta}{B}$.

Now $r_{a/b} = \left| \dfrac{A/B - a/b}{A/B} \right| \approx \left| \dfrac{\alpha}{A} - \dfrac{\beta}{B} \right|$. But for any two numbers $|x - y| \leqslant |x| + |y|$, so $|\alpha/A - \beta/B| \leqslant r_a + r_b$.

5 $\sin a = \sin(A - \alpha) = \sin A \cos \alpha - \cos A \sin \alpha \approx \sin A - \alpha \cos A$. Hence $(\sin A - \sin a)/\sin A \approx \alpha \cot A$.

6 (i) Absolute error is $|\alpha/A - \alpha/a| = |\alpha/A| \times |(a - A)/A| \times |A/a|$

$$\approx r_a^2,$$

because $|A/a| \approx 1$.

(ii) Relative error is absolute error divided by r_a, and so it is $\approx r_a$, from (i).

Exercise 4A

1 (i) Negative at -2, positive at -1, negative to 4, positive at 5. Hence roots near -1.5, -0.5, 4.5. Intersections of cubic and quadratic confirm this. Graphics calculator gives roots at -1.4, -0.59, 4.95 approximately.

(ii) Negative at -5, positive from -4 to -1, zero at 0, negative to 4, positive at 5. Hence roots near $-4.5, 0, 4.5$. Intersections of $y = x$ and $y = \tan x$ are at $x = 0$, and near $x = \pm\frac{3}{2}\pi$, $x = \pm\frac{5}{2}\pi$ and so on. Graphics calculator confirms the values.

(iii) Positive at all integers from -6 to 6; negative at ± 7. Hence roots near ± 6.5. Graphics calculator in fact finds roots at $x = \pm 0.79$, ± 0.59, ± 7.1, ± 6.9, and every 2π thereafter.

2   Area of triangle $= a^2 \sin \frac{1}{2}\theta \cos \frac{1}{2}\theta$, where a is radius. Area of shaded area $= \frac{1}{2}a^2\theta - a^2 \sin \frac{1}{2}\theta \cos \frac{1}{2}\theta$. Equation to solve is $\sin\theta - \frac{1}{2}\theta = 0$, θ in radians. Solution is $\theta = 1.895$, radians, or 108.6 degrees.

3   Splitting as $y = x^2$ and $y = 10\cos x - 10$ is reasonable in this case. Usually signs will be a bad method. Graphics method will suggest a double root.

Exercise 4B

1   13 calculator iterations gave $1.127\,016\,653$. The staircase is between graphs of $y = x$ and $y = \frac{1}{10}x^2 + 1$, starting at $x = 1$.

2   25 computer iterations gave $0.414\,213\,562\,4$. The cobweb is between graphs of $y = x$ and $y = \frac{1}{2}(1 - x^2)$, starting at $x = 0.1$.

3   35 computer iterations of $x_{n+1} = \sqrt{(10x_n - 10)}$ starting at $x_0 = 9$ gave $8.872\,983\,346$.

4   Roots are near -4, 1, 3.
(i) $x_{n+1} = \{12(x_n - 1)\}^{1/3}$, $x_0 = 3$, gives the root $2.768\,734$.
(ii) $x_{n+1} = (x_n^3 + 12)/12$, $x_0 = 1$, gives the root $1.115\,749$.
(iii) $x_{n+1} = -\sqrt{(12 - 12/x_n)}$, $x_0 = -4$, gives the root $-3.884\,484$.

5   The root is near $x = -1.5$. The iteration $x_{n+1} = 1/x_n^3 - 1$ from $x_0 = -1.5$ gives the root $-1.380\,278$.

Exercise 4C

2   Solution is $x_n = \left(A - \dfrac{1}{1+\alpha} \right)(-\alpha)^n + \dfrac{1}{1+\alpha}$. If $|\alpha| > 1$, then $|x_n| \to \infty$; if $|\alpha| < 1$, $x_n \to \dfrac{1}{1+\alpha}$.

3   Take the iteration to be $x_{n+1} = F(x_n)$, with root X. Then the graph of $y = F(x)$ near X is almost a straight line of slope $F'(X)$. Then using the result of question 2, you get convergence for a straight line of slope between -1 and 1. Hence you expect convergence if $|F'(X)| < 1$ (and if you start the iteration near enough to X for the slope to be small enough at the starting point also).

Exercise 4D

1    $x_{10} = 0.811\,362\,435\,1$, $x_{11} = 0.826\,165\,090\,7$, $x_{12} = 0.812\,637\,820\,3$. Then the better estimate is $x_0^* = x_{10} - (x_{11} - x_{10})^2/(x_{12} - 2x_{11} + x_{10}) = 0.819\,096\,963\,3$.

2    $x_1^* = 0.819\,241\,668\,8$, $x_2^* = 0.819\,109\,185\,0$, $x_0^{**} = 0.819\,172\,506\,2$.

3    $K \approx -0.915\,541$, $x_n - X \approx K^n(x_0 - X)$. Estimate $x_0 - X$ by $x_0 - x_0^{**} = -0.019\,172\,5$. Thus you need $|K|^n \approx 10^{-10}/0.019\,172\,5$. Taking logarithms gives $n \approx (-10\ln 10 - \ln 0.019\,172\,5)/\ln|K| \approx 216$. (The root here is actually $0.819\,172\,513\,4$, so x_0^{**} is a good estimate.)

Exercise 5A

1   $x = -12.35$, $y = 73.93$, $z = -61.85$; 0, -5×10^{-3}, 6×10^{-3}.

2   (i) Replacing the second row needs 1 division, 3 multiplications and 2 subtractions. Replacing the third row needs the same. Replacing the third row again takes 1 division, 2 multiplications and 2 subtractions. Solving the equations in turn takes 3 divisions, 3 multiplications and 3 subtractions. The total for the 3×3 case is thus 6 divisions, 11 multiplications, 11 subtractions.
(ii) Similar counting for the 4×4 case shows 10, 26, 26 operations.
(iii) For the $n \times n$ case the same counting methods, and use of standard sums like Σr and Σr^2, give

$$\tfrac{1}{2}n(n+1), \quad \tfrac{1}{6}n(2n^2 + 3n - 5), \quad \tfrac{1}{6}n(2n^2 + 3n - 5)$$

operations.

3   (a) $x = -12.09$, $y = 72.45$, $z = -60.42$; 0, 0, 0.01.
(b) $x = -60.80$, $y = 72.88$, $z = -12.18$; 0, 0, 0.
(c) The answers in (a) are closest to the correct answers; yet the answers in (b) satisfy the equations best. The diagonal elements in the reduced form are
1 1, 0.0833, 0.0054   (product 4.498×10^{-4})
(a) 0.3333, -0.0417, 0.0331   (product 4.600×10^{-4})
(b) 0.2, 0.0208, 0.1099   (product 4.572×10^{-4}).
Division by a very small (and rounded) diagonal element will cause inaccuracy.

4   $-99.99\ldots$, $2279.99\ldots$, $-11\,339.99\ldots$, $19\,039.99\ldots$, $-10\,799.99\ldots$
(Clearly, the correct solution is -100, 2280, $-11\,340$, $19\,040$, $-10\,800$.) Residuals 0, -2×10^{-8}, -3×10^{-8}, -1×10^{-7}, -2×10^{-8}.

Exercise 5B

1   Question 1 in Exercise 5A used (almost) partial pivoting, yet did not give the best answer. See Section 5.4(c) for an explanation of why the result in question 3(a) was better.

2   (a) $x = 2\,666\,666.333$, $y = -3.999\,999$, $z = 1$. Product of pivots $= 3.8\ldots \times 10^{-13}$.
(b) Gauss elimination reduces the third equation to

$$(\tfrac{15}{13} - \tfrac{3}{7} \times 10^{-6} + 2 \times 10^{-12})z = \tfrac{15}{13} - \tfrac{3}{7} \times 10^{-6} + 6 \times 10^{-12}.$$

and terms in 10^{-12} are lost.
(c) $x = 2\,666\,666.162$, $y = -3.999\,998\,486$, $z = 1$.
(d) $x = 2.666\,666\,333$, $y = -3.999\,999$, $z = 1$ without interchange of columns; as in (c) with interchange.

3   (i) Two comparisons are needed in the first column, and later one comparison in the second column. When the largest element in a column has been found, at most a whole row must be interchanged, of 4 elements in the first case, and 3 in the second.
(ii) Similarly $3 + 2 + 1$ comparisons and three interchanges, of 5, 4, and 3 elements.
(iii) Similarly $\tfrac{1}{2}n(n-1)$ comparisons, and $\tfrac{1}{2}(n-1)(n+4)$ interchanges.

Exercise 5C

1   See the solution to Exercise 5A, question 3. In each case one or more pivots is much smaller in size than the coefficients in the equations. Similarly the product of the pivots

is small. The equations are somewhat ill-conditioned, and working with four figure arithmetic gives solutions whose second figure is not always accurate.

2 $x = -76.92\ldots$ $y = 110.34\ldots$ Changing a right hand side moves that line sideways a little, and so the point of intersection of the nearly parallel lines moves a long way. Algebraically, a change of 10^{-5} in the right hand side of the first equation is magnified by the small second pivot -5.834×10^{-8} in the Gauss elimination.

3   No. The three pivots (after partial pivoting) are 1, 1, $1 + 10^{-18}$; the product is $1 + 10^{-18}$.

4   Pivots are 0.9900, -0.4133, -0.4114, -0.8368 (with pivoting). Product of pivots $= -0.1409$. Not ill-conditioned. Note that *without* pivoting the second pivot is -1.01×10^{-4}.

5 $n = 1$, product $= 1$, not ill-conditioned
$n = 2$, product $= 0.0833\ldots$, hardly ill-conditioned
$n = 3$, product $= 4.6296 \times 10^{-4}$, rather ill-conditioned
$n = 4$, product $= -1.6534 \times 10^{-7}$, ill-conditioned
$n = 5$, product $= 3.7493 \times 10^{-12}$, very ill-conditioned.
For example, for 5, $x = 125.000$; while for 5.0005, $x = 125.315$, which is a $\frac{1}{4}$% change in x from $\frac{1}{100}$% change in the coefficient.

Exercise 5D

1 $x = -0.5702$, $y = 3.428$, $z = 8.571$; residuals small.
$3 \times$ first equation $+ 4 \times$ second equation $=$ third equation.
Pivots are 5, 0.0666, -7×10^{-5}; product -2.331×10^{-5}.

2 $x = 35.38$, $y = -212.3$, $z = 224.3$; residuals small.
$3 \times$ first $+ 4 \times$ second $-$ third gives $0 = -0.1$.
Pivots as in question 1.

Exercise 5E

1   Use $(A + \delta A)(X + \delta X) = b + \delta b$ together with $Ax = b$ and $\delta A \delta X \approx 0$.

2 $\det A = \pm$ product of pivots $=$ product of eigenvalues $= 0$. Hence one pivot (at least) must be zero.

Exercise 6A

1   Rearrange first as

$$\begin{cases} 2x + y = 2 \\ -x + 2y = 2 \end{cases},$$

and then as

$$\begin{cases} x = -\frac{1}{2}y + 1 \\ y = \frac{1}{2}x + 1, \end{cases}$$

for the Jacobi iteration

$$\begin{pmatrix} x \\ y \end{pmatrix}_{n+1} = \begin{pmatrix} 0 & -\frac{1}{2} \\ \frac{1}{2} & 0 \end{pmatrix}\begin{pmatrix} x \\ y \end{pmatrix}_n + \begin{pmatrix} 1 \\ 1 \end{pmatrix}, \quad \begin{pmatrix} x \\ y \end{pmatrix}_0 = \begin{pmatrix} 1 \\ 1 \end{pmatrix}.$$

Solution is $x = 0.4$, $y = 1.2$. After 21 iterations you get $x_{21} = 0.400\,000\,095$, $y_{21} = 1.200\,000\,29$; 20 iterations is not accurate enough.

2 (i) 52 (computer) iterations gave $x_{52} = -1.999\,999\,093$, $y_{52} = 1.499\,999\,2$, $z_{52} = 0.999\,999\,509$ (solution is -2, 1.5, 1).
(ii) Interchange second and third equations first. Then 29 iterations give $x_{29} = -0.223\,403\,6$, $y_{29} = 2.819\,148\,4$, $z_{29} = 3.053\,190\,9$.
Solution $-0.223\,404\,26$, $2.819\,148\,94$, $3.053\,191\,49$ to 8 d.p.

3 Interchange first and second equations to start. Extremely slow convergence from $(2.4, -\frac{16}{7}, 0)$. On the 16th iteration 1 s.f. is correct; on the 29th, 2 s.f. are correct. It seems as though about 15 iterations per s.f. are needed, so perhaps as many as 100 to 6 s.f. correct. In fact it takes 91 iterations.

4 Multiply out and all but two terms cancel out. $(A - I)^{-1}(A^n - I)$. If $A^n \to 0$ this tends to $(I - A)^{-1}$, and using the formula for x_n gives $x_n \to (I - A)^{-1}b$. Substitute $(I - A)^{-1}b$ into $x - Ax - b$ to get $(I - A)(I - A)^{-1}b - b$, equal to zero.

5 If D is diagonal then the equations have left hand sides $d_1 x, d_2 y, d_3 z, \ldots$ Divide each by the appropriate d to get to 'proper' Jacobi equations.

Exercise 6B

1 (i) $x_{32} = -1.999\,999\,2$, $y_{32} = 1.499\,999\,4$, $z_{32} = 0.999\,999\,7$.
(ii) $x_{16} = -0.223\,403\,8$, $y_{16} = 2.819\,148\,7$, $z_{16} = 3.053\,191\,3$.
As before, convergence has been almost twice as fast.

2 Interchange first and second equations as before. On 6th iteration 1 s.f. is fixed, on 8th iteration 2 s.f. are obtained. This looks like 3 iterations per s.f. (from a bad initial guess). In fact 15 iterations are needed to get 6 s.f. correct.

3 (i), (ii) When A is 4×4, each equation in either method takes 3 multiplications and 3 additions; hence 12 of each in total. When A is $n \times n$ you need $n(n-1)$ of each operation.
(a) Simple Gauss elimination takes (Exercise 5A, question 2) $\frac{2}{3}n^3 + \frac{3}{2}n^2 - \frac{7}{6}n$ operations in total, with an extra $n^2 + n - 2$ for pivoting.
(b) 20 steps of the Gauss–Seidel method takes $20(n^2 - n)$ operations, and may be more economical for larger values of n, e.g. $n = 30$.

4 In both cases convergence is extremely slow.

5 $I - L = \begin{pmatrix} 1 & 0 \\ q & 1 \end{pmatrix}$, $\quad U = \begin{pmatrix} 0 & -p \\ 0 & 0 \end{pmatrix}$, $\quad (I - L)^{-1} = \begin{pmatrix} 1 & 0 \\ -q & 1 \end{pmatrix}$.

Then $\quad (I - L)^{-1}U = \begin{pmatrix} 0 & -p \\ 0 & pq \end{pmatrix} = K$, say. By induction (or otherwise)

$K^n = \begin{pmatrix} 0 & -p(pq)^{n-1} \\ 0 & (pq)^n \end{pmatrix}$, and, since $|pq| < 1$, $(pq)^n \to 0$ as $n \to \infty$.

6   The Gauss elimination form of the equations is

$$\begin{cases} x+py=b \\ 0+(1-pq)y=c-qb. \end{cases}$$

If p and q are both very close to 1, the second pivot is very small and the equations are ill-conditioned. In question 5, $(pq)^n$ tends to zero extremely slowly as $n\to\infty$, so convergence is very slow for Gauss–Seidel iteration.

7   First, take terms corresponding to elements in **D** below the principal diagonal, into **L**, giving say **D'** and **L'**, where **D'** is now diagonal and **L'** lower triangular. Next, in each equation divide by the appropriate diagonal element in **D'**; this converts **D'** to **I**, and **L'**, **U** and **b** to (say) **L''**, **U'** and **b'**. The equations are now

$$(\mathbf{I}-\mathbf{L''})\mathbf{x}_{n+1}=\mathbf{U'}\mathbf{x}_n+\mathbf{b'},$$

which have the correct form.

Exercise 6C

1   $\varepsilon_0=\begin{pmatrix} -0.6 \\ 0.2 \end{pmatrix}$, $\varepsilon_1=\begin{pmatrix} -0.1 \\ -0.3 \end{pmatrix}$, $\varepsilon_2=\begin{pmatrix} 0.15 \\ -0.05 \end{pmatrix}$, $\varepsilon_3=\begin{pmatrix} 0.025 \\ 0.075 \end{pmatrix}$ and so on, using that the solution is $x=0.4$, $y=1.2$. The matrix **A** is

$$\begin{pmatrix} 0 & -\frac{1}{2} \\ \frac{1}{2} & 0 \end{pmatrix},$$

which gives a contraction of $\frac{1}{2}$ in length (in any direction) and a rotation of $\frac{1}{2}\pi$.

2   The lengths l_n, sums of moduli s_n and maximum modulus elements m_n for the error vectors ε_n in this case, are as follows.

n	1	2	3	4	5	6	7
l_n	1.322	0.7773	0.4677	0.2808	0.1702	0.1027	0.0622
s_n	2.217	1.313	0.8048	0.4830	0.2935	0.1771	0.1073
m_n	0.9960	0.5775	0.3077	0.1875	0.1049	0.0660	0.0392

n	8	9	10	20	30
l_n	0.0376	0.0228	0.0138	9.024×10^{-5}	5.971×10^{-7}
s_n	0.0648	0.0392	0.0237	1.556×10^{-4}	1.030×10^{-6}
m_n	0.0239	0.0144	0.0087	5.723×10^{-5}	3.800×10^{-7}

Each of these measures of the size of ε_n is tending to zero at about the same rate.

3 The equations are the Gauss–Seidel version of those done in Section 6.1.

n	0	1	2	3	4
ε_n	$\begin{pmatrix} 0.075 \\ 0.025 \\ 0.250 \end{pmatrix}$	$\begin{pmatrix} -0.125 \\ 0.125 \\ -0.050 \end{pmatrix}$	$\begin{pmatrix} 0.025 \\ -0.025 \\ 0.010 \end{pmatrix}$	$\begin{pmatrix} -0.005 \\ 0.005 \\ -0.002 \end{pmatrix}$	$\begin{pmatrix} 0.001 \\ -0.001 \\ 4 \times 10^{-4} \end{pmatrix}$
length	0.2622	0.1837	0.03674	7.348×10^{-3}	1.470×10^{-3}
ratio	–	0.7006	0.2	0.2	0.2

The rate-of-convergence constant $K = 0.2$ for all $n \geqslant 2$.

4 This is for the Jacobi version of the iteration, with $\|\varepsilon_n\|_1$ equal to the sum of the moduli of the components.

n	0	1	2	3	4	5
$\|\varepsilon_n\|_1$	0.350	0.330	0.067	0.0647	0.01485	0.012563

This norm also decreases, and in an irregular fashion.

5 $\varepsilon_n = X - x_n = X - (Ax_{n-1} + b)$. But $X = AX + b$, because X is the solution. Hence $\varepsilon_n = A(X - x_{n-1}) = A\varepsilon_{n-1}$. This similarly equals $A^2\varepsilon_{n-2}$, and so on.

Exercise 6D

1 (i) $A = \begin{pmatrix} 0 & -0.8 & -0.1 \\ -0.4 & 0 & 0.5 \\ -0.5 & -0.1 & 0 \end{pmatrix}$.

Row sums of moduli are 0.9, 0.9, 0.6. Hence convergence by Theorem 6.1.

(ii) $A = \begin{pmatrix} 0 & -\frac{3}{7} & -\frac{2}{7} \\ -\frac{1}{4} & 0 & \frac{1}{4} \\ -\frac{2}{5} & \frac{1}{5} & 0 \end{pmatrix}$.

Largest row sum of moduli is $\frac{5}{7}$. Hence convergence by Theorem 6.1.

Theorem 6.2 also shows convergence for these two examples; there is no need to use Theorem 6.3.

2 The matrix

$$A = \begin{pmatrix} 0 & -\frac{1}{5} & \frac{3}{5} \\ \frac{5}{7} & 0 & -\frac{3}{7} \\ 1 & -1 & 0 \end{pmatrix},$$

and neither of Theorems 6.1 and 6.2 gives any result.

The equation for the eigenvalues of $\mathbf{A}$ is $35\lambda^3 + 11\lambda + 12 = 0$, whose roots are approximately -0.55 and $0.28 \pm 0.74j$. All of these have modulus less than 1, so convergence is assured by Theorem 6.3(a).

3   In this case $(\mathbf{I} - \mathbf{L})^{-1}\mathbf{U} = \begin{pmatrix} 0 & -p \\ 0 & pq \end{pmatrix}$. The equation for the eigenvalues is $\lambda^2 - pq\lambda = 0$, so the eigenvalues are 0 and pq. Hence, by Theorem 6.3(b), convergence is assured if $|pq| < 1$.

4   $\mathbf{A}^2 = \mathbf{U}\mathbf{\Lambda}\mathbf{U}^{-1}\mathbf{U}\mathbf{\Lambda}\mathbf{U}^{-1} = \mathbf{U}\mathbf{\Lambda}^2\mathbf{U}^{-1}$; proceed by induction to $\mathbf{A}^n$. By direct multiplication, $\mathbf{\Lambda}$ is diagonal, with entries being the squares of those in $\mathbf{\Lambda}$. Thus if eigenvalues are all less than 1 in modulus, $\mathbf{\Lambda}^n \to \mathbf{0}$ as $n \to \infty$, and so $\mathbf{A}^n \to \mathbf{0}$ also. Hence by the result of Exercise 6C, question 5, the error $\mathbf{\varepsilon}_n \to \mathbf{0}$ and the iteration converges.

5   Any component in $\mathbf{\varepsilon}_{n+1}$ is a sum of terms arising from a row of $\mathbf{A}$ and the components of $\mathbf{\varepsilon}_n$, by matrix multiplication. Hence its modulus

$$\leqslant \Sigma |\text{element of row of } \mathbf{A}| \times | \text{ component of } \mathbf{\varepsilon}_n|$$

$$\leqslant \text{maximum} |\text{component of } \mathbf{\varepsilon}_n| \times \Sigma |\text{row of } \mathbf{A}|.$$

Therefore $\max |\text{component of } \mathbf{\varepsilon}_n| \leqslant C \max |\text{component of } \mathbf{\varepsilon}_n|$, and by induction

$$\max |\text{component of } \mathbf{\varepsilon}_n| \leqslant C^n \max |\text{component of } \mathbf{\varepsilon}_0|,$$

which $\to 0$ as $n \to \infty$ because $C < 1$. Hence the iteration converges.

6   The proof can be illustrated by the example when $\mathbf{A}$ is a 3×3 matrix. Take

$$\mathbf{\varepsilon}_{n+1} = \begin{pmatrix} u \\ v \\ w \end{pmatrix}, \quad \mathbf{A} = \begin{pmatrix} a & b & c \\ d & e & f \\ g & h & i \end{pmatrix}, \quad \mathbf{\varepsilon}_n = \begin{pmatrix} p \\ q \\ r \end{pmatrix}.$$

Then from the equations for u, v, w separately you get

$$\begin{cases} |u| \leqslant |a||p| + |b||q| + |c||r| \\ |v| \leqslant |d||p| + |e||q| + |f||r| \\ |w| \leqslant |g||p| + |h||q| + |i||r|; \end{cases}$$

and hence

$$|u| + |v| + |w| \leqslant K(|p| + |q| + |r|)$$

because of the condition on column sums of moduli. That is,

$$\|\mathbf{\varepsilon}_{n+1}\|_1 \leqslant K\|\mathbf{\varepsilon}_n\|_1 \leqslant K^2\|\mathbf{\varepsilon}_{n-1}\|_1 \leqslant \ldots \leqslant K^n\|\mathbf{\varepsilon}_1\|_1,$$

so that the error $\to 0$ as $n \to \infty$.

7   Very similar proofs apply for Gauss–Seidel iteration.

Exercise 6E

1   Iteration starting from $\mathbf{u}$ whose elements are 1 give the ratio $|\mathbf{A}^{n+1}\mathbf{u}|/|\mathbf{A}^n\mathbf{u}|$ to be 1.618 after seven iterations. The eigenvalue equation here is $\lambda^3 - 2\lambda - 1 = 0$ and use of a graphic calculator gives eigenvalues -1.05, -0.62, 1.62 approximately.

2   We need $x_{10} - (x_{15} - x_{10})^2/(x_{20} - 2x_{15} + x_{10}) = 1.0504$. Note that starting from x_{15} may be less accurate, as only 1 figure remains in the denominator.

3 $\mathbf{Au} = \alpha \mathbf{Ae}_1 + \ldots + \mu \mathbf{Ae}_m = \alpha \lambda_1 \mathbf{e}_1 + \ldots + \mu \lambda_m \mathbf{e}_m$ because the $\mathbf{e}$'s are eigenvectors. Repeat many times to get

$$\mathbf{A}^n \mathbf{u} = \lambda_1^n \left\{ \alpha \mathbf{e}_1 + \beta \left(\frac{\lambda_2}{\lambda_1} \right)^n \mathbf{e}_2 + \ldots \mu \left(\frac{\lambda_m}{\lambda_1} \right)^n \mathbf{e}_m \right\}.$$

If λ_1 is the largest modulus eigenvalue, this becomes nearly $\lambda_1^n \alpha \mathbf{e}_1$ for large values of n. Hence $|\mathbf{A}^{n+1} \mathbf{u}| / |\mathbf{A}^n \mathbf{u}| \to |\lambda_1|$.

Exercise 6F

1 Iteration only converges for $|a| < 0.354$, and is slow for $|a| > 0.1$. Looking at row (or column) sums of moduli would suggest Gauss elimination unless $|a| < 0.01$.

2 The largest row sum of moduli for the iteration matrix is 0.9, so elimination is to be preferred.

Exercise 6G

1

n	1	2	3	4	5	10	15	20	25
s_n	19.60	19.23	18.89	18.57	18.27	17.04	16.11	15.38	14.76
w_n	20.13	20.24	20.33	20.39	20.43	20.44	20.19	19.80	19.33
p_n	19.67	19.35	19.06	18.79	18.53	17.42	16.55	15.83	15.20

2

$$\begin{pmatrix} 0 & 0 & 6 \\ \frac{1}{3} & 0 & 0 \\ 0 & \frac{1}{2} & 0 \end{pmatrix}.$$

You can do this example by numerical iteration, *or* by working with eigenvalues and eigenvectors. Working numerically I found:

(i)

n	1	2	3
f_n	600	900	1000
s_n	333	200	300
t_n	150	167	100

(ii)

n	1	2
f_n	1200	1200
s_n	400	400
t_n	200	200

The results in (i) return every three years. Those in (ii) are constant.

3 At the end of their second year, beetles produce one egg each, at the end of their third year, three each. Half of the beetles survive into their second year, a third of these into their third year.

(i)

n	1	2	3	4	5	6	7	8	9	10
f_n	600	800	800	700	800	750	750	775	750	762
s_n	500	300	400	400	350	400	375	375	388	375
t_n	100	167	100	133	133	117	133	125	125	129

This iteration is converging rather slowly.

(ii)

n	1	2	3	4	5	6	7	8	9	10
f_n	1000	1000	1100	1000	1050	1050	1025	1050	1038	1038
s_n	600	500	500	550	500	525	525	512	525	519
t_n	133	200	167	167	183	167	175	175	171	175

The convergence appears to be towards a constant times 6, 3, 1.

4   This may be investigated by numerical experiment, or by looking at the corresponding equations (e.g. when $c = 0.1$ there is obviously a solution $s_n = w_n = p_n$, for all n), or from the eigenvalues. The eigenvalue equation here is

$$\lambda^3 - 2.7\lambda^2 + (2.43 - 0.1c)\lambda - (0.729 - 0.09c) = 0.$$

For $c = 0.1$ the eigenvalues are $1, 0.9, 0.8$ and (almost) any initial population will tend to a steady state.
   For $c = 0.11$ the eigenvalues are $0.8, 0.9$ approximately and 1.005.
   Since the largest eigenvalue exceeds 1, the population grows without bound.
   For $c = 0.09$ the corresponding results are $0.8, 0.9$ and 0.995, and the population eventually dies out.

5   The equation is $\lambda^3 - \frac{1}{2}\lambda - \frac{1}{2} = 0$ or $(\lambda - 1)(\lambda^2 + \lambda + \frac{1}{2}) = 0$. The roots are 1 and $-\frac{1}{2} \pm \frac{1}{2}j$ $\left(\text{modulus } \dfrac{1}{\sqrt{2}}\right)$. The eigenvector for $\lambda = 1$ is (any multiple of)

$$\begin{pmatrix} 6 \\ 3 \\ 1 \end{pmatrix},$$

and so the population should tend to some multiple of this vector, which is what was seen in question 3.

6   The eigenvalues are $1, -\frac{1}{2} \pm j\sqrt{3}/2$. All three have modulus 1, so the population does not die out or increase in the long run. Since $\lambda^3 = 1$ for the complex roots, the population will go through a cycle of length three years (if it is not steady). Since the eigenvector for $\lambda = 1$ is $\begin{pmatrix} 6 \\ 3 \\ 1 \end{pmatrix}$, a population in these ratios remains steady. These results were observed in question 2.

Exercise 7A

1   The following computer run results in this case.

n	0	20	40	60	80	100	120
u_n	5	19.6	64.0	136.7	185.3	201.4	205.4
v_n	195	180.8	137.9	67.6	20.5	4.9	1.1

2   The equations reduce to $u+v=\frac{1}{2}a$, $u+v=\frac{1}{2}b$. So you must have $a=b$, and then for any value of $u(<\frac{1}{2}a)$ the appropriate v is $\frac{1}{2}a-u$. You may check this with, e.g.

$$a=b=300 \text{ and (i) } u_0=100,\ v_0=50,\ \text{(ii)}\ u_0=10,\ v_0=140.$$

3   Since $a=b$, adding the equations gives

$$z_{n+1}=a-z_n.$$

The methods of Chapter 2 give

$$z_n=A(-1)^n+\tfrac{1}{2}a.$$

This agrees with the result of question 2 for the steady solution with $A=0$.

4   The equations in this case can be rewritten as

$$\begin{cases} \frac{1}{11}u_{n+1}=\dfrac{30u_n}{u_n+v_n}-\frac{1}{11}u_n \\[2mm] \frac{1}{10}v_{n+1}=\dfrac{30v_n}{u_n+v_n}-\frac{1}{10}v_n. \end{cases}$$

So if you put $w_n=\frac{1}{11}u_n+\frac{1}{10}v_n$ and add, you get $w_{n+1}=30-w_n$. The solution of this is $w_n=A(-1)^n+15$, which gives

$$10u_n+11v_n=B(-1)^n+1650;$$

the straight line graph results by using the initial values to find B. Substituting $v_n=150-10u_n/11$ gives the unpleasant equation

$$u_{n+1}=\frac{330u_n}{150+u_n/11}-u_n.$$

Exercise 7B

1   The steady state is $X=(bg+kh)/(ab-kl)$, $Y=(gl+ah)/(ab-kl)$. With the figures given $X\approx108.63$, $Y\approx79.80$. I started with $x_0=109$ and $y_0=80$ and found the following computer run.

n	0	1	2	3	4	5
x_n	109	109.2	110.1	111.7	115.5	123.9
y_n	80	80.5	81.2	83.0	86.8	95.4

It is clearly unstable. Algebraically, the eigenvalues of the matrix $\mathbf{A}$ relating $\begin{pmatrix} \delta_{n+1} \\ \varepsilon_{n+1} \end{pmatrix}$ to $\begin{pmatrix} \delta_n \\ \varepsilon_n \end{pmatrix}$, where $x_n = X + \delta_n$ and $y_n = Y + \varepsilon_n$, satisfy

$$\lambda^2 - (2 - a - b)\lambda + \{(1-a)(1-b) - kl\} = 0.$$

If $|(1-a)(1-b) - kl| > 1$ the product of the eigenvalues exceeds 1, and so at least one must have modulus > 1, and so there is instability. Small values of k and l (representing fear) lead to stability.

2   The equation is $w_{n+1} = 2.2w_n - 233$, which has solution

$$w_n = A(2.2)^n + 233/1.2.$$

Fitting the initial condition gives $w_n \approx 4.83(2.2)^n + 194.2$.

3   Starting from $x_0 = 115.9$ and $y_0 = 83.9$ I reached $x_9 = 3514$, $y_9 = 3481$ for 1918. The model must be inappropriate, as such large sums are a large part of the gross national product.

4   The equation is $z_{n+1} = 0.6z_n + 53$, with solution $z_n = A(0.6)^n + 53/0.4$. Fitting the initial value $z_0 = x_0 - y_0 = 32$ gives

$$z_n = x_n - y_n = -100.5(0.6)^n + 132.5.$$

But from question 2

$$w_n = x_n + y_n = 4.83(2.2)^n + 194.2.$$

Hence

$$\begin{cases} x_n = 2.42(2.2)^n - 50.2(0.6)^n + 163.4 \\ y_n = 2.42(2.2)^n + 50.2(0.6)^n + 30.8. \end{cases}$$

Exercise 7C

1   The three battles have different outcomes, using computer runs.
(i) On day 55, y_n is negative while $x_n = 32.3$.
(ii) The two forces remain in the ratio 2 to 1, while both decrease; by day 100, $x_n = 5.7$, $y_n = 2.8$.
(iii) On day 83, x_n is negative while $y_n = 7.8$.
In the formulas for x_n and y_n:
(i) $\frac{1}{2}x_0 - y_0 > 0$, so $y_n \to 0$; (ii) $\frac{1}{2}x_0 - y_0 = 0$, so $x_n = 2y_n$; (iii) $\frac{1}{2}x_0 - y_0 < 0$, so $x_n \to 0$.
Using the values:
(i) $y_n = 24.25(0.98)^n - 2.75(1.02)^n$, zero at $n = 54.7$ days;
(ii) $x_n = 43(0.98)^n$, $\to 0$ as n increases, but slowly;
(iii) $x_n = 41.5(0.98)^n - 1.5(1.02)^n$, zero at $n = 83.0$ days.

2   With $x_0 = 50$ I reached $x_{100} = 0.7$, $y_{100} = 390$.
With $x_0 = 100$ I reached $x_{100} = 4.2$, $y_{100} = 244$.

3   Not easily explained here. Wait until Chapter 18.

Exercise 7D

1   The steady state solution has $u_{n+1} = u_n = U$, say, and $v_n = v_{n+1} = V$. Solving the equations gives $U = (1-p)/q$, $V = (a-1)/b$.

With these initial values, which give a point near the steady state values, the point (u_n, v_n) spirals away, going round once every 14 steps, approximately.

2 Substitute $x_n = A^n x_0$, $x_{n+1} = A^{n+1} x_0$ into $x_{n+1} - A x_n$ to show it satisfies the equation; it also satisfies the initial value if we define $A^0 = I$.

3 (i) See Exercise 6D, question 4.
(ii) It follows that $A^n = U^{-1} \Lambda^n U$, and substituting in (i) gives $x_n = U^{-1} \Lambda^n U x_0$. Therefore $U x_n = \Lambda^n U x_0$. That is, for example,

(first row of $U \times$ column x_n) $= \lambda_1^n$ (first row of $U \times$ column of x_0),

and similarly for other rows of U. In other words we have

$$\begin{cases} \alpha x_n + \beta y_n = \lambda_1^n (\alpha x_0 + \beta y_0) \\ \gamma x_n + \delta y_n = \lambda_2^n (\gamma x_0 + \delta y_0) \end{cases}$$

from which you can solve for x_n and y_n, the components of x_n.

Exercise 8A

1967 is clearly exceptional, and is better excluded. Your line should pass close to the average point.

Exercise 8B

(i) We need to choose a to minimise

$$|\mathbf{r}|^2 = (y_1 - ax_1)^2 + (y_2 - ax_2)^2 + (y_3 - ax_3)^2.$$

Differentiate with respect to a, and put the derivative equal to zero for a stationary value. This gives

$$-2x_1(y_1 - ax_1) - 2x_2(y_2 - ax_2) - 2x_3(y_3 - ax_3) = 0$$

so that

$$a = \frac{\Sigma x_i y_i}{\Sigma x_i^2}, \ i \text{ running from 1 to 3 in summations.}$$

Check that this does give a minimum, using a second derivative.
(ii) $|\mathbf{r}|^2 = \Sigma y^2 - 2a\Sigma xy + a^2 \Sigma x^2$

$$= (\Sigma x^2)\{a - (\Sigma xy)/(\Sigma x^2)\}^2 + \Sigma y^2 - (\Sigma xy)^2/(\Sigma x^2).$$

Hence choose $a = (\Sigma xy)/(\Sigma x^2)$ as before for a least sum of squares of residuals.

Exercise 8C

1 (a) For all 15 innings $a = 27.49$, $b = 103.39$.
(b) Excluding 1967 $a = 27.55$, $b = 46.37$.
Notice the difference to b made by one extra 'exceptional' value.
(a) $|\mathbf{r}|^2 = 1\,015\,819$, $\sqrt{(|\mathbf{r}|^2/15)} = 260.2$.
(b) $|\mathbf{r}|^2 = 375\,898$, $\sqrt{(|\mathbf{r}|^2/14)} = 163.9$.

2 Use the nine pairs of marks to give $a = 0.9249$, $b = -7.7039$. The estimate is $94a + b = 79.24$. A measure of likely error is provided by $\sqrt{(|\mathbf{r}|^2/9)} = 8.34$, so the estimate for student 4 should be 'between 71 and 88'.

Exercise 8D

1 $H = \sum_{i=0}^{n-1} (p+iq) = np + q \sum_{0}^{n-1} i = np + \frac{1}{2}n(n-1)q.$

$B = n.$

$A = \sum_{0}^{n-1} (p+iq)^2 = np^2 + n(n-1)pq + q^2 \sum_{0}^{n-1} i^2 = np^2 + n(n-1)pq + \frac{1}{6}n(n-1)(2n-1)q^2.$

Hence $AB - H^2 = \frac{1}{12}n^2(n^2-1)q^2.$ Similarly $BG - HF = \frac{1}{12}qsn^2(n-1)^2.$

2 Using unrounded information and $a=0$, $b=0.412$ gives $|r|^2 = 1.306 \times 10^{-3}$, $\sqrt{(|r|^2/5)} = 0.016$; similarly $a = -1$, $b = 0.412$ gives $|r|^2 = 5.363 \times 10^{-3}$, $\sqrt{(|r|^2/5)} = 0.033$. As with other cases of ill-conditioning, the residuals are small.

Exercise 8E

1 (i) For all the years $\begin{cases} 14\,473a + 451b = 444\,529, \\ 451a + 15b = 13\,950. \end{cases}$

Excluding 1967 $\begin{cases} 13\,573a + 421b = 393\,499, \\ 421a + 14b = 12\,249. \end{cases}$

(ii) $\begin{cases} 95\,337a + 901b = 81\,236, \\ 901a + 9b = 764. \end{cases}$

2 $r^T r = y^T y - a x^T y - a y^T x + a^2 x^T x$. Differentiate with respect to a to find when the least value occurs, and note that $x^T y = y^T x$ for *any* vectors (of the same length). This gives $ax^T x = x^T y$ as the normal equation.

3 The matrix A has n rows and 2 columns if there are n data points. Hence $A^T A$ is the product of a $2 \times n$ matrix with an $n \times 2$ matrix, and so is a 2×2 matrix for any n. Similarly y has n entries, so $A^T y$ is a 2×1 matrix, i.e. a vector with 2 entries, for any n.

Exercise 8F

1 $a = 51.5$, $b = 697.0$; residuals 13, 8, 25, -22, -83, 15, 44. Residuals are positive, then negative, then positive. A better model would be a curve which was concave upwards, e.g. $y = Ax^c$.

2 (i) $a = \Sigma xy/\Sigma x^2 = 30.7$ for all years, 29.0 excluding 1967. Residuals for $a = 30.7$ are -103, -127, 780, 299, -151, -48, 246, -299, -36, 73, -168, -148, -3, 37, -263. The residual for 1967 is so large as to distort the whole calculation; it is 3 standard deviations away, and should probably be excluded. For $a = 29.0$ the residuals are -44, -71, 352, -122, 16, 292, -236, -12, 112, -122, -77, 53, 110, -209; there seems to be no particular organisation in them. $\sqrt{(|r|^2/14)} = 165$.

(ii) Excluding 1967, $s = 1.02$, $p = 26.3$. The residuals are -17, -45, 378, -102, 41, 294, -209, 6, 135, -97, -49, 79, 138, -183; and $\sqrt{(|r|^2/14)} = 164$.

To judge from the standard deviation $\sqrt{(|r|^2/14)}$, all the models are about equally good; but it does seem better to have no runs for no innings, so I prefer $y = 29.0x$.

3 $\begin{pmatrix} \Sigma x^2 & \Sigma x^3 \\ \Sigma x^3 & \Sigma x^4 \end{pmatrix} \begin{pmatrix} a \\ b \end{pmatrix} = \begin{pmatrix} \Sigma xy \\ \Sigma x^2 y \end{pmatrix}.$

For this example $\Sigma x^2 = 1164$, $\Sigma x^3 = 24\,786$, $\Sigma x^4 = 561\,348$, $\Sigma xy = 202\,800$, $\Sigma x^2 y = 4\,338\,314$.

Hence $a = 161.58$, $b = 0.5938$; the small coefficient of x^2 shows that the data form roughly a straight line. The residuals are -30, -33, -42, -45, -41, -25, 25; these are large, mainly because the model insists on going through $(0,0)$. The power law $135.2x^{1.084}$ is much the best fit of the models tried.

4   The normal equations are $\begin{cases} (\Sigma x^2)l + (\Sigma xy)m = \Sigma x \\ (\Sigma xy)l + (\Sigma y^2)m = \Sigma y \end{cases}$, where $\Sigma x = 901$, $\Sigma x^2 = 95\,337$, $\Sigma y = 764$, $\Sigma y^2 = 69\,876$, and $\Sigma xy = 81\,236$. These give $l = 0.014\,308$, $m = -0.005\,700\,5$. Rearranging gives the line $y = 2.51x - 175.42$, which is totally different from the one calculated with residuals parallel to the y-axis.

5   Least squares fitting of $y = ax + b + r$ is done using the normal equations $A^T A a = A^T y$. But the raw equations are $Aa + r = y$, and multiplying by A^T gives $A^T A a + A^T r = A^T y$. Combining these equations shows that $A^T r = 0$, which translates back to $\Sigma r = 0$, $\Sigma xr = 0$. But in Section 8.4(c) the equations are $Y = aX + b + R$; so in a similar fashion

$$\Sigma R = 0 \quad \text{and} \quad \Sigma XR = 0.$$

Now these residuals R are $\ln Y - a \ln X - b$, and the ones given are $y - cx^s = r$; there is no reason for $\Sigma r = 0$. Similarly, for $y = ax + bx^2$ you do not get $\Sigma r = 0$.

Exercise 8G

1 $\begin{pmatrix} \Sigma x^4 & \Sigma x^3 & \Sigma x^2 \\ \Sigma x^3 & \Sigma x^2 & \Sigma x \\ \Sigma x^2 & \Sigma x & n \end{pmatrix}$, $A^T y = \begin{pmatrix} \Sigma x^2 y \\ \Sigma xy \\ \Sigma y \end{pmatrix}.$

2 $\Sigma x = 21$, $\Sigma x^2 = 91$, $\Sigma x^3 = 441$, $\Sigma x^4 = 2275$, $\Sigma x^2 y = 86\,696$, $\Sigma xy = 19\,326$, $\Sigma y = 5961$, $n = 7$.

Solving the normal equations gives

$$a = 6.49, \; b = 12.61, \; c = 729.41.$$

Exercise 9A

1

Δf	$\Delta^2 f$	$\Delta^3 f$	$\Delta^4 f$	$\Delta^5 f$	$\Delta^6 f$	$\Delta^7 f$	$\Delta^8 f$
-19							
	-2						
-21		1					
	-1		-2				
-22		-1		5			
	-2		3		-10		
-24		2		-5		17	
	0		-2		7		-25
-24		0		2		-8	
	0		0		-1		11
-24		0		1		3	
	0		1		2		-6
-24		1		-1		-3	
	1		0		-1		9
-23		1		-2		6	
	2		-2		5		
-21		-1		3			
	1		1				
-20		0					
	1						
-19							

2

x	$f(x)$	Δf	$\Delta^2 f$	$\Delta^3 f$	$\Delta^4 f$
-4	-95				
		51			
-3	-44		-22		
		29		6	
-2	-15		-16		0
		13		6	
-1	-2		-10		0
		3		6	
0	1		-4		0
		-1		6	
1	0		2		0
		1		6	
2	1		8		0
		9		6	
3	10		14		
		23			
4	33				

All cubics with integer coefficients have $\Delta^4 f = 0$.

3	x	$f(x)$	Δf	$\Delta^2 f$	$\Delta^3 f$	$\Delta^4 f$
	$-\pi$	-49.745				
			26.561			
	$-\frac{3}{4}\pi$	-23.184		-11.188		
			15.373		2.908	
	$-\frac{1}{2}\pi$	-7.811		-8.280		-3×10^{-3}
			7.093		2.905	
	$-\frac{1}{4}\pi$	-0.718		-5.375		3×10^{-3}
			1.718		2.908	
	0	1.000		-2.467		-2×10^{-3}
			-0.749		2.906	
	$\frac{1}{4}\pi$	0.251		0.439		1×10^{-3}
			-0.310		2.907	
	$\frac{1}{2}\pi$	-0.059		3.346		1×10^{-3}
			3.036		2.908	
	$\frac{3}{4}\pi$	2.977		6.254		
			9.290			
	π	12.267				

Errors of maximum size $\frac{1}{2} \times 10^{-3}$ in $f(x)$ combine randomly to give larger errors in later columns.

4 (i) For example, $0.3980 - 2 \times 0.4554 + 0.5118 = -0.001$.

   (ii) $$\Delta J_0(x) = J_0(x+0.1) - J_0(x)$$
   $$\Delta J_0(x+0.1) = J_0(x+0.2) - J_0(x+0.1)$$
   and so $$\Delta^2 J_0(x) = J_0(x+0.2) - J_0(x+0.1) - \{J_0(x+0.1) - J_0(x)\}$$
   $$= J_0(x+0.2) - 2J_0(x+0.1) + J_0(x).$$

Exercise 9B

1 Better values of $\Delta^3 J_0$ are

$$42, 39, 42, 41, 42, 40, 36, 35.$$

Values of $\Delta^4 J_0$ are still almost entirely due to rounding, $\Delta^4 J_0 \approx 0$.

2	J_0	5118	4554	3980	3400	2818	2329	1666	1104	0555	0025	-0484
	Δ		-564	-574	-580	-582	-489	-663	-562	-549	-530	-509
	Δ^2			-10	-6	-2	93	-174	101	13	19	21
	Δ^3				4	4	95	-267	275	-88	6	2

3

n	1	2	3	4	5	6	7	8	9	10
r	1414	1715	1918	2051	2124	2208	2256	2294	2324	2348
Δr		301	203	133	73	84	48	38	30	24
Δ²r			-98	-70	-60	11	-36	-10	-8	-6
Δ³r				28	10	71	-47	26	2	2

The entries 71 and −47 are clearly wrong; 10 and 26 might be. This suggests an error in 2124; it should in fact be 2142, and the entries in the triangle should be

$$2142; \; 91, \, 66; \; -42, \, -25, \, -18; \; 28, \, 17, \, 7, \, 8.$$

Exercise 9C

1 The line is $y = -0.509x + 1.2241$, giving $y = 0$ at $x = 2.405$ and $y = -0.0983$ at $x = 2.6$. Correct values are 2.4048 and −0.0968. Using the more accurate values for $J_0(x)$ from Exercise 9B, question 1, gives $y = -0.5089x + 1.223\,87$; the root is then given as 2.4049 and $J_0(2.6) = -0.0993$. There is no gain in using more figures when you should be using a cubic to represent $J_0(x)$, and not a straight line.

2 Using the more accurate versions of J_0 and a Gauss elimination package I found the cubic interpolation formula

$$J_0(x) \approx 0.058\,333x^3 - 0.313x^2 - 0.025\,783x + 1.060\,870.$$

This gives $J_0(2.6) \approx -0.096\,785$, and $J_0(2.404\,823) \approx 0$. (The product of the pivots was 1.2×10^{-5}, rather small compared to the coefficients in the equations.)

3 Construct a difference table.

x	1	2	3	4	5	6
f	2000	1000	667	500	400	333
Δf		-1000	-333	-167	-100	-67
Δ²f			667	166	67	33
Δ³f				-501	-100	-34

There is no sign of a line of approximately zero differences, so you cannot expect to get a good interpolating polynomial. In fact $f(x) = 1/(5x)$.

4 The equations for a, b, c are

$$\begin{cases} a(p-q)^2 & +b(p-q) & +c = f \\ ap^2 & +bp & +c = g \\ a(p+q)^2 & +b(p+q) & +c = h. \end{cases}$$

If you take the first plus the third, minus twice the second, you find

$$a = (f - 2g + h)/(2q^2).$$

The occurrence of q^2 in the denominator shows ill-conditioning. Otherwise, Gauss elimination gives a product of pivots $-2q^3$.

Exercise 9D

1 Linear, $y = 0.812 + \dfrac{x - 1.1}{0.6} \times 1.219$.

   Quadratic, add $-\frac{1}{2} \times 0.284 \left(\dfrac{x - 1.1}{0.6} \right) \left(\dfrac{x - 1.7}{0.6} \right)$.

   Cubic, add $-\frac{1}{6} \times 0.929 \left(\dfrac{x - 1.1}{0.6} \right) \left(\dfrac{x - 1.7}{0.6} \right) \left(\dfrac{x - 2.3}{0.6} \right)$. Values 1.482, 1.517, 1.436.

2 The contribution from the second difference term is 0.068, which is of no real importance since $y \approx 47.54$. It is a small term because $\Delta^2 f$ is small for this function.

Exercise 10A

1 (i) The slope is $2 \cos 1$, by calculus; value 1.080 604 612.
   (ii) Values 0.994 727 5; 1.072 172 0, 1.079 762 9, 1.080 520 4, 1.080 595, 1.080 592, 1.080 52.
   (iii) Values 1.078 804 5, 1.080 586 6, 1.080 604 4, 1.080 604 6, 1.080 604 3, 1.080 605, 1.080 59.
   The first formula requires $h = 10^{-5}$ for the best accuracy, giving (almost) 6 d.p. correct. The second formula achieves 7 d.p. of accuracy at $h = 10^{-4}$. For very small h both formulas lose accuracy.

2 (i) The errors are 0.005 435, 5.5432×10^{-4}, 5.5543×10^{-5}, 5.5333×10^{-6} for $h = 10^{-n}$, $n = 1, 2, 3, 4$ for the first formula, and -1.236×10^{-4}, -1.234×10^{-6}, -1.167×10^{-8} for $n = 1, 2, 3$ for the second. The errors are (roughly) $0.054h$ and $-1.2 \times 10^{-2} h^2$.
   (ii) Errors 8.59×10^{-2}, 8.43×10^{-3}, 8.42×10^{-4}, 8.42×10^{-5} for $n = 1, 2, 3, 4$ for the first formula, i.e. $0.84h$; and 1.80×10^{-3}. 1.80×10^{-5}, 1.84×10^{-7} for $n = 1, 2, 3$ for the second, i.e. $0.18h^2$.

3 Solving three equations gives

$$A = \frac{1}{2h^2} \{f(a + h) - 2f(a) + f(a - h)\},$$

$$2Aa + B = \frac{1}{2h} \{f(a + h) - f(a - h)\}.$$

The second of these is the slope of the quadratic at $x = a$.

4 (i) $J_0'(2.25) \approx \dfrac{1}{0.3} \{J_0(2.4) - J_0(2.1)\} = -0.5470$, $h = 0.15$

   (ii) $J_0'(2.25) \approx \dfrac{1}{0.1} \{J_0(2.3) - J_0(2.2)\} = -0.5482$, $h = 0.05$

   (iii) Put $J_0'(2.25) = -0.5470 + (0.15)^2 A$ from (i) and $J_0'(2.25) = -0.5482 + (0.05)^2 A$ from (ii). Eliminate A to get $J_0'(2.25) = -0.5484$.

Exercise 10B

1   (i) $-2\sin 1 = -1.682\,941\,96$

(ii)

h	0.1	0.03	0.01	0.003
formula	$-1.681\,540$	$-1.682\,816$	$-1.682\,928$	$-1.682\,941$
error/h^2	$-0.140\,198$	$-0.140\,263$	$-0.140\,896$	$-0.144\,776$

(iii)

2   (i) $f''(3) = -\frac{1}{9}$

(ii)

h	0.1	0.03	0.01	0.003
formula	$-0.111\,172\,8$	$-0.111\,116\,7$	$-0.111\,111\,7$	$-0.111\,11$
error/h^2	$0.006\,177\,2$	$0.006\,160\,5$	$0.005\,888\,9$	$-0.123\,457$

(iii)

As far as $h = 0.01$ the formula gets more accurate as h decreases, and the error is about $0.006h^2$. When h gets too small there is too much loss of accuracy, due to subtraction of almost equal quantities in the formula; consequently error/h^2 increases in size.

3   To find $f'''(a)$ you might use $\dfrac{1}{2h}\{f''(a+h) - f''(a-h)\}$, with formulas for $f''(a+h)$ and $f''(a-h)$ being

$$f''(a \pm h) \approx \frac{1}{h^2}\{f(a \pm 2h) - 2f(a \pm h) + f(a)\}.$$

This gives

$$f'''(a) \approx \frac{1}{2h^3}\{f(a+2h) - 2f(a+h) + 2f(a-h) - f(a-2h)\}.$$

Alternatively, you could fit a cubic to the five points (for $x = a, a \pm h, a \pm 2h$) and hence get the same result.

The formulas:

(i) are symmetric about a for even derivatives.
(ii) are antisymmetric for odd derivatives,
(iii) are invariant under $h \mapsto -h$.
(iv) have denominators whose power of h is the order of the derivative.

4 $\dfrac{1}{2h}\{f(0+h) - f(0-h)\} = h^{-2/3}$,   as   an   estimate   of   '$f'(0) = \pm\infty$'.

$\dfrac{1}{h^2}\{f(0+h) - 2f(0) + f(0-h)\} = 0$ is no use because '$f'(0) = \pm\infty$'; and '$f''(0) = \pm\infty$'

also. The formulas in the text only apply to smooth functions, and $x^{1/3}$ is not smooth enough (sketch its graph).

5 $\Delta^2 f$, starting from $a - h$, is $f(a+h) - 2f(a) + f(a-h)$.

Exercise 10C

1   Estimate $0.232\,447$, value $e^{-1} - e^{-2} = 0.232\,544\ldots$

2   The sum is $he^{-(1+h/2)}(1-e^{-1})/(1-e^{-h})$. Hence the error is $(e^{-1}-e^{-2})\times$ $\left\{1-\dfrac{he^{-h/2}}{1-e^{-h}}\right\}$. If you use the approximation $e^x \approx 1+x+\frac{1}{2}x^2$ you get that the error is approximately

$$-\tfrac{1}{8}h^2(e^{-1}-e^{-2})/(1-\tfrac{1}{2}h).$$

3   The error in the trapezium rule will be proportional to h^2, so try $h=0.01$ for a start, then $h=0.005$. The values for these estimates are 1.570 788 and 1.570 794, which is 1.5708 to 4 d.p.

5   (a)

h	0.01	0.005	0.001
estimate	0.750 121 9	0.750 048 6	0.750 005 7

    (b)

h	0.01	0.005	0.001
estimate	0.749 405	0.749 764	0.749 972

$f(x)=x^{1/3}$ is a continuous curve, but its derivative at 0 is 'infinite'. The errors are approximately proportional to $h^{1/3}$. The rectangle method does not use the value where the curve is not smooth, so does a little better than you might expect.

Exercise 10D

1   Estimate is 0.232 544 287, error $-1.290\,39 \times 10^{-7}$. Far more accuracy for a slightly more complicated program.

2   Since the error is some constant times h^4, try $h=0.01$ and $h=0.02$. The estimates are both 1.570 796 327, which is correct to 9 d.p. The errors in this estimate are smaller than you might have expected; for the reason, see Chapter 17.

3   Sample values, with their errors, are

h	0.1	0.05	0.01	0.005
estimate	0.755 911 43	0.753 610 77	0.750 931 46	0.750 496 14
|error|	0.005 911 43	0.003 610 77	9.314×10^{-4}	4.9614×10^{-4}

The errors appear to be proportional to $h^{0.85}$, approximately.

Exercise 10E

1   (a) By rectangles: $h=0.01$, integral $=1.3095$
                             $h=0.001$, integral $=1.3187$.

(b) Split as $\displaystyle\int_0^1 x^{-1/3}(\cos x - 1)dx + \int_0^1 x^{-1/3}\,dx$, and use Simpson with $h=0.01$; integral $=1.321\,22$.

(c) Put $t^3 = x$ and use Simpson on $\displaystyle\int_0^1 3t\cos t^3\,dt$ with $h=0.01$; integral $=1.321\,223\,1$.

2 (a) Errors 352×10^{-8} for $h=0.1$, 26×10^{-8} for $h=0.05$. If you assume error $\approx Ah^k$, then these give $k \approx 3.8$.

(b) Errors 1173×10^{-8} for $h=0.01$, 188×10^{-8} for $h=0.05$, giving $k \approx 2.6$.

(c) $x^{-1/3}\{(1+x^3)^{1/2}-1\} \approx \frac{1}{2}x^{8/3}$ for small x, using the binomial expansion of $(1+x^3)^{1/2}$. Similarly $x^{-1/3}(\cos x - 1) \approx -\frac{1}{2}x^{5/3}$, using $\cos x \approx 1 - \frac{1}{2}x^2$. The former is 'smoother' at $x=0$, so the convergence is quicker.

3 Write $A = \displaystyle\int_0^{\pi/2} (\sin x)^{-1/2}\, dx + \int_{\pi/2}^{\pi} (\sin x)^{-1/2}\, dx = A_1 + A_2$ say.   Then

$A_1 = \displaystyle\int_0^{\pi/2} x^{-1/2}\, dx + \int_0^{\pi/2} \{(\sin x)^{-1/2} - x^{-1/2}\}\, dx$. In A_2 make the substitution

$x = \pi - t$ to get $A_2 = A_1$. Thus $A = 2A_1$. Now $\displaystyle\int_0^{\pi/2} \{(\sin x)^{-1/2} - x^{-1/2}\}\, dx$

$= 0.115\,429\,3$ using Simpson's rule with $h = \pi/200$, and so $A = 5.244\,115$.

4 $A = \displaystyle\int_0^1 x^{1/2}\, dx + \int_0^1 x^{1/2}(\cos x - 1)\, dx = 0.531\,203$, using Simpson and $h=0.02$ on the

second integral. To get the same accuracy using Simpson directly on $\displaystyle\int_0^1 x^{1/2}\cos x\, dx$

requires $h = 10^{-4}$.

5 (a) Use $x = t^2$ to get $\displaystyle\int_0^1 2t^2 \cos t^2\, dt$, for which Simpson is very efficient.

(b) Yes, with sufficient ingenuity. Put $\displaystyle\int_0^{\pi/2} (\sin x)^{-1}dx = \int_0^{\pi/4} (\sin x)^{-1/2}\, dx +$

$\displaystyle\int_{\pi/4}^{\pi/2} (\sin x)^{-1/2}\, dx$. In the first put $\sin x = t^2$ to get $\displaystyle\int_0^{2^{-1/4}} 2(1-t^4)^{-1/2}\, dt$, which can be

done by Simpson, as can the second integral.

Exercise 11A

1 (i) $y = \frac{1}{3}x^3 + \frac{2}{3}$, for all x.

(ii) $x = 2 - 2\cos t$, for all t.

(iii) This is $\dfrac{dy}{dx} = 1 - \dfrac{2}{x+2}$, $x \neq -2$; you need separate results for $x > -2$ and $x < -2$;

$$\begin{cases} y = x - 2\ln(x+2) + A \text{ for } x > -2, \\ y = x - 2\ln(-x-2) + B \text{ for } x < -2. \end{cases}$$

Note that A and B need not be equal.

(iv) $y = \frac{1}{2} + \displaystyle\int_0^x e^{-t^2}\, dt$.

2 The equation is $d^2y/dt^2 = -g$, y being height, with $dy/dt = 0$ and $y = h$ at $t = 0$. One integration gives $dy/dt = -gt + 0$; a second gives $y = -\frac{1}{2}gt^2 + h$.

Exercise 11B

1 (i) $y = \dfrac{1}{1 - \frac{1}{2}x^2}$, $-\sqrt{2} < x < \sqrt{2}$.

(ii) $y=e^{(1-x^3)/3}$, all x.

(iii) Since $v(0)=10$, the separation solution is best written as $-\displaystyle\int\frac{dv}{v^2-1}=\int dt$. This

integrates to give $\ln\left(\dfrac{v+1}{v-1}\right)=\ln\frac{11}{9}+2t$. Rearranging gives $v=(11e^{2t}+9)/(11e^{2t}-9)$,

for $t>\frac{1}{2}\ln\frac{9}{11}$.

(iv) $\displaystyle\int\left(\frac{1}{p}+\frac{1}{100-p}\right)dp=\int 10\,dt$, $p=\dfrac{300e^{10t}}{97+3e^{10t}}$,   all t.

(v) $y=\tan(x+\tan^{-1}a)$, $-\frac{1}{2}\pi<x+\tan^{-1}a<\frac{1}{2}\pi$.

2   (i) The hyperbolas $xy=c$, for different values of the constant c (positive, negative, or zero).

(ii) The hyperbolas $x^2-y^2=k$, for different values of k.

3   Suppose the hole has (cross sectional) area a; then water flows out of it at rate av; this causes the surface in the barrel (of area A, say) to fall at rate dh/dt, and so

$$-A\,dh/dt=av;$$

the negative sign comes because dh/dt is positive when h increases. Thus $dh/dt=-av/A$; but $v=ch^{1/2}$ is given, so that

$$dh/dt=-kh^{1/2}.$$

The solution is $h=(1-\frac{1}{2}kt)^2$, for $0<t<2/k$.

4   The solution is $p=p_0e^{-rt}$ for some constant p_0, which is the initial number of atoms.

Half are left when $\frac{1}{2}=e^{-rt}$. The half-life is therefore $\dfrac{1}{r}\ln 2$.

5   Measure positive speed as downwards. Then positive acceleration is downwards, and the resistance acts upwards in the negative direction, so that $dv/dt=g-kv^2$. The separation solution is

$$\int\frac{dv}{g/k-v^2}=\int k\,dt$$

(writing it this way because v starts small, i.e. less than $(g/k)^{1/2}$). This integrates as

$$\ln\left\{\frac{(g/k)^{1/2}+v}{(g/k)^{1/2}-v}\right\}=2(kg)^{1/2}t+C.$$

Take $t=0$ to be when he starts with $v=0$, so that $C=0$. Then

$$v=\left(\frac{g}{k}\right)^{1/2}\frac{e^{2(kg)^{1/2}t}-1}{e^{2(kg)^{1/2}t}+1}$$

which tends to $(g/k)^{1/2}$ as $t\to\infty$.

6   The solution reduces to

$$p=\frac{3.9ae^{at}}{a+3.9b(e^{at}-1)}.$$

Choose a and b by trial and error to match up to the data in Chapter 1, using 10 years as the unit of time. You get quite a good fit with $a=0.318$, $b=0.0017$.

Exercise 12A

1 $\int \dfrac{dy}{4-3y} = \int dx$ gives $-\frac{1}{3}\ln(4-3y) = x + C$. Note that since $y=1$ is given we do not want $\ln(3y-4)$ here. Fitting the initial value gives $C=0$. Rearrange to get $y = \frac{4}{3} - \frac{1}{3}e^{-3x}$, for all x.

2 (i) CF Ae^{3x}; try PS ae^x, and by substitution $a = -2$. Use the boundary condition on $Ae^{3x} - 2e^x$ to find $A=4$, so $y = 4e^{3x} - 2e^x$, for all x.
(ii) CF $Ae^{x/2}$; PS $ax+b$ where $a=12$ and $b=-16$; $A=4e^{1/2}$ and so $y = 4e^{(1-x)/2} + 12x - 16$.
(iii) CF Ae^{-t}; PS ae^{2t} where $a=1$; $A=-1$, so $x = e^{2t} - e^{-t}$.
(iv) CF Ae^{-4t}; PS $a\sin t + b\cos t$, where $a = \frac{5}{17}$, $b = -\frac{14}{17}$; general solution (no boundary condition given) is $Ae^{-4t} + \frac{5}{17}\sin t - \frac{14}{17}\cos t$.
(v) CF Ae^t. The PS here needs a term in e^{2t}; it cannot have a term in e^t alone, as that is in the CF, so the PS is $ae^{2t} + bte^t$, where $a=3$ and $b=-2$ are found by substitution.
(vi) CF Ae^{-3x}. The PS comes in two parts, one for x^2 and one for $\cos x$, so it has the form

$$ax^2 + bx + c + \alpha\cos x + \beta\sin x.$$

Substitution, and matching up the various terms, gives $a = \frac{1}{3}, b = -\frac{2}{9}, c = \frac{2}{27}, \alpha = \frac{3}{10}$, $\beta = \frac{1}{10}$. Finally, fitting the boundary condition gives $A = -\frac{11}{270}$ and so

$$y = -\tfrac{11}{270}e^{-3x} + \tfrac{1}{3}x^2 - \tfrac{2}{9}x + \tfrac{2}{27} + \tfrac{3}{10}\cos x + \tfrac{1}{10}\sin x.$$

3 Try $ax^2 + bx + c$ and get $a=1$, $b=1$, $c=1$. The CF is Ax^{-2}. The solution is $y = -3x^{-2} + x^2 + x + 1$.

Exercise 12B

1 (i) The equation may be written as

$$\frac{d}{dx}\{ye^{-3x}\} = 4e^x e^{-3x} = 4e^{-2x}.$$

Hence $ye^{-3x} = -2e^{-2x} + A$ and $y = -2e^x + Ae^{3x}$. You find A from the boundary condition as before.
(ii) $\dfrac{d}{dx}\{ye^{x/2}\} = (6x+4)e^{x/2}$. Now $\int (6x+4)e^{x/2}\,dx = (12x-16)e^{x/2}$, on integrating by parts, and so

$$ye^{x/2} = (12x-6)e^{x/2} + A.$$

Using the boundary condition gives $y = 4e^{(1-x)/2} + 12x - 16$.
(iii) $\dfrac{d}{dt}\{xe^t\} = 3e^{3t}$, so that $xe^t = e^{3t} + A$. Fitting the condition gives $x = e^{2t} - e^{-t}$.
(iv) $\dfrac{d}{dt}\{xe^{4t}\} = (2\sin t - 3\cos t)e^{4t}$. Integration by parts is needed here:

$$\int \sin t\, e^{4t}dt = -\cos t\, e^{4t} + \int 4\cos t\, e^{4t}\,dt$$

$$= -\cos t\, e^{4t} + 4\sin t\, e^{4t} - 16\int \sin t\, e^{4t}\,dt,$$

so that $\int \sin t\, e^{4t}\, dt = (-\tfrac{1}{17}\cos t + \tfrac{4}{17}\sin t)e^{4t}$.

Similarly

$$\int \cos t\, e^{4t}\, dt = (\tfrac{1}{17}\sin t + \tfrac{4}{17}\cos t)e^{4t},$$

giving $x = \tfrac{5}{17}\sin t - \tfrac{14}{17}\cos t + Ae^{-4t}$.

(v) $\dfrac{d}{dt}\{xe^{-t}\} = 3e^t - 2$ so that $x = 3e^{2t} - 2te^t + Ae^t$.

(vi) $\dfrac{d}{dx}\{ye^{3x}\} = x^2 e^{3x} + \cos x\, e^{3x}$. Integrating by parts gives $y = \tfrac{1}{3}x^2 - \tfrac{2}{9}x + \tfrac{2}{27} + \tfrac{1}{10}\sin x + \tfrac{3}{10}\cos x + Ae^{-3x}$. Fitting the condition at $x = 0$ gives $A = -\tfrac{11}{270}$.

2   (a) Intelligent guesswork has to be *very* intelligent here.

(b) $\dfrac{d}{dx}\{ye^x\} = \dfrac{e^x}{1+e^x}$ and so $ye^x = \displaystyle\int \dfrac{e^x}{1+e^x}\,dx + A$.

The substitution $t = e^x$ simplifies the integral to $\displaystyle\int \dfrac{1}{1+t}\,dt = \ln(1+t) = \ln(1+e^x)$. Hence

$$y = e^{-x}\ln(1+e^x) + Ae^{-x},$$

and fitting the condition gives $A = 0$. The solution holds for all x since $e^x > 0$.

Exercise 12C

(i) $r(x) = x$, $s(x) = xe^{-x}$, i.e. $\dfrac{d}{dx}\{xy\} = xe^{-x}$. Hence $y = -e^{-x} - e^{-x}/x + A/x$, and the condition shows that we must have $A = 3 + 2e^{-1}$. The solution is for $x > 0$.

(ii) $r(x) = e^{x^2}$, $s(x) = xe^{x^2}$, i.e. $\dfrac{d}{dx}\{ye^{x^2}\} = xe^{x^2}$. Hence $y = \tfrac{1}{2} + Ae^{-x^2}$, and the condition gives $A = \tfrac{1}{2}$.

(iii) $r(x) = e^{-x}/x$, $s(x) = (x - x^2)e^{-x}$. Integration by parts gives $y = x^2 + x + 1 + Axe^x$. The given condition does not determine the value of A: this is because at $x = 0$ the equation does not tell you the value of dy/dx on the solution curve.

(iv) $r(x) = \cos^3 x$, $s(x) = \cos^2 x \sin x$. Hence $y = -\tfrac{1}{3} + \dfrac{A}{\cos^3 x}$, for some suitable domain such as $-\tfrac{1}{2}\pi < x < \tfrac{1}{2}\pi$.

(v) $r(x) = (1-x)^{1/2}$, $s(x) = (1-x)^{1/2}$. Hence $y = -\tfrac{2}{3}(1-x) + A(1-x)^{-1/2}$, for $x < 1$. If you want the solution for $x > 1$, then you must use $r(x) = (x-1)^{1/2}$, $s(x) = (x-1)^{1/2}$ and $y = \tfrac{2}{3}(x-1) + B(x-1)^{-1/2}$.

Exercise 12D

1   The equation is $\dfrac{dN}{dt} + tN = t$, or $\dfrac{d}{dt}\{e^{t^2/2}N\} = te^{t^2/2}$. This integrates to give $N = 1 + Ae^{-t^2/2}$. Hence the fish stock reaches a constant level quite quickly.

2   The equation is $\dfrac{dN}{dt} + (bn - a)N = (bn - a)N_1$, or

$$\frac{d}{dt}(N - N_1) + (bn - a)(N - N_1) = 0.$$

If you put $N - N_1 = Z$ (say), this solves by separation:

$$\int \frac{1}{Z} dZ = -\int (bn - a) dt = -s(t), \text{ say.}$$

Thus $N - N_1 = (N_0 - N_1)e^{-s(t)}$, on using $N = N_0$ initially, and taking $s(t)$ to be an integral from $t = 0$. Then if $s(t) > 0$, it is clear that $N \to N_1$ as t increases, and the policy works. One way of ensuring $s(t) > 0$ is to adjust the membership to keep $bn - a > 0$ at all times.

3   The equation is $\dfrac{dN}{dt} + a\dfrac{t}{t+1}N = (t+1)^a$. Using an integrating factor gives $\dfrac{d}{dt}\{Ne^{at}(t+1)^{-a}\} = e^{at}$. Hence $N = \dfrac{1}{a}(t+1)^a\{(a-1)e^{-at} + 1\}$, using the initial condition. The fish stock must eventually rise, like $a^{-1}(t+1)^a$, as $a > 0$ and so $e^{-at} \to 0$.

Exercise 12E

1   $\displaystyle\int \frac{0.1}{1-t} dt = -0.1\ln(1-t)$ and so $r(t) = e^{-0.1\ln(1-t)} = (1-t)^{-0.1}$. The equation becomes $\dfrac{d}{dt}\{v(1-t)^{-0.1}\} = u(1-t)^{-1.1} - g(1-t)^{-0.1}$ which   integrates   to   give

$v = 10u + \dfrac{10g}{9}(1-t) + A(1-t)^{0.1}$. Assuming that $v = 0$ at $t = 0$ gives the required formula.

2   If u is too small (i.e. mass is ejected slowly from the rocket), and if no allowance is made for the launch pad holding the rocket up, then the rocket will sink initially, i.e. $v < 0$.

3   (a) Mathematically, $(1-t)^{0.1}$ is not real for $t > 1$.
    (b) Physically, the mass has all been ejected at $t = 1$, there is no rocket left.

4   The integrating factor is $(m_0 - \alpha t)^{-k/\alpha}$, and the equation is

$$\frac{d}{dt}\{v(m_0 - \alpha t)^{-k/\alpha}\} = u\alpha(m_0 - \alpha t)^{-1-k/\alpha} - g(m_0 - \alpha t)^{-k/\alpha}.$$

This integrates to give (if $\alpha \neq k$)

$$v(m_0 - \alpha t)^{-k/\alpha} = \frac{u\alpha}{k}(m_0 - \alpha t)^{-k/\alpha} + \frac{g}{\alpha - k}(m_0 - \alpha t)^{1-k/\alpha} + A.$$

Taking $v = 0$ at $t = 0$ gives

$$v = \frac{u\alpha}{k}\{1 - (m_0 - \alpha t)^{k/\alpha}\} + \frac{g}{\alpha - k}\{(m_0 - \alpha t) - (m_0 - \alpha t)^{k/\alpha}\}.$$

Exercise 12F

1   The effective area of leaf $e(t)L$ is reduced by the disease by a factor $d(t)$, say, which starts at 0 and increases to $\frac{1}{2}$ (say). The equation becomes

$$\frac{dM}{dt} = \frac{k}{a}d(t)\,e(t)\,M - \frac{k}{a}d(t)\,e(t)\,S(t).$$

The disease function $d(t)$ could be modelled in many ways, e.g. as $c(t/t_0 - 1)$, using t_0 as the start of the disease.

2   Realistic models for this equation are hard to integrate explicitly; numerical methods are called for. However, you could make progress with the equation

$$\frac{dM}{dt} = \frac{1}{1+t}M - \frac{t^2}{(t^2+1)(1+t)},$$

which has roughly the right characteristics.

Exercise 12G

1   $\Delta\{F(n)\} = F(n+1) - F(n)$ by definition, so $\Delta\{r(n)u_n\}$ must have the form stated. So to get $\Delta\{r(n)u_n\} = s(n)$ to be the same equation as $u_{n+1} + p(n)u_n = q(n)$ requires (on division by $r(n+1)$) both $-\dfrac{r(n)}{r(n+1)} = p(n)$ and $\dfrac{s(n)}{r(n+1)} = q(n)$.

These are the same as the required equations.

2   The succession of equations

$$\begin{cases} r(1)u_1 = r(0)u_0 + s(0) \\ r(2)u_2 = r(1)u_1 + s(1) \\ \quad\cdots \\ r(n)u_n = r(n-1)u_{n-1} + s(n-1) \end{cases}$$

is given. Using them in turn gives

$$r(n)u_n = r(n-1)u_{n-1} + s(n-1) = \{r(n-2)u_{n-2} + s(n-2)\} + s(n-1)$$
$$= r(1)u_1 + s(1) + s(2) + \ldots + s(n-1).$$

Hence u_n has the form stated, since $r(1)u_1$ is some constant.

3   From question 1 the equation for $r(n)$ is $r(n+1) = \dfrac{n+1}{n}r(n)$. This can be solved step-by-step to find $r(n) = An$ for any constant A. Then $s(n) = \dfrac{1}{n+1}A(n+1)$ from question 1, as required. The equation for u_n now has solution (from question 2)

$$u_n = \frac{1}{An}\left\{\sum_{i=1}^{n-1}A + \text{constant}\right\} = \frac{n-1}{n} + \frac{B}{n}$$

for any constant B, as can easily be checked.

4   The equation is $u_{n+1} - nu_n = -n/(n+1)$ with $u_1 = 1$. The corresponding equation for $r(n)$ is $r(n+1) = \dfrac{1}{n}r(n)$, which easily has solution $r(n) = \dfrac{A}{(n-1)!}$. Then

$s(n) = -\dfrac{n}{n+1}\dfrac{A}{n!} = -\dfrac{nA}{(n+1)!}$. The solution formula in question 2 now gives

$$u_n = (n-1)!\left\{\sum_{i=1}^{n-1} -\dfrac{i}{(i+1)!} + B\right\}.$$

This in fact (but not at all obviously) gives the same answer as in Section 2.4.

Exercise 13A

1 (i) The equation becomes $\dfrac{1}{a}z^{-1+1/a}\dfrac{dz}{dx} + 2z^{1/a} = (x+1)z^{2/a}$, or

$\dfrac{dz}{dx} + 2az = a(x+1)z^{1+1/a}$. Choose $a = -1$ to simplify this to $\dfrac{dz}{dx} - 2z = -x-1$, which

has solution $z = Ae^{2x} + \frac{1}{2}x + \frac{3}{4}$. So finally $y = z^{-1} = \{Ae^{2x} + \frac{1}{2}x + \frac{3}{4}\}^{-1}$.

(ii) The equation reduces similarly to $\dfrac{dz}{dx} - 3axz = axz^{1+2/a}$, and $a = -2$ gives

$\dfrac{dz}{dx} + 6xz = -2x$. The integrating factor here is e^{3x^2}, so that $\dfrac{d}{dx}\{ze^{3x^2}\} = -2xe^{3x^2}$.

From this you find $z = Ae^{-3x^2} - \frac{1}{3}$ and finally $y = \{Ae^{-3x^2} - \frac{1}{3}\}^{-2}$.

2 Use $y = z^{1/(1-k)}$ and $\dfrac{dy}{dx} = \dfrac{1}{1-k}z^{-1+1/(1-k)}\dfrac{dz}{dx}$ to reduce the equation to

$\dfrac{dz}{dx} + (1-k)pz = (1-k)q$, which is linear in z. The two previous examples are of this

kind, with $k = 2$ and 3.

3 Making the substitution gives $\dfrac{dz}{dx} - 1 = z^2 - 2$ or $\dfrac{dz}{dx} = z^2 - 1$. This solves by separation

of variables as

$$\int \dfrac{1}{z^2-1}\,dz = \int dx.$$

Since $\dfrac{1}{z^2-1} = \dfrac{\frac{1}{2}}{z-1} - \dfrac{\frac{1}{2}}{z+1}$ the solution is given by $\ln\left|\dfrac{z-1}{z+1}\right| = 2x + A$ (no initial values

are given, so it is not known if $z > 1$, $-1 < z < 1$ or $z < -1$ is appropriate).
Consequently $z = (1 \pm Ce^{2x})/(1 \mp Ce^{2x})$, where $C = e^A$, and $y = z - x - 1$.

4 $y = \dfrac{1}{x}z$ requires that $\dfrac{dy}{dx} = \dfrac{1}{x}\dfrac{dz}{dx} - \dfrac{1}{x^2}z$, and so the equation becomes

$\dfrac{dz}{dx} - \dfrac{1}{x}z + \dfrac{1}{x}z = z^3$. This can be separated, with solution $-\dfrac{1}{2z^2} = x + A$, or

$z = \dfrac{1}{\sqrt{(C-2x)}}$, on putting $2A = -C$. Hence $y = \dfrac{1}{x\sqrt{(C-2x)}}$ for a domain which makes

this real and does not include $x = 0$.

5 (i) The substitution $e^{y-x} = z$ looks promising. That is, $y = x + \ln z$, and $\dfrac{dy}{dx} = 1 + \dfrac{1}{z}\dfrac{dz}{dx}$.

The equation becomes $\dfrac{dz}{dx} = z^2 - 2z$, which is separable, giving $\int \dfrac{1}{z^2-2z}\,dz = \int dx$. Use

the identity $\dfrac{1}{z^2-2z} = -\dfrac{\frac{1}{2}}{z} + \dfrac{\frac{1}{2}}{z-2}$ to integrate this as $\ln\left|\dfrac{z-2}{z}\right| = 2x + A$, and as in question 3 you find $z = \dfrac{2}{1 \mp Ce^{2x}}$, and finally $y = x + \ln\left\{\dfrac{2}{1 \mp Ce^{2x}}\right\}$, for a suitable domain.

(ii) The substitution $z = x + y$ gives $\dfrac{dy}{dx} = -1 + \dfrac{dz}{dx}$ and so $\dfrac{dz}{dx} = 1 - \sin^2 z = \cos^2 z$.

Solving this separable equation leads to $\tan z = x + C$ and then to

$$y = \tan^{-1}(x + C) - x$$

for some suitable domain.

Exercise 13B

1   Rewrite the equation as

$$\frac{dx}{dy} = \frac{1 - x^2 y^2}{xy^3},$$

or $xy^3 \dfrac{dx}{dy} = 1 - x^2 y^2$. Now put $\tfrac{1}{2}x^2 = z$ so that $x\dfrac{dx}{dy} = \dfrac{dz}{dy}$, which reduces the equation to

$$y^3 \frac{dz}{dy} + 2zy^2 = 1.$$

This is linear with integrating factor y^2, so that

$$\frac{d}{dy}\{y^2 z\} = \frac{1}{y}.$$

Integrating this leads to $z = \dfrac{1}{y^2}\ln|y| + \dfrac{C}{y^2}$ and so

$$x = \sqrt{\left(\frac{2}{y^2}\ln|y| + \frac{2C}{y^2}\right)},$$

for a suitable domain. Note that it is not possible to deduce an expression for y in terms of x from this.

2   Inversion gives $xy\dfrac{dx}{dy} = x^2 - y^4$, and then the substitution $\tfrac{1}{2}x^2 = z$ gives $y\dfrac{dz}{dy} = 2z - y^4$, which is linear. The integrating factor is y^{-2}, leading to

$$\frac{d}{dy}\{z/y^2\} = -y.$$

This solves as $z = Ay^2 - \tfrac{1}{2}y^4$, or $x = \sqrt{(2Ay^2 - y^4)}$. You can rearrange this as $y^4 - 2Ay^2 + x^2 = 0$, which can be solved for y in terms of x (it is a quadratic in y^2) for some suitable domain.

Exercise 13C

1   In all three parts use $\dfrac{dy}{dx} = x\dfrac{dz}{dx} + z$.

(i) The equation becomes $x\dfrac{dz}{dx} = \dfrac{z}{1+z} - z = -\dfrac{z^2}{1+z}$. This separates to give

$\int \dfrac{1+z}{z^2}dz = -\int \dfrac{1}{x}dx$, and so $-\dfrac{1}{z}+\ln|z| = -\ln|x|+A$. This may be rewritten as $|x| = Ce^{-1/z}|z|$, or $x^2 = C|y|e^{-x/y}$; the domain must be such that $y>0$ or $y<0$.

(ii) The equation becomes $x\dfrac{dz}{dx}-z+z=1$, so that at once $z=\ln|x|+A$ and $y = x\ln|x|+Ax$. The original equation was linear and could be solved to give this answer directly.

(iii) The equation becomes $x\dfrac{dz}{dx}+z=e^z+z$, which separates to give $\int e^{-z}dz = \int\dfrac{1}{x}dx$. Hence $-e^{-z} = \ln|x|+A$, or $y = -x\ln\{\ln(C/|x|)\}$ for x between 0 and C.

2   As before the equation becomes

$$t\dfrac{dz}{dt}+z = \dfrac{-2z}{1+z^2} \quad \text{or} \quad t\dfrac{dz}{dt} = -\dfrac{z(3+z^2)}{1+z^2}.$$

This separates to give $\int \dfrac{1+z^2}{z(3+z^2)}dz = -\int\dfrac{1}{t}dt$. The first integral needs the identity

$\dfrac{1+z^2}{z(3+z^2)} = \dfrac{1}{3}\left\{\dfrac{1}{z} + \dfrac{2z}{3+z^2}\right\}$, and the result is eventually $|x|(3t^2+x^2)=C$.

3   From $y = x^{-1/2}v$ you find $\dfrac{dy}{dx} = x^{-1/2}\dfrac{dv}{dx} - \frac{1}{2}x^{-3/2}v$, so that the equation becomes $\dfrac{dv}{dx} - \dfrac{1}{x}v = \dfrac{1-v^2}{2xv}$. Further reduction gives the separable equation $x\dfrac{dv}{dx} = \dfrac{1+v^2}{2v}$, from which you can find $1+xy^2 = B|x|$. Clearly $x>0$ is intended since $x^{1/2}$ is suggested, so $y = \pm\sqrt{(B-1/x)}$.

Exercise 13D

1   Differentiate to get $\dfrac{d^2y}{dx^2}\left\{x - \left(\dfrac{dy}{dx}\right)^{-2}\right\} = 0$. Hence

either $\dfrac{d^2y}{dx^2} = 0$, which gives $y=mx+c$, and substitution in the equation shows that $c = \dfrac{1}{m}$;

or $x = \left(\dfrac{dy}{dx}\right)^{-2}$ which solves as $y = \pm2x^{1/2}+A$, and substitution in the equation gives $A=0$.

2   Differentiation gives $\dfrac{d^2y}{dx^2}\left\{x - f'\left(\dfrac{dy}{dx}\right)\right\} = 0$. As before,

either $\dfrac{d^2y}{dx^2} = 0$, leading to $y=mx+f(m)$;

or $x = f'\left(\dfrac{dy}{dx}\right)$, and putting $\dfrac{dy}{dx} = m$ here and in the original equation gives the values of x and y parametrically as $x = f'(m)$, $y = mf'(m)+f(m)$.

3 In this case $f(m)=\frac{1}{4}m^4$, so that the solutions (from question 3) are the family of lines $y=mx+\frac{1}{4}m^4$ and the singular solution given by

$$x=m^3, \ y=m^4+\frac{1}{4}m^4.$$

You may eliminate m to write the singular solution as $y=\frac{5}{4}x^{4/3}$.

4 Here $f(m)=m^2-\frac{2}{3}m^3$ so the solutions are the family of lines $y=mx+m^2-\frac{2}{3}m^3$ and the singular solution $x=2m-2m^2$, $y=2m^2-2m^3+m^2-\frac{2}{3}m^3=3m^2-\frac{8}{3}m^3$. It is not very convenient to eliminate m in the singular solution.

Exercise 14A

1 Do not keep too many figures, as Euler's method is not very accurate.

x	0.1	0.2	0.3	0.4	0.5	0.6	0.7	0.8	0.9	1.0	1.1	1.2
y	0.900	0.820	0.758	0.712	0.681	0.663	0.657	0.661	0.675	0.697	0.728	0.765

2 The exact solution is $y=2e^{-x}+x-1$ (the equation is linear), whose graph is concave upwards, i.e. dy/dx is increasing as x increases. Euler's method uses a gradient at the left hand end of each interval, which is therefore too small. Hence the Euler solution in this case lies below the true solution.

3 For Euler's method $y_{n+1}=y_n+h(y')_{\text{at} x_n}$. Use the equation to get $(y')_{\text{at} x_n}=x_n-y_n=nh-y_n$. Hence the difference equation is $y_{n+1}=(1-h)y_n+nh^2$, and $y_0=1$ is required since $y=1$ when $x=0$. This difference equation is linear, with solution

$$y_n=2(1-h)^n+nh-1.$$

Replace nh by x to get a form that looks more like the solution of the differential equation, $2\left(1-\dfrac{x}{n}\right)^n+x-1$. If n is large $\left(1-\dfrac{x}{n}\right)^n\approx e^{-x}$ (for x not large).

4 The error at $x=1$ is $2e^{-1}-2(1-h)^{1/h}$; similarly at $x=2$ it is $2e^{-2}-2(1-h)^{2/h}$

h	0.1	0.05	0.02	0.01	0.001
Error at 1	0.0384	0.0188	0.0074	0.0037	3.68×10^{-4}
Error at 2	0.0275	0.0136	0.0054	0.0027	2.71×10^{-4}

5 h	0.1	0.05	0.02	0.01	0.001
$y(1)$	1.128 4	1.125 6	1.123 7	1.123 06	1.122 43

6 $dy/dx=0$ on the curve $y=1/x$. For $y>1/x$ you have $dy/dx<0$; and for $y<1/x$, $dy/dx>0$. The curve rises initially, reaching a maximum when it crosses $y=1/x$.

Thereafter it goes down towards the curve $y = 1/x$, but cannot cross it (you would need both $dy/dx < 0$ and $dy/dx = 0$ if it crossed).

h	0.1	0.05	0.02	0.01	0.001
$y(3)$	0.337 62	0.337 71	0.337 77	0.337 79	0.337 802 6

7   You should find $y(10)$ to be large and negative.

Exercise 14B

1   (i)

	$x = 1$	2	3	4
$h = 0.1$	0.971 46	1.208 24	1.766 83	2.508 82
0.01	0.975 85	1.222 17	1.781 03	2.522 33
0.001	0.976 16	1.223 48	1.782 41	2.523 66

(ii) Use $h = 0.01$ on the integral in

$$y = \frac{1}{1+x^2}\left\{1 + \int_0^x (1+t^2)t^{1/2}\, dt\right\}$$

to get 0.976 15, 1.223 61, 1.782 56, 2.523 80.

(iii) The equation is linear with integrating factor $1 + x^2$ and solution $y = (1 + \frac{2}{3}x^{3/2} + \frac{2}{7}x^{7/2})/(1 + x^2)$. The values are

x	1	2	3	4
y	0.976 19	1.223 62	1.782 56	2.523 81

(Simpson's rule does not give very high accuracy here because the integrand $(1+t^2)t^{1/2}$ is not smooth at $t = 0$, and so a small value of h is needed, or else a modified method (as in Chapter 10).)

2   (i)

	$x = 1$	2	3	4
$h = 0.1$	0.774 02	1.102 44	1.189 38	0.172 69
0.01	0.780 12	1.112 69	1.164 40	0.118 64
0.001	0.780 81	1.113 69	1.161 93	0.113 32

(ii) Using $h = 0.01$ again with an extra $\sin t$ in the integrand gives 0.780 88, 1.113 80, 1.161 66, 0.112 73. These values should be close to the correct values, as the integrand is smoother at $t = 0$ (because $\sin t$ is zero there). (There is no explicit formula for the solution in this case.)

Exercise 14C

1

x	0.1	0.2	0.3	0.4	0.5	0.6
y	0.91	0.838 05	0.782 44	0.741 60	0.714 15	0.698 81
Error	-3.25×10^{-4}	-5.88×10^{-4}	-7.99×10^{-4}	-9.64×10^{-4}	$-0.001\,1$	$-0.001\,2$
Euler error	0.010	0.017	0.024	0.029	0.032	0.035

x	0.7	0.8	0.9	1.0	1.1	1.2
y	0.694 42	0.699 95	0.714 46	0.737 08	0.767 06	0.803 69
Error	$-0.001\,2$	$-0.001\,3$	$-0.001\,3$	$-0.001\,3$	$-0.001\,3$	$-0.001\,3$
Euler error	0.036	0.038	0.038	0.039	0.038	0.037

2

h	0.1	0.05	0.02	0.01	0.001
$y(1)$	1.120 66	1.121 94	1.122 29	1.122 34	1.122 36

3
$$y = 2e^{-x} + x - 1 \text{ and } dy/dx = -2e^{-x} + 1$$

(i) $y'(0.3) = -0.481\,636$ (ii) $y'(0.4) = -0.340\,640$
(iii) $y(0.3) = 0.781\,636$ (iv) $y_{\text{inter}} = 0.733\,473$

$\dfrac{dy}{dx}$ at $x = 0.4$ and y_{inter} is $-0.333\,473$, which differs from the result in (ii) by 7.167×10^{-3}, of much the same size as h^2.

4

	$h = 0.1$	0.05	0.02	0.01
$x = 1$	1.120 7	1.121 9	1.122 3	1.122 3
2	0.586 0	0.584 5	0.584 1	0.584 1
3	0.347 8	0.338 0	0.337 8	0.337 8
4	$-7.580\,5$	0.606 9	0.251 0	0.251 0
5	-28.210	-11.866	0.204 5	0.200 3
6	-58.678	-42.433	23.756	0.166 8
7	-101.10	-84.874	-19.301	0.402 6
8	-157.49	-141.28	-75.818	-76.278
9	-229.87	-213.66	-148.23	-148.69
10	-320.24	-304.03	-238.61	-239.07

Notice how much all the solutions eventually differ from the expected values of $1/x$.

5 The solution is $y = e^{2x}$, which is concave upwards, with a gradient increasing with x. The predicted value y_{inter} is below the solution curve, and gives too small a value for the gradient at x_{new}; the average gradient at $(x_{\text{old}}, y_{\text{old}})$ and $(x_{\text{new}}, y_{\text{inter}})$ is too small, and so y_{new} is below the solution curve.

The solution, by separation, is $y = \frac{1}{4}(\ln x)^2$. But y_{inter} is always given as 0 since $(dy/dx)_{old}$ is zero if y is zero; hence the improved Euler method gives $y = 0$ for all x. The equation is not linear, and $y(x) = 0$ (for all x) is its singular solution.

Exercise 15A

1 (i) Use an integrating factor $e^{-x^2/2}$ to rewrite the equation as $\dfrac{d}{dx}\{ye^{-x^2/2}\}$ $= -xe^{-x^2/2}$. The solution is $1 + Ae^{x^2/2}$; if you have the condition $y = 1$ at $x = 0$ then $A = 0$, but if $y = 1 + 10^{-9}$ at $x = 0$ then $A = 10^{-9}$ and the solution is

$$y = 1 + 10^{-9} e^{x^2/2}.$$

Hence the solution $y = 1$ is unstable, as starting from a slightly different initial condition gives a very different result by (say) $x = 10$.
(ii) Starting at $y = 1$ gave $y = 1$ at $x = 5$, for $h = 0.01$. Starting at $y = 1 + 10^{-9}$ gave $y = 1.0001319$ at $x = 5$.

2 Using $h = 0.01$ and the various initial values I found the following

$x = 0$		0.1	0.2	0.3	0.4	0.5
$y = 0.12$	0.120 00	0.119 60	0.118 35	0.116 18	0.112 99	0.108 70
$\frac{10}{81}$	0.123 46	0.122 90	0.121 24	0.118 49	0.114 68	0.109 85
0.13	0.130 000	0.129 16	0.126 71	0.122 87	0.117 90	0.112 03

The solutions start at most 0.01 apart, and end at most 0.003 33 apart; they are converging, and the solution is stable. The solution graphs are getting closer together. You can solve the equation exactly as $y = \frac{1}{9}\cos x + \frac{1}{81} + Ae^{9\cos x}$; no small error can grow huge.

3

x	0	1	2	3	4	5	6
|diff|	10^{-9}	10^{-8}	3.9×10^{-8}	1.4×10^{-7}	4.8×10^{-7}	1.59×10^{-6}	5.05×10^{-6}
ratio		10	3.9	3.6	3.4	3.3	3.2

A constant ratio would mean exponential growth.

4 Let $y = z^3$ to get $\dfrac{dz}{dx} - z = -2\dfrac{x}{\pi}$. This has solution $z = Ae^x + \alpha x + \beta$, where $\alpha = \beta = 2/\pi$ by substitution. Hence

$$y = \{Ae^x + 2(x+1)/\pi\}^3.$$

This clearly grows exponentially if $A \neq 0$.

5

f	Δf	$\Delta^2 f$
1.000		
	2.767	
3.767		0.678
	3.445	
7.212		0.611
	4.056	
11.268		0.537
	4 593	
15.861		0.491
	5.084	
20.945		0.474
	5.558	
26.503		0.517
	6.075	
32.578		

6   Put $y=y_0+\delta$ in the equation $\dfrac{dy}{dx}-3y=-6\left(\dfrac{x}{\pi}\right)^{1/2}y^{2/3}$. Then note that $(y_0+\delta)^{2/3}=y_0^{2/3}(1+\delta/y_0)^{2/3}\approx y_0^{2/3}+\frac{2}{3}y_0^{-1/3}\delta$, from the binomial theorem. Most terms in y_0 cancel out because y_0 satisfies the equation, leaving the required equation for δ. Values of the bracketed term are

x	0	1	2	3	4	5	6
Term	3.00	1.55	1.35	1.26	1.20	1.17	1.15

From $x=1$ to $x=6$ you therefore have $\dfrac{d\delta}{dx}\approx 1.25\delta$, whose solution is $\delta\approx Ae^{1.25x}$.

Exercise 15B

1   Using $h=0.01$ (and the improved Euler method) gives

x	0	1	2	3	4	5	6	7
$y=1.01$		1.129 0	0.584 8	0.337 8	0.251 0	0.200 3	0.166 8	0.402 6
1.00		1.122 3	0.584 1	0.337 8	0.251 0	0.200 3	0.166 8	0.402 6
0.99		1.115 8	0.583 4	0.337 8	0.251 0	0.200 3	0.166 8	0.402 6

The solutions converge quite rapidly, and then leave the curve $y=1/x$ almost together, between $x=6$ and $x=7$.

2	x	9	^{5}	10	^{5}	11	^{5}	12	^{5}
	$y - 1/x$	1.695×10^{-5}		1.001×10^{-5}		0.621×10^{-5}		0.402×10^{-5}	

So far y is slowly converging to $1/x$.

x	12.2	12.4	12.6	12.8
$y - 1/x$	0.370×10^{-5}	0.342×10^{-5}	0.318×10^{-5}	91.637×10^{-5}

The divergence from $1/x$ starts near 12.7 when $h = 0.001$.

Exercise 15C

1   The solution of this equation is $y = \tan(\frac{1}{2}x^2 + \frac{1}{4}\pi)$, with asymptote at $x = \sqrt{(\frac{1}{2}\pi)}$. The errors with $h = 0.001$ are small up to $x = 1.2$. At $x = 1.25$, just before the true asymptote, I found $y = 232.5756$ with error 8.4936. Overflow was reported after $x = 1.257$, $y = 2.6229 \times 10^{57}$. This is slightly beyond the true asymptote at $x = 1.2533$.

2   Just after $x = 0.935$, $y = 4.008 \times 10^{79}$ the computer reports overflow. Equation (i) has solution $y = \tan(x + \frac{1}{4}\pi)$, with an asymptote at $x = \frac{1}{4}\pi = 0.7854$. Equation (ii) has solution $y = \tan(\frac{1}{2}x^2 + \frac{1}{4}\pi)$, with an asymptote at $x = 1.2533$. The equation under discussion has slope less than $1 + y^2$ and greater than $x + xy^2$ because $0 < x < 1$ in the calculation. Hence the solution curve fits between the solution curves for (i) and (ii), and so must go to infinity, i.e. have an asymptote, between 0.7854 and 1.2533.

3   Using $x_{\text{old}} = 1.41$, $y_{\text{old}} = 16\,298.654\,72$ and the equation, gives $(dy/dx)_{\text{old}} = 7\,724\,740.556$; consequently $y_{\text{inter}} = 93\,546.060\,28$ and $(dy/dx)_{\text{inter}} = -32\,398\,879.41$. The average slope is $-12\,337\,069.43$, so that y_{new} is $-107\,072.039\,6$.

Exercise 16A

1   (i) We need to solve $\frac{1}{4}h^4 = hc^3$; so $c = 0.629\,96h$, which is indeed between 0 and h.
    (ii) Solve $e^2 - e = e^c$ to get $c = \ln(e^2 - e) = 1.541\,32$, between 1 and 2.

2   (i) We need to solve $\sin 1.2 - \sin 1 = 0.2\cos(1 + 0.2\theta)$. This gives $\theta = 0.504\,238$.
    (ii) We need to solve $e^{-1} - e^{-1-h} = he^{-(1+\theta)}$ or $e^{-\theta h} = (1 - e^{-h})/h$. Thus $\theta = -\frac{1}{h}\ln\left\{\frac{1 - e^{-h}}{h}\right\}$.

3   Clearly $\int_a^{a+h} \cos x\,dx = \sin(a + h) - \sin a$, and from the Mean Value Theorem for integrals $\int_a^{a+h} \cos x\,dx = h\cos(a + \theta h)$. Hence $\sin(a + h) - \sin a = h\cos(a + \theta h)$, for some value of θ between 0 and 1. Now $\sin(a + h) - \sin a = 2\cos(a + \frac{1}{2}h)\sin\frac{1}{2}h \approx h\cos(a + \frac{1}{2}h)$. Hence, for small h, $\theta \approx \frac{1}{2}$.

Exercise 16B

1 (i) $f(a+h)$ here has value $(a+h)^2$; similarly $f(a)=a^2$ and $f'(a+\frac{1}{2}h)=2(a+\frac{1}{2}h)$. The identity $(a+h)^2=a^2+2h(a+\frac{1}{2}h)$ shows the result to be true.
(ii) In this case $f(a+h)=p(a+h)^2+q(a+h)+r$, $\quad f(a)=pa^2+qa+r$, $f'(a+\frac{1}{2}h)=2p(a+\frac{1}{2}h)+q$ (because $f'(x)=2px+q$) and the required identity is

$$p(a+h)^2+q(a+h)+r=pa^2+qa+r+h\{2p(a+\frac{1}{2}h)+q\}.$$

2 (i) $c=\ln(e^2-e)=1.541\,3$. The corresponding Mean Value Theorem statement is $e^{a+h}-e^a=he^c$, $a<c<a+h$, with values $a=1$, $h=1$; and indeed c lies between 1 and 2.

(ii) Remember that $\dfrac{d}{dx}\tan x=\sec^2x$, so that the Mean Value Theorem for tan is $\tan(a+h)-\tan a=h\sec^2(a+\theta h)$. Now take $a+h=\frac{1}{3}\pi$, $a=\frac{1}{4}\pi$, $c=a+\theta h$ to get the required statement. The value of c is $0.929\,77$, which is indeed between $\frac{1}{4}\pi$ and $\frac{1}{3}\pi$ (close to half-way between).

3 From the Mean Value Theorem $e^{a+h}=e^a+he^{a+\theta h}$, since $\dfrac{d}{dx}e^x=e^x$. Hence $e^{a+\theta h}=(e^{a+h}-e^a)/h$, for some θ between 0 and 1. That is $e^{\theta h}=(e^h-1)/h\approx 1+\frac{1}{2}h$, using the approximation. Consequently $1+\theta h\approx 1+\frac{1}{2}h$, $\theta\approx\frac{1}{2}$.

4 $f(a+h)=|\frac{1}{4}|=\frac{1}{4}$, $f(a)=|-\frac{1}{2}|=\frac{1}{2}$, and so $f(a+h)-f(a)=-\frac{1}{4}$. This is not the value of the slope of $|x|$ for any value of x. The function $|x|$ is not smooth between $-\frac{1}{2}$ and $\frac{1}{4}$, so the Mean Value Theorem does not apply to it.

5 (ii) From the Mean Value Theorem, $f(b)=f(a)+(b-a)f'(c)$, where c is between a and b. But $f(a)=f(b)$, so $f'(c)=0$.
(iii) The slope of the graph of f has a largest value $M\geqslant 0$ between a and b, and a smallest value $m\leqslant 0$; if the slope were always positive or always negative you could not have $f(b)=f(a)$. Since the slope is assumed continuous, it must be zero at one or more points, which is Rolle's theorem. Can you see any hidden assumptions in this argument?

6 Consider the graph of $f(x)=x^2$ and the three points

$$\text{A: }(a,a^2),\quad \text{B: }(a+h,(a+h)^2),\quad \text{C: }(a+\tfrac{1}{2}h,(a+\tfrac{1}{2}h)^2).$$

Then **1**(i) asserts that chord AB is parallel to the tangent at C. Now consider the graph of $g(x)=\sqrt{x}$ and the corresponding points

$$\text{A: }(a^2,a),\quad \text{B: }((a+h)^2,a+h),\quad \text{C: }((a+\tfrac{1}{2}h)^2,a+\tfrac{1}{2}h).$$

Then **1**(i) asserts that chord AB is parallel to the tangent at C. But C is less than half way from A to B because (for $h>0$)

$$(a+\tfrac{1}{2}h)^2<\tfrac{1}{2}\{a^2+(a+h)^2\}.$$

Hence $\theta<\frac{1}{2}$ in $g(a+h)=g(a)+hg'(a+\theta h)$.
Using that $g(x)=\sqrt{x}$ gives $\sqrt{(a+h)}=\sqrt{a}+\frac{1}{2}h(a+\theta h)^{-1/2}$; you can solve this to get

$$\theta=\frac{h}{4\{\sqrt{(a+h)}-\sqrt{a}\}}-\frac{a}{h}.$$

Exercise 16C

1 The formula is $x_{n+1}=x_n-\dfrac{x_n^4+x_n^3-1}{4x_n^3+3x_n^2}$. Starting with $x_0=0.8$ gives the sequence

0.819 758 064 5,   0.819 173 040 7,   0.819 172 513 4,   0.819 172 513 4   with   errors 0.019 172 513 4, $-5.855\,511\,16 \times 10^{-4}$, $-5.272\,61 \times 10^{-7}$; $|e_{n+1}/e_n^2| = 1.593$ and 1.538, so it is quadratic convergence.

2   (i) First order convergence to $\sqrt{2}$, errors halving at each step.
    (ii) As for (i).
    (iii) Direct to the root -3 in one step.
    (iv) Jump to 20.6057, thereafter convergence to $\sqrt{2}$ as in (i).
    (v) Quadratic convergence to -3.
    The graph cuts the x-axis at -3 and is tangent to it at $\pm\sqrt{2}$.

3   The iteration $x_{n+1} = x_n + 2(1 + \cos x_n)/\sin x_n$, $x_0 = 0.5$, gives $x_n = 8.332\,635$, $9.548\,061$, $9.424\,622$, $9.424\,778$,   with   errors $\varepsilon_n = 1.092\,143$, $-0.123\,283$, $1.563\,8 \times 10^{-4}$, 9.939×10^{-8} from the root 3π. The convergence is not quadratic; the curve is not smooth near $x = 3\pi$, so the usual rules do not apply.

4   The iteration is $x_{n+1} = x_n + 4(1 + \cos x_n)/\sin x_n$, $x_0 = 0.5$. It spends some time near 5π, then some near 7π, and so on. It never approaches any root of the equation $(1 + \cos x)^{1/4} = 0$. The graph of $(1 + \cos x)^{1/4}$ has a cusp at each root, with infinite derivative there.

5   Method (i) was used in 1 and took 4 iterations to get a small error. Method (ii) uses $x_0 = 0.8$, $x_1 = 0.822\,070\,691\,4$, $x_2 = 0.819\,237\,750\,4$ to get $x_0^* = 0.819\,175\,187\,5$ by Aitken's method; two more iterations give $x_1^* = 0.819\,172\,112\,0$, $x_2^* = 0.819\,172\,573\,7$; another use of Aitken's method gives $x_0^{**} = 0.819\,172\,513\,4$. In this case method (ii) is less efficient; it could be a better method to use if the derivative of the function was hard to find.

Exercise 16D

1   (i) Substitution gives $\frac{1}{4} = \frac{1}{2}3\theta^2$, so $\theta = \sqrt{\frac{1}{6}}$, clearly between 0 and 1.
    (ii) $(1+x)^3 = 1 + 3x + \frac{1}{2}x^2 \times 6(1 + \theta x)$ is required. This gives $\theta = \frac{1}{3}$.

2   The theorem gives $\ln(1+x) = \int_1^{1+x} \frac{1}{t}\,dt = x - \frac{1}{2}x^2/(1 + \theta x)^2$, $0 < \theta < 1$. If $|x| < 10^{-3}$, then $|\frac{1}{2}x^2/(1 + \theta x)^2| < \frac{1}{2} \times 10^{-6}/(1 - 10^{-3})^2 = 5.01 \times 10^{-7}$.

3   $x_1 = X + h - f(X+h)/f'(X+h)$. Now use $f(X+h) = f(X) + hf'(X) + \frac{1}{2}h^2 f''(X + \theta h)$, and $f'(X+h) = f'(X) + hf''(X + \phi h)$ from the ordinary Mean Value Theorem applied to f'; and also use $f(X) = 0$ as X is the root of the equation. Thus

$$\text{error} = X - x_1 \approx -h + \{hf'(X) + \tfrac{1}{2}h^2 f''(X)\}/\{f'(X) + hf''(X)\}.$$

Rearrange, using the standard approximation $(1+\alpha)^{-1} \approx 1 - \alpha$, to get the error to be approximately $-\frac{1}{2}h^2 f''(X)/f'(X)$.

4   $\int_a^{a+h} \cos x \, dx = h \cos a - \frac{1}{2}h^2 \sin(a + \theta h)$.   Hence $-\frac{1}{2}\sin(a + \theta h) = (-h\cos a + \sin(a+h) - \sin a)/h^2$ as   required.   Now $\sin(a+h) - \sin a = 2\cos(a + \frac{1}{2}h)\sin\frac{1}{2}h \approx h \cos(a + \frac{1}{2}h)$ and so the right hand side above $\approx (\cos(a + \frac{1}{2}h) - \cos a)/h$. Use trigonometric formulas again to get $-\frac{1}{2}\sin(a + \frac{1}{4}h)$ approximately. And so $\theta \approx \frac{1}{4}$ when h is small.

5   The rate of increase of the slope of $y = f(x)$ has least value m (say) and the greatest value M (say) and is assumed to be continuous. If the quadratic has rate of increase of slope m

it will lie below (or on) $y=f(x)$ and so have a smaller (or equal) area; if it has rate of increase of slope M it will be too high and have too large an area. Thus you need to use an intermediate rate of increase of slope, which will be $f''(c)$ for some c between a and $a+h$. That is, the quadratic

$$y=f(a)+(x-a)f'(a)+\tfrac{1}{2}(x-a)^2f''(c)$$

has the same area, and so (by integrating y),

$$\int_a^{a+h} f(x)\,dx = hf(a)+\tfrac{1}{2}h^2f'(a)+\tfrac{1}{6}h^3f''(a+\theta h), \quad 0<\theta<1.$$

Replace f by f' and carry out the integration to get the second result.

Exercise 16E

1   (i) $\ln(1+x)=x-\tfrac{1}{2}x^2+\tfrac{1}{3}x^3-\ \ldots\ +(-1)^{n+1}\dfrac{x^n}{n}+(-1)^{n+2}\dfrac{x^{n+1}}{(n+1)(1+\theta x)^{n+1}}$,

   $0<\theta<1$.

   (ii) $e^x=1+x+\dfrac{x^2}{2!}+\dfrac{x^3}{3!}+\ \ldots\ +\dfrac{x^n}{n!}+\dfrac{e^{\theta x}x^{n+1}}{(n+1)!}$, $0<\theta<1$.

   (iii) $\qquad (1+x)^k=1+kx+\dfrac{k(k-1)x^2}{2!}+\ \ldots\ +\dfrac{k(k-1)\ldots(k-n+1)x^n}{n!}$

   $\qquad\quad +\dfrac{k(k-1)\ldots(k-n)(1+\theta x)^{k-n-1}x^{n+1}}{(n+1)!}$, $0<\theta<1$.

2   (i) The error in $\ln(1+x)\approx x-\tfrac{1}{2}x^2+\tfrac{1}{3}x^3-\tfrac{1}{4}x^4$ is $\dfrac{x^5}{5(1+\theta x)^5}$; this has largest size
   $\tfrac{1}{5}\times 10^{-5}/(0.9)^5=3.39\times 10^{-6}$.
   (ii) Similarly the error is $e^{\theta x}x^5/5!$ with largest value 9.21×10^{-8}.
   (iii) Similarly the error is $k(k-1)\ldots(k-4)(1+\theta x)^{k-5}x^5/120$; its largest size depends on k. If $k\geqslant 5$ it is $k(k-1)\ldots(k-4)1.1^{k-5}\times 10^{-5}/120$, and if $k<5$ it is $k(k-1)\ldots(k-4)0.9^{k-5}\times 10^{-5}/120$.

3   $$f(a+h)=f(a)+hf'(a)+\tfrac{1}{2}h^2f''(a)+\tfrac{1}{6}h^3f'''(a+\theta h)$$

   from Taylor's theorem, and

   $$f(a-h)=f(a)-hf'(a)+\tfrac{1}{2}h^2f''(a)-\tfrac{1}{6}h^3f'''(a-\phi h)$$

   similarly, with $0<\phi<1$.
   Subtracting gives

   $$f(a+h)-f(a-h)=2hf'(a)+\tfrac{1}{6}h^3\{f'''(a+\theta h)+f'''(a-\phi h)\}$$

   and the last term $\approx\tfrac{1}{3}h^3f'''(a)$ if h is small and if f''' is continuous.
   Using longer Taylor theorems and adding gives the second result, in a similar fashion.

4   For $f(x)=x^{11/3}$ we have $f'(x)=\tfrac{11}{3}x^{8/3}$, $f''(x)=\tfrac{88}{9}x^{5/3}$, $f'''(x)=\tfrac{440}{27}x^{2/3}$. Hence (a suitable) Taylor's theorem gives

   $$x^{11/3}=0+0+0+\dfrac{1}{3!}x^3\,\tfrac{440}{27}(\theta x)^{2/3},\ 0<\theta<1.$$

   That is, $\theta^{2/3}=\tfrac{163}{440}$, so that $\theta=0.223\,4$.
   There can be no higher order Taylor theorem here, because higher derivatives do not exist at $x=0$.

5 By experiment you can find that the remainders tend to 0
(i) for $-1<x<1$, (ii) for all x, (iii) for $-1<x<1$.

Exercise 16F

1 Substitute $y=ax+bx^2+cx^3$ (which has $y=0$ at $x=0$) and get $a+2bx+3cx^2=x-(a^3x^3+\text{higher terms})/x$. Thus we choose a, b, c to satisfy $a=0$ (coefficient of x^0), $b=\frac{1}{2}$ (coefficient of x), $c=-\frac{1}{3}a^3=0$ (coefficient of x^2). The approximate solution is thus

$$y\approx\tfrac{1}{2}x^2 \text{ near } x=0.$$

2 Substitution gives $b+2cx+3dx^2+4ex^3=(b+cx+dx^2+ex^3)^2-x$. Equating coefficients now gives $b=b^2$, $2c=2bc-1$, $3d=c^2+2bd$, $4e=2be+2cd$. The only solution is

$$b=0,\ c=-\tfrac{1}{2},\ d=\tfrac{1}{12},\ e=-\tfrac{1}{48}.$$

At $x=\frac{1}{4}$ the term ex^4 contributes only -8.14×10^{-5}, so you would expect to have an answer correct to (at least) 4 decimal places.

3 Use $y\approx ax+bx^2+cx^3+dx^4$ near $x=0$. Substitution gives $a+2bx+3cx^2+4dx^3\approx x(a+bx+cx^2+dx^3)^2+1$. Comparing coefficients gives $a=1$, $b=\frac{1}{2}a^2$, $c=\frac{2}{3}ab$, $d=\frac{1}{4}(b^2+2ac)$. The approximate solution is thus $y\approx x+\frac{1}{2}x^2+\frac{1}{3}x^3+\frac{11}{48}x^4$. Starting at $x=0.01$ and $y=0.010050335$ should give an accurate answer. Or you could start at $x=0$ and $dy/dx=1$ from the approximate solution.

4

x	1	2	3	4	5	6	7
y	1.122 36	0.582 63	0.337 26	0.250 69	0.200 12	0.166 66	0.117 16

using $h=0.01$ and the second order Euler method. This is slightly better than the improved Euler method in this case.

Exercise 16G

1 (i) The left hand side is $\cos a-\cos(a+h)$, directly. The right hand side is
$$\int_a^{a+h}\sin(2a+h-X)\,dX=[\cos(2a+h-X)]_a^{a+h}=\cos a-\cos(a+h) \text{ also.}$$
(ii) Similarly, each side is $e^{a+h}-e^a$.

2 $R_n=\displaystyle\int_0^h\frac{x^n}{n!}f^{(n+1)}(a+h-x)\,dx$

$=\displaystyle\int_a^{a+h}\frac{(X-a)^n}{n!}f^{(n+1)}(2a+h-X)\,dX$ on putting $x=X-a$.

3 Use Taylor's theorem in the form

$$f(x)=f(a)+(x-a)f'(a)+\ldots+\frac{(x-a)^{n-1}}{(n-1)!}f^{(n-1)}(a+\phi(x-a))$$

where $0 < \phi < 1$ and ϕ may well depend on $x - a$. Integrate from a to $a + h$ to get

$$\int_a^{a+h} f(x)\,dx = hf(a) + \tfrac{1}{2}h^2 f'(a) + \ldots + \int_a^{a+h} \frac{(x-a)^{n+1}}{(n-1)!} f^{(n-1)}(a + \phi(x-a))\,dx.$$

Now use an argument like that in (a)(iii) to change the last term to $\dfrac{h^n}{n!} f^{(n-1)}(a + \theta h)$, $0 < \theta < 1$.

Exercise 17A

1   For this F you have the Mean Value Theorem

$$\tfrac{1}{10}(x-t)^2 + 1 = \tfrac{1}{10}x^2 + 1 - t\tfrac{1}{5}(x - \theta t),$$

from which $\theta = \tfrac{1}{2}$ (for all x and t). Now $|e_1/e_0| < 1$ if $|F'(X - \theta e_0)| < 1$. This gives $-5 < X - \tfrac{1}{2}e_0 < 5$ as the condition for $|e_1|$ to be smaller than $|e_0|$, and this can be rearranged as $-X - 10 < x_0 < -X + 10$. Since $X = 1.1270\ldots$ in this case the requirement is $-11.127 < x_0 < 8.873$. In fact you do *not* get convergence for $-11.127 < x_0 < -8.873$ because x_1 then falls outside 8.873, even though e_1 is reduced in size. From symmetry the interval of convergence is $-8.873 < x_0 < 8.873$.

2   In this case $F'(x) = -\tfrac{1}{3}(x+1)^{-4/3}$ and $|F'(-1.40)| = 1.131$, while $|F'(0.82)| = 0.150$. Hence convergence to the root near 0.82 will occur, but not to the root near -1.40.

3   Here $F'(x) = 3x^2 - 2x - 1$ and so $F'(1) = 0$. The iteration equation is $X - e_{n-1} = F(X - e_n) = F(X) - e_n F'(X) + \tfrac{1}{2}e_n^2 F''(X - \theta e_n)$, using Taylor's theorem. Since we are using $X = 1$ and $F(X) = 1$ and $F'(X) = 0$ we get $e_{n+1} = -\tfrac{1}{2}e_n^2 F''(X - \theta e_n)$. Since $F''(1) = 4$ you may expect to get convergence if $|e_0| <$ about $\tfrac{1}{2}$, because then e_1 should be less than e_0, and so on. Numerical trial shows that you get convergence for $0.469 < x_0 < 1.414$.
$F'(\sqrt{2}) = 2.17$, $F'(-\sqrt{2}) = 7.83$, so expect convergence to neither of these roots. This is confirmed by numerical trial.

Exercise 17B

1	x	-1	-0.9	$-0.844\,239$	$-0.820\,883$	$-0.816\,061$
	Error	0.184 15	0.084 15	0.028 385	0.005 029 3	$2.077\,2 \times 10^{-4}$

x	$-0.815\,853\,394\,8$	$-0.815\,853\,515\,4$
Error	$3.794\,01 \times 10^{-7}$	4.5×10^{-11}

n	0	1	2	3	4
e_{n+1}/e_n^2	2.481	4.008	6.242	8.212	8.793

$-f''/2f'$ at the root $= 8.818$, which is close to the final value of e_{n+1}/e_n^2.

2 $-1, -0.87, -0.822\,034\,356\,8, -0.815\,881\,117\,5, -0.815\,853\,515\,5$. The iteration ends after 4 steps instead of 6, so it is a little faster.

3 From the calculations in the text

$$e_{n+1} \approx e_n - e_n \frac{f'(X) - \tfrac{1}{2}e_n f''(X)}{f'(X) - e_n f''(X)}$$

so that if $f'(X) = 0$ you get $e_{n+1} \approx \tfrac{1}{2}e_n$, provided that $f''(X) \neq 0$.

4 Expand $f(x_n) = f(X - e_n)$ as $f(X) - e_n f'(X) + \tfrac{1}{2}e_n^2 f''(X - \theta e_n)$. Since $f(X) = f'(X) = 0$ you have approximately $e_n = \pm\{2f(x_n)/f''(x_n)\}^{1/2}$; $f/f'' > 0$ in most cases near a root, and use $\pm$ according to which works. Thus the new estimate of X is $x_{n+1} = x_n \pm \{2f(x_n)/f''(x_n)\}^{1/2}$. Analysis like that in the text shows that

$$|e_{n+1}| \approx \tfrac{1}{3}e_n^2 |f'''(x_n)/f''(x_n)|.$$

Using the $-$ sign gives the following

x	2	1.602 64	1.443 82	1.415 15	1.414 214 532
Error	$-0.585\,8$	$-0.188\,4$	$-0.029\,6$	-9.315×10^{-4}	$-9.694\,4 \times 10^{-7}$

Exercise 17C

1 For any initial value you find $x_0 \to -x_0 \to x_0$, so there is no convergence. This is because $f'(x) = \tfrac{1}{2}\operatorname{sgn} x(|x|)^{-1/2}$ gives the iteration to be $x_{n+1} = x_n - 2\operatorname{sgn} x_n|x_n| = -x_n$.

2 Here $f'(0) = \tfrac{5}{3} \times 0^{2/3} = 0$, and $f''(\theta x) = \tfrac{10}{9}(\theta x)^{-1/3}$; the equation is therefore $x^{5/3} = \tfrac{5}{9}x^2(\theta x)^{-1/3} = \tfrac{5}{9}\theta^{-1/3}x^{5/3}$, true for $\theta = (\tfrac{5}{9})^3$. Newton–Raphson iteration here is

$$x_{n+1} = x_n - \frac{x_n^{5/3}}{\tfrac{5}{3}x_n^{2/3}} = \tfrac{2}{5}x_n,$$

so that it converges to zero, but not quadratically. The justification follows the text in (b), since this function has a suitable Taylor theorem involving a second derivative.

3 $1 + \cos(3\pi - y) = 1 - \cos y \approx \tfrac{1}{2}y^2$ if y is small, i.e. if x is near 3π. Thus $\sqrt{(1 + \cos x)} \approx |y|/\sqrt{2}$ for x near 3π, and $f'' \to 0$ as $x \to 3\pi$. Hence the error analysis in (b) cannot apply. For $(1 + \cos x)^{1/4}$ the curve near $x = $ odd multiple of π is approximately $2^{-1/4}|y|^{1/2}$, and the consequent iteration turns out to be approximately that in **1**.

Exercise 17D

1 $f'(a) = 3a^2$, and $\frac{1}{h}\{f(a+h) - f(a)\} = \frac{1}{h}\{3a^2h + 3ah^2 + h^3\}$. The error is therefore

$$-3ah - h^2 \approx -\tfrac{1}{2}h \times 6a = -\tfrac{1}{2}hf''(a). \quad \text{Similarly} \quad \frac{1}{2h}\{f(a+h) - f(a-h)\} = 3a^2 + h^2,$$

giving error $h^2 = -\tfrac{1}{6}h^2 f'''(a)$.

2 $f(a-h) = f(a) - hf'(a) + \tfrac{1}{2}h^2 f''(a - \theta h)$. Hence

$$\frac{1}{h}\{f(a) - f(a-h)\} = f'(a) - \tfrac{1}{2}hf''(a - \theta h),$$

and the error is approximately $\tfrac{1}{2}hf''(a)$.

3 $f(a\pm 2h)=f(a)\pm 2hf'(a)+2h^2f''(a)\pm\frac{4}{3}h^3f'''(a)+\frac{2}{3}h^4f^{(4)}(a)$ with remainder terms approximately $\pm\frac{4}{15}h^5f^{(5)}(a)$. Consequently $f(a+2h)-f(a-2h)\approx 4hf'(a)+\frac{2}{3}h^3f'''(a)+\frac{8}{15}h^5f^{(5)}(a)$, and in a similar fashion $f(a+h)-f(a-h)\approx 2hf'(a)+\frac{1}{12}h^3f'''(a)+\frac{1}{60}h^5f^{(5)}(a)$. Thus the expression given $\approx f'(a)-\frac{1}{30}h^4f^{(5)}(a)$, and the error $\approx\frac{1}{30}h^4f^{(5)}(a)$.

4 Use $f(a\pm h)=f(a)\pm hf'(a)+\frac{1}{2}h^2f''(a)\pm\frac{1}{6}h^3f'''(a)$ with remainder terms approximately $\frac{1}{24}h^4f^{(4)}(a)$, to get the required result. Then $f(a+2h)-2f(a)+f(a-2h)\approx 4h^2f''(a)+\frac{4}{3}h^4f^{(4)}(a)$. Taking

$$\frac{1}{12h^2}\{-f(a+2h)+16f(a+h)-30f(a)+16f(a-h)-f(a-2h)\}$$

gives $f''(a)$ with an error almost zero. Using longer forms of Taylor's theorem shows that the error is proportional to $h^4f^{(6)}(a)$, approximately.

5 Taylor theorems including terms in h^4 give

$$f(a+h)+\tfrac{3}{2}f(a)-3f(a-h)+\tfrac{1}{2}f(a-2h)\approx 3hf'(a)+\tfrac{1}{4}h^4f^{(4)}(a).$$

It looks as though you get an accurate value of $f(a+h)$ from $f'(a)$ (found from the differential equation) and previously calculated values of f. However the method may be unstable, as in Section 19.4(*b*), and you need some starting values.

Exercise 17E

1 $f''(x)=e^{-x}$, with largest value 1 in $0\leqslant x\leqslant 4$. Hence the error is no larger than $\frac{1}{24}\times 4\times h^2$. In fact it should be considerably smaller, as a *typical* value of $f''(x)$ is more like $e^{-1.5}=0.2231$.

h	0.5	0.25	0.1	0.05
Value	0.971 5	0.979 13	0.981 275	0.981 582 1
Error	0.010 2	0.002 55	4.089×10^{-4}	$1.022 5\times 10^{-4}$
Error/h^2	0.040 6	0.040 8	0.040 9	0.040 9

2 $|\text{Errors}|/h^2=3.07\times 10^{-2}$ for h down to 0.005, after that still close to 3×10^{-2}. Here $f''(x)=(-2+4x^2)e^{-x^2}$, with largest size 2 in the interval, average size nearer 1. The $|\text{errors}|/h^2$ are certainly less than $2\times\frac{1}{24}=0.083$.

Exercise 17F

1 In this case $f''=2$ and the error estimate is $-\frac{1}{6}h^2$. The trapezium rule here gives the estimate

$$\tfrac{1}{2}h\{0^2+2h^2+2(2h)^2+\ldots +2(n-1)^2h^2+n^2h^2\}$$

where $h=1/n$. This is $h^3\sum_{i=1}^{n}i^2-\tfrac{1}{2}h^3n^2=h^3\sum_{i=1}^{n}i^2-\tfrac{1}{2}h$. Now $\sum_{1}^{n}i^2=\tfrac{1}{6}n(n+1)(2n+1)$ and so the estimate of the integral is $\tfrac{1}{6}(1+h)(2+h)-\tfrac{1}{2}h=\tfrac{1}{3}+\tfrac{1}{6}h^2$. Since the actual value of $\int_{0}^{1}x^2\,dx$ is $\tfrac{1}{3}$, the error estimate is exactly correct.

2 (i)

h	$\frac{2}{3} \times$ rectangle $+ \frac{1}{3} \times$ trapezium	Simpson
$\pi/40$	0.500 000 125 0	0.500 001 696 1
$\pi/80$	0.500 000 006 7	0.500 000 105 8

(ii) Using the figures in Sections 10.3 and 10.4 gives the errors to be

h	$\frac{2}{3}R + \frac{1}{3}T$	S
0.1	5.7×10^{-8}	82×10^{-8}
0.05	1×10^{-8}	5×10^{-8}

Thus in each case the new estimate is considerably better than Simpson's rule.

Exercise 17G

1 $f^{(4)}(x) = (12 - 48x^2 + 16x^4)e^{-x^2}$. This has largest size 12 in $0 \leqslant x \leqslant 1$. Hence the error must be less than $\frac{1}{180} \times 12h^4 = h^4/15$. Figures for $|\text{error}|/h^4$ from Section 10.4 are

h	0.25	0.1	0.05
$|\text{error}|/h^4$	0.0080	0.0082	0.0080

This is much less than $\frac{1}{15}$; the typical value of $f^{(4)}(x)$ is much less than 12, as $f^{(4)}(x)$ is negative for about half of the interval.

2 (i) $I = \displaystyle\int_{-h}^{h} \{f(0) + xf'(0) + \frac{1}{2}x^2f''(0) + \frac{1}{6}x^3f'''(0) + \frac{1}{24}x^4f^{(4)}(\theta x)\}\,dx$

(ii) $f(\pm h) = f(0) \pm hf'(0) + \frac{1}{2}h^2f''(0) \pm \frac{1}{6}h^3f'''(0) + \frac{1}{24}h^4f^{(4)}(\pm\theta_{\pm}h)$ where $\theta_{+} = \phi$ and $\theta_{-} = \lambda$ gives the required answer on substitution in S.

(iv) The integral lies between $m\displaystyle\int_{-h}^{h}\frac{1}{24}x^4\,dx$ and $M\displaystyle\int_{-h}^{h}\frac{1}{24}x^4\,dx$, where m and M are the smallest and largest values of $f^{(4)}$. Assuming continuity of $f^{(4)}$, the integral must be $\frac{1}{60}h^5$ times some intermediate value of $f^{(4)}$, say $f^{(4)}(\mu h)$. Similarly the bracketed terms lie between $2m$ and $2M$, and hence can be written as $2f^{(4)}(\psi h)$.

3 $f^{(4)}(x) = (\cos x + 3 - 7\sin^2 x - 6\sin^2 x \cos x + \sin^4 x)e^{\cos x}$. A graph of $f^{(4)}(x)$ gives $f^{(4)}_{\max} = 4e$, $f^{(4)}_{\min} \approx -3$, and a typical value of at most 1. The largest possible error size is therefore $(2e/15)h^4$, and a likely error size is about $\frac{1}{30}h^4$. Values of I are

h	0.01	0.05	0.10
I	7.195 275 016	7.195 274 921	7.195 273 463
$|\text{Error}|/h^4$	—	0.015 2	0.015 53

and the errors are about $\frac{1}{60}h^4$.

Exercise 18A

1 Since $u_{n+1}-u_n=au_n/(u_n+v_n)-2u_n$ we should try the equations $\dfrac{du}{dt}=\dfrac{au}{u+v}-2u,$

$\dfrac{dv}{dt}=\dfrac{bv}{u+v}-2v.$

The answers will probably be much the same as before.

2 For example $df/dt=-af+brf$ gives a natural death rate a of foxes when there is no food, and an increase proportional to fox numbers when there is food available, the increase depending on the quantity of food. The rabbit equation might be $dr/dt=pr-qr^2-erf$, giving an increase of rabbits (up to $r=p/q$) in the absence of foxes, and a loss of rabbits due to their becoming fox food.

3 If y/x is large some guerillas may despair; if a fraction cy/x do, then the appropriate equation is $dx/dt=-axy-cy$. But other models might well fit better to reality.

4 (i) If n now refers to hours since the start of the battle, we have to use $x_{n+1}=x_n-ay_n/12$ and $y_{n+1}=y_n-bx_n/12$, since the death rates per hour are only a twelfth of those per day.
(ii) Similarly $dx/dt=-ay/12$ and $dy/dt=-bx/12$.

5 (i) Those who recover are those who were infected some days ago, so that dR/dt should relate to earlier values of I, say at time T earlier: $dR/dt=cI(t-T)$, which is not an easy equation.
(ii) $a=c$, those who cease to be ill become those who have recovered, unless some die of the disease.
(iii) New people enter the population by migration from other areas, and others leave; extra terms can be put in the equations for this.
(iv) Some 'susceptibles' do not catch the disease even if exposed to it.
(v) Diseases are often not as simple as the models of them.

Exercise 18B

1 (a) The formal expressions of the solutions, e.g.
$$\begin{cases} x(t)=30\,000(e^{0.02t}+e^{-0.02t})-20\,000(e^{0.02t}-e^{-0.02t}) \\ x_n=30\,000(1.02^n+0.98^n)-20\,000(1.02^n-0.98^n), \end{cases}$$
are extremely similar, and are equally easy to use.
(b) The numerical values predicted at later times match quite well to start with, but slightly less well later on. E.g.

n	x_n	$x(t)$	y_n	$y(t)$
5	56 237	56 294	17 078	17 095
10	53 044	53 151	14 332	14 361
25	46 579	46 813	6 884	6 920
40	44 365	44 722	102	106

The solutions are equally easy to produce and use.

2 Using the combination $w = b^{1/2}x + a^{1/2}y$ and $z = b^{1/2}x - a^{1/2}y$, for which the equations are $dw/dt = -(ab)^{1/2}w$ and $dz/dt = (ab)^{1/2}z$ gives the solutions

$$\begin{cases} 2b^{1/2}x = (b^{1/2}X - a^{1/2}Y)e^{(ab)^{1/2}t} + (b^{1/2}X + a^{1/2}Y)e^{-(ab)^{1/2}t} \\ 2a^{1/2}y = -(b^{1/2}X - a^{1/2}Y)e^{(ab)^{1/2}t} + (b^{1/2}X + a^{1/2}Y)e^{-(ab)^{1/2}t}. \end{cases}$$

Clearly if $b^{1/2}X - a^{1/2}Y > 0$, y becomes zero; i.e. x wins if $bX^2 > aY^2$, as required.

3 (i) $w = x + y$ satisfies $dw/dt = 5w$, and $z = x - y$ satisfies $dz/dt = z$. Hence $x + y = (X + Y)e^{5t}$ and $x - y = (X - Y)e^t$, giving

$$x = \tfrac{1}{2}(X + Y)e^{5t} + \tfrac{1}{2}(X - Y)e^t, \quad y = \tfrac{1}{2}(X + Y)e^{5t} - \tfrac{1}{2}(X - Y)e^t.$$

(ii) $w = x + 2y$ satisfies $dw/dt = 7w$, and $z = x - 2y$ satisfies $dz/dt = 3z$. The solution is

$$\begin{cases} x = \tfrac{1}{2}(X + 2Y)e^{7t} + \tfrac{1}{2}(X - 2Y)e^{3t} \\ y = \tfrac{1}{4}(X + 2Y)e^{7t} - \tfrac{1}{4}(X - 2Y)e^{3t}. \end{cases}$$

(iii) $\dfrac{d}{dx}(\alpha y + \beta z) = (\alpha + b\beta)y + (a\alpha + \beta)z$. This has the form $\dfrac{dw}{dx} = \lambda w$ if $\alpha + b\beta = \lambda\alpha$ and $a\alpha + \beta = \lambda\beta$. Eliminating α (or β) shows there is a solution if $\lambda^2 - 2\lambda + 1 - ab = 0$, i.e. $\lambda = 1 \pm \sqrt{(ab)}$. Then $\alpha/\beta = \dfrac{\lambda - 1}{a} = \pm\sqrt{\left(\dfrac{b}{a}\right)}$ gives the appropriate combinations, e.g. $b^{1/2}y \pm a^{1/2}z$ (or any multiple of these).

4 $dW/dt = -aR$, $dR/dt = bW$. If you proceed by combinations as in question **3**(iii) you find $\lambda^2 = -ab$, and correspondingly you get imaginary exponentials for W and R. It is easier to follow the suggested line and try

$$R = \alpha \cos \omega t + \beta \sin \omega t.$$

Since R is zero at $t = 0$, $\alpha = 0$. Substitution in the equations gives $W = \dfrac{1}{b}\omega\beta \cos \omega t$ and $\dfrac{1}{b}\omega^2\beta = a\beta$. Hence $\omega^2 = ab$ and the solution is $W = \beta\sqrt{(a/b)}\cos\{t\sqrt{(ab)}\}$, $R = \beta \sin\{t\sqrt{(ab)}\}$, until $t = \tfrac{1}{2}\pi/\sqrt{(ab)}$.

5 You find that $b\,dx/dt - ay\,dy/dt = 0$, i.e. $\dfrac{d}{dt}(bx - \tfrac{1}{2}ay^2) = 0$. That is $bx - \tfrac{1}{2}ay^2 = $ constant, which is a set of parabolas. If $bX > \tfrac{1}{2}aY^2$, then the constant is positive, and $x > 0$ when $y = 0$, i.e. the guerillas win.

6 Add the three differential equations to get $\dfrac{d}{dt}(I + S + R) = (c - a)I$. But $I + S + R = N$, a constant, and so $(c - a)I = 0$; hence $c = a$, since $I \neq 0$ during the infection.

7 (i) $\dfrac{d}{dt}\cosh t = \dfrac{1}{2}\dfrac{d}{dt}(e^t + e^{-t}) = \tfrac{1}{2}(e^t - e^{-t}) = \sinh t$.

(ii) $\cosh^2 t = \tfrac{1}{4}(e^{2t} + 2 + e^{-2t})$; $\sinh^2 t = \tfrac{1}{4}(e^{2t} - 2 + e^{-2t})$ and so $\cosh^2 t - \sinh^2 t = 1$.

(iii) $\cosh 2t = \tfrac{1}{2}(e^{2t} + e^{-2t}) = \cosh^2 t + \sinh^2 t$, using the results in (ii).

Exercise 18C

1 (i) $\dfrac{d}{dt}(x + y) = 0$ and so $x + y = $ constant $= 3$, the value at $t = 0$. Also $\dfrac{d}{dt}(x - y) = 2(x - y)$

and so $x-y=-e^{2t}$ (using $x-y=-1$ at $t=0$). Hence $x=\frac{3}{2}-\frac{1}{2}e^{2t}$ and $y=\frac{3}{2}+\frac{1}{2}e^{2t}$.

(ii) $\ddot{y}=\dot{y}-\dot{x}=\dot{y}-(x-y)$. But $x=y-\dot{y}$ and so $\ddot{y}=2\dot{y}$ or $\dfrac{d^2y}{dt^2}=2\dfrac{dy}{dt}$. Integrating once

gives $\dfrac{dy}{dt}=2y+\text{constant}$, and using the second equation gives $dy/dt=1$ at $t=0$, so

$dy/dt=2y-3$. Solving this first order equation gives $y=\frac{3}{2}+\frac{1}{2}e^{2t}$ again, and from $x=y-\dot{y}$ you find $x=\frac{3}{2}-\frac{1}{2}e^{2t}$.

(iii) $\ddot{x}=\dot{x}-\dot{y}=\dot{x}-(y-x)$. But $y=x-\dot{x}$ and so $\ddot{x}=2\dot{x}$. Rewrite this as $v\,dv/dx=2v$, so that $dv/dx=2$. This has solution $v=2x+k$. Now $v=\dot{x}=-1$ when $t=0$, and then $x=1$. Hence we have $v=2x-3$. Rewrite this as $dx/dt=2x-3$, which is first order. The solution is as before.

2   (a) By elimination $\ddot{y}=-2\times10^{-5}y\dot{y}$. Hence $\dot{y}=-10^{-5}y^2+k$. Using initial values gives

(i) $\dot{y}=3.6-10^{-5}y^2$, which has solution $y=600(4+e^{-0.012t})/(4-e^{-0.012t})$.

(ii) $\dot{y}=-10^{-5}y^2$, which has solution $y=1000/(1+t/100)$.

(b) By combination you find $0.2x-10^{-5}y^2=\text{constant}$, which returns you to the previous route. This shows that $x=0$ when $y=\sqrt{(3.6\times10^5)}$, i.e. as $t\to\infty$ in case (i) and at $t=200/3$ in case (ii).

3   This is $v\dfrac{dv}{dx}+n^2x=0$, and so $\frac{1}{2}v^2+\frac{1}{2}n^2x^2=\text{constant}$, say $\frac{1}{2}n^2k^2$. Consequently $v=\pm n\sqrt{(k^2-x^2)}$. Choose the $+$ sign without any real loss, and derive

$$\int\frac{dx}{\sqrt{(k^2-x^2)}}=nt+\text{constant}.$$

That is, $x=k\sin(nt+c)$. We now choose k and c to match the initial conditions.

(i) $c=\frac{1}{2}\pi$, $k=a$, giving $x=a\cos nt$.

(ii) $c=0$, $k=U/n$, giving $x=(U/n)\sin nt$.

4   Differentiate the second equation and replace $\dot{I}$ by using the first:

$$\ddot{S}=-b\dot{I}S-bI\dot{S}=-bS(-aI+bIS)-bI\dot{S},$$

as required.

Rewrite the second equation as $I=-\dot{S}/(bS)$, and substitute this in the above equation to get

$$\ddot{S}=-a\dot{S}+bS\dot{S}+\dot{S}^2/S.$$

We replace $\ddot{S}$ by $T\,dT/dS$ in the usual way to find $dT/dS=-a+bS+T/S$, which is linear in T. Solving with an integrating factor gives

$$T=-aS\ln S+bS^2+CS,$$

which is hard to solve for S in terms of t.

Exercise 18D

1   Here $\dfrac{dy}{dx}=\dfrac{bx}{ay}$, which integrates via $\displaystyle\int ay\,dy=\int bx\,dx$ to give solution curves ay^2-bx^2+C. If $bX^2>aY^2$ (using initial values X and Y) then $C<0$ and $x>0$; thus the x-army wins when $bX^2>aY^2$, as before.

2   In this case $\dfrac{dy}{dx} = \dfrac{bx}{axy+cy}$, which separates as $\displaystyle\int y\,dy = \int \dfrac{bx}{ax+c}\,dx$.

This leads to the relation

$$\tfrac{1}{2}y^2 - \tfrac{1}{2}y_0^2 = \frac{b}{a}(x-x_0) - \frac{bc}{a^2}\ln\left(\frac{ax+c}{ax_0+c}\right).$$

The guerilla force is beaten if $x=0$ for $y>0$, that is if

$$\tfrac{1}{2}y_0^2 - \frac{bx_0}{a} - \frac{bc}{a^2}\ln\left(\frac{c}{ax_0+c}\right) > 0.$$

This is the required condition.

3   Division followed by separation of variables leads to $\displaystyle\int bW\,dW = \int(-aR+c)\,dR$. This solves as $bW^2 + a(R-c/a)^2 = $ constant, which are ellipses centred at $W=0$ and $R=c/a$; only the part in the first quadrant is needed.

4   Since $W = \dot{R}/b$, the equation in question **3** can be written as

$$\dot{R} = (ab)^{1/2}\{k^2 - (R-c/a)^2\}^{1/2}.$$

(You can also get there by eliminating W from the original equations.) Solving this separable equation gives

$$R = c/a + k\sin\{(ab)^{1/2}t + \alpha\},$$

to which the conditions $R=0$ and $W=W_0$ (i.e. $\dot{R}=bW_0$) at $t=0$ must be applied to find k and α. The solution is finally

$$R = \frac{c}{a}(1 - \cos(ab)^{1/2}t) + \left(\frac{b}{a}\right)^{1/2}W_0\sin(ab)^{1/2}t,$$

until R reaches its maximum value; this is part of a displaced sine curve, through the origin.

5   By division $dS/dR = -bS/a$ (since $c=a$, as above). This solves as $S = S_0 e^{-bR/a}$. Again by division $dI/dR = -1 + bS/a = -1 + (bS_0/a)e^{-bR/a}$. Integrating this, with the appropriate constant of integration, gives

$$I = -R - S_0 e^{-bR/a} + N.$$

Finally $dR/dt = aI$ is $dR/dt = a\{N - R - S_0 e^{-bR/a}\}$.

6 R can only increase, and $dR/dt = 0$ when $R + S_0 e^{-bR/a} = N$. This must occur before $R = N$, because $S_0 e^{-bR/a} > 0$, and so $R < N$ when R reaches its largest value.

Exercise 18E

1 $u = u_0 e^{(a-1)t}$, $v = v_0 e^{(p-1)t}$, where $a>1$ and $p<1$. Take an easy example like $a=2$, $p=\tfrac{1}{2}$ to see that the curves are rather like rectangular hyperbolas, coming down near the v-axis and out along the u-axis.

2   If bv is much greater than $a-1$, then the first equation is approximately $du/dt = -buv$. Similarly $dv/dt = quv$. These solve (by combination or division) as $u/b + v/q = $ constant, straight lines at an angle to the two axes.

3   By division $\dfrac{dM}{dL} = \dfrac{bM}{aL}$, if $L \neq M$. This solves as $M = kL^{b/a}$. Now $M \leqslant L$, inevitably, and this can only happen if $b/a \geqslant 1$. For $b/a > 1$ the curves are like parabolas open upwards until they meet the line $L = M$; after that $L = M$ is followed, if it is reached.

     $M(t)$ increases rapidly at first, then more slowly; similarly for $L(t)$. If $b = 2a$, $M = kL^2$ and $dL/dt = a(L - kL^2)$. This solves as $L = \dfrac{ce^{at}}{1 + kce^{at}}$, which confirms the shape; in this case $L \to 1/k$ and $M \to 1/k$ as $t \to \infty$, so that $L = M$ is not reached in a finite time.

4   The equations reduce to $dx/dt = -b(1-p)y/q$ and $dy/dt = qx(a-1)b$ when terms in xy are neglected. Write these as $dx/dt = -\alpha y$, $dy/dt = \beta x$ with $\alpha, \beta > 0$. Division gives $\alpha y^2 + \beta x^2 = $ constant by solving an equation for dy/dx, and these are ellipses. Then substitution gives, for example,

$$dy/dt = \beta(k^2 - \alpha y^2/\beta)^{1/2}$$

which solves in terms of sines (or cosines) of a constant times t. Similarly for x.

Exercise 18F

1   The period is 23.48.
(i) A long oval reaching out to $u = 45\,000$ and in to $u = 560$, with the largest v being 1750.
(ii) u reaches its maximum soon after $t = 4$, regains its starting value near $t = 7$, then reaches its minimum near $t = 14$.
(iii) A similar shaped curve, starting at its minimum.

2   $b = 0.08$ gives a light attack; there is 10% infection at 60 days, and growth is little affected. $b = 0.20$ gives a very heavy attack; there is 75% infection near 35 days and growth effectively stops around then. Realistic values depend on the weather and application of fungicides.

3   (i) $b = 10^{-4}$ (little infection of the population), duration about 40 days, 878 left uninfected.
(ii) $b = 3 \times 10^{-4}$, duration 95 days, 397 left.
(iii) $b = 10^{-3}$ (great infection), duration 45 days, 8 left uninfected.

4   Using $b = 3 \times 10^{-4}$ (the longest lasting case above) leaves less than one infectious person on board by 23 days. Note that quarantine originally meant isolation for forty days.

Exercise 19A

1   (i) $u_n = A(-2)^n + B(-1)^n$. The initial values give $A = -3$, $B = 4$.
(ii) $u_n = A\,2^n + B$. Initial values give $A = 1$, $B = 0$.
(iii) $u_n = A(\tfrac{1}{4} + \tfrac{1}{2}\sqrt{3})^n + B(\tfrac{1}{4} - \tfrac{1}{2}\sqrt{3})^n$, $A = \tfrac{1}{2} + \tfrac{7}{12}\sqrt{3}$, $B = \tfrac{1}{2} - \tfrac{7}{12}\sqrt{3}$.
As $n \to \infty$ (i) approaches $(-3)(-2)^n$, (ii) approaches 2^n, (iii) approaches $(\tfrac{1}{2} + \tfrac{7}{12}\sqrt{3})(\tfrac{1}{4} + \tfrac{1}{2}\sqrt{3})^n$, i.e. $1.51 \times (1.116)^n$, since other terms do not increase in size as n increases.

2   (a) The auxiliary equation is $c^2 - 4c + 0 = 0$, so $c = 4$ or 0. Hence the solution is $A \times 4^n + B \times 0^n = A \times 4^n$.
(b) The equation is $v_{n+1} = 4v_n$, and using methods in Chapters 1 and 2 the solution is $v_n = 4^n v_0$. Thus $u_{n+1} = 4^n v_0 = 4^{n+1} \times \tfrac{1}{4}v_0$, and so $u_n = 4^n \times \tfrac{1}{4}v_0$, i.e. a constant times 4^n as in (a).

3 $x_{n+2} = x_{n+1} - 0.04y_{n+1} = x_{n+1} - 0.04(y_n - 0.01x_n)$ using the second equation. Now $0.04y_n = x_n - x_{n+1}$ from the first equation, and so

$$x_{n+2} - 2x_{n+1} + 0.9996x_n = 0.$$

The auxiliary equation gives $c = 1 \pm \sqrt{0.0004} = 1.02$ or 0.98, and so $x_n = A(0.98)^n + B(1.02)^n$. From this $x_0 = A + B$ and $x_1 = 0.98A + 1.02B$; but the first equation gives $x_1 = x_0 - 0.04y_0$, so that A and B can be found in terms of x_0 and y_0:

$$A = \tfrac{1}{2}x_0 - y_0, \quad B = \tfrac{1}{2}x_0 + y_0.$$

Exercise 19B

1 (i) $c^2 + 2c + 5 = 0$ gives $c = -1 \pm 2j$, and so $r = \sqrt{5}$, $\theta = 116.6°$ (note that $\tan\theta = -2$ here, but $\theta \neq \tan^{-1}2$, because $\cos\theta = -1/\sqrt{5}$ and $\sin\theta = 2/\sqrt{5}$). The solution is $5^{n/2}(A\cos n\theta + B\sin n\theta)$ and fitting the given values gives $A = 0$, $B = 1$; i.e. $u_n = 5^{n/2}\sin n\theta$.
(ii) Here $r = \sqrt{5}$, $\theta = 63.4°$ and $u_n = 5^{n/2}\sin n\theta$ again (but with the new θ value).
(iii) $c = -\tfrac{1}{4} \pm \tfrac{1}{2}j$, $r = \tfrac{1}{4}\sqrt{5}$ and $\theta = 116.6°$. Fitting the initial values to $u_n = (\tfrac{1}{4}\sqrt{5})^n(A\cos n\theta + B\sin n\theta)$ gives $u_n = 4(\tfrac{1}{4}\sqrt{5})^n\sin n\theta$.
(iv) $c = \pm 2j$, $r = 2$ and $\theta = \tfrac{1}{2}\pi$. $u_n = 2^n\sin(\tfrac{1}{2}n\pi)$.

2 $\cos(n+2)\theta - 2p\cos(n+1)\theta + \cos n\theta = \cos n\theta(\cos 2\theta - 2p\cos\theta + 1) + \sin n\theta(-\sin 2\theta + 2p\sin\theta)$. If $p = \cos\theta$ then each bracket is zero, and so $\cos n\theta$ is a solution.
Let $p = \cos\theta$ for some θ between 0 and $\tfrac{1}{2}\pi$. Then $A\cos n\theta$ is a solution. But so will $B\sin n\theta$ be a solution, as they go together for this type of equation (*or* verify this by substitution). So we have $u_n = A\cos n\theta + B\sin n\theta$, and fitting the values gives

$$u_n = a\cos n\theta + \frac{b - a\cos\theta}{\sin\theta}\sin n\theta.$$

3 We have $W_{n+2} = W_{n+1} - bR_{n+1} = W_{n+1} - b(R_n + aW_n)$; but $bR_n = W_n - W_{n+1}$ and so $W_{n+2} - 2W_{n+1} + (1+ab)W_n = 0$. *Either* solve this directly, or use the previous solution $R_n = W_0(a/b)^{1/2}(1+ab)^{n/2}\sin n\theta$, together with $W_n = (R_{n+1} - R_n)/a$ and the trigonometric formula for $\sin(n+1)\theta$.

4 For $u_{n+2} + 9u_n = 0$ the solution is $u_n = 3^{n-1}\sin\tfrac{1}{2}n\pi$. For $u_{n+2} - 9u_n = 0$ we have solution $u_n = \tfrac{1}{6}\{3^n - (-3)^n\}$. Now $\sinh n\theta = \tfrac{1}{2}(e^{n\theta} - e^{-n\theta})$ and the second term is the reciprocal of the first, which is not the case in u_n. So it cannot be done easily.

Exercise 19C

1 (i) $c^2 + 4c + 4 = 0$ gives $c = -2$, so the solution has the form $u_n = A(-2)^n + nB(-2)^n$, from the work above. Fitting the values gives $u_n = (-2)^n\{1 + (\tfrac{1}{2}a - 1)n\}$.
(ii) Let $v_n = u_{n+1} + 2u_n$ so that $v_{n+1} + 2v_n = 0$. The latter has solution $v_n = C(-2)^n$. Next solve $u_{n+1} + 2u_n = C(-2)^n$ by the methods of Section 2.5 (see question 3 in Exercise 2D). The solution is $u_n = D(-2)^n - \tfrac{1}{2}Cn(-2)^n$. Fitting the values gives the solution as in (i).

2 $v_{n+1} - bv_n = 0$ is $u_{n+2} - (a+b)u_{n+1} + abu_n = 0$ and so we need $a + b = 3$, $ab = 2$; one solution is $a = 2$, $b = 1$ (the other is $a = 1$, $b = 2$). The solution of $v_{n+1} = v_n$ is $v_n = A$, and the solution of $u_{n+1} - 2u_n = A$ is $u_n = 2^nB - A$.

3 $c^2 - 2ac + 1 = 0$ has roots (i) $c = a \pm \sqrt{(a^2 - 1)}$ for $a^2 > 1$, (ii) $c = a \pm j\sqrt{(1 - a^2)}$ for $|a| < 1$, and (iii) $c = 1$ for $a = 1$. The solutions are

(i) $(a^2 - 1)^{-1/2}\{(a + \sqrt{(a^2 - 1)})^n - (a - \sqrt{(a^2 - 1)})^n\}$,

(ii) $2a(1 - a^2)^{-1/2} \sin n\theta$, where $\sin \theta = \dfrac{1}{a}\sqrt{(1 - a^2)}$,

(iii) $2n$.

Exercise 19D

1 (i) $3c^2 + 4c + 1 = 0$ gives $c = -1$ or $-\tfrac{1}{3}$, so the complementary function is $A(-1)^n + B(-\tfrac{1}{3})^n$. The particular solution is 2, so the general solution is $2 + A(-1)^n + B(-\tfrac{1}{3})^n$. Fitting the values gives $A = -\tfrac{1}{2}$, $B = -\tfrac{3}{2}$.
(ii) $c = 1$ or $-\tfrac{1}{3}$; complementary function $A + B(-\tfrac{1}{3})^n$. The particular solution cannot be a constant, so try Cn; substitution shows $C = 16$, giving the general solution $16n + A + B(-\tfrac{1}{3})^n$. Fitting the values gives $A = -\tfrac{39}{4}$, $B = -A$.
(iii) $c = -1$ or $\tfrac{1}{5}$; complementary function $A(-1)^n + B(\tfrac{1}{5})^n$; particular solution $\tfrac{5}{2}$; general solution $\tfrac{5}{2} + A(-1)^n + B(\tfrac{1}{5})^n$, $A = -\tfrac{5}{6}$, $B = -\tfrac{5}{3}$.
(iv) $c = -1$; complementary function $A(-1)^n + nB(-1)^n$; particular solution $\tfrac{1}{4}$; general solution $\tfrac{1}{4} + A(-1)^n + nB(-1)^n$, $A = -\tfrac{1}{4}$, $B = -\tfrac{5}{2}$.

2 $3 \times \tfrac{1}{6}(n+2)^2 - 6 \times \tfrac{1}{6}(n+1)^2 + 3 \times \tfrac{1}{6}n^2 = 0n^2 + 0n + 1$. $c = 1$, so the general solution is $\tfrac{1}{6}n^2 + A + Bn$, $A = -1$, $B = \tfrac{17}{6}$.

3 The equation is $v_{n+1} - v_n = 4$, which has solution $v_n = A + 4n$. So next solve $u_{n+1} - u_n = A + 4n$. By the methods of Chapter 2, it has solution $u_n = B + An + 2n^2 - 4 = C + An + 2n^2$.

Exercise 19E

1 CF is $A + B(-2)^n$.
(i) Since there is a constant in the CF, try $an^2 + bn$ as PS. Substitution gives
$$a(n+2)^2 + b(n+2) + a(n+1)^2 + b(n+1) - 2an^2 - 2bn = n + 1,$$
for all $n \geq 0$. This is $n(6a - 1) + 5a + 3b - 1 = 0$. Hence $a = \tfrac{1}{6}$ and $b = \tfrac{1}{18}$ give the PS and the GS is $A + B(-2)^n + \tfrac{1}{6}n^2 + \tfrac{1}{18}n$.
(ii) Substituting in the formulas in the text gives the same result.
(iii) Split the equation as
$$u_{n+1} - u_n = v_n, \quad v_{n+1} + 2v_n = n + 1.$$
Solve the latter as $v_n = C(-2)^n + \tfrac{1}{3}n + \tfrac{2}{9}$, by the usual methods. The equation $u_{n+1} - u_n = C(-2)^n + \tfrac{1}{3}n + \tfrac{2}{9}$ has CF A and PS $B(-2)^n + an^2 + bn$, where $B = -\tfrac{1}{3}C$ and where a and b are found by substitution.

2 Substitution gives $6Dn + 2C + 6D = n + 1$ (for all $n \geq 0$), and so $D = \tfrac{1}{6}a$, $C = \tfrac{1}{2}(b-1)$.

3 CF is $A + B(-\tfrac{1}{4})^n$. Expect a PS $an^2 + bn$; substitution gives $a = \tfrac{2}{5}$, $b = \tfrac{34}{25}$, so the GS is $A + B(-\tfrac{1}{4})^n + \tfrac{2}{5}n^2 + \tfrac{34}{25}n$. Fitting the values gives $A = -\tfrac{226}{125}$, $B = \tfrac{476}{125}$. For large n the term $\tfrac{2}{5}n^2$ dominates the solution.

4 (i) $c = 1$ is not a root of the auxiliary equation, so $an^2 + bn + d$ is a suitable guess. Substitution shows that $a = \tfrac{1}{2}$, $b = -\tfrac{2}{3}$, $d = \tfrac{14}{18}$.
(ii) $c = 1$ is a root of the auxiliary equation, so try $an^3 + bn^2 + dn$, because there is another root also. Substitution gives $a = \tfrac{1}{4}$, $b = -\tfrac{9}{16}$, $d = \tfrac{47}{32}$.

Exercise 19F

1   (i) CF $A(-4)^n + B2^n$. Try PS $C3^n$, and substitute to find $C = \frac{1}{7}$. Hence GS $u_n = A(-4)^n + B2^n + \frac{1}{7}3^n$, and fitting values gives $A = -\frac{1}{7}$, $B = 0$.

(ii) CF $A5^n + B(-1)^n$. Try PS $C\sin\frac{1}{2}n\pi + D\cos\frac{1}{2}n\pi$ and substitute to find $\sin\frac{1}{2}n\pi\{-C + 4D - 5C\} + \cos\frac{1}{2}n\pi\{-D - 4C - 5D\} = 2\sin\frac{1}{2}n\pi$, for all $n \geq 0$. Using $n = 0$ and $n = 1$ (or by comparing coefficients) gives $-C + 4D - 5C = 2$, $-D - 4C - 5D = 0$, so that $C = -\frac{9}{39}$, $D = \frac{2}{13}$, and the GS is $A5^n + B(-1)^n - \frac{3}{13}\sin\frac{1}{2}n\pi + \frac{2}{13}\cos\frac{1}{2}n\pi$. Fitting values gives $A = \frac{1}{78}$, $B = -\frac{1}{6}$.

(iii) CF $A(-3)^n + B$. Try PS $C3^n$, because 3^{n+1} is just 3×3^n, and find $C = \frac{1}{4}$. Fitting values to GS gives $\frac{3}{8}(-3)^n + \frac{3}{8} + \frac{1}{4}3^n$.

(iv) Auxiliary equation $c^2 + 1 = 0$, so the CF is $A\cos\frac{1}{2}n\pi + B\sin\frac{1}{2}n\pi$. Hence for PS try $an\cos\frac{1}{2}n\pi + bn\sin\frac{1}{2}n\pi$, where $a = -\frac{1}{2}$ and $b = 0$. The GS is therefore $A\cos\frac{1}{2}n\pi + B\sin\frac{1}{2}n\pi - \frac{1}{2}n\cos\frac{1}{2}n\pi$, and fitting the given values results in $u_n = \cos\frac{1}{2}n\pi + \sin\frac{1}{2}n\pi - \frac{1}{2}n\cos\frac{1}{2}n\pi$.

(v) The CF is $A3^n + B(-1)^n$ so take $an3^n$ as PS. Substitution gives $a = \frac{1}{36}$. Fitting the conditions leads to $A = \frac{11}{48}$, $B = \frac{37}{48}$.

(vi) The auxiliary equation is $(c - 3)^2 = 0$, so the CF is $A3^n + Bn3^n$, and hence the PS must be $dn^2 3^n$. Substitute this in the equation to find $d = \frac{1}{18}$. Fitting the conditions gives $A = 0$, $B = -\frac{1}{18}$.

2   $n = 0$ gives $2Br^2 + pBr = a$; $n = 1$ gives $3Br^2 + 2pBr - (pr + r^2)B = a$. Both equations are the same, and give $B = a/(2r^2 + pr)$.

3   The first equation is satisfied by $\cos n\theta$ and $\sin n\theta$ if $\cos\theta = c$, $\sin\theta = \sqrt{(1 - c^2)}$. The second equation has CF $A\cos n\theta + B\sin n\theta$ and PS $an\cos n\theta + bn\sin n\theta$. Substitution gives (after the use of trigonometric formulas)

$$a\{\cos(n+2)\theta - \cos n\theta\} + b\{\sin(n+2)\theta - \sin n\theta\} = 2\sin n\theta.$$

Further manipulation gives

$$\cos n\theta\{a(\cos 2\theta - 1) + b\sin 2\theta\} + \sin n\theta\{b(\cos 2\theta - 1) - a\sin 2\theta - 2\} = 0.$$

Using $n = 0$ and 1, or equating coefficients to zero, since this has to hold for all n, gives $a = -\cot\theta$ and $b = -1$; in terms of c, $a = -c/\sqrt{(1 - c^2)}$.

4   Substitution gives $C = \frac{1}{2}ar^{-2}$.

5   Elimination of W_n gives the second order equation

$$R_{n+2} - 2R_{n+1} + (1 + ab)R_n = az_n$$

whose CF (as in Section 19.1(b)) is

$$r^n(A\cos n\theta + B\sin n\theta)$$

where $r = (1 + ab)^{1/2}$ and $\theta = \tan^{-1}\{(ab)^{1/2}\}$.

(i) The PS is the constant p/b. Initial values $R_0 = 0$, and a given value of W_0 (and so $R_1 = aW_0$) are fitted by $A = -p/b$ and $B = (aW_0 - p/b)/(r\sin\theta) + (p\cot\theta)/b = W_0(a/b)^{1/2}$.

(ii) The PS is of the form Cs^n, and substitution gives $C = aq/\{s^2 - 2s + (1 + ab)\}$. Initial values are fitted by $A = -C$ and $B = W_0(a/b)^{\frac{1}{2}} + C(1 - s)/(ab)^{1/2}$: note that this reduces to the solution to (i) when $s = 1$, as it should.

Solutions for W_n come from $W_n = (R_{n+1} - R_n)/a$.

6   (a) The auxiliary equation is $c^2 - 4c + k = 0$, which has real and distinct solutions for

$k < 4$, equal roots if $k = 4$, and complex conjugate roots for $k > 4$. Therefore there are the following cases:
(i) $k = 3$, $c = 1$ and 3, $CF = A + B\,3^n$.
(ii) $k < 4$, $k \neq 3$, $CF\ Ac_1^n + Bc_2^n$, $c_{1,2} = 2 \pm \sqrt{(4 - k)}$.
(iii) $k = 4$, $CF\ A\,2^n + Bn2^n$.
(iv) $k > 4$, $CF\ k^{n/2}\{A \cos n\theta + B \sin n\theta\}$, $\cos \theta = 2/k^{1/2}$, $\sin \theta = k^{-1/2}\sqrt{(k - 4)}$.
(b) The appropriate forms of PS are (i) $Cn + D\,2^n$, (ii) $C + D\,2^n$, (iii) $C + Dn^2\,2^n$, (iv) $C + D\,2^n$, where the values of C and D (found by substitution) are (i) $C = -\frac{1}{2}, D = -1$; (ii) $C = 1/(k - 3)$, $D = 1/(k - 4)$; (iii) $C = 1$, $D = \frac{1}{12}$; (iv) as for (ii).
(c) The values of A and B come from the initial conditions and are (i) $A = -\frac{1}{4}, B = \frac{5}{4}$; (ii) $A + B = (7 - 2k)/(k^2 - 7k + 12)$, $A - B = (k - 2)/\{(k - 3)\sqrt{(4 - k)}\}$; (iii) $A = -1$, $B = \frac{11}{6}$; (iv) $A = (7 - 2k)/(k^2 - 7k + 12)$, $B = (k - 2)/\{(k - 3)\sqrt{(k - 4)}\}$.

Exercise 19G

1 (i) CF is $A(-4)^n + B$, so if A is ever non-zero in a numerical solution, the CF will grow rapidly in size, i.e. the solution is unstable. Numerical calculation matches $u_n = -1/(n - 1)$ very closely to start with. But by $n = 21$ the computed result will be badly wrong. The exact solution is indeed $-1/(n - 1)$ here, but rounding errors cause A and B to become non-zero.
(ii) Numerical solution gives a sequence of numbers gradually decreasing to 1; the solution is stable (starting with $u_1 = 1.01$ gives a very similar series of numbers). In fact u_n approaches $1 + 1/n$ as n gets large.

2 The solution of the modified equation is $-4(\frac{1}{2})^n - \frac{16}{3}(-\frac{1}{2})^n + \frac{4}{3}$, which converges to $\frac{4}{3}$ as n gets large; the solution is not the same as for the unmodified equation, but it shows the stability for large n.

3 Take $x_{\text{old}} = nh$, $y_{\text{old}} = y_n$, $y_{\text{new}} = y_{n+1} = y_{\text{old}} + h(-\pi y_n + x_n)$. Then we have $y_{n+1} = y_n(1 - h\pi) + nh^2$. The solution of this equation is $y_n = A(1 - h\pi)^n + nh/\pi - 1/\pi^2$. This is a stable solution provided that $|1 - h\pi| < 1$, so certainly it is stable if h is small.

4 The auxiliary equation is $c^2 - c - \frac{1}{2} = 0$, $c = \frac{1}{2}\{1 \pm \sqrt{3}\}$. Now $\frac{1}{2}(1 + \sqrt{3}) > 1$, so the term $A\{\frac{1}{2}(1 + \sqrt{3})\}^n$ in the CF becomes very large if $A \neq 0$ (and the $1/(n^2 + 1)$ terms will ensure that rounding errors come into a numerical solution). The solution is unstable.

Exercise 20A

1 Adding gives $R_{n+1} + W_{n+1} = U_{n+1} = U_n - \frac{1}{10}V_n$. Subtracting gives the other equation.
The eigenvalues for the R, W equations come from $\lambda^2 - 2\lambda + \frac{101}{100} = 0$, $\lambda = 1 \pm \frac{1}{10}j$, $\begin{pmatrix} 1 \\ j \end{pmatrix}$; and for $\lambda = 1 - \frac{1}{10}j$, $\begin{pmatrix} 1 \\ -j \end{pmatrix}$, any multiples. For the U, V equations the eigenvalues are the same, and the eigenvectors are interchanged.

2 The eigenvalue equation is $\lambda^2 - 2\lambda + (1 + ab) = 0$, with solutions $\lambda = 1 \pm j\sqrt{(ab)}$. For $\lambda = 1 + j\sqrt{(ab)}$ the eigenvector is $\begin{pmatrix} \sqrt{a} \\ j\sqrt{b} \end{pmatrix}$, for $\lambda = 1 - j\sqrt{(ab)}$ the eigenvector is $\begin{pmatrix} \sqrt{a} \\ -j\sqrt{b} \end{pmatrix}$.

3 The three separate equations are $f_{n+1} = s_n + 3t_n$, $s_{n+1} = \frac{1}{2}f_n$, $t_{n+1} = \frac{1}{3}s_n$. Since $f_{n+3} = s_{n+2} + 3t_{n+2}$ and $s_{n+2} = \frac{1}{2}f_{n+1}$ and $t_{n+2} = \frac{1}{3}s_{n+1} = \frac{1}{6}f_n$, we have $f_{n+3} = \frac{1}{2}f_{n+1} + \frac{1}{2}f_n$

as the third order equation. The auxiliary equation is $c^3 = \frac{1}{2}c + \frac{1}{2}$, with roots $1, -\frac{1}{2} \pm \frac{1}{2}j$. The eigenvalue equation is

$$\det \begin{pmatrix} -\lambda & 1 & 3 \\ \frac{1}{2} & -\lambda & 0 \\ 0 & \frac{1}{3} & -\lambda \end{pmatrix} = 0$$

or $\lambda^3 - \frac{1}{2}\lambda - \frac{1}{2} = 0$, giving the same values as for c.

4   The equations are $f_{n+1} = u_n$, $u_{n+1} = v_n$, $v_{n+1} = \frac{1}{2}u_n + \frac{1}{2}f_n$, with matrix

$$\begin{pmatrix} 0 & 1 & 0 \\ 0 & 0 & 1 \\ \frac{1}{2} & \frac{1}{2} & 0 \end{pmatrix}.$$

The eigenvalues are still $1, -\frac{1}{2} \pm \frac{1}{2}j$, with eigenvectors now

$$\begin{pmatrix} 1 \\ 1 \\ 1 \end{pmatrix}, \quad \begin{pmatrix} 1 \\ -\frac{1}{2} + \frac{1}{2}j \\ -\frac{1}{2}j \end{pmatrix}, \quad \begin{pmatrix} 1 \\ -\frac{1}{2} - \frac{1}{2}j \\ \frac{1}{2}j \end{pmatrix} \quad \text{for } \lambda = 1, \ -\frac{1}{2} + \frac{1}{2}j, \ -\frac{1}{2} - \frac{1}{2}j$$

respectively.

For the matrix in question 3 the eigenvectors are

$$\begin{pmatrix} 6 \\ 3 \\ 1 \end{pmatrix}, \quad \begin{pmatrix} 1-j \\ -1 \\ \frac{1}{3}(1+j) \end{pmatrix}, \quad \begin{pmatrix} 1+j \\ -1 \\ \frac{1}{3}(1-j) \end{pmatrix}.$$

Exercise 20B

1   $M = \begin{pmatrix} 0.8 & 1.4 \\ 1.4 & 0.8 \end{pmatrix}$. The eigenvalues are 2.2, -0.6 and the eigenvectors are $\begin{pmatrix} 1 \\ 1 \end{pmatrix}$ and $\begin{pmatrix} 1 \\ -1 \end{pmatrix}$, and so $U = \begin{pmatrix} 1 & 1 \\ 1 & -1 \end{pmatrix}$, $U^{-1} = \begin{pmatrix} \frac{1}{2} & \frac{1}{2} \\ \frac{1}{2} & -\frac{1}{2} \end{pmatrix}$.

$U^{-1}MU = \begin{pmatrix} \frac{1}{2} & \frac{1}{2} \\ \frac{1}{2} & -\frac{1}{2} \end{pmatrix}\begin{pmatrix} 2.2 & -0.6 \\ 2.2 & 0.6 \end{pmatrix} = \begin{pmatrix} 2.2 & 0 \\ 0 & -0.6 \end{pmatrix} = \Lambda$, diagonal matrix of eigenvalues.

Then

$$U\Lambda^n U^{-1} = \begin{pmatrix} 1 & 1 \\ 1 & -1 \end{pmatrix}\begin{pmatrix} (2.2)^n & 0 \\ 0 & (-0.6)^n \end{pmatrix}\begin{pmatrix} \frac{1}{2} & \frac{1}{2} \\ \frac{1}{2} & -\frac{1}{2} \end{pmatrix}$$

$$= \begin{pmatrix} 2.2^n + (-0.6)^n & 2.2^n - (-0.6)^n \\ 2.2^n - (-0.6)^n & 2.2^n + (-0.6)^n \end{pmatrix}.$$

Consequently

$$x_n = \frac{1}{2}\{2.2^n + (-0.6)^n\}x_0 + \frac{1}{2}\{2.2^n - (-0.6)^n\}y_0$$

and

$$y_n = \frac{1}{2}\{2.2^n - (-0.6)^n\}x_0 + \frac{1}{2}\{2.2^n + (-0.6)^n\}y_0.$$

2    $U = \begin{pmatrix} 6 & 1-j & 1+j \\ 3 & -1 & -1 \\ 1 & \frac{1}{3}(1+j) & \frac{1}{3}(1-j) \end{pmatrix}$ and $U^{-1} = -\dfrac{1}{10}j \begin{pmatrix} \frac{2}{3}j & \frac{4}{3}j & 2j \\ -2+j & 1-3j & 9+3j \\ 2+j & -1-3j & -9+3j \end{pmatrix}.$

3              $U^{-1}u_{n+1} = z_{n+1} = U^{-1}MU(U^{-1}u_n) + U^{-1}K$

$$= \Lambda z_n + K, \text{ say.}$$

The CF for this equation for z_n is $\Lambda^n a$, for any constant vector a; and a PS is $(I-\Lambda)^{-1}K$. Hence the GS is

$$z_n = \Lambda^n a + (I-\Lambda)^{-1}K.$$

Finding a from a given value of z_0 gives

$$a = z_0 - (I-\Lambda)^{-1}K,$$

so that

$$Uz_n = u_n = U\Lambda^n\{z_0 - (I-\Lambda)^{-1}K\} + U(I-\Lambda)^{-1}K$$

$$= U\Lambda^n U^{-1}u_0 + U(I-\Lambda^n)(I-\Lambda)^{-1}U^{-1}k.$$

This has assumed that $(I-\Lambda)^{-1}$ exists, i.e. that no eigenvalue of M is equal to 1. It has also assumed a full set of independent eigenvalues for M.

4   The last equation gives $w_n = A$, a constant. Then $v_{n+1} - v_n = A$ has the solution $v_n = B + An$. And $u_{n+1} - u_n = B + An$ has the solution $u_n = C + Bn + \frac{1}{2}An^2$, for any constants A, B, C. Here the matrix M has only one eigenvalue, $\lambda = 1$, and only one

eigenvector $\begin{pmatrix} 0 \\ 0 \\ 1 \end{pmatrix}$. So the matrix U does not exist.

Exercise 20C

1   Here $M = \begin{pmatrix} 2 & 1 \\ 2 & 3 \end{pmatrix}$; $\lambda = 4, 1$; eigenvectors $\begin{pmatrix} 1 \\ 2 \end{pmatrix}$ and $\begin{pmatrix} 1 \\ -1 \end{pmatrix}$, so U is as given. The matrix

$E = \begin{pmatrix} e^{4t} & 0 \\ 0 & e^t \end{pmatrix}$, and the solution is

$$x = UEU^{-1}x_0 = \frac{1}{3}\begin{pmatrix} 1 & 1 \\ 2 & -1 \end{pmatrix}\begin{pmatrix} e^{4t} & 0 \\ 0 & e^t \end{pmatrix}\begin{pmatrix} 1 & 1 \\ 2 & -1 \end{pmatrix}\begin{pmatrix} x_0 \\ y_0 \end{pmatrix}$$

$$= \begin{pmatrix} \frac{1}{3}(e^{4t} + 2e^t)x_0 + \frac{1}{3}(e^{4t} - e^t)y_0 \\ \frac{1}{3}(2e^{4t} - 2e^t)x_0 + \frac{1}{3}(2e^{4t} + e^t)y_0 \end{pmatrix}.$$

2   Eliminating y gives $\ddot{x} - 5\dot{x} + 4x = 0$. Now put $z = \dot{x}$ and you have the two equations $\dot{x} = z$, $\dot{z} = 5z - 4x$, which have the given matrix M. The eigenvalues are 4 and 1 as before, and the eigenvectors are $\begin{pmatrix} 1 \\ 4 \end{pmatrix}$ and $\begin{pmatrix} 1 \\ 1 \end{pmatrix}$ respectively. Therefore $U = \begin{pmatrix} 1 & 1 \\ 4 & 1 \end{pmatrix}$.

3   Substitution of $x = -M^{-1}k$ shows that this is a PS. The CF for this equation is the solution of $dx/dt = Mx$, which from the methods of this section is UEA for any constant vector A. Hence the GS is $x = UEA - M^{-1}k$. This has assumed that U exists (which it will do if M has distinct eigenvalues) and that M^{-1} exists (which it will do if zero is not an eigenvalue of M).

4   Using the given forms for **x** and **k** gives, on substituting,

$$p\mathbf{e}_1 = \mathbf{M}(tp\mathbf{e}_1 + q\mathbf{e}_2 + r\mathbf{e}_3) + \alpha\mathbf{e}_1 + \beta\mathbf{e}_2 + \gamma\mathbf{e}_3.$$

But $\mathbf{Me}_1 = \mathbf{0}$, corresponding to eigenvalue 0, and $\mathbf{Me}_2 = \lambda_2\mathbf{e}_2$, $\mathbf{Me}_3 = \lambda_3\mathbf{e}_3$. Hence $p\mathbf{e}_1 = \lambda_2 q\mathbf{e}_2 + \lambda_3 r\mathbf{e}_3 + \alpha\mathbf{e}_1 + \beta\mathbf{e}_2 + \gamma\mathbf{e}_3$. This determines the constants in the PS: $p = \alpha$, $q = -\beta/\lambda_2$, $r = -\gamma/\lambda_3$.

Exercise 21A

1    $d^2Z/dt^2 = \dot{V}$, so the given equation of motion can be rewritten as $\dot{V} = b(1 - aZ) - cV|V|$, where $\dot{Z} = V$. The program is based on

$$Z_{\text{inter}} = Z_{\text{old}} + h\dot{Z}_{\text{old}}, \quad V_{\text{inter}} = V_{\text{old}} + h\dot{V}_{\text{old}}$$

where $\dot{Z}_{\text{old}}$ and $\dot{V}_{\text{old}}$ come from the equations, and then

$$Z_{\text{new}} = Z_{\text{old}} + \tfrac{1}{2}h(\dot{Z}_{\text{old}} + \dot{Z}_{\text{inter}}), \quad V_{\text{new}} = V_{\text{old}} + \tfrac{1}{2}h(\dot{V}_{\text{old}} + \dot{V}_{\text{inter}}).$$

2   Maximum height about 255 m, after 162 s; next at rest at 247 m, at time 213 s. This used the crude value $h = 1$.

3   If the burner is not used, then heat is lost from the canopy and so buoyancy will be reduced; this has not been modelled. If the burner is used, then this ought to be included in the modelling; to pretend that the burner is used just enough to maintain buoyancy is unrealistic. There will usually be a breeze horizontally. The use of a linear variation of density with height may be a poor model. The drag due to relative motion may well not be exactly proportional to speed squared. The numbers chosen are not likely to be accurate. But on the whole the results seem quite plausible.

Exercise 21B

1   (i) Use times $t = rh$, $r = 0, 1, 2, \ldots$ Put $Z(rh) = Z_r$. Then using standard derivative formulas gives

$$\frac{Z_{r+1} - 2Z_r + Z_{r-1}}{h^2} + c\frac{(Z_{r+1} - Z_{r-1})^2}{4h^2} - b(1 - aZ_r) = 0$$

as the discretised equation, for $r = 1, 2, \ldots$
(ii) $Z_0 = 0$ is given. Now $Z_1 = Z(h)$ and Taylor's theorem is $Z(h) = Z(0) + h\dot{Z}(0) + \tfrac{1}{2}h^2\ddot{Z}(0) + \tfrac{1}{6}h^3\dddot{Z}(0) + $ a remainder term in h^4. From the given conditions, $\dot{Z}(0) = 0$; from the equation $\ddot{Z}(0) = b$. From the equation differentiated again, $\dddot{Z}(0) = 0$. Hence we take $Z_1 = \tfrac{1}{2}bh^2$, to be a consistent approximation.

2   Rearranging the equation in (i) above gives the quadratic $Z_{r+1}^2 + PZ_{r+1} + Q = 0$, $r = 1, 2, \ldots$, with $P = 4/c - 2Z_{r-1}$ and $Q = Z_{r-1}^2 + \{4Z_{r-1} - 8Z_r + 4h^2b(aZ_r - 1)\}/c$. The required solution is $Z_{r+1} = \{-P + (P^2 - 4Q)^{1/2}\}/2$ so that $Z_{r+1} > 0$ when $r = 1$. The maximum value of Z is 255 m, reached at 162 s, as before, again using $h = 1$.

3   No. $P \approx -470$, $Q \approx 54\,822$, $P^2 - 4Q \approx 1599$, and there is no difficulty in calculating the next value of Z.

4   (i) X increases from $t = 4.09$ to 4.095; this is physically impossible for an emptying pipe.
(ii) C has reached such a small size by $t = 4.09$ that after then it is smaller than h^4 ($= 6.25 \times 10^{-10}$), and its value in the approximation $X_{r+1}^2 - BX_{r+1} + C \approx 0$ is too small to give an accurate value for X_{r+1}.

Exercise 21C

1 The graph is a rounded off version of:

straight line from $(0,0)$ to $(0.75, -0.36)$, plus a half parabola
from $(0.75, -0.36)$ to $(1,0)$.

2 A direct calculation of the fourth derivative is an awful task, liable to error. If you calculate $f''(a+h)$, $f''(a)$, $f''(a-h)$, then $f^{(4)}(a) \approx \{f''(a+h) - 2f''(a) + f''(a-h)\}/h^2$. Each second derivative can be found similarly from function values at appropriate points. Using $h=0.001$ you find $f^{(4)}(0.99) \approx 2.4 \times 10^9$. There is an even easier method at 0.01, because near there $x^{80/9} \approx 10^{-18}$ which is negligible in comparison with x. Hence $f^{(4)}(0.01) \approx \frac{105}{16}(0.01)^{-9/2} \approx 6.6 \times 10^9$. To make the error in Simpson's rule small you need a small value for $h^4(b-a)\max|f^{(4)}|/180 \approx 3.7 \times 10^7 \times h^4$. So you need h as small as 1 or 2×10^{-3}. It is probably easier to use several values of h in Simpson's rule, rather than do the above estimation.

3 (i) Write d^2Z/dt^2 as $V\,dV/dZ$, and then as $\frac{1}{2}dW/dZ$ where $W=V^2$. This gives the required equation.

(ii) Integrating factor e^{2cZ}, so that $We^{2cZ} = \int 2b(1-aZ)e^{2cZ}dZ$. Hence

$$W = \left(\frac{ab}{2c^2} + \frac{b}{2}\right)(1 - e^{-2cZ}) - \frac{ab}{c}Z.$$

(iii) CF is Ae^{-2cZ}, and PS is $\alpha Z + \beta$ where $\alpha = -ab/c$ and $\beta = b/c + \frac{1}{2}ab/c^2$ by substitution. The value of A is found from the initial value.

(iv) $W=0$ (or $V=0$) when $Z=M$, given by

$$\left(\frac{ab}{2c^2} + \frac{b}{c}\right)(1 - e^{-2cM}) = \frac{ab}{c}M,$$

i.e.

$$(1 + 2c/a)(1 - e^{-2cM}) = 2cM.$$

For $c=0.1$ and $a=0.004$ this has solution $M=255$; in fact if $1+2c/a$ is large, the solution is inevitably almost exactly $(1+2c/a)/(2c)$ because the equation for M can be written as $e^{-m} = 1 - m/(1 + 2c/a)$, $m = 2cM$.

(v) We now have $dZ/dt = V = W^{1/2} = \{R(1 - e^{-2cZ}) - abZ/c\}^{1/2}$, where $Z=0$ at $t=0$ and $Z=M$ at $t=T$ (say). This separable equation integrates, using $Z=0$ at $t=0$ and $Z=M$ at $t=T$ (say), as $T = \int_0^M \{R(1 - e^{-2cZ}) - abZ/c\}^{-1/2}\,dZ$.

(vi) The time for the first $\frac{1}{10}$ m is easily worked out by a Taylor series in the original equation: substitute $Z = \alpha t^2 + \beta t^3 + \gamma t^4$ (because $Z = \dot{Z} = 0$ at $t=0$) and find $\alpha = \frac{1}{2}b$, $\beta = 0$, $\gamma = -\frac{1}{12}(\frac{1}{2}a + b^2c)$. Then solving the quadratic for t when $Z=0.1$, with the previous values of a, b, c, gives $t=0.448$ s.

The time from $Z=0.1$ to $Z=254.9$ (i.e. just less than M) can be done by Simpson's rule. With $h=0.1$ the estimate is 158.310 793 9 and with $h=0.2$ it is 158.361 442 7. Assuming that these results fit a formula $A + Bh^4$ (where A is the correct value of the integral) gives that the integral is 158.307 417 3.

The time from 254.9 to 255 is calculated by the change of variables $Z = M - x$ in the integral. The main terms in M all sum to give zero from the definition of M; other terms involving M are all in terms of $e^{-2cM} \approx 0$. So the integral reduces to $\int_0^{0.1} (abx/c)^{-1/2}$ $dx = 2(ab/c)^{-1/2}(0.1)^{1/2} = 3.162$.

Finally, the total time is the sum of the three parts, 161.917 s, which agrees well with the early estimates.

The improved Euler method on the differential equation is easy and accurate in this case; followed in simplicity by the discretisation method.

Exercise 22A

1   The equation is $d^2x/dt^2 + 33\frac{1}{3}x = 16\frac{2}{3}$, with $x = 0.4$ and $\dot{x} = 0$ at $t = 0$. The CF (from Exercise 18C, question 3) is of the form $k\sin(nt + c)$, where $n^2 = 33\frac{1}{3}$. The PS is just $\frac{1}{2}$, and so the GS is $\frac{1}{2} + k\sin(nt + c)$. Fitting the initial conditions gives $y = \frac{1}{2} - 0.1\cos nt$, $n = 5.7735$.

2   The period is $2\pi/n = 1.088$ s.

3   Since $h = r^2\,d\theta/dt$, $h = 25 \times 0.24 = 6$. Differentiate $d\theta/dt = h/r^2$ to get $d^2\theta/dt^2 = -(2h/r^3)\,dr/dt$, and hence at the time of observation $dr/dt = -1$ AU per year.

4   We have to solve $d^2r/dt^2 - 36/r^3 = -41/r^2$ with $r = 5$ and $dr/dt = -1$ at $t = 0$. Experience in Chapter 21 suggests that solving the pair of equations

$$\frac{dr}{dt} = v, \quad \frac{dv}{dt} = \frac{36}{r^3} - \frac{41}{r^2}$$

with $r = 5$ and $v = -1$ at $t = 0$ by the improved Euler method will be easiest and accurate enough. With step length $h = 0.005$ (but with $h = 0.001$ near $v = 0$) I found $v = 0$ at $r = 0.4780$ (at $t = 1.659$), and $r = 1$ at times $t = 1.543$ and $t = 1.775$.

In fact, for this equation you can find v explicitly in terms of r by using $d^2r/dt^2 = v\,dv/dr$ and integrating once to get

$$v^2 = 2E - 36/r^2 + 82/r,$$

with E found from initial values as -6.98. This gives $r = 0.4779$ when $v = 0$; it also gives the maximum value of r to be 5.396 AU.

5   To get a really good equation here would be a very large task. Suppose the buoy is a vertical cylinder of cross-sectional area A and mass M. Let the height of its base above the sea floor be z, and height of the wave be y. Then the buoyancy force on the cylinder is $\rho g(y - z)A$, by Archimedes' theorem. Some sea water will be forced to move vertically by the vertical motion of the buoy, say a volume V. There will also be a frictional resistance force F between buoy and water. All this together gives an equation of motion

$$M\,d^2z/dt^2 = -Mg + \rho g(y - z)A - V\rho\,d^2z/dt^2 - F.$$

You might take $y = a\sin\omega t$; you might guess at V; you might assume F to be proportional to A and ρ and $\dot{z}^2$. The numbers to use would be hard to find.

Exercise 22B

Pressures are in metres of water. There is a gain of 8 through the pump, a loss in long pipes and also in each radiator. There is a change between floors due to gravity. When the pump is not running the pressures are all 14.0 on the upper floor, 16.5 on the lower.

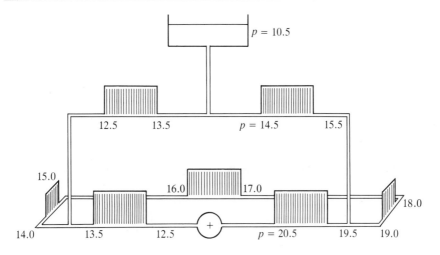

Exercise 22C

1   Voltage × current = power, so current = 0.02/6 amperes. Since current × resistance = voltage, resistance = 36/0.02 = 1800 ohms. Current = rate of flow of charge, so charge = $(0.02/6) \times 3600 \times 300 = 3600$ coulombs.

2   (i) The same current flows through each resistance, so the voltage drop is Ir for the first and IR for the second. By Kirchhoff's second law $V = Ir + IR$ and so $V/I = r + R$. For a single resistance S you would have $V/I = S$. Hence $S = r + R$: resistances in series add directly.

(iii) Let the currents through r and R be J and $I - J$ respectively (no loss at the junction, Kirchhoff's first law). Using the second law $V = Jr$ (through r) and $V = (I - J)R$ (through R). Hence $V/r + V/R = I$. But for a single resistance S, $V/S = I$. Therefore

$$\frac{1}{S} = \frac{1}{r} + \frac{1}{R},$$

the law for combining two resistances in parallel.

3   (i) As in question 2(i) the current is I throughout, and using Kirchhoff's second law gives $V = L_1 dI/dt + L_2 dI/dt + L_3 dI/dt$. For a single inductance L, $V = L dI/dt$. Hence $L = L_1 + L_2 + L_3$.

(ii) The charges generated must all be $\pm Q$; hence by Kirchhoff's second law $V = Q/C_1 + Q/C_2 + Q/C_3$. For a single capacitor C, $V = Q/C$. Hence

$$\frac{1}{C} = \frac{1}{C_1} + \frac{1}{C_2} + \frac{1}{C_3}.$$

(iii) As in question 2(ii) set up currents I_1, I_2, I_3 through the inductors L_1, L_2, L_3; by Kirchhoff's first law $I = I_1 + I_2 + I_3$ is the current from the generator. By Kirchhoff's second law

$$V = L_1 dI_1/dt, \ V = L_2 dI_2/dt, \ V_3 = L_3 dI_3/dt.$$

and so $dI/dt = V/L_1 + V/L_2 + V/L_3$. For a single inductor $dI/dt = V/L$. Consequently

$$\frac{1}{L} = \frac{1}{L_1} + \frac{1}{L_2} + \frac{1}{L_3}.$$

For three capacitors in parallel, the charges are $\pm Q_1$ on C_1, $\pm Q_2$ on C_2, $\pm Q_3$ on C_3; and $Q_1 + Q_2 + Q_3 = Q$ has passed through the generator. Using Kirchhoff's second law gives

$$V = Q_1/C_1, \quad V = Q_2/C_2, \quad V_3 = Q_3/C_3$$

so that $Q = Q_1 + Q_2 + Q_3 = V(C_1 + C_2 + C_3)$. For a single capacitor C you have $Q = VC$, and so

$$C = C_1 + C_2 + C_3$$

for capacitors in parallel.

4 By Kirchhoff's first law the current in R is $I - J$. We have, from Kirchhoff's second law,

$$Q/C + L\,dI/dt = V_0 \cos \omega t$$

$$R(I - J) + L\,dI/dt = V_0 \cos \omega t;$$

subtracting these two equations, and then differentiating gives

$$R(dI/dt - dJ/dt) = (1/C)\,dQ/dt.$$

Replace dI/dt from the first equation and J from the equation $J = dQ/dt$: this gives the required result.

5 We have $Q = V_0 C \cos \omega t - LC\,dI/dt$ in question 4, so that $J = -\omega V_0 C \sin \omega t - LC\,d^2I/dt^2$. Substitute this in the second equation in question 4 to get

$$LRC\,d^2I/dt^2 + L\,dI/dt + RI = V_0 \cos \omega t - \omega RCV_0 \sin \omega t.$$

Exercise 22D

1 (i) Differentiating the x equation gives

$$\ddot{x} = -ax\dot{y} - a\dot{x}y - c\dot{y} = -ax(-bx) + a\dot{x}^2/(ax+c) - c(-bx),$$

on eliminating $\dot{y}$ using the second equation and y using the first equation. That is,

$$\frac{d^2x}{dt^2} = \frac{a}{ax+c}\left(\frac{dx}{dt}\right)^2 + abx^2 + bcx.$$

The substitution $d^2x/dt^2 = v\,dv/dx$, where $v = dx/dt$, gives a linear equation for $w = v^2$: $dw/dx = 2aw/(ax+c) + 2abx^2 + 2bcx$, which can be solved for w.
(ii) From the first equation $d^2L/dt^2 = adL/dt - adM/dt$, and also $M = L - (1/a)\,dL/dt$. Now using the second equation gives

$$\frac{d^2L}{dt^2} = a\frac{dL}{dt} - ab\left(L - \left(\frac{dL}{dt}\right)\Big/a\right)\frac{dL}{dt}\Big/(aL)$$

$$= b\left(\frac{dL}{dt}\right)^2\Big/(aL) + (a-b)\frac{dL}{dt}.$$

Putting $\dfrac{d^2L}{dt^2} = V\,dV/dL$ reduces this to (if $V \neq 0$)

$$\frac{dV}{dL} = \frac{bV}{aL} + a - b$$

which is an easy linear equation for V in terms of L.
(Note that $x(t)$ and $L(t)$ are rather hard to find.)

2   We have $d^2T/dt^2 = -a\,dT/dt + b\,d\theta/dt$ and also $b\theta = b\theta_0 + dT/dt + a(T-T_0)$, from the first equation. Using the second equation gives

$$d^2T/dt^2 = -a\,dT/dt + bcT + bk\theta_0 - (c+k)(b\theta_0 + dT/dt + aT - aT_0).$$

This is the second order equation for T,

$$\frac{d^2T}{dt^2} + (a+c+k)\frac{dT}{dt} + (ac+ak-bc)T = -bc\theta_0 + (ac+ak)T_0.$$

3   The equations are $\dot{\mathbf{x}} = \mathbf{Mx}$, with $\mathbf{M} = \begin{pmatrix} -a & 0 & 0 \\ a & -b & 0 \\ 0 & b & 0 \end{pmatrix}$, $\mathbf{x} = \begin{pmatrix} x \\ y \\ z \end{pmatrix}$. The eigenvalue

equation is $\lambda^3 + (a+b)\lambda^2 + ab\lambda = 0$, with solutions $\lambda = 0, -a, -b$ and eigenvectors

$\begin{pmatrix} 0 \\ 0 \\ 1 \end{pmatrix}, \begin{pmatrix} b-a \\ a \\ -b \end{pmatrix}, \begin{pmatrix} 0 \\ 1 \\ -1 \end{pmatrix}$ respectively. Hence $\mathbf{U} = \begin{pmatrix} 0 & b-a & 0 \\ 0 & a & 1 \\ 1 & -b & -1 \end{pmatrix}$ and

$\mathbf{U}^{-1} = \begin{pmatrix} 1 & 1 & 1 \\ \dfrac{1}{b-a} & 0 & 0 \\ -\dfrac{a}{b-a} & 1 & 0 \end{pmatrix}$. The matrix $\mathbf{E} = \begin{pmatrix} 1 & 0 & 0 \\ 0 & e^{-at} & 0 \\ 0 & 0 & e^{-bt} \end{pmatrix}$, and the solution is

$\mathbf{x} = \mathbf{UEU}^{-1}\mathbf{x}_0$. This reduces to the same solution as in Section 22.4(c).

Exercise 23A

1   The equation factorises as $\left(\dfrac{d}{dx} + 6\right)\left(\dfrac{d}{dx} - 2\right)y = f(x)$, so we solve $\dfrac{dz}{dx} + 6z = f(x)$ and

then $\dfrac{dy}{dx} - 2y = z$.

(i) $z = Ae^{-6x}$, $y = Be^{2x} - \frac{1}{8}Ae^{-6x}$.
(ii) $z = Ae^{-6x} + 1$, $y = Be^{2x} - \frac{1}{8}Ae^{-6x} - \frac{1}{2}$.
(iii) $z = 1$, using the values at $x = 0$ to find A; then $y = \frac{1}{2}e^{2x} - \frac{1}{2}$.
(iv) Fit both values to the formula for y in (ii) and get

$$A = (1-e^2)/(\tfrac{1}{4}e^2 + \tfrac{3}{4}e^{-6}), \quad B = \tfrac{1}{2} + \tfrac{1}{8}A.$$

2   The equation factorises as $\left(\dfrac{d}{dx} + 2\right)\left(\dfrac{d}{dx} - 1\right)y = e^x$, and so we solve first $\dfrac{dz}{dx} + 2z = e^x$

as $z = Ae^{-2x} + \frac{1}{3}e^x$. Next we must solve $dy/dx - y = Ae^{-2x} + \frac{1}{3}e^x$. By earlier methods this gives $y = -\frac{1}{3}Ae^{-2x} + Be^x + \frac{1}{3}xe^x$. Fitting the given values gives the solution to be $y = \frac{1}{9}e^{-2x} - \frac{1}{9}e^x + \frac{1}{3}xe^x$.

3   The equation factorises as $\left(\dfrac{d}{dx} + 1\right)\left(\dfrac{d}{dx} + 1\right)y = e^{-x}$. Solving $dz/dx + z = e^{-x}$ gives

$z = Ae^{-x} - xe^{-x}$. Then solving $dy/dx + y = Ae^{-x} - xe^{-x}$ gives $y = Be^{-x} - Axe^{-x} - \frac{1}{2}x^2e^{-x}$.

4 Solve first $dz/dx - 4z = 6x$ to get $z = A'e^{4x} - \frac{3}{2}x - \frac{3}{8}$. Then solve $dy/dx + 3y = A'e^{4x} - \frac{3}{2}x + \frac{3}{8}$ to find $y = B'e^{-3x} + \frac{1}{7}A'e^{4x} - \frac{1}{2}x + \frac{1}{24}$, which is the same as found earlier, with different names for the constants in the solution.

5 (i) The equation is $\left(\dfrac{d}{dx} - \dfrac{1}{x}\right)\left(\dfrac{d}{dx} - 1\right)y = x$. Solve $\dfrac{dz}{dx} - \dfrac{1}{x}z = x$ to get $z = Ax + x^2$.

Then $y = -x^2 - (2+A)(x+1) + Be^x$.

(ii) This equation is $\left(\dfrac{d}{dx} - \tan x\right)\left(\dfrac{d}{dx} + 1\right)y = \sin x$. Solve $\dfrac{dz}{dx} - z\tan x = \sin x$ by an integrating factor:

$$\frac{d}{dx}(z\cos x) = \cos x \sin x = \tfrac{1}{2}\sin 2x.$$

Hence $z = A\sec x - \frac{1}{4}\cos 2x$. No progress seems likely with $dy/dx + y = A\sec x - \frac{1}{4}\cos 2x$.

Exercise 23B

1 (i) Substitute $y = Ae^{kx} + Be^{lx}$ into $\dfrac{d^2y}{dx^2} - (k+l)\dfrac{dy}{dx} + kly = 0$.

(ii) Substitute $y = Ae^{kx} + Bxe^{kx}$ into $\dfrac{d^2y}{dx^2} - 2k\dfrac{dy}{dx} + k^2y = 0$.

(iii) Substitute $y = e^{kx}(C\cos sx + D\sin sx)$ into $d^2y/dx^2 - 2k\,dy/dx + (s^2 + k^2)y = 0$.

2 (i) $m^2 + m - 6 = 0$, $(m+3)(m-2) = 0$, $y = Ae^{-3x} + Be^{2x}$.

(ii) $m^2 - 4m + 4 = 0$, $(m-2)(m-2) = 0$, $y = Ae^{2x} + Bxe^{2x}$.

(iii) $m^2 + 6m + 9 = 0$, $(m+3)(m+3) = 0$, $y = Ae^{-3x} + Bxe^{-3x}$.

(iv) $m^2 + 4m = 0$, $m = \pm 2j$, $y = C\cos 2x + D\sin 2x$.

(v) $m^2 + 4m + 5 = 0$, $m = -2 \pm j$, $y = e^{-2x}(C\cos x + D\sin x)$.

(vi) $m^2 + 2m + 5 = 0$, $m = -1 \pm 2j$, $y = e^{-x}(C\cos 2x + D\sin 2x)$.

3 Four factors: $\left(\dfrac{d}{dx} - 2\right)\left(\dfrac{d}{dx} + 2\right)\left(\dfrac{d}{dx} - 1\right)\left(\dfrac{d}{dx} + 1\right)y = 0$, four integrations, four constants of integration. The auxiliary equation is $m^4 - 5m^2 + 4 = 0$, solutions $m = \pm 2$, ± 1. Solution of the equation is $y = Ae^{-2x} + Be^{2x} + Ce^{-x} + De^x$.

4 Again, four of everything. The auxiliary equation is $m^4 - 1 = 0$, i.e. $(m^2 - 1)(m^2 + 1) = 0$, so its solutions are $m = \pm 1$, $\pm j$. The equation has solution

$$y = Ae^x + Be^{-x} + C\cos x + D\sin x;$$

or, if you prefer, $A'\cosh x + B'\sinh x + C\cos x + D\sin x$.

5 (i) $y'' - 2y' - 3y = 0$, $m^2 - 2m - 3 = 0$, $y = Ae^{3x} + Be^{-x}$.

(ii) $y'' - 4y = 0$, $m^2 - 4 = 0$, $y = Ae^{2x} + Be^{-2x}$.

(iii) $4y'' + 20y' + 25y = 0$, $4m^2 + 20m + 25 = 0$, $(2m+5)^2 = 0$, $y = Ae^{-5x/2} + Bxe^{-5x/2}$.

(iv) $y'' - 2y' + 3y = 0$, $m^2 - 2m + 3 = 0$, $y = e^{-x}(C\cos x\sqrt{2} + D\sin x\sqrt{2})$.

Of these, only equation (ii) looks easily soluble.

6 (i) The complementary function satisfies $\left(\dfrac{d}{dx} - \dfrac{1}{x}\right)\left(\dfrac{dy}{dx} - y\right) = 0$, as in question 5 of Exercise 23A. Solve $\dfrac{dz}{dx} - \dfrac{z}{x} = 0$ to get $z = Ax$. Then solve $\dfrac{dy}{dx} - y = Ax$ to get $Be^{-x} - A(x+1)$, which is the CF.

(ii) The homogeneous equation factorises as $\left(\dfrac{d}{dx}+\dfrac{\alpha}{x}\right)\left(\dfrac{d}{dx}+\dfrac{\beta}{x}\right)y=0,$ where $a=\alpha+\beta,\ b=\alpha\beta-\beta,$ i.e. (eliminating α)

$$\beta=\tfrac{1}{2}\{a-1\pm\sqrt{((a-1)^2-4b)}\},\quad \alpha=\tfrac{1}{2}\{a+1\mp\sqrt{((a-1)^2-4b)}\}.$$

Solving $\dfrac{dz}{dx}+\dfrac{\alpha z}{x}=0$ gives $z=Ax^{-\alpha},$ and solving $\dfrac{dy}{dx}+\dfrac{\beta y}{x}=Ax^{-\alpha}$ gives $y=Bx^{-\beta}+Cx^{1-\alpha},$ which is the CF of this equation.

Exercise 23C

1 (i) CF is $Ae^{(-2+\sqrt{3})x}+Be^{(-2-\sqrt{3})x}$ so seek a PI of the form $ax^2+bx+c.$ Substitution shows that $a=1,\ b=-6,\ c=23.$
(ii) CF is $Ae^{-4x}+B,$ so PI cannot have a term in x^0; try ax^3+bx^2+cx and get $a=\tfrac{1}{12},$ $b=\tfrac{3}{16},\ c=\tfrac{5}{32}.$
(iii) CF is $Ax+B,$ so PI cannot have terms in x or x^0; try $ax^4+bx^3+cx^2$ and get $a=\tfrac{1}{12},\ b=\tfrac{1}{3},\ c=\tfrac{1}{2}.$

2 The particular integral will be a polynomial $ax^{n+2}+bx^{n+1}+cx^n,$ where n is the smallest integer (positive or zero) for which x^n is *not* in the complementary function.

Exercise 23D

1 (i) Auxiliary equation $m^2+2m-3=0$ has roots $-2,1$; so Ae^{-x} is *not* in the CF, and ce^{-x} will be a PI, with $c=-1$ found by substitution.
(ii) Here Ae^x is the CF and so it cannot be a suitable PI. Try $cxe^x,$ and find $c=\tfrac{2}{3}$ by substitution.
(iii) Auxiliary equation $m^2-6m+8=0$ has roots 4 and 2, so try PI $ce^{-2x}.$ Substitution gives $c=\tfrac{1}{2}.$
(iv) Try cxe^{4x} since Ae^{4x} is in the CF, and find $c=2.$
(v) Auxiliary equation $m^2-8m+16=0$ has root $m=4$ only, so the CF is $Ae^{4x}+Bxe^{4x}$; try PI ce^{-x} and find $c=\tfrac{1}{25}.$
(vi) Try cx^2e^{4x} as this has the lowest power of x not in the CF; substitution gives $c=6.$
(vii) Auxiliary equation $m^2-4m+4=0$ gives a CF $Ae^{2x}+Bxe^{2x}$; the right hand side of the equation is not in the CF, and since derivatives of 'polynomial times exponential' will always be 'another polynomial times the same exponential' we should try $(ax+b)e^x$ as PI. Substitution gives $a=1,\ b=3.$
(viii) Since the CF contains both Ae^{2x} and $Bxe^{2x},$ try cx^2e^{2x} as PI. Substitution gives $2ce^{2x}=8xe^{2x},$ so this is *not* a suitable guess. Try instead ax^3e^{2x} and get $a=\tfrac{4}{3}.$
If the right hand side is a polynomial times an exponential the PI will also be a (different) polynomial times the same exponential; the degree will be the same, or one higher, or two higher, depending on whether the CF does *not* contain, *does* contain, or contains x *times*, the exponential.

2 (i) Try $ae^x+be^{2x}+ce^{3x},$ since none is in the CF, and get $a=\tfrac{1}{3},\ b=\tfrac{2}{7},\ c=\tfrac{3}{13}.$
(ii) Substitution and rearrangement soon proves this result.

Exercise 23E

1 (i) Auxiliary equation $m^2+2m+2=0$ does not have roots $\pm2j,$ so $\sin 2x$ is not in the CF. Hence try $a\cos 2x+b\sin 2x$ as PI and find $a=-\tfrac{3}{5},\ b=-\tfrac{3}{10}.$

(ii) For a similar reason try $a\cos x+b\sin x$ as PI and get $a=-\frac{6}{5}$, $b=\frac{3}{5}$.

(iii) Here the CF is $A\cos x+B\sin x$, so try $ax\cos x+bx\sin x$ as PI. Substitution gives $a=-\frac{3}{2}$, $b=2$.

(iv) The right hand side is not in the CF. Try $a\sin(x+s)$, or something equivalent, and get $a=\frac{1}{3}r$.

(v) The CF contains both $\cos 2x$ and $\sin 2x$, so the PI cannot. The easiest form to try is $cx\sin(2x+s)$, when substitution rapidly gives $c=\frac{1}{4}r$.

2 (i) Since $\cos 3x=\cos 2x\cos x-\sin 2x\sin x=4\cos^3 x-3\cos x$, the right hand side is $\frac{1}{4}(\cos 3x+3\cos x)$. For $\frac{1}{4}\cos 3x$ the PI has the form $ax\sin 3x$, because $\cos 3x$ and $\sin 3x$ are in the CF; for $\frac{3}{4}\cos x$ the PI has the form $b\cos x$. Substitution of $ax\sin 3x+b\cos x$ shows that $a=\frac{1}{24}$, $b=\frac{3}{32}$.

(ii) Since $\cos x\sin 2x=\frac{1}{2}(\sin 3x+\sin x)$ the PI has the form (as in (i) above) $ax\cos 3x+b\sin x$, and you find that $a=\frac{1}{12}$, $b=\frac{1}{16}$.

Exercise 23F

1 All this needs is careful calculation of derivatives.

2 Even more, very careful calculation is needed. You get six equations for the coefficients a, b, c, p, q, r and these solve in pairs to get $a=-\frac{4}{17}$, $p=\frac{1}{17}$; then $b=\frac{152}{17^2}$, $q=-\frac{4}{17^2}$; finally $c=-\frac{2480}{17^3}$, $r=-\frac{26}{17^3}$ (I hope).

3 (i) $e^{-2x}\cos x$ is not part of the CF, so try $ae^{-2x}\cos x+be^{-2x}\sin x$ as a PI. Substitution gives $a=\frac{3}{30}$, $b=-\frac{3}{40}$.

(ii) The right hand side is $-\frac{1}{2}e^{-x}(\cos 2x-1)$, and $e^{-x}\cos 2x$ is part of the CF. So try $axe^{-x}\cos 2x+bxe^{-x}\sin 2x+ce^{-x}$ as PI. You find that $a=0$, $b=-\frac{1}{8}$, $c=\frac{1}{8}$.

Exercise 23G

(i) Factorise the left hand side: $\left(\dfrac{d}{dx}+a\right)\left(\dfrac{d}{dx}+b\right)y=x^2\ln x$, for some constants a and b.

Then you need to solve first $\dfrac{dz}{dx}+az=x^2\ln x$, and later $\dfrac{dy}{dx}+by=z$. The solution of the

first equation, using an integrating factor, is $ze^{ax}=\displaystyle\int x^2\,e^{ax}\ln x\,dx$. You can improve this a

bit by two integrations by parts, but not enough. There is no simple PI in this case.

(ii) This is similar: $\displaystyle\int e^{ax}\tan x\,dx$ is not elementary.

Exercise 23H

(i) The CF is Ae^x+Be^{5x}. The PI has the form cxe^x, where $c=-\frac{1}{4}$. The GS is $y=Ae^x+Be^{5x}-\frac{1}{4}xe^x$ and the conditions are $3=Ae+Be^5-\frac{1}{4}e$ and $4=Ae+5Be^5-\frac{1}{2}e$. These solve to give $A=\frac{3}{16}-\frac{11}{4}e^{-1}$, $B=\frac{1}{16}e^{-4}-\frac{1}{4}e^{-5}$.

(ii) The CF is Ae^x+Be^{-x}. The PI has the form ax^2+bx+c, and is $-2x^2-4$. The GS is $y=Ae^x+Be^{-x}-2x^2-4$, and the conditions are $Ae+Be^{-1}=6$ and $Ae-Be^{-1}-4=1$. These give $A=\frac{11}{2}e^{-1}$, $B=\frac{1}{2}e$.

(iii) The CF is $e^{-x}(A\cos 3x+B\sin 3x)$ and the PI is $-\frac{6}{85}\cos x+\frac{27}{85}\sin x$. The conditions give $A=\frac{6}{85}$, $B=\{e(6\cos 1-27\sin 1)-6\cos 3\}/(85\sin 3)$.

(iv) The CF is $Ae^{-5x} + Be^x$. The PI is -2. Thus the GS is $y = Ae^{-5x} + Be^x - 2$. This is bounded as x gets large only if $B = 0$. The other condition is that $3 = A - 2$, so $A = 5$.

(v) The CF is $A\cos x + B\sin x$ and the PI is of the form $ax^2\sin x + bx\cos x$, and you find $a = b = \frac{1}{4}$ by substitution. The conditions give $A = 0$ and $-B\sin 2 + \frac{3}{2}\cos 2 - \sin 2 = 2$, so that $B = (\frac{3}{2}\cos 2 - \sin 2 - 2)/\sin 2$.

Exercise 23I

1   (i) CF is $A\cos x + B\sin x$, PI is $x^2 - 2$, GS is $y = A\cos x + B\sin x + x^2 - 2$. Conditions give $A = 2$ (using $y = 0$ at $x = 0$) and $A = 2 - 4\pi^2$ (using $y = 0$ at $x = 2\pi$). There is *no* solution.

(ii) The general solution is $A\cos x + B\sin x + x$, and the conditions are $A = 0$, $B + 1 = 1$. The solution is $y = x$.

(iii) The conditions are $A = 0$ and $A + 1 = 1$; there is no restriction on B, and $y = B\sin x + x$ is a solution for any B.

2   The GS is $e^{-x}(A\cos x + B\sin x) + \frac{1}{2}$, and the conditions are $A + \frac{1}{2} = 0$, $-e^{-\pi}A + \frac{1}{2} = k$. These are both true only if $k = \frac{1}{2} + \frac{1}{2}e^{-\pi}$. The solution is then $y = e^{-x}(-\frac{1}{2}\cos x + B\sin x) + \frac{1}{2}$, for any value of B.

3   (i) If $a \neq 1$ there is a solution $x = \dfrac{a-b}{a-1}$, $y = \dfrac{b-1}{a-1}$.

(ii) If $a = 1$ and $b \neq 1$ there is *no* solution.

(iii) If $a = 1$ and $b = 1$ the solution is $x = t$, $y = 1 - t$ for any value of t.

Case (i) is like many differential equation problems, e.g. question 1(ii) above, where there is a solution and it is unique. Case (ii) is like question 1(i) – in special cases there may be *no* solution. Case (ii) is like question 1(iii) – there may be an infinite set of solutions.

Exercise 23J

1   The equations are $dx/dt = -0.055y$, $dy/dt = -0.01x$ and appropriate initial conditions are $x = 67.3$, $y = 18.7$ (after the last reinforcements). The equations combine to $d^2y/dt^2 = 5.5 \times 10^{-4}y$, with $y = 18.7$ and $\dot{y} = -0.673$ at $t = 0$. The solution is $y = Ae^{0.02345t} + Be^{-0.02345t}$, and fitting the values gives $A = 5.00$, $B = -23.7$. The time at which $y = 0$ can then be calculated as $(\ln 4.74)/0.0469 = 33.2$ days. This is not quite the same as was calculated using the difference equations in Section 7.3.

2   The equations are $dW/dt = -aR + c$, $dR/dt = bW$, which combine to $d^2R/dt^2 + abR = bc$. The solution is $R = A\cos(ab)^{1/2}t + B\sin(ab)^{1/2}t + c/a$. The initial conditions are $R = 0$ and $\dot{R} = bW_0$ at $t = 0$, so the required solution is $R = (c/a)\{1 - \cos(ab)^{1/2}t\} + (b/a)^{1/2}W_0\sin(ab)^{1/2}t$. This will certainly not hold after $W = 0$; it may not be valid before that if the plant has finished its growing season. The time when $W = 0$ is found from the time when $\dot{R} = 0$, which is given by $\tan(ab)^{1/2}t = -(ab)^{1/2}W_0/c$. The appropriate solution is $t = (ab)^{-1/2}\{\pi - \tan^{-1}((ab)^{1/2}W_0/c)\}$.

3   All we need is the PI, and we seek it in the form $A\cos(\omega t - \delta)$. Substituting this in the equation, which is $\ddot{J} + \omega\dot{J} + \omega^2J = J_0\cos\omega t$ when the stated values are used, gives $-\omega^2A\sin(\omega t - \delta) = J_0\cos\omega t$. Thus the amplitude A is J_0 and the phase lag δ is $\frac{1}{2}\pi$.

4   The CF is $Pe^{\{-\frac{1}{2}A+\sqrt{(\frac{1}{4}A^2-B)}\}t}+Qe^{\{-\frac{1}{2}A-\sqrt{(\frac{1}{4}A^2-B)}\}t}$ and the PI is C/B. If $B<0$, then $\sqrt{(\frac{1}{4}A^2-B)}>\frac{1}{2}A$, and the first term in the CF has an exponential which increases rapidly in size as t increases. The only way to avoid this is by having $P=0$: this *can* be done, by taking $\theta=\theta_0+Q+C/B$ at $t=0$ and also $d\theta/dt=-Q\{\frac{1}{2}A+\sqrt{(\frac{1}{4}A^2-B)}\}$ at $t=0$.

5   The solution is $y=Ae^{-at}+Be^{-bt}$, from the second order equation. If you solve $dy/dt+by=aNe^{-at}$ you get $y=\{aN/(b-a)\}e^{-at}+Be^{-bt}$, which is the same, since A is any constant. In particular, if $y=0$ at $t=0$, and $x=N$ at $t=0$, both solutions are
$$y=\frac{aN}{b-a}e^{-at}-\frac{aN}{b-a}e^{-bt}.$$

6   (i)   CF is $e^{-Kt}\{A\cos(\sqrt{8})Kt+B\sin(\sqrt{8})Kt\}$.
    (ii) CF is $e^{-Kt}(At+B)$.
    (iii) CF is $Ae^{-(1-\frac{1}{3}\sqrt{8})Kt}+Be^{-(1+\frac{1}{3}\sqrt{8})Kt}$.
    All of these decrease in size to zero as t increases, because all the exponentials are negative.

Exercise 24A

1   (i) Yes. The CF is Ae^{-at} which rapidly goes to zero. The impedance is $j\omega+a$, so that $Z=(\omega^2+a^2)^{1/2}e^{j\delta}$ where $\delta=\tan^{-1}(\omega/a)$. The steady-state response is
$$\frac{F_0}{(\omega^2+a^2)^{1/2}}\cos(\omega t-\delta).$$
    (ii) No, (iii) No, because the CF does not tend to zero as t increases in either case.

2   (i) $Z=4j+3$, so that $Z_0=5$ and $\delta=\tan^{-1}\frac{4}{3}$. The solution has steady state $\frac{2}{5}\cos(\omega t-\delta)$.
    (ii) Expect a particular integral $a\cos4t+b\sin4t$, and substitute to get $-4a+3b=0$ and $3a+4b=2$. These solve as $a=\frac{6}{25},b=\frac{8}{25}$ to give the steady state $\frac{6}{25}\cos4t+\frac{8}{25}\sin4t$.
    (iii) The equation is $\dfrac{d}{dt}(xe^{3t})=2e^{3t}\cos4t$. On the right integrate by parts twice, to get the steady state solution again.
    I think that (i) is easiest, followed by (ii), and then (iii).

3   $Z=-9+6j+10=\sqrt{37}e^{j\delta}$ with $\delta=\tan^{-1}6$.   The   response   is $(1/\sqrt{37})\{\cos(3t-\delta)+\cos(3t-\delta-\frac{1}{2}\pi)\}$.

4   (i) Suitable only for (i) and (ii) of that question, as in the other cases the CF does not tend to zero. In the first case we have $Z=4j-2=\sqrt{20}e^{j\delta}$ where $\tan\delta=-2$ (and $-\frac{1}{2}\pi<\delta<0$ to get $\cos\delta>0$ and $\sin\delta<0$); this gives the response as $(3/\sqrt{20})\cos(2x-\frac{1}{2}\pi-\delta)$. In the second case $A=1+2j=\sqrt{5}e^{j\delta}$ with $\tan\delta=\frac{1}{2}$; the response is $(3/\sqrt{5})\cos(x-\frac{1}{2}\pi-\delta)$. The responses are better put in terms of $\sin(2x-\delta)$ and $\sin(x-\delta)$.
    (ii) Impedance $Z=-L\omega^2+jL\omega/RC+1/C$
$$=\{(L\omega^2-1/C)^2+(L\omega/RC)^2\}^{1/2}e^{j\delta}$$
    with $\tan\delta=L\omega/(R-LRC\omega^2)$. The response for Q is then $(V_0/Z_0)\cos(\omega t-\delta)$.
    (iii) $Z=N^2-\omega^2 2jK\omega=\{(N^2-\omega^2)^2+4K^2\omega^2\}^{1/2}e^{j\delta}$, with $\tan\delta=2K\omega/(N^2-\omega^2)$. The steady state response is $(b/Z_0)\cos(\omega t-\delta)$.

5   (i) Does the CF $\to0$ as n increases? It is $A(-a)^n$, so 'yes' if $|a|<1$. Can we take another

equation $v_{n+1} + av_n = F_0 \sin kn$ and add one to j times the other? Yes, and we get

$$w_{n+1} + aw_n = F_0 e^{jkn}.$$

The PI should be a multiple of e^{jkn}, say ce^{jkn}; substitute to get $c(e^{jk} + a) = F_0$. So the 'impedance' in this case is $e^{jk} + a = Z_0 e^{j\delta}$ when you take

$$Z_0 = (1 + a^2 + 2a\cos k), \quad \tan\delta = \sin k/(a + \cos k).$$

The response is then the real part of $(F_0/Z_0)e^{j(kn-\delta)}$, i.e. $(F_0/Z_0)\cos(kn-\delta)$.
(ii) If the CF $\to 0$ as n increases, which requires

$$|-p \pm \sqrt{(p^2 - q)}| < 1,$$

then the same theory can be used. The impedance will be $Z = e^{2jk} + 2pe^{jk} + q$, for which Z_0 and δ can be calculated (with some difficulty), and the steady state response will be $(F_0/Z_0)\cos(kn-\delta)$.

Exercise 24B

1   (i) Impedance is $R + \dfrac{1}{j\omega C + 1/j\omega L} = 1 + \pi j/(10 - 10^{-4}\pi^2)$.

    (ii) $Z = \dfrac{1}{j\omega C} + \dfrac{1}{1/R + 1/j\omega L} = -\dfrac{j}{10^{-4}\pi} + \dfrac{\pi}{\pi - 10j} = \dfrac{\pi(\pi + 10j)}{\pi^2 + 100} - \dfrac{10^4 j}{\pi}$.

2 |Impedance| for C is $10^4/\pi$, for R is 1, for L is $\pi/10$. For impedances in parallel the result has modulus near the smaller value – the current goes through the easy way, via the smaller impedance. Hence you get the largest impedance from L and R in parallel, and C in series with that (as in Fig. 5(b)). And the smallest comes from C and R in parallel, and L in series with that.

       Largest: $|Z| = 3182.8$, $\tan\delta = -35\,431.5$ (and $-\frac{1}{2}\pi < \delta < 0$)

       Smallest: $|Z| = 1.048\,09$, $\tan\delta = 0.313\,845$

       Intermediate: $|Z| = 1.048\,20$

3
$$Z = j\omega L + \frac{R}{1 + j\omega CR} = j\omega L + \frac{R(1 - j\omega CR)}{1 + \omega^2 C^2 R^2}$$

$$= R/(1 + \omega^2 C^2 R^2) + j\{\omega L - \omega CR^2/(1 + \omega^2 C^2 R^2)\}.$$

For $L = 0$ this gives $Z_0 = R/(1 + \omega^2 C^2 R^2)^{1/2}$ and $\tan\delta = -\omega CR$. Consequently the response is $I = \{V_0(1 + \omega^2 C^2 R^2)^{1/2}/R\}\cos(\omega t - \delta)$. The answer to question 5 of Exercise 22C, in the case $L = 0$, is $I = (V_0/R)\cos\omega t - \omega C V_0 \sin\omega t$; the two are in fact the same.

4   (i) R, C, L are all in parallel, so

$$Z = S + \frac{1}{1/R + j\omega C + 1/j\omega L} = S + \omega LR\{\omega L - j(\omega^2 LRC - R)\}/\{\omega^2 L^2 + (\omega^2 LRC - R)^2\}.$$

From this it is possible to calculate Z_0 and δ, especially if numerical values are given for S, R, C, L, ω. Then the response is $(V_0/Z_0)\cos(\omega t - \delta)$.
(ii) Take currents J through R, K through C, $I - J - K$ through L (to satisfy

Kirchhoff's first law). Then the second law is satisfied by (for example)

$$\begin{cases} SI + JR = V_0 \cos \omega t, \quad SI + Q/C = V_0 \cos \omega t \quad \text{where } dQ/dt = K, \\ SI + L\dfrac{d}{dt}(I - J - K) = V_0 \cos \omega t. \end{cases}$$

You now need to eliminate J, K, Q to leave an equation for I. You then find the PI by the usual methods.

Exercise 24C

1 Impedance $Z = 36 - \omega^2 + \frac{1}{10}j\omega$, $Z_0 = \{(36 - \omega^2)^2 + \omega^2/100\}^{1/2}$, $\tan \delta = \frac{1}{10}\omega/(36 - \omega^2)$. Steady state response $(0.36/Z_0)\cos(\omega t - \delta)$. The elastic is slightly more resistant to stretching; there is a small resistance force proportional to velocity; the height of the support above the floor wobbles a bit, so that $36h(t) - 18 = 0.36\cos \omega t$, i.e. $h = \frac{1}{2} + 0.01\cos \omega t$.

2 General shape is like Fig. 9, but sharper. Amplitude is very small for $\omega < 4$ or $\omega > 8$, and is only large from $\omega = 5.8$ to 6.2. The maximum amplitude is 0.6.

3 $Z = N^2 - \omega^2 + 2jK\omega$, $Z_0 = \{(N^2 - \omega^2) + 4K^2\omega^2\}^{1/2}$, $\tan \delta = 2K\omega/(N^2 - \omega^2)$. The response amplitude is b/Z_0 and this is large near $N = \omega$. At $N = \omega$ the response amplitude is $\frac{1}{2}b/(K\omega)$, which is much larger than b if $2K\omega$ is very small. Now ω is fixed at 2π per day, i.e. $\omega = 7.27 \times 10^{-5}$. And $K = 9\mu/(2\rho_0 r^2)$, with $\mu/\rho_0 \approx 10^{-6}$ in SI units. Thus $2K\omega \approx 7 \times 10^{-10}/r^2$. There will therefore be resonance if r is smaller than 3×10^{-4} metres, say. But this does depend on having very nearly the correct value of N.

4 $Z = 10^8 - \omega^2 + 2 \times 10^{-4}j\omega$, $Z_0 = \{(10^8 - \omega^2)^2 + 4 \times 10^{-8}\omega^2\}^{1/2}$, and the response amplitude is $10^3 V_0/Z_0$. There will be resonance near $\omega = 10^4$ if $10^3 V_0/Z_0$ is much greater than V_0 there. At $\omega = 10^4$, $10^3 V_0/Z_0 = \frac{1}{2}10^3 V_0$, so there is indeed resonance.

Exercise 24D

1 (i) The auxiliary equation (i.e. trying Ax^m) is $m(m-1) - 4m + 6 = 0$ with solutions $m = 2, 3$. The solution is therefore $Ax^2 + Bx^3$, and fitting the conditions gives $y = Ax^2 + (1 - A)x^3$, for any value of A.
(ii) $m^2 + 5m + 6 = 0$, solution $Ax^{-2} + Bx^{-3}$, $y = x^{-2} - x^{-3}$.
(iii) $m = 1 \pm 2j$, solution $x\{A\cos(2\ln x) + B\sin(2\ln x)\}$ and fitting the conditions gives $A = 0$, $B = \frac{1}{2}$.
(iv) $m = 1$ only, solution $Ax + Bx \ln x$, conditions giving $A = 0$, $B = 0$.

2 $\dfrac{dy}{dx} = \dfrac{dt}{dx}\dfrac{dy}{dt} = \dfrac{1}{x}\dfrac{dy}{dt} = e^{-t}\dfrac{dy}{dt}$. Then $\dfrac{d^2y}{dx^2} = \dfrac{d}{dx}\left(\dfrac{dy}{dx}\right) = \dfrac{dt}{dx}\dfrac{d}{dt}\left(\dfrac{dy}{dx}\right) = e^{-t}\dfrac{d}{dt}\left(e^{-t}\dfrac{dy}{dt}\right)$

$= e^{-2t}\left(\dfrac{d^2y}{dt^2} - \dfrac{dy}{dt}\right)$. Making these substitutions $\dfrac{d^2y}{dx^2} + \dfrac{a}{x}\dfrac{dy}{dx} + \dfrac{b}{x^2}y = 0$ becomes

$\dfrac{d^2y}{dt^2} + (a-1)\dfrac{dy}{dt} + by = 0$.

3 The equation is converted to $\dfrac{d^2y}{dt^2} + 2a\dfrac{dy}{dt} + a^2y = 0$, which has the solution $Ae^{-at} + Bte^{-at}$. Converting back gives $Ax^{-a} + Bx^{-a}\ln x$.

4 See question 6 of Exercise 23B for the factorisation. In this case one factorisation is $\left(\dfrac{d}{dx}+\dfrac{3}{x}\right)\left(\dfrac{dy}{dx}+\dfrac{3y}{x}\right)=x^2+2$. Solve first $\dfrac{dz}{dx}+\dfrac{3z}{x}=x^2+2$

to get $z=\frac{1}{6}x^3+\frac{1}{2}x+Ax^{-3}$; then solve $\dfrac{dy}{dx}+\dfrac{3y}{x}=\frac{1}{6}x^3+\frac{1}{2}x+Ax^{-3}$ to get $y=\frac{1}{42}x^4+\frac{1}{10}x^2+Ax^{-2}+Bx^{-3}$.

(The other factorisation is $\left(\dfrac{d}{dx}+\dfrac{4}{x}\right)\left(\dfrac{dy}{dx}+\dfrac{2y}{x}\right)$.)

5 (i) The left hand side converts to $e^{-2t}\left(\dfrac{d^2y}{dt^2}+5\dfrac{dy}{dt}+6y\right)$, and the right hand side converts to e^{-kt}. Hence the equation becomes $\dfrac{d^2y}{dt^2}+5\dfrac{dy}{dt}+6y=e^{(k+2)t}$. The CF is $Ae^{-2t}+Be^{-3t}$; so if $k+2\ne-2$ or -3, the PI is $e^{(k+2)t}/(k^2+9k+20)$, which converts back to $x^{k+2}/(k^2+9k+20)$. If $k=-4$ the PI is te^{-2t}, if $k=-5$ it is $-te^{-3t}$; these convert to $x^{-2}\ln x$ and $-x^{-3}\ln x$.

(ii) Solve first $\dfrac{dz}{dx}+\dfrac{32}{x}=x^k$ to get PI $\dfrac{1}{k+4}x^{k+1}$ if $k\ne-4$ and $x^{-3}\ln x$ if $k=-4$. Then solve $\dfrac{dy}{dx}+\dfrac{3y}{x}=z$ to get PI $\dfrac{1}{(k+4)(k+5)}x^{k+2}$ if $k\ne-4$ or -5; $x^{-2}\ln x$ if $k=-4$; $-x^{-3}\ln x$ if $k=-5$.

(iii) The guess cx^{k+2} is intelligent, and works for $k\ne-4$ or -5. Until you have the experience of (e.g.) questions 2 or 3 above, the guess $cx^{-2}\ln x$ or $cx^{-3}\ln x$ may be rather hard to make.

Exercise 24E

2
$$J_{3/2}(x)=\left(\frac{2}{\pi x}\right)^{1/2}\left\{\frac{1}{x}\sin x-\cos x\right\}.$$
$$J_{-3/2}(x)=\left(\frac{2}{\pi x}\right)^{1/2}\left\{\sin x+\frac{1}{x}\cos x\right\}.$$

Exercise 24F

1 Put $y=x^2A(x)$ and substitute to find that $(4x^3+3x^2)A'+x^3(x+1)A''=0$. This is $\dfrac{d}{dx}\left\{x^3(x+1)\dfrac{dA}{dx}\right\}=0$, and so $\dfrac{dA}{dx}=\dfrac{B}{x^3(x+1)}$. This can be integrated using partial fractions to get $A=B\ln\{x/(x+1)\}+B/x-\frac{1}{2}B/x^2$; the second solution is thus $Bx^2\ln\{x/(x+1)\}+Bx-\frac{1}{2}B$.

2 Put $y=A(x)/x$ to get $\dfrac{d^2A}{dx^2}=-\dfrac{1}{x+1}\dfrac{dA}{dx}$. This has solution $\dfrac{dA}{dx}=\dfrac{B}{x+1}$, and so $A=B\ln(x+1)$; second solution $(B/x)\ln(x+1)$.

3 Put $y=xe^{-x}A(x)$ and get $\dfrac{d^2A}{dx^2}=\left(1-\dfrac{2}{x}\right)\dfrac{dA}{dx}$. This solves as $\dfrac{dA}{dx}=Be^x/x^2$, which has no easy formula for its integral.

4 It is satisfied by $A(x^3 + x)$. So try $y = A(x)(x^3 + x)$ and find

$(x^3 + x)d^2A/dx^2 + 2(3x^2 + 1)dA/dx = 0$, which is $\dfrac{d}{dx}\left\{(x^3 + x)^2 \dfrac{dA}{dx}\right\} = 0$. Hence

$\dfrac{dA}{dx} = \dfrac{B}{x^2(x^2+1)^2} = \dfrac{B}{x^2} - \dfrac{B}{x^2+1} - \dfrac{B}{(x^2+1)^2}$. This can, with trouble, be integrated to

give $A = -\dfrac{B}{x} + \dfrac{\frac{1}{2}Bx}{1+x^2} - \frac{1}{2}B\tan^{-1}x$, so that the second solution is

$\frac{1}{2}Bx^2 - B(x^2+1) - \frac{1}{2}Bx(x^2+1)\tan^{-1}x$.

5 Trial and error leads to the first solution Ax^2. Then putting $y = A(x)x^2$ gives

$\dfrac{d^2A}{dx^2} = -\left(1 + \dfrac{3}{x}\right)\dfrac{dA}{dx}$; hence $\dfrac{dA}{dx} = Be^{-x}/x^3$, and no further progress can be made.

Exercise 25A

1 The initial speed of the bullet, given as 1772 miles an hour, is very close to 2600 feet per second; it may be a rounded version of a real speed between (say) 2580 and 2620 feet per second. Similarly the speed at 400 yards may easily be inaccurate by ± 10 miles per hour; and the distance of 400 yards to the airliner may be a crude estimate, being truly somewhere between 350 and 450 yards.

2 $du/dt = -ku$ and $dv/dt = -kv - g$. These solve as $u = u_0 e^{-kt}$, $v = (v_0 + g/k)e^{-kt} - g/k$. The initial values are $u_0 = 792\cos\alpha$, $v_0 = 792\sin\alpha$, where α is the initial inclination of the trajectory.

Rewrite the horizontal equation of motion as $u\,du/dx = -ku$; this has solution $u = u_0 - kx$. Taking $u_0 = 792$, and $u = 541$ at $x = 366$, gives $k = 0.686$; this is reasonable since α is small and so $\cos\alpha \approx 1$. (On this model the bullet stops at $x = 1155$ m, which is rather small.)

3 It is speed relative to the air that gives the resistance force.
(i) $du/dt = -k(u+10)\{(u+10)^2 + v^2\}^{1/2}$, $dv/dt = -kv\{(u+10)^2 + v^2\} - g$, where u is speed relative to the ground and $u + 10$ is speed relative to the air (horizontally).
(ii) We now need the other horizontal component of velocity w (say) as the bullet is blown sideways by the wind. The appropriate equations are

$$du/dt = -ku\{u^2 + v^2 + (w-10)^2\}^{1/2},$$
$$dv/dt = -kv\{u^2 + v^2 + (w-10)^2\}^{1/2} - g,$$
$$dw/dt = -k(w-10)\{u^2 + v^2 + (w-10)^2\}^{1/2}.$$

4 Rewrite the approximate equation as $u\,du/dx = -ku^2$, so that $u = u_0 e^{-kx}$. Fitting the constants gives $k = 1.04 \times 10^{-3}$. On this model the speed at 1 km is 280 m/s, at 2 km it is 99 m/s.

5 No, you could hit the aircraft by shooting at a large angle to the ground also. It is made unique by asking for the smaller angle α.

Exercise 25B

1 Using $h = 0.01$ I found $k = 3.9397$.

2 (i) $y = A\sin\pi x$ for any value of A. (ii) No solution exists.

3 (i) Starting with different slopes dy/dx at $x=0$ gives non-zero values at $x=1$ (due to arithmetic and formula errors) which are proportional to the initial slope.
(ii) You need a huge initial slope to get $y=1$ at $x=1$: with $h=0.01$ I found the necessary initial slope to be -6081. *For* $h=0.001$ the slope needed to be $-608\,100$.

4 The resistance force is $3.485 \times 10^{-4}(u^2+v^2)$, and the mass is 41×10^{-3}, so the equations to solve are

$$\frac{du}{dt} = -8.5 \times 10^{-3}u(u^2+v^2)^{1/2}, \quad \frac{dv}{dt} = -8.5 \times 10^{-3}v(u^2+v^2)^{1/2} - g$$

with $u_0 = 75 \cos \alpha$ and $v_0 = 75 \sin \alpha$ at $t=0$, and also $x=y=0$ at $t=0$, $x=140$, $y=0$ at $t=T$. We need to find suitable values for α.
Using $h=0.1$ gives $\alpha=22°$ and $\alpha=50°$; using $h=0.02$ gives $\alpha=21.2°$ and $\alpha=51.1°$. The times of flight for these angles are 3.98 s and 7.36 s respectively, and the angles at landing are $-40.5°$ and $-73.5°$.

5 Take horizontal and vertical components of the forces on the ball to get

$$m\,du/dt = -ku(u^2+v^2)^{1/2} - l\omega v(u^2+v^2)^{1/2}$$
$$m\,dv/dt = -kv(u^2+v^2)^{1/2} + l\omega u(u^2+v^2)^{1/2},$$

where k is the constant in the resisting force and l the constant in the lift force. The spin equation is $d\omega/dt = -s\omega$, where s is a constant.

Exercise 25C

1 The first equation is separable and gives $u=u_0/(1+u_0kt)$. The second equation is linear and may be put as

$$\frac{d}{dt}\{(1+u_0kt)v\} = -g(1+u_0kt).$$

This solves as $v=\{v_0 + \frac{1}{2}g/u_0k)\}/(1+u_0kt) - \frac{1}{2}g(1+u_0kt)/(u_0k)$.

2 Solving $dx/dt=u=u_0/(1+u_0kt)$ gives $x=k^{-1}\ln(1+u_0kt)$. For small values of z, $\ln(1+z)\approx z-\frac{1}{2}z^2$ (Taylor approximation). Hence $x \approx k^{-1}(u_0kt - \frac{1}{2}(u_0kt)^2)$ $= u_0t - \frac{1}{2}u_0^2 kt^2$. The solution of $du/dt = -ku_0^2$ is $u=u_0 - ku_0^2 t$, so that $x=u_0t - \frac{1}{2}ku_0^2 t^2$ from this approximate equation too (which should be useful for small t).

3 Solving $\quad dy/dt=\{v_0 + \frac{1}{2}g/(u_0k)\}/(1+u_0kt) - \frac{1}{2}g(1+u_0kt)/(u_0k) \quad$ gives
$$y = \left(\frac{v_0}{u_0k} + \frac{\frac{1}{2}g}{u_0^2 k^2}\right)\ln(1+u_0kt) - \frac{gt}{2u_0k} - \frac{1}{4}gt^2. \text{ For small } t, \ y \approx v_0t - \frac{1}{2}gt^2 - \frac{1}{2}u_0v_0kt^2.$$
Solving the approximate equation $dv/dt = -g - ku_0v_0$ gives the same result.

4 From the solution for x, $t=(e^{kx}-1)/u_0k$. Substituting in the solution for y gives
$$y = \left(\frac{v_0}{u_0} + \frac{\frac{1}{2}g}{u_0^2 k}\right)x - \frac{\frac{1}{2}g}{u_0^2 k^2}(e^{kx}-1) - \frac{\frac{1}{4}g}{u_0^2 k^2}(e^{kx}-1)^2.$$

5 The solution of $dv/dx + kv = -(g/u_0)e^{kx}$ is
$$v = \left(v_0 + \frac{g}{2ku_0}\right)e^{-kx} - \frac{g}{2ku_0}e^{kx},$$

so that $dy/dx = \left(\dfrac{v_0}{u_0} + \dfrac{g}{2ku_0^2}\right) - \dfrac{g}{2ku_0^2}e^{2kx}$. Integrating this, with $y=0$, gives the same result as in question 4.

6 $\sec^2\theta \dfrac{d\theta}{dx} = \dfrac{1}{u}\dfrac{dv}{dx} - \dfrac{v}{u^2}\dfrac{du}{dx}$; now use $\sec^2\theta = 1 + \tan^2\theta$ and the equations in the text to get $(1+v^2/u^2)\,d\theta/dx = -g/u^2$, and hence $d\theta/dx = -g/w^2$.

Similarly $w\dfrac{dw}{dx} = u\dfrac{du}{dx} + v\dfrac{dv}{dx} = -kw - \dfrac{g\tan\theta}{w}$. That is, $\dfrac{1}{w}\dfrac{dw}{dx} = \tan\theta\dfrac{d\theta}{dx} - k$, which integrates as $w = A\sec\theta\,e^{-kx}$; from the initial values $A = w_0\cos\alpha = u_0$. Return to the equation for $d\theta/dx$ to get $d\theta/dx = -(g/u_0^2)\cos^2\theta\,e^{2kx}$, which integrates to give $\tan\theta = \tan\theta_0 - g/(2ku_0^2)(e^{2kx}-1)$. This is the same as in question 5. You get w in terms of x from $w = u_0\sec\theta\,e^{-kx}$.

Exercise 26A

1 (i) The discretised equations, for $r=1,2,3,4$ and $h=0.2$, are

$$\frac{y_{r+1}-2y_r+y_{r-1}}{h^2} + rhy_r = 0$$

with $y_0=0$ and $y_5=1$. In matrix form they are

$$\begin{pmatrix} -1.992 & 1 & 0 & 0 \\ 1 & -1.984 & 1 & 0 \\ 0 & 1 & -1.976 & 1 \\ 0 & 0 & 1 & -1.968 \end{pmatrix}\begin{pmatrix} y_1 \\ y_2 \\ y_3 \\ y_4 \end{pmatrix} = \begin{pmatrix} 0 \\ 0 \\ 0 \\ -1 \end{pmatrix}.$$

(ii) The difference equation, for $r=1,2,3,4$ and $h=0.2$, is

$$(1+h)y_{r+1} - (2-h^2)y_r + (1-h)y_{r-1} = h^2,$$

with $y_0=1$ and $y_5=0$. In matrix form

$$\begin{pmatrix} -1.96 & 1.2 & 0 & 0 \\ 0.8 & -1.96 & 1.2 & 0 \\ 0 & 0.8 & -1.96 & 1.2 \\ 0 & 0 & 0.8 & -1.96 \end{pmatrix}\begin{pmatrix} y_1 \\ y_2 \\ y_3 \\ y_4 \end{pmatrix} = \begin{pmatrix} -0.76 \\ 0.04 \\ 0.04 \\ 0.04 \end{pmatrix}.$$

2 (i) The differential equation has solution $Ae^{-x} + Bxe^{-x} + 1$, and fitting the values gives $y = 1 - xe^{1-x}$.
(ii) The difference equation has solution $C(1.2)^{-r} + D(0.8)^r + 1$, and fitting the values gives $y_r = 1 - 13.477\,53\{(1.2)^{-r} - (0.8)^r\}$.

(iii)

r	1	2	3	4
x	0.2	0.4	0.6	0.8
$y - y_r$	0.004\,143	0.004\,929	0.003\,906	0.002\,062

The errors are about $\frac{1}{10}h^2$ in size; error/solution $\approx \frac{1}{2}h^2$ in general size, as the solution has average value about $\frac{1}{4}$.

3 $\frac{1}{h^2}(y_{r+1}-2y_r+y_{r-1})+r(y_{r+1}-y_{r-1})=1$ (with $y_0=1$, $y_{10}=0$ and $h=0.1$) for $r=1$ to 9. That is,

$$(1+0.01r)y_{r+1}-2y_r+(1-0.01r)y_{r-1}=0.01$$

for $r=1$ to 9, with $y_0=1$ and $y_{10}=0$.

Exercise 26B

1 (i) $y_1=0.2170$, $y_2=0.4323$, $y_3=0.6407$, $y_4=0.8337$. Errors are expected to be around 0.03, so there is no need for many decimal places.

(ii) $y_1=0.55075$, $y_2=0.26622$, $y_3=0.10100$, $y_4=0.02082$, as you will have found in question 2 of Exercise 26A.

2 The equations to solve have matrix form

$$\begin{pmatrix} -2 & 1.01 & 0 & 0 & \cdots & 0 & 0 \\ 0.98 & -2 & 1.02 & 0 & \cdots & 0 & 0 \\ 0 & 0.97 & -2 & 1.03 & \cdots & 0 & 0 \\ \vdots & \vdots & \vdots & \vdots & & \vdots & \vdots \\ 0 & 0 & 0 & 0 & & 0.91 & -2 \end{pmatrix} \begin{pmatrix} y_1 \\ y_2 \\ y_3 \\ \vdots \\ y_9 \end{pmatrix} = \begin{pmatrix} -0.98 \\ 0.01 \\ 0.01 \\ \vdots \\ 0.01 \end{pmatrix}.$$

$y_1=0.8184$, $y_2=0.6504$, $y_3=0.4987$, $y_4=0.3656$, $y_5=0.2524$, $y_6=0.1666$, $y_7=0.1001$, $y_8=0.0508$, $y_9=0.0181$. Errors should be about 0.005 is size.

Exercise 26C

1 With $h=\pi/8$ you get the matrix in the text back again, and $y(\pi)=1$ changes the last element in the column of right hand sides to 0.0561. Solving gives $y_r=1$ for $r=0$ to 8, which is certainly *one* solution of the equation; the real solution is $y=1+A\sin x$ for *any* value of A. The numerical solution is 'trying' to make the last equation $0y_7=0$, but inaccuracies in the discretisation prevent this.

2 (i) Integrating once gives $\dfrac{dy}{dx}=\displaystyle\int_0^x K(s)\,ds+C=I(x)+C$, say. Integrating again gives

$$y=\int_0^x I(t)\,dt+Cx+D.$$

The conditions give $D=0$ and $C=A-\displaystyle\int_0^1 I(t)\,dt$; thus y exists for all x, since all reasonable functions have integrals (even if only numerically), and it is uniquely found in terms of A.

(ii) The discretised equations are

$$y_{r-1}-2y_r+y_{r+1}=h^2K_r, \quad r=1,2,\ldots,n-1$$

with $y_0=0$ and $y_n=A$, where $h=1/n$ and K_r is the value of $K(x)$ at $x=rh$. Gauss elimination on the matrix gives pivots -2, $-\frac{3}{2}$, $-\frac{4}{3}$, $-\frac{5}{4}$, ..., $-\dfrac{n}{n-1}$; these are all greater than 1.

3 (i) At $x=1$ and $y=0$ you have $d^2y/dx^2=xy=0$, so that the rate of change of slope is 0, and the solution is like a straight line; say it has slope m (>0). By $x=1.1$ you have $y\approx0.1m$ and so $d^2y/dx^2=1.1\times0.1m$; that is, the slope is increasing at rate $0.11m$, and so the curve starts to go up faster than the line of slope m. The further on you go, the faster the slope increases.

(ii) Shooting with the modified Euler method, $h=0.01$, and initial slope 7.88, gives

x	1	1.2	1.4	1.6	1.8	2
y	0	1.588	3.254	5.105	7.288	10.00

The final slope is 15.32, a considerable increase.

(iii) The discretised equation is

$$y_{r-1}-(2+h^2+rh^3)y_r+y_{r+1}=0$$

with $y_0=0$, $y_n=10$. Using $h=0.2$ gives values at 1.2, 1.4, 1.6, 1.8 very close to those in (ii).

Exercise 26D

1

$$L=\begin{pmatrix} 1 & 0 & 0 & 0 & 0 & \ldots & 0 \\ \frac{1}{2} & 1 & 0 & 0 & 0 & \ldots & 0 \\ \frac{1}{3} & \frac{2}{3} & 1 & 0 & 0 & \ldots & 0 \\ \frac{1}{4} & \frac{1}{2} & \frac{3}{4} & 1 & 0 & \ldots & 0 \\ \frac{1}{5} & \frac{2}{5} & \frac{3}{5} & \frac{4}{5} & 1 & \ldots & 0 \\ & & & \ldots & & & \\ \frac{1}{9} & \frac{2}{9} & \frac{3}{9} & \frac{4}{9} & \frac{5}{9} & \ldots & 1 \end{pmatrix}, B=\begin{pmatrix} -2 & 1 & 0 & \ldots & 0 \\ 0 & -\frac{3}{2} & 1 & \ldots & 0 \\ 0 & 0 & -\frac{4}{3} & \ldots & 0 \\ & & \ldots & & \\ 0 & 0 & 0 & \ldots & 1 \end{pmatrix}$$

$$U-\begin{pmatrix} -\frac{1}{2} & -\frac{1}{3} & -\frac{1}{4} & -\frac{1}{5} & \ldots & -\frac{1}{10} \\ 0 & -\frac{2}{3} & -\frac{1}{2} & -\frac{2}{5} & \ldots & -\frac{1}{5} \\ 0 & 0 & -\frac{3}{4} & -\frac{3}{5} & \ldots & -\frac{3}{10} \\ 0 & 0 & 0 & -\frac{4}{5} & \ldots & -\frac{2}{5} \\ & & \ldots & & & \\ 0 & 0 & 0 & 0 & \ldots & -\frac{9}{10} \end{pmatrix}.$$

2

$$UL=-\frac{1}{10}\begin{pmatrix} 9 & 8 & 7 & 6 & 5 & 4 & 3 & 2 & 1 \\ 8 & 16 & 14 & 12 & 10 & 8 & 6 & 4 & 2 \\ 7 & 14 & 21 & 18 & 15 & 12 & 9 & 6 & 3 \\ 6 & 12 & 18 & 24 & 20 & 16 & 12 & 8 & 4 \\ 5 & 10 & 15 & 20 & 25 & 20 & 15 & 10 & 5 \\ 4 & 8 & 12 & 16 & 20 & 24 & 18 & 12 & 6 \\ 3 & 6 & 9 & 12 & 15 & 18 & 21 & 14 & 7 \\ 2 & 4 & 6 & 8 & 10 & 12 & 14 & 16 & 8 \\ 1 & 2 & 3 & 4 & 5 & 6 & 7 & 8 & 9 \end{pmatrix}.$$

3

$$\text{In this case } \mathbf{A} = \begin{pmatrix} 4 & 1 & 0 & 0 & \dots & 0 \\ -2 & 4 & 2 & 0 & \dots & 0 \\ 0 & -3 & 4 & 3 & \dots & 0 \\ 0 & -4 & 4 & 4 & \dots & 0 \\ & & \dots & & & \\ 0 & 0 & 0 & 0 & \dots & 4 \end{pmatrix}, \mathbf{k} = \begin{pmatrix} 0 \\ 0 \\ 0 \\ 0 \\ \vdots \\ -1-9h^2 \end{pmatrix}.$$

$$\mathbf{T}^{-1}\mathbf{A} = - \begin{pmatrix} 2 & 2 & 2 & 2 & 2 & 2 & 2 & 2 & 2 \\ 0 & 3 & 4 & 4 & 4 & 4 & 4 & 4 & 4 \\ 0 & 0 & 4 & 6 & 6 & 6 & 6 & 6 & 6 \\ 0 & 0 & 0 & 5 & 8 & 8 & 8 & 8 & 8 \\ 0 & 0 & 0 & 0 & 6 & 10 & 10 & 10 & 10 \\ 0 & 0 & 0 & 0 & 0 & 7 & 12 & 12 & 12 \\ 0 & 0 & 0 & 0 & 0 & 0 & 8 & 14 & 14 \\ 0 & 0 & 0 & 0 & 0 & 0 & 0 & 9 & 16 \\ 0 & 0 & 0 & 0 & 0 & 0 & 0 & 0 & 10 \end{pmatrix}.$$

The maximum row sum of moduli is 46; since $h^2 = 0.01$ the maximum for $h^2\mathbf{T}^{-1}\mathbf{A}$ is 0.46, so convergence of an iterative scheme is certain (but probably not very fast).

$$\mathbf{T}^{-1}\mathbf{k} = (\tfrac{1}{10} + \tfrac{9}{10}h^2)(1 \quad 2 \quad 3 \quad 4 \quad 5 \quad 6 \quad 7 \quad 8 \quad 9)^{\mathrm{T}}.$$

The iteration to be used is

$$\mathbf{y}_{n+1} = -h^2\mathbf{T}^{-1}\mathbf{A}\mathbf{y}_n + \mathbf{T}^{-1}\mathbf{k},$$

and a sensible starting vector is (from previous work) something like

$$(0.3 \quad 0.5 \quad 0.7 \quad 0.9 \quad 1.0 \quad 1.1 \quad 1.2 \quad 1.1 \quad 1.0)^{\mathrm{T}}.$$

Gauss–Seidel and Jordan iteration are the same here because of the shape of $\mathbf{T}^{-1}\mathbf{A}$. You could use simple back substitution here, but you are asked to use iteration. Six iterations give convergence to 0.2709, 0.5257, 0.7500, 0.9320, 1.0642, 1.1432, 1.702, 1.1499, 1.0900. Correct values from $y = xe^{1-x^2}$ are 0.2691, 0.5223, 0.7453, 0.9266, 1.0585, 1.1379, 1.1657, 1.1467, 1.0883.

Outline solutions to revision exercises

Have you looked at the relevant section of text?

Revision exercise A

1 Add up

$$\begin{cases} f(n) & -f(n-1)=g(n-1) \\ f(n-1)-f(n-2)=g(n-2) \\ \quad\quad\quad \cdots \\ f(2) & -f(1) \quad =g(1) \end{cases}$$

to get the required answer.

Take $f(n)=u_n/n$ and $g(n)=n$ and note that $f(1)=1$ in this case; $f(n)=\sum_{r=1}^{n-1} r+1$ so that $u_n=\tfrac{1}{2}n^2(n-1)+n$.

2 $u_{n+1}+(n+1)n!$ so that the result follows. The CF here satisfies $u_n=(n-1)u_{n-1}=(n-1)(n-2)u_{n-2}=\ldots=A(n-1)!$, so that the GS is $n!+A(n-1)!$ The condition gives $A=-1$ (taking $0!=1$ as usual).

3 (a) $u_n=(n-1)^2u_{n-1}=(n-1)^2(n-2)^2u_{n-2}=\ldots=C\{(n-1)!\}^2$.
   (b) If $v_1=0$, then $v_3=0$, $v_5=0$, and so on for all odd numbers. Now take n to be even; then

$$v_n=(n-1)(n-2)v_{n-2}=(n-1)(n-2)(n-3)(n-4)v_{n-4}=\cdots$$
$$=(n-1)!v_2=4(n-1)!$$

4 (a) Interest $rx_n/100$, repayment b.
   (b) CF is $A(1+r/100)^n$, PS is $100b/r$; fitting the condition at $n=0$ gives the required solution.

   (c) $x_n=0$ when (solving) $\left(1+\dfrac{r}{100}\right)^n=\dfrac{100b}{100b-x_0r}$. This gives $n=-\ln(0.1)/\ln(1.12)=20.32$.

5 (a) Solution of $x_{n+1}=ax_n$ is Ca^n; if $x_0=\alpha$, then $x_n=\alpha a^n$, which tends to either $+\infty$ or $-\infty$ as n increases.
   (b) Solution is $y_n=D(-a)^n-1/(1+a)$ and fitting $y_0=\beta$ gives $y_n=\{\beta+1/(1+a)\}(-a)^n-1/(1+a)$. In general $|y_n|\to\infty$ because $a^n\to\infty$; you *could* have a very large and $\beta=-1/(1+a)$ and then $y_n=-1/(1+a)$ for all n (but in this case it is not a correct approximate equation). Solutions cannot stay near 1.

(c) $x_n = -ax_{n-1}^2$ and so $x_{n+1} = -a^3 x_{n-1}^4$. Consequently $x_n = -a^3 x_{n-2}^4 = -a^7 x_{n-3}^8 = \ldots = -a^{2^n-1} A^{2^n}$, so $x_n \to -\infty$.

(d) $4x_n(1 - x_n) = 4\sin^2(2^n\theta)\cos^2(2^n\theta) = \sin^2(2^{n+1}\theta) = x_{n+1}$.

6   Substitution, followed by collection of real and imaginary parts, gives

$$(u^3 - 3uv^2 + pu^2 - pv^2 + qu + r) + j(3u^2v - v^3 + 2puv + qv) = 0.$$

From the imaginary part you get $v^2 = 3u^2 + 2pu + q$. Substitution in the real part gives the result.

(i)   The real root lies between 5 and 6, using change of sign. Eleven iterations of $x_{n+1} = (3x_n^2 + 9x_n + 9)^{1/3}$, $x_0 = 5$, (which has $F'(5) \approx \frac{1}{2}$, giving convergence) leads to the root $x = 5.1072$; iterations beyond that show that it is correct to 4 decimal places.

(ii) In this case u satisfies $8u^3 - 24u^2 + 36 = 0$. This has a root near -1. The iteration $u_{n+1} = -\sqrt{(\frac{1}{3}u_n^3 + \frac{3}{2})}$ converges to $-1.053\,62$.

(iii) Then $v = \pm\sqrt{(3u^2 - 6u - 9)} = \pm 0.8075$.

7 (i) $\alpha = \dfrac{-b + \sqrt{(b^2 - 4ac)}}{2a}$ and $\alpha' = \dfrac{-(b+\varepsilon) + \sqrt{\{(b+\varepsilon)^2 - 4ac\}}}{2a}$. Using a binomial

expansion, and omitting squares of ε, gives $\alpha' \approx \alpha + \dfrac{\varepsilon}{2a}\{-1 + b(b^2 - 4ac)^{-1/2}\}$.

Now $\dfrac{\alpha}{\beta - \alpha} = -\frac{1}{2} + \frac{1}{2}b\sqrt{(b^2 - 4ac)}$, so the result for ε_1 follows. Similarly (or by a

symmetry argument) $\varepsilon_2 \approx \dfrac{\varepsilon}{a}\dfrac{\beta}{\alpha - \beta}$.

(ii) α is well calculated by $\frac{1}{2}\{100 + \sqrt{(10^4 - 4)}\} = 99.990$, to 5 s.f. β is best calculated from $\alpha\beta = 1$, so that $\beta = 1.0001 \times 10^{-2}$ to 5 s.f. Estimates are $\alpha + k\alpha/(\beta - \alpha)$ and $\beta + k\beta/(\alpha - \beta)$, with α and β as found.

8 (a) (i) $-P - Q - R \leqslant z \leqslant P + Q + R$.

(ii) $a + \delta a = 2\{s + \delta s - (u + \delta u)(t + \delta t)\}/(t + \delta t)^2$. Simplify this by using that products of errors are approximately zero, and that $(t + \delta t)^{-2} = t^{-2}(1 + \delta t/t)^2 \approx t^{-2}(1 - 2\delta t/t)$. This gives

$$a + \delta a \approx \frac{2(s - ut)}{t^2}\left\{\left(1 + \frac{\delta s - u\delta t - t\delta u}{s - ut}\right)\left(1 - \frac{2\delta t}{t}\right)\right\}$$

$$\approx \frac{2(s - ut)}{t^2}\left\{1 + \frac{\delta s - u\delta t - t\delta u}{s - ut} - \frac{2\delta t}{t}\right\}.$$

The formula for δa follows. Putting the numbers in gives $\delta a \approx \frac{1}{8}\delta s - \frac{1}{2}\delta u - \frac{3}{4}\delta t$, and $-0.021 \leqslant \delta a \leqslant 0.021$ (to 3 s.f.).

(b) $w + \delta w \approx \dfrac{xy}{\sqrt{z}}\left\{1 + \dfrac{\delta x}{x} + \dfrac{\delta y}{y} - \dfrac{1}{2}\dfrac{\delta z}{z}\right\}$, as in part (a)(ii). Hence

$\dfrac{\delta w}{w} \approx \dfrac{\delta x}{x} + \dfrac{\delta y}{y} - \dfrac{1}{2}\dfrac{\delta z}{z}$. Now $\left|\dfrac{\delta x}{x}\right| \leqslant \frac{1}{2}\%$ for the given rounding, and similarly for

the others. So $\left|\dfrac{\delta w}{w}\right| \leqslant 1\frac{1}{4}\%$.

9 (a) Value at 1.6 is 0.399, at 2.8 it is -2.130, so there is a root between. Now at 2.2 the value is -0.583, so the root is in $[1.6, 2.2]$. Take $x_2 = 1.9$, half way between,

and get the value -0.007. Thus the root is in $[1.6, 1.9]$, and we take $x_3 = 1.75$, where the value is 0.218, giving the root to be in $[1.75, 1.90]$. Then x_4 must be taken as 1.825. Each bisection halves the interval, whose initial length is 1.2; so using x_n gives an interval of length $1.2 \times 2^{-n+1}$. This is $< 10^{-3}$ when $n \geqslant 12$.

(b) (i) $|F'(1.1)|$ for $F(x) = 2\cos x$ is $2\sin 1.1 = 1.782$, divergence.

(ii) $|F'(1.1)|$ for $F(x) = \cos x + \frac{1}{2}x$ is $\sin 1.1 - \frac{1}{2} = 0.391$, convergence.

(iii) $|F'(1.1)|$ for $F(x) = \frac{2}{3}(\cos x + x)$ is $\frac{2}{3}(1 - \sin 1.1) = 0.0725$, convergence.

Draw curve $y = \cos x + \frac{1}{2}x$ and line $y = x$. A cobweb diagram is needed. The required iteration is $x_{n+1} = \frac{2}{3}(\cos x_n + x_n)$ with $x_0 = 1$, $x_2 = 1.0296$, $x_3 = 1.0298$ gives the root as 1.030 to 4 s.f.

10 (a) $u_1 = 1.122\,07$, $u_2 = 1.109\,88$, $u_0^* = 1.1 + (0.022\,07)^2/0.034\,26 = 1.114\,22$.

(b) $2.5\sin 2.5 - 1 = 0.496$, $3\sin 3 - 1 = -0.577$, hence the root is between 2.5 and 3.0.

$$u + e_{n+1} = -\sin^{-1}\left(\frac{1}{u + e_n}\right) + \pi \approx u - e_n/(u^2 \cos u).$$

Hence $e_{n+1} \approx -e_n/(u^2 \cos u)$ as   required. $-(2.5^2 \cos 2.5)^{-1} = 0.200$, $-(3^2 \cos 3)^{-1} = 0.112$. Hence $|e_{n+1}/e_n| \leqslant 0.2$ in the interval, and $e_n \to 0$ as n increases, and v_n therefore tends to u.

11   Small changes in coefficient give much larger changes in solutions; or a very small determinant, or some very small pivots (compared to coefficient sizes).

$x = (kd - bl)/(ad - bc)$, $y = (al - kc)/(ad - bc)$.   If $|ad - bc| \ll |d|$ then $|(\delta k)d/(ad - bc)| \gg \delta k$, similarly for $|c|$ and changes in solution for y. If $|b|$ or $|a|$ is large compared with $|ad - bc|$, then small changes in l give large changes.

For these equations $|ad - bc| = 1$ and $|d| = 24 \gg 1$, so the first condition holds.

The region of possible solutions is bounded by the two pairs of parallel lines

$$\begin{cases} 2x - 7y = 19.5 \text{ or } 20.5 \\ 7x - 24y = 68.5 \text{ or } 69.5. \end{cases}$$

The four vertices of this parallelogram are found from solutions of pairs of equations, to be

$$(-12.5, -6.5), \ (-5.5, -4.5), \ (11.5, 0.5), \ (18.5, 2.5).$$

12 (a)   The third pivot is 6.336×10^{-4}, the determinant is 9.550×10^{-4}, and both are much less than typical coefficient sizes (from 0.3 to 1.6). Small inaccuracies in any of the numbers can lead to large changes in the solution; you get fewer significant figures of accuracy than you work to.

(b)   The equations can be written as

$$\begin{pmatrix} x \\ y \\ z \end{pmatrix} = \begin{pmatrix} 0 & -0.1 & 0.2 \\ -0.1 & -0.2 & 0.15 \\ 0.2 & -0.15 & 0.2 \end{pmatrix} + \begin{pmatrix} 1 \\ 2 \\ 3 \end{pmatrix}.$$

The row (or column) sum of moduli for the matrix has largest value 0.55 which is <1, hence convergence of either method.

$$\mathbf{x}_1 = \begin{pmatrix} 1.4 \\ 1.175 \\ 4.3203 \end{pmatrix}, \quad \mathbf{x}_2 = \begin{pmatrix} 1.7466 \\ 1.8144 \\ 4.5268 \end{pmatrix}.$$

(c)   If $a = 0.31$, $a\sqrt{(45/4)} = 1.0398$. Since this is >1, Jacobi iteration will not converge.

13 |Determinant| $= 0.004\,400$, much less than a typical product of elements, so the equations are ill-conditioned. The equations cannot be arranged with largest elements on the principal diagonal. $x = -0.55$, $y = 1.59$, $z = 0.55$.

14

$$\begin{pmatrix} p \\ c \\ a \\ r \end{pmatrix} = \begin{pmatrix} 0.95 & 0.05 & 0 & 0 \\ 0.05 & 0.85 & 0.05 & 0 \\ 0 & 0.10 & 0.94 & 0.02 \\ 0 & 0 & 0.1 & 0.98 \end{pmatrix} \begin{pmatrix} w \\ x \\ y \\ z \end{pmatrix}.$$

Rewrite this ready for iteration as

$$\begin{pmatrix} w \\ x \\ y \\ z \end{pmatrix} = \begin{pmatrix} 0.05 & -0.05 & 0 & 0 \\ -0.05 & 0.15 & -0.05 & 0 \\ 0 & -0.10 & 0.06 & -0.02 \\ 0 & 0 & -0.01 & 0.02 \end{pmatrix} \begin{pmatrix} w \\ x \\ y \\ z \end{pmatrix} + \begin{pmatrix} p \\ c \\ a \\ r \end{pmatrix}.$$

An iterative scheme will converge, from the row (or column) sum of moduli ($\leqslant \frac{1}{4}$). For example, using Jacobi iteration and $\mathbf{w}_0 = (200 \quad 1000 \quad 200 \quad 50)^{\mathsf{T}}$ gives $\mathbf{w}_1 = (160 \quad 1130 \quad 111 \quad 49)$. Use $\mathbf{w}_1$ on the right in the matrix equation.

15   The normal equations are $\mathbf{A}^{\mathsf{T}}\mathbf{A}\mathbf{a} = \mathbf{A}^{\mathsf{T}}\mathbf{y}$, where in this case

$$\mathbf{A} = \begin{pmatrix} x_1^3 & x_1 & 1 \\ \vdots & \vdots & \vdots \\ x_n^3 & x_n & 1 \end{pmatrix}, \quad \mathbf{a} = \begin{pmatrix} a \\ b \\ c \end{pmatrix}, \quad \mathbf{y} = \begin{pmatrix} y_1 \\ \vdots \\ y_n \end{pmatrix}.$$

Hence

$$\mathbf{A}^{\mathsf{T}}\mathbf{A} = \begin{pmatrix} \Sigma x^6 & \Sigma x^4 & \Sigma x^3 \\ \Sigma x^4 & \Sigma x^2 & \Sigma x \\ \Sigma x^3 & \Sigma x & n \end{pmatrix}$$

and $\mathbf{A}^{\mathsf{T}}\mathbf{y} = (\Sigma x^3 y \quad \Sigma xy \quad \Sigma y)^{\mathsf{T}}$. These are the given equations. With the given figures $n = 5$, $\Sigma x = 0$, $\Sigma x^3 = 0$, $\Sigma x^2 = 10$, $\Sigma x^4 = 34$, $\Sigma x^6 = 130$, $\Sigma y = 9.9$, $\Sigma xy = -10.9$, $\Sigma x^3 y = -33.7$. The normal equations have solution $a = 0.233$, $b = -1.88$, $c = 1.98$, to 3 s.f.

16 $f(0) = 1, f(1) = -1.2874$; linear interpolation gives $a_1 = 1/2.2874 = 0.4372$. Similarly, using $f(0.5) = 0.2096$, you get $a_2 = 0.5 + (0.2096/1.4970) \times 0.5 = 0.5700$, and

$a_3 = 0.5803$, $a_4 = 0.5866$. It could be (but is not so in this case) that the sequence of a_n had a limit more than 0.01 beyond a_4, even though $a_4 - a_3 < 0.01$.

17

f	Δf	$\Delta^2 f$	$\Delta^3 f$
1.0914			
	−2828		
8086		457	
	−2371		−290
5715		167	
	−2204		+910
3511		1077	
	−1127		−886
2384		191	
	−936		+312
1448		503	
	−433		8
1015		511	
	78		9
1093		520	
	598		13
1691		533	
	1131		11
2822		544	
	1675		
4497			

Evidently 3511 is incorrect, and affected figures are underlined. A correction of about 300 is needed. Replacing 3511 by 3811 (a misread figure?) gives the new figures

		10
	467	
	−1904	10
3811	477	
	−1427	14
	491	
		12

$\Delta f = 0$ at $x \approx 5.5 + 433/511 \approx 6.35$, using differences at 5.5 and at 6.5. Since $\Delta^4 f \approx 0$, cubic interpolation should be used to find $f(6.35)$; since $\Delta^3 f$ is rather small, quadratic would be good enough.

18    $g(x) = 3ax^2 + (3a + 2b)x + (a + b + c)$; $h(x) = 6ax + (6a + 2b)$; $k(x) = 6a$. $f'(x + \frac{1}{2}) = g(x) - \frac{1}{4}a$, $f''(x + 1) = h(x)$, $f'''(x) = k(x)$. The figures underlined in the table are given, and $k(x) = 6$ for all x.

x	f	g	h	k
0	$\underline{1}$			
		$\underline{5}$		
1	6		-2	
		3		$\underline{6}$
2	9		4	
		7		6
3	16		10	
		17		
4	33			

From the given values $f(1), g(1), h(1), k(1)$ can be found; then $f(2), g(2), h(2)$; then $f(3)$, $g(3)$; finally $f(4)$. Use the values at $x=0$ to find $a=1$, $b=-4$, $c=8$, $d=1$.

19 Find the entries in the order $y(5)=-0.16$, $\Delta y(4)=-0.2125$, $\Delta^2 y(4)=0.17$, $\Delta^2 y(3)=0.095$ (because $\Delta^2 y$ is linear for a cubic), $\Delta^2 y(1)=-0.055$, $\Delta^3 y(1,2,3)=0.075$, $\Delta y(3)=-0.3075$, $\Delta y(2)=-0.3275$, $\Delta y(1)=-0.2725$, $y(1)=0.96$, $y(3)=0.36$ (which checks).

$$y(2.6)\approx 0.6875+0.6\times(-0.3275)=0.491.$$

Value at $x=1$ gives $a=0.96$. Value at $x=2$ gives $a+b=0.6875$ and so $b=-0.2725$. Similarly $c=-0.0275$, $d=0.0125$, $y(2.6)=0.4928$. The percentage error in the estimate is 0.365.

Revision exercise B

1 Integrate by parts twice to show the result:

$$\int_0^1 x^2 e^x \, dx = [x^2 e^x]_0^1 - \int_0^1 2xe^x dx = e - 2e + \int_0^1 2e^x dx = e - 2.$$

The trapezium rule gives 0.745 40 (5 s.f.) and the correct answer is 0.718 28, so it is about 3.8% too high. The graph of $x^2 e^x$ is concave upwards, so the approximating trapezia are always above the curve.

2 The calculation gives 0.1884, or 0.19 to 2 d.p. The correct answer can be found from the substitution $x=e^t$, followed by integration by parts twice, to be $2(\ln 2)^2 - 4\ln 2 + 2 = 0.188\,317$.

3 This can be evaluated 'exactly', i.e. in terms of ln and $\sqrt{\ }$, giving (after some effort) the value 1.019 923. Using Simpson's rule with $h=0.02$ gives 1.019 924, which is easy to do if you have the program to hand and a computer.

4 (i) The integrand cannot be evaluated at $x=0$.
   (ii) The range of integration cannot be cut up into a finite number of sections of finite length.

$$\int_0^1 \frac{e^x}{\sqrt{x}}dx = [2e^x\sqrt{x}]_0^1 - \int_0^1 2e^x\sqrt{x} \, dx = 2e - \int_0^1 2e^x\sqrt{x} \, dx,$$

and the last integral can be evaluated numerically (though not easily with high accuracy as the function is not smooth at $x=0$: further integrations by parts would help).

$$\int_1^\infty \frac{e^{-x}}{1+x^2}\,dx = \int_{\pi/4}^{\pi/2} e^{-\tan\theta}\,d\theta$$ on substituting $x=\tan\theta$; this integral is of an

apparently smooth function over a finite interval, and it can easily be estimated. For four intervals (i.e. $h=\pi/16$) the result is 0.096 115 38; for eight intervals it is 0.096 685 48. Unfortunately the errors here are *not* proportional to h^4 (because $e^{-\tan\theta}$ has no useful Taylor series about $\theta=\frac12\pi$), and so the best estimate here is 0.0967. In fact (using $h=\pi/128$ and $h=\pi/256$) gives the value 0.096 652 48.

5   (i) $J\approx 2.178\,40$ (using accurate calculation and rounding at the end).
  (ii) $J\approx 2.178\,44$ similarly. You will get different answers from hand calculations retaining only 5 d.p. in each function value.
  The integrand is smooth in $[0,1]$ and so the error $=Ah^4$. Solving $J_1=J+Ah_1^4$ and $J_2=J+Ah_2^4$ gives $J=(h_1^4J_2-h_2^4J_1)/(h_1^4-h_2^4)=(16J_2-J_1)/15$. So a better estimate is $J\approx 2.178\,44$. Since J_2 is only known to 5 d.p., you cannot get a better estimate than this by this means. In fact using longer versions of J_1 (2.178 404 612) and J_2 (2.178 442 316) enables the estimate $J\approx 2.178\,444\,83$ to be found, which is accurate to 6 d.p. despite J_1 and J_2 only having 4 d.p. accuracy.

6	x	$f(x)$	Δf	$\Delta^2 f$	$\Delta^3 f$
	1	1409			
			654		
	2	2063		91	
			745		−22
	3	2808		69	
			814		−28
	4	3622		41	
			855		−24
	5	4477		17	
			872		−118
	6	5349		−101	
			771		244
	7	6120		143	
			914		−295
	8	7034		−152	
			762		67
	9	7796		−85	
			677		−20
	10	8473		−105	
			572		−23
	11	9045		−128	
			444		
	12	9489			

The underlined figures are suspect. Changing 6120 to 6210 changes them to:

$$-28$$
$$-11$$
$$861 \qquad -26$$
$$6210 \qquad -37$$
$$824$$
$$-25$$
$$-62$$
$$-23$$

This gives an effectively constant value for $\Delta^3 f$, as required for a cubic.

Use Simpson's method to get an estimate of 2.7006. Each function value is in error (due to rounding) by up to 5×10^{-5}, so the total error from this cause could be as much as 3×10^{-4}. There is no truncation error in using Simpson's rule on a cubic function, so the answer may be inaccurate by up to 3×10^{-4}.

7 Put $I_1 \approx I + Ah_1^2$ and $I_2 \approx I + Ah_2^2$. The solution is $I \approx (4I_2 - I_1)/3$. Let the function values at the ends be f_a and f_b and at the mid point be f_m. Then $I_1 = \frac{1}{2}(f_a + f_b)$ and $I_2 = \frac{1}{4}(f_a + 2f_m + f_b)$. The value for the estimate is $(4I_2 - I_1)/3 = \frac{1}{6}(f_a + 4f_m + f_b)$, as for Simpson's rule.

$T_{0,1} \approx 0.750\,43$ (to 5 d.p.). From what is now known you can calculate $T_{1,0}$, $T_{1,1}$, $T_{1,2}$; and then $T_{2,0}$, $T_{2,1}$; and finally $T_{3,0}$. The error terms are of order $(h/2^m)^{2i+2}$ where h is the original interval width. Since $h = 0.8$ here the powers of h are of less concern than the power of 2. Consequently $T_{1,2}$ is likely to be the best estimate; it is 0.757 52, which is indeed correct to 5 d.p. $T_{2,1}$ and $T_{3,0}$ give the same result.

8 (a) The differential equation is $dh/dt + h/T = k$.
 (b) It is a linear (or separable) equation with solution $Ae^{-t/T} + kT$. Fitting the initial value gives $h = kT(1 - e^{-t/T})$.
 (c) $h_{max} = kT = 40$ and $T = 10$; hence the height at 15 years is 31 m.
 (d) The graph starts as a line of slope 4, and tends to $h = 40$ as $t \to \infty$.

9 The differential equation for the growth of the population is $dP/dt = k(P_M - P)(P - P_C)$. This equation is separable, with solution

$$\ln\left(\frac{P - P_C}{P_M - P}\right) = (kt + K)(P_M - P_C), \quad P_C < P < P_M.$$

Using the given values gives $K = -\frac{1}{9500}\ln 94$, $k = \frac{1}{47500}\ln(47/9) = 1.7399 \times 10^{-4}$. Starting at $P = 400$ requires the solution to have a new form,

$$\ln\left(\frac{P_C - P}{P_M - P}\right) = (kT + L)(P_M - P_C), \quad P < P_C.$$

The value of L is, from the new starting condition (at $t = 0$ say), $-\frac{1}{9500}\ln 96$. Then $P = 0$ occurs at $kt = \frac{1}{9500}\ln(24/5)$, i.e. at $\frac{1}{5}\ln(\frac{24}{5})/\ln(\frac{47}{9})$ years after the epidemic, or 4.74 years.

10 The differential equation is $dT/dt = k(T_0 - T)$. The solution is $T = T_0 + (100 - T_0)e^{-kt}$. Fitting the given values leads to $T_0 = 28$ and $k = \frac{1}{10}\ln 1.2 = 0.018\,23$. The temperature is $50\,^\circ$C when $t = 10\ln(36/11)/\ln 1.2 = 65.03$ minutes.

11 $4\dfrac{dx}{dt} = 0.08 - 0.12x$ expresses volume changes in the container. The solution is $x = Ce^{-3t/100} + \frac{2}{3}$. If $x = 0.1$ at $t = 0$ then $0.1 = C + \frac{2}{3}$; when $x = 0.5$, t is given by $Ce^{-3t/100} = 0.5 - \frac{2}{3}$. Solving for t, you get $t = 40.8$ s.

12 The population equation is $dP/dt = (aP - m)P$. The equation is separable and has solution $(aP - m)/P = Ke^{mt}$. Using the initial value shows that $K = (aP_0 - m)/P_0$, and rearranging gives

$$P = \frac{mP_0}{aP_0 - (aP_0 - m)e^{mt}}.$$

The population is going to become infinite if $aP_0 - m > 0$, at a time given by $aP_0 - (aP_0 - m)e^{mt} = 0$; i.e.

$$t = -\frac{1}{m}\ln\left(1 - \frac{m}{aP_0}\right).$$

13 The equation is $\dfrac{d}{dt}(ve^{4t}) = e^{2t}$, so that $ve^{4t} = \frac{1}{2}e^{2t} + C$, and the general solution is $v = \frac{1}{2}e^{-2t} + Ce^{-4t}$.

14 The equation may be rewritten as $\dfrac{d}{dx}(x^3 y) = x^6$, so that x^3 is an integrating factor for it. Hence $x^3 y = \frac{1}{7}x^7 + C$ and $y = \frac{1}{7}x^4 + Cx^{-3}$. Using the condition gives $y = \frac{1}{7}x^4 + \frac{6}{7}x^{-3}$.

15 The equation may be rewritten as $\dfrac{d}{dx}(y\cos x) = -2\sin 2x$. Integrating gives $y\cos x = \cos 2x + C$, and the condition shows that $C = 1$. Thus $y = 2\cos x$ finally (which is easily checked). The equation does not determine dy/dx at $x = \pm\frac{1}{2}\pi$ ('$0 \times \infty$'), so the solution is appropriate for $-\frac{1}{2}\pi < x < \frac{1}{2}\pi$.

16 $\dfrac{d}{dx}(x^{-3}e^{x^2/2}y) = -3x^{-4}e^{x^2/2}y + x^{-2}e^{x^2/2}\dfrac{dy}{dx}$, and so the equation may be written as

$$\frac{d}{dx}(x^{-3}e^{x^2/2}y) = -2x^{-3};$$

that is, $x^{-3}e^{x^2/2}$ is an integrating factor. The solution is

$$y = xe^{-x^2/2} + Cx^3 e^{-x^2/2},$$

and the condition requires that $C = -1$. The value at $x = 2$ is $-6e^{-2} = -0.812$.

17 The equation may be written as $\dfrac{d}{dx}(y\sec x) = \sin 2x$, because $\dfrac{d}{dx}\sec x = \sec x\tan x$, so $\sec x$ is an integrating factor. The solution is $y = -\frac{1}{2}\cos 2x\cos x + C\cos x$, and C has value $\frac{1}{2}$ to give $y = 0$ when $x = \pi$. This may be rewritten as $y = \cos x(1 - \cos^2 x)$; now $t(1 - t^2)$ has its maximum at $t = 1/\sqrt{3}$, so y has its maximum at $x = \cos^{-1}(1/\sqrt{3}) = 0.955$, which lies between 0 and $\frac{1}{2}\pi$. The maximum has value $2/(3\sqrt{3})$.

18 The equation is $\dfrac{d}{dt}(ve^{kt}) = (a + b\sin\omega t)e^{kt}$. Integrate this as

$$ve^{kt} = \int_0^t (a + b\sin\omega s)e^{ks}\, ds,$$

where the lower limit ensures that $v(0) = 0$.

The equation for the motion is ('force = mass × acceleration')

$$\frac{dv}{dt} = -g - kv + E \sin \omega t, \quad 0 \leqslant t \leqslant \pi/\omega.$$

Using the result above,

$$v(t) = e^{-kt} \int_0^t (-g + E \sin \omega s) e^{ks} \, ds$$

and so $v(\pi/\omega) = e^{-k\pi/\omega} \left(-\frac{g}{k} e^{ks} + \frac{Ee^{ks}(k \sin \omega s - \omega \cos \omega s)}{\omega^2 + k^2} \right)_0^{\pi/\omega}$. That is, the final speed is

$$-\frac{g}{k}(1 - e^{-k\pi/\omega}) + \frac{E\omega}{\omega^2 + k^2}(1 + e^{-k\pi/\omega}).$$

19 The equation of motion is $(m_0 - \alpha t)dv/dt = -kv + c\alpha$ because the mass remaining is $m_0 - \alpha t$. The equation can be written as

$$\frac{d}{dt}\{v(m_0 - \alpha t)^{-k/\alpha}\} = \alpha c(m_0 - \alpha t)^{-1 - k/\alpha}.$$

Integrating this gives

$$v = K(x_0 - \alpha t)^{k/\alpha} + \alpha c/k.$$

Fitting $v = 0$ at $t = 0$ gives $K = -(\alpha c/k)m_0^{-k/\alpha}$, and so $v = (\alpha c/k)\{1 - (1 - \alpha t/m_0)^{k/\alpha}\}$, for $0 \leqslant t \leqslant m_0/\alpha$ (i.e. while the fuel is burning).

20 (i) Solving $dI/dt = bI$ gives $I = I_0 e^{bt}$. Then the other equation can be integrated, with result $D = (aI_0/b)e^{bt} + C$; fitting the initial value gives the required formula for D.

(ii) The 'mass × acceleration = force' equation is $49\, dv/dt = 196e^{-t/2} - 5gv$. Taking $g = 9.8$ gives the required equation. The solution is $v = Ae^{-t} + 8e^{-t/2}$, and the condition shows that $A = -8$. Thus v is $8(e^{-t/2} - e^{-t})$.

The maximum of v occurs when $e^{-t/2} = \frac{1}{2}$, $t = 2 \ln 2 = 1.38$; the value of v is then 2. v increases from zero at $t = 0$ to its maximum, then decreases to zero, having the values 0.60 at $t = 5$ and 0.05 at $t = 10$.

21 (i) Verify by substitution. General solution $rd^n/(d - c) + Ac^n$.

(ii) Using (i), the solution is $A\left(1 + \dfrac{a+s}{100}\right)^n + \dfrac{100b}{a}\left(1 + \dfrac{s}{100}\right)^n$; A is found, from $u_0 = 100$, to be $100(1 - b/a)$. Putting in the values gives

$$u_n = -60(1.08)^n + 160(1.03)^n,$$

which is zero when $n = \dfrac{\ln(16/6)}{\ln(1.08/0.03)} = 20.7$ years.

(iii) The solution is

$$u = Ce^{(a+s)t/100} + \frac{100b}{a}e^{st/100},$$

where $C = 100(1 - b/a)$ follow from $u = 100$ at $t = 0$. Then $u = 0$ when $\dfrac{b}{a} = \left(\dfrac{b}{a} - 1\right)e^{at/100}$, independent of s. (In fact this gives $t = 20 \ln(8/3) = 19.6$ years.)

22 The equation is $\dfrac{d\theta}{dt} = k(T_1 - \theta) - \frac{1}{6}k(\theta - T)$.

The equation to solve is $\dfrac{d\theta}{dt} + \frac{7}{6}k\theta = kT_1 - \frac{1}{3}kT_0 + \frac{1}{6}kT_0 e^{-kt/6}$, with $\theta = -T_0$ at $t = 0$. The CF is $Ce^{-7kt/6}$. The PI for the constant on the right hand side is $\frac{6}{7}T_1 - \frac{2}{7}T_0$; the PI for the exponential is $\frac{1}{6}T_0 e^{-kt/6}$. Hence the general solution has the form stated. (Using the initial condition gives the value of C.)

23 $dz/dx = \alpha y^{\alpha-1}\,dy/dx$ so that $2(1+x^2)\alpha y^{\alpha-1}\,dy/dx + 3xy^\alpha = 3(x^3+x)y^{\alpha/3}$. Choose $\alpha = \frac{3}{2}$ to get the required form:

$$\frac{dy}{dx} + \frac{x}{1+x^2}y = x, \quad \text{or} \quad \frac{d}{dx}\{(1+x^2)^{1/2}y\} = x(1+x^2)^{1/2}.$$

The solution is therefore $y = \frac{1}{3}(1+x^2) + C(1+x^2)^{-1/2}$. The condition gives $C = \frac{2}{3}$, so finally

$$z = \{\tfrac{1}{3}(1+x^2) + \tfrac{2}{3}(1+x^2)^{-1/2}\}^{3/2}.$$

24 $dz/dx = -2e^{-2y}\,dy/dx$, and the equation becomes

$$-x\frac{dz}{dx} = z - e^{-x} \quad \text{or} \quad \frac{d}{dx}(xz) = e^{-x}.$$

This solves as $z = (-e^{-x} + C)/x$, and using $z = 1$ at $x = 1$ gives $C = 1 + e^{-1}$. Hence $y = -\frac{1}{2}\ln\{(1 + e^{-1} - e^{-x})/x\}$. This requires $x > 0$.

25 $dy/dx = -(1/u^2)\,du/dx$ and so $du/dx - u/x = -x$ follows. This is $\dfrac{d}{dx}\left(\dfrac{u}{x}\right) = -1$, so that $u = Ax - x^2$, or $y = \dfrac{1}{Ax - x^2}$. The condition requires that $A = 2$. The solution will hold for $0 < x < 2$; the graph has vertical asymptotes at $x = 0, 2$.

26 Here $dy/dx = (1/u)\,du/dx$ and the equation becomes

$$\frac{du}{dx} - \frac{u}{x} = 1 \quad \text{or} \quad \frac{d}{dx}\left(\frac{u}{x}\right) = \frac{1}{x}, \quad \text{solution } u = x\ln x + Ax.$$

Fitting the condition gives $A = e$, so that $y = \ln(ex + x\ln x)$. For $ex + x\ln x > 0$ we need $\ln x > -e$, $x > e^{-e}$, since $x > 0$.

27 $dy/dx = -\frac{1}{2}z^{-3/2}\,dz/dx$ and the equation becomes $x^3\,dz/dx + 4x^2 z = -2$, or $\dfrac{d}{dx}(x^4 z) = -2x$. Hence $z = -x^{-2} + Ax^{-4}$, and since $z = 4$ at $x = 1$, $A = 5$. Therefore $z = 5x^{-4} - x^{-2}$, and

$$y = \frac{x^2}{\sqrt{(5 - x^2)}}.$$

The graph is parabolic near $x = 0$, and has vertical asymptotes at $x = \pm\sqrt{5}$.

28 (i) $\dfrac{d}{dx}(x^3 w) = 0$ and so $w = Cx^{-3}$.

(ii) Separation of variables gives $\displaystyle\int \frac{dy}{1 - y^2} = \int dx$, and so

$$\tfrac{1}{2}\ln\left(\frac{1+y}{1-y}\right) = x + D.$$

The condition requires $D=-1$, and $y=\dfrac{e^{2(x-1)}-1}{e^{2(x+1)}+1}$.

Substitution shows that $c=2$ or $c=-1$ is needed.

$$\frac{dy}{dx}=-\frac{1}{z^2}\left(\frac{dz}{dx}\right)^2+\frac{1}{z}\frac{d^2z}{dx^2}-\frac{3}{2x^2}, \quad y^2=\frac{1}{z^2}\left(\frac{dz}{dx}\right)^2+\frac{3}{zx}\frac{dz}{dx}+\frac{9}{4x^2}.$$

Put $w=\dfrac{dz}{dx}$ to show (using (i)) that $\dfrac{dz}{dx}=\dfrac{C}{x^3}$, and hence that $z=-\dfrac{C}{2x^2}+D$.

Consequently $y=\dfrac{1}{D-\frac12 C/x^2}\times\dfrac{C}{x^3}+\dfrac{3}{2x}$. The condition is that $D=-\frac14 C$, so that finally

$$y=\frac{3}{2x}-\frac{6}{x+3}.$$

29 Here $\dfrac{dz}{dx}=\dfrac{y}{1+x^2}$ and so $(1+x^2)\dfrac{dz}{dx}+2xz=3x^2+2x+1$. That is,

$$\frac{d}{dx}\{(1+x^2)z\}=3x^2+2x+1, \quad z=\frac{x^3+x^2+x+A}{x^2+1}.$$

Now the substitution requires $z=0$ when $x=0$, so $A=0$, and

$$z=x+1-\frac{1}{1+x^2}, \quad \text{so that} \quad y=(1+x^2)\left\{1+\frac{2x}{(x^2+1)^2}\right\}$$

$$=1+x^2+\frac{2x}{1+x^2}.$$

Revision exercise C

1 (i) The graph decreases from $+\infty$ at $p=0$ to -1.5 at $p=2$. The root is near $p=1.3$.

For $F(p)=5\ln p$, $F'(1.3)=3.8$; since this is >1, the iteration cannot converge to p_s.

For $p_{n+1}=e^{p_n/5}$ the corresponding derivative has value $1/3.8=0.26$; hence this iteration will converge to p_s if it is started reasonably near it. For example starting at $p_0=1.3$ gives

$$p_1=1.296\,93, \quad p_2=1.296\,13 \text{ (to 6 s.f.).}$$

Then Aitken's method gives $p_0^*=1.3-(0.003\,07)^2/0.002\,27=1.295\,85$. Thus $p_s=1.296$ to 3 d.p.

(ii) $y_{\text{inter}}=1+0.1\times1=1.1$, $x_{\text{new}}=0.1$, $(dy/dx)_{\text{inter}}=0.6234$;
$y_{\text{new}}=1+\frac12\times0.1\times(1+0.6234)=1.0812$.

(iii) $\Sigma h^2=0.0529$, $\Sigma h^4=1.7064\times10^{-3}$, $\Sigma t=12.46$, $\Sigma h^2t=0.1757$, $n=4$. Hence $D=4.0272\times10^{-3}$, $A=2.9716$, $B=10.8428$. The estimate is 2.97.

2 $y_5=1.129\,48$ from a computer program.

3 Using the given formula,

$$y_1\approx y_0+\tfrac12 h\{y_0 P(x_0)+Q(x_0)+y_1 P(x_1)+Q(x_1)\}.$$

Solve this for y_1:

$$y_1 \approx \frac{y_0 + \frac{1}{2}h\{y_0 P(x_0) + Q(x_0) + Q(x_1)\}}{1 - \frac{1}{2}h P(x_1)}.$$

Use the same method from y_n to y_{n+1}, with $P(x) = \sin x$ and $Q(x) = x$.

$$y_{n+1} \approx \frac{y_n + \frac{1}{2}h\{y_n \sin x_n + x_n + x_{n+1}\}}{1 - \frac{1}{2}h \sin x_{n+1}}.$$

Replace x_{n+1} by $x_n + h$ and rearrange to obtain the result. $y(1.1) = 1.200\,571$, $y(1.2) = 1.435\,989$.

4 (i) $\displaystyle\int_{y_0}^{y_2} \frac{dy}{dx}\,dx = y_2 - y_0$, and also $= \displaystyle\int_{y_0}^{y_2} f(x,y)\,dx$. Using Simpson's rule on the

second integral gives $\frac{1}{3}h\{f(x_0, y_0) + 4f(x_1, y_1) + f(x_2, y_2)\}$, as required.

(ii)   In this case $y_2 \approx y_0 + \frac{1}{30}\{\frac{1}{2} - x_0 y_0 + 4(\frac{1}{2} - x_1 y_1) + \frac{1}{2} - x_2 y_2\}$. Solve this for y_2 to get the required formula.

(iii) $y(0) = 1$, $y'(0) = \frac{1}{2}$ from the equation. Differentiating the equation repeatedly gives $y'' = -y - xy'$ so that $y''(0) = -1$; $y''' = -2y' - xy''$ so that $y'''(0) = -1$; $y^{(4)} = -3y'' - xy'''$ so that $y^{(4)}(0) = 3$.
    Consequently $y \approx 1 + \frac{1}{2}x - \frac{1}{2}x^2 - \frac{1}{6}x^3 + \frac{1}{8}x^4$, and if $x = 0.1$ this gives $y_1 = 1.044\,85$ to 5 d.p.

(iv)   From the formula in (ii) $y_2 = 1.078\,88$; and using a similar formula gives $y_3 = 1.101\,58$.

5   Use $\dfrac{d}{dx}\sec x = \sec x \tan x$ and $\tan^2 x = \sec^2 x - 1$. A proof by induction is not asked here, but in essence one must be used: every time you differentiate twice, any power of $\sec x$ is converted into a (short) polynomial in $\sec x$, from the first result. And $f^{(2n+1)}(x)$ must have a factor $\tan x$, so that $f^{(2n+1)}(0) = 0$.
    From the initial result $f''(x) = 2\sec^3 x - \sec x$, using $k = 1$. Differentiate twice more: $f^{(4)}(x) = 24\sec^5 x - 18\sec^3 x - (2\sec^3 x - \sec x)$. Differentiate once more to get the result.
    $\sec x = 1 + \frac{1}{2}x^2 + \frac{5}{24}x^4 + R_5$, from Taylor's theorem and the values of derivatives found above. $|f^{(5)}(\xi)|_{\max} = $ value at $0.3 = 25.6846$. Hence $|R_5|_{\max} = 5.201 \times 10^{-4}$ (to 4 s.f.).

6   $f(x - \frac{1}{4}) \approx f(x) - \frac{1}{4}f'(x) + \frac{1}{32}f''(x)$, $f(x - \frac{1}{2}) \approx f(x) - \frac{1}{2}f'(x) + \frac{1}{8}f''(x)$, on neglecting remainder terms. Hence $F = \alpha f(x) + \beta f(x - \frac{1}{4}) + \gamma f(x - \frac{1}{2})$ has the form required. The conditions given are

    (a) $\alpha + \beta + \gamma = 1$,   (b) $\frac{1}{4}\beta + \gamma = 0$ and $\frac{1}{4}\beta + \frac{1}{2}\gamma < 0$,   (c) $\frac{1}{4}\beta + \frac{1}{2}\gamma = -1$.

Solving these gives $\alpha = 7$, $\beta = -8$, $\gamma = 2$ (and so this system would encourage you to score zero in April!).

7   $y(x + h) \approx y(x) + hy'(x)$, and so y_{r+1} (defined as $y(x_r + h)) \approx y_r + hy'_r$. Hence the result.
    Use $y_{r+1} = y_r + hy'_r$ twice, with y'_r evaluated as $x_r^2 - y_r/x_r$. This gives $y(1.1) = 1 + 0.1 \times 0 = 1$ and $y(1.2) = 1 + 0.1 \times 0.3009 = 1.030$ to 2 d.p.
    The error in the first formula is proportional to h, that in the second to h^2 (for small h). Now $h = 0.2$ in $y_{r+1} = y_{r-1} + 2hy'_r$ is to be used. The results, starting from $y(1.2) = 1.030$, are $y(1.4) = 1.233$, $y(1.6) = 1.462$, $y(1.8) = 1.891$, $y(2.0) = 2.338$ (all to 3 d.p.). The solution of the differential equation (which can be written as $\dfrac{d}{dx}(xy) = x^3$) is $y = \frac{1}{4}(x^3 + 3/x)$, so that $y(2) = 2.375$ is the exact solution.

8 $y(\pm h) \approx y(0) \pm hy'(0) + \frac{1}{2}h^2 y''(0) \pm \frac{1}{6}h^3 y'''(0) + \frac{1}{24}h^4 y^{(4)}(0)$. Hence $(y_1 - 2y_0 + y_{-1})/h^2$
$\approx y_0''(0) + \frac{1}{12}h^2 y^{(4)}(0)$.
(i)   The leading term in the truncation error is $\frac{1}{12}h^2 y^{(4)}(0)$.
(ii) The maximum error (due to rounding) in the left hand side is $4E/h^2$.

$$f''(1.00) \approx \frac{1}{(0.1)^2}\{f(1.1) - 2f(1) + f(0.9)\} = -0.840\,769\,9$$

$$f''(1.00) \approx \frac{1}{(0.05)^2}\{f(1.05) - 2f(1) + f(0.95)\} = -0.841\,295\,6.$$

You have

$$f''(1) \approx -0.840\,769\,9 - \frac{1}{12}(0.1)^2 y^4(0)$$

and

$$f''(1) \approx -0.841\,295\,6 - \frac{1}{12}(0.05)^2 y^4(0).$$

Eliminating $y^4(0)$ gives $f''(1) \approx -0.841\,471$.

Both estimates are -0.84, so no improved value can be found. The rounding error is now (at most, from above) 8×10^{-3}. The truncation error is at most 7×10^{-4}.

9 $f(x+h) = f(x) + hf'(x) + \frac{1}{2}h^2 f''(\xi)$ from Taylor's theorem, hence the result.

$$\alpha f(x) + \beta f(x+h) + \gamma f(x+2h) = (\alpha + \beta + \gamma)f(x) + (\beta + 2\gamma)hf'(x) + \frac{1}{2}h^2(\beta + 4\gamma)f''(x)$$
$$+ \frac{1}{6}h^3\{\beta f'''(\lambda) + 8\gamma f'''(\mu)\}$$

where $x < \lambda < x + h$ and $x < \mu < x + 2h$. Choose $\alpha = -\frac{3}{2h}$, $\beta = \frac{2}{h}$ and $\gamma = -\frac{1}{2h}$ to reduce the expansion to

$$f'(x) + \frac{1}{3}h^2\{f'''(\lambda) - 2f'''(\mu)\}$$

and the error will have size approximately $\frac{1}{3}h^2 f'''(x)$, and certainly no larger than h^2 times the maximum of $f'''(x)$ in $(x, x+2h)$.
   $f'' = 0.217\,15$.   The   maximum   rounding   error   is 2×10^{-5},   being $5 \times 10^{-8} \times (\frac{3}{2} + 2 + \frac{1}{2})/h$.

10 $y(0.1) = 1 + 0.1y'(0) + \frac{1}{2}(0.1)^2 y''(0) + \dots$ By differentiating the equation you find $y''(0) = 2$, $y'''(0) = -4$, $y^{(4)}(0) = 20$, $y^{(5)}(0) = -112$. Thus $(1/5!)(0.1)^5 y^5(0) \approx 10^{-5}$ so neglect terms beyond that in $y^{(4)}(0)$. This gives $y(0.1) \approx 0.9094$. Then use $y(x+h) = y(x-h) + 2hy'(x)$, first from $x = 0.1$, then $x = 0.2$, and so on, with $h = 0.1$; this gives $y(0.2) = 0.8366$, $y(0.3) = 0.7774$, $y(0.4) = 0.7337$, $y(0.5) = 0.7018$.
   To get a better answer you need a better starting value at $x = 0.1$, which means more terms in the MacLaurin (Taylor) series. The error of the formula $y(x+h) = y(x-h) + 2hy'(x)$ is approximately $\frac{1}{6}h^2 f'''(x)$, which is about 3×10^{-2} per step. Thus a better answer can only be found (using this method) with a smaller value of h.

11 Put $x \approx a + by + cy^2$ and use the Taylor series for e^y (and also for e^{y^2}) to get $y \approx 1 - ke^a\{1 + (b+1)y + \frac{1}{2}(b+1)^2 y^2\}(1 + cy^2)$. That is:

$$(1 - ke^a) + y\{-1 - ke^a(b+1)\} + y^2\{-ke^a(\frac{1}{2}(b+1)^2 + c)\} \approx 0.$$

Equating coefficients of powers of y gives $e^a = 1/k$, $a = -\ln k$, $b = -2$, $c = -\frac{1}{2}$.
   Differentiating $y = 1 - ke^x e^y$ gives $y' = -ke^x e^y - ke^x e^y y'$ so   that $y' = -ke^x e^y/(1 + ke^x e^y)$. Put $x = 0$ and $y = \lambda$, and use $ke^\lambda = 1 - \lambda$ to get

$y'(0) = (\lambda - 1)/(2 - \lambda)$. Put $ke^{x+y} = 1 - y$ to get $y' = \dfrac{y-1}{2-y} = -1 + \dfrac{1}{2-y}$. Hence

$y'' = \dfrac{y'}{(2-y)^2}$, and so $y''(0) = y'(0)/(2-\lambda)^2 = (\lambda - 1)/(2-\lambda)^3$.

In the first expansion $k = 0$ is excluded. In the second $\lambda \neq 2$, which requires $k \neq -e^{-2}$.

12 $y'' = -x^{1/2}y' - \tfrac{1}{2}x^{-1/2}y$ so that $y''(1) = -y'(1) - \tfrac{1}{2}y(1)$, and using the given equation $y'(1) = -1$. Thus $y''(1) = 0$. Consequently $y(1.1) \approx 2 - 0.1 = 1.900$.

Using the given equation, the prediction formula is

$$y_{n+1} = (1 - hx_n^{1/2} + \tfrac{1}{2}h^2 x_n - \tfrac{1}{4}h^2 x_n^{-1/2})y_n + (h - \tfrac{1}{2}h^2 x_n^{1/2}).$$

Using $y = 1.9$ and $x = 1.1$ (and $h = 0.1$) gives $y(1.2) = 1.8019$. Proceeding similarly gives $y(1.3) = 1.7066$. To 3 d.p., 1.802 and 1.707.

This is the standard derivative approximation $y'(a) = \{y(a+h) - y(a-h)\}/(2h)$ applied at $a = x_n + h$, i.e. at the $(n+1)$th point. Using $y'(1.1) = 1 - 1.9\sqrt{1.1}$ and $y(1) = 2$ gives $y(1.2) \approx 1.8015$, and a similar calculation gives $y(1.3) \approx 1.7053$.

13 The Taylor series method is

$$y_{n+1} \approx y_n + hy'_n + \tfrac{1}{2}h^2 y''_n + \tfrac{1}{6}h^3 y'''_n,$$

where $y'_n = x_n^2 - \cos y_n$, $y''_n = 2x_n + y'_n \sin y_n$, $y'''_n = 2 + y''_n \sin y_n + y'^2_n \cos y_n$. Thus $y'_0 = 0$, $y''_0 = 2$, $y'''_0 = 2$ and $y(1.2) = y_1 = 0.0400$ and similarly $y(1.4) = y_2 = 0.1795$. To 3 d.p., $y(1.2) = 0.040$, $y(1.4) = 0.180$.

14 See Section 17.3.

15 For the first part, see Sections 14.1 and 14.3, using the derivations from approximations for integrals.

The Euler formula gives $y_1 \approx y_0 + h(x_0^3 + y_0/x_0) = 1.1$. The corrector formula applied once gives

$$y_1 \approx y_0 + \tfrac{1}{2}h\{(x_0^3 + y_0/x_0) + (x_1^3 + 1.1/x_1)\} = 1.105\,13$$

and applying it again replaces 1.1 by 1.105 13 to get $y_1 \approx 1.105\,25$ (a third application would give 1.105 256, but there is no point, there are other errors of larger size in the method: the correct value is 1.105 169).

Using this method repeatedly gives (using a computer program) $y(1.1) \approx 1.221\,54$, $y(1.15) \approx 1.349\,95$, $y(1.2) \approx 1.491\,59$, $y(1.25) \approx 1.647\,64$. The correct value is 1.647 14.

16 Using the equation, $y'' = 2x + 2yy'$, $y''' = 2 + 2y'^2 + 2yy''$, $y^{(4)} = 6y'y'' + 2yy'''$; hence $y'(0) = 1$, $y''(0) = 2$, $y'''(0) = 8$, $y^{(4)}(0) = 28$. The expansion is therefore $y \approx 1 + x + x^2 + \tfrac{4}{3}x^3 + \tfrac{7}{6}x^4$, and $y(0.1) \approx 1.111\,45$, which is y_1. The formula gives $y_2 = y_0 + 2h(x_1^2 + y_1^2) = 1.249\,06$. Proceeding in a similar fashion gives $y_3 = 1.431\,48$, $y_4 = 1.676\,89$, $y_5 = 2.025\,87$. Using the extra error gives $Y_2 = 1.259\,06$, $Y_3 = 1.446\,50$, $Y_4 = 1.705\,53$, $Y_5 = 2.070\,27$; the increase in the estimate of y_5 is 0.044 to 3 d.p.

17 (i) $\tfrac{1}{3}h\{k(x_0+h)^4 + 4kx_0^4 + k(x_0-h)^4\} = 2khx_0^4 + 4kx_0^2h^3 + \tfrac{2}{3}kh^5$.
$\tfrac{1}{5}k\{(x_0+h)^5 - (x_0-h)^5\} = 2khx_0^4 + 4kx_0^2h^3 + \tfrac{2}{5}kh^5$.
The error has size $(\tfrac{2}{3} - \tfrac{2}{5})kh^5 = \tfrac{4}{15}kh^5$; $\tfrac{1}{90}h^5 p^{(4)}(x) = \tfrac{4}{15}kh^5$ also. The same error occurs in each strip (since $p^{(4)}(x)$ is a constant), so the total error is $\tfrac{1}{90}nh^5 p^{(4)}(x)$, as required.

(ii) Here $b - a = \tfrac{1}{2}\pi$, $f^{(4)}(\xi) = -\sin\xi$, with largest size 1 in the interval. It is required to have $\frac{1}{2}\pi h^4|\sin\xi|/180 < 5\times10^{-5}$, and using the largest value of $|\sin\xi|$ gives $h < 0.275$. This gives > 5.71 strips, i.e. 7 ordinates are needed.

The result is $1.000\,026\,3$, in error by 2.6×10^{-5}.

18 $22 - \ln x$ decreases in $[1.5]$ and so does $1/x^4$. Hence $f^{(4)}(x)$ decreases and has its largest value at $x=1$, which is 22. We require $4\times h^4 \times 22/180 < 5\times10^{-9}$; this needs $h < 0.010\,06$.

With $h=10^{-2}$ there are function evaluations at 401 points; at the two end ones the multiplier is 1, at 200 the multiplier is 4, and at 199 the multiplier is 2. So in the summation the maximum error has size $(2+800+398)\times10^{-10}$. In the final value the maximum error is therefore this times $h/3$, which is 4×10^{-10}.

19 (i) $I = [\frac{1}{3}px^3 + \frac{1}{2}qx^2 + rx]_a^b;\ (b-a)f\!\left(\dfrac{a+b}{2}\right) = (b-a)\{\frac{1}{4}p(a+b)^2 + \frac{1}{2}q(a+b)+r\}.$

Multiplying out, the difference $I-$ approximation $= \frac{1}{12}p(b-a)^3$.

(ii)   For an interval of length $(b-a)/n$ the error is $\frac{1}{12}p(b-a)^3/n^3$. Hence for n such intervals the error is $\frac{1}{12}p(b-a)^3/n^2$. Clearly $\varepsilon_{kn} = \varepsilon_n/k^2$, since $b-a$ is kept constant.

(iii) $J_1 = 0.9(\sin 0.45)/0.45 = 0.869\,931.$

(iv) $J_3 = 0.3(\sin 0.15)/0.15 + 0.3(\sin 0.45)/0.45 + 0.3(\sin 0.75)/0.75 = 0.861\,509.$

Assuming $J_n = J + A/n^2$ gives $J \approx (9J_3 - J_1)/8 = 0.860\,456.$

(v) $J \approx (9J_9 - J_3)/8 = 0.860\,471.$ In fact $J = 0.860\,470\,71$ to 8 d.p.

20   Roots at about $-0.75,\ 0.35,\ 1.88$.

(i) $x_{n+1} = x_n^3 - \frac{3}{2}x_n^2 + \frac{1}{2}$ has $F'(x) = 3x^2 - 3x$ and at $x = \frac{1}{3}$ this is $-\frac{2}{3}$.

(ii) $x_{n+1} = \frac{2}{3}x_n^2 - x_n^2 + \frac{1}{3}x_n + \frac{1}{3}$ has $F'(x) = 2x^2 - 2x + \frac{1}{3}$, value $-\frac{1}{9}$ at $x = \frac{1}{3}$. Both converge. The latter converges much faster.

From $x_0 = 0.33$, you get $x_4 = 0.3554 = x_5$. You could use $x_0,\ x_1,\ x_2$ and Aitken's method; or you could use $x_{n+1} = \frac{1}{10}(2x_n^3 - 3x_n^2 + \frac{4}{3}x_n + 1)$, which has $F'(\frac{1}{3}) = 0$.

From $x_0 = -0.75$ you get $x_1 = -0.744\,68$, $x_2 = -0.744\,64$; hence this root is -0.7446 to 4 d.p. From $x = 1.88$ you get $x_1 = 1.889\,32$ and $x_2 = 1.889\,23$, hence 1.8892 to 4 d.p.

21   Look for local extreme values: they occur when $6x^2 + 6x = 0$, i.e. at $x = 0$ and -1. At 0 the value is -4, at -1 it is -3; since they have the same sign there is only one real root. The value at 1 is 1, so the root lies between 0 and 1.

$x_0 = 1$ gives $x_1 = 0.9167$ and $x_2 = 0.9108$. Newton–Raphson errors satisfy $e_{n+1}/e_n^2 \approx$ constant. Here $e_1/e_0^2 \approx 1$, and so $e_2 \approx e_1^2 \approx 36\times10^{-6}$. Hence x_2 is accurate enough (in fact $x_3 = 0.9108$ also), giving the root as 0.911 to 3 d.p.

If the iteration converges it does so to x satisfying
$$x = \tfrac{1}{2}\{x + \sqrt{(\tfrac{4}{3} - \tfrac{2}{3}x^3)}\}.$$

Simplifying this gives $2x^3 + 3x^2 - 4 = 0$.

For the iteration, $F'(x) = \frac{1}{2} + \frac{1}{4}(-2x^2)(\frac{4}{3} - \frac{2}{3}x^3)^{-1/2}$.

(i) $F'(1) = -0.112$; this has modulus much less than 1, so convergence is sure.

(ii)   The right hand side of the iteration is not real for $x_0 = 2$.

22 (i) $\dfrac{d}{dx}(e^{x\ln a}) = \ln a\,e^{x\ln a} = a^x \ln a.$

(ii)   Like e^x, but passing through $(-1, \frac{1}{2})$, $(1, 2)$, $(2, 4)$. $\displaystyle\int_0^b e^{x\ln 2}\,dx = 1$ and so

$\dfrac{1}{\ln 2}(e^{b\ln 2} - 1) = 1$. Consequently $b = \dfrac{1}{\ln 2}\{\ln(1 + \ln 2)\} = 0.76$ to 2 d.p.

(iii)   Values at 4 and 5 are -3 and 4 for $2^x - 3 - x^2$. Draw on $y = 3 + x^2$ (passing through $(0, 3)$, $(1, 4)$ and so on); there is only one intersection. $x_0 = 4.5$ gives $x_1 = 4.593$ and $x_2 = 4.588$, so to 2 d.p. the root is 4.59.

23 (a) $x_{n+1} = x_n - \dfrac{x_n^m - a}{mx_n^{m-1}}$ gives the required result. Start from $x_0 = 2$ (say) and get $x_1 = 1.8$, $x_2 = 1.745$, $x_3 = 1.741$; result is 1.74 to 2 d.p. as you can check from your calculator.

(b)   Taking values at 0.8 and 0.9 gives 0.278 and -0.133. Try $x_{n+1} = (1 + \sin x_n - \tan x_n)^{1/4}$. $F'(0.85) \approx 0.34$, so there will be convergence. Start at 0.87 (from the values above) for x_0, and find $x_1 = 0.8723$ and $x_2 = 0.8708$. The result is 0.87 to 2 d.p.

   You are being asked for a cobweb diagram based on $y = x$ and $y = (1 + \sin x - \tan x)^{1/4}$; the latter starts at 1, and remains very close to there until after $x = \frac{1}{2}$, when it starts to curve downwards.

24 $x^2 + 3x + 3 = (x + \frac{3}{2})^2 + \frac{3}{4}$, which must be positive.
   $dy/dx = 6x^2 + 18x + 18 = 6(x^2 + 3x + 3) \geq \frac{9}{2}$; a positive gradient ensures that the graph cuts the x-axis once only.
   At $x = 0$, $y = -10$; at $x = 1$, $y = 19$. Hence there is an intersection between $x = 0$ and $x = 1$, at $x = 0 + 10/29 = 0.345$.
   $x_{n+1} = x_n - (2x_n^3 + 9x_n^2 + 18x_n - 10)/(6x_n^2 + 18x_n + 18)$, with $x_0 = 0.345$, gives $x_1 = 0.4508$, $x_2 = 0.4462$ and $x_3 = 0.4462$ also. The root is 0.45 to 2 d.p.

25 (a)   For convergence $|f'(X)| < 1$; for divergence $|f'(X)| > 1$. Draw staircase or cobweb diagrams based on these two cases.
   $X + \varepsilon_{n+1} = f(X + \varepsilon_n) = f(X) + \varepsilon_n f'(X + \theta \varepsilon_n)$ for some θ in $(0, 1)$. Since $X = f(X)$, this gives $|\varepsilon_{n+1}/\varepsilon_n| = |f'(X + \theta \varepsilon_n)|$. Thus errors will decrease in size if $|f'(X + \theta \varepsilon_n)| < 1$ for all the points reached in the iteration. It is sufficient to have $|f'(x)| < 1$ in the symmetrical interval of length $2(X - x_0)$ centred on X, i.e. of extent $|\varepsilon_0|$ on each side of the root X.

(b)   It is normally quadratically convergent (when $f(x)$ is smooth and $f'(X) \neq 0$). The iteration here is $x_{n+1} = x_n + \dfrac{1 + \cos x_n}{\sin x_n}$.

$x_0 = 3.14$	$\varepsilon_0 = -1.592\,654 \times 10^{-3}$
$x_1 = 3.140\,796\,327$	$\varepsilon_1 = -7.963\,266 \times 10^{-4}$
$x_2 = 3.141\,194\,491$	$\varepsilon_2 = -3.981\,625\,9 \times 10^{-4}$
$x_3 = 3.141\,395\,572$	$\varepsilon_3 = -1.970\,815\,9 \times 10^{-4}$
$x_4 = 3.141\,493\,113$	$\varepsilon_4 = -9.954\,059 \times 10^{-5}$

$\varepsilon_{n+1} \approx \frac{1}{2}\varepsilon_n$ because $f'(X) = 0$. For the new iteration, $x_{n+1} = x_n + \dfrac{4(1 + \cos x_n)}{\sin x_n}$.

$x_0 = 3.14$	$\varepsilon_0 = -1.592\,654 \times 10^{-3}$
$x_1 = 3.143\,185\,308$	$\varepsilon_1 = 1.592\,654 \times 10^{-3}$
$x_2 = 3.139\,999\,998$	$\varepsilon_2 = -1.592\,656 \times 10^{-3}$
$x_3 = 3.143\,185\,310$	$\varepsilon_3 = 1.592\,656 \times 10^{-3}$
$x_4 = 3.139\,999\,996$	$\varepsilon_4 = -1.592\,658 \times 10^{-3}$

This curve is not smooth at $x = \pi$. It has a symmetrical cusp there.

26 Since $\phi(x) = x - f(x)/f'(x)$ we have

$$\phi'(x) = 1 - f'(x)/f'(x) + \{f(x)f''(x)\}/\{f'(x)\}^2$$
$$= \{f(x)f''(x)\}/\{f'(x)\}^2.$$

But $f(X) = 0$ since X is the root. Hence $\phi'(X) = 0$.

Similarly $\phi''(x) = \{f'(x)f''(x)\}/\{f'(x)\}^2 +$ terms in $f(x)$. Hence $\phi''(X) = f''(X)/f'(X)$. Now it has been assumed that $f'(X) \neq 0$, and for very few equations $f(x) = 0$ is it true that $f''(X) = 0$, so in general $\phi''(X) \neq 0$.

Use the Mean Value Theorem on

$$X + e_{r+1} = \phi(X + e_r)$$

with $\phi'(X) = 0$, and also $X = \phi(X)$, to get

$$e_{r+1} \approx \tfrac{1}{2} e_r^2 \, \phi''(X).$$

This is $e_{r+1} \approx k e_r^2$, with $k = \tfrac{1}{2}\phi''(X)$. The Newton–Raphson process is usually quadratically convergent.

Revision exercise D

1 The auxiliary equation is $c^2 - 6c + 9 = 0$, $c = 3$ only. Hence the CF is $(A + Bn)3^n$, and the PS must have the form $u_n = k$. Substitution shows that $k = \tfrac{1}{2}$. The GS is $(A + Bn)3^n + \tfrac{1}{2}$, and using the given values gives $A = \tfrac{1}{2}$, $B = (\alpha - 2)/3$. The solution becomes large and positive if $\alpha \geqslant 2$.

2 The CF (using the auxiliary equation) is $A(-2 + \sqrt{3})^n + B(-2 - \sqrt{3})^n$. The PS is $\tfrac{1}{6}c$. The GS is $A(-2 + \sqrt{3})^n + B(-2 - \sqrt{3})^n + \tfrac{1}{6}c$. Since $|-2 + \sqrt{3}| < 1$ and $|-2 - \sqrt{3}| > 1$ you must have $B = 0$ to give u_n a finite size as $n \to \infty$. Then $u_0 = 0$ requires $A + \tfrac{1}{6}c = 0$. The solution is $u_n = \tfrac{1}{6}c\{1 - (-2 + \sqrt{3})^n\}$, which $\to \tfrac{1}{6}c$ as $n \to \infty$.

3 $2\cos\theta\cos(n+1)\theta = \cos(n+2)\theta + \cos n\theta$, and so the result follows.

The CF is $A\{c + \sqrt{(c^2 - 1)}\}^n + B\{c - \sqrt{(c^2 - 1)}\}^n$ and the conditions give $A + B = 1$,

$$c + (A - B)\sqrt{(c^2 - 1)} = 0. \text{ Hence } A = \frac{-c + \sqrt{(c^2 - 1)}}{2\sqrt{(c^2 - 1)}}.$$

No: $u_1 = c > 1$, while $|\cos\theta| < 1$.

4 Using the given values, for $n = 0$: $-6 + a = -2$, so that $a = 4$; and for $n = 1$: $27 - 6a + b = 6$, so that $b = 3$.

The CF for $u_{n+2} + 4u_{n+1} + 3u_n = 8n - 2$ is $A(-3)^n + B(-1)^n$. The PS is (by trial) $n - 1$. The GS is $A(-3)^n + B(-1)^n + n - 1$. Using the values gives $A = -1$, $B = 2$. Check: $n = 3$ gives $u_3 = 27$.

5 The auxiliary equation is $c^2 - ac - b = 0$, $c = \tfrac{1}{2}\{a \pm \sqrt{(a^2 + 4b)}\}$. Hence the solution is $u_n = A\{\tfrac{1}{2}a + \sqrt{(\tfrac{1}{4}a^2 + b)}\}^n + B\{\tfrac{1}{2}a - \sqrt{(a^2 + b)}\}^n$.

When $a + b = 1$, $c = \tfrac{1}{2}\{a \pm (a - 2)\} = a - 1$ or 1 and the solution is $u_n = A(a - 1)^n + B$. Now $0 < a < 1$, since $a + b = 1$ and both a and b are > 0. Hence $u_n \to B$ as $n \to \infty$.

6 (i) The auxiliary equation has the single root $c = 3$. Hence the equation is $u_{n+2} - 6u_{n+1} + 9u_n = 0$, or its equivalent.

(ii) The CF is $A4^n + B2^n$. Put $nv_n = u_n$ to see that $nv_n = A4^n + B2^n$ and so $v_n = (A4^n + B2^n)/n$. Fitting the values gives $A = -\tfrac{4}{3}$, $B = \tfrac{2}{3}$.

7 $u_n = A2^n + B$, and the conditions give $A = 2$, $B = -3$. Rewrite the equation as $(n+2)!v_{n+2} - 3(n+1)!v_{n+1} + 2n!v_n = 0$, and put $n!v_n = u_n$ to show that $v_n = (2^{n+1} - 3)n!$.

8 We have $B_{n+2}=2B_{n+1}-\frac{1}{4}W_{n+1}$; substitute for W_{n+1} in this, and also use $W_n=8B_n-4B_{n+1}$ from the first equation.

The solution for B_n is $A(\frac{17}{8})^n+B(\frac{7}{8})^n$. Fitting the values $B_0=4$ and $B_1=5$ (using $W_0=12$ and the first equation) gives $B_n=\frac{6}{5}(\frac{17}{8})^n+\frac{14}{5}(\frac{7}{8})^n$.

9 (i) $y=Ae^x-x-1$, and $A=0$ from the condition.

(ii) The equation is $y_{n+1}-2hy_n-y_{n-1}=2nh^2$, which has CF $A\{h+\sqrt{(1+h)^2}\}^n+B\{h-\sqrt{(1+h^2)}\}^n$ and PS $-nh-1$. Fitting the conditions gives $A=B=0$, and the solution is $y_n=-nh-1$; the correspondence is nh to x between the difference equation and the corresponding differential equation.

10 See Section 22.4(b) and Exercise 23J, question 4. The equation for $x=\theta-\theta_0$ is
$$\frac{d^2x}{dt^2}+2p\frac{dx}{dt}+qx=r,$$
where p and q are given to be positive. The CF is $Ae^{m_1t}+Be^{m_2t}$ where $m_{1,2}=-p\pm\sqrt{(p^2-q)}$ if $p^2>q$; or it is $e^{-pt}(C+Dt)$ if $p^2=q$; or it is $e^{-pt}[E\cos\{t\sqrt{(q-p^2)}\}+F\sin\{t\sqrt{(q-p^2)}\}]$ if $p^2<q$. In all cases the CF $\to0$ as $t\to\infty$ and only the PI remains, which is $ac(T_0-\theta_0)/(ac+ak-bc)$. Hence $\theta\to\theta_0+ac(T_0-\theta_0)/(ac+ak-bc)$ as $t\to\infty$.

11 See Section 22.4(c) and Exercise 23J, question 5.

The equation for z is $\dot{z}=\mu y$. The solution for x is $x_0e^{-\lambda t}$. Then solve
$$\dot{y}+\mu y=\lambda x_0e^{-\lambda t} \qquad \text{to} \qquad \text{get} \qquad y=\left(y_0-\frac{\lambda x_0}{\mu-\lambda}\right)e^{-\mu t}+\frac{\lambda x_0}{\mu-\lambda}e^{-\lambda t}. \qquad \text{Finally}$$
$$x=\int\mu y\,dt=-\left(y_0-\frac{\lambda x_0}{\mu-\lambda}\right)e^{-\mu t}-\frac{\mu x_0}{\mu-\lambda}e^{-\lambda t}+x_0+y_0+z_0.$$ In the given case $y_0=z_0=0$ and so
$$x=x_0e^{-\lambda t}, \qquad y=\frac{\lambda x_0}{\lambda-\mu}(e^{-\lambda t}-e^{-\mu t}), \qquad z=\frac{x_0}{\mu-\lambda}(\lambda e^{-\mu t}-\mu e^{-\lambda t})+x_0.$$

$\frac{dy}{dt}=0$ happens when $\lambda e^{-\lambda t}=\mu e^{-\mu t}$, $t=\{\ln(\mu/\lambda)\}/(\mu-\lambda)$. $x(t)$ decreases to zero as $t\to\infty$; $y(t)$ increases to a maximum and then decreases to zero; $z(t)$ increases and tends to x_0 as $t\to\infty$.

12 Auxiliary equation $m^2+4m+3=0$, $m=-3$ or -1; CF $Ae^{-3x}+Be^{-x}$. The PI has the form $ax+b$, and substitution gives $a=3$, $b=-4$. The GS is thus $Ae^{-3x}+Be^{-x}+3x-4$, and the given conditions require $A=-\frac{3}{2}$, $B=\frac{15}{2}$.

13 Auxiliary equation $m^2+4m+4=0$ has the single root $m=-2$. The CF is $(A+Bx)e^{-2x}$. The PI must therefore be cx^2e^{-2x}, and substitution shows that $c=\frac{1}{2}$. The GS is therefore $(A+Bx)e^{-2x}+\frac{1}{2}x^2e^{-2x}$, and the conditions give $A=1$ and $B=2$.

14 The CF is $Ae^{-4x}+Be^x$. Consequently the PI has the form axe^x+b, where $a=1$ and $b=-2$ by substitution. The GS is $Ae^{-4x}+Be^x+xe^x-2$, and the given values require $A=\frac{1}{3}$, $B=-\frac{1}{3}$.

15 (a) CF is $Ae^{m_1x}+Be^{m_2x}$, $m_1=-1+\sqrt{(1-c)}$, $m_2=-1-\sqrt{(1-c)}$. The PI is $x/c-2/c^2$. The solution is therefore
$$y=Ae^{m_1x}+Be^{m_2x}+x/c-2/c^2.$$

(b) CF is now $(C+Dx)e^{-x}$, and the PI is $x-2$. That is
$$y=(C+Dx)e^{-x}+x-2.$$

16 CF is $e^{-x}(A\cos x + B\sin x)$. PI has the form $a\cos 2x + b\sin 2x$ and $a = -\frac{1}{10}$, $b = \frac{1}{5}$ by substitution. The GS is the sum of these, and from the initial values $A = \frac{1}{10}$, $B = -\frac{3}{10}$.
From the equation, $(d^2y/dx^2)_{x=0} = 1 - 2(dy/dx)_0 - 2y_0 = 1$.
For large x, $y \approx -\frac{1}{10}\cos 2x + \frac{1}{5}\sin 2x$.

17 CF is $A\cos nt + B\sin nt$, PI is g/n^2. Thus the GS is $A\cos nt + B\sin nt + g/n^2$, and the initial conditions give $A = 2g/n^2$, $B = 0$; that is, $x = (g/n^2)(1 + 2\cos nt)$.
A particle of unit mass hangs on a piece of elastic. d^2x/dt^2 is the mass-acceleration; n^2x is the upward force due to elasticity when the elastic is stretched by a length x; g is the weight (of unit mass).

18 (i) For $0 < k < 3$ the solution is $e^{-kt}[A\cos\{t\sqrt{(9-k^2)}\} + B\sin\{t\sqrt{(9-k^2)}\}]$, with $A = 0$, $B = (9-k^2)^{-1/2}$ following from the initial conditions. This is a damped oscillation, which starts by increasing from $x = 0$.

  (ii) For $k = 3$ the solution is $e^{-kt}(Ct + D)$, with $D = 0$ and $C = 1$ to satisfy the initial conditions. The graph rises to a maximum of $\frac{1}{3}e^{-1}$ at $t = \frac{1}{3}$, and then decreases towards zero, without ever reaching it.

  (iii) For $k > 3$ the solution is $Ee^{-\{k+\sqrt{(k^2-9)}\}t} + Fe^{-\{k-\sqrt{(k^2-9)}\}t}$, with $F = -E = \frac{1}{2}(k^2-9)^{-1/2}$ to satisfy the conditions. The graph is similar to the previous one.

19 The CF is $Ae^{2x} + Be^x$ and the PI is $e^{ax}/(a^2 - 3a + 2)$, for $a \neq 1$ and $a \neq 2$. Satisfying the conditions requires $A = -\dfrac{1}{a-2}$ and $B = \dfrac{1}{a-1}$, so $y = \dfrac{e^x}{a-1} - \dfrac{e^{2x}}{a-2} + \dfrac{e^{ax}}{(a-1)(a-2)}$.
The solution becomes

$$y = \frac{1}{\varepsilon}e^x + e^{2x}(1-\varepsilon)^{-1} - \frac{1}{\varepsilon}e^x e^{\varepsilon x}(1-\varepsilon)^{-1}.$$

Now use $(1-\varepsilon)^{-1} \approx 1 + \varepsilon$ and $e^{\varepsilon x} \approx 1 + \varepsilon x$, neglecting terms in ε^2 and higher. Then $y \approx e^{2x}(1+\varepsilon) - xe^x - e^x + \varepsilon xe^x$. Letting $\varepsilon \to 0$ gives the answer.

20 (a) The general solution is $Ae^{2x} + Be^{-2x} + 3$.

  (b) The general solution is $C2^n + D(-2)^n + 4$.

21 (a) The equation is $\dfrac{d}{dx}\{(1+x^2)^{1/2}y\} = (1+x^2)^{-1/2}$, so that $(1+x^2)^{1/2}y = \sinh^{-1}x + C$, i.e. $y = (1+x^2)^{-1/2}\{C + \sinh^{-1}x\}$. Fitting the value at $x = 0$ gives $y = (1+x^2)^{-1/2}\{1 + \sinh^{-1}x\}$.

  (b) The CF is $Ae^x + Be^{ax}$ and the PI is e^{-2x}, in the case when $a \neq 1$ and $a \neq 2$. Fitting the values to the GS gives $y = (e^{ax} - e^x)/(a-1) + e^{-2x}$.

22 (a) The equation is $\dfrac{d}{dx}\{ye^{-x}/x\} = 2e^{-x}$, which has solution $y = Axe^x - 2x$.

  (b) The CF is $B\cos 2x + C\sin 2x$, and the PI is $\frac{1}{3}\cos x$.

23 (a) $k = -4$ because the roots of the auxiliary equation must be ± 2. Then since 3 is the PI, $n = -12$.

  (b) This equation separates as $\int\dfrac{1}{y^2}dy = -\int\dfrac{1}{x^2}dx$, so the solution is $-\dfrac{x}{1+Cx}$. Fitting the condition gives $C = 0$, solution $y = -x$.

24 (a) The equation is $\dfrac{d}{dx}\left(\dfrac{y}{x}\right) = x$, with solution $y = \frac{1}{2}x^2 + Cx$. Fitting the value gives $C = \frac{1}{2}$, $y = \frac{1}{2}x(1+x^2)$.

(b) CF is $e^{-x/2}\{A\cos(\tfrac{1}{2}x\sqrt{3})+B\sin(\tfrac{1}{2}x\sqrt{3})\}$. The PI has the form $a\cos x+b\sin x$, and substitution shows that $a=-1$ and $b=3$,

25 (a)   The equation is $\dfrac{d}{dt}\{(1+t^2)u\}=t(1+t^2)$, with solution
$u=(A+\tfrac{1}{2}t^2+\tfrac{1}{4}t^4)/(1+t^2)$. Fitting the condition gives $A=1$.

(b)   The CF is $e^{-2x}(A+Bx)$. The PI is 1. The GS is $e^{-2x}(A+Bx)+1$. The conditions are satisfied if $A=B=-1$.

26 (a) $dy/dx=\pm x^{1/2}y^{1/2}$. By separation $y^{1/2}=\pm\tfrac{1}{3}x^{3/2}+A_{\pm}$. Fitting the condition gives $y=\tfrac{1}{9}x^3$ or $y=(2-x^{3/2})^2/9$. $dy/dx=\pm\tfrac{1}{3}$ at P, so the angle is $2\tan^{-1}\tfrac{1}{3}=37°$.

(b)   CF is $e^{2x}(A+Bx)$ in both cases. When $k=1$ the PI is e^x. When $k=2$ the PI must have the form cx^2e^{2x}; substitution shows that $c=\tfrac{1}{2}$. So, (i) the GS is $e^{2x}(A+Bx)+e^x$, and (ii) the GS is $e^{2x}(A+Bx)+\tfrac{1}{2}x^2e^{2x}$.

27 (i)   The equation is $\dfrac{d}{dx}(y\cosh x)=\cosh x$ and so the GS is $y=A\,\mathrm{sech}\,x+\tanh x$. Fitting the condition gives $A=1$.

(ii)   If $z=y^3$, then $3y^2\dfrac{dy}{dx}=\dfrac{dz}{dx}$ and $6y\left(\dfrac{dy}{dx}\right)^2+3y^2\dfrac{d^2y}{dx^2}=\dfrac{d^2z}{dx^2}$. Hence the equation becomes $\dfrac{d^2z}{dx^2}+3\dfrac{dz}{dx}+2z=0$. The GS of this is $z=Ae^{2x}+Be^x$, and so $y=(Ae^{2x}+Be^x)^{1/3}$.

28 (a) $\ddot{x}=\dot{y}-4\dot{x}=-4x-4\dot{x}$, i.e. $\ddot{x}+4\dot{x}+4x=0$. The GS of this is $e^{-2t}(At+B)$, and fitting the conditions ($\dot{x}=1$ at $t=0$ from the first equation) gives $x=te^{-2t}$. Then $y=\dot{x}+4x=e^{-2t}(1+2t)$.

(b) $\dot{w}=\dot{u}+\dot{v}=-(u+v)^2=-w^2$. So $w=(t+A)^{-1}$; and $w=1$ when $t=0$, so $w=(1+t)^{-1}$. Now $\dot{v}=-\tfrac{1}{2}v^2-uv=-v(u+v)+\tfrac{1}{2}v^2$, i.e. $\dot{v}+wv=\tfrac{1}{2}v^2$, so that $\dot{v}+(1+t)^{-1}v=\tfrac{1}{2}v^2$.
Put $v=z^{-1}$, $\dot{v}=-z^{-2}\dot{z}$, and the equation becomes

$$\frac{dz}{dt}-(1+t)^{-1}z=-\tfrac{1}{2}.$$

This may be written as $\dfrac{d}{dt}\left\{\dfrac{z}{1+t}\right\}=-\dfrac{1}{2(1+t)}$, and its solution is therefore $z=C(1+t)-\tfrac{1}{2}(1+t)\ln(1+t)$. Since $v=1$ at $t=0$, the condition on z is $z=1$ at $t=0$, and so $C=1$.

We now have $v=\dfrac{1}{(1+t)\{1-\tfrac{1}{2}\ln(1+t)\}}$, and $u=w-v$, so

$u=\dfrac{\tfrac{1}{2}\ln(1+t)}{(1+t)\{1-\tfrac{1}{2}\ln(1+t)\}}$. Each holds until $1=\tfrac{1}{2}\ln(1+t)$, i.e. $t=e^2-1$.

29 The equation of motion is

$$M\frac{d^2z}{dt^2}=-n^2(z-z_0)-Mg-\lambda Mn\left(\frac{dz}{dt}-a\sin pt\right)$$

where the terms on the right hand side are restoring force, weight and resistance to relative motion. Since it can float at rest at height z_0, $n^2z_0=Mg$, and the equation reduces to $\ddot{z}+\lambda n\dot{z}+(n^2/M)z=a\lambda n\sin pt$. Since $\lambda>0$ (it is a resistance) the CF decays to zero as $t \to \infty$. The PI is of the form $A \cos pt + B \sin pt$; substituting (and using $p = nM^{-1/2}$) gives $A = 0$, $B = aM^{1/2}/n$.

30 The GS is $Ae^{4t} + Be^{-4t}$, and fitting the conditions gives $x = (\frac{1}{2}a - \frac{1}{8}b)e^{4t} + (\frac{1}{2}a + \frac{1}{8}b)e^{-4t}$. If $a > 4b$ then both coefficients are positive, and since exponentials are positive, $x > 0$ for all t. The solution of $dx/dt = 0$ is given by $(2a - \frac{1}{2}b)e^{8t} = (2a + \frac{1}{2}b)$, i.e. $t = \frac{1}{8}\ln\{(2a + \frac{1}{2}b)/(2a - \frac{1}{2}b)\}$, which is a (real) time > 0 since $a > \frac{1}{4}b$ and since $2a + \frac{1}{2}b > 2a - \frac{1}{2}b$.

The equations for the forces are

$$dx/dt = -2y, \quad dy/dt = -8x.$$

Then $d^2x/dt^2 = -2dy/dt = 16x$. In the above solution, take $a = x_0$ and $b = 2y_0$; then if $x_0 > \frac{1}{2}y_0$, x is never zero, but dx/dt becomes zero at some time, i.e. $y = 0$ and the A-force wins.

31 (i) The equation for the motion is $dx/dt = k(A - x)$. Solving this by separation, with $x = A$ at $t = 0$, gives $\ln(1 - x/A) = -kt$, i.e. $x = A(1 - e^{-kt})$. As $t \to \infty$, $x \to A$, so it travels a finite distance. Note that $dx/dt = kA$ at $t = 0$ is satisfied automatically.

(ii) The equation is $dv/dt = k(U - v)$ or $\dfrac{d^2x}{dt^2} + k\dfrac{dx}{dt} = kU$. The CF is $B + Ce^{-kt}$ and the PI is Ut. Thus the GS is $B + Ce^{-kt} + Ut$, and fitting the initial values gives $x = Ut + (A - U/k)(1 - e^{-kt})$. As $t \to \infty$ the second term is finite, but the first is unbounded.

32 The equation expresses the statement

'moment of inertia × rate of increase of angular velocity = total couple acting',

and is therefore $\frac{1}{10}ma^2 \, d\omega/dt = -k\omega + \frac{1}{2}\rho ca^3 U^2$. When $U = U_0$, there is a solution which has $\omega = \text{constant} = \frac{1}{2}\rho ca^3 U_0^2/k$.

Now $(U_0 + u \cos nt)^2 = U_0^2 + \frac{1}{2}u^2 + 2U_0 u \cos nt + \frac{1}{2}u^2 \cos 2nt$, and so the equation is

$$\frac{d\omega}{dt} + \frac{10k}{ma^2}\omega = \frac{5\rho ca}{m}\{(U_0^2 + \frac{1}{2}u^2) + 2U_0 u \cos nt + \frac{1}{2}u^2 \cos 2nt\}.$$

The CF for this linear equation is $\omega_1 = Ae^{-pt}$, where $p = 10k/(ma^2)$. The PI has a constant term corresponding to the first term on the right hand side, $\omega_3 = \dfrac{ma^2}{10k} \times \dfrac{5\rho ca}{m}(U_0^2 + \frac{1}{2}u^2) > \frac{1}{2}\rho ca^2 U_0^2/k$. The other terms in the PI come from the $\cos nt$ and $\cos 2nt$ terms on the right, and so $\omega_2 = p \cos nt + q \sin nt + P \cos 2nt + Q \sin 2nt$, where p, q, P, Q are found by substitution.

33 (a) The equation for mass-acceleration is $4\dot{v} = -(28v + 24x)$, and $v = \dot{x}$, so $\dfrac{d^2x}{dt^2} + 7\dfrac{dx}{dt} + 6x = 0$. The GS here is $Ae^{-6t} + Be^{-t}$, and fitting the values gives $A = -1$, $B = 5$. Thus $x = 5e^{-t} - e^{-6t}$, and $x = 0$ when $e^{-5t} = 5$, $t = \frac{1}{5}\ln\frac{1}{5}$ s.

(b) $dP/dt = -kP$ and so $P = P_0 e^{-kt}$. Using the values $e^{-3k} = \frac{1}{2}$, so that $k = \frac{1}{3}\ln 2$. The value at 8 years from new is then (in pounds) $8000e^{-8k} = 8000 \times 2^{-8/3} = 1260$.

34 (i) The mass-acceleration equation is $mdv/dt = -mg - (mg/W^2)v^2$. Put $dv/dt = v\,dv/dx = \frac{1}{2}d(v^2)\,dx$ to get the required equation.

(ii) $\dfrac{dv}{dx} = (-ac + B)e^{-ax} \cdot \dfrac{dy}{dx} + ay = b$ follows. Clearly $y = c$ at $x = 0$.

(iii)   Using (ii) (and the uniqueness of initial value solutions of linear equations) gives $v^2 = -W^2 + (U^2 + W^2)e^{-2gx/W^2}$. At the maximum height X, $v=0$, and so
$$X = \frac{W^2}{2g} \ln\left(1 + \frac{U^2}{W^2}\right).$$

35   When θ is small, $\sin\theta \approx \theta$, so $\ddot{\theta} + (2\mu/I)\dot{\theta} + (n^2/I)\theta = (2\mu/I)\dot{\phi}$; that is, $\lambda = 2\mu/I$, $k^2 = n^2/I$. In the given case $\lambda = n/I^{1/2}$, and $k = n/I^{1/2} = \lambda$.

In this case $\phi = 0$, so solve $\ddot{\theta} + 2k\dot{\theta} = 0$ with $\theta = \theta_0$ and $\dot{\theta} = 0$ at $t=0$. The GS is $e^{-kt}(A + Bt)$ and the initial conditions require $A = \theta_0$, $-kA + B = 0$, i.e. $B = k\theta_0$. The solution is $\theta = \theta_0 e^{-kt}(1 + kt)$.

Solve, during $0 \leqslant t \leqslant T$, $\ddot{\theta} + 2k\dot{\theta} + k^2\theta = 2k\pi/2T$; the initial values are $\theta = \dot{\theta} = 0$ at $t=0$. The GS here is $e^{-kt}(C + Dt) + \pi/(kT)$ and the initial values are fitted by $C = -\pi/(kT)$, $D = -\pi/T$.   That   is, $\theta = \dfrac{\pi}{kT}\{1 - e^{-kt}(1 + kt)\}$ and $\dot{\theta} = \dfrac{\pi}{T}e^{-kt}\{(1 + kt) - 1\}$; this gives $\dot{\theta} \geqslant 0$, and so $\theta <$ its ultimate value for this solution, which is π/kT. Finally, if $kT/\pi > 10$, $\theta < \frac{1}{10}$, and $\sin\theta \approx \theta$ is a good approximation.

36   Extra acceleration term is $k(\dot{y} - V)$, so that $\ddot{x} = \alpha(y - x - L)/L + k(\dot{y} - V)$. Put $k = \beta/V$ to get $\ddot{x} + \alpha x/L = \alpha y/L + \beta \dot{y}/V - (\alpha + \beta)$. Substituting $\dot{x} = \dot{y} = V$, $x = Vt - L$, $y = Vt$ shows that this is a solution.

(a)   Initial values are $\dot{x} = V$, $x = 0$ at $t=0$, when $y = L$. The equation for x is $\ddot{x} + \alpha x/L = -\alpha$, on taking $\beta = \alpha$. The GS of this equation is $A\cos\{(\alpha/L)^{1/2}t\} + B\sin\{(\alpha/L)^{1/2}t\} - L$. Fitting the values gives $A = L$, $B = (L/\alpha)^{1/2}V$. There is a crash if $x = L$. Now the maximum value of $A\cos\theta + B\sin\theta$ is $\sqrt{A^2 + B^2}$, so there is no crash if $L^2 + LV^2/\alpha < 4L^2$, i.e. $\alpha > \frac{1}{3}V^2/L$.

(b) $\dot{y} = V - b\omega \sin\omega t$, so the equation for x is
$$\ddot{x} + \alpha x/L = \alpha Vt/L + (\alpha b/L)\cos\omega t - (\beta b\omega/V)\sin\omega t.$$

If $\omega = (\alpha/L)^{1/2}$ there will be resonance and the oscillation in x will be unbounded.

37   The CF is $e^{-3t}(A\cos 4t + B\sin 4t)$ and the PI is $V_0(\frac{1}{25} - \frac{1}{20}e^{-t})$. Fitting the conditions to the GS gives $A = \frac{1}{100}V_0$ and $B = -\frac{1}{200}V_0$, i.e. $V = \frac{1}{200}V_0 e^{-3t}(2\cos 4t - \sin 4t) + \frac{1}{100}V_0(4 - 5e^{-t})$. The graph is flat (locally) at $t=0$, then rises with a positive gradient at all times, approaching $V_0/25$ as $t \to \infty$.

38   For the diver at rest at $x = L$ you need the effective weight λMg equal to the upthrust $\rho Vg = \rho cg/(P_1 + \rho gL)$. This gives P_1 the value required.

The equation of motion is
$$M\ddot{x} = \lambda Mg - \rho cg/(P + \rho gx) - k\dot{x},$$
so that $\alpha = \frac{1}{2}k/M$, $\beta = \lambda g$, $f(x) = \dfrac{\rho cg}{M(P + \rho gx)}$.

From the earlier work $f(L) = \lambda Mg$, when $P = P_1$; and $f'(L) = \dfrac{\rho^2 cg^2}{M(P_1 + \rho gL)^2}$, by differentiating. Hence the equation is replaced by $\ddot{x} + 2\alpha\dot{x} - \gamma^2(x - L) = 0$ where $\gamma^2 = \dfrac{\rho^2 cg^2}{M(P_1 + \rho gL)^2}$.

The GS is $Ae^{m_1 t} + Be^{m_2 t} + L$, where $m_{1,2} = -\alpha \pm \sqrt{(\alpha^2 + \gamma^2)}$. Fitting the condition gives $x = A(e^{m_1 t} - e^{m_2 t}) + L$. One of $m_{1,2}$ is positive, the other negative; as t increases, the positive exponential term increases rapidly, and the direction the diver moves in depends on the sign of A, i.e. on the sign of $\dot{x}$ at $x = L$. A more direct argument is that if the diver is moved up slightly from $x = L$, the pressure is lower, so V is greater, and so the upthrust is larger – hence it moves further from $x = L$. A similar argument holds for downward motion.

39   The volume out of the water is $x/36$ (m³) so the volume in the water is $A - x/36$. Hence the upthrust is $\rho g (A - x/36) = 10^4 (A - x/36)$. In equilibrium the upthrust equals the weight, and so $10^4(A_0 - 10^{-3}) = 800$, i.e. $A_0 = 8.1 \times 10^{-2}$.
   His equation of motion is

$$80\ddot{x} = 10^4(8.1 \times 10^{-2} + a \sin \omega t - x/36) - 20\ddot{x} - 200\dot{x}$$

which can be rearranged as $\ddot{x} + 2\dot{x} + 100x/36 = 8.1 + 100a \sin \omega t$.
   The CF of this equation is $e^{-t}\{A\cos(\tfrac{4}{3}t) + B\sin(\tfrac{4}{3}t)\}$. The PI is $8.1 \times 36/100 + p\cos \omega t + q\sin \omega t$, where (by substitution)

$$p = \frac{-200a\omega}{(\omega^2 - \tfrac{25}{9})^2 + 4\omega^2}, \quad q = \frac{200a(\tfrac{25}{9} - \omega^2)}{(\omega^2 - \tfrac{25}{9})^2 + 4\omega^2}.$$

(Notice that this gives resonance, and quite a large motion vertically, if $\omega = \tfrac{5}{3}$, i.e. a period of about 3.8 s for his breathing. Try it!)

40   The equation is $y'' + (P/B)y = Pd/B$, and its GS is $C\cos\{(P/B)^{1/2}x\} + d$. Fitting the values gives $y = d(1 - \cos \alpha x)$, where $\alpha^2 = P/B$.
   The deflection at $x = l$ is given to be d. Hence $d = d(1 - \cos \alpha l)$, and when $P = \pi^2 B/(9l^2)$ the value of $\cos \alpha l$ is $\tfrac{1}{2}$; that is, $d = \tfrac{1}{2}d$, so that $d = 0$. But when $P = P_c$ the equation for the deflection at $x = l$ is $d = d$, and any value of d is allowed.
   Replace d by $d + a$ in the solution of the equation to get $y = (d + a)(1 - \cos \alpha x)$. Now consider $x = l$, where $y = d$, to derive $d\cos \alpha l = a(1 - \cos \alpha l)$. The solution becomes $y = a(1 - \cos \alpha x)/\cos \alpha l$, if $\cos \alpha l \neq 0$.

Revision exercise E

1   Let $y = ax^3 + bx^2 + cx + d$. Then $y(x + h) - 2y(x) + y(x - h)$ can be worked out from $a(x + h)^3 - 2ax^3 + a(x - h)^3 +$ etc. to be $6axh^2 + 2bh^2$. On division by h^2 you get $y''(x)$.
   Discretise the equation (for $r = 1, 2, 3$) as

$$(V_{r-1} - 2V_r + V_{r+1})/h^2 - rhV_r = 0, \quad V_0 = 1, \quad V_4 = 3,$$

(where $V_r = V(hr)$). This gives the set of equations

$$\begin{cases} -2.001V_1 & + V_2 & & = -1 \\ V_1 - 2.002\ V_2 + & V_3 = & 0 \\ & V_2 - 2.003\ V_3 = -3. \end{cases}$$

The solution is (by Gauss elimination) $V_1 = 1.4950$, $V_2 = 1.9915$, $V_3 = 2.4920$ (to 4 s.f.).

2 $dz/dx = d^2y/dx^2$ and so $d^2y/dx^2 = -2yz/x = -2x^{-1}y\,dy/dx$.

$$(dy/dx)_{\text{old}} = 1.2384, \quad (dz/dx)_{\text{old}} = -1.5766$$

$$y_{\text{inter}} = y_{\text{old}} + h(dy/dx)_{\text{old}} = 1.1423$$

$$z_{\text{inter}} = z_{\text{old}} + h(dz/dx)_{\text{old}} = 1.0807.$$

Then $x_{new} = 1.7$ and $(dy/dx)_{inter} = 1.0807$, $(dz/dx)_{inter} = -1.4523$, and

$$\begin{cases} y_{new} = y_{old} + \frac{1}{2}h\{(dy/dx)_{old} + (dy/dx)_{inter}\} = 1.1345, \\ z_{new} = z_{old} + \frac{1}{2}h\{(dz/dx)_{old} + (dz/dx)_{inter}\} = 1.0870. \end{cases}$$

The normal equations are $\begin{pmatrix} \Sigma h^4 & \Sigma h^2 \\ \Sigma h^2 & 3 \end{pmatrix}\begin{pmatrix} a \\ b \end{pmatrix} = \begin{pmatrix} \Sigma h^2 y \\ \Sigma y \end{pmatrix}$ for fitting the model $y = ah^2 + b$. Here $\Sigma h^2 = 0.0725$, $\Sigma h^4 = 2.206 \times 10^{-3}$, $\Sigma y = 3.068$, $\Sigma h^2 y = 0.0743$. Consequently $b = 1.0143$, which is the estimated value of $y(1.6)$ as $h \to 0$.

3 (a) $\dfrac{dy}{dx} = \dfrac{dy}{du}\dfrac{du}{dx}$ (by the chain rule) $= -\dfrac{1}{x^2}\dfrac{dy}{du}$. Hence $\dfrac{d^2y}{dx^2} = \dfrac{2}{x^3}\dfrac{dy}{du} - \dfrac{1}{x^2}\dfrac{d}{dx}\left(\dfrac{dy}{du}\right)$.

Now $\dfrac{d}{dx}\left(\dfrac{dy}{du}\right) = \dfrac{du}{dx}\dfrac{d}{du}\left(\dfrac{dy}{du}\right) = -\dfrac{1}{x^2}\dfrac{d^2y}{du^2}$. Substituting in the equation gives

$\dfrac{d^2y}{du^2} + \dfrac{dy}{du} - 6y = 10$. This has the GS $y = Ae^{-3u} + Be^{2u} - \frac{5}{3}$, so $y = Ae^{-3/x} + Be^{2/x} - \frac{5}{3}$.

(b) Put $\dfrac{d^2y}{dx^2} = p\dfrac{dp}{dy}$ to get the separable equation $py\dfrac{dp}{dy} = 1 + p^2$. This has the solution $p = \pm\sqrt{(Ay^2 - 1)}$, where $A > 0$ for a real solution. This too separates, giving

$\displaystyle\int \dfrac{a}{\sqrt{(y^2 - a^2)}}dy = \pm\int dx$, where $A^{-1} = a^2$. The easiest solution formula is $y = a\cosh\{(c \pm x)/a\}$.

4   If $a^2 > 4b$ the GS is $Ae^{m_1 t} + Be^{m_2 t}$, where $m_{1,2} = \frac{1}{2}\{-a \pm \sqrt{(a^2 - 4b)}\}$. If $a^2 = 4b$ the GS is $e^{-at}(Ct + D)$. If $a^2 < 4b$ the GS is $e^{-at}(E\cos pt + F\sin pt)$, $p = \sqrt{(4b - a^2)}$.

(i) a cannot be negative, or else the second and third solutions above are unbounded as $t \to \infty$. If b is negative, then $a^2 - 4b > a$, and $-a + \sqrt{(a^2 - 4b)}$ is positive, which allows unbounded solutions in the first case.

(ii) If $x = e^t$, $\dfrac{dy}{dx} = \dfrac{dt}{dx}\dfrac{dy}{dt} = \dfrac{1}{x}\dfrac{dy}{dt}$; then $\dfrac{d^2y}{dx^2} = -\dfrac{1}{x^2}\dfrac{dy}{dt} + \dfrac{1}{x}\dfrac{d}{dx}\left(\dfrac{dy}{dt}\right)$. But

$\dfrac{d}{dx}\left(\dfrac{dy}{dt}\right) = \dfrac{dt}{dx}\dfrac{d}{dt}\left(\dfrac{dy}{dt}\right) = \dfrac{1}{x}\dfrac{d^2y}{dx^2}$, and so $\dfrac{d^2y}{dx^2} = -\dfrac{1}{x^2}\dfrac{dy}{dt} + \dfrac{1}{x^2}\dfrac{d^2y}{dt^2}$. Making the

substitutions, the equation becomes $\dfrac{d^2y}{dt^2} + \dfrac{dy}{dt} - 6y = 0$. This has GS $Ae^{2t} + Be^{-3t}$ and so the GS is $Ax^2 + Bx^{-3}$. Fitting the conditions gives $A = 3$, $B = -1$.

5 (a) Integrate twice to get $y = \frac{1}{6}x^3 - x + \frac{2}{3}$.

(b) Make the substitition to get $x\, dz/dx - 2z = 0$, which can be put as $\dfrac{d}{dx}(z/x^2) = 0$.

Thus $z = Ax^2$, and using the conditions gives $A = 1$. Now solve $\dfrac{dy}{dx} + 2y = x^2$; this

can be written $\dfrac{d}{dx}(e^{2x}y) = x^2 e^{2x}$, whose solution is $y = Be^{-2x} + \frac{1}{2}x^2 - \frac{1}{2}x + \frac{1}{4}$.

6 Substitition, and checking the conditions, verifies that $\cos 2x$ is a solution.
$\dfrac{d}{dx}\left(\dfrac{f''}{f}\right) = \dfrac{ff''' - f'f''}{f^2} = 0$ from the equation (if $f \neq 0$). Consequently $f''/f = A$, or $f'' - Af = 0$.

7   $y'=u'v+uv'$ and $y''=u''v+2u'v'+uv''$.   Thus   the   equation   becomes
$u''+u'(2v'/v+p)+u(v''/v+pv'/v+q)=0$. Hence if you choose v from $v'/v+\frac{1}{2}p=0$, the
required form appears. You need $\ln v=-\frac{1}{2}\int p(x)\,dx$, and once v has been found,
substitition gives $f(x)=v''/v+pv'/v+q$.

   In this case $\ln v=-\frac{1}{2}\int 4x\,dx$, $v=e^{-x^2}$, $f(x)=1$ and the equation has reduced to
$u''+u=0$,   solution $A\cos x+B\sin x$.   Then $y=e^{-x^2}\,(A\cos x+B\sin x)$,   and   the
conditions give $A=1$, $B=2$.

8   Here $y'=A+2Be^{2x}$ and $y''=4Be^{2x}$. So $xy'-y=B(2x-1)e^{2x}=\frac{1}{4}(2x-1)y''$. This can
be arranged as

$$(1-2x)\frac{d}{dx}\left(\frac{dy}{dx}-2y\right)+2\left(\frac{dy}{dx}-2y\right)=0.$$

Put $z=\dfrac{dy}{dx}-2y$ and the equation is $(1-2x)\dfrac{dz}{dx}+2z=(1-2x)^2$. This can be written as
$\dfrac{d}{dx}\left(\dfrac{z}{1-2x}\right)=1$, whose solution is $z=x+A(1-2x)$. The given values show that
$A=-1$, and so $z=3x-1$. Now solve $dy/dx-2y=3x-1$; the CF is Be^{2x} and the PI is
$-\frac{3}{2}x-\frac{1}{4}$. Again using the initial values shows that $B=\frac{5}{4}$, and the solution is
$y=\frac{5}{4}e^{2x}-\frac{3}{2}x-\frac{1}{4}$.

9   The CF is Ae^x+Be^{-x}, hence the PI has the form cxe^x, and substitution shows that
$c=1$. The boundary values give $A=-\frac{1}{2}$, $B=\frac{1}{2}$.
   The equation is replaced by $h^{-2}(f_r-2f_{r-1}+f_{r-2})-f_r=2e^{rh}$, with $f_0=f_1=0$. That
is, $(1-h^2)f_r-2f_{r-1}+f_{r-2}=2h^2e^{rh}$, $2\leqslant r\leqslant n$. Substitution shows that the PI is
$2e^{2h}/\{(1-h^2)e^{2h}-2e^h+1\}$. The auxiliary equation is $(1-h^2)c^2-2c+1=0$, with
solutions $(1+h)^{-1}$, $(1-h)^{-1}$. The GS is therefore as required. The given conditions
show that $k+a+b=0$ and $ke^h+a/(1+h)+b/(1-h)=0$.

10   Using the equations for $r=1$ and $r=2$ gives $-1.64y_1+y_2=0.04$ and
$y_1-0.64y_2=0.04$. The solutions are $y_1=-1.3226$, $y_2=-2.1290$.
   The GS is $A\cos 3x+B\sin 3x+\frac{1}{9}$, and the conditions give $A=-\frac{1}{9}$,
$B=-(1-\cos 3)/(9\sin 3)$. The formula for f'' has error approximately $h^2f^{(4)}/12$. Now
$f^{(4)}(x)=81\,(A\cos 3x+B\sin 3x)$, so that the error at 0.2 has size 0.264 and at 0.4 the
error is 0.405.

11   The CF is $e^{-2x}(Ax+B)$ and the PI is $\frac{1}{4}(x-1)$. The conditions require $A=-\frac{1}{4}e^2$,
$B=\frac{1}{4}e^2$.
   The equation becomes

$$y_{n+1}-2y_n+y_{n-1}+2(y_{n+1}-y_{n-1})+4y_n=n,$$

as required. The CF is $A(-1)^n+B(\frac{1}{3})^n$ because the auxiliary equation factorises as
$(c+1)(3c-1)=0$. The PS must have the form $an+b$, and substitution shows that
$a=\frac{1}{4}$, $b=-\frac{1}{4}$.
   For large values of x, $f(x)\approx\frac{1}{4}(x-1)$; for large values of n, $y_n\approx\frac{1}{4}(n-1)$. Hence $f(x)$
and y_n are nearly equal (in the given sense) for large n.

Revision exercise F

1 Reduce the size of the square EFGH a bit (say to half each side), and then push it down on the plane ABCD: this gives an equivalent network.

There is symmetry across the plane ACGE, and also across the plane BDHF. Thus the currents are as follows: AD, BC and DC: all i_1; GC: i_2; EF, EH, FG, HG: i_3. No current along BF or DH. One choice of the equations is

$$\left.\begin{array}{ll} \text{Along ABC} & i_1+i_2=V \\ \text{Round AEFB} & i_2+i_3-i_1=0 \\ \text{Along AEFGC} & 2i_2+2i_3=V \\ \text{At A} & 2i_1+i_2-I=0 \end{array}\right\} \text{ i.e. } \mathbf{M}=\begin{pmatrix} 1 & 1 & 0 & 0 \\ -1 & 1 & 1 & 0 \\ 0 & 2 & 2 & 0 \\ 2 & 1 & 0 & -1 \end{pmatrix}, \mathbf{E}=\begin{pmatrix} V \\ 0 \\ V \\ 0 \end{pmatrix}.$$

Solving the equations gives $I=\frac{4}{3}V$, a resistance of $\frac{3}{4}\Omega$.

2 The resistance of one string of lights is Nr/n; for n such strings in parallel the resistance is Nr/n^2, and so for the whole system it is $R+Nr/n^2$. Hence $I=E/(R+Nr/n^2)$, and since $ni=I$, $i=E/(nR+Nr/n)$. The power used in each light is i^2r, so the total power used in the lights is $P=NE^2r/(nR+Nr/n)^2$. The minimum of $2n+180/n$ occurs (either using differentiation or trials) at $n=9$ or 10 (n must be an integer), and so $n=10$ because it must be a factor of 60.

3 The other currents are: $x+y$ through the battery, $x-z$ in BC, $y+z$ in DC. Equations for (i) the circuit through battery and ADC, (ii) round ABD, (iii) round BDC are $x+7y+4z=30$, $4x-2y+z=0$, $-2x+4y+7z=0$. Solutions are $x=3$, $y=5$, $z=-2$ amperes. The power is $30\times8=240$ watts.

4 Let the current through the resistance $2R$ be J_n. Then $I_{n+1}=I_n-J_n$. Also $2RJ=V_{n+1}$ and $V_{n+1}=V_n-I_nR$. Reorganising these gives

$$\begin{pmatrix} V_{n+1} \\ I_{n+1} \end{pmatrix}=\begin{pmatrix} 1 & -R \\ -1/(2R) & \frac{3}{2} \end{pmatrix}\begin{pmatrix} V_n \\ I_n \end{pmatrix}.$$

From the CF two independent solutions are $A2^n$, $B(\frac{1}{2})^n$. The first is unbounded as $n\to\infty$, the second decreases to zero, and hence is the relevant one.

5 The basic equations are $V_{n+1}=V_n-I_{n+1}=I_n-V_n/S$. Eliminating I_{n+1} (and using $I_n=(V_n-V_{n+1})/R$) gives the required equation. The auxiliary equation is $m^2-(e^\lambda+e^{-\lambda})m+1=0$ which has roots e^λ and $e^{-\lambda}$ (by substitution). Hence

$$V_n=Pe^{n\lambda}+Qe^{-n\lambda}=\tfrac{1}{2}(P+Q)(e^{n\lambda}+e^{-n\lambda})+\tfrac{1}{2}(P-Q)(e^{n\lambda}-e^{-n\lambda})$$

$$=A\cosh n\lambda+B\sinh n\lambda$$

by choosing $A=P+Q$, $B=P-Q$. Fitting the conditions at $n=0$ and $n=N$ gives the answer.

6 The equation for the current is $0.2dI/dt+I=10\sin(100\pi t)$ for $t\geqslant0$, with $I=0$ at $t=0$. The impedance of the circuit is $0.2\times100\pi j+1$. The CF is Ae^{-5t} and the PI is $(10\sin100\pi t-200\pi\cos100\pi t)/(1+400\pi^2)$. Fitting the initial value gives $A=200\pi/(1+400\pi^2)$.

7 The equations for the circuit are $20I+100Q=50\sin\omega t$ and $I=dQ/dt$. Hence $dQ/dt+5Q=\frac{5}{2}\sin\omega t$.   The   CF   is Ae^{-5t} and   the   PI   is $(25\sin\omega t-5\omega\cos\omega t)/(50+2\omega^2)$. The value of A, from $Q=0$ at $t=0$, is $5\omega/(50+2\omega^2)$.

8   The equation for the circuit is $0.25dI/dt + Q = 0.25 \sin \omega t$, where $I = dQ/dt$. Hence the equation for I is $d^2I/dt^2 + 4I = \omega \cos \omega t$. In case (i) the solution is $A \cos 2t + B \sin 2t + \frac{1}{3} \cos t$. In case (ii) the solution is $C \cos 2t + D \sin 2t + \frac{1}{4} t \sin 2t$. Fitting the conditions $I = 0$ and $dI/dt = 0$ (from the first equation) at $t = 0$ gives (i) $A = -\frac{1}{3}$, $B = 0$ and (ii) $C = 0$, $D = 0$.

9   Round the loop $Q/10^{-3} - 10^{-2}\dot{J} = 0$, and $\dot{Q} = I - J$. Hence $\ddot{J} = 10^5(I - J)$. Through the generator, $RI + 10^{-2}\dot{J} = V_0 \sin(100\pi t)$, and eliminating I gives $\ddot{J} + (10^3/R)\dot{J} + 10^5 J = (10^5 V_0/R)\sin(100\pi t)$. You can *either* find the PI *or* use impedances. For the latter, Z for the circuit is $-(100\pi)^2 + (10^3/R)100\pi j + 10^5$, so that $|Z| = \sqrt{\{(10^5 - 10^4\pi^2)^2 + 10^{10}\pi^2/R^2\}} \approx 10^5\pi/R$ in the given case. Hence the current amplitude is V_0/π.

10   The current through C is both $I - J$ and $\dot{q}$, where q is the charge on the capacitor. But $V = q/C$, hence $\dot{V} = (I - J)/C$; also $V = JR$ and $E = LdI/dt + V$. Eliminating V and I gives the required equation.

     The equation is $\ddot{J} + 4\dot{J} + 4J = 40E_0 + 40\varepsilon \sin 2t$, and $J = \dot{J} = 0$ at $t = 0$. The solution is $10E_0 + 5\varepsilon\{(1 + 2t)e^{-2t} - \cos 2t\}$.

11   The equation is $LdI/dt + rI = V$ for $t \geqslant 0$, with solution $I = (V/r)(1 - e^{-rt/L})$. In the special case $I = \frac{1}{2}(1 - e^{-10t})$, and at $t = 0.23$, $I = 0.450$. After then the current decays to zero as it flows round the loop.

12   (a) $V_1 = V_2 + RI_1$, $I_1 = I_2 + V_2/(j\omega L)$. Rearranging gives

$$\begin{pmatrix} V_2 \\ I_2 \end{pmatrix} = \begin{pmatrix} 1 & -R \\ \dfrac{1}{j\omega L} & 1 + \dfrac{R}{j\omega L} \end{pmatrix} \begin{pmatrix} V_1 \\ I_1 \end{pmatrix}, \text{ or } \mathbf{M} = \begin{pmatrix} 1 & -R \\ j/(\omega L) & 1 - jR/(\omega L) \end{pmatrix}.$$

     (b) $\sqrt{j} = \pm(1 + j)/\sqrt{2}$, as can be seen by squaring both sides. Hence the GS of the equation is $A \exp\left\{\left(\dfrac{1+j}{\sqrt{2}}\right)\left(\dfrac{r}{\omega l}\right)^{1/2} x\right\} + B \exp\left\{-\left(\dfrac{1+j}{\sqrt{2}}\right)\left(\dfrac{r}{\omega l}\right)^{1/2} x\right\}$. Fitting $V = V_0$ at $x = 0$ and $V \to 0$ as $x \to \infty$ gives the required solution.

13   A frequency of f Hz corresponds to $e^{j2\pi ft}$. The impedance is

$$20 + \{(2\pi fj \times 0.05) + 1/(2\pi fj \times 0.02)\}^{-1} = 20 + \frac{10\pi f}{250 - \pi^2 f^2}j.$$

     The largest impedance magnitude comes from $f^2 = 250/\pi^2$; no current through AB.

14   Resistor 2; capacitor $1/(j\omega)$; inductor $4j\omega$. The total impedance is $2 + \{j\omega + 1/(4j\omega)\}^{-1} = 2 + 4\omega j/(1 - 4\omega^2)$. $I = 0$ when $\omega = \frac{1}{2}$, as the magnitude of the impedance is infinite. $|Z| = \sqrt{\{4 + 16\omega^2/(1 - 4\omega^2)^2\}}$, and $V_0/|Z|$ is to be plotted: it starts at 2 when $\omega = 0$, has a cusp at 0 when $\omega = \frac{1}{2}$, then rises up to reach 2 again for large ω.

Index

See also the list of Contents and the Summary at the end of each Chapter.